D1192701

This study examines the extent of Bible reading in medieval England, and in particular the place of the Lollard translations. Miss Deanesly shows that the medieval church tolerated translation in principle, but distrusted it in practice, because of its associations with Lollardy. She examines wills, library catalogues and episcopal registers where the existence of translations might be noted. She concludes that mystical writings in English were far more widely read than the Bible.

CAMBRIDGE STUDIES

IN

MEDIEVAL LIFE AND THOUGHT

Edited by G. G. COULTON, M.A.
Fellow of St John's College, Cambridge
and University Lecturer in English

# THE LOLLARD BIBLE

# THE LOLLARD BIBLE

## AND OTHER MEDIEVAL
## BIBLICAL VERSIONS

BY

MARGARET DEANESLY, M.A.,

MARY BATESON FELLOW, NEWNHAM COLLEGE, CAMBRIDGE

CAMBRIDGE

AT THE UNIVERSITY PRESS

1920

REPRINTED

1966

PUBLISHED BY
THE SYNDICS OF THE CAMBRIDGE UNIVERSITY PRESS
Bentley House, 200 Euston Road, London, N.W.1.
American Branch: 32 East 57th Street, New York, N. Y. 10022
West African Office: P.M.B. 5181, Ibadan, Nigeria

*Publisher's Note*
Cambridge University Press Library Editions are reissues of out-of-print
standard works from the Cambridge catalogue. The texts are unrevised
and, apart from minor corrections, reproduce the latest published edition.

*First published* 1920
*Reprinted* 1966

*First printed in Great Britain at the University Press, Cambridge
Library of Congress Catalogue Card Number: 20–16787
Reprinted in the United States of America*

# GENERAL PREFACE

THERE is only too much truth in the frequent complaint that history, as compared with the physical sciences, is neglected by the modern public. But historians have the remedy in their own hands; choosing problems of equal importance to those of the scientist, and treating them with equal accuracy, they will command equal attention. Those who insist that the proportion of accurately ascertainable facts is smaller in history, and therefore the room for speculation wider, do not thereby establish any essential distinction between truth-seeking in history and truth-seeking in chemistry. The historian, whatever be his subject, is as definitely bound as the chemist "to proclaim certainties as certain, falsehoods as false, and uncertainties as dubious." Those are the words, not of a modern scientist, but of the seventeenth century monk, Jean Mabillon; they sum up his literary profession of faith. Men will follow us in history as implicitly as they follow the chemist, if only we will form the chemist's habit of marking clearly where our facts end and our inferences begin. Then the public, so far from discouraging our speculations, will most heartily encourage them; for the most positive man of science is always grateful to anyone who, by putting forward a working theory, stimulates further discussion.

The present series, therefore, appeals directly to that craving for clearer facts which has been bred in these times of storm and stress. No care can save us altogether from error; but, for our own sake and the public's, we have elected to adopt a safeguard dictated by ordinary business commonsense. Whatever errors of fact are pointed out by reviewers or correspondents shall be publicly corrected with the least possible delay. After a year of publication, all copies shall be provided with such an erratum-slip without waiting for the chance of a second edition; and each fresh volume in this series shall contain a full list of the errata noted in its predecessors. Thus, with the help of our critics, we may reasonably hope to put forward these monographs as roughly representing the most accurate information obtainable under present conditions. Our facts being thus secured, the reader will judge our inferences on their own merits; and something will have been done to dissipate that cloud of suspicion which hangs over too many important chapters in the social and religious history of the Middle Ages.

G. G. C.

4 *March* 1920

# AUTHOR'S PREFACE

THE history of mediaeval translations of the Vulgate, their place in the social history of the time, and the attitude of authority towards them, was suggested to me by Mr G. G. Coulton as a subject needing investigation. I should like here to express my gratitude to him for continuous help and criticism during the years in which I have been engaged on the work, for much kindness, and for many suggestions.

I wish especially to thank Miss A. C. Paues for kind and valuable help, as also Miss Hope Allen, Mr E. J. Thomas, Mr P. S. Allen and the officers of the University Press. I should like finally to thank the councils of Merton College, Oxford, and Trinity College, Cambridge, for permission to print certain manuscripts.

With regard to the method of this study, though I have often cited encyclopedias and certain reference manuals in order to save space in suggesting bibliography, yet I have always tried to cite original authorities in dealing with any disputed or disputable point. Mediaeval surnames are usually printed according to the modern form of the place name, save in cases where a particular form of spelling has already become widely accepted.

MARGARET DEANESLY

4 *March* 1920

# PREFATORY NOTE, 1966

SINCE *The Lollard Bible* was published in 1920, there has been much research into Lollard history between Wycliffe's day and the Reformation, and fresh light has been thrown, incidentally, on the Lollard use of the scriptures. No book however, using all the new evidence, has dealt expressly with this subject.

One book, nevertheless, is pre-eminent as shedding light on the matter: Mr J.A.F. Thomson's *The Later Lollards*, 1965, which has, besides its geographically comprehensive account of Lollard history, an excellent and up-to-date bibliography of all the printed and unprinted sources. Mr Thomson quotes many instances showing that the mere possession of English books, and specially of English scriptures, might make a man suspect of heresy. He refers also to the secret meetings of the Lollards for Bible reading. Two other books which should not be passed over are A.B. Emden's *Biographical Register of the University of Oxford*, 1957–9, an instrument for tracing Lollard careers, and Mr J. Robson's *Wyclif and the Oxford Schools*, 1961, which expounds Wycliffe's ultra-realist philosophy, and his contention that "the Bible" was one divine thing, a Platonic exemplar existing in the mind of God before the creation, of equal sanction throughout. Such teaching, erratically followed, may lie behind one Lollard's claim that the Old Testament was of more authority than the New.

As to the Wycliffite authorship of the English Bible: though Forshall and Madden's monumental study, *The Wycliffe Bible*, 1850, has not been re-edited, work has been done on the Wycliffite texts and an "intermediate version" between Hereford's and Purvey's is now recognized and so named, or else described as "the most revised and idiomatic form of the Earlier Version". For the bibliography of work on the Biblical text, see *The Year's Work in English Studies*, Vols. xxxvii (1956), p. 84; xli (1960), p. 66; xlii (1961) pp. 70–1; xliv (1963), p. 28.

As defending the writing of theology in English, involved in the use of English scriptures, bishop Pecock's *Reule of Crysten Religioun* is of interest, and was edited in 1927 by

W.C. Greet in the E.E.T.S., O.S. 171. Pecock claims that he is as much entitled to write about high and divine matters in English as to preach about them, when "who may take, take he!". His philosophy was far from ultra-realist: the Bible, he says, is in the main reasonable, but where it "does not conform to the very, moral, truth of reason", reason may not be gainsaid; though the reader may "accept the explanation of expositors of that which he will not believe by credence."

M. DEANESLY

196, Clarence Gate Gardens,
London, N.W.1.

# CONTENTS

## CHAPTER I

### *The problem of the Middle-English Bible, and the aim of this study*

## CHAPTER II

### *The prohibitions of vernacular Bible reading in France, Italy and Spain*

# CHAPTER III

*The prohibitions of vernacular Bible reading in the Holy
Roman Empire and the Netherlands, before 1400*

# CHAPTER IV

*Bible reading in the Empire and the Netherlands
c. 1400–1521*

# CHAPTER V

*Translations of parts of the Vulgate in England before Wycliffe*

# CHAPTER VI

*Pre-Wycliffite biblical study by clerks: (a) the higher clergy, friars, monks*

# CHAPTER VII

*Pre-Wycliffite biblical study by clerks: (b) parish priests*

# CHAPTER VIII

## *Pre-Wycliffite Bible reading by lay people*

# CHAPTER IX

## *Wycliffe as the instigator of a vernacular Bible*

# CHAPTER X

## *The two versions of the Wycliffite Bible, and the evidence of the* General Prologue *as to the authorship of the second version*

# CHAPTER XIII

### *Bible reading by the orthodox, 1408–1526*

# CHAPTER XIV

### *The Lollards and English Bible reading*

# APPENDIX I

## APPENDIX II: DOCUMENTS

# CONTRACTIONS

| | |
|---|---|
| ADB, | *Allgemeine Deutsche Biographie*. Leipzig. 1875. |
| AM, | *Acts and Monuments*, Foxe, J. 1843; life by G. Townsend. |
| CE, | *Catholic Encyclopedia*. New York. 1907. |
| CHEL, | *Cambridge History of English Literature*. |
| CPL, | *Calendar of Papal Letters*. Public Record Office. |
| CPR, | *Calendar of Papal Registers*. Public Record Office. |
| CVD, | *Catalogi Veteres Librorum Ecclesiae Cathedralis Dunelmensis*. Surtees Society. 1839. |
| CYS, | Canterbury and York Society Publications. |
| DH, | *Diocesan Histories*. S.P.C.K. |
| EB, | *Encyclopedia Britannica*. Cambridge. 1910. |
| EDR, | *Ely Diocesan Remembrancer*. (Extracts from episcopal registers.) |
| EETS, ES, | Early English Text Society, Extra Series; EETS, OS, Original Series. |
| EHR, | *English Historical Review*. |
| EV, | Early version of Wycliffite Bible. |
| FM, | *The Holy Bible: made from the Latin Vulgate by John Wycliffe and his followers*. Oxford. 1850. |
| FZ, | *Fasciculi Zizaniorum Magistri Johannis Wyclif cum tritico*. Shirley, W. W. 1858. |
| HH, | Herzog-Hauck. *Realencyclopädie*. Leipzig. 1903. |
| HJ, | *Historisches Jahrbuch*. |
| HZ, | *Historische Zeitschrift*. |
| LV, | Later version of Wycliffite Bible. |
| MBVP, | *Magna Bibliotheca Veterum Patrum*. De la Bigne, Cologne. 1618. |
| MLN, | *Modern Language Notes*. |
| MLR, | *Modern Language Review*. |
| NED, | *New English Dictionary*, ed. Murray, J. A. H. Oxford. 1888. |
| PL, | *Patrologia Latina*. Migne. 1844. |
| RHT, | *Royal Historical Society Transactions*. |
| RS, | Rolls Series, *Chronicles and Memorials*. |
| SH, | *Schaff-Herzog Encyclopedia of Religious Knowledge*. New York. 1908. |
| SS, | Surtees Society Publications. |
| TE, | *Testamenta Eboracensia*. Surtees Society. |
| TV, | *Testamenta Vetusta*. Nicolas, N. H. London. 1826. |
| V, | Vigouroux, F. *Dictionnaire de la Bible*. Paris. 1912. |
| VCH, | *Victoria County History*. |

*Anec. Hist.* *Anecdotes Historiques, tirées du recueil inédit d'Etienne de Bourbon.* Lecoy de la Marche, A. Paris. 1877.

*Archaeol.* *Archaeologia.*

*Ann. Trevir.* *Annales Trevirenses.* Brower, C. Liège. 1670.

Barclay. *The Ship of Fools,* trans. Barclay, A. Edinburgh. 1874.

Berger. *La Bible française au moyen âge.* Berger, S. Paris. 1884.

Bernard, *Cat.* *Catalogi Librorum Manuscriptorum Angliae et Hiberniae.* Bernard. 1697.

*Bibliom.* *Bibliomania in the Middle Ages.* Merryweather, F. S. London. 1849.

*Boekzaal.* *Boekzaal der Nederduytsche Bybels.* Le Long, I. Amsterdam. 1732.

*Book of Faith.* *Reginald Pecock's Book of Faith.* Morison, J. Cambridge. 1909.

Busch. *Des Augustinerpropstes Johannis Busch Chronicon Windeshemense und Liber de Reformatione Monasteriorum.* Grube, K. Halle. 1886.

*Bury.* *The Abbey of S. Edmund at Bury.* James, M. R. 1905.

*Canterbury.* *Ancient libraries of Canterbury and Dover.* James, M. R.

Capes. *English Church in the fourteenth and fifteenth centuries,* Capes, W. W. London. 1903.

*Cat. of Rom.* *Catalogue of Romances in the Department of Manuscripts in the British Museum.* Vols. I and II, Ward, H. L. D.; vol. III, Herbert, J. A. 1910.

Carleton Brown. *A Register of Middle English Religious and Didactic Verse.* Carleton Brown. Oxford. 1916, pt I.

*C.C.C. Descrip. Cat.* *A Descriptive Catalogue of the manuscripts of Corpus Christi College, Cambridge.* James, M. R. Also the catalogues of other Cambridge colleges.

*Chaire Fran.* *La Chaire Française au Moyen Âge.* Lecoy de la Marche, A. Paris. 1886.

*Chester Plays.* *Chester Plays.* Deimling, H. EETS, ES, 62.

*Codex Apoc.* *Codex Apocryphus Novi Testamenti.* Fabricius, J. A. Hamburg. 1703.

*Conc. Germ.* *Conciliae Germaniae.* Hartzheim, J. Cologne. 1763.

Cook. *Biblical quotations in Old English prose writers.* Cook, A. S. 1898. Second Series, 1903.

*Crise Scol.* *La Crise Scolaire au début du xiiie siècle et la fondation de l'ordre des Frères Prêcheurs.* Mandonnet, P. in *Revue d'histoire ecclésiastique.* Jan. 1914, 34–50.

Cutts. *Parish priests and their people in the middle ages in England.* Cutts, E. L. S.P.C.K. 1898.

Dacheux. *Jean Geiler de Kaysersberg, 1478–1510.* Dacheux, L. Paris. 1876.

Denis. *Codd. Theol. Lat. Bib. Vienn.* Denis, M. 1793.

*De Verit.* *De Veritate Sacrae Scripturae.* Wyclif Soc., ed. Buddensieg, R. 1905.

*Die Deut. Bibelüber.* *Die Deutsche Bibelübersetzung der mittelalterlichen Waldenser in dem codex Teplensis und der ersten gedrückten deutschen Bibel nachgewiesen.* Haupt, H. Würzburg. 1885.

*Doct.* *Thomae Waldensis Doctrinale Antiquitatum Fidei catholicae ecclesiae.* Venice, ed. Blanciotti, F. B. 1757.

*Early Linc. Wills.* *Early Lincoln Wills,* 1280–1547. Gibbons, A. Lincoln. 1888.

*Ec. Reg.* *Synopsis of Romish Corruptions in the Church* (i.e. *Ecclesiae Regimen*); ed. Forshall, J. 1851.

*Educ. Char.* *Educational Charters and Documents.* Leach, A. F. Cambridge. 1911.

*Eng. Franc. Hist.* *Studies in English Franciscan History.* Little, A. G. Manchester. 1917.

*Fabricius.* *Bibliotheca Mediae et Infimae Latinitatis.* Fabricius, J.

*Fasc. Rer. Exp.* *Fasciculus Rerum Expetendarum et Fugiendarum.* Brown, E. 1690.

*Fasti.* *Fasti Ecclesiae Anglicanae.* Le Neve, J. 1854.

*Frere, Visit.* *Visitation Articles and Injunctions.* Frere, W. H. Alcuin Club Collections. 1910.

*Friedjung.* *Kaiser Karl IV und sein Antheil am geistigen Leben seiner Zeit.* Friedjung, H. Vienna. 1876.

*Gairdner.* *Lollardy and the Reformation in England.* Gairdner, J. London. 1908. 4 vols.

*Gem. Ec.* *Selections from Giraldus Cambrensis.* Skeel, C. A. J., S.P.C.K. 1918.

*Gieseler.* *Compendium of Ecclesiastical History,* trans. Hull, J. W. Edinburgh. 1886. 5 vols.

*Gir. Cambren.* *Giraldi Cambrensis Opera.* RS. 8 vols.

*Gottlieb.* *Ueber Mittelalterliche Bibliotheken.* Gottlieb, T. Leipzig. 1890.

*Harney.* *De sancta scriptura linguis vulgaribus legenda: rationabile obsequium Belgii Catholici, per Martinum Harney, adversus quaedam scripta D. Antonii Arnaldi.* Louvain. 1693.

*Hellwald.* *Geschichte der Niederländischen Litteratur.* Hellwald, F. and Schneider, L. Leipzig. 1887.

*Henry IV.* *History of England under Henry IV.* Wylie, J. H. 1884.

*Hentsch.* *De la littérature didactique du moyen âge s'adressant spécialement aux femmes.* Hentsch, A. A. Cahors. 1903.

*Hermits.* *Hermits and Anchorites of England.* Clay, R. M. (Antiquary's Series.)

*Horstmann.* *Richard Rolle of Hampole and his followers.* Horstmann, C. 1896.

*Incendium.* *Incendium Amoris of Richard Rolle of Hampole.* Deanesly, M. 1915.

*Inq.* *History of the Inquisition in the Middle Ages.* Lea, H. C. 3 vols. London. 1906.

*Inq. Neer.* *Corpus Documentorum Inquisitionis Neerlandicae.* Fredericq, P. Ghent. 1896.

*Janssen.* *History of the German People at the close of the Middle Ages.* Janssen, J. London. 1905; or other ed. where stated.

*Jonckbloet.* *Geschichte der Niederländischen Litteratur.* Jonckbloet. W. J. A., trans. Berg, W. Leipzig. 1879.

Jostes, *Die Waldenser*. *Die Waldenser und die vorlutherische deutsche Bibelübersetzung*. Münster. 1885.

Jourdain. *L'Éducation des Femmes au moyen âge*. Jourdain, C. Mémoires de l'Institut nat. de France, acad. des inscriptions, XXVIII. 79–134.

Kehrein. *Zur Geschichte der deutschen Bibelübersetzung vor Luther*. Kehrein, J. Stuttgart. 1851.

Keller. *Die Waldenser und die Deutschen Bibelübersetzungen*. Keller, L. Leipzig. 1886.

Kern. *Album H. Kern*. Leyden. 1903.

Kingsford. *Chronicles of London*. Kingsford, C. L. Oxford. 1905.

*Knighton*. *Chronicon Henrici Knighton*. Lumby, J. R. RS, 9, 1889.

*Lambeth*. *Manuscripts in the Library of Lambeth Palace*. James, M. R. 1900.

*Lanterne*. *The Lanterne of Liȝt*. Swinburn, L. M. 1917. EETS, OS, 151.

*La Tour-Landry*. *The Book of the Knight of La Tour-Landry*. Wright, T. EETS, OS, 33.

*Lay Folks MB*. *Lay Folks Mass Book*. Simmons, T. F. EETS, OS, 71. 1879.

*Lib. Sent. Thol*. *Liber Sententiarum Inquisitionis Tholosanae*. Limborch, P. Amsterdam.

*Linc. Dioc. Docs*. *Lincoln Diocesan Documents*. Clark, A. EETS, OS, 149.

*London Wills*. *Calendar of Wills proved and enrolled in the Court of Husting, London, 1258–1688*. Sharpe, R. R. London. 1889.

Lounsbury. *Studies in Chaucer*. Lounsbury, T. R. London. 1892. 3 vols.

Love's *Mirrour*. *The Mirrour of the Blessed Lyf of Iesu Crist*. Powell, L. F. Oxford. 1908.

Madan, *Sum. Cat*. *Summary Catalogue of Western MSS*. Madan, F.

Mansi. *Sacrorum Conciliorum Collectio*. Ed. Mansi.

Martène, *Thes*. *Thesaurus novus Anecdotorum*. Martène, E. Paris. 1717. 4 vols.

Martène, *Vet. Mon*. *Veterum Scriptorum et Monumentorum amplissima collectio*. Martène, E. and Durand, A. 1733. 9 vols.

*Monast*. *Monasticon Anglicanum*. Dugdale, W. Ed. Cayley, J. 1846.

More, Dialogue. *Workes of Sir Thomas More*. London. 1557. *A Dialogue concerning heresies*, pp. 105 ff.

Mosheim. *De Beghardis et Beguinabus commentarius*. Mosheim, T. L., ed. Martini, G. H. Leipzig. 1790.

*Myroure*. *Myroure of our Ladye*. Blunt, J. H. EETS, ES, 19.

*North Country Wills*. Ed. Clay, J. SS, 116.

*Op. Evang*. *Opus Evangelicum*. Wyclif Soc. Loserth, J. 1895.

*Parker Coll*. *Sources of Archbishop Parker's Collection of MSS*. James, M. R. 1899.

Paues, 1902. *A Fourteenth Century English Biblical Version*. Paues, A. C. Cambridge. 1902.

Paues, 1904. *Id*. Cambridge. 1904.

*Paul, Ep.* *Pauline Epistles.* Powell, M. J. EETS, ES, 116.

*Polem. Works.* *Polemical Works.* Wyclif Soc. Buddensieg, R. 1883.

Pollard. *Fifteenth Century Prose and Verse.* Pollard, A. W. 1903.

Preger. *Beiträge zur Geschichte der Waldesier im Mittelalter.* Preger, W. Munich. 1875.

Putnam. *Censorship of the Church of Rome.* Putnam, G. H. 1906.

*Rel. Antiq.* *Reliquiae Antiquae.* Halliwell and Wright. London. 1841.

*Repressor.* *The Repressor of Over Much Blaming of the Clergy.* Ed. Babington, C. 2 vols. RS, 1860.

*Research Ed.* *Some Results of Research in the History of Education in England.* Leach, A. F. 1914. *Brit. Acad. Proc.* vol. VI.

Reusch. *Index der Verbotenen Bücher.* Reusch, H. Bonn. 1883.

Revius. *Daventria Illustrata.* Revius, J. Leyden. 1651.

*Rom.* *Romania.*

*Sel. Eng. Works.* *Select English Works of John Wyclif.* Arnold, T. 1869.

*Som. Med. Lib.* *Somerset Mediaeval Libraries.* Williams, T. W. *Som. Archaeol. Soc.* 1897.

Stevens, *Monast.* Two additional volumes to the *Monasticon Anglicanum* by Stevens, J. London. 1723.

Summers. *Our Lollard Ancestors.* Summers, W. H. London. 1904.

*Syon.* *Catalogue of the Library of Syon Monastery.* Bateson, M. Cambridge. 1908.

*Tepler Bibel.* *Die Tepler Bibelübersetzung.* Jostes, F. Münster. 1886.

*Test. Scots.* *New Test. in Scots.* Law, T. G.

Trevelyan. *England in the age of Wycliffe.* Trevelyan, G. M. 1899.

*Univs.* *Universities of Europe in the Middle Ages.* Rashdall, H. 1895.

Ussher. *The Whole Works of the Most Reverend James Ussher.* Elrington, C. R. Dublin. 1847. 16 vols.: vol. XII. pp. 154 ff.: *Historia Dogmatica de Scripturis et Sacris Vernaculis.*

*Walden. Ursprung.* *Der Waldensische Ursprung des Codex Teplensis: gegen die Angriffe von Dr F. Jostes verteidigt von Dr Hermann Haupt.* Würzburg. 1886.

Walther. *Die Deutsche Bibelübersetzung des Mittelalters.* Walther, W. Brunswick. 1889.

Wells. *A Manual of the Writings in Middle English,* 1050–1400. Wells, J. E. Yale Univ. Press. 1916.

*Westminster.* *Manuscripts of Westminster Abbey.* Robinson, A. and James, M. R. 1908.

Wiegand. *De Ecclesiae Notione quid Wiclif docuerit.* Wiegand, F. Leipzig. 1891.

Wilkins. *Concilia.* Wilkins, D. 1738.

Witzel. *De Fr. Rogero Bacon eiusque sententia de rebus Biblicis.* Witzel, P. T., O.F.M. Quaracchi. 1910.

# Cambridge Studies in Medieval Life and Thought

## ERRATA FOR VOLUME I

# THE LOLLARD BIBLE

Very few corrections have been made which affect the argument of the book. The most serious is on p. 181, l. 3, where the medieval chronicler's reference is perfectly correct (Gen. xlvii. 22), and the charge of Bible ignorance is therefore unfounded. Certain bibliographical corrections, for which I am grateful to my critics, will be found in their place ; they seem to leave my main argument almost untouched.

p. xviii, l. 15. *For* "Frere, W. H." *read* "Frere, W. H. and Kennedy, W. W. M."

p. 2, l. 1. *For* "unity of Christendom" *read* " unity of western Christendom."

pp. 10, n. 1, 29, and *infra passim*, *read* bishop, *for* archbishop, of Metz.

p. 54, l. 20. There does appear to be satisfactory evidence that this Valencia, 1477, Bible was published. See Brit. and For. Bible Society's *Hist. Cat. of printed Bibles*, No. 8646. Since this catalogue was printed, the compilers kindly inform me, the specimen of the last leaf of this Bible has reappeared : see *La Biblia Valenciana de Bonifacio Ferrer* in *Revista de Archivos, Bibliotecas y Museos, organo del Cuerpo Facultativo del Ramo*, Tercera época año xiii, Sept.—Oct. 1909, pp. 234–248, by L. Tramoyeres Blasco. See also K. Haebler in *Revue Hispanique*, tom. xxi, No. 60 (Dec. 1909), pp. 371–387.

p. 59, l. 16 "same towns." Add : the existence of a rich burgher class in the latter was favourable both to lay devotional movements in the thirteenth and fourteenth centuries, and the early development of printing in the fifteenth.

p. 64, l. 10. I am indebted to the Rev. A. C. Moule for a reference to a contemporary Chinese translation of the New Testament. The Minorite, John of Monte Corvino went to the east as missionary about 1280 : in 1305 he wrote to his superiors, recounting his successes, and asking for help. He had baptized large numbers, trained a school of 40 pagan boys, whom he had bought, to say the Latin office with him, built a church and caused 6 pictures from the Old and New Testaments to be placed in it " for the instruction of the simple," and translated into Chinese the New Testament and the psalter, "and I keep it and read it and preach with it open in front of me, as if in testimony of the Law of Christ." He had also arranged with the local potentate to have the divine office translated, so that it might be sung everywhere throughout his lands in Chinese ; and he said mass in his presence in Chinese, according to the Latin rite. (The Jesuits were given papal permission to say mass in Chinese as lately as the seventeenth century.) The Pope, to whom the letter was sent, commended John's labours, without referring to the translation, and made him archbishop of Peking. There is nothing in the account to indicate that the translation was circulated to lay people, or even the children trained as clerks in the school. See *Jour. of the Royal Asiatic Soc.*, 1914, pp. 533–599.

p. 69, n. 4. *For* the date of Grosseteste's death, *read* " 1253."

p. 91, l. 26 and *passim*. *Doctrine*. From S. Augustine's use of *doctrina* in this tract, the word would be better translated "learning" or "scholarship."

p. 123, l. 19. Walther was probably wrong in attributing this significance to the absence of printers' names : in the four early editions the absence of name is not abnormal, while that of 1485 was a Strassburg book, where such absence of name continued late.

p. 123, n. 3. Though this Bible is without printer's name, it is in Mentel's types.

p. 125, l. 36. No German Bibles were printed in the town of Mainz itself : but the edict of 1486 apparently succeeded in restricting their publication in other towns in the archbishopric, to which it certainly applied. Between 1466 and 1486 there were 10 High German editions in the archbishopric, or one in two years; between 1486 and 1522 there were 4, or one in nine years, although printed books of other kinds were more frequent in the later than the earlier period.

p. 133, l. 13. *For Ecclesiastical History*[4] *read* "letter of his disciple Cuthbert[4]."

p. 135, n. 2. *For* "RHT, vii." *read* "RHT, xvii."

p. 136. Aelfric seems to have been the scribe only, not the author.

p. 138, l. 8. *For* "monastery" *read* "monks or canons." The word "minstre" occurs in the A.S. account of Leofric's bequest, but has several meanings in A.S. of this period, and should not, probably, in this case be translated "monastery."

p. 140, ll. 1–13. Dr Henry Bradley informs me that the extant south-east midland Genesis and Exodus were of literary, not popular, origin, and quite unconnected with Caedmon. The poem on Adam and Eve is also of literary origin. See Wells 318; review in *Scottish Hist. Rev.*, Oct., 1920.

p. 141, n. 2. This sermon of Grosseteste's, sometimes called the *De Cura Pastorali*, is extant in various MSS.; Bodley, 36, 801, etc.

p. 142, n. 4. See J. C. Fox on this *Earliest French Apocalypse* in the MLR, vii. 445. The passages about preaching there cited as suggesting a Dominican authorship appear to be all taken from the common and interlinear glosses. Gilbert de la Porrée's Latin comment is not now extant: but Hugh of St Cher, who wrote his *Postillae* on the Apocalypse at about the same date as the author of the Anglo-Norman Apocalypse, attributed one to him. (*Postillae*, 1600, Venice ed., vii. 364.)

p. 143, l. 10. Mr J. C. Fox kindly informs me that he has compared these inscriptions from Berkeley chapel (for which see *Bristol and Gloucs. Archaeol. Soc.*, 1876, 138–46) with the prose Apocalypse, and finds that this is their source.

p. 143, l. 11. See Mr J. C. Fox's article on the rhymed Apocalypse in MLR, viii. 338.

p. 152, n. 2. Mainz, vi. "534–401" to "334–401."

p. 164, n. 2. These are references to books possessed by friary libraries: the only complete friary library catalogue which has been so far discovered is that of the Austin friars of York.

p. 173, l. 24. William Giffard, "chaplain of the church of S. Edward," may have written his French rhymed Apocalypse for the nuns of Shaftesbury. See MLR, viii. 349 for his high birth and noble connexions.

p. 174, l. 2. The *Consuetudines Cluniacenses* give full directions for the reading of the whole Bible *in ecclesia* and *in refectorio*: see Mr Little's valuable review in EHR, Jan. 1921, p. 124.

p. 174, l. 27. *For* "fifty" *read* "five hundred, according to tradition."

p. 177, l. 4. *For* "1291" *read* "1254."

p. 178, ll. 16–17. Lecturing on the *Sentences* was the duty of a B.D. The statement should imply only that Aureoli became bachelor of theology in 1316.

p. 183, l. 1. *For* "possessed a copy of" *read* "is once credited with the authorship of."

p. 185, l. 24. *For* "Chandos" *read* "de Wyche."

p. 185, l. 25. *For* "1299" *read* "1280," when Nicholas died.

p. 186, n. 2. For these entailed Vulgates, see Mr Little in EHR, Jan. 1921, p. 124.

p. 187, l. 12. It is unknown whether the English Dominicans were bound by their constitutions to direct Dominican nuns: but it is known that there was only one such house of nuns (at Dartford).

p. 204, l. 2. William Giffard, "chaplain of the church of S. Edward," who turned the Anglo-Norman prose Apocalypse into rhyme, belonged to a noble and prominent family: see *supra*, note on p. 173.

p. 207, n. 1. *For* "authoress's" *read* "anchoress's."

pp. 213–14, quotation: transpose "endauntës" and "enchauntës."

p. 221. French Bible owners: add John, earl of Warrenne, +1347. "I leave to sir William of Warrenne my son, my Bible which I have had made in French, and after his death let it stay in the house where he will be prior, in perpetual memory of me." TE, i. 43.

p. 235, l. 15. *For* Holborn, see *infra*, p. 287.

p. 238, l. 12. *For* "John xxii." *read* "John xxiii."

p. 251, l. 3. *For* "that of Wycliffe" *read* "the Wycliffite."

p. 253, l. 9. *For* "midland" *read* "northern or midland"; see review in *Scottish Hist. Rev.*, Oct. 1920.

p. 268, l. 8. *For* "only lecturers" *read* "chief lecturers."

p. 283, l. 10. *For* "monk" *read* "Dominican."

p. 287, l. 14. Palmer belonged to the London Dominicans: but the latter had sold their Holborn (Lincoln's Inn) site in 1286.

p. 291, l. 22. Peter Payne was M.A., not regent master of theology, in 1406.

p. 330, n. 1. In 1414 Thomas Langley, bishop of Durham, wishing to endow the no doubt previously existing grammar school of Durham cathedral, founded two chantries, whose chaplains were to give instruction in grammar and song, freely to the poor, and to the rest, for fees. Of the two chaplains first appointed, one was an M.A., one not. This foundation, however, should perhaps be distinguished from such private chantries as founded new centres of instruction. See VCH, *Durham*, i. 371. The great majority of the chantry priests of Oxfordshire are described as "well learned."

p. 365, l. 13. For mention of English Bible-reading at Lollard trials of the period, see the striking evidence, c. 1472, in the recently published Hereford register (CYS): cf. *Reg. Stanbury*, iv. 118–128.

p. 369, l. 10. *For* "bishop of Hereford" *read* "the martyrologist."

p. 371, l. 3. *For* 1609 *read* 1611.

p. 380, l. 19. *For* "Purvey in prison" *read* "Purvey's haereticum libellum." There is much uncertainty about the date of Lavenham's death. Leland, in *Commentarii de Scriptoribus Britannicis*, 1709, ii. 399, places it in 1383 at Winchester: but his original MS. (*Top. Gen.* c. 4, p. 284, in the Bodleian) shews that he was in some doubt, from using two conflicting sources: and suggests that the source which Leland preferred, placing the death at Winchester, had no date of death. For other reasons it appears likely that Lavenham lived as late as 1391 (the date of S. Bridget's first canonization), or that there was another Richard Lavenham, who was confused with him.

p. 384, l. 17, "1783" *for* "1793."

p. 384, l. 31, "Malou" *for* "Malon."

p. 392 (3) *Testamenta Eboracensia*. Add one French Bible, and in totals on pp. 397, 398.

p. 403, l. 19. *For* "modum" *read* "medium."

p. 408, l. 20. *For* "iter" *read* "iterum."

p. 409, l. 13. Emend: [rationabiliter] malitiarum [refrenatio].

p. 411, l. 15. Emend: sententiam priorem [de] capite... [addat] ad.

p. 411, l. 16. Emend: [secundam] sententiam.

p. 411, l. 17. Emend: de capite [dici].

p. 411, l. 29. *For* "portenda" *read* "portanda."

p. 417, ll. 32-3 "pincernae:" a pun on Butler's own name.

p. 420, l. 9. *For* "praevaricandum?" *read* "peccandum?"

p. 424, l. 21. Emend, for Urri [viri].

p. 427, l. 23. Emend: quod [propter] Graecarum.

p. 434, l. 25. "Verum" should not agree with "meritum," but begin the next sentence.

p. 442, n. 3. See *supra*, p. 141, n. 2.

M. DEANESLY

*October* 1921

# CHAPTER I

## *The problem of the Middle-English Bible, and the aim of this monograph.*

§ 1. When sir Thomas More wrote in his *Dialogue*[1] that he himself had seen English Bibles, fair and old, in the houses of his friends, and that such Bibles had been licensed for their use by the bishops, he was unwittingly preparing the ground for a later controversy: that of the origin and history of the translations long and justly known as the Wycliffite Bible. Several points have been raised by his words: Were these translations the work of Wycliffe and his immediate followers? Or were they, as has been suggested, the authorised versions of orthodox catholics, made before Wycliffe's time[2]? Was the reading of all English Bibles viewed with suspicion and disapproval by the Church, or did her disapproval extend only to translations savouring of heresy? What, in short, is the history of Bible reading by the laity in England, and what place do these translations known as the Wycliffite Bible take in it? The questions are of more than antiquarian interest: they are part of the history of vernacular translations of the Bible in Europe.

§ 2. This larger subject was most closely linked in the middle ages with those of the liberty of private judgment, and the unity of Christendom. The liberty of the individual to interpret Christianity afresh for himself, from the study of her original records, and to interpret it, if he liked, in a manner different from that of the united body of instructed opinion, had not yet been conceded. This liberty to reinterpret Christianity, to form fresh Christian bodies or sects, depended altogether on the right to study the original records, and to make them accessible in translations to the unlettered masses whose conversion was wished.

---

[1] *Workes of Sir Thomas More*, London, 1557, *A Dialogue concerning heresies*, ff. 105–288. The *Dialogue* is a controversial work directed against Tindale.

[2] The view put forward by cardinal Gasquet in *The Old English Bible and other Essays*, London, 1897 and 1908; see appendix 1, p. 382.

It is scarcely doubtful that the unity of Christendom was preserved till the sixteenth century only by force. Had lay people
in the thirteenth century been allowed the right to read the
gospels for themselves, or exposed to the temptation to do so,
and had they generally been able to read, reinterpretation
would inevitably have followed, and Christendom would have
been divided in that century instead of the sixteenth[1]. It has
been maintained that it was the scarcity of books before the
invention of printing, and not the discouragement of the Church,
which actually prevented lay Bible reading, and its result, reinterpretation: but the history of such bodies as the Waldensians
makes this doubtful. They obviated the lack of books by
memorising the gospels; and, but for their suppression by the
inquisition, and their exclusion from all orthodox universities
and schools, they would have formed permanent bodies outside
the Church. The question of the unity of Christendom depended
on the possibility of the reinterpretation of Christianity, and
this depended on the accessibility of the original Christian records to the masses. It was only to these books that a sectarian
teacher could appeal against the traditional teaching of the
Church. He might be able to read the Vulgate himself: his
hearers could not: therefore he prepared, and appealed to, translations in their mother tongue. It is thus true to say that the
history of vernacular translations, and the attitude of the
Church towards them, is not a matter of merely antiquarian
interest, but the central strand in the history of the unity of
Christendom.

§ 3. The old fashioned tradition on the subject of the Wycliffite
Bible was that it was the work of Wycliffe himself, and that the
ecclesiastical authorities forbade the use of all English translations before the Reformation. Modern study has modified this
view: but that which has most confused the issue has been the
opinion of sir Thomas More. More's *Dialogue*, the work in which
he discussed the subject of English Bibles, is still accessible only
in a sixteenth century edition; but certain passages from it have
been largely quoted, though never the whole chapter dealing
with the subject. The first English edition of the New Testament, Tindale's, was printed at Cologne and Worms in 1525,

[1] Cf. *Univs.* I. 71 n.

and introduced into England in 1526: Tindale's controversial
works were being introduced at the same time. More, as the
councillor and chancellor of Henry VIII, wrote his *Dialogue* in
1528 to refute the new teaching on the subject of images,
prayer to the saints, "and many other things, by the t'one
begun in Saxony, and by the t'other laboured to be brought into
England[1]." The "many other things" included the subject of
biblical translations, and the withholding of the scriptures from
the laity, to which he devoted the sixteenth chapter of the third
book. He referred here to the provincial council of Oxford,
1408, wherein archbishop Arundel had forbidden the making of
a translation of the text of holy scripture, or the reading of any
such translation, made in the time of John Wycliffe, or since[2].
In connexion with this, More touched upon the subject of

---

[1] Sub-title of *Dialogue*, p. 105, *Workes of Sir Thomas More*, 1557.

[2] Wilkins, III. 317. "*Ne quis texta S. Scripturae transferat in linguam
Anglicanam*. Statuimus igitur atque ordinamus, ut nemo deinceps aliquem
textum sacrae scripturae auctoritate sua in linguam Anglicanam vel aliam
transferat, per viam libri, libelli aut tractatus, nec legatur aliquis huiusmodi
liber, libellus aut tractatus jam noviter tempore dicti Johannis Wycliffe,
sive citra compositus, sive in posterum componendus, in parte vel in toto,
publice vel occulte." Cardinal Gasquet's assertion that "aliquem textum"
"can only mean 'any passage'" (1897 ed. p. 169), is contrary to historical
evidence. The word *textus* is used very commonly

(1) for a liturgical gospel book, cf. the "textus of S. Dunstan," *Som. Med.
Lib.* 89; Britwold's textus, *id.* 49; one of 1122, *id.* 39; and those referred to
page 185, n. 3;

(2) less frequently for a particular biblical verse, *Dialogue*, III. "to lay and
confer one text with another"; *Myroure*, 71;

(3) frequently, as here, for the substance or version of a particular book:
the "texts" of the Vulgate at the date offered great variety, and a translator
might well be in doubt which to use as the basis of his version. The word
is used in this sense of the Lollard versions in Trevenant, *Reg.* 148, in a letter
of 1397: "neque libros Anglicos secundum nudum textum de sacra scriptura
sinistre extractos"; by Lyndwood in his gloss on the passage: "Although it
be the plain text of sacred scripture that is so translated." Gundulph, bishop
of Rochester, wrote out "the text of the Vulgate," *Bibliom.* 60; Gerson complained, c. 1415, of those who thought "holy scripture should be believed in
its bare text without any interpretation"; "appeal to the bare text of scripture," see pp. 104–6; Matthias of Janov, c. 1390, spoke of "the study of the
text of the most holy Bible," see p. 91; a Dutch gospel-harmonist, 1350–1400,
"I made one fair history out of the texts of the four gospels," see p. 115 n.; the
Oxford synod of 1408 forbade grammar masters to go beyond "explaining
the text grammatically," see p. 295. The prohibition of "aliquem textum s.
scripturae" simply made it clear to contemporaries that no one was to
translate the Bible, or its books, from any Latin or French version; the
translation of Bible stories in the narrator's own words was not, on the other
hand, covered by Arundel's prohibition.

Wycliffe's Bible, and the attitude of the Church towards translations in his day: but we cannot properly estimate More's evidence
unless we realise that the matter with which he was vitally
concerned, and about which he was really well informed, was
Tindale's translation, and not Wycliffe's.

The character of the Messenger, More's interlocutor in the
*Dialogue*, is that of a promising young student, inclined towards
the ideas of the New Learning, and ready to agree with the
plausible arguments of the man in the street. He professes to
set forth the murmurings of reasonable men of small understanding, who are attracted by some of the new teaching, or, at
least, consider heretics are in some points hardly dealt with.
The value of the Messenger's arguments is that More himself
states them, as representing the attitude of many of the
orthodox and ignorant at the time of the burning of Tindale's
New Testament in 1526: and, as such, they agree with the
teaching and knowledge of such an orthodox teacher as Roger
Edgeworth[1], in Mary's reign. The man in the street thinks the
Bible ought to be accessible in English: so do the Messenger,
Edgeworth, and, to some extent, More. The man in the
street knows of no existent manuscript English Bible except
Wycliffe's: neither do the Messenger nor yet Edgeworth: but
the scholar and nobleman, More, has seen English Bibles in
the houses of the great, which, since they are orthodox,
cannot, he thinks, be Wycliffe's. The man in the street
believes that the clergy keep the scriptures from the laity: so
do Edgeworth and the Messenger: but sir Thomas More is
scholar enough to be able to quote the provincial council of
Oxford, and Lyndwood, in support of his contention that
they do not do so altogether.

The description of the Messenger's personal attitude to the
scriptures is interesting. Some men believe, he says, that
Tindale's New Testament was burnt at Paul's Cross, not be-

---

[1] Cf. *Eve of Reformation*, Gasquet, F. A., London, 1890, 245. Roger Edgeworth knew of no existent orthodox English translation: "I have ever borne
in mind, that I thought it no harm, but rather good and profitable, that holy
scripture should be had in the mother tongue, and withheld from no man
that was apt and meet to take it in hand, specially if we could get it well
and truly translated, which will be very hard to be had." *Sermons*, London,
Caly, 1557, f. 31.

cause of the faults declared to be found in it, but to disguise the
fact that none such were found[1]:

And that, for none other intent but for to keep out of the people's
hands all knowledge of Christ's gospel, and of God's law, except so
much only as the clergy themselves list now and then to tell us. And
that, little as it is, and seldom shewed, yet as it is feared, not well
and truly told, but watered with false glosses, and altered from the
truth of the very words and sentence of scripture, only for the maintenance of their authority. And for the fear lest this thing should
evidently appear to the people, if they were suffered to read the
scripture themselves in their own tongue, was, (as it is thought), the
very cause, not only for which the New Testament translated by
Tindale was burned, but also that the clergy of this realm hath
before this time by a constitution provincial prohibited any book
of scripture to be translated into the English tongue, fearing men
with fire as heretics who should so presume to keep them, as though
it were heresy for a Christian man to read Christ's gospel. And
surely sir, quoth he, some folk that think this dealing of the clergy
to be thus, and good men to be mishandled for declaring the truth,
and the scripture' self to be pulled out of the people's hands[2], lest they
should perceive the truth, be led in their minds to doubt whether
Luther himself, (of whose opinions, or at the least of whose works,
all this business began), wrote indeed so evil as he is borne in hand.

After this prologue, More devotes three chapters to the instruction of the Messenger on the subject of biblical translations,
the first to explaining the enactment of the council of Oxford in
1408, the others to shewing that the laity might use such translations under certain restrictions[3]. There was no constitution,
said More, which positively forbade the people to have any
scripture translated into our tongue:

For ye shall understand that the great arch heretic, Wycliffe,
whereas the whole Bible was long before his days by virtuous and
well learned men translated into the English tongue, and by good
and godly people with devotion and soberness well and reverently
read, took upon of a malicious purpose to translate it of new[4]. In

---

[1] More, *Dialogue*, 109.
[2] Erasmus supported this view of the Messenger, see pp. 384–7, and it is
justified also by the wording of the episcopal injunctions of 1538, see
pp. 348–9.
[3] *Dialogue*, lib. III. cc. 11, 14, 15, 16; pp. 224–6, 233–47.
[4] This sentence, with the words "long before his day," is quite consistent
with a reference to the Anglo-Saxon gospels, etc., which had become so out-
worn in language, that Wycliffe, "translated it of new." The next sentence
is typical of More's description of Wycliffe's text, as he imagined it, from the
analogy of Tindale's.

which translation he purposely corrupted the holy text, maliciously planting therein such words, as might in the readers' ears serve to the proof of such heresies as he went about to sow: which he not only set forth with his own translation of the Bible, but also with certain prologues and glosses which he made thereon....After that it was perceived what harm the people took by the translation, prologues and glosses of Wycliffe's, and also of some other, that after him holp to set forth his sect: then for that cause, and forasmuch as it is dangerous to translate the text of scripture out of one tongue into another[1], as holy S. Jerome testifieth, forasmuch as in translation it is hard alway to keep the same sentence whole: it was, I say, for these causes at a council holden at Oxford, provided upon great pain, that no man should from thenceforth translate into the English tongue, or any other language, of his own authority, by way of book, libel, or treatise: nor no man openly or secretly any such book, libel or treatise read, newly made in the time of the said John Wycliffe: or that should be made any time after, till the said translation were by the diocesan, or if need should require, by a provincial council approved....For I trow that in this law ye see nothing unreasonable. For it neither forbiddeth the translations to be read that were already well done of old before Wycliffe's days, nor damneth his because it was new, but because it was naught: nor prohibiteth new to be made, but provideth that they shall not be read if they be mismade, till they be by good examination amended, except they be such translations as Wycliffe made and Tindale, that the malicious mind of the translator had in such wise handled, it were as it were labour lost to go about to mend them.

To this the Messenger replies:

"I long by my troth," quoth he, "and even sit on thorns, till I see that constitution. For not myself only, but every man else hath ever taken it for otherwise....I suppose," quoth he, "that this opinion is rather grown another way, that is to wit, that the clergy, though the law serve them not therefore, do yet in deed take all translations out of every lay man's hand. And sometime, with those that be burned or convicted of heresy, they burn the English Bible without respect, be the translation old or new, bad or good."

"Forsooth," quoth I, "if this were so, then were it, in my mind, not well done. But I believe ye mistake it. Howbeit, what ye have seen I cannot say; but myself have seen, and can shew you, Bibles fair and old written in English, which have been known and seen by the bishop of the diocese[2], and left in laymen's hands, and

[1] From this point, More is quoting from the constitutions of Oxford, 1408.
[2] More had no doubt seen English biblical translations in noblemen's libraries, or perhaps those of nunneries. He was closely in touch with the London Carthusians, for between 1499 and 1503 he had attended their daily offices and shared their ascetic practices, while undecided as to his vocation:

women's[1], to such as he knew for good and catholic folk.  But of truth, all such as are found in the hands of heretics, they use to take away[2]."

In the next chapter, More explains that translations were allowed from the earliest days of the Church, and that he for his part would favour their being allowed now, under proper supervision.

he had probably seen the English Bible of the Sheen Charterhouse (a later version, without heretical prologues or glosses, see FM I. xlvii).  He was also the special friend of at least one Brigittine monk of Sion, Richard Whitford, and Sion was presented in 1517 with an early version of the Wycliffite Bible, also perfectly orthodox.  Whether More inferred from the constitutions of 1408 that the Bibles he had seen had been licensed by the bishop for individual use, or whether he actually knew this to have been the case, is doubtful: episcopal licenses may have been verbal: and no English written ones have survived. (For remains of a note that an English Bible had been "overseen and read" for a woman by two doctors, see p. 336.)  The earliest surviving written license to use a vernacular Bible of which I am aware (apart from that in the *Myroure*, see p. 339), is that of the Spanish archbishop and inquisitor general Tavera to the duchess of Soma, c. 1539, allowing her to use an Italian Bible for a year only; printed *Span. Inq.* III. 575.

[1] *Dial.* 233-4.  For More's next account of the burning of Richard Hun's Bible, not because it was in English, but because it contained a prologue of great and manifest heresy, see p. 14, n. 3.  Cardinal Gasquet's assertion (1897 ed. p. 129) that "in the edition of Wycliffite scriptures published by Forshall and Madden we shall look in vain for any trace of these errors," has been shewn to be unfounded by the reviewer in the *Church Quarterly Review*, Jan. 1901, pp. 265-298, and a very slight examination of the *General Prologue* to the O. Test. confirms this.  Cardinal Gasquet notices (*id.* 117) that "there is no room for doubting" that this prologue and the translation are the work of the same hand.

[2] That the licensed reading of English Bibles could not have been general, even among the upper classes, is indicated by Cranmer, in his preface to the second (1540, Richard Grafton) edition of the Great Bible.  Though anxious to commend the book, and to shew that the reading of English Bibles was not unlawful, he does not mention any custom of English Bible reading for the last hundred years, but divides English thinkers on the question into: those who opposed it and those who misused it.  It would have been natural for him to mention that some few pious folk had used the English Bible profitably within the last hundred years, had they been numerous, for he was in want of precedents.  He wrote that the English Bible "may be both the better accepted of them which hitherto could not well bear it, and also the better used of them which heretofore have misused it.... In the former sort be all they that refuse to read, or to hear read, the scripture in the vulgar tongues: much worse, they also let or discourage the other from the reading or hearing thereof.  Such is the nature of custom... and therefore I can well think them worthy pardon, which at the coming abroad of scripture doubted and drew back.... And yet if the matter should be tried by custom, we might also allege custom for the reading of scripture in the vulgar tongue, and prescribe the more ancient custom.  For it is not much above one hundred years ago," etc. (See continuation, p. 12, n.)

Methinketh that the constitution provincial of which we spake right now, hath determined this question already. For when the clergy therein agreed that the English Bibles should remain, which were translated afore Wycliffe's days, they consequently did agree that to have the Bible in English was no hurt.

These passages have been quoted to shew More's view on the subject of pre-Wycliffite versions, and the existence of English Bibles in his own day by the license of the bishop. But he does not deny that men commonly took the constitution of 1408 as prohibiting the use of translations in general, and that, though he himself has seen English Bibles, they are nevertheless not common.

"Sir," quoth the Messenger, "yet for all this I can see no cause why the clergy should keep the Bible out of laymen's hands, that can no more but their mother tongue."

"I had weened," quoth I, "that I had shewed you plainly, that they keep it not from them...."

"Ye say well," quoth he, "but yet, as women say, somewhat it was alway that the cat winked when her eye was out. Surely it is not for nought that the English Bible is in so few men's hands, when so many would so fain have it[1]."

More agrees that this is true; but the authorities fear that it is chiefly the heretics who wish to have it. Yet it strikes him as curious that, though the constitutions of 1408 did not forbid the making of translations, no catholic scholar had ever ventured to make one.

"And surely how it hath happed, that in all this while God hath either not suffered, or not provided, that any good virtuous man hath had the mind in faithful wise to translate it, and thereupon either the clergy, or at the least wise, some one bishop to approve it: this can I nothing tell."

"I am sure," quoth the Messenger, "ye doubt not but that I am full

---

[1] *Dial.* 241. Cf. Erasmus' assertion, p. 387, that many theologians even in Germany, where opinion was far more liberal towards vernacular Bibles than in England, denied the right of the laity to read the Bible. Erasmus recommends that lay people should be warned to use it with reverence and humility: "but as to those people who simply banish the divine books from the hands of lay people, I know not by what spirit they are led. Their decision is contrary to the example of Christ and the Apostles. The greatest doctors of the Church advise that course from which they would deter us; and reckon that most praiseworthy which they execrate as impious." *Opera*, 1706, v. 729.

and whole of your mind in this matter, that the Bible should be in our English tongue. But yet that the clergy is of the contrary, and would not have it so, that appeareth well, in that they suffer it not to be so[1]."

Enough has perhaps been quoted to shew that sir Thomas More gives, in his *Dialogue*, evidence of two kinds, both equally valuable. In the first place, he states the belief of his unenlightened contemporaries: in the second, he gives his own expert opinion. In the first place, the Messenger's views are his own picture of the belief of a young and intelligent lay scholar of his day,—certainly not those of a man who counted himself a Lutheran; he represents the "man in the street" in that he has not, like More, inquired into the authority of his belief about the prohibition of translations, but simply shares it with the mass of his contemporaries. More states then that, rightly or wrongly, it was about 1528 generally believed that the council of Oxford had forbidden the making or using of translations of the Bible, and that the clergy would not suffer such translations to be in lay people's hands.

Secondly, More gives his own views on the desirability and history of English translations,—those of a devout and instructed catholic, an eminent lawyer defending his case, and a fervent admirer of the New Learning. They are the views of the friend of Erasmus[2], of one of the most liberal and brilliant scholars of the day: and it would be rash to assume that they coincided at all points with those of the representative politician or bishop of the time, let alone the representative parish priest. More's personal evidence can, now, be analysed from these three points of view, for which it has very differing values. It is that of a lawyer who has looked up his authorities: of a most liberal but strictly orthodox scholar: and of a historian. The three questions, what is the value of More's statements as a lawyer, as a liberal catholic, and as a historian, must be answered separately, or much confusion will arise.

As to law, More was undoubtedly right. The only authorities he studied were the constitutions of Oxford, and Lyndwood's comments thereon: but his conclusion was sound. He did not quote the *Decretals* of Gregory IX on the subject of biblical

[1] *Id.* 241.        [2] See p. 11.

translations[1], as he might perhaps have been expected to do: but thought it sufficient to quote rightly the English constitution which was the subject of such general misunderstanding and comment.

His views as a devout catholic and humanist scholar are also valuable: but they are, in all probability, more liberal than those of the average churchman of his day; and they were much less liberal than they are sometimes represented. To a scholar like More, imbued with the Renaissance reverence for original authorities and first principles, it was impossible to overlook the practice of the Church of the first nine centuries with regard to biblical translations. The gospels were written in the vulgar tongue: S. Jerome had translated them into the vulgar tongue of his day: therefore to More it was just as desirable now that

---

[1] For the letter of Innocent III to the archbishop of Metz, partly embodied therein, see pp. 31–2. The original letter was distinctly hostile to translations, and interpreted in that sense by the pope's legates: but the portion in the *Decretal*, *Cum ex injuncto*, dealt mainly with conventicles and lay preaching, and as such received the attention of commentators. The *Cum ex injuncto* and the commentators' glosses were well known to inquisitors, but they interpreted "lay preaching" as including the recitation of vernacular translations of the Bible, and the possession of such translations as giving rise to lay preaching. (For the commentators, and Eymeric's *Directorium Inquisitorum* see p. 34.) The Dutch lawyers of Cologne, 1398, were the first to argue that the *Cum ex injuncto* was in reality favourable to translations of the simpler parts of the Bible. I have not found any manual for inquisitors mentioning the whole letter to Metz, as distinguished from the *Cum ex injuncto* (Pegna, the 1607 editor of the *Direct. Inq.* mentions it, p. 100), but the inquisitors had no need to do so, for they were usually granted all the powers granted to the inquisition at Toulouse, 1229, which included that of suppressing translations. More may have considered the *Cum ex injuncto* not to the point, and either been unaware of the hostile decisions of provincial councils, or disregarded them. Erasmus who supported the popularisation of the scriptures much more ardently than More, had evidently had some "canonical" prohibition objected to him by his opponents, probably this letter of Innocent III. He replied to the monk who denied the lawfulness of biblical translations: "Moreover, if any constitution of our forefathers that the common people ought not to have the sacred books, was issued, that ought to be adjudged a remedy given for reasons of time and place. For my part, this is not clear to me: and yet nevertheless, it may have occurred that such a constitution was issued, directed against the arrogance of certain unlettered people. It is certainly clear that it has not been confirmed by public custom. For of late the common people have the sacred books translated into the vulgar tongue, and read them openly" (*Erasmi Opera*, Leyden, 1706, IX. 785). Erasmus wrote ten years after the publication of Luther's N. Test., and even before that time vernacular gospel books, etc. had been more plentiful in Germany than elsewhere in Europe. More was most closely in touch with Erasmus before the subject of vernacular Bibles had become a burning question.

the devout should be able to read in their mother tongue such portions of the Bible as their simplicity could comprehend. The scheme by which he proposed to accomplish this end can be examined later in his *Dialogue*; though it was that of one of the most liberal churchmen of his day, its limits were very narrow. More did not propose that, in practice, more than the devout of the upper classes should have English Bibles. Could not the bishop, he said, give an English Bible, or such part of it as he might see fit, to those of the faithful in his diocese whom he personally knew to be fit to profit by it? The books should be returned at death to the bishop, who would thus have a personal knowledge of those who used them. In practice, this scheme could hardly have been democratic.

More had been the friend of Erasmus since 1498, and cannot fail to have been influenced by his views as to the desirability of popularising knowledge of the scriptures: and yet their attitude to the question is widely different. More wished for a regularisation of the old scheme of a diocesan license for each reader of an English Bible, though he wished the bishop to present the Bible at his own expense[1] to the reader during his life-time. The desire of Erasmus was for the accessibility of the scriptures to all, and in the references to the subject among his different works, there is no question of an episcopal license, or even that of the confessor, though "they do well who warn the common people that they should make use of the sacred volumes with religious fear, and not trust rashly to their own judgment[2]." More wrote his *Dialogue* in 1528: and in 1529 a translation of a work of Erasmus called the *Exhortation to the diligent study of scripture* was brought into England, where the wishes expressed for the general knowledge of the Bible were different from More's.

I would to God that the ploughman would sing a text of the scripture at his plough-beam; and that the weaver at his loom with this would drive away the tediousness of time. I would the wayfaring man with this pastime would expel the weariness of his journey. And to be short, I would that all the communication of the Christian should be of the scripture; for in a manner, such are we ourselves, as our daily tales are[3].

[1] *Dial.* 245.         [2] *Erasmi Opera*, 1706, Leyden, v. 729.
[3] For the continuation of this and other extracts from Erasmus' works in defence of translations, and for the 1527 condemnation of them at Paris, see appendix, pp. 384–7.

The very year before More published his *Dialogue*, the theological faculty at Paris had condemned a catena of the propositions of Erasmus, where he defended the general use of biblical translations, and the views of More in the *Dialogue* are much more in accordance with the censure, than with Erasmus' propositions. More wished to perpetuate the mediaeval system of infrequent and licensed Bible reading by the upper classes: Erasmus wished, like the Waldensians and the Lollards, that men of all classes, husbandmen, smiths, weavers, plough boys, and even women, should be free to find in vernacular Bibles "the quick and living image of His most holy mind, yea, and Christ Himself, healing, dying, rising again."

More's authority as a historian is less than his authority as a lawyer, and much less than his authority as a saint, with which it is sometimes confused. He had only the linguistic and historical equipment of his contemporaries: much too little linguistic or historical knowledge to be able to assign an old English manuscript to a particular century. His only authority for his statements about the Wycliffite Bible is, quite clearly, the constitutions of 1408: he adds to that his own inferences therefrom, and a perfectly natural, but inaccurate guess, that the text of the actual Wycliffite Bible must have been heretical. It is quite easy to reconstruct the process by which More arrived at his conclusions about old English Bibles. It was patent to him, to start with, that there was nothing wrong in biblical translations themselves[1], since, for instance, that of S. Jerome was in universal use. He found next that the constitutions of Oxford did not forbid translations as such, but mentioned the existence of pre-Wycliffite ones[2]. More had no historical knowledge to tell

---

[1] This was far from being patent to many mediaeval minds: as for instance to the two very learned Dominican and Franciscan friars who contended for the opposite view in Henry IV's reign; see pp. 401–37; 297 n.

[2] The following criticism of More's belief applies also to Cranmer's, who said in the preface to the 1540 edition of the English Bible (see p. 7, n. 2), "It is not much above one hundred years ago since Scripture hath not been accustomed to be read in the vulgar tongue within this realm, and many hundred years before that it was translated and read in the Saxon tongue, which at that time was our mother's tongue: whereof there remaineth yet divers copies found lately in old abbeys, of such antique manners of writing and speaking that few men now been able to read and understand them. And when this language waxed old and out of common use, because folk

him that those responsible for the constitutions had in mind, in all probability, Bede's translation of S. John's gospel, with which they were acquainted through Higden; or principally, existence of unreadable manuscripts of Anglo-Saxon gospels; or finally, that already fairly widely known book, Richard Rolle's English psalter[1]. There were actually in existence in 1408 a few solitary manuscripts of partial translations of the New Testament made in Wycliffe's day, and quite possibly by orthodox catholics: but it would be very rash, and contrary to probability, to assume that those who drew up the constitutions of 1408 had a modern specialist's knowledge of these sparse manuscripts[2]: or that they knew even vaguely that contemporary translations existed which were not due to the Wycliffite school. Had they known of them, they would most certainly have required their submission for episcopal approbation, as they did of any future translations. But it was perfectly natural for More (who had no means of knowing what early fourteenth century translations actually existed), to think that English translations did exist in

should not lack the fruit of reading, it was again translated in the newer language. Whereof yet many copies remain and be daily found." Cranmer's authority here was almost certainly, like More's, the constitution of 1408. Gairdner, *Loll.* I. 104, emphasises the point that "Cranmer does not even hint that the newer translations were due to Wycliffe." Cranmer was no more likely than sir Thomas More to know to whom the translations were due: had he suspected them to be due to any particular orthodox translator, he would certainly have said so, for his preface aimed at proving the lawfulness of the use of vernacular scriptures. If he had any suspicion that the English fifteenth century versions were connected with Wycliffe, he would certainly not have mentioned the suspicion in such a preface: but there is no need to suppose that he had. It is noticeable, however, in this connexion, that sixteenth century apologists who were anxious to give all the examples of earlier translations by orthodox writers, or those used by the orthodox, never quote anything later than Hampole's psalter (written before 1349, popular by c. 1370). J. Foxe wished to give a historical example of an early translation: but what he chose to print was *The Gospels of the fower Evangelistes, translated in the olde Saxons' time out of Latin into the vulgar toung of the Saxons*, London, 1571.

[1] Ed. Bramley, H. R., Oxford, 1884.

[2] For partial biblical translations contemporary with the Wycliffite versions, see chapter XII, p. 299. There are two main points to notice about such translations: first, they are not clearly earlier than the Wycliffite, but broadly speaking, contemporary. Secondly, they were unknown, compared to the Wycliffite versions: one or two MSS. only survive of each, as against the 170 MSS. of the Wycliffite versions mentioned by Forshall and Madden (*The Holy Bible: made from the Latin Vulgate by John Wycliffe and his Followers*, Oxford, 1850), in addition to which others are now known.

the age preceding Wycliffe: and perfectly natural for him to draw the inference that the English Bibles he had himself seen were the descendants of such orthodox versions. These Bibles were in the hands of the orthodox, and were therefore, he argued, free from heresy. Since Wycliffe's Bible had been condemned, doubtless it was because its text, like Tindale's, was heretical: it could not therefore have been the parent of the Bibles he had seen: the originals of these must have been the pre-Wycliffite translations implied in the constitutions of 1408. This seemed certain to him, because, curious as the fact might be, no translations had been approved by the bishops since[1]; and he could not conceive the possibility of an episcopal license to read a Wycliffite version.

The preoccupation of his mind with Tindale's New Testament explains this unquestioning assumption. He had, earlier in the *Dialogue*, commented on Tindale's controversial translations of parts of the scriptures[2]. More certainly stated that the heresy in the only Wycliffite Bible he had himself examined, Richard Hun's Bible, was in the prologue[3]: and that the Wycliffites wrote heretical prologues and glosses[4] to their text: but it did not strike him that there might have been perhaps nothing to quarrel

[1] See p. 319.

[2] "For first he would make the people believe that we should believe nothing but plain scripture, in which point he teacheth a plain pestilent heresy. And then would he with his false translation make the people ween further that such articles of our faith as he laboureth to destroy, and which be well proved by holy scripture, were in holy scripture nothing spoken of, but that the preachers have all this fifteen hundred year misreported the gospel, and Englished the scripture wrong, to lead the people purposely out of the right way." *Dialogue*, 223.

[3] More was present at the examination of Richard Hun in the Tower in 1514. He says in the *Dialogue*, 240, "For surely at such time as he was denounced for an heretic, there lay his English Bible open, and some other English books of his, that every man might see the places noted with his own hand, such words and in such wise, that there would no wise man, that good were, have any doubt after the sight thereof, what naughty minds the men had, both he that so noted them, and he that so made them. I remember not now the specialities of the matter, nor the formal words as they were written. But this I remember well, that besides other things framed for the favour of divers other heresies, there were in the prologue of that Bible, such words touching the blessed sacrament as good Christian men did much abhor to hear, and which gave the readers undoubted occasion to think that the book was written after Wycliffe's copy, and by him translated into our tongue." For Richard Hun, see pp. 369–70.

[4] See pp. 259–66.

with in the Wycliffite translation of the text itself[1]. His assumption that the text itself was heretical was a quite unconscious assumption, based on the analogy of Tindale's New Testament. He would have been surprised to learn that the English Bibles he had seen in his friends' houses were merely the Wycliffite text, with the prologue omitted: but could he have known that orthodox catholic historians have now identified the translations used in some Italian nunneries in his own day as descendants of Waldensian originals[2], and that many philological specialists believe the same phenomenon to have occurred in Germany[3], he need not have been surprised. To expect from Sir Thomas More, however, accurate historical or linguistic knowledge of the relation of the manuscripts he had seen to the Wycliffite Bible would be to expect an anachronism. His view as to the legal aspect of the matter was right: his scheme for the distribution of Bibles is most interesting evidence as to what the best mind of that day wished in the matter: his evidence as to contemporary belief in the absolute prohibition of all translations is valuable: but his theory as to the origin of such English Bibles as he had seen, though natural, was wrong. There is almost historical certainty that, though found in the houses of the faithful, they were the Wycliffite texts, and that there was no important biblical translation, whole or partial, made in the fourteenth century before the days of Wycliffe's influence.

[1] No contemporary of Wycliffe accused the Lollards of mistranslating the text of the Bible: Walden's reference to Wycliffe, *Doct*. III. 12, as a "falsifier of scripture," is, as the context shews, only an attack on certain Wycliffite theories based on an interpretation of certain biblical verses. In 1397 the Lollards were blamed in a royal letter for translating the "bare text" of holy scripture, not for mistranslating it, see p. 288. In a contemporary anti-Lollard poem quoted *Lanterne*, EETS, OS, 151, 143, the Lollards are vaguely accused of misinterpretation:

> Ther the Bibelle is al myswent,
> To jangle of Job or Jeremie,
> That construen hit after her entent
> For lewde lust of Lollardie.

But the editor can find only Lollard glosses, not inserted as part of the translated text, in support of the accusation, see *id*. 143. For the absence of accusation of partizan translation by opponents of earlier Waldensian French or German translations, see pp. 30–1; for modern acknowledgment of their literal accuracy, S. Minocchi in V, *Italiennes* [*Versions*], p. 1022.

[2] See *Italiennes* [*Versions*] *de la Bible*, V, III. 1020; and cf. chapter II, p. 44.

[3] See pp. 64–8.

§ 4. More's evidence has been here criticised at length, because without it some modern theories as to the nature and number of old English translations, and the attitude of the Church towards them, could scarcely have been put forward. The present explanation of his evidence is here suggested as a theory, which it is hoped to prove in the following chapters. No effort seems to have been made as yet to put the study of English biblical translations into its proper European background, although the comparison of the efforts of English Lollards to spread vernacular scriptures with those of the continental Lollards, and the Brethren of the Common Life, at the same date, is most illuminating. A vivid light is thrown on the history of translations in England by continental prohibitions of translations, the efforts of thirteenth and fourteenth century inquisitors to suppress them, and their defence by more liberal minded catholics. England was under the same canon law as the continent: and the precedent of earlier provincial constitutions applied to us as much as to other European countries. The thirteenth century inquisition was never introduced into England to suppress Lollardy: but the old inquisition of heretical pravity had existed long before that century, under episcopal and papal direction, and it existed alongside with it. The episcopal inquisition used in England against the Lollards differed little in authority and method from that inquisition, which was carrying on so vigorous a campaign against the Lollards or Beghards of the low countries at the time of Wycliffe's death: Foxe's *Acts and Monuments* is a record very similar to that of the inquisitor of Toulouse. Again, the attitude of the orthodox in Germany towards biblical translations in the fifteenth century throws much light on the attitude of the orthodox in England.

The English sources for the history of English biblical translations, and the attitude of the Church towards them include six groups. There is the evidence of contemporaries as to the making of any translation, or their lack of knowledge of particular translations, shewn by their omission in any list of such which they give. There are the existent manuscripts of English Bibles, which afford evidence as to different translations, and indications as to their possession by clerks or laymen, men or women, heterodox or orthodox. There are contemporary wills, large numbers of which already exist in printed collections: numbers sufficiently large to give a fairly secure index of the relatively frequent ownership of Latin, French and English Bibles and devotional books (for these last are interesting for comparison's sake). There are very many contemporary catalogues of the libraries of individuals, colleges, monasteries, etc., in which one would expect to find mention of English Bibles if they had existed in any considerable number. Episcopal registers also afford evidence on the subject, in the shape of occasional wills, and the records of heresy trials, which throw light on the connexion between possession of an English Bible and heresy. Finally, the enactments of diocesan and provincial synods afford light on the educational level reached by the clergy, and help to decide the question whether the Sunday gospel was ever directly translated at mass.

# CHAPTER II

## The prohibition of vernacular Bible reading in France, Italy and Spain

§ 1. The attitude of the mediaeval Church towards translations of the Bible is not easy to define: both because it underwent considerable modification between the tenth and the sixteenth centuries, and because it was always connected in practice with the right of the laity to inquire into high and divine matters[1], and to preach without episcopal license[2]. As a result of this connexion, the attitude of the Church to biblical translations was determined by the status of the translator and the purpose of the translation: if this translation were made for some king or exalted personage, or by some solitary student, and remained a hallowed but practically unused volume in a royal or monastic library, no objection was taken to the translation as such: but if the translation was used to popularise a knowledge of the biblical text among lay people, prohibition immediately followed. This was certainly the case till the end of the fourteenth century throughout Europe, and it was a course that found a majority of advocates in most European countries down to the Reformation, and many orthodox champions later. From the end of the fourteenth century lay people of the upper classes could usually obtain license from their confessors to use translations of parts of the Bible, as they could obtain other

[1] It was for this reason that Maerlant states that he incurred the enmity of the clergy for his translation of the *Historia Scholastica* into Dutch verse. See p. 72. For the explicit statement of this point of view, see the letters of Gregory VII and Innocent III, pp. 24, 31.

[2] In the case of the Waldensians, see for instance the indictment of their unauthorised preaching in Alanus de Insula's *De Fide Catholica contra hereticos*, lib. II. c. 377, in PL 210, c. 305–400. The Waldensians presume to preach, he says, though they are laymen and illiterate, while even learned Cistercian monks do not preach, because they are not licensed and sent thereto by the bishop. At the disputation at Narbonne, again, held in 1190 between the orthodox and the Waldensians, the discussion turned on the right of the Waldensians to expound, not to read, translations of the scriptures. *Inq.* I. 78. See also pp. 31–3; and for the repression of preaching without episcopal license in England, pp. 283, 295..

minor dispensations; but, broadly speaking, those who desired to obtain such dispensations were few, since Bible reading was not recommended as an ordinary pious practice for the laity, till quite the close of the middle ages. Till that period, the broad distinction remains, that the Church took no notice of the making of biblical translations as such, but forbade all attempts at their popularisation, and this from quite worthy motives and deliberate judgment as to the inexpediency of such a course.

In nearly all European countries, parts of the Bible were translated into verse or prose, almost from the time of the barbarian invasions: indeed, in the case of Ulphilas's translation of the gospels, from a time prior to the migration of the Goths. In most cases the psalter, the foundation of the divine office, was translated early, and the translation of parts of the New Testament almost always preceded parts of the Old. After Peter Comestor, canon of Troyes, had about 1150 compiled his *Historia Scholastica*[1], translations of this work were more frequent, and more copied, than translations of portions of the Bible itself[2]. This was largely through the very great popularity of the *Historia Scholastica* in its Latin form, and no doubt also because such a work was considered safer than the literal translation of the sacred text. But these cases of translations, loose or literal, glossed or unglossed, of single biblical books or of the *Historia Scholastica*, remained merely literary curiosities[3]: they were not,

---

[1] See p. 177. A summary in Latin of the historical books of the Old and New Testaments, together with historical information from secular writers.

[2] Manuscripts of the French *Bible historiaulx* are more frequent than translations of the Bible itself: this was a free translation made by Guyart Desmoulins, canon of Aire in Artois, c. 1291–4. Maerlant translated it into Dutch, c. 1271.

[3] For accounts of the different vernacular versions, see the articles on *Françaises* [*Versions*], *Vaudoises*, *Allemandes*, *Italiennes*, *Danoises*, *Suédoises et Scandinaves*, *Espagnoles*, in V with the bibliographies; also the corresponding articles in HH, CE, and SC. See also in *Dominicains: (travaux des) sur les saintes écritures*, and the corresponding articles on *Franciscains*, *Chartreux*, etc. In the learned article, *Dominicains: (travaux des) etc.*, P. Mandonnet brings out clearly that the friars, as missionaries, were sometimes torn between the needs of the souls they shepherded, and the official condemnation of vernacular Bibles. "Torn between the very real need of coming to the aid of the faithful, and the prohibition of the hierarchy, the Dominicans hesitated a little, but gave way here and there to the first consideration.... This kind of uncertainty must explain, we believe, to a large extent, why so few translators' names remain attached to their works,

for instance, among the books normally studied in monastic libraries,—a class which can be defined with very great certainty from the numerous monastic catalogues which have come down to us[1]. Translations for royal personages were made at some period in nearly all European countries; in France, the Dominicans prepared a translation of the greater part of the Old Testament for king John the Good, about 1355[2], and Raoul de Presles revised for Charles V the old thirteenth century French Bible prepared by the stationers, or booksellers, of the university of Paris. This was just at the time when the Wycliffite versions were appearing in England. The same text was used in preparing a translation of the Sunday epistles and gospels for queen Jeanne of Burgundy, wife of Philip VI. In Norway Hakon V ordered the translation of the historical books of the Bible early in the fourteenth century; in Bohemia, a beautifully illustrated German Bible was prepared for the emperor Wenzel, between 1389 and 1400, while his daughter Anne possessed the gospels in Latin, German and Slavonic, and the princess Marguerite, daughter of Charles IV, who married Louis, king of Hungary and Poland, had a psalter in Latin, Polish and German.

Copies of these or similar translations were sometimes possessed by princes, nobles, and the owners of large collections of manuscripts, but the translations had no influence on the instruction of the secular clergy, the great body of regulars, or of the laity. The lower and middle classes could not, of course,

especially in the realm of translations of scripture, the authors being liable to trouble on account of their literary paternity....Nevertheless, there is no religious order which has not to its account, in the middle ages, a fairly large number of biblical translations." In the detailed account of the works of the Dominicans in the different countries, P. Mandonnet, however, sometimes overrates the Dominicans' share in issuing or encouraging translations: his chief claim, that the Dominicans prepared the thirteenth century Paris Bible is explicitly traversed by Mangenot in the article on *Françaises* [*Versions*] in V; for his inference from the prohibition of the chapter general in 1242 see p. 37; and note also that his citations of Dominican translators come in most cases from the late middle ages, after the invention of printing. For his estimate of the work of Dominicans in Germany, and the prevalence of translations in German convents, he has been misled by too much reliance on the work of F. Jostes: V, II. 1470, for which cf. p. 117 n.

[1] For a summary of the manuscript and printed sources of continental monastic and other libraries, see Gottlieb; it is hoped to print shortly the list of c. 75 mediaeval English catalogues consulted for this work.

[2] CE, *Versions of the Bible, French*. The Dominicans were Jean de Sy, Jean Nicolas, William Vivien, and Jean de Chambly.

have read them for themselves: but there is no evidence that they were used in instructions by the parish priests till the middle of the fifteenth century at earliest[1]. It is characteristic, indeed, of mediaeval sermons and books of instruction, that the translations of single biblical texts are always in the author's own words, not in the words of such translations as existed. Against the existence of vernacular translations as such, while they remained comparatively unused, the Church made no protest.

Much light is thrown upon the comparative rarity of biblical study, even among the upper classes, by a comparison of the advice given in didactic treatises to lay people, throughout the middle ages. A recent collection has been made of 114 such treatises addressed to women[2], from the time of S. Jerome to the Reformation; but most of them come from the eleventh to the fifteenth centuries; they are written in Latin, French, Italian, English, Spanish, Catalan, etc., and give a good idea of the duties and ideals held up to women of each rank and social class, both secular and religious. Women of all classes are exhorted again and again to the practices of piety,—prayer, early rising, attendance at mass, saying of the hours, submission to husbands, care for the poor, nursing of the sick; women of high rank are, in addition, urged to learn to read, and study good and virtuous books, lives of the saints, etc.: but only in a single treatise, written in 1394, is a woman advised to read the Bible itself. In this tract[3], written by a member of the higher bourgeoisie of Paris, the husband writes an instruction for his wife on her secular and sacred duties, and advises her to read "the Bible and the *Lives of the Fathers*, which he possesses in French." The date of the tract is very interesting, for it is that

---

[1] For certain exceptions in the case of the Gottesfreunde and the Brethren of the Common Life, see pp. 76, 89.

[2] *De la littérature didactique du moyen âge s'adressant spécialement aux femmes.* Hentsch, A. A., Cahors, 1903.

[3] *Id.* 141, *Le Ménagier de Paris.* The greater merchants of Paris were people of considerable importance, and their daughters had exceptional chances of education: they might not only have private teaching, as elsewhere, but they could attend grammar schools kept by women, a phenomenon apparently unique in Europe, and certainly without parallel in England. There were, apparently, 21 such schools in Paris about 1380. see Jourdain, 127.

of the twenty years before the council of Constance, when the use of the vernacular languages for literature had been making great strides all over Europe, and had been applied even to the sacred books: while the consequent outburst of reinterpretation or heresy had not yet turned the attention of the orthodox to the need of severely limiting vernacular scriptures. It is remarkable that this should be the solitary instance[1]: especially as these didactic tracts must, from the nature of things, have been written for women who could read or write;—in nearly all cases, they are dedicated to some one of exalted birth. The tracts help us also to estimate how low in the social scale the ability to read descended: one interesting manual, written between 1307 and 1315 in rhymed Provençal, actually discusses this question[2]. The advice given in it is carefully graded according to the rank of the hearer; the daughters of kings and emperors are advised to learn to read and write well, because they will have later to govern many lands. The second class is formed of the daughters of marquises, dukes, counts and barons,—these also should be taught to read: while the third class, composed of the daughters of squires, judges, "solemn doctors" and gentlemen of similar rank, causes the writer great perplexity. Opinions differ, he says, as to whether they should be taught to read or write: but he himself decides in the negative. With the daughters of merchants and craftsmen he has no difficulty at all: no one suggests that reading or writing would be good for them, or for the classes beneath them. Thus, while there are undoubted records of the making of biblical translations for orthodox princes and princesses in the middle ages, orthodox didactic manuals shew plainly that the reading of them was not a normal practice even among the educated laity,—a very small minority of the population.

---

[1] Apart from a tract of S. Jerome's, Miss Hentsch (38, S. Aldhelm's *De laude virginitatis*) gives no direct evidence that the nuns addressed read the Bible, as she implies, p. 38, but merely shews that S. Aldhelm himself was very familiar with it. Instances of exhortation to the reading of devotional books, saints' lives, etc., are on pp. 52, 133, 135, 150, 154, 181, 191, 199, 216, 225. Neither S. Louis, writing c. 1271, nor Anne de France, the daughter of Louis XI, writing c. 1504 advised their daughters to read the biblical text, though Anne specifies in some detail the books she advises: see *id.* 80, 199.

[2] That of the much-travelled Italian, Francesco da Barberino, 1264–1348, *id.* 106.

On the broad question of the popularisation of biblical translations, their possession by unlettered or little lettered people,
and their use for the instruction of unlettered people, the mind
of the mediaeval Latin Church was never quite unanimous. The
first time the question of the lawfulness of vernacular versions
of the scriptures was raised was in connexion with the debatable
land between the Eastern and Western Churches, and the real
importance of the question was political: Greek or Slavonic
offices or scriptures would draw the population towards the
East, Latin towards the West. Bulgaria was Christianised from
Byzantium and accepted Eastern Christianity in 869[1]; Moravia
was also converted by missionaries of the Eastern Church, Cyril
and Methodius, but Methodius went to Rome about 879, and
obtained from John VIII permission to use Slavonic as the
language of the Church; after which Moravia accepted Latin
Christianity. Methodius had already translated parts of the
Bible into Slavonic[2], and papal permission was given both to
use this version, and to sing mass and the divine office in
Slavonic[3]. The Eastern Church continued to use vernacular
scriptures and offices,—though the retention of Old Slavonic
rendered them in time as little understandable to the uneducated[4] as Latin ones,—but the Latin Church withdrew the
permission to use Slavonic as soon as her position in this district
was firmly established. This withdrawal was the occasion of the
first distinctively mediaeval pronouncement on the undesirability
of biblical translations: but the main pronouncement was
directed against vernacular offices.

This occurs in a letter of Gregory VII to Vratislaus, king of
Bohemia, written in 1079: it shews in germ the subsequent
divided opinion of the Church at large, with the mass of ortho-

---

[1] *Russian Church Hist.*, Frere, W. H., 1918, 4.

[2] *Id.* 10, 32; *Eastern Church*, Stanley, A. P., 1869, 310.

[3] *Acta Concil.*, Hardouin, J., Paris, 1714, VI. pt i. p. 86. "Nor is there any
objection, against either singing mass in the Slavonic tongue, or reading
the holy gospel, or the sacred lessons of the Old and New Testament, well
translated and interpreted,...We command therefore, that in all the
churches in your land, the gospel shall be read in Latin, for the greater
honour: and afterwards read translated into the Slavonic tongue in the
hearing of the people, who understand no Latin." In 879, *id.* 61,
Methodius had been forbidden to celebrate mass in Slavonic.

[4] See Frere, 89–94, for the struggle over the revision of the service books.

doxy hostile to such a course. Vratislaus wrote to the pope to
ask for permission for his monks to recite the divine office in
Slavonic, and Gregory answered prohibiting such a measure.
He gave as his reason for this, that such a course would necessi-
tate the translation of portions of the divine scripture:

> Since your excellency has asked that we would allow the divine
> office to be said among you in Slavonic, know that we can by no
> means favourably answer this your petition. For it is clear to those
> who reflect often upon it, that not without reason has it pleased
> Almighty God that holy scripture should be a secret in certain places,
> lest, if it were plainly apparent to all men, perchance it would be
> little esteemed and be subject to disrespect; or it might be falsely
> understood by those of mediocre learning, and lead to error. Nor does
> it avail as an excuse that certain religious men have patiently
> suffered the simple folk who asked for it, or have sent them away
> uncorrected: since the primitive Church allowed many things to pass
> unheeded, which, after Christianity had grown stronger, and when
> religion was increasing, were corrected by subtle examination. Where-
> fore we forbid what you have so imprudently demanded of the autho-
> rity of S. Peter, and we command you to resist this vain rashness with
> all your might, to the honour of Almighty God[1].

This refusal shews that there were already advocates of biblical
translations, in so far as these were involved in the translation
of the divine office[2], in the persons of the religious whom Vratislaus had quoted as favouring his request, which they did, no
doubt, from missionary motives; but the hostile pronouncement
of Gregory himself remained the opinion of the Church at large.
The question of reciting the divine office in the vernacular was
not of sufficient practical importance for this letter to be included in the *Decretum* of Gratian, so that it retained only the
authority of an apostolic rescript: it had not, that is, universally
binding canonical authority, but could be quoted as a precedent[3].

Gregory wrote this letter in 1079. Just a hundred years later
John Beleth, rector of the theological schools at Paris, composed
his *Rationale Divinorum Officiorum*, which became the chief
liturgical authority of the next century. He gave as the reason

---

[1] PL 148, c. 555.

[2] This consisted entirely of the psalms and biblical passages, apart from
the hymns for the hours, and the patristic homilies at mattins.

[3] CE, article on *Decretals*.

for his work, the general lack of understanding of the services, due to ignorance of Latin on the part of both priests and people. He begins:

In the primitive Church it was prohibited that any should speak, unless there were some one to interpret. For what, I ask, does speech profit, if it is not understood? Assuredly, nothing. Hence there grew in certain parts of the Church the laudable custom, that when the gospel had been read according to the letter [in Latin], forthwith it was explained to the people in the vulgar tongue. But what shall we say of our own times, if scarcely or not at all there may be found any man who understands what he reads or hears read, or who truly perceives what he sees done or does himself? We must lament with the prophet, etc.[1]

It is not clear whether Beleth here had in mind the old Gallican custom of translating the gospel at mass[2], or whether he was referring to Eastern custom: but his long and detailed description of the reading of the gospel at mass shews that no such custom of translation obtained in his own day, in the Western Church.

§ 2. The question of popular Bible reading for the laity did not arise till a hundred years after Gregory VII, though from that time onwards it was continuously demanded by heretical sects down to the Reformation. From the last quarter of the fourteenth century also it was advocated by a certain stream of orthodox opinion in central Europe. The original demand was connected with the rise of the Waldensians in southern France, about 1180. The century had already seen the rise of many heresies in southern Europe, some of the wilder ones due partly to Eastern influences, travelling with the returning crusaders; but the Waldensian movement was original, and, like the Lollard movement later, was based upon the desire to approximate the Christian polity to the more obvious features of apostolic Christianity. It was inspired by the lay reading of the New Testament. The Dominican inquisitor, Etienne de Bourbon, whose convent was at Lyons, describes how he knows of the origin of the Waldensians from a certain priest, rich and honoured in

---

[1] PL 202, c. 13: for an O.F. translation, see *Bull. de la soc. des anc. textes franç.* 1884, p. 84, where "translated" in the prologue is rendered "en-romançast."

[2] See p. 213 n.

Lyons, called Bernardus Ydros, who wrote for money certain translations for Peter Waldo:

A certain rich man of the city (Lyons), called Waldo, was curious when he heard the gospel read, since he was not much lettered, to know what was said. Wherefore he made a pact with certain priests, the one, that he should translate to him the Bible: the other, that he should write as the first dictated. Which they did; and in like manner many books of the Bible, and many authorities of the saints, which they called *Sentences*. Which when the said citizen had often read and learned by heart, he proposed to observe evangelical perfection as the apostles observed it; and he sold all his goods, and despising the world, he gave all his money to the poor, and usurped the apostolic office by preaching the gospel, and those things which he had learned by heart, in the villages and open places, and by calling to him many men and women to do the same thing, and teaching them the gospel by heart....Who indeed, being simple and illiterate men and women, wandered through villages and entered houses and preached in open places, and even in churches, and provoked others to the same course[1].

When through their boldness, Etienne says, many errors arose, the archbishop of Lyons summoned them and forbade them to meddle with the scriptures, either by exposition or preaching. They were declared heretics and schismatics by the papal edict of Verona in 1184, and later at the fourth Lateran council of 1215, but defied the excommunication of the Church, and continued to travel about disguised in Provence and Lombardy, joining themselves to other heretics,—notably in Italy, with the Cathari or the Patarini.

The account of another contemporary is interesting, since it is that of an Englishman who actually saw the earliest Waldensian translations. Walter Map wrote his book, *De Nugis Curialium*, between the years 1181–1192[2]. He travelled to the third Lateran council in 1179, and tells us that:

We saw the Waldensians at the council celebrated at Rome under pope Alexander III. They were simple and illiterate men, named after their leader, Waldo, who was a citizen of Lyons on the Rhone: and they presented to the lord pope a book written in the French tongue, in which were contained a text and gloss on the psalter, and on very many other books of both testaments. These besought with

[1] *Anec. Hist.* 291.
[2] *Walter Map, De Nugis Curialium*, James, M. R., Oxford, 1914, p. xxvi.

great urgency that authority to preach should be confirmed to them, for they thought themselves expert, when they were scarcely learned at all.... For in every small point of the sacred page, so many meanings fly on the wings of virtue, such stores of wealth are accumulated, that only he can fully exhaust them whom God has inspired. Shall not therefore the Word given to the unlearned be as *pearls before swine*, when we know them to be fitted neither to receive it, nor to give out what they have received? Away with this idea, and let it be rooted out. *The ointment ran down from the head, even to the skirts of his clothing*: waters flow from the spring, not from the mud of public ways[1].

Map goes on to relate how he himself was set to examine two Waldensians, and soon exposed their lack of theological learning, by entrapping them into giving an answer to one of his questions, which though they did not know it, was heretical and Nestorian. His condemnation of the Waldensian desire to preach[2] certainly implies that of the study of the divine "Word" by the unlearned[3]. The accounts of both Etienne de Bourbon and Map shew that there was no complete Waldensian translation of the Bible at this date[4], but only those of particular books, probably, in most cases, with a gloss or comment; the glossed psalter they presented was almost certainly the old Anglo-Norman psalter,

[1] *De Nugis*, 60.

[2] Waldensian "preaching" consisted largely of the recitation of passages of the gospels, etc., in the vernacular: see p. 39 for the evidence on this point of the record of the Inquisitor of Toulouse.

[3] The manuscript from which the *De Nugis Curialium* is edited belonged to John Wells, monk of Ramsey, who was for 13 years the prior of Gloucester Hall, the Benedictine college at Oxford, and died in 1388. He "determined," or gave academic judgments, against both Wycliffe and Nicholas Hereford on certain theological points: and it is interesting to find that he was aware of the earlier papal refusal to countenance the Waldensian biblical translations. *De Nugis*, p. viii.

[4] Berger, 35. Keller, 72. "Waldensian" as applied to a MS. may refer either to doctrinal or linguistic characteristics: in the first sense, the MS. may be either Provençal, Italian, Catalan, etc. No MS. of Waldo's original translations in the dialect of the Lyonnais remains to us; the earliest Provençal fragment is c. 1200 (Harl. 2928, which has 5 chapters of S. John, and the rest of the MS. liturgical). The Waldensians had however a Provençal version in the thirteenth century, which remains to us, and which influenced the "Vaudois" or Piedmontese version of the fourteenth century, parts of which remain to us. V, *Vaudoises* [*Versions*]. The other early "Waldensian" translations which remain to us are a "Plenarium," or glossed Sunday epistles and gospels, from Metz, in the Lorraine dialect, see p. 30, and a thirteenth century old Italian, or Catharan, translation, see p. 43. There is also a thirteenth century Provençal gospel harmony, or life of Christ, *La Nobla Leyczon*, see *Cat. of Ashburnham MSS.* 1853, MS. 110.

and not a fresh translation in the Provençal dialect of the Lyonnais[1]; and, as the later Waldensians were never agreed as to the number of the canonical books[2], and attached nothing like the same importance to a knowledge of the Old Testament as they did to the New, there never was a complete Waldensian translation. But there is no doubt that the right of the laity to draw inferences from a knowledge of the New Testament gained through translations was the foundation of the Waldensian position. The Waldensian lower classes, like the orthodox lower classes, could not read: but extraordinary stress was laid on memorising parts of the New Testament, and Waldensian "sermons" often consisted of the recitation of such memorised passages: Waldensian "schools" or conventicles were gatherings where the slightly lettered, or the already taught, could teach such passages to others. As is often the case with those who have not been taught to read, their power of memory was very great, and all the Sunday gospels would often be learned by heart.

As with the Lollards later, the extent to which individual Waldensians, or small groups of Waldensians, departed from orthodox teaching, differed very widely. They accepted the usual articles of the faith, or the creed, and the seven sacraments[3], but some doubted of the validity of a sacrament administered by an unworthy minister. Some however, like the later Lollards, rejected the doctrine of transubstantiation, and the discipline of the Church as regards fasting and the necessity of confession. They ordained their own ministers or "magistri," and, according to Etienne de Bourbon, despised offerings to saints, plain song, and the divine office, saying that "they had seen God laugh at those who sang to Him what they wished to say[4]." By all Waldensians, the taking of an oath was regarded as forbidden by the New Testament,—a point through which they were often detected by the inquisitors, who administered the oath on the gospels before hearing their evidence. Many also were pacifists, holding it unlawful to take life in battle, or even in process of justice. They were not a completely unlettered

[1] Berger, 37.                    [2] Keller, 72.
[3] Cf. the statement on these points demanded from Waldensian ordinands: Walden. Ursprung, 9.
[4] Anec. Hist. 297.

party[1], for there is evidence that some orthodox priests[2] and many Franciscan tertiaries[3] joined them; certainly some lay nobles were "hereticated" or admitted as Waldensian magistri, and others protected them[4]; the archbishop of Metz denounced two Waldensian masters of arts and a certain "scholasticus" from the pulpit[5]. There was communication also between the heads of the movement in France, Italy and Spain[6], and it seems likely that the heretical "schools" at Milan gave some more intellectual teaching than the instruction in the text of the gospels afforded by every little midnight meeting of Waldensians; one convert from Waldensianism who became a Dominican and an inquisitor had attended them for eighteen years[7]. But nevertheless, Waldensianism never gained a hold at any university, as the Lollard movement did in its earlier stages at Oxford. The instruction of the laity was carried on by the "magistri" or by the laity themselves, and chiefly by means of vernacular gospels, epistles, and other biblical books: by means of which the Waldensian teachers, "arguing falsely from the letter," as their opponents said, supported the main points of their doctrine. It was for this reason that vernacular Bibles and vernacular "scriptures," in the wider mediaeval sense, were burned by in-

[1] For the dispute as to the learning of Waldensians somewhat later, see *Die Waldenser und die vorlutherische deutsche Bibelübersetzung*. Jostes, F., Münster, 1885, 7–, and *Walden. Ursprung*, 1–7.

[2] *Lib. Sent. Thol.* 253; *Walden. Ursprung*, 16.

[3] The tertiaries on the Rhine were infected with Waldensianism, see p. 70, and in Spain were forbidden to read vernacular scriptures, see p. 49. For heretical tertiaries, probably rather "spiritual Franciscans" than Waldensians, see *Lib. Sent. Thol.* 298, 299, 301, 381.

[4] Anon. of Passau in MBPV, XIII. 299, of the Waldensians: "there was none who dared to hinder them, on account of the power and number of those who supported them." David of Augsburg says that in 1250 a powerful prince joined them, *Walden. Ursprung*, 7. Cf. also Robert, dauphin of Auvergne, †1234, who wrote Provençal verse, and diligently collected and read all the books of the heretics,—only, as he affirmed to the Dominican inquisitor who visited him, to render himself the firmer in the catholic faith; he submitted finally to making a bonfire of his library, since the Dominicans were not satisfied with his explanation. *Anec. Hist.* 276. In the *Ann. Trevir.* II. 106, the success of the Waldensians in Metz about 1207 is ascribed to civil strife.

[5] *Id.* 106.

[6] The "magistri" at Metz in 1208 came from the Pyrenees, *Ann. Trevir.* II. 106, while the connexion between the heretics of Provence and Lombardy was close.

[7] He had learnt by heart the N.T. and much of the O.T. *Anec. Hist.* 280.

quisitors, and prohibited by archbishops and provincial synods wherever Waldensianism spread: not because the translations were themselves regarded as false or heretical[1], as was the case with the Reformation versions.

The original cradle of Waldensianism in France was the Lyonnais: from hence it spread into two chief areas, Lorraine and the border district between France and the Empire, where the division of secular power was favourable to its existence: and south-westward into the Mediterranean provinces of France, particularly the bishoprics of Toulouse and Narbonne. After the original suppression of the Waldensians at Lyons c. 1180–90, the next great repressive effort was made against the towns of Lorraine, from about 1192–1208; and the next, and never perfectly successful effort, in the south of France, from about 1229 onwards.

The most important papal decision in the middle ages concerning biblical translations was connected with the repressive measures in Lorraine. In 1192 these began in Toul, where the archbishop ordered all the heretics called "Vaudois" to be brought in chains before his episcopal seat[2]. By 1199 they had become dangerous also in Metz, for a chronicler says that:

There was also breeding and swarming in the city of Metz a sect called Waldensians, and certain abbots were sent there to preach, who burnt certain books translated from Latin into Romance, and extirpated the aforesaid sect[3].

In July 1199 the archbishop wrote to Innocent III, to obtain confirmation of the repressive measures he wished to take. Innocent answered with two letters, one to the faithful at Metz, one personally to the archbishop. In the first he deplored that

---

[1] Writers against the Waldensians like Etienne de Bourbon and Alain de Lisle make no accusation of the falsity of their translations; the Anon. of Passau is the only writer who accuses the translators of inaccuracy through insufficient learning, MBVP, XIII. 299, and he does not suggest that their mistranslations had any doctrinal significance.

[2] Martène, *Thes.* IV. 1180; cf. Berger, 39.

[3] *Chronica Albrici, Mon. Germ., Script.* XXIII. 878. *Chaire Fran.* 238, on the strength of Innocent III's letter to the archbishop of Metz in 1199 about Waldensian translations, has the sentence: "Before 1199 translations of the gospels and epistles, accompanied by commentaries, circulated in certain dioceses [of France]," which is misleading, as implying an orthodox origin of the practice, and omitting to mention the subsequent burning of the translations by the papal inquisitors. See also p. 39 n.

certain heretics had resisted their parish priests, alleging reasons from the scriptures[1]:

The bishop of Metz has signified to us that both in his city and in his diocese a multitude of laymen and women, led to a large extent by a desire of understanding the scriptures, have had translated for themselves the gospels, epistles of S. Paul, the psalter, the moralisation on Job[2], and many other books in the French tongue. They intend that with this translation, made thus at their own discretion (would that it had been made with prudence as well), laymen and women shall presume to hold forth on such matters, and to preach to each other.... Now although the desire of understanding holy scriptures, and zeal for exhorting in accordance with them, is not to be reprehended but rather commended, yet in this matter certain laymen appear to be justly accused: because they hold secret conventicles, usurp to themselves the office of preaching, elude the simplicity of priests, and scorn the company of those who cling not to these things.... The secret mysteries of the faith ought not therefore to be explained to all men in all places, since they cannot be everywhere understood by all men: but only to those who can conceive them with a faithful mind; for what says the apostle to simple people? *Even as babes in Christ I have fed you with milk and not with meat....* For such is the depth of divine scripture, that not only the simple and illiterate, but even the prudent and learned, are not fully sufficient to try to understand it. *For many seek and fail in their search*[3], whence it was of old rightly written in the divine law, that *the beast which touched the mount should be stoned*: lest, apparently, any simple and unlearned person should presume to attain to the sublimity of holy scripture.... *Seek not out the things that are above thee.* For what says the apostle? *Not to think more highly than one ought to think, but to think soberly....* Although learning is most necessary for priests for the sake of teaching,...nevertheless simple priests ought not to be despised, even by scholastics, since the priestly ministry ought to be honoured in them.

In any case, Innocent concluded, the office of reproving unsuitable priests did not belong to the laity, and he exhorted the faithful to withdraw themselves from such errors, lest severer measures should be taken. At the same time, he wrote to the archbishop, warning him against either tolerating heretical pravity, or trying to gather in the tares before the harvest, and

[1] PL 214, cc. 695-9. Dated 12 July, 1199; *Epistolarum Innocentii III*, Baluzius, S., 1682, tom. I. p. 432.

[2] The work of Gregory the Great.

[3] An often quoted version of psalm 64, 6 (Vulgate, 63, 7), *Quia multi defecerunt scrutantes scrutinio.*

especially lest impatience should turn the misguided zeal of unlettered men into heresy. He asked for further information
about the way of life of these heretics who held secret conventicles, and especially about the origin of the biblical translation,
before taking further steps:

> We are completely ignorant of the opinions and way of life of those
> who have thus translated the holy scriptures, or of those who teach
> them this translation (neither of which could be done without a
> knowledge of letters).... Warn them to desist from those things which
> appear blameworthy, and not to claim for themselves the office of
> others. Enquire diligently, who was the author of this translation;
> what was his intention: the faith of those who use it: the reason of
> their teaching: whether they venerate the apostolic see and the catho-
> lic Church: so that...we may the better understand what ought to
> be decreed.

We do not possess the archbishop's answer, giving Innocent
the required information, but it must have been sent between
July and December 1199, for on December 9th Innocent issued
a commission to the abbot of Cîteaux and two other Cistercian
abbots, to assist the archbishop of Metz in suppressing heresy[1].
This commission throws much light on the interpretation his
earlier letter to Metz had been given by contemporaries, as condemning the lay use of vernacular scriptures: the three abbots
were so certain he had condemned them that they burnt all
biblical translations found in the hands of the Vaudois[2]. The long
string of quotations, "*Cast not pearls before swine,....Seek not out
the things which are above thee,*" had been taken as discountenan-
cing the use of the Waldensian translations, as they were probably
intended to do. This was in accordance with the whole tenor of
the letter: and indeed, Innocent, in his commission to the three
abbots, spoke as if he had already condemned the translation,
though he had actually only condemned its users. He told the
abbots that at Metz:

> No small multitude of laymen and women presume to hold forth
> among themselves at secret conventicles, in order to learn a certain
> translation of holy scripture,...even when prohibited: they despise
> those who differ from them, and study the said translation as much as

[1] PL 214, c. 699.
[2] Albéric de Trois Fontaines, in *Mon. Germ.*, *Scriptores*, XXIII. 878.

heretofore. They are to be condemned for holding secret conventicles
...and refusing the fellowship of those who do not receive the said
translation[1].

The abbots were to go to Metz, and, with the archbishop,
summon before them "those who favour these things and
adhere to the aforesaid translation[2],"—with the result that
they burnt all that they could find of such books.

The measures taken, however, were not completely successful;
in 1201 the pope sent the cardinal bishop, Guido of Praeneste,
to Cologne as his legate, to aid in suppressing heresy[3], and in
1207–8 archbishop Bertram of Metz again had trouble with the
Waldensians, particularly with two "magistri" and a "scholasticus" who had travelled to Metz from the Pyrenees[4]. From
Metz and Lorraine the heretics spread into the Empire, where
they were found in considerable numbers in Strassburg in 1211,
in Bavaria and Austria in 1218, and at Trier and Mainz in 1231.

The part played by Innocent in dealing with the Waldensians
at Metz is of great interest. He displayed a broader mindedness
than the local archbishop[5], but ended by confirming what the
latter desired: the suppression of the translation. His letters dealt
with "vernacular scriptures" in the wider sense, but included
the translation of biblical books, since it explicitly mentioned
their names; there was no written prohibition, but the whole
tenor of the letter, with its string of citations, "Cast not pearls
before swine," etc., was hostile. There seems no doubt that at
the time Innocent's letters were regarded as giving papal sanction to the condemnation of biblical translation; contemporaries
interpreted the first letter by the action of the three abbots who

[1] This was not wonderful, since all the faithful were bidden to report
cases of heresy among their numbers to their parish priests. The recantation
of a heretic before the inquisition had to be accompanied by whatever
information he possessed about his fellow heretics, or those whom he had,
at the time, "believed to be good and honest men."

[2] All three letters of Innocent deal with the subject of lay preaching, as
much as lay study of the scriptures: but this sentence, and the whole letter,
shew that the primary mark of the Waldensians was that they used a
certain translation of the scriptures, and taught it to each other verbally in
secret conventicles. See pp. 38–41.

[3] *Ann. Trevir.* II. 98.          [4] *Id.* II. 106.

[5] P. Mandonnet believes that the Curia was always more favourable than
the local bishops to popular religious movements among laymen, as in this
case: see V, II. 1467.

were Innocent's commissioners. These had been told to summon before them—first in the list of heretical symptoms—"those who favour these things and adhere to the aforesaid translation"; as the Metz chronicler says, "they burnt certain books translated from Latin into Romance[1], and extirpated the aforesaid sect."

Part of Innocent's letter of 1199 was embodied in the *Decretal* of Gregory IX and became of universal canonical application: but the string of citations, "Cast not pearls before swine," etc., was omitted, and the letter, known as *Cum ex injuncto*[2] became chiefly a prohibition of conventicles and lay preaching. As such it was interpreted by the official commentators[3], without direct reference to the subject of biblical translations. In this form it was known to the inquisition and all canonists: and yet inquisitors acted on the theory that biblical translations were forbidden, and other theologians stated as a fact of common knowledge that it was canonically forbidden to the laity to have the sacred books in the vernacular[4]. Thirteenth century inquisitors certainly burnt or confiscated biblical translations wherever they found them, not only in those provinces where their possession was expressly forbidden by the local synod. It is therefore very

---

[1] French, not German; the dialect of Lorraine. Berger believes, with great probability, that the translations of the "epistles and gospels" was that of the Sunday epistles and gospels. He believes that an existent early thirteenth plenary (for plenary, see *infra* p. 39, n. 4) in the Lorraine dialect, of Messine provenance, was one of these Waldensian books. Berger, 40. We possess also an early thirteenth century manuscript of the *Moralities on Job* of S. Gregory, in a dialect very near to that of the Lorraine dialect of the plenary; *id.* 42. "Romance" in Godefroi, *Dictionnaire de l'Ancienne Langue française*, is defined as having two meanings, (1) French as opposed to Latin, (2) a work in the vulgar tongue of any Latin nation. Thus the earl of Warwick bequeathed in 1359 his library of "romances," including French gospels and a psalter, etc. (*Bibliom.* 193); and the synod of Tarragona, 1233, absolutely forbade the possession of the Bible in "Romance," probably referring either to Catalan, or Provençal, or the vulgar tongue; cf. p. 48, n. 1. In nearly all cases, however, "Romance" means vernacular French.

[2] *Corpus Iuris Canonici*, Friedberg, A., Leipzig, 1881, pars ii. c. 785; =*Decretal. Gregor. IX*, lib. v. tit. vii. cap. xii.

[3] For convenience, see them as cited (the *Glossa ordinaria*, Hostiensis, and Johannes Andreae) by the inquisitor general of the kingdom of Aragon, the Franciscan Eymeric. He completed his famous manual, the *Directorium Inquisitorum*, in 1376; for the *Cum ex injuncto* and glosses, see F. Pegna's 1607, Venice, ed. of Eymeric's *Direct. Inq.*, index of glossators; also pp. 100 and 565, where Pegna gives the full form of Innocent's letter, though Eymeric comments only on the *Cum ex injuncto*.     [4] See p. 84.

difficult not to believe that Innocent III's letter of 1199 was one
of the foundations of the action of the inquisitors and the belief
of the theologians. It was available as a precedent in its original
hostile form till the pontificate of Gregory IX, and, although
incorporated in its less hostile form in this pope's *Decretal*, it was
rendered unnecessary by the prohibition of Toulouse during this
pontificate. This prohibition was of wider than provincial
application, and specially confirmed by the presence of Gregory
IX's legate. The powers there granted to the inquisition were
generally mentioned in the commissions of later inquisitors as
granted to them also, in addition to particular ones given at the
time: so that, after 1229, inquisitors who found the use of biblical
translations giving rise to heresy could have suppressed them in
reliance on this and later provincial constitutions, even if they
were not aware of the full form of Innocent III's letter to Metz.
It was not till 1398 that certain Dutch lawyers, writing out of
opposition to the inquisition, boldly claimed that the *Cum ex
injuncto* itself implied a commendation of German books of
edification, in the words "the desire of understanding holy
scriptures and...exhorting in accordance with them is not to
be reprehended but rather commended[1]."

Waldensianism spread from Metz not only into the Empire,

[1] During the struggle over the lawfulness of vernacular Bibles, and their
promiscuous reading by the laity, at the Reformation, this letter of Innocent III was explicitly quoted as a "Decree" forbidding such translations
and use. Luther printed his German New Testament in 1521: Erasmus wrote
in defence of popular Bible reading: and the theological faculty in Paris
condemned his propositions in 1527. They said that his refusal to prohibit
the laity from reading any book of the O.T. was rash and impudent, since
by a decree of the apostolic see the reading of many such books was "long
ago" prohibited to the laity: the same causes for prohibiting their reading
still existed, as when Innocent III drew up a "decree" about these matters
(a fragment of which is incorporated in his own words in the *De haereticis*,
as the *Cum ex injuncto*). Erasmus answered that if the decree of that pope,
or any other, had at any time been issued against the rashness of men, he
did not consider that it was now binding on the whole Church. See also
p. 10 n. Harney, 214, says of this letter of Innocent III: "Neither then nor
since has there been any constitution which applies to the whole Church,
directly and clearly, in this matter: but Spaniards took measures for Spain,
Frenchmen for France, Belgians for the Netherlands.... To speak strictly
[of the *Cum ex injuncto*], it does not touch the matter in hand, for the pope
did not (there at least) censure the reading of scripture by the laity in the
vulgar tongue, or forbid women to read it in any medium: but he condemned their reading it, if it led to the despising of priests, or the usurpation
of the office of preaching."

but westward into the Ile de France. In 1210 the archbishop of Sens, Pierre de Corbeil, the bishop of Paris, and certain other bishops, issued an edict for the burning of certain heretics, and the confiscation of all books of a theological nature written in French:

> We command concerning books of theological nature written in Romance, that they shall be handed over to the diocesan bishops, including *Credos* and *Paternosters* in Romance (except lives of the saints), and this before the feast of the Purification: and that all their possessors shall be regarded as heretical[1].

There is no record that the edict was promulgated at a provincial synod: Paris, Sens and Metz were not far distant from each other, and the edict seems to have been issued in accordance with the measures taken by papal authority to suppress heresy at Metz.

The alarming development of heresy in the south of France had given rise to the labours of the Dominican order, and the efforts of these friars were, throughout the thirteenth and fourteenth centuries, chiefly responsible for its repression, partly by personal preaching, partly by raising the standard of theological education through their "studia," partly by a vigorous use of the powers of the inquisition. In 1229 a synod was held at Toulouse: the see was not yet an archbishopric, but the synod was of far wider than provincial authority[2], for its decrees were confirmed by the archbishops of Narbonne, Bordeaux and Auch, many bishops and other prelates, and—more important still—by the legate of the apostolic see, Bonaventura, cardinal deacon of S. Angelo; also by the count of Toulouse and many secular barons. It was decreed that[3]:

> *Lay people shall not have books of scripture, except the psalter and the divine office: and they shall not have these books in the vulgar tongue.* Moreover we prohibit that lay people should be permitted to have

---

[1] *Chartularium Universitatis Parisiensis*, Denifle, H., Paris, 1889, I. 70.

[2] H. Reusch, in his *Index der Verbotenen Bücher*, Bonn, 1883, has a good and clear section on mediaeval prohibitions of biblical translations in synods, but underrates the authority of the synod of Toulouse, and ignores the decrees at Béziers: cf. I. 43. He was also unaware of the prohibition at Trier, 1231, and the imperial edict of 1369. For emphasis on the papal confirmation of the edicts of Toulouse, see Harney, 183, who says the synod was of "greater than provincial authority," and Hegelmaier, 135.

[3] Mansi, XXIII. 197.

books of the Old or New Testament, except perchance any should
wish from devotion to have a psalter, or a breviary for the divine
office, or the hours of the blessed Virgin: but we most strictly prohibit their having even the aforesaid books translated into the vulgar
tongue.

There is evidence that the severe decrees of Toulouse and
Paris were not merely regarded as exceptional local measures
to deal with heresy. The Dominican order itself was not limited
to any locality, and its rules would bind men of all nationalities,
but a learned Dominican of the seventeenth century himself
points out "that he could not doubt that it was according to
the spirit of S. Dominic, and of this council, that it was decreed
in the Dominican constitutions, distinction 2, cap. 15, text. 3,
that the lay brothers should not have a psalter," since the order
of friars preacher was instituted in the same region at the same
time[1]. That individual preachers made some effort to translate
books of edification, probably not the biblical text itself, is
shewn however by the general prohibition of such action issued
by the Dominican chapter-general in 1242, at Bologna, in the
words[2]:

Neither shall any brother for the future translate sermons, or collations, or other holy scriptures.

The words do not imply that the prohibition was inspired by
a previous translation of the canonical books themselves, but
it doubtless covered them; the context shews also that such
translations of holy books as had been made, were for the use
of houses of nuns or tertiaries. The Dominicans at the time were

[1] Harney, 184.

[2] For the decree, see Martène, *Thes.* IV. c. 1684, Reichert's *Mon.
Ord. Fratrum Predica.* III. 24. For German Dominicans and nunneries,
see p. 77. There is no evidence that in this case the Dominican translations
had been inspired by general missionary zeal for the instruction of the faithful laity. Though missionaries such as the friars had doubtless more occasion
than other classes to consider the expedient of biblical translations, such
an expedient was not encouraged by orthodoxy in the thirteenth and fourteenth centuries. In 1311 it was enacted, for the furtherance of the conversion of Jews and heathen, that two professors should be appointed at the
Roman Curia, Oxford, Bologna and Salamanca, skilled in Hebrew, Arabic
and Chaldean, to translate books in these tongues into Latin, for the sake
of those who should eventually be missionaries to such peoples: but no
provision or mention was made for providing translations of the Vulgate
into any foreign tongue. Gieseler, IV. 195. For the keeping of the decree see
*Eng. Franc. Hist.* 217.

anxious that the brothers should not waste their energies by the direction of convents of sisters: some provinces continued this policy, though in Germany there was a marked change later in the century.

A long list of anti-heretical measures was again issued by the provincial council for Narbonne, held at Béziers in 1246. Chapter XXXVI enacted that certain officials

Shall see that it is rigorously carried out that theological books shall not be kept, either by the laity in Latin, or by them or by clerks in the vulgar tongue. The penalties for the aforesaid matters shall be, etc....and they shall extirpate all other things which tend to heresy[1].

In view of the evidence given before inquisitors, "theological books" in this clause was certainly held to cover biblical translations. This is clearly shewn by the account which Etienne de Bourbon, himself an inquisitor, gives of the heretics of south France, about the period of the synods of Toulouse and Béziers[2]. The signs by which heretics may be known, he says, are first, their presumptuous and unwarrantable usurpation of the office of preaching, and teaching of holy doctrine,

And especially of the gospels and other books of the New Testament, which they learn firmly by heart in the vernacular, and mumble the one to the other....For when they approach the house of simple men (for they shun the able and the learned), they say they know some good prayers, and they have fair forms of prayer, which they first say and teach, and then the gospel in the vulgar tongue, which they tell and go over according to the literal text, not merely expounding the honest meaning of the words, whenever they find those who are curious and willing to learn. For I myself have seen a young cowherd, who for the space of only a year stayed in the house of a certain Waldensian heretic, who learned by heart and retained with such diligent attention and careful repetition in his mind what he heard, that within that year he had learnt and remembered forty of the Sunday gospels (without counting the feast days), and he had learnt all these in his own tongue word for word, apart from other words of sermons and prayers. For I have seen some lay people who were so imbued with their teaching, that they could repeat by heart much of the evangelists, as for instance Matthew or Luke, and especially those things which are said there of the instruction and words of the Lord, so that they would hardly miss a word there, but repeat them in order:

---

[1] Mansi, XXIII. 724.  [2] 1229 and 1246: Etienne died in 1261.

which matter I relate because of their diligence in evil, and the negligence of catholics in good, for very many are so unmindful of their
soul and their salvation, that they scarcely know their *Paternoster*
or *Credo*, or teach them to their families[1].

That the decisions of Toulouse and Béziers continued in force
is also shewn in the register of Bernard Gui, who was vicar of the
Dominican province of Toulouse, and "inquisitor general of
heretical pravity in the kingdom of France, and specially in the
parts about Toulouse[2]" from 16 Jan. 1307 to 1323,—a man who
between 1308 and 1323 pronounced 930 sentences as inquisitor,
and sent 114 heretics to the flames[3]. In the confessions of the
Waldensians,—not the only heretical sect dealt with,—there are
several explicit references to the reading of translations, generally of the epistles and gospels: several references which shew
that the reading of such books was the sign by which the de-
ponent recognised the reader as a heretic: and very numerous
references to the reading of Waldensian books whose nature is
not specified, though analysis of the confessions shews that they
were the same described by other members of the conventicle as
"epistles and gospels." A certain Bernard of Toulouse confessed
that he had seen two heretics, father and son, in his house, and
heard the son "read in a certain book of the gospels and epistles,
as he said"; another woman heard the same two heretics read
the gospels and epistles from a certain book[4]; others heard them

[1] *Anec. Hist.* 307–9.                    [2] *Lib. Sent. Thol.* 273, 279.
[3] *Les frères prêcheurs en Gascogne*, Paris, 1885, 386.
[4] *Lib. Sent. Thol.* 10. It is noteworthy that in this inquisitor's record, as
in AM and elsewhere, reference is so often made to the use of "gospel and
epistle books," or what were later loosely called "plenaries," by the heretics:
Etienne de Bourbon expressly states that they learned "the Sunday gospels
and epistles" by heart. This shews that the argument sometimes put forward that particular manuscript plenaries could not have been made for
use by French or German Waldensians, or Lollards, because they set no
store on liturgical books, is false: the evidence shews again and again that
books of liturgical gospels and epistles were the form in which Bible reading
heretics used the sacred text more often than not. Foxe, in AM, IV. 201, is
naïvely surprised that the heretic Hun, who possessed a Lollard Bible
with the heretical prologue, and was formally condemned after death, went
to daily mass. No doubt many early Waldensians and Lollard heretics did
the same, or, at least, went on Sundays and festivals. The Lollard Purvey
would scarcely have agitated for the reading of a translation of the liturgical
gospels and epistles at mass (see p. 272), if he had not contemplated the
attendance of his followers. The word "plenary" is derived from *liber
plenarius, missale plenarium*, which in the ninth century denoted the com-

also "read in a certain book." Another man first suspected another of heresy from "seeing him reading in a certain book... and he heard him speak excellently about God, and from the epistles and gospels[1]," and a woman heard another heretic "read many words from the epistles and gospels[2]." A certain William

went to a house with others and sat round the fire, and there was there a certain man whom he did not know, and then that man pulled out a certain book and read many words from the book, and it seemed to him that the words were from the gospels, and immediately when he, William, heard this, he thought and believed that that man was one of the heretics[3].

Two others confessed that the Waldensians "preach from the gospels and epistles and other sacred scriptures, which they corrupt by their explanation like masters of error who know not how to be disciples of truth, since preaching and exposition of holy scripture is completely forbidden to laymen[4]." A priest who had joined the Waldensians, and was afterwards burnt as a relapsed heretic, confessed that he had associated with Waldensians, and that "he knew and saw and heard that the Waldensians preach sometimes after supper at night from the gospels and epistles in the vulgar tongue[5]." Another man "had seen in the house of his father and mother a certain old man, whom he did not know, and in the presence of himself and others of the household the old man drew out a certain book and began reading to them many words[6]." A woman saw two men sitting in a certain house by firelight, and one of them said holy words, and then the other opened a book, and read many words from it; and one of them told her that they were friends of God, and then she suspected their actions, because of their words, and because they read from the book[7]. The heretics often confessed merely

plete Latin missal, with the *sacramentarium*, *graduale* and *lectionarium*. By the thirteenth century, however, the name had come to mean collections of Sunday or feast day epistles and gospels, without the mass prayers, and very often with glosses, or comments (postillae). Such plenaries were sometimes in the vernacular, and were for private use only: there was never an official issue of a Latin or vernacular plenary. See *Plenarien* in HH.

[1] *Lib. Sent. Thol.* 23.       [2] *Id.* 113.       [3] *Id.* 148.
[4] *Id.* 264.              [5] *Id.* 254.       [6] *Id.* 106.
[7] *Id.* 108. The use of the term "friend of God" of a Waldensian at Toulouse before 1261 is interesting: they probably had some influence on the "Friends of God" in the Empire in the next century. See p. 75. "Friend of God" is also the meaning of "Bogomil,"—a Bulgarian heretic.

that they had heard Waldensian preaching, or, in the usual formula, "heard their words, admonitions and preaching": but the entries shew that this preaching consisted very largely of Bible reading. One man went to the house of a certain old man, a heretic, "and heard there his preaching, which he used to read in a certain book[1]"; "the younger heretic used to read in a certain book those words which he said and taught[2]." Another man has been in the cellar of a certain house by moonlight, and heard one of the heretics who was reading in a certain book some words about God[3]. Many other entries state that he or she "had seen the heretic reading in a book," or had themselves "read in the books of the heretics[4]": in any case, the register shews that the reading of biblical translations was regarded as very serious evidence of heresy.

§ 3. Three points stand out in connexion with the history of popular Bible reading in Italy. First, the Waldensians and a kindred sect were strong in Lombardy, and it is generally admitted that existent manuscripts of Italian biblical translations go back to versions made and popularised by them early in the thirteenth century[5]; this is not disputed, as it is for instance in the case of the earliest German versions. Secondly, we have no evidence of the express prohibition of such versions by any Italian synod. Thirdly, since the inquisition was used against the Bible reading heretics in Italy as well as France and Germany in the thirteenth century, it is not likely that Romance versions were considered suitable for the laity earlier than in any other European country.

The Waldensians spread from the south of France into Italy at an early date, and very soon coalesced with the existent Lombard heretics, known as the Cathari[6] or Patarini. The Patarini had originally, about 1085, been an orthodox party in Milan, the followers of the deacon Arialdus, an extreme opponent of clerical marriage. Manichaean heresy had, however, existed

---

[1] *Lib. Sent. Thol.* 112.          [2] *Id.* 140.          [3] *Id.* 107.
[4] Cf. *id.* pp. 10, 12, 54, 61, 66, 101, 110, 137, 138, 170, 180, 186, 197; for a man who made a burse to carry a heretic's book, p. 50; for those who took charge of heretics' books, pp. 50, 170, 186, 197.
[5] Cf. S. Berger, *La Bible italienne au moyen âge, Rom.* xxiii. (1894), 358–431; and V, *Italiennes* [*Versions*], iii. 1018, 1020.
[6] Cathari = the original of the German "ketzer" or heretic.

both in eastern and western Europe from S. Augustine's day, and about 1150 Italian heretics of this type, the Cathari, appropriated the name Patarini, and became partly confounded with them; similar Manichaean or dualistic sects existed in the Balkans as the Bogomils, or "friends of God," and in France as the Albigensians. The Cathari or Patarini had already been condemned as heretical by the decree of the third Lateran council of 1179[1], when Peter Waldo had presented his trans-lations, and asked in vain for confirmation of his way of life. He and his followers were not condemned as heretics in the decrees of this council: but in 1184[2] Lucius III did condemn both the "poor men of Lyons," and the Italian Cathari, and ordered the setting up of an inquisition for heresy in each parish of the infected districts, both in France and Italy. From this time there was very close connexion between the Waldensians and the Cathari, and they were for a time united in one organisa-tion. The Cathari, however, owing to original Manichaean influence, always tended to deviate more widely from orthodoxy than the Waldensians: but they borrowed from them a devotion to the study of vernacular versions of the Bible. The Walden-sians seem, in return, to have borrowed from them the sacrament of the "consolamentum," by which a postulant was "haereti-cated" or "made perfect": at this ceremony S. John's gospel was laid on the postulant's head, with certain prayers, and he became a Waldensian elder, bound to a life of poverty and preaching. The Cathari in Lombardy, like the Waldensians, held "schools" or conventicles for the memorising of the gospel text, etc., and their headquarters at Milan,—the original home of the Patarini,—formed the most famous of all the so-called Waldensian schools. The emperor Otto IV, on his way to Rome in 1209 to receive the imperial crown, issued at the prayer of the bishop of Turin an imperial edict against the "heretical Walden-sians, and all who sow the tares of falsehood in the diocese of Turin[3],"—tares that were sown by the same methods as in Provence and Lorraine.

[1] Mansi, XXII. 231.  [2] *Id.* XXII. 476.

[3] *Monumenta Historiae Patriae*, edita iussu ·Regis Caroli Alberti, Turin, 1840, IV. 487; "zizaniam seminant falsitatis": ecclesiastical comparisons of heretics to "tares" go back much earlier than papal or episcopal compari-sons of *Lollard* and *lolium*, cf. pp. 31, 83.

The group of translations which was the result of heretical propaganda was made about the middle of the thirteenth century, and is based, as can be seen from the arrangement of their chapters, on a family of Latin manuscripts which were not used in the fourteenth or fifteenth centuries[1]. They are not due to any one translator, but are of a popular character; we possess mid-fourteenth century manuscripts, the marginal notes of which indicate lay ownership or even authorship. The earliest existent translations are an early thirteenth century copy of the gospels in old Italian, with portions of a Catharan ritual[2]. The earliest Italian psalters are fourteenth century, and are based on the old Norman psalter, which was one of the biblical books presented to the pope at the third Lateran, in 1179[3]. The Tuscan or Lombardic gospels are clearly founded on the Waldensian Provençal texts, even following the Provençal when that departs from the Vulgate rendering[4]; the same is the case with the Tuscan texts of the Acts, Pauline and Catholic epistles, and the Apocalypse. There is no evidence for the possession of these translations by orthodox lay people in the thirteenth century, but we have a copy of the gospels copied by a political prisoner in 1369 at the request of a Venetian nobleman[5], and other slightly later manuscripts copied by laymen. The earliest case of work by a friar upon a translation is that of Domenico Cavalca, who died in 1342, and who added a gloss to an already existent translation of the Acts of the Apostles[6]: there is no evidence, however, that he intended it for lay use. There is other evidence that in the fifteenth century the friars possessed copies or wrote modernised versions of the old Italian texts. The evidence, however, is much too scanty for such a statement as that the friars were the chief agents in popularising biblical translations in Italy in the middle ages: we actually know only

---

[1] V, III. 1015.  
[2] Id. v. 774.  
[3] Id. III. 1020; Berger, 77.  
[4] V, III. 1020.  
[5] Rom. XXIII. 387; V, III. 1018.  
[6] V, III. 1017. This article on Italiennes [Versions] contradicts itself on pp. 1016 and 1022 as to the work of Dominicans on the Bible in the thirteenth and fourteenth centuries. There is no mention in the earlier list of translators to justify the statement "that towards the end of the thirteenth century the translation of the O.T., apart from the psalms and the sapiential books, was exclusively the work of certain Franciscans or Dominicans," p. 1022.

that Cavalca paraphrased the Acts before 1342, that Nicholas de Neridono, a Dominican, copied an Italian Bible in 1466[1], that another fifteenth century friar wrote a Venetian psalter, that two manuscripts belonged to Dominican convents, one 1363–1414, the other in 1472, and that there are a few traces of the possession of translations by individual Dominicans or Franciscans in the fifteenth century[2].

With the exception of Cavalca, the earliest Italian friars to undertake the work of translation were those of the late middle ages, after the invention of printing. In 1477 Marino of Venice helped issue a fresh edition of the Bible, with Nicholas de Lyra's expositions; at about that date Bartholomew of Modena, an inquisitor, translated or re-edited the psalter, and in 1474 Frederick of Venice prepared for publication the Apocalypse with a comment. It is however notable, and in contrast to the early printed editions in Germany, that the first Italian printed Bible was the work of a religious, the Camaldolese Benedictine Nicolo di Malherbi[3]. The latter says in his preface that many ancient partial translations existed, all anonymous: he made a very free use of such translations, following, however, in the main the usual Italian text, and printed his edition interspersed with many glosses; this, printed at Venice, was very often reprinted.

Historical references to mediaeval Italian translations are few. Dante wrote his *De Vulgari Eloquentia* about 1320, but without reference to biblical translations, such as might have been hoped for in the chapter devoted to the subjects for which the vulgar tongue is fitting[4]. There is however a very interesting passage in Passavanti's *Trattato della Scienza*, which shews that this Dominican, who died in 1357, was not in favour of the study of holy scripture by lay people, or of the increase of such translations into the vernacular: and this though he contends eagerly

---

[1] *Rom.* XXIII. 363; V, III. 1015–19: cf. Mandonnet's description of the work of Dominicans in Italy, *id.* II. 1466. Cavalca did not translate the text of the Acts, as Mandonnet says, but used an earlier translation, cf. III. 1017; the other friars he quotes are all of late fifteenth century date.

[2] V, III. 1022–.

[3] *Rom.* XXIII. 364. Parallel cases are the issue of the Dutch Cologne Bible in 1480, especially for religious, and a possible edition at Valencia, 1477, by the Dominican Borrell.

[4] *De Vulgari Eloquentia*, trans. Ferrers Howell, A. G., London, 1890.

for the knowledge of holy scripture by all people "according to their degree," and himself published his manual on *Penance* in Italian for the instruction of the simple. He says that:

Each Christian is bound to have some knowledge of holy scripture, and each according to the state and condition and rank that he holds: for in one manner should the priest and guide of souls know it, and in another manner the master and doctor and preacher: those who ought to step down into the deep sea of scripture, and know and understand the hidden mysteries, so as to be ready for the instruction of others, and to be prepared to render a reason, as the apostle says, for the things of the faith and of scripture, to whoever shall ask it. And in yet another manner the laity and unlettered parish priests are bound to have it: to whom it is sufficient to know in general the ten commandments, the articles of the faith, the sacraments of the Church, the sins, and ecclesiastical ordinances: the doctrine of the holy gospel, as far as is necessary to their salvation, and as much as they hear from their rectors and the preachers of the scriptures and the faith: not searching them subtly, nor putting the foot down too deeply into the sea of scripture, which not all people can do, nor ought they to wish to scan it: because very often one slips and drowns oneself in incautious and curious and vain researches. But each one ought to know, and study to know, as much as befits his office, and the status which he holds[1].

Throughout this tract on *Knowledge*, Passavanti uses the term "holy scriptures" or "the scriptures" very loosely, generally to include both the canonical and patristic books, though once,

[1] *Lo Specchio della vera penitenza*, Passavanti, J., ed. Polidori, Florence, 1863. The *Trattato della Scienza* is one of Passavanti's separate tracts, found in the MSS. and in the early editions at the end of *Lo Specchio*, and treated as part of it. The passage quoted is pp. 278–9. The whole tract on *Knowledge* is very interesting, but quite normally mediaeval in tone: there is nothing to shew that the clergy in Italy were more progressive or liberal in their attitude to vernacular scriptures, or other subjects, than in other European countries c. 1350. The attitude is almost precisely similar to friar Butler's tract, of c. 1399: see p. 290. Great emphasis is laid on the need of an instructed priesthood for the instruction of the laity, the examples of S. Dominic, S. Jerome, etc. being quoted. Not only masters and doctors ought to study holy scriptures, but other priests according to their condition: for in them we read what we ought to believe, to hope for, to love, and to do (p. 284). "First, we should seek for divine knowledge in the scriptures of the holy prophets and the holy gospels, and the apostles;...we ought to read books of holy doctors, approved by the Church, which expound the scriptures wisely: and not to seek it in books of philosophy and worldly poets;...as the eyes are bound to care for and supervise the other members, so are doctors and preachers bound to supervise the people: and as blindness of the eyes is a scandal to all the body, so the ignorance of priests and doctors is a scandal and a danger to all the body of holy Church " (p. 291).

clearly to mean only the canonical. He discusses the existent translations of "the scriptures," probably as including both canonical and patristic books, in his day, and decides that they should be read only with very great caution, since they were often false, and especially since they could translate only the literal, and not the moral, allegorical and mystical meanings.

In certain books of scriptures and of the doctors which are translated into the vulgar tongue, one may read, but with great caution: because many of them are found false and corrupt, either through the fault of the scribes, who do not generally fully understand them, or through the fault of the translators, who do not understand the deep passages of the scriptures, or the subtle and obscure sayings of the saints, and do not explain them according to the interior and spiritual understanding, but only the rind of the letter, according to grammar, when they turn them into the vulgar tongue. And because they have not the spiritual understanding, and because our vulgar tongue is lacking in the right words, they expound it often coarsely and rudely, and often not truly. In short, it is too perilous: for they may fall so easily into error[1].

Apart from that, he observes, they debase the scriptures; some envelope them in rhetorical and trivial glosses; some abbreviate them, like the French and Provençal scribes, some obscure them in dark language, like the Germans, Hungarians and English; some make them trifling and crude like the Lombards; some use ambiguous words like the Neapolitans; some make them rugged

---

[1] *Trat. d. Scienza*, 289. With Passavanti's dicta on translations should be compared the preface of an anonymous, but probably noble and lay, translator of the gospels into Tuscan, or reviser of the current translation into contemporary Tuscan: the work dates from the early fifteenth, or possibly even the late fourteenth century, and the author, with his insistence on the scholastic difficulties in the work of translation, offers a strong resemblance to his contemporary, Purvey. "I beg each man who wishes to transcribe this book of the gospels in the vulgar tongue, that he take care to preserve the words literally as he finds them written down, and not to change them: because little syllables and articles like *lo, la, lo propheta, la scriptura*, and such like words and syllables,—when they are put down or taken away, do more to change the meaning than other people would believe. And grammar alone is not sufficient for translation, but theology and exposition of holy doctors are required, and therefore I tell you all this, that what has been done may not be wasted. And because scripture speaks in many places like the centre of a wheel; and it is clear that there are words which should be supplied to help the unlettered: so that others may not misunderstand, and believe that the meaning of the text is changed when I supply or explain any word which shall be necessary, and where it is understood, I underline such words and sentences, so that it may be known which words are in the text and which are not." *Rom.* XXIII. 408.

with harsh accents, like the Romans; all others like the maritime
people, rustics, and dwellers in the Alps, coarsen them; the
Tuscans and Florentines perhaps least badly. Those who wish
to translate must not merely know grammar, but be experts in
theology and have knowledge of holy scriptures: they must
be rhetoricians and exercised in the vulgar tongue, and have
the spirit of holy devotion:

Otherwise they commit many faults, and many are already committed. And it is very necessary that they should be prohibited
from making any more translations into the vulgar tongue: and those
which are made should be corrected by those who have the wisdom
to do it well[1].

As in other European countries, and in accordance with the
sentiments expressed by Passavanti, such biblical translations
as were in use in the fifteenth century were those incorporated
into devotional books, rather than used as separate works.
Versions of the penitential psalms are found, and a comparatively
large number of manuscripts of gospel harmonies—or lives of our
Lord[2],—which in England, Spain and Germany were thought the
orthodox mediaeval form of the knowledge of the New Testament suitable for lay people; we have also four fifteenth century
plenaries, and a few single gospels or biblical books, laden with
glosses and paraphrases[3]. It is noticeable however that Savona-
rola, the Dominican reformer who set such great stress on
biblical study for the friars who followed him, who was such an
ardent biblical student himself, and who did all he could to encourage the study of the learned languages as an aid to biblical
interpretation, never advocated the use of biblical translations.
This, in a popular reformer who laid such great stress on the
popular adoptance of an apostolic life, and who died as late as
1498, would seem to shew that, like Gerson, Geiler von Kaysersberg, and Ximenes, he was unfavourable to them.

There is thus very little evidence, in spite of the absence of
prohibition by synod, that orthodox opinion even tolerated
biblical translations before the end of the fourteenth century,
or that it regarded them with favour from that time till the
invention of printing: though it is quite possible that vernacular

[1] *Trat. d. Scienza*, 289.                    [2] Cf. pp. 148–54.
[3] *Rom.* XXIII. 412.

versions were occasionally found in convents of Dominican nuns and friars in the fifteenth century.

§ 4. The Waldensian movement spread also from Toulouse into the north of Spain: in which country first the Waldensians were condemned to death by burning, where the first edict of the civil power was passed against them, and where the prohibition of lay Bible reading was maintained till the Reformation. The Waldensians were banished from Aragon in 1194, and condemned to death by burning in 1197. In 1233 James I of Aragon presided at the provincial synod of Tarragona[1], assisted by the archbishop and five bishops, and enacted twenty-six ordinances for the support of the inquisition and the extirpation of heresy. The first of the twenty-six was that:

No man shall possess books of the Old or New Testament in Romance. And if any possess such, let him hand them over to the episcopal seat to be burnt within eight days of the publication of this constitution; and whosoever shall not do this, be he clerk or layman, shall be held suspect of heresy, until he shall have purged himself.

The edict applied to the kingdom of Aragon: but it doubtless guided the action of the inquisition throughout the peninsula. It has been contended that this prohibition of vernacular Bible reading was allowed to lapse "in about forty years[2]": but this is exceedingly doubtful, from the later prohibitions and the nature of the remaining Spanish translations. It is difficult to believe that it did lapse, for in 1317 the provincial synod of Tarragona[3] enacted that:

---

[1] Martène, *Vet. Mon.* VII. 123, gives the date as 1233; Reusch misdates as 1276; cf. V, II. 1952. Probably both the synod of Trier, 1231, and this synod of 1233 were local efforts to carry out the policy of the synod of Toulouse, 1229, under its impressive papal and local sanctions. For *Romance*, see p. 34, n. 1.

[2] Suggested in V, II. 1952, 1956, but contradicted in Reusch, I. 43. C. H. Lea, in *Span. Inq.* 1907, III. 528 (followed by Putnam, II. 23), thinks that "from the thirteenth to the sixteenth century there was no proscription of vernacular Bibles in Spain," but he appears to take this from Villanueva's *De la leccion de la sagrada Escritura*, Valencia, 1791 (as he does the statement about Borrell's Bible, III. 52). This work was written by a catholic anxious for a more liberal attitude to vernacular scriptures in Spain at his own date, and anxious to shew that the pre-Reformation Spanish Church was not hostile to them: but he quoted only post-Reformation authorities, and was not specially well-informed about the earlier period.

[3] Mansi, XXV. 627–; cc. II. and III.

No Béguinus or Béguina shall hold, possess, or read theological books in the vulgar tongue, except books which contain only prayers, and we enjoin that those who have such books shall be compelled by ecclesiastical censure to hand them over to the diocesan bishop.

These Béguines, or lay people living under a rule, were at the time suspected of heresy: but it was also enacted that those who were actually Franciscan tertiaries "shall not have theological books in the vulgar tongue." In the Empire and the Netherlands at a later date, it was just this class of devout lay people, unable to read the Latin scriptures, who were first allowed to use vernacular plenaries[1], or books of scripture: so that it is most unlikely that ordinary lay people were at the date allowed to use books prohibited to the privileged tertiaries.

Between the years 1317, however, and about 1470, there is no direct reference to the use of vernacular Bibles by lay people in Spain, and no prohibition. Although heresy of the Waldensian type may have persisted to some extent in Aragon, the great enemy of orthodoxy in Spain was always Judaism and Judaising Christians: and there is no evidence that these used vernacular versions of the Old Testament as a means of propaganda. The Spanish Jews had such translations, and to a noticeably far greater extent than the orthodox of Castile, as is explained later: but they were apparently the property of the scholarly and the wealthy, as was the case with biblical translations used by Christian nobles of other countries at the time. Biblical translations were not therefore a source of anxiety to orthodox Christians, anxious chiefly to combat Judaism: but there is no evidence that orthodox lay people possessed biblical translations, at this time, any more than in the other European countries. The evidence from remaining manuscripts is quite the other way: and there is no reference to the value of reading translations of the scriptures in any Spanish manual of piety or instruction. There is no evidence of prohibition for this period: but the burden of proof for their use (by any except a very few princes and nobles) lies on those who assert that they were thus used[2].

---

[1] For meaning of plenary, see p. 39, n. 4.

[2] Spanish monastic and other library catalogues are plentiful, but have not been specially examined for mention of biblical translations: those adduced in Gottlieb, however, contain no such examples.

There is a reference, however, to a prohibition of biblical translations in Spain, with the special confirmation of pope Paul II, by cardinal Pacheco, the most learned Spanish doctor to attend the council of Trent. The historian of that council says:

Cardinal Pacheco noticed that among dangers to the sacred books should be considered the custom of turning them into the common national tongues, and communicating them thus translated to the ignorant people. To whom Cardinal Madrucci answered, urbanely indeed but ardently, saying the Germans would be offended, where it was accepted that the Fathers wished to deprive the people of the sacred oracles, which, according to the apostle's warning, should never depart from the lips of the faithful. And when Pacheco objected that this had been interdicted in Spain with the special confirmation of Paul II, Madrucci answered: "Paul II and any other Pope might be deceived in judging what was profitable or not, but not so Paul the apostle, in the passage alleged...." But certainly the argument of Madrucci is not fully satisfactory[1].

Pacheco tried, we are told, at the council of Trent, to have extended to the whole Church this statute of Ferdinand and Isabella, which they had imposed on Spain on account of the wicked Jews; but Madrucci opposed this successfully[2].

Pacheco's assertion about the old statute is possibly correct, for Paul II, who died in 1471, was much concerned to suppress heresy in Spain, particularly of course that of the Judaisers. The earlier inquisition into heresy in Aragon had been carried out by the royal power and the local bishops: but in 1451 the

---

[1] *Conc. Tridentini Hist.*, Pallavicino, S., 1717, lib. VI. p. 211, Pacheco, †1560, and Madrucci, †1561, are called by Pallavicino the most respected doctors from Germany and Spain respectively, to attend the council of Trent. The passage concludes: "For certainly, while heretics were publishing their false doctrines in the speech of the fatherland, it was needful to afford some antidote to those streams by which the poison was spread: but it was not therefore permissible that in that tempest all the parts of the Bible should flow forth in the vulgar tongues to the people: for in them may be found certain passages open in appearance, but profound in fact, which could at first sight appear to favour heretics;...but this would not be likely to happen with other religious books of a different kind." Passages from Alphonso a Castro (see p. 51), who wrote c. 1539, and Pallavicino, who wrote c. 1656, are quoted at length, not only for their evidence about the edict of c. 1471, but to shew that Reformation and post-Reformation catholic historians did not regard the repugnance of the pre-Reformation church to promiscuous Bible reading as a matter for apology or minimisation. See Staphylus, appendix, and p. 104 n. 1.

[2] Harney's discussion of Pallavicino, 223.

king of Castile applied to Nicholas V for a delegation of the
papal inquisitorial power to punish heretics[1]. Nicholas V readily
appointed two inquisitors, with full powers to do all acts
necessary for the suppression of heresy, and since this included
the powers granted to the inquisitors at Toulouse, 1229, and
other synods, they had the power to enforce the prohibition of
vernacular scriptures, though there is no evidence that they were
specially concerned with them. This inquisition, dependent as
it was on a weak king, never achieved much: but between 1451
and 1474 Fray Alonzo de Espina and others left no stone un-
turned to procure a fresh and more powerful establishment of
the inquisition. Paul II was pope between 1464 and 1471, and
was anxious for the establishment of an effective inquisition,
such as was actually accomplished by his successor: and though
we do not possess the prohibition of biblical translations confirmed by him, whose existence was asserted by Pacheco, it is
not impossible that the king of Castile did apply for and receive
such confirmation, in connexion with the inquisition.

There is further evidence for a fresh royal prohibition of
vernacular scriptures in Castile, Leon and Aragon between 1479
and 1504,--the years between the marriage and death of
Isabella of Castile. It is noticeable that, just when orthodox
opinion in other countries was beginning to change, Ferdinand
and Isabella issued an edict, prohibiting under heavy penalties
the translation or possession of the sacred text. Alphonso a
Castro, the friar Minor who was confessor to Charles V, addressed
the council of Trent on the subject of vernacular scriptures, and
he published a work against heresy in 1539. In the latter he
states that[2]:

The third parent and origin of heresy is the translation of the sacred
books into the vernacular, when it often happens that they are read
by mankind without distinction of persons.... If therefore heresy
arises from a perverse understanding of the scriptures, what could
more incite to heresy than the reading by the common people of that
which they cannot in the least understand? For it is difficult to
believe that untaught people should understand what the most
learned of men can scarcely grasp by long study and daily examina-

[1] *Span. Inq.* I. 147.
[2] *Opera Alphonsi a Castro Zamorensi: Adversus omnes haereses*, Paris, 1571,
lib. I. c. 13, col. 80.

tion.... *Nolite sanctum dare canibus*, etc. Wherefore most right and praiseworthy was it, that there came the edict of the most illustrious and catholic king of Spain, namely Ferdinand, and his wife Isabella, which prohibited under the heaviest penalties anyone from translating the sacred books into the vernacular, or on any pretext to keep such a translation.... From this cause came the Waldensians... and from the same reason sprang the Beghards, etc., all men untaught, and quite ignorant of letters.

Ferdinand and Isabella were married in 1479, and were most anxious to clear their kingdoms from all heretics, especially Judaisers. They applied to Sixtus IV for permission to establish an inquisition against heresy, with the fullest powers and the special guarantee and protection of the crown. This royal inquisition was introduced into Castile in 1480, Catalonia 1486, and Aragon 1487, with papal license and approval: and the royal edict mentioned by Alphonso a Castro was probably issued in connexion with this establishment of the inquisition. It was probably thought necessary to the completion of their powers, as in the imperial edict of 1369[1].

Whether or no there were any express confirmation of the prohibition of vernacular Bible reading between the royal and synodal edict of 1234, and the royal and papal edicts of c. 1471–1480, there is not a scrap of evidence that popular Bible reading was ever practised by the faithful between those dates. The edict of 1317 about tertiaries renders it improbable, as does the special severity of the Spanish attitude towards such scriptures at the Reformation and later; and the evidence from existent manuscripts confirms this view[2].

The earliest evidence of the existence of vernacular Bibles in Spain, the prohibition of 1233, probably refers to Catalan versions. The history of the earliest Spanish versions is obscure, but the earliest existent manuscripts are founded on an ancient Visigothic Latin text of the New Testament[3], which suggests a connexion of origin with the early Waldensian-Provençal translations. The tradition that the earliest Spanish translations go

---

[1] See p. 83

[2] For a short but valuable article on Spanish Bibles, see S. Berger in SH; also V, *Catalanes* [*Versions*], *Espagnoles* [*Versions*]; for the absolute prohibition of the printing of vernacular Bibles by the Spanish Inquisition after the council of Trent, V, II. 1956, and *Span. Inq.* III. 528.

[3] *Les Bibles Castillanes*, Berger, S. in *Rom.* XXVIII. 398.

back to a complete Bible translated at the command of Alphonso the Wise of Castile (1252–1286), is now shewn to be due to the fact that Alphonso actually had the *Historia Scholastica* translated into Castilian. This translation, "simply a historical work, and in no sense a history of the Bible[1]," kept less closely to the biblical text than the *Bible Historiale* in France: it was known as the *Historia General*, was probably inspired by the making of the French translation, and had a parallel history. Just as in France the Anglo-Norman psalter and Apocalypse, and then other partial biblical translations, were interpolated into the manuscripts of the *Bible Historiale*, so in Spain partial translations were also interpolated: but they were no part of the original work. The interpolations from the Old Testament seem to have been of Jewish origin, for they are founded on the Hebrew text: the oldest Spanish translation, in the Aragonese dialect, has the Pentateuch and the psalter, translated by master "Hermannus Allemannus," who actually lived in the reign of Alphonso the Wise at Toledo, and made also Latin translations of Aristotle from the Arabic[2]. The interpolations from the New Testament, founded on the Visigothic Latin text, date in existent manuscripts from about 1300–1350: but may also go back to the reign of Alphonso the Wise, and have been made under Waldensian influence. In any case, such translations as existed were in the libraries of princes and nobles only, and were never used for the popular instruction of the faithful. Thus there was in Spain, from about 1284, a Spanish *Historia General*, several partial translations of the Old Testament made by Jews from the Hebrew[3], and a translation of the New Testament made from the Visigothic Latin text. It says little for the encouragement of translations by orthodoxy in Spain, that no translations were made from the Vulgate at all. The earliest Spanish translation of the Bible founded on the Vulgate was that provided by cardinal Quiroga for Philip II[4].

---

[1] *Rom.* 366.                        [2] *Id.* xxviii. 390.

[3] See *id.* 360–408, and V, ii. 1954, where five anonymous translations of the Jewish Old Testament are mentioned: another however was the O. Test. prepared by the Rabbi Moses Arragel for the nobleman Luis de Guzman in 1422, the catholic glosses being added by a Franciscan.

[4] Mandonnet, in V, ii. 1469, states that the Dominican Jean Lopez translated the Sunday gospels into Castilian, c. 1490: but compare *id.* ii. 1956.

The Catalan versions were more plentiful, and probably go back to the prohibited "Romance" versions of 1233, for the earliest existent ones (fourteenth century) were connected in origin with the Waldensian-Provençal scriptures[1]. The Dominican Romeu de Sabruguera, who was provincial of Aragon 1312–1313, translated the psalter into Catalan, and has been supposed to have translated the whole Bible: but this was probably a mistake due to his production of a "rhymed Bible," extending to the psalms and parts of the gospels of SS. Matthew and John[2]. There is also an interesting reference to a translation of the Bible by the Carthusian Boniface Ferrer, who was prior general of the whole order from 1402 till his death in 1417. There is no improbability in a learned Carthusian's having translated some part of the Bible[3] at the date, for use by religious and specially nuns: but there is very great improbability in his having intended it for general use by lay people. In any case, there are no remaining manuscripts of such a translation, as might have been expected. This version is further said to have been edited and printed by the Dominican Jayme Borrell in 1477 at Valencia: but of this edition also "no exemplar or bibliographical datum[4]" remains. Apart from the insufficient evidence as to the existence of this printed edition, the papal and royal prohibition of vernacular Bibles c. 1471 is difficult to reconcile with such a fact[5].

It is interesting to compare the attitude of authority in

[1] See Berger in SC, and for bibliography, V, II. 346.

[2] See C. Douais in V, II. 346. This ascription of the psalter to Sabruguera is interesting to compare with the edict of Bologna, 1242, forbidding Dominicans to translate the holy scriptures, in the wider sense: and with the prohibition of vernacular scriptures for tertiaries in 1317.

[3] Or, more probably, re-edited old translations, as was done in Italy in the fifteenth century.

[4] Berger in SH. Cf. also V, II. 1957, 1961, where it is stated that the Franciscan Ambrose de Montesino edited in 1512 the gospels and epistles for the year: "but the prohibition existed already in fact at this epoch, as Francis de Enzinas affirmed in 1543 in a preface to a Spanish version of the N. Test." For this preface, see Appendix, *infra*: Enzinas states that for twenty years past there has been sharp debate and quarrels about vernacular scriptures, and men of much zeal have striven to prevent the printing of such books: in Spain is prohibited what is with reason conceded to all other nations.

[5] Though not impossible. The version may have been printed for the use of religious, and children training to be religious, like the Cologne Bible of 1480 (see p. 121): and its issue may have occasioned the prohibition. But the whole evidence for its existence is insufficient; copies of the Cologne Bible remain: those of the Valencia Bible do not.

England and in Spain with regard to the instruction of the laity in the scriptures, at the beginning of the fifteenth century. England was troubled with Bible reading heretics, while in Spain Waldensianism had nearly died out, and the enemies of the faith were the Jews. Thus in England Arundel issued his prohibition in 1408, and in 1409 confirmed the Carthusian Love's *Life of Christ* for the reading of the faithful; in Spain there was reassertion of the old prohibitions, and the Carthusian Ferrer perhaps did something in the way of biblical translation: but the popular reading-book of the laity became, not this translation, but the *Life of Christ*, written in 1409 by the Franciscan bishop of Perpignan, Francis Ximenes[1]. It was a parallel effort of authority to supply the laity with a safe vernacular substitute for the holy scriptures. Thus there is no evidence from existent manuscripts to shew that the prohibition of vernacular Bibles lapsed between 1233 and the reign of Ferdinand and Isabella. There are no cases of Spanish manuals recommending Bible reading to the laity, and no cases of Spanish epistle and gospel books being found in lay ownership, as occurs in Germany between 1500 and the Reformation. No doubt noblemen in some cases had Spanish versions of the *Historia Scholastica*: but there is no evidence that orthodox opinion in Spain was as far advanced even as in Germany in favour of the use of biblical translations.

§ 5. The history of biblical translations and their prohibitions presents peculiar features in the Holy Roman Empire: but some characteristics of the attitude of the mediaeval Church towards them in France, Italy and Spain, where the movement for popular Bible reading first spread, may now be noticed.

In regions unaffected by heresy, there was no formal opposition to biblical translations as such; but their use, or rather their

---

[1] See V, II. 2392. The subject of gospel harmonies, written from the time of Tatian in Greek and Latin for the study of the learned, and from the time of the *Heliand* in vernacular verse or prose, is very large, and has as yet received little attention from modern critics. For Latin gospel harmonies see V, II. 2113. The *Heliand* was a life of Christ in the language of the Germanic conquerors of Gaul in the ninth century (see *Bibliom.* 166): no modern work has as yet been written on vernacular harmonies from this date, but such a work would probably shew that they were relatively popular for the instruction of lay people. For an early Waldensian example, see p. 27, n. 4; for early Italian, Dutch, French and English ones, Index.

possession was in fact confined to a few kings and princes, or doctors of the university.

But manuals of instruction, whether for the laity or for the clergy, never refer to any religious duty of acquiring acquaintance with the contents of the biblical books, either by personal study or by listening to translations, until the last quarter of the fifteenth century,—that is, until the spread of humanistic ideas, and the multiplication of unlicensed printed vernacular Bibles, had made such a course inevitable. When the masses of the people were illiterate, and the libraries of even great princes usually so small, it may seem obvious that manuals would not recommend Bible study: but we sometimes meet with assertions that the " mediaeval Church " encouraged a personal study of the scriptures, even by means of vernacular versions, supported perhaps by a solitary reference of very late fifteenth century date[1].

On the other hand, the instruction of the laity was at least as pressing a problem to the Roman Curia as to the Waldensian heretics, and it would be false to imagine that it received no attention at their hands. The expedient of using biblical translations was a very obvious one, and would have seemed particularly safe, for instance, in the instruction of the secular clergy in the diocesan theology and grammar schools: and it is impossible to imagine that it was never even considered. There would have been no difficulty in issuing an approved translation in the language of any country, if the general reading of the literal text of the Bible by the laity had been regarded as desirable: but there is not the slightest evidence that such a step was ever taken.

It is nevertheless quite clear what steps were taken to meet the difficulty: they consisted of measures to obtain a better educated clergy, who should be able to instruct their parishioners[2]: this is obvious in the decrees of the fourth Lateran council of 1215[3],

---

[1] Cf. the generalisations by some of the authors of articles on vernacular versions in Vigouroux; by cardinal Gasquet; by Janssen, in *Hist. of the German People at the Close of the Middle Ages*, London, 1905, I. 23; by F. Jostes, etc. Such writers seem not to realise all the documentary evidence that exists for the mediaeval suspicion of lay Bible reading.

[2] Innocent III had commented on the duty of the faithful not to despise unlettered priests, in his letter to the faithful at Metz. See p. 31.

[3] Mansi, XXII. 979–.

and the policy can be traced later. The decisions of that council are very largely concerned with heresy,—Waldensian, Catharan and others,—and the means of dealing with it; the action of the inquisition was strengthened, and yearly confession to the parish priest was made obligatory, in order that he might be personally responsible for the orthodoxy of his flock. But the chief curative measures were those to secure better preaching and a better educated clergy:

Among those things which pertain to the salvation of Christendom, the food of the word of God is known to be chiefly necessary to it. Wherefore, since it often happens that bishops, on account of their manifold occupations...not to speak of lack of learning (which in them is altogether shameful, nor for the future, to be tolerated), are not sufficient by themselves to minister to the people the word of God,....we ordain a general constitution that bishops are to maintain and send out competent preachers, etc.[1]

Mention was also made of the clause of the third Lateran council by which a competent benefice was to be set aside by each cathedral chapter to maintain a schoolmaster, who should instruct gratuitously the clerks of that church, and also other poor scholars; this clause however had not been observed (owing to the difficulty of enforcing the setting aside of the benefice), and the decrees now confirmed it, and added that it should apply to other collegiate churches of sufficient means as well as cathedrals; and that both masters of grammar (Latin) and of theology were to be maintained[2]. The enactment was not more successful than its forerunner, and it was left to the Dominican order to improve the level of clerical learning, by the teaching given in their "studia generalia" and "studia particularia[3]": but the decree indicates the end which was always aimed at by the mediaeval Church in dealing with heresy,—the better education of the clergy, and not the self-education of the laity through the spread of vernacular versions of the Bible.

[1] Mansi, XXII. 998: cap. x.
[2] *Id.* 999: cap. xi.
[3] See *Crise Scol.* 35–49.

# CHAPTER III

## *The prohibition of vernacular Bible reading in the Holy Roman Empire and the Netherlands, before* 1400

§ 1. More material exists for the study of the attitude of the mediaeval Church to biblical translations[1] within the mediaeval Empire than in France, Italy or Spain, because contemporary thought was there more exercised with the subject. It seems likely that this was partly due to the weakness of the Emperor as compared with other secular rulers, which led both to progressive thought within orthodox circles, and to the survival of heresy without. One chronicler asserts that the heretics of the Rhine district took advantage of the civil war between rival claimants to the Empire; and possibly the relative prosperity and independence of the German free towns fostered religious societies of lay people, with their frequent mediaeval development into heresy. In any case, the orthodox section of the community which advocated the use of biblical translations took its rise in Germany, gained toleration for its attitude earlier there than elsewhere, and after 1500 was fairly strong. At that date the use of such translations was practised within only very limited circles in France, Spain, England and Italy. The forwardness of the Empire in this matter was due also to its comparatively early reception of the ideas of the Renaissance, and, of course, the development of printing. In Italy the Renaissance had been earlier still: but it had produced no religious movement as it did in Germany, and particularly, no religious movement among laymen, such as might have led to a demand for biblical translations. In Germany, on the other hand, the work done by early Béguines and Franciscans had produced religious movements among laymen long before 1400. But, whatever the cause, orthodox champions of vernacular scriptures arose earlier in Germany than elsewhere.

---

[1] Cf. T. M. Lindsay, *Hist. of Ref.* 1915, II. 147–152 for some account of pre-Reformation vernacular scriptures in Germany, and HH II. 700–13.

A continuous demand for popular Bible reading was made by different sects and religious movements in the same geographical region,—the western border of the Empire, or upper and lower Rhine country. The Waldensians about 1200 were strong in Toul, Metz, Strassburg and Cologne, whence they spread into the eastern portions of the Empire. The early orthodox Béguine communities of the upper and lower Rhine became infected by Waldensian and other heretical teaching, and were constantly accused of heresy in the thirteenth and fourteenth centuries. The German mystics and Friends of God,—both orthodox and comparatively favourable to vernacular Bibles, had their centres in the towns of the upper Rhine, or the Oberland. The Brethren of the Common Life, the outstanding mediaeval orthodox champions of German devotional books, influenced both Netherlands and Oberland: and finally, the earliest printed vernacular Bibles came from the presses of the same towns.

In the late fourteenth and fifteenth centuries, much more evidence is found for a demand for vernacular Bibles in this region, than for one by particular classes or orders throughout Europe. In Italy, Spain and Germany, there is some evidence that Franciscan and Dominican convents possessed copies of biblical translations between 1450 and 1521, and that Franciscans, Dominicans or Carthusians took some little part in the revision or publication of vernacular Bibles[1]: but the only early champions of popular Bible reading shared in one or other of the movements of this region,—that of the Friends of God or the Brethren of the Common Life especially. Not the Empire as a whole, whose rulers were probably no more friendly to translations than other kings, but the upper and lower Rhine country, was the first district of Europe to obtain toleration for popular Bible reading.

The struggle itself differed from that carried on in England by the Lollards. On the continent, the demand was always for "German scriptures" in the wider mediaeval sense, and not for German Bibles: so that, while it was more successful than in England, it had to contend partly for what in England was not

[1] Cf. the Dominican Rellach, who intended to "publish" a German translation before the invention of printing, c. 1459–61, see p. 117: but his training and sphere of work were in the Oberland.

denied,—the use of vernacular books of devotion. It never asked, as the Lollards did, for a complete translation of the Bible, but only for that of its more "plain and open parts." Again, it never asked for the encouragement of Bible reading apart from the license of the confessor; and, down to 1450, there is very little evidence that it advocated a general use of biblical translations at all, but only for convents of women, or those lay people known as the Friends of God who were under very close religious direction. The strength of the movement in Germany, at the end of the fourteenth and early fifteenth centuries, was this: that it contended for the encouragement of the laity proper to use German books of edification and sermons, the use of which was generally not questioned in England or France[1].

§ 2. The Waldensians at Metz were subjected to other attacks in 1207–8[2], and, probably in consequence, dispersed eastward into the Empire, particularly into Cologne and Strassburg. They had been found at Liège, the centre of the preaching of the founder of the Béguines, in 1203: they were at Strassburg in 1211, and eighty of them were burned in that year. Nothing is said of the translations used in the brief notices of their existence at Cologne and Strassburg, while we know that the Romance versions confiscated at Metz were in the French dialect of Lorraine.

The earliest record of the use of German translations by the Waldensians comes from a chronicler of Trier in the year 1231. Franciscan and Dominican friars had been working in Germany against the heretics since 1225[3], but in 1231 Gregory IX[4] again sent legates to carry on the work of Guido of Praeneste and the three Cistercian abbots. The chief of these legates was the Dominican, Conrad of Marburg, the celebrated confessor of S. Elizabeth of Hungary, and through his energy three years of persecution followed, as a chronicle of Trier relates[5]. The archbishop of Trier held a synod for the suppression of the Waldensian heretics in 1231; three heretics were presented at it, and

---

[1] For the controversy over the translation of S. Bernard's sermons at an earlier date, see *Chaire Fran.* 237.

[2] *Ann. Trevir.* II. 106.    [3] *Id.* II. 121.    [4] *Id.* II. 127.

[5] *Prodromus Historiae Trevirensis*, Hontheim, Augsburg, 1757, II. 796; =*Gesta Trevir.* c 103; cf. Mansi, Supp. 2, 977.

one was burnt. The acts of the synod have perished: but it was a reflex of the synod of Toulouse in 1229, assembled similarly for the suppression of Bible reading heretics and the strengthening of the inquisition, so that the passage of some prohibition of German scriptures at it is very probable. In Spain the synod of Tarragona, 1233, was a similar reflex of that of Toulouse, and its prohibition of vernacular scriptures was stringent[1]. At any rate, the confiscation of German Bibles by inquisitors followed immediately. "In the year 1231," said another chronicler, "three schools of heretics were taken in the city of Trier. And there were many who belonged to these sects, and many of them were instructed in holy scripture which they used translated into German[2]." The evidence of contemporary and later inquisitors shews that these German scriptures were as much prohibited in Germany as in France and Spain, and the probability is that the prohibition dated from the synod of Trier, 1231; though it may have rested only on the general conferment on the inquisitors of the powers granted them at Toulouse, 1229[3].

An anonymous inquisitor of Passau[4] wrote a tract on heresy[5] about 1260, and spoke from intimate knowledge of the heretics: he had been frequently present at their examination, and he reckoned that in the diocese of Passau alone there were forty-one "schools" or conventicles of heretics; some towns had more than one, but he mentions thirty-four towns or villages which possessed at least one. He gives most details about his own diocese of Passau, but mentions the number and power of the Waldensians elsewhere:

In all the towns of Lombardy and Provence, and in other kingdoms and countries, there were more schools of heretics than of theologians, and many hearers. And they used to hold public disputations and summon the people to hear them in courts; and they preached in the fields and in houses, and there was none who dared to hinder them, on account of the power and number of those who supported them.

He explains the six causes of heresy; the third is that they have translated the New and Old Testament into the vulgar tongue, and this they teach and learn:

---

[1] See p. 48.     [2] Mansi, XXIII. 241.     [3] See p. 37
[4] Formerly known as Reiner the Dominican, cf. Preger, 7, on his identity
[5] MBVP, XIII. 298.

For I have heard and seen a certain unlettered countryman who used to recite Job word for word, and many others who knew the whole New Testament perfectly[1].

The second is the heretic's diligence in teaching and learning these biblical translations:

All, men and women, cease not to teach and learn, night and day. The workman, who toils by day, learns or teaches at night....They teach and learn without books,...and even in leper-houses....To those who excuse themselves, saying that they cannot learn, they say: "Learn only one word a day, and in a year's time you will learn three hundred, and thus you will grow proficient." What I say is true.

The fifth cause is their insufficient doctrine; for they hold as fables whatever a doctor of the Church teaches which cannot be proved by the text of the New Testament, contrary to the teaching of the Church. After the discourse on these causes of heresy, he gives a list of questions for the help of his fellow inquisitors in the examination of heretics, and it is significant that the first and primary question is whether the suspected heretic has ever heard or learned the words of the German gospels, etc.:

First, if he has learned any holy words, and when he began to learn, and from whom? Has he ever taught them to lay people[2]?

This inquisitor's experience and recommendations shew that undoubtedly these translations existed, though condemned, in south Germany, in the period between 1231 and 1260.

[1] MBVP, XIII. 299; cf. 300. "They say also that Latin prayers do lay people no good....Also that what is not proved by the text of the Bible is fabulous. They say too that holy scripture has the same effect in the vulgar tongue as in Latin, wherefore they consecrate in the vulgar tongue, and administer the sacraments. Also, they know the text of the New Testament and a great part of the Old, by heart, in the vulgar tongue: and they despise the Decretals and the Decrees and the sayings and expositions of the saints, and adhere only to the biblical text. And they refuse to acknowledge the mystical sense of holy scripture," etc.

[2] *Id.* 308. This inquisitor is the only writer, as far as I am aware, who questions the accuracy of the Waldensian translations. He does not accuse them of perversion, but only of textual blunders arising through ignorance. His tract is in Latin, but he particularises the German words of the translation which are blunders: and says that the heretics even confuse *sui* and *sues* (i.e. *porci*), in the text *In propria venit et sui eum non receperunt* (John, i. 11), a confusion actually found also in another French translation. The modern assertion that the prohibitions of Waldensian scriptures were due only to their wilful mistranslations is not justified: it is not mentioned by contemporaries. The dependence of particular doctrines on particular texts and their translation only became a matter of controversy in the sixteenth century. Cf. *supra* p. 30, n. 1.

The writings of the Minorite, David of Augsburg, are also evidence for the work of the inquisition in Germany against the Waldensians, or the "pauperes de Lugduno." He belonged to the south German Minorite province, was the pupil of Berthold of Regensburg, and acted as inquisitor for some years: he died in 1272[1]. The burning of German heretics had begun again in 1265, and the inquisition was active in Austria and Bavaria between 1250 and 1270. David says that the early followers of Peter Waldo began, though laymen, to preach the gospel:

And because they presumed to interpret the words of the gospel in a sense of their own, not perceiving that there were any others, they said that the gospel ought to be obeyed altogether according to the letter: and they boasted that they wished to do this, and that they only were the true imitators of Christ.... This was their first heresy, contempt of the power of the Church[2].... They give all their zeal to lead many others astray with them: they teach even little girls the words of the gospels and epistles, so that they may be trained in error from their childhood[3].... They do not receive the Old Testament as of faith, but they learn only certain passages from it, in order to attack us and defend themselves, saying that, when the gospel came, all the old things passed away. And similarly they pick out the words of SS. Augustine, Jerome, Gregory, Ambrose, John Chrysostom, Isidore, and short passages from their books, in order to prove their illusions and to resist us. And they very easily lead simple people astray, by dressing up their sacrilegious doctrine with fair passages from the saints; but they pass over in silence those passages of the saints which seem to contradict them, and by which their error is refuted. They teach their docile and fluent disciples to repeat the words of the gospels and the sayings of the apostles and other saints by heart, in the vulgar tongue, so that they may know how to teach others and lead the faithful astray.... All their boasting is about their singularity; for they seem to be more learned than other men, because they have learnt to say by heart certain words of the gospels and epistles in the vulgar tongue. For this reason they esteem themselves superior to our people, and not only to lay people, but even to literate people; for they are fools, and do not understand that a school boy of twelve years old often knows more than a heretical teacher of seventy: for the latter knows only what he has learnt by heart, while the former, having learnt the art of grammar, can read a thousand Latin books, and to some extent understand their literal meaning[4].

[1] Cf. Preger, 8, who prints the complete form of the tract, which is given incompletely in Martène, *Thes.* v. 1777–.
[2] Preger, 26.  [3] *Id.* 33.
[4] *Id.* 29. For a discussion of this evidence see *Die deutsche Bibelüber.* 18–.

Both inquisitors thus agree that the use of biblical translations was the mainspring, in Germany as in France, Italy and Spain, of the Waldensian heresy: while the whole tenor of their evidence, and especially the circumstance that the first question to be put to a heretic by the inquisition was, whether he knew any biblical words by heart, shews that the use or knowledge of such translations was prohibited. That Waldensian heretics used German translations of the New Testament and parts of the Old from 1231, and throughout the thirteenth century, is also beyond dispute.

§ 3. The origin of the existent manuscripts of the old German translation of the New Testament, and part of the Old, is much disputed; a great deal of controversial literature on the subject has appeared in pamphlets and periodicals in Germany from 1885 onwards[1]. It is certain at any rate that all the early German printed Bibles follow a text derived, as regards the New Testament and part of the Old, from a group of late fourteenth century manuscripts, and that this text is followed in the majority of the manuscript plenaries, or collections of the epistles and gospels, with glosses. There was, that is to say, a German translation of the New Testament at least, which was sufficiently widely known to be copied in all the plenaries and early printed Bibles, and to be translated into Low Dutch. The oldest and most remarkable manuscripts of this translation are those at Wolfenbüttel, Freiberg and Tepl[2], all written shortly before or after 1400, the oldest being the New Testament which belongs to the cloister of Tepl in Bohemia[3]. Controversy has raged as to whether the prototype of the manuscript was the work of an orthodox or a Waldensian translator: possession of the translation in other manuscripts can be traced to both

---

[1] There is a good bibliography at the end of *Allemandes [Versions]* in V. See especially Keller; the above quoted works of H. Haupt contending for a Waldensian origin; and F. Jostes' *Die Waldenser und die vorlutherische Bibelübersetzung*, Munster, 1885; Haupt, *Walden. Ursprung des Codex Teplensis*, Würzburg, 1886; and W. Walthers' *Die Deutsche Bibelübersetzung des Mittelalters*, Brunswick, 1889, as leaving the question undecided.

[2] Cf. W. Walther, HJ, XII. 687; and F. Jostes in HJ, XV. 771-, XVIII. 136.

[3] *Grundriss der Germanischen Philologie*, Paul, H., Strassburg, 1901–9, II. I. p. 354. Though this is the oldest complete New Testament, the same translation is found in older plenaries: cf. MSS. 532, 4878, 66, 157, 58 at Munich, cited by Haupt, *Walden. Urs.* 26.

Waldensians and orthodox, and so has little significance as to
origin. It seems probable that the actual Tepl manuscript was
copied by an orthodox scribe, since it has directions to shew
which parts of the gospels correspond to the special gospels for
the three masses for Christmas Day[1]. It is true that from the
earliest times Waldensians used the Sunday and saints' day
gospels in translations[2], perhaps more even than the continuous
text of the New Testament; but between 1380–1400 it is more
likely that this use indicated an orthodox owner. It is also likely
that the manuscript was copied in a monastery: not merely on
the grounds that it is written in several hands[3], which might even
more easily prove that it was copied for a university stationer
or bookseller than in a monastic scriptorium, but because, at the
date, orthodox opinion was beginning to allow the use of biblical
translations in German monasteries, more readily than to lay
people[4]. The real question, however, is as to the origin of its
prototype; for, when linguistic knowledge was so slight, and
translations never bore their authors' names, there is no difficulty
whatever in supposing that an orthodox scribe copied a text
which 150 years earlier had been Waldensian in origin, or *vice
versa*. The first Waldensians incorporated the old Norman psalter
in the book of translations they presented at the third Lateran
council[5]: the fifteenth century Dominicans in Italy certainly
used the old Waldensian translations: there was not, before the
Reformation, any question as to the orthodoxy of the contents
of particular translations, only as to the propriety of their
existence[6]. Two points, however, stand out in connexion with
the original of the Tepl manuscript:

i. The earliest Waldensian (Provençal) translations were made
anterior to the issue and general acceptance of the famous Paris
revision of the Vulgate, of the thirteenth century. The earliest
existent Waldensian texts, Provençal, Catalan and Italian, were
founded on a Latin Bible, the use of which prevailed widely
in the Visigothic kingdom of Narbonne, up to the thirteenth

---

[1] *Tepler Bibel.* 40; *Walden. Urs.* 15; Keller, c. iii.
[2] See p. 34.        [3] Jostes, *Die Waldenser*, 8.
[4] See pp. 109, 121.       [5] See pp. 27–8.
[6] Keller's endeavours to read heretical meanings into the German translation at Tepl shews a lack of historical perspective: see Keller, 83–.

century, but was afterwards completely superseded by the Paris Vulgate[1]. It is characterised by a set of peculiar readings, amounting to over thirty, in the Acts of the Apostles, and these readings appear, as S. Berger pointed out, in the early Provençal, Catalan and Italian Bibles. They appear also in the Tepl manuscript: and S. Berger, whose authority is very high, gave it as his opinion that the prototype of the Tepl manuscript was translated from such a Latin version, or even from a very early Provençal version[2]: he therefore concluded that the Tepl manuscript was of Waldensian origin[3]. This remains the chief positive argument for such an origin: for, although scholars can parallel particular variant readings from other manuscripts, their number and coincidence with the Visigothic Vulgate has not been satisfactorily explained by any theory save that of S. Berger[4]. The question is not: Is it more probable that an orthodox or a heretical translator made the German translation shortly before 1400? but, Is it more probable that a Waldensian or an orthodox person made its prototype, since he used as his basis a particular Latin version which was not in use much after 1200, or the Provençal translation founded on it? The absence of record of the making of an orthodox translation at the date, and the certain knowledge that the greater part of the New Testament then

---

[1] *Walden. Urs.* 30–.

[2] Earlier than existent manuscripts: cf. Walther, 191.

[3] *Walden. Urs.* 31. S. Berger in *Revue Historique*, XXX. 1. 1886, p. 168, traced the textual resemblances between the Tepl MS., particularly the Acts, and earlier Waldensian (Provençal) texts, and concluded: "From so many resemblances, none of which by itself would suffice to establish a certainty, but the accumulation of which leaves scarcely room for doubt, we must conclude that according to all probability...this, the most important German Bible of the middle ages, appears to have been translated in part, by the efforts of the Waldensians, from an original written in one of the Provençal dialects."

[4] Walther, in his long and laborious work on the mediaeval German Bible, agrees that the original of the Tepl MS. was much older than the Tepl MS. itself, and that the Tepl manuscript has remarkable resemblances to the Romance translations. He is unwilling however to accept S. Berger's conclusion (see p. 191), though his alternative theories are unconvincing, and unaccompanied by evidence. "Why," he asks, "if there is some resemblance between the French and German versions, should the French not have corrected theirs from the German? Or why should not either of them, in preparing a Romance or German version, have used an already existent catholic version?" We have, however, excellent historical evidence as to how the earliest Provençal translations were prepared, cf. Etienne de Bourbon in *Anec. Hist.* 291, and pp. 26–7 of this book.

existed in Waldensian translations, makes the theory of a Waldensian origin at least probable. The argument, that a Waldensian translation would not have been used by the orthodox 150 years later, certainly has no strength. In any case, the strongest argument for the antiquity of origin of the original of the Tepl manuscript, is S. Berger's verdict on its Latin source.

ii. Controversy has also raged as to the nature of the tracts which accompany the biblical translations in the Tepl manuscript, and which have been claimed to prove, not merely a Waldensian original, but even Waldensian possession of the manuscript itself. The Latin tracts are patristic and inconclusive: they may or may not have been copied from the same manuscript as the translation, and in any case both Waldensians and orthodox used patristic literature in support of their doctrine[1]. The other two tracts are curious. They are in German, which says something for an early association with the ancestors of the Tepl translation, and they consist of a list of the seven sacraments and the seven articles of the faith, both with short expositions[2]. That on the seven sacraments may have been originally orthodox or Waldensian, since many Waldensians acknowledged the seven sacraments, and some accepted them at the hands of orthodox priests: arguments from the order of the sacraments in the tract are inconclusive, for it is very doubtful whether there was a recognised order either among Waldensians or orthodox at the date. The tract on the articles of the faith, however, has a very marked verbal resemblance to those demanded from Waldensian ordinands, as contained in an early manuscript: the seven articles in both are indistinguishable in orthodoxy from the catholic seven articles, but the verbal resemblance is much closer than between the Tepl articles and any other orthodox catechism or articles with which controversialists have compared them[3]. The significant feature however is the date of origin to which the number of the articles point. The division of the creed into articles or clauses was

[1] Cf. Jostes, *Die Waldenser*, 9–; *Walden. Urs.* 1–9; for Waldensians and patristic literature, David of Augsburg, in Preger, 29, etc.
[2] Jostes, *Die Waldenser*, 10–; *Walden. Urs.* 9–18.
[3] *Id.* 11–13.

primitive[1] and arbitrary: the division into seven, or the doubled number, fourteen, had no particular relation to the structure of the creed, but was an arbitrary summary of its contents under the number denoting perfection: the whole creed was divided into seven, or seven clauses were assigned to both the godhead and the humanity. The division into seven goes back at least to the third century, and it is likely that it was superseded by the division into fourteen in the thirteenth, or early fourteenth century. English manuals and catechisms in the fourteenth century certainly teach twelve or fourteen articles of the faith[2]: and it is probable that this was the continental custom. The synod of Var in 1368 set forth fourteen articles of the faith for the instruction and guidance of parish priests of little learning[3], as do the majority of fourteenth century manuals and catechisms. It is thus certain that the division of the creed into seven articles goes back to a period anterior to the fourteenth century, and probable that it was only used in the fourteenth century as a verbal and traditional rendering of an older form: it had been generally superseded by the fourteen articles. This would seem to shew a very early origin for the Tepl tract, quite possibly at about the date of the original translations themselves, and it strengthens the argument for the antiquity of those translations. Thus the Latin source of the earliest German biblical translations, and the antiquity, and probably Waldensian nature, of a tract accompanying the Tepl version, both point towards the early thirteenth century as the date of the first German translations; a date at which the historical evidence is much stronger in favour of a Waldensian than an orthodox origin.

§ 4. The Rhine valley and Rhine mouth seem from the twelfth century onward to have been the scene of religious movements among laymen, of the association of lay people in communities for the purpose of leading a devout life, and, (closely connected with this), of the tendency of such communities to deviate into heresy, through the "mediocre learning," as

---

[1] The creed of Origen at Alexandria, A.D. 230, and the creed used at the baptism of Palmatius, Rome, c. A.D. 220, were both divided into seven clauses.

[2] See pp. 196–9. I have not found a manual or catechism of the date which divides the creed into seven articles.

[3] Mansi, XXVI. 486.

their enemies said, of the local leaders of the movements. While Peter Waldo was getting the gospels translated for himself at Lyons, Lambert le Bègue (the Stammerer) was preaching in the Netherlands. Gilles d'Orval, a religious of Liège, the town where Lambert himself preached, wrote in 1251 a chronicle of the city; he says that Lambert, the founder of the Beghards, "although he was but little instructed in the study of letters," was a celebrated preacher at Liège, c. 1167–91: he incurred, however, the displeasure of the bishop, and when he was imprisoned in the castle of Rivogne in consequence, "and had been kept some little time in captivity, he translated the Acts of the Apostles into French[1]." Another chronicler states "he was a fervent preacher of the new devotion which filled Liège and the neighbouring regions,"—a phrase curiously reminiscent of the contemporary description of the Brethren of the Common Life as the "founders of the new devotion." Lambert translated many books, especially the lives of the saints and the Acts of the Apostles[2]; the Acts and a life of our Lady were probably in verse[3]. His career as a popular preacher, founder of communities and translator of scriptures, bears remarkable resemblance to that of Gerard Groot (or, the Great), the founder of the Brethren of the Common Life. Though orthodox himself, the resemblances in his story with that of the early Lollards is also curious, while it is certain that the name Lollard was copied from that applied to the Beghards[4], or followers of Lambert, early in the fourteenth century. Beghard, or the Latin, Beguinus, was derived from Lambert's own surname:

[1] *Mon. Germ., Scrip.* XXV. 12: lib. iii. § 43; and Berger, 49.
[2] *Mon. Germ., Scrip.* XXIII. 855.
[3] *Inq. Neer.* II. 365, 25.
[4] The English word *beggar* is probably derived through O.F. *bégard* from the Flemish *beggaert*, a follower of Lambert le Bègue; the form *beggaert* being derived either directly from Bègue with the masc. ending *ard, hard,* or from the Latinised *Beguinus,* with *ard.* The earliest English example is *beggares,* in the *Ancren Riwle* of 1225, and the word *beg* means always, to ask alms, (not, to be a lay preacher). There is no Flemish word *beg,* to ask alms. See NED. Grosseteste, †1265, knew of these lay preachers: he told the Franciscan William of Nottingham that "there was a higher degree of poverty than mendicancy, namely to live of one's own labour; hence, he said that the Béguines are of the most perfect and holy religion, (religious order), because they live of their own labour and do not burden the world with exactions." (*Eng. Franc. Hist.* 87.) The Wycliffites were great students of Grosseteste.

Lollard, from a Flemish word meaning to "mumble" or "mutter[1]."

Beghard, Beguinus or Beguina had at first no opprobrious significance, but in 1209, and from then onwards, the Beghards received various ecclesiastical condemnations. This was due partly to the looseness of their organisation and wandering life, partly to suspicion of contamination by heretical pravity. The Waldensian heretics had in fact come to Lambert's own city of Liège in 1203[2], and the similarity of their life of lay piety to that of the Beghards probably led to a mutual influence upon each other. But the term Lollard, which had always a heretical implication, was not applied to the Beghards till the beginning of the fourteenth century, when they had fallen seriously into disrepute. "Lollard" was applied to Wycliffe's followers and poor priests from the resemblance of their wandering life, and doubtful orthodoxy, to those of the Beghards or Lollards of the Netherlands (one of whom had been burned, as a "Lollard," as early as 1322), and whose existence as a band of "wandering and hypocritical fellows[3]" had been noticed in Brabant as early as 1309. These societies of devout lay people, living without monastic rule, were disliked by the regular religious, not only on account of their dubious orthodoxy, but as rival associations:

And thus they are plainly wont to say: if this man or woman desire to remain a virgin, why does he or she not enter our religion? What is such a person doing in the world? Why does he or she not fly to the cloisters of nuns or monks from the midst of Babylon[4]?

[1] Lollen or lullen, see NED; Gieseler, IV. 159; and in *Anec. Hist.* 307, the Waldensians "learn the gospels by heart in the vernacular and mumble the one to the other." This meaning of Lollard,—a heretical Flemish lay preacher,—was undoubtedly that implied by the Irish Cistercian monk, Henry Crump, who caused a disturbance in 1382 by calling the Wycliffites "Lollards," in a sermon preached in the church of S. Mary the Virgin (FZ 311). But ecclesiastics connected the derivation with *lolium*, the tares sown among the wheat; and the populace, and even Wycliffites themselves, with the ME *loll* (lounge, sprawl). Cf. the Wycliffite preacher who said "the most blessed Loller" was Christ Himself, "lolled between two thieves" (p. 274), and the examples in NED.

[2] SH, *Waldo.*

[3] *Hypocritae gyrovagae*, Gieseler, IV. 159.

[4] *Id.* n. 2. For those in Italy, n. 3; in France, in 1321, *Lib. Sent. Thol.* 298; and for the Dominican prohibition of biblical translations made by the friars for houses of nuns or Béguines in 1242, *supra* p. 37; those in Spain, p. 49.

So strong was this feeling, that the term "Béguines" was applied even to Franciscan and Dominican tertiaries, not only of the Rhine country, but in France, Spain and Italy[1].

As associations of devout but unlettered lay people, the Beghards and Béguines were a class to whom vernacular scriptures would have been specially useful, and there is evidence that vernacular books were popular among them. They were infected with Waldensianism at an early period, very shortly after Lambert's own death: and there are some indications that among the vernacular books they used were translations of the canonical scriptures.

A bishop of Doornik in the late twelfth century issued an ordinance, commanding all parish priests to proclaim as heretics publicly and frequently at mass, all those who, among other crimes, "translate the psalter[2]." In 1310 the archbishop of Trier condemned the Béguines because "they feign themselves to the unlearned to be expounders of holy scripture[3]." In that same year a very learned Dutch Béguine, Margaret Porete, was condemned and burned at Paris: she had held heretical tenets, and made a translation of holy scripture[4].

Some Béguines also were infected with the heresies of the Brethren of the Free Spirit, and the Fraticelli, and studied the books of Peter John Olivi, and especially his exposition of the Apocalypse, in the vernacular, as the inquisitor of Toulouse frequently ascertained; later Beghards studied other heretical and semi-heretical books in the vernacular[5]. The Béguine movement, though influenced both by the German mystics and by the Brethren of the Common Life, nevertheless remained a parallel movement down to the beginning of the fifteenth century.

There are other evidences that early Dutch translations of the Bible were received with hostility by the hierarchy, besides Lambert's Acts of the Apostles, composed in prison. In 1271 Jakob van Maerlant, a Dutch poet and layman, translated,—not the Bible itself, but—Peter Comestor's *Historia Scholastica*

---

[1] *Lib. Sent. Thol.* 299, 300, 313, 316, 318, 325.
[2] *Inq. Neer.* I. 149.
[3] *Id.* I. 155.
[4] *Id.* II. 64.          [5] See p. 82.

into Dutch verse[1]. This work was later translated by clerks into French and German for royal or noble students, without exciting opposition: but Maerlant was himself a layman, and seems to have intended his translation,—a very free one,—for popular use. He complained in a later poem that there was far greater eagerness to read tales of Tristram and Lancelot, Perceval and Galahad than the gospel, "which is too hard for us, because it is so true and righteous: and mark now a clear and certain token,—he who would so gladly hear it, for him it may easily be deemed unfitting[2]." Maerlant incurred ecclesiastical censure of some sort for his translation of the *Rijmbijbel*, and the tradition of this was sufficiently widely spread to be known to an English writer of the fourteenth century. Maerlant himself mentions it in a subsequent translation of the *Speculum Historiale*, in which he omitted to translate the biblical portions, either because he had already translated them, or a large part of them, in the *Rijmbijbel*, or (as he himself hints), because such translations were unacceptable to ecclesiastics. He says in the *Spiegel Historiael*, I. 3, that he will give only the main facts of his original, omitting the theological portions and learned discussions,

because they are too hard for the lay people: and also I am afraid about it, that the papacy might take it amiss, if I should wish to undertake this. And I have been subjected to attacks from this source, because I have made known to the lay people secret things out of the Bible[3].

---

[1] *Rijmbijbel*, ed. David, J., Brussels, 1858–9; cf. Jonckbloet, I. 228–. Maerlant's poem, *Die Clausule van der Bible*, is only a hymn to, or life of, our Lady. For the view that opposition to the *Rijmbijbel* was due only to its lay authorship, see Hellwald 115; *Hist. of Flemish Literature*, Delepierre, London, 1860, 39.

[2]
> Truffe van minnen ende van stride
> Leest men dar de werelt wide;
> Die ewangelie es ons te zwaer,
> Om dat soe recht seit ende waer.
> Merct een tekin harde clare:
> Wie so gherne horen tware,
> Hem mach lichte niet gescien,
> Men sabre noch duegt an zien.

*Leven van Sint Franciscus*, Tideman, J., Leyden, 1847; *Werken uitgegeven door de Vereeniging ter bevordering der oude Nederlandsche Letterkunde*, Vierde Jahrgang, Derde aflevering; p. 4.

[3]
> want den leeken eist te swaer;
> ende occ mede hebbic vaer,

Maerlant's pupil, Jan de Weert, himself a layman, mentions the opposition his master had incurred, in his *Disputation between Jan and Roger*[1]:

> Because he unbound the Bible into Dutch:
> And because he exposed himself for his poem's sake:
> For this they were wroth.

The matter is referred to in the tract in favour of biblical translations, written in England at the end of the fourteenth century, probably by John Purvey:

> It was heard of a worthy man of Almain, that some time a Fleming, (his name was Jacob Merland), translated all the Bible into Flemish. For which deed he was summoned before the pope of great enmity: and the book was taken to examination and truly approved. It was delivered to him again, in confusion to his enemies[2].

It is thus certain that some sort of storm was raised against Maerlant by the publication of the *Rijmbijbel*, no doubt by the local ecclesiastics. In his earlier and famous poem, the *Wapene Martijn*[3], he had lamented over the decadence of the world in his day, and specially over the evil condition of the Church, and the ignorance and idle lives of the clergy. These were naturally hostile to him afterwards: Maerlant said, in his preface to the

> dat des dat paepscap belgen soude,
> of ic mi dies onderwinden woude.
> Ende anderwaerven ebbic gewesen
> in haer begripen van desen,
> want ik leeken weten dede
> uter byblen die heimlichede.

Quoted *Tepler Bibel.* 36; printed in *Spiegel historiael*, Amsterdam, 1849; cf. Jonckbloet, I. 229.

[1] As quoted by Jostes, 36:
> Want die Bibele hi in Dietsche ontbant,
> Ende voor sijn dicht thooft hi boot,
> Voor dies hadde toren.

With slight variations in *Denkmäler altniederländischer Sprache und Litteratur*, Kausler, E., Leipzig, 1866, III. 16; and in Jonckbloet, I. 229. Jan de Weert lived at Ypres, was a doctor of medicine, and died about 1362. He was a great admirer of Maerlant, and also a translator: his chief work was the translation of the *Speculum Peccatorum* into Dutch, as the *Nieuwe Doctrinael* of *Spiegel der Sonde*, c. 1351. For his other works, cf. *Biographisch Woordenboek der Nederlanden*, Van der Aa, Haarlem, 1877, xx. 96.

[2] Printed in Appendix.

[3] *Jacob van Maerlant's Strophische Gedichte*, Verwijs, E., Gröningen, 1879, XI-; cf. *Maerlant's Werken beschoud. als Spiegel van de dertiende Eeuw*, Jan te Winkel, Ghent, 1892, 68; 183–200. For Maerlant's laments about the clergy of his day, cf. also his *Der Kerken Claghe*, in the *Strophische Gedichte*.

*Rijmbijbel*, that he had enemies who were ever ready to attack him[1]. It is significant also that for years after the publication of the *Rijmbijbel* in 1271 nothing appeared from Maerlant's pen, though both before and after these years his output was large and regular. It is quite possible that his enemies appealed to the Curia about the matter, for appeals to Rome in the thirteenth century were regular, and often occasioned by quite minor matters. Maerlant may have actually travelled to Rome, or authority to deal with the matter may have been sent to the local bishop of Utrecht, John of Nassau. Maerlant's reference to the "papacy" in his *Spiegel Historiael* is, moreover, precise, and would scarcely have been used if no appeal to Rome had been made at all. If he actually travelled to Rome to defend his *Rijmbijbel*, and obtained an assurance that it was harmless, coupled with a warning not to meddle with high matters in the future, both his own words in the *Spiegel* and Purvey's form of the tradition would be easily understood. The Curia was less ready to condemn translations than the local bishops, the *Rijmbijbel* was after all only a translation of the *Historia Scholastica*, and the authorities at Rome had not been annoyed, like those at Utrecht, by the popularity of the *Wapene Martijn*.

Nearly a hundred years later, another layman undertook the work of translating the *Historia Scholastica* into prose, in 1358[2]. His preface shews that, at the date, the majority of the clergy still regarded Innocent III's letter and the synodal decisions as prohibiting biblical translations. The author states his intention of translating the Bible for popular edification:

And yet I know well that it shall be much begrudged among the clergy. Now, that they may well understand the usefulness thereof, know that... because it torments some clerks, that men should unbind the secrets of scripture to the common people: and they refuse to know, that the apostles of Christ preached and wrote their teaching in all tongues and speeches to the people[3].

---

[1] Quoted te Winkel, 66:

> Die altoes versch ende nuwe
> Talrestont sijn daertoe gerust
> Dat hem emmer begripens lust
> Mijn gedicht ende mine wort.

[2] For prose versions, V, *Néerlandaises* [*Versions*], IV. 1549; HH, III. 119; *Boekzaal*, 235–9.

[3] Quoted in full, *Boekzaal*, 367–9; partially, *Tepler Bibel*. 36. Actually the author translated only the O. Test. portion of the *Hist. Schol.*, which he

Similar references to the state of clerical opinion at the time are too numerous and important for us to belittle the opposition of these clerks as that of a "few zealots[1]."

§ 5. The German mystics of the upper Rhine in the fourteenth century gave the first important impetus towards the use of vernacular Bibles from the side of orthodoxy. The Beghards were suspected of heresy: Maerlant had been a layman: but many of the *Gottesfreunde* were Dominicans or Franciscans, and therefore of trustworthy orthodoxy. It is true that direct advice to lay people to use translations comes rather from the later "Friends of God," when the movement had already become partly heretical, or from the lay side of the movement, which was accused of heresy at an early stage: but the work of the most unimpeachably orthodox "Friends of God" did a very great deal indirectly for the sanction of vernacular Bibles, by encouraging the practice of meditation among the laity as a primary duty.

Denifle has shewn that the real significance of the German mystics, the Dominicans Eckhart, Tauler, Suso, and the other Gottesfreunde, was not the originality of their thought,—even in Eckhart's case,—but their popularisation of scholastic mystical teaching by means of vernacular sermons and vernacular writings[2]. Through these, the mystical theology of the pseudo-Dionysius, of S. Augustine, S. Bonaventura and the Victorines first reached a wide lay public: and this led eventually to a demand for biblical translations which devout lay people could use for meditation. The fact is hardly (as Eicken expresses it)[3] that teaching as to the duty of striving after immediate communion with God led by analogy to the desire for an immediate acquaintance with His Word; for the early

seems to have regarded as equivalent to a glossed text of the Bible: "It has long been in my mind, that I would gladly translate the foundation of the scripture out of Latin into Dutch, because I hope that many holy men who are ignorant of clergy shall profit by it" (*Boekzaal*, 368). The book was first printed in 1477 at Delft (*id.* 365), with the names of the printers, but not the last editor.

[1] *Tepler Bibel*. 36; Jonckbloet, I. 241; Hellwald, 102, 115.

[2] *Meister Eckhart's Lateinische Schriften, und die Grundsanschauung seiner Lehre*, in *Archiv für Litteratur- und Kirchen-Geschichte des Mittelalters*, II. (1886), 416–.

[3] *Geschichte und System der Mittelalterlichen Weltanschauung*, Eicken, H., Stuttgart, 1887, 786.

followers of the Friends of God were taught to lay far greater stress on guidance by a Friend of God, or enlightened spiritual director, than on a personal study of the scriptures:

"Dear Christian men," said an early Friend of God, perhaps Nicholas of Bâle, "I advise you in all truth that you learn to be able to fight against all vices,...and whoever is not yet well prepared to fight, let him seek out such men as are well learned in the eternal truth, and ask them to teach him to fight against all vices: and let him also gladly hear sermons and read good little books, through which men may also become well instructed[1]."

"It would be well for such men, who wish to live to the truth," said Tauler, "to have a Friend of God, to whom they could submit themselves, and who would direct them according to the Spirit of God;...such men ought to seek an experienced Friend of God, even twenty miles round, who would know the right way and guide them aright[2]."

But, on the other hand, it was certain that teaching which encouraged lay people to imitate "religious" in the practice of meditation and attention to God, would soon need to provide material for such meditation. For a Benedictine monk or a Dominican friar, the material had always been the Vulgate: the sanction of German scriptures for nuns or tertiaries who could not read Latin, and finally for lay people, followed naturally, more especially when their use was only demanded for those under close religious direction.

Meister Eckhart, or "the Master," as he was called by his followers[3], died in old age in 1327, after being provincial of the Dominican order in Saxony since 1304. His chief works remain as vernacular sermons, no doubt preached chiefly in convents of Dominican nuns. Denifle has pointed out the importance of the constitutions for the reform of these houses in the German provinces in 1281. Dominican convents of women were especially numerous and important in Germany, and most of all on the upper Rhine, and the care of these obviously involved a great labour to the friars' convents. In 1252 Innocent IV had removed the charge of all of them except two from the Dominican order,

---

[1] Printed in C. Schmidt's *Johannes Tauler von Strassburg*, Hamburg, 1841, 231.

[2] *The Inner Way*, Hutton, A. W., London, 1909, 174.

[3] *Archiv*, II. 529.

to leave the brothers more free for preaching, etc.[1] (just as in 1242 the chapter general had sought to interdict the friars from being visitors to, or in charge of, women's convents). The example of this pope however was not followed[2], the care of them was again committed to the brothers, and in 1281 Hermann of Minden, the provincial, drew up constitutions for the reform of the houses, and their direction by the friars. "Ye shall give heed," it was provided, "that the sisters lack not the word of God, but that it shall be preached to them frequently, according as befits their learning, by learned brothers[3]." It was further enacted that the lecturers at the Dominican studia, and the masters of arts, were to lecture to the sisters, and that these sermons were to take place on vigils rather than on saints' days or Sundays, in order that the people should not be attracted from the houses of the brethren, or from their parish churches, on those days,—a provision which clearly shews that lay people were admitted to hear the sermons, probably in the sisters' antechapels. This provision was carried out, and the most learned of the brothers were sent to preach to the sisters: a circumstance which was the main cause of the spread of mystical ideas among the laity. Many of the German mystical sermons were thus delivered, including those of Eckhart and Tauler; the brothers preached the theology they had themselves learned, but "sicut eruditioni ipsarum convenit," in German. Denifle claims that a large number of women in the Dominican convents came from the highest burgher class, and some from the nobility[4]: their intelligence was not slight, and fitted them to profit by such sermons[5]. Such was the genesis of German mystical preaching

---

[1] *Archiv*, II. 642.

[2] To Denifle's regret: he sees a connexion between this burden on the brothers, and the paucity of Dominican theologians in Germany in the fourteenth century; *id.* 645. There was exactly the same problem in the Franciscan order; nearly a century earlier, it meets us among the Praemonstratensians.

[3] *Id.* II. 645, 650.

[4] *Id.* II. 647.

[5] The Dominicanesses at Nuremberg had more than one volume of Eckhart's sermons, c. 1469, and many other sermons: some taken down by one of the sisters during the sermon; cf. p. 112. Mediaeval writers like Rolle, the author of the *Cloud of Unknowing*, and Hilton give such frequent warnings that their metaphors must not be understood literally, that the need of some degree of education in the hearers of mystical discourses is apparent.

within the Dominican order, afterwards copied sporadically by other orders: Strassburg was thus a centre of German mysticism, because it had seven convents of Dominican nuns. The sermons influenced not only the nuns, but the laity who frequented their chapels, to whom the friars were also confessors and directors; and in the fourteenth century the term "Friend of God" was used, not of the members of a particular religious association, but of those who aspired to a life of mystical piety, whether religious, secular priests or lay people.

The leader of the movement in its early stages was a layman, Nicholas of Bâle, who was influential between 1330 and 1382, and acted as spiritual director to four other laymen who lived with him, and also to Tauler in his youth[1], and to Rulman Merswin of Strassburg. Nicholas himself had been a young knight, had been converted, and given himself to the study of the saints' lives in German. He was regarded by Tauler as a man of the greatest holiness, and only at the end of his career incurred suspicion of heresy, through confusion with the Beghards. He evaded the inquisition for a time, but was finally burned as a heretic,—and as a "Friend of God," not as a Beghard,—in 1397[2]: one of the most celebrated of his pupils, Martin of Mainz, a Benedictine monk of Reichenau, having suffered in 1393. Other Friends of God were also burnt, before and after this date;—there was enough burning of Beghards and Friends of God at this time to justify any English Lollard's fear of the same fate for years before the *De Haeretico Comburendo* statute of 1401. The movement was throughout regarded with some jealousy by the clergy, on account of its lay element: but it may fairly be considered orthodox until brought into disrepute by the speculations of Rulman Merswin, a layman who founded a religious community near Strassburg, and was condemned as a heretic in 1382, though his community survived him.

Between 1300 and 1350, when verse translations and homilies upon the Sunday gospels were being prepared in the north of England, and a verse *Legendary*, or lives of the saints, in the

---

[1] Gieseler, IV. 186; Friedjung, 185. See also Denifle's researches on the early Gottesfreunde, Tauler and Merswin in *Das Buch von geistlich Armuth*, Munich, 1877, preface, and *Tauler's Bekehrung*, 1879.

[2] The exact date is disputed.

south, parallel work was going forward among the Friends of God in Germany. A German gospel harmony, with the epistles for Sundays and saints' days, dates from 1367[1]: but a later manuscript incorporates the preface of a biblical translator of about 1340[2]. The latter was a layman of the Gottesfreunde type, who believed that biblical translations would be useful to lay people, but was much opposed by orthodox scholars and ecclesiastics for such a belief, and for engaging on the work of translation; the opposition he mentions is like that of the Dutch translator of the *Historia Scholastica*[3], but he describes his enemies more vividly and at greater length. A translation in prose of the Sunday gospels and epistles was also apparently prepared by the Gottesfreunde about 1340[4]: it may go back to earlier collections made by the immediate followers of Eckhart for German nuns: and these again may have been founded on the Waldensian translations condemned by German inquisitors about 1250, and earlier. The collection of c. 1340 is contemporary and has been connected with the work of another Friend of God, Hermann of Fritzlar[5]. The latter collected, between 1343 and 1349, a set of prose sermons on the lives of the saints, in which the mystical teaching of Eckhart is intermingled, and wrote a preface to them, with illustrations from his own travels in Italy, Spain and Germany. His sharp reproaches of worldly priests and teachers are similar to those of Nicholas of Bâle, and the above-mentioned translator; and he made use of earlier material in apparently the same way as the collector of the Sunday epistles and gospels.

There is thus a certain amount of direct evidence that the Friends of God, orthodox or semi-orthodox, advocated the use of biblical translations by the laity. Nicholas of Bâle, or one of his early followers, urges the reading of German books of piety

---

[1] This is the earliest plenary quoted by Haupt in the list of MSS. cited in *Walden. Urs.* 26.

[2] Printed p. 118. The translator apparently belonged to the same period as Nicholas of Bâle, and Hermann of Fritzlar, but he may have been slightly later.

[3] See p. 74.

[4] See ADB, VIII. 118, and Keller, 47.

[5] See HH. His *Buch von der Heiligen Leben* followed an earlier compilation, perhaps by the Dominican, Gieseler von Schlotheim, lector at Cologne and Erfurt, and the latter used a still earlier one, c. 1337.

in 1356: it is noticeable both that he is not mainly concerned
with biblical translations (though he may have included such
books as German plenaries among the books he considered
useful), and that there were many "great teachers" of the time
who considered German books of edification, of any sort, unlawful for the laity,—-an opinion stated as common knowledge
in an imperial edict of 1369. After the passage quoted earlier,
the tract continues:

> But some teachers say, that German books are harmful to Chris-
> tianity. That in one way is very true, and in another way not true.
> In one way it would certainly be good that certain books should not
> be turned into German, the books that have many glosses, for such
> books do not appertain to lay people. For you will take a part of them,
> and expound it according to your carnal manners, and you cannot
> get the matter clear, and so you go astray: and such glossed books
> are proper for the priesthood. But such little books as this little book
> is, and also other German books which are of this kind, and moreover
> not written contrary to the holy scriptures,—such German books are
> very useful and very good for simple people, and you shall not let
> the great teachers deprive you of them (for those teachers themselves
> are full of the scriptures and the doctrine of God); if they seek them-
> selves, in the honour of this world, more than God. But where you find
> teachers who seek not themselves, them shall you gladly obey,...
> and such counsel is, moreover, not contrary to holy scripture, for the
> holy scripture and the Holy Ghost are in union one with another[1].

The next reference is more explicit. Otto of Passau, a Franciscan lector at Bâle, wrote in 1386 a book of allegorical and
mystical piety, called the *Four and twenty elders, or the Golden
Throne*, in reference to the Elders of the Apocalypse[2]. Nothing
is known of Otto except what he himself tells us in the preface[3];
the book was regarded as orthodox and became intensely
popular, though it appeared just at the time when the Gottes-

---

[1] C. Schmidt's *Tauler*, 231.

[2] *Die vier und zwanzig Alten, oder der guldin Tron*, Antony Sorg,
Augsburg, 1480, to which the references are given, the later editions being
unfoliated. A modernised edition was printed in 1835 at Landshut, as the
tenth volume of the *Leitstern auf der Bahn des Heils*, entitled *Die Krone der
Aeltesten*.

[3] See *Boekzaal*, 322, and E. Schroeder's article in *Gött. Gel. Anz.* 1888,
p. 251. This article, while treating of the attitude of religious orders to
biblical translations, confuses the authorship of the *Four and twenty elders*,
attributing it on p. 255 to Otto of Passau, and on p. 257 to John Nider, the
Dominican. This article is probably the source of the error in HH, where
John Nider is said to have written a book called *Four and twenty elders*.

freunde movement was declining into heresy[1]. The preface
states that the book is addressed to all the Friends of God,
clerical and lay, male and female,—that is, it was intended for
the devout section of the population only. Certain sections deal
with the holy scriptures[2], their great usefulness, and the obligation of man to follow them; and in one place the author gives the
first mediaeval approbation of biblical translations by a religious:

I advise you also with all diligence, to read the scriptures of the
Old and the New Testaments oftentimes with reverence and earnest-
ness, either in German or in Latin, if you understand Latin[3].

The advice is one of great interest, but it proceeded from the
participator in a certain movement and was addressed to a
certain class, and cannot therefore be quoted as representative
of the general opinion of the friars or the clergy at the time. If
it were so, it would be paralleled in the very numerous contemporary manuals and works of piety.

§ 6. The Beghards, as has been said, dragged on a rather
precarious existence during the fourteenth century. Restrictions
had been placed upon them by three synods from 1269 to 1281:
and a sweeping condemnation was passed against them by the
synod of Béziers in 1299. They were again condemned at
Cologne in 1306, and in 1310 the synod of Trier passed a decree
against "those who under a pretext of feigned religion call themselves Beghards... and, hating manual labour, go about begging,
holding conventicles, and posing among simple people as inter-
preters of scripture[4]." An attempt was made at Vienne in 1311
to suppress them, as the main instruments in the spread of
heresy: and between 1366 and 1378 a fresh and serious attempt
was made to suppress them in Germany, by Urban V and
Gregory XI, aided by the "pfaffenkaiser," Charles IV.

[1] The authorities quoted are the Bible, the Fathers, "those heathen writers
whom the Church does not condemn," and S. Elizabeth of Schönau.
[2] 1480 ed. f. ciii.: "Der xiiii alte leret von gotlicher geschrifft und gotlicher
kunst." f. cix.: "Von der heiligen geschrifft wie man jr volgen sol." f. cx.:
"Was die heilig geschrifft grossen nucz schafft."
[3] Id. f. cxi.: "Ich rat dir auch mit allem fleiss das du die geschrifft der
alten und der newen ee dick und vil mit andacht und mit ernst lesen solt,
es sei in teütsch oder in Latein, ob du Latein verstandest."
[4] Mansi, xxv 261: "Seque fingunt coram personis simplicibus exposi-
tores sacrarum scripturarum." The Waldensian influence had thus survived
in the Beghards of the Rhine country in 1310.

It was recognised, in this outburst of persecution, that heretical beliefs had been spread by German "scriptures," including glossed plenaries and other books of homilies and semi-mystical devotion. Certain Friends of God at least had contended for German epistles and gospels, against the opinion of the main body of the clergy; and some had already been burned as Beghards and heretics. The Béguines who approximated to the Brethren of the Free Spirit had used the condemned works of Berengarius and John Peter Olivi; and other Béguines had used the German sermons of Eckhart to support their pantheistic heresies. Eckhart's works had been condemned by bull in 1329[1], as a result of this confusion, though a later bull had tacitly ignored the earlier condemnation. It was probably against the works of Eckhart that the reiteration of the prohibition of German scriptures was largely directed, either because they were still considered heretical by some theologians (though studied with the greatest reverence in some Dominican convents), or because their doctrine was considered utterly unsuitable for the uninstructed laity,—a qualification which was constantly recognised by mystical writers in the vernacular themselves, in the fourteenth and fifteenth centuries. A champion of German scriptures in 1398 expressly excepted

those books which in the style of their writing differ from that of the doctors of the Church: and this is said because of certain German books which have a new, profane, and abusive mode of speech, and certain of them are entitled: *Of Eckhart*, or the *Sermons of Eckhart*[2].

John Nider[3] the Dominican also described certain Beghards[4] at the time of the council of Bâle, who

use subtle, sublime, spiritual and metaphysical words, such as the German tongue can hardly express, so that scarcely any man, even an educated man, can fully understand them; and in these they wrap up lofty sentences about spirit, abstraction, various lights, divine persons, and the grades of contemplation.

And certain German books, full of their subtle sermons, plainly do

---

[1] Raynaldi, *Ann. Eccles.*, Lucca, 1750, V, 450.

[2] See p. 75.

[3] A Swabian and a reformer, belonging to the convent of Bâle; †1438.

[4] In his *Formicarius*, or *Myrmecia Bonorum*; in the 1611 edition, lib. iii. c. v. p. 215; cf. Schroeder in *Gött. Gel. Anz.* 1888, p. 255. For the same argument against translations in England, see pp. 289–94.

good service to their evil intention, and use such expressions; and some of the books were written foolishly and rashly, or were allowed to be copied,—unless I much mistake; and there are some at least which are obviously falsely ascribed to certain honest and ancient doctors of religion by certain Beghards or heretics. For they hide the poison of their depravity beneath the cloak of such words, and express the venom of their malignant heresy by means of them.

Against such books of subtle sermons, and the translations undertaken by the laymen of the Gottesfreunde movement, a sweeping measure of prohibition was enacted by the emperor. Charles IV had always been a staunch supporter of the Church and ecclesiastics, and was himself interested in devout literature, legends of the saints[1], etc.: but it was not till 1369 that his interview with Urban V at Rome led him to undertake a campaign against German books of piety. The pope had already made a fresh attempt to suppress heresy in Germany by means of the inquisition: in 1367 he sent Walter Kerling[2], and three other Dominicans, as inquisitors under papal authorisation, and called on all German prelates to support them: one heretic was burnt at Erfurt and seven elsewhere. When the Emperor was returning from Rome in 1369, he issued from Lucca, at the request of the pope[3], a number of bulls in support of the inquisition, assuring to it privileges and protection which it had never before received in Germany[4]. The fourth of such edicts issued within a week dealt with the subject of German books at great length. It was addressed to the Dominican inquisitor Walter Kerling, to Louis de Caligula, and two other Dominicans to be chosen by Walter Kerling as fellow inquisitors. After the usual reference to the tares (zizania), which the enemy of man had sown in the Lord's field, and which should be rooted up by the faithful, it proceeded[5]:

---

[1] See Friedjung, 149.  [2] Id. 194.

[3] Id. 195; and Mosheim, 368. The first of the group of imperial edicts issued in support of the inquisition in 1369 was promulgated "opitulante Domino Deo ac domino nostro summo pontifice mandante." Friedjung states that these edicts were aimed against the heretical Beghards, and the "last remains of the Waldensian heretics," p. 196.

[4] 10 June, 1369, jurisdiction of the inquisition increased indefinitely: six great nobles appointed its protectors: order for the confiscation of a third part of a heretic's goods to be confiscated to the inquisition; 11 June, 1369, all houses of Beghards and Béguines to be suppressed; 17 June, 1369, the last unconditional edict modified in favour of the orthodox and old established Beghard houses; 17 June, 1369, edict against German devotional books; cf. Friedjung, pp. 194–9.

[5] Mosheim, pp. 368–75; Inq. III. 612.

Wherefore, since we have received trustworthy information that there are in Germany sermons, treatises and other books written in the vulgar tongue, which are used by lay people, or those who are almost lay people[1]: and that these books are generally harmful, erroneous, and infected with the leprosy of heresy: and that the lay people who read them do not understand them in a safe and good sense[2]: and that they wish to know through their own understanding more than it befits them to know, and not soberly and according to the measure of faith: and that they turn away their ears from hearing the truth, and turn themselves instead to error, through him who is the father of lies.... Wherefore we strictly enjoin and command all the venerable archbishops, bishops...and all clerics secular and regular...and all dukes, princes, marquesses etc....and each and every man, on their obedience to the Holy Roman Empire:...that ye assist the said inquisitors and their deputies to demand and confiscate such books, treatises, sermons, pamphlets, leaves, bound books, etc., written in the vulgar tongue, from all men, whatsoever their rank: and any other books written in any other manner, which are suspected of containing heretical errors, which books might give occasion to certain seducers of souls to preach and teach errors. And all these are to be taken from all persons, secular and regular, and chiefly from lay people (and the more especially, since it is not lawful, according to canon law, for lay people of either sex to read any books whatsoever of holy scripture written in the vulgar tongue[3]), so that such books may be examined: lest through a false understanding men should be led into heresy or error, even as many Beghards and Béguines in these days are, alas, led into error and heresies. And ye shall lend your counsel and effectual help, with all your powers and with devout minds, to punish those who are rebellious and disobedient with the penalties set forth below, according to the style of the inquisition,... for the effectual prevention of books of this kind.... And ye shall lend your counsel and effectual help that the aforesaid books should be presented to the inquisitors to be burned[4].

[1] "Personas laycas vel pene laycas." *Laicus* in mediaeval Latin frequently bears the sense of *unlettered*: as here.

[2] This and the following sentence are such as were frequently used in arguments against biblical translations, by those who claimed that a translation of the bare text did not give the subsidiary mystical understandings, and was dangerous. See Index, Textus.

[3] "Praesertim cum laycis utriusque sexus, secundum canonicas sanctiones, etiam libris vulgaribus quibuscunque de sacra scriptura uti non liceat." Mosheim, p. 370.

[4] Martini printed this edict from Mosheim's unpublished work, and collated it with a MS. at Helmstadt: see p. 368, and *Inq. Neer.* I. 215–17. The names of the witnesses to this group of edicts leave no reason to doubt their genuineness. The edict is perhaps the "antique statute" referred to in certain statutes made for Dutch tertiaries by the chapter-general at Utrecht: the copy was made by the warden of the Barbara-Kloster at Delft before 1585: "Renovatum est illud antiquum statutum, quod cantica

It is noticeable that this very stringent edict was addressed to the inquisitor to whom the Emperor had, shortly before, "confirmed and approved all the powers and privileges of inquisitors in Lombardy, France, Toulouse, Carcassonne, Italy, Gallia, Germany and elsewhere[1]."

The decree of 1369 had an indirect result in the breach between Charles IV and Henry von Mügeln[2], who in one sense compares with the Englishman, Richard Rolle, and in another with Maerlant. Like Maerlant, he was a layman and court poet,—one of the most famous amongst the meistersingers. He wrote some verses descriptive of the contents of the Bible: and then, like Rolle, and at about the same stage of the development of the vernacular tongue, he prepared a translation of the psalter, with glosses. Rolle wrote his psalter before 1349: von Mügeln sometime between 1345 and 1370. It is significant that both chose the psalter for translation, and both thought it necessary to afford a gloss as well. Rolle chose the gloss of Peter Lombard[3], von Mügeln the postill of Nicholas of Lyra,—a much more up-to-date choice. Lyra was a Franciscan, with a great reverence for the Hebrew text of the Old Testament, and considerable knowledge of Hebrew. Von Mügeln's choice of Lyra's postill for the gloss made his work fairly popular and simple, since Lyra made no attempt to give a fourfold interpretation to each passage: but there is no indication that his translation was made specially for lay people. He had lived for a long time at Prague, enjoying the favour of Charles IV, but, after the issue of the 1369 edict against German scriptures, he fell into disfavour and left the court.

It is noticeable, in contrast to Charles IV's edict, that his

canticorum, Biblia ac etiam novum testamentum, ante annos aliquot impressa, non legentur, iuxta mandatum imperiale, nec detinebuntur in conventibus sororum" (*Hist. Episcopatuum foederati Belgii*, Van Heussen, Antwerp, 1755, I. 413). The reference may however be to the imperial edicts (1529, 1533 or 1550) of Charles V, prohibiting the making or use of translations of the Bible: see Harney, 212, 218.

[1] Mosheim, 345. This is significant as shewing that provincial decrees, passed for the strengthening of the inquisition, were not purely local in effect, but were regarded as precedents. As Kerling was expressly given the powers of the inquisitors in Toulouse, it was certainly within his right to enforce the decree of Toulouse, 1229, against biblical translations.

[2] Walther, 589, 718; cf. *infra*, p. 145.

[3] See p. 146.

successor, the Emperor Wenzel, had more liberal ideas about translations. He is said to have ordered a certain Martin Rotlev to translate the Bible, and a late fourteenth century manuscript exists, known as the Wenzel Bible, though it contains only the Old Testament[1]. The translation, however, is related to that in other manuscripts, and goes back to a common original, now lost. The book was not meant for popular use, and was not widely copied: it was probably meant for the possession of the Emperor or some exalted personage.

Like the earlier decrees of Toulouse, Paris, etc., the imperial edict clearly prohibited German translations of the Bible, plenaries, service books, psalters, sermons, books of mystical instruction, and not only these, but (if strictly interpreted) such orthodox manuals as books of vices and virtues, confession books, etc.,—since these, like Eckhart's sermons, could be regarded by a zealot as "de sacra scriptura tractantes." It was, in fact, an attempt to revive the policy of the synod of Toulouse: but at a date when the growth of orthodox vernacular manuals made such a sweeping prohibition impossible. In England it would have rendered illegal Rolle's psalter, the *Prick of Conscience*, and the *Ayenbite of Inwyt*, while in Germany the development of German plenaries and orthodox manuals was more advanced. Etienne de Bourbon could enforce such a decree, because orthodox French manuals in the thirteenth century were still so rare as to be possessed only by the great: Walter Kerling could scarcely do so, and it was possibly at his request for further instruction, possibly at the petition of Nicholas of Bâle himself[2], that a fresh edict was issued by Gregory XI in 1375, the rescript *Ad Apostolatus*[3]. This was much less sweeping than the imperial edict:

Since it has come to our apostolic ears, that in some regions in which ye exercise the office of inquisitors of heretical pravity, there are certain simple laymen, for the most part illiterate, who read or have read to them certain books of sermons written in the vulgar tongue, which are said to contain heretical errors: and that these laymen usurp to themselves the office of preaching, and publicly

---

[1] See F. Jelinck, *Sprache der Wenzelbibels*, Görz, 1899; and *Amer. Jour. of Phil.* XXI. 62–75, *The Wenzelbibel*, by W. Kurrelmeyer.

[2] Friedjung, 198.

[3] Mosheim, 378; *Inq. Neer.* I. 237.

propound doctrine which they know not, because they have not learnt it: and that through reading and hearing what they do not understand, become masters of error rather than disciples of truth: Since therefore books of this kind in the vulgar tongue are too dangerous, and since it is not lawful to preach except for those to whom it is expressly granted,...we command your discretion by the apostolic authority, that you cause such books to be brought forward and exhibited to you, in those places in which ye exercise the office of the inquisition, in order that you may diligently examine them among you; and ye shall condemn by apostolic authority those books, or those parts of them, in which ye shall find heretical errors. And ye shall announce them to be erroneous and heretical to the people in sermons, and by the apostolic authority prohibit for the future any such lay person from presuming to preach, or any other man from daring to write, buy, sell, or possess condemned books or sermons of this kind, or to say that he believes any dogma written in them, or in anywise to disclose it[1].

Moreover, the words *secundum canonicas sanctiones* express the belief that biblical translations[2] were generally prohibited,—a belief held by the majority of ecclesiastics down to the last quarter of the fourteenth century, and by a very important number of them, even in Germany, to a later date. This prohibition is referred to as a matter of common knowledge, for which proof is unnecessary. The canon law, like the common law in England, was primarily unwritten and traditional, to be decided by cases tried in the ecclesiastical courts. By this time it had become almost entirely written, the earlier traditional law having been further elaborated by papal legislation, as English common law was gradually limited and defined by statute law; and it was, finally, expressed in the great ecclesiastical codes, the *Decretum* of Gratian, and the *Decretals* of Gregory IX, the *Liber Sextus*, etc. The words "canonical sanctions" might refer to any such expression of the canon law, as interpreted by commentators of acknowledged authority, or to synodal edicts. But the common knowledge here appealed to was probably that of the confiscation and burning of vernacular scriptures by the inquisition, from which the inference was obvious that "canonical sanctions" lay behind their action. These sanctions were not

---

[1] Friedjung, 198.
[2] Compare also the frequent condemnation of vernacular prayer-books in the examinations of suspected Lollards, *infra*: and the fact that a Dutch theologian found occasion for defending the usefulness of vernacular prayers, p. 95.

simply the prohibitions of provincial synods, binding only within the province itself, for the inquisitor of Passau's evidence shews that German Bibles were regarded as evidence of heresy in other provinces than Trier, and this is confirmed by that of David of Augsburg for Austria and Bavaria, and the wide powers given to Walter Kerling himself. Not merely were the decisions of local synods cumulative in effect as precedents, but, wherever the inquisitors worked, the sanction of the synod of Toulouse in this matter seems to have lain behind them. For most people, assistance at a book-burning was a far more frequent source of education than the study of the decisions of provincial synods, and it was to knowledge thus gained that the edict of 1369 appealed. In any case, the words are those of the Emperor's responsible advisers, and not merely of a few "fanatics or zealots."

# CHAPTER IV

## Bible reading in the Empire and the Netherlands
### c. 1400–1521

§ 1. At the end of the fourteenth century a fresh movement, the "New Devotion," arose in the Netherlands, and sought to establish a devout community life, not under religious vows like those of the monks, and not supported by mendicancy like the friars. This movement of the "Brethren of the Common Life" struggled to increase devotion among lay people, and it succeeded in converting a large section of orthodox German opinion to the usefulness of German and Dutch books of scriptures for this purpose. The "New Devotion" was founded through the exertions of Gerard Groot, who died in 1384: and it took shape in the formation of houses of Brethren or Sisters of the Common Life, as at Deventer, or of canons regular under the influence of Groot's teaching, as at Zwolle. The strength of the movement lay largely in its insistence on learning among the brethren or canons themselves, and their zeal for secular education. It was not merely their devotion, but their intellectual ability that enabled the founders of the New Devotion to save themselves from being confounded with the heretical Beghards, and to protect themselves from the attacks of their enemies: their learning also of course largely protected them not merely from the punishment for heresy, but from heresy itself. Nevertheless, they were at first bitterly attacked as "Lollards" and heretics, both on account of their zeal for the use of German books of devotion by the laity, and through the jealousy of many regulars, who regarded any life in community not under the three religious vows as necessarily "Beghardist" and "Lollard."

In 1398 the Brethren of the Common Life summoned to their house in Deventer a gathering of the law school at Cologne and other friendly ecclesiastics, to obtain from them legal pronouncements, or "determinations," on the many points for which the inquisition attacked them. The most important was that on the lawfulness of the manner of community life which they practised, and which the new communities of sisters practised under their direction. But second in the list of determinations[1], both for length and importance, came a joint determination of the doctors on the lawfulness of the use of German "scriptures" in the wider sense, including biblical translations, by the laity. The librarian at the house of Deventer at the time was Gerard Zerbolt[2], or Gerard of Zutphen, and it is more than likely that in such a capacity he acted as secretary to the conference of doctors, and possibly even had some share in the drawing up of their joint determination. From the fact that a seventeenth century editor[3] printed the determination, in a slightly altered form, from a manuscript which he calls "the book of Gerard Zerbolt," the tract has long been ascribed to this brother. The earliest manuscript, however, states quite clearly[4] that when certain

---

[1] The determinations exist in four MSS. (1) Royal Library at the Hague, MS. 355, the earliest, (2) Burgundian Library at Brussels, MS. 2285–2301, quarto, (3) Helmstadt MS., see Mosheim, 433–, (4) Cologne MS., see HH, III. 478. Jostes printed the list of the determinations, and that on vernacular scriptures, in HJ, XI. 14–22; 709–17, without stating from which MS. he was printing: but Dr Byvanck, librarian at the Royal Library, the Hague, finds that his version is identical with that of the Hague MS. Mosheim used this MS. also, and his editor Martini collated his transcript with the Helmstadt MS. Mosheim printed, not this determination on vernacular scriptures, but some of the others more directly defending the brethren's manner of life against the inquisition, and also the inquisitor's comments upon them; for the documents in this heresy trial, see *Inq. Neer.* II. 176–84.

[2] See Jostes, *Die Schriften des Gerhard Zerbolt von Zutphen* in HJ, XI. (1890), 1–; Revius, 41.

[3] Revius.

[4] The list of doctors' names is given in the title of the determination on vernacular scriptures, which comes second on the list, and not at the beginning, as responsible for the whole set of determinations. The first (see HJ, XI. 4) is a tract "from the sayings of the saints and the determinations of the doctors" on the mode of life of the brethren; the second, this tract with the doctors' names; the third and fourth are attributed to Everard Foec; the fifth, a direct attack on the inquisitors of Cologne, is by a "certain devout and learned man" who prefers to remain anonymous; the sixth is the determination of abbot Arnold. Jostes regards the list of nine lawyers as responsible for the whole set of determinations, and imagines that one of them must have been responsible for the tract on vernacular scriptures: he inclines to abbot Arnold, while others have ascribed it to Everard Foec. But since this special tract is attributed jointly in the MS. to the nine lawyers, it is superfluous to ask which of them was the author, and misleading to call the tract anonymous (HJ, XI. 14). Abbot Arnold's concurrence in it makes him, as far as is known, the next religious after Otto of Passau to approve of German Bibles,—but he excluded the Apocalypse as unsuitable for the laity, while Otto's work is based upon it.

doctors were assembled at Deventer in 1398 to give the brethren
their verdict on certain doubtful points, nine of them, whom it
mentions by name, concurred in giving this determination on
the lawfulness of vernacular scriptures. Of these nine, three
were doctors of law, three doctors of decretals, or canon law,
and three licentiates in law[1]. All were men of position and influence, and probably all were secular priests except the abbot
Arnold of Dyckeninghe. With their decision concurred "many
others," whose names are not given.

There are no grounds for supposing that the university of
Cologne had been especially influenced in its attitude to biblical
translations by the spread of Wycliffite teaching, as was the
case at Prague. It was almost certainly influenced by the earlier
liberal teaching of the Waldensians, Beghards and Friends of
God, and it was certainly no friend of the inquisition introduced
by Charles IV: these influences and motives to some extent
account for the readiness of the doctors to support the Brethren
of the Common Life in the matter. It is interesting to compare
their pronouncement with the words of Matthias of Janov, a
doctor of Prague, who held the same views on many disputed
points as Wycliffe, and died in 1394. He had the greatest
reverence for the sacred text, and, though he did not suggest
its popularisation, would perhaps have been ready to agree with
the doctors of Cologne in their determination.

"And because I read blessed Augustine[2]," he says, "in the book
*Of Christian Doctrine*, and Jerome, who says that the study of the text
of the most holy Bible is, first and last and above all things, necessary
to each man desiring to attain to a knowledge of theological truth:
and that the Bible is the first and fundamental matter, and ought so
to be, to each lettered Christian: immediately my soul was joined
to the Bible in a perpetual love. For I confess that from my youth

---

[1] "Of Hermann Stakelwegghe, provost of S. George in Cologne, John de
Novo Lapide,' canon of Aachen, John called Bau scholasticus of Mechlin,
doctors of law: and of Arnold abbot of Dyckeninghe, Gerhard of Gröningen,
John of Wercborch, doctors in decretals: and of Ralph ' de Rivo ' dean of
Tongres, licentiate in law; and of Tielman Eckhart of Attendorn, licentiate in
law, advocate of the church of Cologne. With whose Responses concur Master
Everard Foec, dean of S. Saviour at Utrecht, licentiate in both laws, and
many others." Mosheim, 433; *Inq. Neer.* II. 177.

[2] Gieseler, IV. 240. Purvey, the editor of the second version of the Wycliffite Bible, had the same devotion to Augustine's *O Christian Doctrine*;
see pp. 281, 303.

it has not departed from me, even to old age, neither in the way, nor
when I was occupied, nor when I was at leisure.  And in all my perplexity, in every doubtfulness, I ever found in and through the Bible
sufficing and enlightening help and consolation to my soul: and in all
my perturbations, persecutions and sadnesses I fled in all cases to the
Bible, which, as I have said, walks ever with me, as my best beloved.
...And when I saw that many men carried with them everywhere
the relics and bones of divers saints, for their especial defence and
singular devotion, I chose for myself the Bible as my elect, the companion of my pilgrimage, to bear ever with me.''

Matthias limited the necessity of a knowledge of the text of
the Bible to theological students, even though he took up a
Wycliffite position in many of his other writings.  To what extent
the doctors of other German universities would have sided with
the lawyers of Cologne or with the chancellor of the university
of Paris, whose hostile attitude will be mentioned later, is
doubtful: but there would probably have been more liberal
opinion among the learned for the ten years before the council
of Constance than later.  No doubt many potential German
Bibles burned with Hus.

The determination of the lawyers of Cologne and the abbot of
Dyckeninghe is headed thus:

*It is asked whether it is lawful for lay people to read or possess sacred
books written in the vulgar tongue, or translated out of Latin into the
vulgar tongue*[1]?
To which it is briefly answered: that to read such books is lawful
and meritorious, provided they do not contain heresies or errors,
and especially if they treat clearly of plain subjects, and do not
disagree with the books of the saints, either in the style of the writer,
or in likeness of reasoning.  Which is thus proved: if lay people ought
not to read such books, it must be either because they are lay people
and unlettered, and it is not lawful or suitable for such people to read
or study holy scripture: or else it is because, though it is not prohibited for lay people to read holy scripture itself, yet it is unlawful
or evil to read or have holy scripture in the vulgar tongue.  But neither
of these two can be proved: nay more, each of them is out of accordance with the sayings of the saints, and contrary and repugnant to
their counsels: and this can be declared in many manners.

The arguments given in the determination are then collected
quite symmetrically under these two heads: and it is of especial
interest that Innocent III's letter to Metz, as incorporated in the

---

[1] HJ, XI. 14.

*Decretal* of Gregory IX[1], is dealt with under the first head. That is, the nine doctors allege it to prove that holy books may be read by the laity: but not to prove that the canonical scriptures may be read in the vulgar tongue; a conclusive evidence as to their opinion on the letter. To prove that it is lawful and suitable for lay people to read holy scripture (in the wider sense), they quote this letter of Innocent III[2], and passages from SS. Augustine, Chrysostom, Jerome (who exhorted "not only a lay woman, but over and above that, a married woman," to study the scriptures), Gregory, etc.; and, like Maerlant, they lament that "there are many lay people to-day, who constantly read the *Song of Roland* and the *Trojan War*, and other foolish and unprofitable fables: and indeed it would be beneficial to them to expend that labour on reading and understanding divine scriptures."

The doctors then pass to the second contention: that holy scripture may be translated into the vernacular, "and first, about the canonical scriptures." Here, they do not allege the letter of Innocent III to Metz, as indeed, considering the letter as a whole, they could scarcely do; but they point out that the whole canonical scriptures were at first written in the language of the people for whom they were intended, and not in Latin; that the saints translated them for the benefit of the heathen to whom they preached,—as S. Bartholomew is said to have done in India; and that holy scripture was translated into Latin, not in order that it might be hidden to certain people through their ignorance, but expressly that it might be generally open to all. They conclude, that the Hebrews, Chaldeans, Syrians, Arabs, Goths (for whom Ulphilas translated the holy scriptures), the Egyptians, Russians, and Armenians have the holy scriptures in their vulgar tongues, "and perhaps, if any man inquired more diligently, he would find that they exist in every language under heaven: what then is the reason that holy scripture may be read in the tongues of so many nations, and yet not in the German language?"

---

[1] See p. 31.

[2] Or rather, the sentence "the desire of understanding divine scriptures is not to be reprehended but rather commended," omitting the passages following, "Cast not pearls before swine," etc.

This academical decision is in marked contrast with the contemporary judgements of distinguished Franciscan and Dominican friars in England[1]. The arguments in favour of vernacular scriptures are very similar to those given in the determination for biblical translations which is probably by an English Lollard[2]: but, while the English thesis leaves the affirmative conclusion unqualified, the Dutch one goes on to give five careful limitations. First, the vernacular writings must not contain heresy, for the letter of Gregory XI in 1375[3] was directed against such books; secondly, they must deal with simple subjects, for children should be fed with milk and not with meat; thirdly, they must deal openly with the subject, and not figuratively, like many books of the Old Testament (the prophetical books and others), and some of the New Testament (like the Apocalypse and others), such as simple people cannot properly digest; fourthly, they must be similar in style to the books of the doctors of the Church, because "there are German books which have a new, profane and abusive manner of speech, some of which are called *Of Eckhart*, or the *Sermons of Eckhart*"; and lastly, the meaning must agree with the books of the saints, and care should be taken to see that they are properly translated.

This determination was probably of great service to the Brethren of the Common Life in their efforts to instruct lay people and houses of sisters by means of German books and pamphlets, and in their defence against the inquisitors. In another of these determinations of 1398, Everard Foec, dean of S. Saviour's at Utrecht, defended the brethren "against a certain person who used publicly in his sermons to attack the devout persons dwelling in [the brethren's] congregations." The next is a defence "by a certain devout and learned man," "of those devout persons of both sexes in the province of Cologne, whom the inquisitors of heretical pravity have molested and slandered for their customs and manner of life[4]." The Brethren

---

[1] See pp. 289–94.  [2] See Appendix.
[3] Described as "illud rescriptum apostolicum quod incipit *Ad Apostolatus*"; see p. 86.
[4] Mosheim prints, p. 443, "*The observations of the Inquisitor of Belgium on the Responses of the Masters of Cologne.*" It seeks to expose "the falsehoods of the sect of the Gerardists (followers of Gerard Groot), who declare themselves protected by the determination of the Masters of Cologne. Extracts

of the Common Life succeeded in obtaining approval of their manner of life from the council of Constance; but the question of the lawfulness of German devotional books remained open. The brethren maintained their right to teach by these means, but they had to struggle for it. On the one hand, the determination found a fresh editor, who may or may not have been himself one of the brethren, within a few years of 1398, and was incorporated in a popular and orthodox volume of sermons about 1466. On the other, the records of the brethren themselves contain evidence of the struggle, down to about the middle of the fifteenth century.

To complete the history of the determination of 1398 first: it is found in a slightly altered form in an early fifteenth century manuscript, "the book of Gerard Zerbolt," from which Jacobus Revius printed his history of Deventer in 1651. The manuscript comes from the library of Deventer, and it is therefore likely that the editor himself was one of the brethren; Revius states that he made two extracts, *De libris Teutonicalibus*[1], one of which is substantially the 1398 determination, the other[2] a short and interesting tract on the lawfulness and profitableness of using German prayers instead of Latin ones, by those who knew no Latin. The editor changes the strictly logical form of the earlier determination by substituting a preface of his own for

from the acts of the Inquisition will therefore be given by Master Eylardus Schoeneveld, friar preacher, in 1399 inquisitor for Saxony, in Utrecht, and the surrounding neighbourhood." The extracts, whether obtained from "Gerardists" examined by the inquisition, or in depositions given against them, dealt with the life in the Brethren and Sisters' communities: i.e. the sisters say grace in the vernacular, listen in silence to reading during the whole meal, and have every Sunday a sermon read to them in the vulgar tongue by a sister; certain learned Carthusians object to their manner of life. "They have certain pieces of information in defence of their order against the inquisitors, which I judge to be the aforesaid determinations of the doctors of Cologne, made impertinently enough on their behalf, and with evil intention translated into the vulgar tongue, with the authorities and citations." (The Dutch translations exist also in the original MSS.) Cf. *Inq. Neer.* II. 184. This quarrel with the Dominicans of the inquisition probably accounts for the hostility of M. Grabow, and the opponents of Busch. It is interesting that this determination for vernacular scriptures was expressly obtained as a defence against the inquisition.

[1] Revius, 41; for a list of editors who have printed from Revius, or referred to the tract, generally, as that of Gerard Zerbolt, see HJ, XI. 1–2.

[2] For this tract see Index, Vernac. prayers. It is found also in two MSS containing the 1398 determination.

the original thesis, which maintained that either (i) it was wrong for lay people to read holy scriptures, or (ii) it was wrong to translate the scriptures into the vernacular. He then copies the references of the original determination to prove its two points, and adds the two points themselves at the end: regardless of the fact that the two sets of citations have no exact relation to the theory maintained in his own preface. It is interesting to compare his own views on the subject, as stated in his preface, with the conclusions of the original determination[1]:

> Since there are some who have small understanding of holy scripture and the sayings of the holy fathers, who believe and state that it is unlawful for laymen, and unlettered people, to read divine scripture and exercise themselves in the sacred page: and since they judge that devotional books written in the vulgar tongue, or translated into it (such books as are solely or mainly intended for lay people), ought to be condemned, and completely avoided and rooted out: therefore, it is profitable to know whether all books of the scriptures and the holy doctors, or which of such books, may lawfully be read by lay people.

The editor then states that two kinds of teaching are found in holy scripture, which (with S. Paul and the author of the Epistle to the Hebrews) he compares to "milk and meat": the simple and open doctrines, and those which are deep and obscure, unsuitable for the simple. Lay people, he says, may read in the vulgar tongue books which deal with matters of the first class: but not those dealing with the second. He defines moreover books included in the first class: "such as the lives and deeds of the saints, the passions and triumphs of the martyrs, and other teaching concerning vices and virtues[2], the glory of the saints and the misery of the damned, and books like these which are plain and open." It is noticeable that whereas the original determination contended for the right of the laity to read the more plain and open books of the Bible, this editor does not: it is noteworthy that his list did not include vernacular plenaries or gospel books. He did not, however, omit the

---

[1] Revius, 41.
[2] Books of *Vices and Virtues* were a distinct class in the middle ages, generally analyses of the seven deadly sins, and the virtues opposed to them. A "book of vices," or a "book of virtues" is considered sufficient title for a mediaeval catalogue or will, cf. TV, 762.

passages of his original citing authorities to prove that some biblical books may be read in the vernacular; on the contrary, when he began to copy the original determination, he copied all the citations. But his own preface agrees exactly with the class of Dutch books for which John Busch, a notable reformer in this movement, contended in the early years of the fifteenth century.

The determination was also used in a very popular collection of sermons written about 1466, by the Augustinian hermit of Osnabruck, Gottschalk [Holen[1]]. The sermon for the second Sunday in Advent deals with the text: *Quaecunque scripta sunt ad nostram doctrinam scripta sunt*, and contains a very short epitome of the determination, occupying not more than one-eighth of the whole sermon. This has three sections, the first shewing the necessity of written scriptures through the frailty of human memory, and the second proving the supernatural character of the canonical scriptures. The third begins by stating that "It is doubted by many whether it is lawful to read and possess sacred books written or translated in the vulgar tongue." The main body of the determination is then summarised very shortly, perhaps because the citations were felt to be too academic for a sermon; but the limitations at the end (that the said books must contain nothing heretical, and must deal only with plain material, and that plainly, and in "a manner according with the writings of the saints") are given in full. The greater part of the last section of the sermon proceeds to deal with the necessity of avoiding pride in the collection of a great multitude of books[2]. The collection was popular: and the inclusion even of the much-abridged determination shews Holen to have regarded the use of translations as lawful.

Meanwhile, the Brethren of the Common Life continued to be the chief champions of Dutch devotional books. But they had to struggle for their opinions, even though they were no advo-

---

[1] Cf. *Sermonum opus exquisitissimum...lectoris patris Gotschalci eremitari diui Augustini professi*, 1517. *Sermo V. Domin. II in Adv.*

[2] This tract, usually attributed to Zerbolt, has also been ascribed to Nicholas von Dinckelspühl, originally through the mistake in Denis, I. 2477, MS. dcxlvii, f. 8; Denis was followed by Aschbach, J., *Gesch. der Wiener Univ.*, Vienna, 1865, I. 440, and by Keller, p. 68. The latter also imagined that the determination opposed translations.

cates of unlicensed Bible reading among the laity[1]. The doctors in 1398 had declared the use of translations of the simpler books of the Bible canonical and lawful, and there is good reason to believe that the brethren actually encouraged their use in the houses of nuns and tertiaries which they directed. But among the laity they only argued for the free use of Dutch books of edification, not the canonical scriptures themselves; though they would, no doubt, have been willing to allow particular penitents to use Dutch or German plenaries. Vernacular lives of Christ[1] were popular and lawful among the devout of the Netherlands, as in other countries: there are indeed, a particularly large number of such manuscripts.

It has been stated that the condemnation of the Dominican Matthias of Grabow, the bitter enemy of the brethren, at the council of Constance in 1415, was a triumph for the defenders of Dutch Bibles[2]: but there is no evidence at all that the Dominican had attacked the brethren on this score, or that the fathers of Constance, including Gerson, who himself opposed vernacular Bibles, would have condemned him for his attack on Dutch scriptures.

An interesting Dutch manuscript was written in 1407 for the library of the canons at Zwolle by John Henricson, who describes himself as "the Warden[3]." He was probably only the scribe, and there is no evidence that the manuscript was intended for the use of lay people: but it contains interesting features. After the Dutch pericope[4],—gospels, epistles and Old Testament lessons,—it contains a translation of S. Paul's epistles, with the preface, possibly of John Henricson, but more probably of the

---

[1] Eicken, 786, misrepresents the brethren's attitude when he says, "from 1400 onwards they made it one of their chief efforts to translate and publish translations of the holy scriptures," if he means canonical scriptures.

[2] *Tepler Bibel.* 38.

[3] Cf. Jostes, *Die Waldenser*, 26, "dit boeck hoert in der clerckehus bynnen Zwollen"; "Here are the four gospels in Dutch. Written by me, John Henricson the warden, an unworthy priest, in the year 1407, the Thursday before the nativity of our Lady." These "four gospels" are actually a pericope, with the O. Test. lessons as well: they are followed by the translation of S. Paul's epistles, and by separate homilies upon them. The preface to the epistles is printed in *Boekzaal*, pp. 235-9; Jostes regards the date of the original translation of the epistles as about 1380. HJ, XI. 12.

[4] See p. 112 n. A pericope is a collection of the sections of holy scripture appointed to be read in church.

earlier translator. It states that S. Paul wrote his letters for all Christians, some in Latin, some in Greek, some in Hebrew, so that all alike could read them[1]:

And thus these epistles, which are profitable and useful to those who understand Latin and Greek and Hebrew, are profitable also for Dutchmen. And it is a strange thing, that we make and come across so many Dutch books, and that these bright and shining epistles, inspired by the spirit of the living God, are not commoner among lay people, who hold Christ's teaching dear; for, next to the gospels, these are the most edifying books that ever were written.... And because the epistles are difficult, and treat of many matters in few words (because Latin is more convenient for speech than Dutch), therefore holy mother Church has come to the help of this difficulty with the teacher's gloss, so that men may the better understand, and not be put to confusion. Also, many matters, as has been explained, are not here told in as few words as in the original.

The words and sentiments should be ascribed, however, to the original translator,—probably some clerk influenced by the Gottesfreunde movement,—and not to the warden at Zwolle.

Many instances shew the value set by the Brethren of the Common Life upon biblical studies among themselves,—not, of course from biblical translations. The first monastery of the brethren, that at Windesheim, was begun in 1386, and one of its chief works was the establishment of a corrected text of the Vulgate,—a work, as in England at the date, necessary for those interested in translations[2]. The chronicle of Windesheim states that William Vornken, the prior, was a man of great piety, "and he was no little esteemed among us, because he was able to make moralisations and mystical interpretations of a part of the Bible, and nearly the whole of the psalter[3]." John Scutken, a brother of Windesheim who died in 1423, translated many service and

---

[1] *Boekzaal*, 282. It is not certain that many contemporaries would have agreed that the Pauline epistles were clear enough material for translation, though books of the Sunday epistles, glossed, appeared later. Cf. the statement of Jacob van Tombe, that because there were many passages hard to be understood in S. Paul's epistles "our holy forefathers wisely decreed that the unlearned laity should not read the Bible: but they themselves selected out of the scriptures books of devotion called *Getydeboexckens*, leaving out the aforesaid passages, and gave them to the laity." *Claer bewys van de warachtige Kerke Cristi*, Antwerp, 1567, p. E 1.

[2] Cf. Busch, p. xix; and cf. Purvey's difficulties in establishing a correct Latin text to translate from, p. 258.

[3] Busch, 331.

devotional books into Dutch, as Gerard Groot[1] had done before him: but he also translated the psalter, the pericope, and perhaps a set of epistles and gospels with sermons.  John Busch also, in his autobiography, shews that much biblical study was pre-scribed in the noviciate at Zwolle[2], where he received the habit in 1419.  Here he read both Old and New Testaments, with the great doctors upon them, till he should be "as clothed in these as the body is in its outward clothing."  When, however, his ceaseless study led to confusion and difficulties, master Arnold of Noethern advised him that he was overstraining his capacities, warning him that

children should be fed with milk and not with meat,... for it is not re-quired that everyone should know the deep things of God and holy scrip-ture, and seek to investigate them: but it is enough for them to live well, to believe well, and to have a good intention to do the will of God[3].

A little later, Busch compares the holy scriptures to a fallen oak tree, from which the different officials of the abbey each carry off the roots, leaves, trunk, oak galls, according to their different needs.  Busch gives a long account of his subsequent career in his *Liber de Reformatione Monasteriorum*, for he, like other Brethren of the Common Life, not only directed new com-munities, but was sent by the bishop to reform houses of the older orders.  He gives one or two instances shewing that German books were used in such reformed convents[4], and the catalogues of such nunneries shew that they included a small number of gospel and epistle books, though of course by far the greater number were German or Dutch sermons, lives of saints, and manuals of devotion.

Busch relates one interesting instance of how he overcame the opposition of a Dominican to the lay use of German books[5].

" A certain lector of the order of friars preachers in the town of Zutphen[6]," he says, "publicly preached, that lay people ought not to

---

[1] There seems no evidence that Groot translated any part of the Bible: but he perhaps translated freely in his sermons: "verbum Dei sanctum Christi evangelium canonicamque scripturam...predicavit." Busch, 252.

[2] A house of Austin canons founded under Groot's influence.

[3] Busch, 708, 9.

[4] *Id*. 730, "more than a hundred congregations of sisters in the diocese of Utrecht used German books"; 732, "two nunneries at Zutphen had Ger-man books read in refectory."    [5] *Id*. 730. (*Lib. de Ref. Monast.* c. iii.)

[6] *Id*. c. iii. p. 730. *Of a lector of the friars preachers, who preached that lay people ought not to have German books.*

have German books, and sermons ought not to be made to the people except in the church or the cemetery. Then I, being but a simple brother in Windesheim, was sent to Zutphen with brother Theoderic William to carry out some business for our monastery; and hearing this, and knowing that more than a hundred congregations of sisters and Béguines in the country round Utrecht had many German books, which they read daily by themselves, or in the hearing of others in the refectory, firmly contradicted this; because they read and listen to German books of this kind in Zutphen, Deventer, Zwolle, Kempen, and everywhere, in the towns and country. I went therefore to the church of the monastery of those friars preachers, and asked for the prior, to whom I said:

'My lord prior, I have heard your lector preach publicly that lay people ought not to have German books. Now he preached this wrongly, and he ought publicly to retract it. For the princes of the land, and the common people, men and women, have many books written in German, and read in them and study them. Even you and your brothers often preach to the people in the vulgar tongue. Do you wish, then, that your sermons should be remembered?' And he answered: 'Certainly.' Then I said: 'If they had them in writing, then they would the better remember them: why therefore ought they not to have books in German?'

Then he answered: 'Many lay people have books in German, namely of Sentences, and the like, which a certain doctor of our order translated from Latin into German: and some have the missal with the canon in German[1], and therefore it is not good for them to have or read books in German.'

To whom I said: 'No, I do not approve of that, that simple lay people, men and women, should have such lofty and divine books in German; nay, for when I have found the canon [of the mass] in German among nuns, I have burnt it. But moral books of vices and virtues, of the incarnation, life and passion of our Lord, of the life and holy conversation and martyrdom of the apostles, martyrs,

---

[1] Cf. the quotations from the *Formulare Inquisitionis*, 1420, in the Staatsarchiv at Münster, Jostes, *Waldenserbibeln*, HJ, xv. (1894), 779. The inquisitor, James of Swabia, wrote to ask for instructions as to his powers with regard to German plenaries, or even German mass books. He had found "complete mass books written in the vernacular among lay people, the canon only excepted, and also other books, namely, expositions of the gospels, and such like." "It is doubtful," he says, "what ought to be done about these books in such times as ours. For it is said that in some places heretical lay people, both men and women, use these books, perchance with the canon, and believe, according to the Waldensian error, that it is lawful for laymen to celebrate and say mass; and the canon may easily be added to these books, and heresies and errors follow, which cannot be so easily extirpated. It is asked therefore, what should be done with these books. Apparently they ought not to be burned, because there is no heresy therein: yet they may give rise to heresies and errors." Cf. the German "mass book" at Nuremberg, p. 112 n. 7.

confessors and virgins, and homilies and sermons of the saints, tending to the reformation of life, the discipline of manners, the fear of hell and the love of the heavenly country,—it is most useful for all people, learned and unlearned, to have and read such books daily. And if you are not willing to admit this, I will myself shew you in writing the sayings of the doctors of holy Church, Augustine, Gregory, Ambrose and Jerome, and of other orthodox teachers, that it is lawful and very useful to have books of this kind.'

And he answered: 'If you produce from manuscripts the sayings of doctors, we too shall produce the sayings of doctors to the contrary.'

Then I spake more plainly: 'My lord prior: as your lector publicly preached before the people that they ought not to have German books, so must he publicly revoke this: or else shall I arrange with the lord bishop of Utrecht and his household, in the great chapter, that neither you nor your lector shall preach any more in the diocese of Utrecht.'

But the prior said: 'It seems to me then, that you have a commission to do this from the bishop of Utrecht. Be at peace: for I will arrange that our lector shall revoke those words.' And when for my part I wished to go to the lector, who was lying upon his bed, the prior said: 'He is a very learned man.' To whom I answered: 'Therefore I would the more gladly speak with him, that he might the better understand his error.' Yet, at the petition of the prior and of the brother whom I had with me, I did not go to the sick man forthwith: because his prior promised me that he should revoke those words.

Another time, when I was going from Deventer in a boat through Yssel towards Zutphen, I questioned the men and women who were sailing with me, what the friars preachers in Zutphen were wont to preach. They answered:

' Our lector sometimes preached, that lay people ought not to have books in German; but he revoked that in this summary fashion: "You good people, when I preach the gospel to you, you forthwith tell it askew to others. Now I spoke to you at another time in a sermon about German books which the laity ought not to have, and I noticed this point: that some women, or even men, sometimes lay German writings beneath the altar cloth, so that mass may be read over them, and when it is finished, they take away such writings, and make with other people many incantations, divinations and auguries. Now I forbade you to have and read such writings. But you may well and lawfully have and read good books and moral books." '

And the people in the boat who said this added, that they had been greatly astonished at this, that he should have revoked what he said in such a way, not knowing who had compelled him to it. But I, hearing this, was well content at his recanting in this manner, because there were two houses of sisters in that town which always read German in refectory at table, while they were eating."

Busch's account of the matter shews the attitude of the Brethren of the Common Life to biblical translations. They were not primarily concerned with the spread of these, but of Dutch devotional books: yet probably their attitude was chiefly instrumental in making orthodox opinion more favourable to biblical translations at the end of the fifteenth century.

§ 2. In the period 1400–1526, however, the most eminent of the brethren's contemporaries, and the most liberal of orthodox reformers, remained hostile to biblical translations. This is most interesting in the case of Jean Gerson, who was so definitely convinced that they were mischievous, that he actually included a proposal for their formal condemnation in his scheme of reform, presented to the council of Constance. Gerson became bachelor of theology in 1384, the year of Wycliffe's death, and from 1395 onwards, when he became chancellor of the university of Paris, he was regarded as the greatest of European scholars and the chief champion of ecclesiastical reform. He was a leading spirit in the council of Pisa, 1409, which deposed the rival popes, and elected the Franciscan, Alexander V. There is some evidence that the latter was connected in some way with the practical suppression of biblical translations in England[1]: but he lost Gerson's support through his championship of the privileges of his own order against the university of Paris. Gerson continued, however, to write and preach that a general council should meet, to heal the schism and reform abuses. When the council of Constance met in 1415, Gerson attended as legate of the French king, and representative of the Gallican church; and his personality and learning gave him an outstanding influence. Though the council succeeded in healing the schism, and in passing a certain number of canons dealing with reform, many other suggestions for reform failed. Among them was that put forward by Gerson in his tract *On communion in both kinds*, where he stated that there were many people who wished that the reading of scripture should be everywhere permitted. To refute these, Gerson discussed the authority of the canonical scriptures, and their manner of exposition, and then gave other arguments against "the heretics" who were opposing him.

[1] See Index and Appendix.

"Now this use of holy scripture by modern men," he says, "as if holy scripture should be believed in its bare text without the help of any interpretation or explanation, is a kind of use which is attended by grave dangers and scandals....Moreover, the errors of the Beghards and the Poor Men of Lyons and the like have sprung from this pestiferous root, and do daily increase: because there are many lay people who have a translation of the Bible into the vulgar tongue, to the great prejudice and scandal of catholic truth, and it is proposed in the scheme of reform that this should be abolished[1]."

Gerson's proposal was not embodied in a decree: but the council passed one which shewed that it still regarded the better education of the clergy, and the improvement of their instruction of the laity, as the great aim,—not the encouragement of the use of biblical translations. It confirmed a proposal of Gerson and Pierre d'Ailly[2], and enacted that, "to counteract the ignorance of those priests who have already been promoted" (as opposed to those still in training), short text-books should be written for cathedrals and important collegiate churches, and should be publicly read in synod, both in Latin and the vulgar tongue. These should give the necessary instruction on the virtues and vices, the creed, the sacraments, the form of confession, etc.

Also, in each of the said churches there ought to be a reader of theology, who shall lecture on the second and third book of the *Sentences*, or who shall take the material in the said books and shall apply it shortly to the exposition and explanation of the epistles and gospels, which are read in church in the course of the year[3].

---

[1] *Tractatus contra haeresim de communione laicorum sub utraque specie*, published at Constance in 1417. Gerson, *Opera*, Du Pin, Antwerp, 1706, I. 459. This tract is quoted by the Dominican friar, Martin Harney, in the tract which he wrote against that of the Jansenist, Antoine Arnauld, on the subject of vernacular scriptures. Harney's learned treatise seeks to establish that the mediaeval Church was right in prohibiting biblical translations. He says that at the council of Constance a certain scheme called the *Reformatorium* was drawn up, so that, inter alia, "the reading of holy scripture in the vulgar tongue should be restrained, at least within due bounds." To prove his statement he gives several quotations from Gerson's writings, "for his single testimony in this matter is worth that of many men, even of many credible witnesses: for he acted in the name of many others, he acted before the whole council of Fathers, and it is obvious that he cannot have acted thus through party zeal, or from any such motive." Harney, 185.

[2] *Magnum oecumenicum constantiense concilium*, V. d. Hardt, H., Helmstadt, 1700, tom. I. pars viii. p. 428, where the decree is coupled with d'Ailly's name. It is given in Gerson's tract, *De Reformatione, in Concilio Constantiensi, Opera*, II. 914: but the expedient had of course been in use in many provinces in the fourteenth century. See pp. 141, 196.

[3] For the complaint of a contemporary that the study of the sacred text

Gerson explained his opposition to biblical translations also in other treatises. In his tract *Against idle curiosity*, he said that

Presumptuous curiosity, and singularity, easily cause a schism in all knowledge, and consequently destroy it. The building of the tower of Babel gives us an example of this, for the division of languages ruined and destroyed it: and even so, on the other hand, does unity of language strengthen the building of the Church....In addition, it follows from the aforesaid points, that the translation of holy books, of our Bible especially, is justly prohibited, except in the case of moralisations and Bible histories. It is easy to find very clear reasons for this[1].

He brought out the same point in a sermon, speaking of a certain heretic, who was

deceived by a false understanding of scripture: even as there are many other men who understand scripture according to their own private opinion, and not according to the exposition of holy doctors, which they know not, or are unwilling to understand and consider. And therefore I take this as evidence, that it is most dangerous to give to simple men, who are quite unlearned, books of the holy scripture translated into French, because they may forthwith fall into many errors by a false understanding[2].

Here Gerson expressed the fundamental objection to biblical translations by the best minds of his century: the translation of the "bare text," unaccompanied by glosses to explain also the secondary interpretations, was too dangerous.

"Even as some good might come," he wrote elsewhere, "of the good and true translation of the Bible into French, if it were soberly understood, even so, on the other hand, innumerable errors and evils would arise if it were badly translated or presumptuously understood, contrary to the exposition of holy doctors. It would be better to be completely ignorant of the matter: even as in medicine and similar sciences it would be better to be completely ignorant than to know little, or to know wrong[3]."

---

was neglected at the universities, cf. Nicholas de Clemanges, "I marvel that the theologians of our time read so negligently the pages of the divine Testaments." Gieseler, IV. 176.

[1] *Lectiones duae contra vanam curiositatem, Opera,* I. 106. The last sentence reads: Rursus sequitur ex praemissis prohibendam esse vulgarem translationem librorum sacrorum, nostrae Bibliae praesertim, extra moralitates et historias.

[2] Harney, 188.

[3] *Decem considerationes contra adulatores principum,* consid. IV. and V.; Harney, 189. Gerson wrote a tract, *De sensu litterali sacrae scripturae et de causis errantium,* which it is interesting to compare with Purvey's treatment

A tract written by a Carthusian, who died in 1470 adopted the same point of view. Jean le Riche (Ioannes Divitis), a Carthusian of Ghent, wrote among other theological works a treatise entitled: *Why it is not always profitable for worldly people to have the books of holy scripture translated into the mother tongue*[1]. The tract itself has perished, or exists only in an unknown manuscript: but its contents can be inferred from its title.

The attitude of fifteenth century orthodoxy in Germany can also be inferred from the silence on the subject of biblical translations of those churchmen most anxious for reform. Their exhortations to the laity did not include advice to study the Bible for themselves, except in a few cases between 1500 and the Reformation. The teaching of Geiler of Kaysersberg was typical of the most liberal and devout opinion of his time, and he urged, as Gerson might have done, the careful instruction of the laity in holy scripture at the hands of the priest, and pronounced against the publication of German Bibles. He himself preached long and eloquently at Strassburg, no doubt basing his sermons on the gospel for the day; and, when he occasionally exhorted the readers of his treatises to be diligent in gaining a knowledge of holy scripture, it was almost certainly this means which he

of the same subject in the preface to his version. Gerson states that, "there is opposition to the truth, in England, in Scotland, in the university of Prague, and in Germany, and even, shameful as it is to admit it, in France. ...And these sowers of heresy, and enemies of truth (truth which they know, or should know, since they call themselves catholics), claim that their sayings are founded upon holy scripture, and on its literal sense; and they say that they follow and recognise scripture only, and reject and despise other constitutions and writings." Therefore he proposes to consider what the literal sense of holy scripture is, and how it is to be investigated and held: and, like Purvey, cites the "seven rules of Ticonius," which had lately been brought into prominence by Nicholas de Lyra, in his commentary on the biblical text. (See p. 181.) Gerson then again mentions that his heretical opponents are to be found in England, "have destroyed the university of Prague, and have even reached Scotland." *Opera*, I. 1–7. Cf. other discourses on the four senses of scripture, II. 350, 365; and his sermon before the council of Constance, inviting the fathers to condemn many errors, including those of Wycliffe and Hus, "which cannot be condemned merely by an appeal to the bare text of scripture, without reference to the expositions of the doctors"; II. 278.

[1] *Quo pacto secularibus non semper conducant libri sacrae scripturae materno idiomate translati*; cf. *Illustrium sacri Cartusiensis ordinis scriptorum catalogus*, Petreius, T., ed. Miraeus, D. A., Cologne, 1609, 161.

had in mind, in the case of lay people. In his book on the *Christian Pilgrimage*, he drew an exact parallel between the duty of receiving at the priest's hand the sacrament of the altar and the word of God.

Elias was fed with the bread of angels, and with water from a pitcher. And thou, O Pilgrim, when thou art weary and failing, refresh thyself ...by receiving bread,...the sacrament of the Eucharist, the body of the Lord,...and drink from the pitcher the water of heavenly wisdom springing forth to everlasting life: that is, the word of God: which water...thou shalt find in the pitcher of holy scripture....Moreover, see that thou drink as from a pitcher of the water of the word of God, only as given thee by the angel, and according to his advice. For there are people who drink of that water of scripture at will and without measure, and not from the hands of the angels of God, who are the priests of the Church, from whose mouth they should acquire the law: but they presume to understand them by their own proper intelligence, like the Waldensians, the Brethren of the Free Spirit, the Bohemians, and other heretics[1].

In some of his sermons Geiler spoke even more plainly on the dangers to which the laity were exposed through the publication of German Bibles:

It is dangerous to put knives into children's hands, for them to cut bread with themselves, for they may cut themselves. So also holy scripture, which contains the bread of God, should be read and explained by such as are already far advanced in knowledge and experience, and will set forth the undoubted meaning. For inexperienced people will easily take harm from their reading....We read the Bible and other scriptures, and do not understand. We have not the skill to read intelligently and according to the true Christian meaning. It is certainly a foolish thing that the Bible is printed in German, for one must understand it quite otherwise than it is written, to do it justice. [A reference to the need of understanding not only the literal, but also the "moral," "allegorical" and "anagogical meaning."] If you have already a book on fencing from which to learn to fight, you cannot fight therewith, till you have learned from a fencing-

---

[1] The *Christenbilgerschaft*, or *Peregrinus*, quoted by L. Dacheux in *Jean Geiler de Kaysersberg*, 1478–1510, Paris, 1876, 226 and 229. This interesting study overstresses the extent to which biblical knowledge was "widespread" in the fifteenth century: see p. 2. Janssen also, in *Gesch. des deutschen Volkes*, 1881, I. 608, is not justified in representing Geiler and S. Brandt as solitary individuals who preached against translations out of excess of paternal solicitude for their flocks: Geiler's pronouncements against the dangers of lay Bible reading are exactly in line with the best mediaeval thought, from Gregory VII to the Reformation.

master. If you have already a cobbler's knife, and have leather ready, and a needle and thread, you still cannot make a shoe, until you have learned. Therefore, if you wish to read the Bible, beware of falling into error[1].

Geiler's attitude is noteworthy, because he lived till 1510, when printed German Bibles had become fairly common, and because he was not a conservative zealot, but a great preacher of reform. Two manuals had already, in 1508 and 1509, begun to recommend the laity to read the Bible in a spirit of piety and humility: but Geiler retained the normal mediaeval fear that such a course was too dangerous.

It is doubtful if Geiler's friend, Sebastian Brandt, viewed the printed German Bibles with much more favour, though he mentioned that Hebrew, Slavonic and Bohemian versions existed[2]. Brandt's famous satirical poem, the *Ship of Fools*, was published first in German in 1494, and achieved an enormous popularity. It was at once translated into Latin, Dutch, English and French, parts of it were sometimes preached from the pulpit, and Geiler delivered public lectures upon it[3]. The section "On the contempt and despising of holy scripture," lamented that though "All lands now are full of holy writ,...the Bible, the teaching of the holy fathers, and many another similar book,...yet no one improves himself therewith[4]," and throughout the section Brandt emphasised the same point. The English verse translation of 1509 lamented that the world was full of:

> Such as despiseth ancient scripture,
> Which provèd is of great authority,
> And hath no pleasure, felicity or cure
> Of godly Prophets which wrote of verity:
> A fool he is, for his most felicity
> Is to believe the tales of an old wife,
> Rather than the doctrine of eternal life[5].

---

[1] "Es ist fast ein bösz Ding das man die bibel zu teütsch trückt, wen man musz sye gar vil anders verston weder es do stot, will man im echter recht thün," *Christlichen Bilgerschaft*, Bâle, 1511, p. 127, quoted J. Kehrein, *Zur Geschichte der deutschen Bibelübersetzung vor Luther*, Stuttgart, 1851, and Janssen, J., *Gesch. des deutschen Volkes*, 1881, I. 609.

[2] Dacheux, 226.

[3] *The Ship of Fools, translated by Alexander Barclay*, ed. Jamieson, T. H., Edinburgh, 1874, introd.

[4] Dacheux, lxxvi.

[5] Barclay, I. 72.

But though Brandt lamented the neglect of scripture, it is doubtful if he would have recommended the unrestricted use of translations, for in his section on "Heretics," he is much of his friend Geiler's opinion as to the danger of false interpretations. Heretics are:

> False prophets, not following the right,
> Which with false hearts, imperfect of credence,
> Not duly worship the law of God almight,
> Nor His holy doctrine with worthy reverence:
> And other such as vary the true sense
> Of Goddis law, expounding other wise
> Than it in the text clear and plainly lies[1].
>
> They holy scriptures rehearse much other wise
> Than the Holy Ghost them uttered first of all[2].

Thus there is a good deal of evidence that catholic reforming opinion, at the beginning of the sixteenth century, was much the same as that of Gerson at the beginning of the fifteenth.

§ 3. Biblical translations were used in women's convents in the fifteenth century more freely than elsewhere, because in such cases they were always used under the direction of the warden or confessor of the house. A fifteenth century Dutch manuscript shews the closeness of this supervision: the sister who had charge of the books was to see that

> If anything in the book appeared to be false, it should be brought before the rector of the house for him to oversee, before it is allowed to be commonly used by the sisters....Great care is to be taken, not to lend books to outside people without the permission of the rector.... Uncommon books are not to be read in refectory till the rector has first seen that their contents are good and profitable....Books are not to be lent to ignorant people[3].

Men's convents occasionally contained biblical translations, but

---

[1] Barclay, II. 225.

[2] *Id.* II. 226. Cf., for quotations from the *Narrenschiff*, Janssen, ed. 1881, I. 609. The poem does notice the danger to faith through misinterpretation of scripture, and in such a manner as to render it very likely that Brandt disapproved of the printed German Bibles; but the main emphasis in the matter is that the world is full of holy books, which all can read, and yet men do not reform their manners.

[3] *Nederlandisch Proza, van de dertiende tot de achtiende eeuw*, ed. V[loten], J. H., Amsterdam, 1851, I. 297–9.

there is much more evidence for their use in women's convents[1], and especially in Holland. Some Dutch convents used German gospel books from 1400 onwards: and between 1450 and 1526 it is quite possible that their use was general, not only in the Netherlands, but in Germany. The evidence for this has, however, been very much exaggerated. Extraordinarily few catalogues of sisters' libraries, compared to those of men's houses, have come down to us. No English nunnery catalogue, for instance, is known, while only one Dutch and one German one are printed and accessible; which, in view of the very numerous survivals of those of men's houses, must shew that the sisters' libraries were relatively infrequent and unimportant. Probably there were many of the less well-governed and well-instructed houses in which very little reading was done at all: and others where the reading was confined to the vernacular sermons, saints' lives, and books of vices and virtues, which form the bulk of the two catalogues which are known to us. The evidence is too slight for certainty, and the diffusion of vernacular Bibles has been overestimated by the mistaken idea that all the items recorded in fifteenth century Dutch catalogues were themselves in Dutch[2]:

---

[1] Isaac de Long, after his extensive search for Dutch biblical MSS., stated that more biblical MSS. came from women's convents than from men's (*Boekzaal*, 335, 336). He considered that surprisingly few examples existed, and that the nuns could have used them little: but, actually, biblical MSS. from the nunneries of other countries are fewer than from Dutch ones. W. Moll, *Kerkengeschiedenis van Nederland voor de Hervorming*, II[2]. 334, says that: "We can say very little about the distribution of our old biblical translations. As to their use by lay people [sic], they were apparently read most in communities of women, in the houses of Béguines, or Sisters of the Common Life; and also in communities of men, which included besides the monks unlettered lay brothers, oblates, etc. It is probable that they existed in many, if not in all convents, from the middle of the fifteenth century, either wholly or in part, for the manuscripts which are found in our public or private libraries give manifold internal evidence of a monastic source." Moll's statement, however, applies to the period, post 1450, when the labours of the Brethren of the Common Life had been largely successful: and does not justify a general assertion that German nunneries freely used biblical translations "in the middle ages"; also, his statement was probably partly due to a misunderstanding of the one nunnery catalogue known to him: see p. 113, n. 5.

[2] Fifteenth century catalogues, whether of the libraries of noblemen, monasteries or princes, were often written in the vernacular,—French, German, English, Dutch, etc. But it is generally quite clear that the bulk of the books, where the language is not stated, were in Latin, and not in the vernacular in which the catalogue was written. The custom, in writing

but nevertheless, there is good ground to believe that the majority of biblical translations used by the orthodox were written for use in houses of women.

The earliest known nunnery catalogue is that of the Dominican nuns of Nuremberg, written between 1456 and 1469. The convent was one of those which prized the works of Eckhart and the early Gottesfreunde, and was directed by the Dominican friars who were their successors. It had been reformed shortly before the making of the catalogue; and, from the size of the library, and the information given in the catalogue about the copying of manuscripts by the nuns, it must have been one of the most learned in Germany. The nuns were drawn from the upper burgher or noble class, and the Dominican rule for nuns, as well as for friars, emphasised the duty of study; we should expect therefore to find Dominican nuns among the best educated of the day. We have both the catalogue of their library, and an interesting note-book of the volumes which were read in refectory throughout the year. The library catalogue includes 350 volumes[1], and a careful note is made as to how each book

a catalogue in Latin, was to leave the language unspecified except in the case of vernacular books, and in most cases this earlier custom seems to have been followed when catalogues came to be written in the vernacular. Such a catalogue frequently states: "this book is written in Romance, or in German, or in Dutch": and in such a catalogue, when the language of certain items is carefully specified, it is much safer to conclude that the other items are in Latin, especially when no translations of such works are known to have existed. Again, if, in such a catalogue, a number of works of the same class are given, and the language of the earlier volumes is not given, while it is stated that the last is "in German" or "in French," it is fairly safe to think that the unspecified ones are in Latin; because it was customary in Latin catalogues thus to append the vernacular copies at the end of the section. The conclusion is not positive, but, in dealing with an otherwise carefully made catalogue, it is fairly safe to assume that some few items would not have been stated to be "in Dutch" or "in German," if all the manuscripts had been in Dutch or in German. For catalogues written in German, whose contents are undoubtedly Latin books, cf. especially Gottlieb, 51 (the chapel of S. Peter at Lucerne); 56 (the spital of the Holy Ghost), where the books are all liturgical; 28 (the Kreuzkirche); 25 (the Elizabethenkirche), 1483. For French catalogues of books mainly in Latin see Gottlieb, 97 (Pierre Cardonnel); 101 (Clairvaux); and lists on pp. 102, 124-6, 134-5.

[1] Cod. Musei Germanici, Nuremberg, Cent. VII. 79, ff. 86-146: *Item die hernach geschrieben puecher hat der Convent hie zu sant Kathereyn zu Nürnverg prediger ordens*, see Gottlieb, 55, no. 131. Jostes printed this most interesting catalogue in *Meister Eckhart und seine Jünger, Collectanea Friburgensia*, fasc. IV. (1895), pp. 113-; but confuses his account of it by considering it as the list of refectory reading-books (cf. p. xxiii). The list of refectory

was obtained: whether it was brought by a sister on admission, copied by one of the sisters, or given by a benefactor. It is written in German, and has been cited as if it recorded a collection of German manuscripts, containing very numerous German biblical translations[1]; but this is clearly a mistake. It is inconceivable that a Dominican convent would have possessed 350 German manuscripts, including a set of "psalters for the choir[2]," and no single volume in Latin, liturgical or otherwise. Moreover, 26 manuscripts are specified as being in German, or as "in Latin and German"; and some are specified as being in "Netherlandish," or "in the speech of the Netherlands[3]." The biblical and gospel books, as in all catalogues, are placed at the beginning of the first section. The language of the first volumes is not given; the last of the biblical books, however, are a psalter in German, and an "Epistle, gospel, and Nicodemus-gospel, and the psalter, the one verse Latin and the other verse German[4]." In all probability, it was only the psalter in this latter volume which had one verse Latin and one German; thus no biblical book except the psalter is stated as being in German at all. The 26 German books mentioned in the catalogue included one book of "sins," —a discourse on the ten commandments, seven mortal sins[5], etc. —one German psalter, two Latin and German psalters, seven books of sermons[6], one "missal" (or, perhaps, antiphoner), for Advent and Lent[7], a tract of S. Augustine, the Dominican Rule

reading-books, from which he prints an extract, is actually in Cod. Musei Germanici zu Nürnberg, Cent. VII. 92, ff. 45–: see Gottlieb, 55, no. 132. It would have been most interesting had Jostes printed this list also, only the title and the first item of which are printed in Gottlieb. As it is, his article does not refer to it, but only to the list of extracts and page references which immediately precedes it. Whether the library catalogue and the refectory lists aré in separate MSS. (Cent. VII. 79 and Cent. VII. 92), or are bound together, as Jostés implies, I am unable to ascertain.

[1] Jostes, *Meister Eckhart*, p. xxiv, and HJ, xv. (1894), 771; xviii. (1897), 133, followed by Mandonnet in V, II. 1470, who states that the Dominicanesses had 15 biblical books, 11 pericopes, and 5 gospel harmonies, in German.

[2] *Meister Eckhart*, 119: section C of the catalogue contains 9 psalters, language unspecified, and the tenth and last is a German psalter.

[3] *Id.* 138, no. IX. and 136, no. XXXI.

[4] *Id.* 119, nos. X., XI.

[5] *Id.* 117, no. VI.

[6] Including no. XXIV. p. 148: a volume of sermons preached by the father confessor of the house, and written out by the sisters.

[7] *Id.* 122, no. XVII.: described as "die mesz" in German for Advent and Lent, and beginning, *Ad te levavi*. Possibly an antiphoner or a pericope: the

in German, two copies of the Rule in German and Latin[1], five books of prayers, two of hymns, two *Lives* of our Lady, and a tract on a psalm[2].

The convent also possessed some German books used specially for reading in refectory: though library books were also used for this purpose. Another manuscript gives a "note book of what shall be read at dinner and at collation throughout the whole year, so that it can be found indicated for every week, and day, and festival, what ought to be read therein[3]." The list gives also the library numbers of the books, and the pages which are to be read, and the notice ends: "Also, after the note-book, the books are written down which are described in the note-book." This list (which begins with Suso's book of the *Eternal wisdom*, in German[4]) has not been printed in full. On Christmas Eve the reading was to be the "prophecy and epistle and gospel for the third mass," or "from the lessons and from the three masses on Christmas Day": perhaps the German translation of the epistles and gospels, etc., which they were about to hear in Latin, or perhaps German discourses upon them.

The other nunnery catalogue is that of the Franciscan tertiaries at Delft. This community was founded through the influence of the Brethren of the Common Life, and was continuously directed by them[5]. It was an offshoot of the Franciscan

word "mesz" is used loosely elsewhere, in the notice about the refectory reading-books, where the reading for Christmas Eve at dinner is to be, "the third mass and the prophecy and epistle and gospel." The only parts of the Missal which could have been read in refectory would have been the epistle and gospel: actually, there is no "prophecy" or "lesson" or O. Test. passage in the three masses for Christmas Day; and the prayers from the missal would not, of course, have been read. Similarly, it is very doubtful if this MS. was a complete German missal, see p. 101.

[1] *Meister Eckhart*, 132, no. XV.; 131, no. I.; 132, no. XVII.; there were also many copies of the Rule in Latin.

[2] These 26 MSS. were, from the incipit or the description, certainly in German: possibly other volumes of sermons, prayers, etc., were also in German. Dr M. R. James, however, who has kindly looked through these two nunnery catalogues for me (see n. 5), considers that the majority of the MSS., where the language is not specified, were in Latin, and that the biblical books at the beginning of the catalogue were certainly in Latin.

[3] See p. 111, n. 1; Gottlieb, 55, *Meister Eckhart*, 114.

[4] Gottlieb, 55, no. 132.

[5] *De Boekerij van het St. Barbara-Kloster te Delft, in de tweede helft der vijftiende eeuw*, Moll, W.; printed in *Kerkhistorisch Archief, verzameld door N. C. Kist en W. Moll*, Amsterdam, 1866, deel 4, 213–28.

tertiaries of S. Agatha at Utrecht, with which house Gerard
Groot was himself connected; the sister of S. Agatha's who had
charge of the books was "to take most great and especial care,
by the advice of the director, that books written either in Latin
or in the vulgar tongue, should be catholic and well translated,
and shall use no profane or abusive manner of speech[1]"; so that
it is evident that the mother house had sisters sufficiently
educated to read Latin, and a director who allowed them to
read Dutch. This is interesting, because the tertiaries at Delft
and Utrecht came probably from a lower social class than the
Dominicanesses at Nuremberg, and it has been questioned
whether they could read Latin books at all[2]. The catalogue is
headed: *These are the study-books which belong to the library of the
Convent of S. Barbara in Delft*; it is written in Dutch, includes
109 manuscripts, and dates from the second half of the fifteenth
century. It is difficult to say with certainty in this case whether
the majority of the books were in Dutch or Latin: the connexion
with the Brethren of the Common Life, and the social class of the
tertiaries, make it much more likely than in the case of the
Nuremberg convent that most of the books were in Dutch. The
list begins with biblical books, of which there are seven[3]: one of
these is stated to be a Flemish gospel book, which renders it
most likely that the others were in Latin. The convent would
almost certainly have possessed a few Latin biblical books for
study: and it would be very probable that they should have had
in Latin four gospel books, glossed and unglossed, the epistles
of S. Paul glossed, part of the Canticles: and in Dutch, a gospel
book. Most of the other books were probably in Dutch.

These two catalogues shew a marked difference in character
from those of men's convents. They are of course smaller, do

---

[1] Moll, 220; the last words recall the determination of 1398, see p. 90.

[2] *Id.* 230; Moll's belief that the majority of the MSS. were in Dutch rests
upon the belief that a knowledge of Latin was very unusual at the mother
house at Utrecht. Busch, however, expressly states that some of "our
sisters" (those directed by the brethren), were good Latinists: Busch, 576.
He mentions, however, four houses of Augustinian nuns, to whom he was
sent to introduce reform, who said the hours of our Lady in German, in
choir: *id.* 549. Cf. Erasmus's statement on the subject, p. 116.

[3] Moll, 224; 1. Gospels and epistles; 2. Gospels with concordances, two
copies; 3. "Een vlaems ewangeliboc"; 4. S. John's gospel, with the exposition; 5. *Gospel of Nicodemus*; 6. S. Paul's epistles, glossed; 10. Three pieces
from the Canticles.

not contain a complete gloss on the Vulgate, or glosses on the separate biblical books, and are almost completely lacking in patristic works. They have relatively many more sermons, pious manuals, and books of mystical devotion, and a larger proportion of vernacular books[1].

Besides these catalogues, another exists, in manuscript only, of the women's cloister at Wonnenstein, in 1498[2]; and, among the list of biblical manuscripts and plenaries quoted by Le Long, there are eight which came from nunneries. Dutch Bible histories, or translations of Peter Comestor, were owned in the fifteenth century by the nuns of S. Margaret at Haarlem; the Franciscan tertiaries of the convent of Sion in Liere, 1412; and the nuns of S. Agnes without the walls at Nymwegen, in 1453[3]. The convent of S. Ursula at Enkhuysen owned the four gospels, or a gospel harmony; and a nun of the canonesses regular of Haarlem near Syl,—sister Mary, the daughter of Jacob Williamson of Dordrecht,—copied the Epistles and Acts in 1447. The

---

[1] Other books of interest in the Nuremberg catalogue are those in section D, p. 119, devoted to gospel harmonies, lives of our Lord, the "Bible history" of P. Comestor, etc.; section B, sermons, including those of Eckhart and Tauler; the large section of "confession books"; an "Abcdarius"; the *Eternal Wisdom*; the *Veni sancte* and *Veni creator* in German; "a treatise against the heretical Waldensians"; several *Imitations*; many saints' lives, etc. The Delft catalogue includes the *Revelations of Mechthild*; the *Passionale* for summer and winter; Cassian's *Collations*; tracts from SS. Bernard, Augustine, etc.; lives of SS. Francis, Barbara, etc.; confession books; a life of our Lord; Ruysbroeck,—the reading of whose treatises would not have been allowed to quite uneducated people; letters of Gerard Groot; a work of Gerard Zerbolt; Sydrach, S. Lydwin of Schiedam's book, etc.; but no book of medicine, like the Nuremberg catalogue. Dutch gospel harmonies, or lives of our Lord, were frequent in convents: cf. that printed by J. Bergsma, *De levens van Jesus in het middelnederlandsch*, Leyden, 1896, in the *Bibliothek van middelnederlandsche Letterkunde*; a harmony founded on that of Victor of Capua. The translator says in his preface: "I greet in our dear Lord God, Jesus Christ, all those who shall read this book, and hear it read, and ask them to pray for me. One of my dear friends prayed me, on a certain time, that I would translate the gospel out of Latin into the Dutch language: and so I made one fair history out of the texts of the four gospels of the life of our Lord Jesus Christ, from the time that He was conceived and born of the holy maiden, our Lady, till that time that He sent His holy Spirit to His disciples"; but actually the text follows Victor of Capua pretty closely, and quotes from his preface. Both the Nuremberg nuns and the Delft tertiaries studied similar Lives, or Gospel Harmonies more than the actual text of the gospel.

[2] Cloister library at S. Gallen, MS. 973, ff. 1–9; cf. Gottlieb, 83.

[3] *Boekzaal*, 249, 250; cf., for the following examples, pp. 277, 286, 287, 291, 294; for gospels of two other Dutch nunneries, Addit. 26659, 26631.

seven canonical epistles and the Apocalypse, written in 1399, was owned then or later by the nuns of S. Denis in Amsterdam. The nunnery at Landen had a glossed plenary, and the convent of S. Ursula at Haarlem another; while the nuns of Brunteshusen had three glossed plenaries in the last half of the fifteenth century[1]. The number is greater than those known to have belonged to men's houses[2], and interesting to compare with the single English example,—the manuscript given to Sion in 1517 by lady Danvers. It is also greater than that of biblical translations proved to belong to lay people at the time: and, together with the other evidence, shews that the chief readers of the German Bible in manuscript were the nuns and tertiaries, especially in the Netherlands[3].

Walther considered it likely that some of the names of scribes or owners on the German manuscript Bibles he examined were those of laymen[4], though he was unable to identify them with certainty. There is one marked difference, however, between the German manuscripts of which he speaks, and the English biblical manuscripts,—both very numerous groups. The German manuscripts give the scribe's name in 19 cases: no English biblical manuscript has one at all, although they are very frequently found in contemporary manuscripts of a different class. The

---

[1] Jostes, *Die Waldenser und die vorlutherische deutsche Bibelübersetzung*, Münster, 1885, 25.

[2] The "library of the order at Wittenberg" in 1434 was catalogued in German as having 31 books, Gottlieb, 83; see Kern, 397, for late fourteenth century catalogue of Roodekloster (Rubea Vallis, in the Netherlands), enumerating 22 Dutch books belonging to the house, the first of which was a gospel book, Gottlieb, 261. The four gospels were copied in 1472 by brother Ghysbert Beynop, for the canons regular of Vredendal, near Utrecht; and two houses of the Brethren of the Common Life had Dutch Bibles,—Hem, near Schoonhoven, and Gouda; cf. *Boekzaal*, 278, 333, 335; cf. also p. 99, *supra*.

[3] Erasmus, writing in defence of vernacular Bibles, says: "In many places there are religious, both men and women, who have the sacred books translated into the vulgar tongue, and read them, and even recite them in chapels, with the connivance of the bishop." (*Opera*, 1706, IX. 786.)

[4] Walther, 725. A MS. containing the five Wisdom books of the O.T. in German, written 1465, although it does not give the translator's or reviser's name, says in a prologue: "Because all lay people do not understand Latin, therefore I will translate these books out of Latin into German"; *id.* 386. Hans Zättelin, of Memingen, *id.* 130, who in 1481 ordered a complete German Bible to be written by Martin Huber, the schoolmaster of the place, was probably a layman; the copy was made from, or corrected from, one of the early printed Bibles.

19 German scribes were all men: there is no reason to be surprised at this (though it might have been natural enough to find some sisters' names among them), for it was of course exceedingly common in the fifteenth century for convents to get manuscripts written for them by professional scribes[1], and some of these books may have been for conventual use. The presence of so large a number of scribes' names reflects the greater security in Germany for the writers of such translations.

§ 4. The first German Bible was printed in 1466. There is no doubt that it and its successors were derived, as far as the New Testament is concerned, from the original of the above mentioned manuscript of about 1400 at Tepl: but there has been much discussion as to intermediate editors, and as to the translators of the Old Testament. During the period of about 1400–1466, a complete translation of the Bible had been made, or older partial translations had been merged in a complete German Bible: for it is not thought likely that the printers of 1466 translated any part themselves, though they may have made verbal changes.

The three earliest manuscripts which contain portions of this text are, as has been mentioned above, those of Tepl, Freiberg and Wolfenbüttel[2], the latter containing most of the Old Testament. Parts of the same Old Testament text are also contained in a Nuremberg manuscript[3] of about 1450; and this manuscript is connected with the name of a Dominican translator or reviser, John Rellach. One or two passages incorporated between the books of the Old Testament[4] give certain details concerning the circumstances which led Rellach, who belonged to a probably Dominican convent in Constance, to undertake the work. The manuscript is confusing: it contains translations of Joshua,

---

[1] Cf. *Bibliom.* 28–31.

[2] For minute analyses of these and other German biblical MSS., see Walther.

[3] Stadtbibliothek, Solgersche Bibl., MS. N. 16: cf. Walther, 147.

[4] For details, see Walther, 148–54. For the theory that Rellach was the original translator of the text used by the early printed editions (which is, however, discredited owing to the existence of the text in earlier MSS.) see Jostes, *Die Waldenserbibeln und Meister Johannes Rellach,* HJ, xv. (1894), 771–95 ; xviii. (1897), 133–45, and the controversial literature which it occasioned, in the bibliography, HH, iii. 65. For the weak point in Jostes' argument, the dating of the pre-Rellach biblical MSS., see HJ, xv. 781.

Judges, Ruth[1], and the three books which follow them in the Vulgate: and intervening passages from different scribes or translators. The preface to the book of Joshua, carelessly copied so that Jerome's preface is confused with the translator's, is that of a layman of the Gottesfreunde type, with a strong prejudice against highly-learned ecclesiastics. If another extract in the same manuscript is his work, as it certainly is in his style, he possessed a special enemy, whose varied and apostate career he describes. There are also passages about Rellach by a fellow-student, one possibly by Rellach himself, and one by a scribe who describes himself as "Peter Zarter, cathedralis [magister]," dated 1471. The ascription to Rellach of the preface by the earlier translator has led to confusion[2], but the mistake is now clear.

The preface of the translator of Joshua, Judges and Ruth is found in two other manuscripts[3], both earlier than that of Nuremberg: and the text is that of the Wolfenbüttel Old Testament. The preface is in a south German dialect, and begins[4]:

This is a foreword against him, who is opposed to the German writing, which is, nevertheless, useful and profitable for men's souls. My enemies have up till now done violence to their own conscience, because they have till now been silent as regards my plan to translate the holy gospel[5] into German. Now however they have taken a different stand, inspired by foolish pride, and they bring forward foolish counsels, and say:

"But what shall we [clergy] now preach, when [lay] men read and listen to the holy scriptures in the German tongue in their rooms and houses?"

Him[6] will I answer from holy scripture, until it is again necessary that we should meet. Now mark that they have objected to me with the more pride, because they think that they themselves excel in holy scripture, and have somewhat noised this abroad: and would that their knowledge were less than it is! For no one accuses the perfect of knowledge, and withholds them from preaching, if they read and strive diligently to strengthen faithful Christians in the word of God.

---

1 Walther, 147; HJ, xv. 777–9; see *supra*, p. 79.

2 Jostes' articles fail to recognise the distinction.

3 Vienna MSS. 2845, 3063: see HJ, xv. 777.

4 *Id.* 777–9; Walther, 147–52.

5 Which would seem to shew that the tract was originally written in connexion with some New Testament translation.

6 The author, or the careless scribe, continually changes from the singular to the plural, with respect to his enemies.

*Woe to you who call good evil, and evil good*: as they do, who in their
pride contradict what learned priests and blessed laymen praise and
call good. It is through pride that these unlearned philosophers and
their followers contradict with their subtlety, and fight against, the
righteous truth: that is, they fight against the holy scriptures and
hinder the spread of their revealing[1].…

And my proud enemies, set about with highmindedness, have held
forth before lords and learned people, desiring to gain their respect:
but thus is their deep folly the more fully known to the people, who
before knew it not. For while they were wisely silent, they were
esteemed prudent and well-learned.…And now they hotly attack
my fitness to deal with the lore of holy scripture: whereof I have good
hope towards God that they shall be confounded and put to silence.
And now they suggest from pride that I am too poor a scholar for
this matter, because I have not been in great places of learning[2]. And
that is true! But the Holy Ghost supplies by His grace what is lacking
in me, and it is also well supplied by the help and counsel of learned
people. For I have known many a man, who has been at places of
learning, and returned as ignorant as he went, unless it be that he has
gained patrons, or learned how to find Easter[3]: for the knowledge of
holy writ is neglected. For the truly learned willingly hear and diligently learn, and gain true knowledge in their own home, when they
ponder what in universities is counted worthless. For it is quite
obvious that there are certain simple lay people who thoroughly and
perfectly understand holy scripture, in all its parts: even as there are
some, who think they know what they have never learned.

The preface to the book of Joshua[4] perhaps describes the same
opponent whom the translator wished to meet again:

"My enemy," he says, "is an apostate monk, who has gone from one
order to another, and now is not living under a rule at all: he has been
an Augustinian,…a parish priest and a Benedictine: no faith is to be
placed in such a man. My lord the bishop of Eichstädt has denounced
him, and exhorted him to return to his cloister."

Both passages, in their denunciation of worldly ecclesiastics who

---

[1] Offenbarung: translation. For a very similar attack by a Friend of God
on learned prelates and "grossen Pfaffen," see the *Buch von geistlicher Armuth*, Denifle, H. S., 180. Denifle has shewn that the book is not Tauler's,
but earlier in date.

[2] Hohen schulen. The term would signify primarily universities, but might
include episcopal theological schools, or Dominican "studia sollemnia."
The statement that the writer had not been to "hohen schulen" tells
strongly against Jostes' theory that this preface is by the Dominican
Rellach, which is untenable on other grounds.

[3] "Di meisterliche goldyne czal": probably a punning reference to the
"golden number" for determining Easter.

[4] Printed HJ, xv. 785–6.

seek to prevent the spread of biblical translations, deny the right of laymen to make them, and hinder the laity from using them, resemble the tract of Nicholas of Bâle against the worldly prelates who "say that German books are harmful to Christianity[1]."

The other abstracts deal with "the master of this book," John Rellach. They state that when the news was brought to Rome of the fall of Constantinople, 1453, "we students" were dismayed and sad, and especially after the eloquent sermon of Leonard of Chios, bishop of Mitylene, describing it[2]. John Rellach, however, declared that S. Peter's ship should never founder: and declared that he would translate the Vulgate into German, till the knowledge of it should be so spread that the Church should be compensated for the loss of the Greek biblical manuscripts. He was ordered, however, to preach the crusade against the Turks, which delayed his plan. Moreover, he himself probably regarded it as perilous, since he answered those who twitted him for delay "that a prophet was a very different person from a commentator[3]." He himself describes his travels in another manuscript[4]: they took him from Rome to Constance, Mainz, Fulda, Marburg, Norway and Finland. He visited S. Bridget's monastery of Vadstena, saw the book of her revelations, and was probably encouraged in his scheme of translation by the favour of the Brigittines for such works. He had begun making an index of the contents of the biblical books, to help the uninstructed laity, in 1450[5]; and, after his return from his travels, he translated Joshua, Judges and Ruth, or revised an earlier translation,—again shewing by his reply to his friends that he considered the action risky[6]. He is called the "master"

[1] See p. 80.

[2] Walther, 151; HJ, xv. 782.

[3] *Id*. 784: "Es ist ain ander ding ze sein ain prophet, und ist noch ain ander ding ain tolmetsch."

[4] Printed HJ, xv. 793–5.

[5] Walther, 151.

[6] HJ, xv. 795. During his travels "the students" had begun the work of translation in Strassburg, Bâle, Speyer and Worms: they asked Rellach, "Master, where is that plan of yours?" To which he answered that the "lamb should become the lion, and that the soldier in arms never proclaims his own valour,"—meaning apparently, that he had not thought it prudent as yet to speak openly of his plans; he then set to work to translate the book of Joshua (using actually an older text).

(owner or translator) of this book in one or two later notices: and as late as 1471 Peter Zarter thought it advisable to state in a note, that the "master of this book" considered Bible study good and profitable for the laity: though he was perhaps quoting, not Rellach, but the preface of the earlier translator embedded in the manuscript. However little original translation was actually due to Rellach, the manuscript shews that there was in 1453 a Swiss Dominican who was anxious to promote the spread of biblical translations.

Between 1466 and 1522, the date of the printing of Luther's New Testament, eighteen editions of the German Bible were printed, fourteen in German, four in Dutch[1]. The publisher of the earliest edition was Mentel of Strassburg[2], of whom we know little, except that he was in favour at the court of the emperor Frederick III, so that no suspicion of heresy attaches to him. The other edition of most interest for the question of the lawfulness of the use of translations is that of Cologne, 1480, which has an interesting preface[3]. This states that highly learned masters of the schools

read and use the translations of S. Jerome, whereas unlearned and simple men, both spiritual and secular, but especially children brought up in monasteries and dedicated to be religious, should use the German translation of the Latin Bible, for the avoiding of idleness, on saints' days, when they have time. Therefore a lover of the salvation of all men, not moved by earthy praise and honour, but by Christian love and virtue, and urged thereto by certain men of good heart: this man, with the help and counsel of many highly-learned men, has had printed at great cost, in the city of Cologne, the German translation of the Latin Bible; which translation was made many years before, and used in manuscripts by many devout men, both in men's and women's convents: and long before this time it has been

---

[1] For descriptions and bibliographies of these editions, see Walther, 113–18. HH, III. 65. The number of editions is large, but not particularly large compared with the number of issues of various popular pious manuals; it is, of course, very much smaller than that of liturgical books in frequent use, like missals and breviaries.

[2] Walther, 204.

[3] *Boekzaal*, 387–92; cf. *Tepler Bibel*. 31; Hain, *3141. The Bible was printed by Henricus Quentell in 1480, though it does not contain his name or the date. See Walther, 655–71 ; and J. Geffcken, *Bildercatechismus des fünfzehnten Jahrhunderts*, Leipsig, 1855, 9. The text was followed by the Lübeck Bible, 1494, which has a similar preface, but added the gloss of Nicholas of Lyra to the text. For the original translator, see *supra*, p. 64.

printed in the Oberland, and in some towns of the Netherlands: and it has spread into many lands, and is bought there with the greatest eagerness at great cost.

This preface almost takes the form of an explanation or apology for the printing of the book, and is interesting as shewing that the editor thought his work would be of chief use to simple priests and religious, and as alleging that German manuscripts had been widely used, not by lay people, but in convents. This agrees with other evidence as to the users of such translations: and the regions cited are those where, long before, the Waldensian heretics, then the Béguines, the Gottes-freunde, and finally the Brethren of the Common Life, had been influential, and friendly to the use of a vernacular literature of devotion.

The history of the early printed German Bibles is of special interest for the attitude of the Church to biblical translations. Such editions are earlier, and much more numerous, than those of any other country. Of course this was partly due to the flourishing condition of the Rhine towns at the time, and to the number and vigour of the printing presses, which had multiplied earlier in the Rhine towns than elsewhere. No doubt, also, the early appearance of printed Bibles in Germany was due to the relaxation in favour of biblical translations, in some orthodox circles, which was strengthened after 1466 by the diffusion of the printed editions. The question is nevertheless very interest-ing: What share did the official ecclesiastical world take in the production of these editions, and what was its attitude towards them?

The two extreme answers to these questions can be put aside. On the one hand, there is no evidence that the editions were the work of a definite sect of heretics, like the Lollards or the Waldensians, and as such condemned by authority. The Hussites had preserved Wycliffe's teaching in Bohemia when it had been almost stamped out in England, and other sects existed, who set store on the lay reading of the Bible: but there is no definite evidence to connect the early printed editions with these sects. On the other hand, it is quite certain that none of these printed Bibles was an official edition[1], approved by

[1] Keller, 67–.

authority: though to issue such an edition would have been as possible to any bishop, as to order the publication of tracts on faith and conduct at diocesan synods, a thing which had often been done in the past.

The chief authority on the history of the German Bible considers, however, that there is evidence that the attitude of ecclesiastical authority was not favourable to the issue of these editions[1]; and such a conclusion agrees with the evidence examined above as to the usual mediaeval attitude towards biblical translations. First, there is no evidence of any change in the carefully considered mediaeval idea, that lay Bible reading, unsupervised by the clergy, was harmful. If John Busch, who held advanced and liberal ideas on the subject, and who only died about 1480, did not approve of unlicensed Bible reading, it is not probable that the majority of German bishops did so in 1466. Secondly, it is noticeable that, while the cloister presses of Germany were turning out a stream of devotional literature, both Latin and German, they never printed any translation of the Bible[2]. Thirdly, the absence of printers' names in the four earliest editions, and in some of the later ones, is strong evidence that the printers expected no thanks from ecclesiastics for their work[3]. Just as Luther's Bible found printers who were not too scrupulous as to the view the Church would take of their work, so the printers of the early German Bibles considered it safest to conceal their names,—even in an edition as late as the tenth, of 1485, at which date the absence of a printer's name is most unusual. Thirdly, the absence of the translator's name, though not as significant as the absence of the printer's, probably shews that the earliest editors were laymen. Walther considers that the first four editions at least were due to the efforts of laymen, and that their anonymity was due partly to suspicion that their enterprise would not be well received[4].

---

[1] Walther, 204, 5.
[2] Falk, *Die Druckkunst im Dienste der Kirche*, Cologne, 1879, 10.
[3] Walther, 205. The publisher (not printer) of the first German Bible, Mentel of Strassburg, was apparently orthodox, see *id*. 204; Putnam, II. 12, states that Anthonius Koberger of Nuremberg, who printed a German Bible in 1483, was a very well-known publisher; and that Christ Froschauer of Zürich, an associate of Zwingli and an ardent reformer, printed a German Bible.
[4] Walther, 206.

Lastly, there is the evidence of the censor's edicts on the subject; and, though these have been interpreted as intending to prevent only bad translations, there is some ground for thinking that the authorities would not have been displeased had they prevented the printing of translations altogether. It is certain in any case that no German Bible was approved by the ecclesiastical censor, as, for instance, were two books from Venice and Heidelberg in 1480, and the Cologne Latin Bible of 1479, which still bear the censor's mark[1]. The most interesting edict is that of Berthold, count of Henneburg, archbishop of Mainz, and archchancellor to the emperor, in 1486[2]. Printing, it states, is useful for the increase of knowledge:

Yet we have found that certain men, inspired by the desire of money or by vain glory, have abused this art: and have perverted what was given for the instruction of humanity to ruin and calumny. For we have seen even books of the divine office, and the mysteries of our religion[3], translated from Latin into German, and handled by the common people, to the degradation of religion. And finally even, how can we express ourselves about the translation even of the canonical books and the precepts of the law[4]? For, if these books should be translated most suitably and prudently by the most prudent and eloquent of men, yet this branch of science is so exceedingly knotty, that even the whole life-time of a most wise and prudent man would scarcely suffice for it. Yet certain rash and ignorant fools dare to translate into the vulgar tongue, and to print, such volumes: for whose translation many learned doctors have confessed that their understanding is too small, because of the great inappropriateness and

---

[1] Reusch, I. 56. Books passed by the censor were marked "Admissum"; "Temptatum"; or "Examinatum admissumque ac approbatum ab alma Universitate studii civitatis Coloniensis, de consensu ac voluntate (censor's name), pro tempore rectoris eiusdem"; see also I. 58, and for a 1491 ordinance by a papal legate, Mansi, *Supp.* VI. 681.

[2] Printed *Codex Diplom. Anecdotorum*, Gudenus, Frankfürt, 1758, IV. 469–72.

[3] i.e. breviaries and missals.

[4] *Sacrorum canonum legumque preceptis*: the remainder of the edict shews that this expression refers to the Bible, and not to a translation, for instance, of the *Decretals*, or some collection of canon laws, for which the next sentence would be quite inappropriate, even if it were less incredible a priori that anybody should translate books of canon law into the vernacular. These were quite useless except to men who could plead in the Latin tongue before ecclesiastical judges. The "books of both laws" is a frequent mediaeval term for the "books of both Testaments,"—the old law, and the new law; see pp. 81 n. 3, 227, 256.

The later reference to the gospels and epistles renders it almost certain that this expression means the Bible.

abuse of words. What shall we say, finally, about works of the other branches of science, with some of which false passages are mingled and false titles given, or when they are sometimes attributed to famous authors, to obtain the more buyers?

Let such translators say, if they have any regard for truth, whether they do this with good or evil mind, and whether the German language is sufficient to treat of these things[1], of which so many great writers both Greek and Latin have written with such exceeding accuracy and skill, both of the highest mysteries of the Christian religion, and of natural philosophy? For it must be confessed that the poverty of our mother tongue is quite insufficient, and that it would be necessary for translators to invent unknown names for things out of their head; or, if they used old names, they would corrupt the true meaning: which we fear the more, because of the great danger in the case of the sacred books. For who would enable simple and uneducated men, and even women, into whose hands copies of the sacred books might fall, to pick out the true meaning[2]? For it is obvious, and certainly no prudent man will deny, that the text of the holy gospels, or the epistles of S. Paul, need much supplementing and exposition by other writers. Yet such books are met with, and even frequently [in the vernacular].

What shall we say then of the translation of those works which rest under the sharpest disapproval of writers of the catholic Church? We might say much: but let the bare mention of them here suffice....

We therefore command and enjoin that no work, of whatever branch of science, art or knowledge, shall be translated from the Greek or Latin or any other tongue into the common German tongue, or, when translated (even with any change of style or title), shall be published or bought, publicly or privately, directly or indirectly: unless both before printing, and between printing and publication, they are licensed to be printed and published by John Bertram of Naumburg[3], in the case of theological books, and...[three other professors in the case of books of law, medicine and arts, respectively], deputed by our letters patent.

This edict seems to have been effective in suppressing the printing of Bibles in Mainz itself for the next ten years: but not altogether in the other big towns of the province, where evasion was probably easier. Yet it is noticeable that after 1488 only three editions of the German Bible appeared in the next thirty years: a number significantly small compared with that of the

---

[1] For the same argument about Italian, see Passavanti, p. 46; about English, friars Butler and Palmer, Appendix.
[2] The backbone of the mediaeval argument: the need of the fourfold interpretation of scripture: cf. p. 288.
[3] Rector of the university of Mainz; cf. Reusch, I. 58.

years 1466–1486[1]. No biblical translation, however, bears the mark of having been approved by Bertram of Naumburg, who should, presumably, have censored all such works till his death in 1515. This is the only edict which refers expressly to biblical translations: but in 1479 the rector of the university of Cologne issued one against all printers, buyers and readers of heretical and erroneous books, "and such things as are hurtful to the Christian religion," and this edict was confirmed and applied to the provinces of Cologne, Mainz, Trier and Magdeburg by pope Alexander VI in 1501[2]. The later censorial edicts do not deal specially with biblical translations, like that at Mainz: but are quoted to shew that censors of erroneous books existed elsewhere in Germany at the time, and that we might have expected to find one or two of the numerous German Bibles bearing their mark of examination, had the ecclesiastical world been generally favourable to such translations. In 1479 a Latin edition of the scriptures was printed at Cologne, with the approbation of the censor of the university[3]: so that the omission of the censor's mark in the Dutch Bible printed at Cologne in 1480 is the more marked. On the whole, however, it was not till printed German Bibles had spread beyond control, that the official attitude to them changed,—and not then in all cases, as we have seen in that of Geiler of Kaysersberg.

§ 5. Lastly, it is interesting to trace the growth of orthodox favour towards biblical translations in the years 1450–1526, the period of the spread of the printed editions. Evidence of this can be found in the edicts of provincial councils, in manuals, and in instances of the ownership of translations by lay people: and (a most important point), in the case of the councils and manuals, it cannot be paralleled in an earlier period.

In the fourteenth and fifteenth centuries, councils and synods had passed many regulations for the preaching of sermons in the vulgar tongue: but the end had always been the instruction of the faithful in the elements of the faith[4], not the translation to them of the Sunday gospel. The value of these sermons at mass

---

[1] Walther, 718.    [2] Reusch, I. 54–6.    [3] Putnam, II. 11.
[4] Canon LVI. of the diocesan synod of Strassburg, 1335, required all parish priests in the sermon at the Sunday mass, to preach and explain the creed to their people in the vulgar tongue. See Dacheux, 7.

was specially emphasised in Germany in the fifteenth century; and, at the end of it, priests were advised to explain the meaning of the Sunday gospel in German. No case is known where a synod enjoined the preliminary reading of the text of the gospel in German, before 1526; although one manual recommended in 1504 that the priest should do this in place of the sermon, if hard pressed for time. At the end of the period, however, there are two cases of synods[1] recommending a close exposition of the text of the gospel: priests were to "expound the honest meaning of the words."

In 1403 the council of Magdeburg, in addition to the universal canonical duty of attendance at mass on Sundays and holy days, laid the faithful under obligation to hear the sermon of their parish priest or his substitute[2]; even as they bound the priest to preach the sermon. In 1445, 1497 and 1504 synods enjoined that parishes with Slav inhabitants must have an assistant priest who could speak that language, or should have the sermon translated for them by an interpreter[3]. The synod of Eichstädt, 1447[4], was the first to recommend a close exposition of the Sunday gospel, and here there is no mention of an actual translation:

We enjoin priests to be cautious in their sermons, and not to utter useless and vain tales, utterly offensive to pious minds, but rather to preach on Sundays and holy days the holy scripture of the Old and New Testament, plainly and intelligibly. First, let them explain the text in the vulgar tongue, as it lies, adding a commentary, or verse by verse, even as they know to be suitable for their people's capacity[5].

The fifteenth century synods do not generally mention the sermon when requiring attendance at mass; but in 1492 that at Schwerin forbade parish priests to be absent on Sundays, thus depriving the faithful of mass and sermon; and at Freysingen[6]

---

[1] Eichstädt and Ratisbon, see *infra*.
[2] *Con. Germ.* v. 697.
[3] Dacheux, 8.
[4] *Con. Germ.* v. 364.
[5] Primo textum, prout jacet, vulgariter exponendo subjunctis postillis vel per membra declarent, veluti plebis capacitati convenire cognoverint.
[6] Dacheux, 8. The preaching of a sermon was certainly general at the end of the century: the synod of Bâle, 1503, and various writers, denounced those who went out into the churchyard during the sermon.

visitors were to ask if the parish priest preached every Sunday. The synod of Ratisbon in 1512 reiterated almost verbatim the decree of the synod of Eichstädt about sermons, but omitted the words emphasising the closeness of the exposition, "as the text lies,... verse by verse[1]." The synod of Meissen, 1504, ordered the priest to "read the Pater and Creed in the vulgar tongue to the people, and teach it them[2]" at the sermon, in language that shews that the synod of Eichstädt did not intend to order "the reading of the gospel in the vulgar tongue" in the sermon.

This is borne out by the advice given in the very popular *Manuale Curatorum*, or manual of parish priests, composed by Ulric Surgant of Altkirch, the parish priest of S. Théodore at Bâle, who died in 1503[3]. The manual gives a list of books suitable for the study of young priests, and analyses preaching under five headings,—the homily, the prone, the sermon proper, etc.:

> But sometimes, if the priest is in great haste or has to say several masses, the parish priest may say to the people: "I shall merely read to you the gospel for the day, without comment or introduction; these are the words of S. Matthew, and this is the meaning, in the vulgar tongue": or, "Instead of a sermon for to-day, I will tell you the gospel for the Sunday, with its meaning, in brief."

The priest is however warned to tell the people that he is only telling them the sense of the words: for he might translate in one way, and there are printed gospels which might translate in another: and laymen or women might read them at home, and say: "My book has not got the text as the preacher says," as if he had said something wrong[4].

From 1470 onwards various German manuals, written for the laity, recommended attendance at the Sunday sermon. In 1470 the *Spiegel der Sünder* went so far as to say that: "Whoever has in his house boys of fourteen and girls of twelve, and neglects to send them to the sermon, sins mortally, as they do in not

---

[1] *Con. Germ.* VI. 112: primo textum subjunctis postillis declarent, veluti plebis capacitati noverint convenire.

[2] Dacheux, 10.

[3] Dacheux, 19, and E. Schröder, *Gött. Gel. Anz.* 1888, 254, for the passages quoted.

[4] "Dis ist der Sinn der Worten: non sine cautela, ideo quia evangelia sint in vulgari impressa; et ille sic, alius sic, vulgarizat, et laici viri seu mulieres in domo prius legentes ista deinde dicerent: liber meus non habet sic textum ut praedicans dixit, quasi male dixisset." Geffcken, *Bildercatechismus*, 10.

going[1]." In 1484 the *Hymmelstrasz* and the *Licht der Seele* both recommended the faithful to go, and to write down what they heard[2]. In 1508 the *Nutzlich...Buchlin,* and in 1509 the *Wurzgärtlein*[3] went further, and recommended the faithful to read the scriptures for themselves, in a spirit of humility: "if you should read them in a spirit of pride, they will be hurtful to you." In 1513 the *Himmelstür*[4] urged that

All that you hear in sermons or through other modes of instruction... should incite you to read with piety and humility the Bible and holy books, which are now translated into German, and printed and distributed in large numbers[5], either in their entirety or in part, and which you can purchase for very little money.

More striking still is the preface to the Bâle plenary of 1514[6]:

Hast thou pious books? Read them on Sunday after the sermon, after supper and in the midst of thy family. There ought to be no man who has not a copy of the holy gospel with him in his house[7].

The number of these exhortations to Bible reading is of course small compared to the stream of such manuals and books of homilies which came from the press[8]: but, since they cannot be paralleled in earlier manuals, which were also very numerous, they are interesting as evidence of the turn of the tide.

Four cases of individual ownership, or copying of biblical translations, might perhaps be noticed. In 1399 Wernerus Dominicus Mynne, possibly a layman, completed the writing of

---

[1] Dacheux, 14; this tract, published Augsburg, 1470, is a confession book, compiled chiefly from three fifteenth century Latin manuals. It is not a German edition of the much older Latin *Speculum Peccatorum*, which was translated into English in the fourteenth century, and which has no reference to sermons. See Geffcken, *Bildercatechismus*, (ii), 47–79, for long extracts from this work, and from many similar contemporary confession books.

[2] Dacheux, 14; *Bildercatechismus*, (ii), 106.

[3] Janssen, I. 59.

[4] *Id.* I. 56.

[5] There were 22 editions of the psalms before 1509, 25 of the epistles and gospels before 1518.

[6] Schroeder, *Gött. Gel. Anz.* 1888, 254.

[7] This is, incidentally, the preface meant to secure customers for the edition of the epistles and gospels, not merely a pious exhortation. That the reading of glossed plenaries was popular, however, is shewn by the issue of 102 editions of gospels and epistles with homilies between 1470–1520. Janssen, I. 54.

[8] Cf. the German manuals of the date in Hentsch: the *Frauenbuechlein*, c. 1500, p. 229, gives many instances from the Bible, but no tract advises the use of German plenaries, etc.

a Dutch plenary in the house of Hugo of Necelhorst[1]. About 1450, or a little later, Elizabeth von Volkensdorf, a daughter of one of the noblest and richest families of upper Austria[2], possessed about fifty German books, of which the catalogue has come down to us. The list included a Bible, a psalter, a gospel-book, an epistle-book, the Apocalypse, a homily on the epistles, and another on the gospel *In Principio*, and two copies of "Our Lady's Bible,"—that is, her life. In 1462 a burgher of Leyden, Willem Heerman, left to the church of S. Peter in that town a complete copy of a Dutch Bible, for the use of "all good pious men, who wish to read therein something profitable[3]"; and in 1474 a Dutch *Bible History* was written for master Hugh Gherytz, a surgeon[4]. These cases, which could perhaps be increased in number by an exhaustive search, contrast with the complete absence of evidence of lay ownership in England, after 1408[5], except among the Lollards; but they do not oppose the conclusion that the greatest users of translations were convents of women.

It seems a fair deduction from the evidence given in this chapter to say that at the beginning of the fifteenth century the orthodox champions of biblical translations were few, and confined to the circle of the Gottesfreunde; that the Brethren of the Common Life were largely influential in extending the use of translations in convents, and of German manuals among the laity; that the printing of German Bibles was done without the approval of the Church, and that though, about 1500, some writers of manuals had begun to approve of their possession by lay people, other orthodox churchmen continued to regret it.

[1] *Boekzaal*, 292.
[2] *Die Bibliothek des Chorherrnstiftes St. Florian*, Czerny, A., Linz, 1874, 237, 8. "Hie ist ze merckhen waz ich Elspet Volchenstorfferin pueher hab deutscher." Cf. Kern, 400.
[3] Moll, *Kerkenges*, II[2]. 335; cf. Jostes, *Waldenser und die vorluther. Bibel*, Münster, 1885, 28.
[4] *Boekzaal*, 251.
[5] Absence of owner's names in the MSS., or in wills.

# CHAPTER V

## Biblical translations before Wycliffe: as known to Wycliffe's contemporaries, and as known to us

§ 1. Between the death of Wycliffe in 1384, and the prohibition of the Wycliffite translations in 1408, there was considerable discussion about the lawfulness of making any translation of the Vulgate. Apart from evidence that such discussion
went briskly forward[1], we have five treatises written between
1380 and 1408 dealing with this subject, occasioned of course by
the Lollard effort to popularise their own biblical translations.
This discussion could not of course ignore the argument from
precedent, so that it affords ample evidence of what Wycliffe's
contemporaries believed about the existence of earlier biblical
translations, and the examples with which they were acquainted.
Three of these treatises were by Lollards, and pleaded for the
lawfulness of translations, while two were by friars, who wrote
against them[2]. There is also an interesting reference to biblical
translations in a non-controversial tract, the *Dialogue between a
Lord and a Clerk*, which John Trevisa prefixed to his English
version of Higden's *Polychronicon* in 1387. Trevisa, chaplain to
lord Thomas of Berkeley, was a professional "turner" or translator, and he recounted in the *Dialogue* how his lord had recommended him to English the *Polychronicon*, and had overcome
his scruples as to whether the popularisation of such a work was
profitable. The "Lord" called to witness the making of earlier
translations of learned works, and included in his catena such
instances as he could give of the translation, in verse or sermon,
of any part of the Bible: he was plainly ignorant of any complete English translation of the Bible, suitable for a precedent.

In the five controversial tracts also, the champions of vernacular Bibles employed the argument from precedent largely,
and their opponents could not altogether ignore it. Both sides

---

[1] Cf. Pollard, 203–8.     [2] Printed, Appendix II.

mentally ran through what they knew of earlier English translations: the Lollard party, like the jurists of Cologne, eagerly
sought for all the instances that they could find, to prove that
translations had been made and used by orthodox Englishmen;
and since at least one of their treatises is the work of a scholar,
the non-reference to any translation immediately preceding the
days of Wycliffe is very strong proof that such translation was
completely unknown. Had any such orthodox translation
existed, and been at all widely used by the faithful between
1350 and 1408[1], it is scarcely conceivable that the two anti-
translation treatises should have been written at all. But these
"anti" treatises did deal with the alleged precedents of Bede's
translations. The importance of the historical references in
these tracts and in Trevisa's *Dialogue* is this: that it enables us
to distinguish clearly between recognised translations and tracts,
and those which existed at the time but were quite unknown,
and without influence. It enables us to see what archbishop
Arundel meant, when he said in 1408 that translations made
before Wycliffe's day should remain lawful: because the translations of which he was thinking were not those which might be
"alleged" by a modern specialist in English literature. We can
reconstruct from these tracts a list of these works, as known to
the contemporaries of Wycliffe and Arundel, both in the periods
before and after the conquest.

§ 2. There was a fairly general concurrence of opinion that
large parts of the Bible had been translated into prose in Anglo-
Saxon times, and the two names with which the translation was
connected were those of Bede and Alfred. Probably the basis
of the idea was the writers' knowledge of some manuscript of
the Anglo-Saxon gospels in one of the abbey libraries: we should
probably have dated the manuscript as written about 1050 or
1100 A.D., as were those now in existence, but fourteenth century
scholars believed them to be much earlier, and connected them
with the names they found mentioned as translators in written
records.

[1] With the exception of the psalter: the translation of which was always
regarded as more permissible than that of other parts of the Bible, and
occurred earlier. The pro-vernacular writers quoted Hampole in their
favour: the anti-vernacular ones did not bring up the point of English
psalters at all.

John Purvey, whose list of historical precedents is by far the largest, mentions that

S. Oswald[1], king of Northumberland, asked of the Scots an holy bishop Aidan to preach to his people: and the king himself interpreted it on English to the people. If this blessed deed be allowed to the king of all holy Church: how not now as well ought it to be allowed a man to read the gospel on English, and do thereafter?

Trevisa says that "Caedmon[2] of Whitby was inspired by the Holy Ghost, and made wonder poesies in English, nigh of all the stories of holy writ."

Three writers mention Bede. "The holy man Beda[3]," says Trevisa, "translated S. John's gospel out of Latin into English," —a statement justified by a passage in the *Ecclesiastical History*[4]. Purvey the Lollard mentions the same precedent:

Venerable Bede...translated the Bible, or a great part of the Bible, whose originals been in many abbeys in England....And Cistrence saith, that the evangely of John was drawn into English by the foresaid Bede, which evangely of John, and other gospels been yet in many places of so old English, that unnethe can any man read them[5].

Palmer the Dominican, when expressly challenged with the precedent of Bede's translation, made two objections:

Even if Bede did translate the whole of holy scripture, nevertheless the Church did not accept his translation, because perchance he erred in it, even as Jerome and nearly all the others who have presumed to translate it. And secondly, I assert that Bede did not translate it, except inasmuch as it was necessary to salvation and easy of understanding; because, according to his own teaching, he could not translate the whole into the barbarian tongue, as I have shewn above[6].

The Franciscan Butler also made a veiled reference to the supposed translations of Bede, quoting first from the third book of Aristotle's *Rhetoric*, "quanto maior est populus, tanto minor vel remotior est intellectus."

"Therefore, though it might have been allowable," he says, "that the common people should be able to read holy scripture at a time when few speaking that tongue were converted to the faith, in what-

---

[1] See p. 441..     [2] Pollard, 206.     [3] *Id.* 206.
[4] *Ven. Bedae Hist. Eccles.*, Plummer, C., 1896, I. lxxv.
[5] See p. 441; Cistrence = Ranulph of Chester, or Higden, author of the *Polychronicon*: which was translated into English by Trevisa.
[6] See p. 435.

ever nation it might be: nevertheless it does not follow that it would be allowable in the same nation nowadays for all in like manner to be able to read the scriptures, as in the days when they were catechumens. And if it can be proved that any recognised or canonized doctor did translate the holy scriptures for any people to read, or even advised them to read, nevertheless it does not follow that it would be allowable nowadays: because one matter remains doubtful, even that saying of Aristotle, that 'the greater the people, the smaller its understanding.' Therefore the best way of knowing God is by reflecting about Him, and by prayerfully entreating Him, and Christians get more good from these two methods than by reading or hearing[1].

Trevisa mentions too that king Alfred[2], "that founded the university of Oxford, translated the best laws into English tongue, and a great deal of the psalter, out of Latin into English"; and Purvey, probably quoting from the same source, says that "Alfred[3] the king ordained open schools of divers arts in Oxford, and he turned the best laws into his mother tongue, and the psalter also."

There is, of course no *a priori* reason why Anglo-Saxon scholars should not have translated the Bible, as fourteenth century critics believed that they did. In a missionary church this should have been useful, not to the unlettered layman, but to the young monks and priests sent out to instruct them. Translations were made for use in the Eastern branch of the Church in the ninth century, and their use was confirmed by the pope in 879; the western feeling against translations did not harden till the time of Gregory VII. Nevertheless there is no evidence that a complete translation, even of the four gospels, was made till the time of Aelfric, in the eleventh century, or that biblical translations were used at all in the Anglo-Saxon period for the regular instruction of monks, priests or laity. Generally speaking, the text of the Bible was studied only by the monks, and it was studied in Latin.

Bede, who died in 735, wrote Latin commentaries on all the books of the Bible, and the story of his completion of an English translation of the gospel of S. John on his death-bed is familiar.

[1] See p. 406.  [2] Pollard, 206.
[3] See p. 441. Anglo-Saxon interlinear glosses on the psalms date from the ninth century: Paues, 1902, x.; but Anglo-Saxon psalters were written as late as the twelfth or thirteenth centuries: cf. Fitzwilliam, 12, the Peterborough psalter of 1260–70. The whole number of remaining manuscripts is, however, small.

He probably translated only about the six first chapters, as is explicitly mentioned by Cuthbert his pupil in a letter. In either case, the translation is not extant, and would have been of little use to any except the monks of his day. These of course did a large amount of missionary and pastoral work: but the secular clergy appear, from Bede's description of them, to have had very little learning. In a letter to bishop Egbert, Bede exhorted him to take especial care in instructing ordinands in

the Catholic faith, which is contained in the apostles' creed and the Lord's prayer, which scripture in the holy gospel teaches us. For it is certain, that all who have learnt the use of the Latin speech, will best learn this in Latin: but make the unlearned, that is, those who know only their own tongue, learn them in their own language, and carefully repeat them; and this should be done, not only in the case of laymen, that is, those hitherto living the secular life, but also in the case of monks and clerks, who know Latin. . . . Wherefore I have myself had both these, that is, the creed and pater noster, translated into the English tongue, for the sake of many priests, who are often unlearned[1].

The words throw light on the learning of secular ordinands of the day, and shew how little likely they were to attempt translations of the Sunday gospel at mass, or anything of the kind[2].

The only translations made by the command of king Alfred were those chapters of the Bible he incorporated in the collection known as Alfred's Dooms, or Alfred's Laws[3]. He began this by an English rendering of Exodus, chapters xx. to xxiii.,—the account of the giving of the law to Moses, and of the Mosaic civil code. This was followed by that passage from Acts xv. which describes the enactment of the council of Jerusalem, and gives the relation of Christianity to the Mosaic law. The other books which Alfred actually selected for translation were not biblical, but such works as Gregory's *Pastoral Rule* and Bede's *Ecclesiastical History*; he and Aethelwold, bishop of Winchester, also ordered the translation of S. Benedict's *Rule*, for the benefit of seculars joining the monasteries. Alfred died in 901: but though we possess twelve manuscripts of English glosses on the

---

[1] Plummer's *Bede*, I. 408.

[2] For the learning of the Anglo-Saxon clergy, cf. R. Graham's *Intellectual influence of English monasticism*, RHT, VII. 24 ff.; and for a priest who knew the old British, or Gaelic, language, *Gesta Abbatum*, RS, 28, I. 26; cf. also *Schools of Med. England*, Leach, A. F., 1915, 51 ff.    [3] Cook, 69.

psalter, some of them from the ninth century, there is nothing
to connect any of them with his name. The belief of Purvey and
Trevisa that he translated a large part of the psalter was due to
the assertion of William of Malmesbury, that he "attempted to
translate the psalter, but died when he had barely finished explaining the first part[1]." This description fits the first translation of the psalms which has come down to us: a translation
actually of the first part, or quinquena, of fifty psalms; this
work originated, however, early in the tenth century[2].

The earlier verbal glosses on the psalter would have been
useful in teaching novices to read the divine office, but word for
word glosses could never have been actually read aloud, because
they did not form consecutive English sentences. This was the
case also with the earliest Saxon gospels which have survived,
the Lindisfarne gospels or old Northumbrian gloss, which was
written about 950 A.D., and the slightly later Rushworth gospels,
or old Mercian gloss. Such works must have been used for
private study only: they could not have been read aloud, in
either church or refectory.

The earliest surviving gospels, which can properly be called a
translation, were the West Saxon gospels of an otherwise unknown Aelfric, monk of Bath, who wrote about 900, or soon
after. There are seven manuscripts of this version, some of a
good deal later date. A more famous Aelfric, the scholarly abbot
of Eynsham, who died c. 1020, wrote both a vigorous paraphrase
of parts of the Old Testament, and a set of homilies on the
Sunday gospels, most of them prefaced by a translation[3].

"I regretted," said Aelfric, "that the English knew not nor had not
the evangelical doctrines among their writings, those men only excepted who knew Latin, and except for those books which king Alfred
wisely turned from Latin into English, which are to be had.... Not
only have we explained the treatise of the gospels in this matter, but
also the lives or passions of saints, for the use of the unlearned[4]."

[1] *Gesta Regum Anglorum*, II. 123.   [2] EB, III. 894.   [3] Cook, II. Ser. viii. 135.
[4] *Homilies of the Anglo-Saxon Church*, Thorpe, B., London, 1844, I. 1–3.
Aelfric exhorted Wulfsine, bishop of Sherborne, that ordinands must possess
the books needful for saying mass, and performing their pastoral duties:
"Before a priest can be ordained he must be armed with the sacred books,
namely a psalter, book of epistles, book of gospels, missal, book of hymns,
manual or Encheiridion, Gerim, passionale, penitentiale, lectionary. These
the diligent priest requires, and let him be careful that they are all accurately
written." *Bibliom*. 47. For opposition to translations, Cook, LXX.

The words shew that Aelfric was not aware of any translation of the gospels at the time, though the West Saxon gospels were already in existence.

Such Saxon gospels as have been preserved in manuscripts date from about 1050–1100, and the question arises as to their original use. References to Saxon gospels occur also in the catalogues of mediaeval libraries, or in lists of Saxon manuscripts written in later treatises: but they are rare. Waltham abbey had two richly bound Anglo-Saxon gospel books in its library at the Dissolution[1]; the Durham book, or the Lindisfarne gospels, another richly bound volume with relics in its cover, is mentioned in the Durham catalogues; and Burton abbey had a copy of the gospel book in Anglo-Saxon[2]. The cathedral priory of Christchurch, Canterbury, had between 1284 and 1331 no less than seventeen English books (out of a total of nearly two thousand)[3], and one of these seventeen was an English "textus" of the four gospels, a twelfth century manuscript we still possess. Three others were a paraphrase of Genesis, some English sermons, and an English Acts of the Apostles,—possibly also a paraphrase, since no manuscript of the Acts in Anglo-Saxon exists. Bath had also the four gospels in Anglo-Saxon about 1100[4], and two English psalters occur in a list of eleven Anglo-Saxon manuscripts which belonged in the twelfth century to either Worcester or Westminster[5]. Glastonbury in 1247 had two Anglo-Saxon books, which, from their position in the catalogue were probably paraphrases, or glossed biblical books[6].

[1] W. Winters, *Hist. notes on MSS. of Waltham Holy Cross*, RHT, VI. 265.

[2] CVD, p. xxxiv; Addit. 23944.

[3] *Canterbury*, xxv. 51. The 17 English MSS. form a separate section in this catalogue. The English textus is probably the eleventh century Royal I. A. 14.

[4] *Parker Coll.* no. CXL.

[5] See *C.C.C. Descrip. Cat.* II. 202, for MS. C.C.C. 367. The list of Saxon MSS. mentions a passionale, two *Dialogues*, a martirologe, two psalters, two *Pastorals*, S. Benedict's *Rule*, the *Vision of Barontus of Pisoia*, and another book.

[6] *Joh. Glaston. Chron.*, Hearne, T., Oxford, 1726, II. 424. The number of English MSS. as mentioned in these catalogues has been much over-estimated, apparently through the idea that the books described as "vetusti". were in English; cf. especially Miss Graham in RHT, VII. 37. All the books, however, were classified as *novus* or *vetustus*, *legibilis* or *illegibilis*: *vetustus* had no reference to language, and was clearly used of Latin books; e.g. II. 423, alia bibliotheca (biblia) integra vetusta sed legibilis; 424, cantica canticorum et

S. Paul's cathedral had in 1295 two Saxon manuscripts, one an Old Testament as far as Zechariah, the other, probably given by bishop Hugh de Orivalle c. 1075, as far as Job[1]. These seven cases are all the references to possible biblical translations to be found in printed monastic and other catalogues[2], save for one case of a "Christes book" in English, which was probably an English gospel; in 1073 Leofric, bishop of Exeter, gave to his monastery "one book of Christ in English[3]." The two tenth century "Christes books" at York, and the four "Christes books" which the abbey at Bury S. Edmunds possessed about 1050[4], were probably in Latin and not English, since they are mentioned in lists of liturgical books, and the language is not specified. Thus the monasteries of Waltham, Durham, Burton, Canterbury, Bath and Exeter are the only known possessors of Saxon gospel books about 1100 A.D.[5]

liber sapientiae, vetusta et sine glosa; quattuor evangelia vetusta et sine glosa, inutilis; 425, epistolae Pauli vetustae et glossatae, inutiles; 424, Iuvencus de evangeliis, vetustus et inutilis; 426, liber de quadriforio b. Augustini, vetustus sed legibilis; Augustinus *de perfectione hominis*, vetustus; Ieronymus, *de consonancia evangeliorum*, vetustissimus; 429, Beda *de arte metrica, de rhetorica, super Lucam*: omnes isti vetusti et quasi inutiles; 430, *Decreta* nova non tamen bona, etc. Thus *vetustus* clearly applies to condition, not language: 426, bonus sed aliquatenus vetus; 437, licet vetusti sint legi tamen possunt (of Latin MSS.). These instances are given because similar mistakes as to the meaning of *vetustus* in other catalogues have probably caused over-estimation of the number of A.S. MSS. Only 8 out of c. 605 codices in the Glaston. cat. of 1247 are mentioned as being in English. These were the two glossed books mentioned above, Orosius, two *Sermons*, a passionale, a medicinale, and another English book: pp. 424, 34, 6, 9, and as correctly quoted in *Somerset Med. Libraries*, Williams, T. W., *Som. Arch. Soc.* 1897, 69. See for king Ine's munificent adornment of the covers of a Latin gospel book at Glastonbury, *Som. Med. Lib.* 48.

[1] *Archaeol.* l. 451, 496. The second MS. had relics in its cover.
[2] Except for one or two sermons and loose paraphrases; Wells, Somerset, had Aelfric's sermons, *Som. Med. Lib.* 117, *Eng. Monast. Lib.*, J. Hunter, 27; for list of 8 A.S. books at Durham, see CVD, 5; 6 A.S. ones at Abbotsbury, *Eng. Mon. Lib.* 8; for an A.S. book, probably Bede's, at Rivaulx c. 1150, *Reliq. Antiq.* ii. 185; for 2 A.S. books at Bury, *Bury*, 23; 1 at S. Augustine's, Canterbury, *Canterbury*, LXXXIV.
[3] *Monast.* ii. 527; *Parker Coll.* 40, MS. cxc. For "Christes book" see *Lay Folks MB*, 155: probably the term was simply a variant for a "gospler" or gospel book, but it may have meant a "textus," or book of the four gospels.
[4] *Lay Folks MB*, 155; *Bury*, 6, in a list made between 1044 and 1065, distinguishing gospel and epistle books.
[5] For givers of Vulgates to monasteries between 661 and 1066, see *Monast.* ii. 13; *Bibliom.* 95, 99, 113, 115, 119, 122, 130, 131, 156; *Yorks. Archaeol. and Top. Jour.* ii. 371; *Som. Med. Lib.* 48, 49, 89; Royal MSS. i. D. iii., i. D. ix.; Titus D. 27.

The rarity of these Saxon gospel books, compared with the fact that not only the great monasteries, but every church and chapel had to be provided with a Latin gospel book[1], is very strong evidence against any general custom of reading the gospel in English after the Latin at mass. Permission to do sc in Slavonic was granted to Methodius, for political reasons: similar papal sanction would apparently have been needed also in England, but it was never given to an English prelate. Had such a custom existed, evidence for it would almost certainly have survived, as it has in the case of the vernacular bidding prayers, said before the sermon. The strongest evidence put forward for the custom has been, that surviving manuscripts of Saxon gospel books are divided by headings, which state that "this is the gospel for a certain Sunday, or week-day." The evidence of the rich bindings has also been called upon to shew that the manuscripts were liturgical books. In face of the other evidence, however, the headings can only have been made for the private study of the monks: had they been meant for liturgical use, the ends of the gospels would, it seems probable, have been inserted also, whereas actually the text sometimes continues uninterruptedly for a chapter or two, after some heading[2]. The translations would have been useful in the preparation of sermons, for the canons of Aelfric recommended the mass priest, on Sundays and mass days, to tell the people the sense of the gospel in English, and then to explain the creed and pater noster, as often as he could[3]. But the canons clearly refer only to translations in the course of the sermon, not to a recognised custom of reading the translated gospel as part of the mass[4].

Popular knowledge of the Bible in the Anglo-Saxon period was based, not on translations, but on sermons, and on the old popular paraphrases attributed to Caedmon,—a poet and

[1] See Aelfric's canons, in *Lay Folks MB*, 155, *id.* 211 for criticism of Lingard's opinion concerning the reading of Saxon gospel books in church, and *id.* XII. for bidding prayers.

[2] Cf. the arrangement in the Saxon gospel book printed by B. Thorpe, *Da Halgan Gospel*, 1842, pp. 73–9, 79–83, 94–6, 119–123, 125–9, where ferias in various weeks after Pentecost have "gospels" of nearly two chapters of S. Mark or S. Luke. Altar books would almost certainly have had the correct endings indicated.

[3] *Lay Folks MB*, 212.          [4] As in Armenia, in 879, see p. 23.

peasant, to whom the verse only, and not the translation of the biblical stories, was due. These poems were intended to be learnt by heart and sung by the people, for whom the memorisation of verse was much easier than prose. It is claimed that a written version of the songs of Caedmon exists in a manuscript, which contains the story of Genesis, Exodus and Daniel, and a poem on Adam and Eve and the fall of man. The earliest manuscript of these songs belongs to the ninth century: but others were copied as late as 1250. Though no doubt poets of much later date contributed to these songs, and the form in some of the manuscripts may be entirely due to them, yet it seems historical to class them as a cycle, which, like so many early group-poems, long existed unwritten before taking final shape. Up till and during the twelfth century, while English was still mainly the language of the serfs and villeins, some knowledge of these Old Testament epics may have been handed down by memory and influenced belief,—just as a poem written about 1400 describes a peasant's religious knowledge as received thus traditionally:

> In Lenten time the parson did him shrive:
> He said: "Sir, canst thou they believe?"
> The ploughman said unto the priest:
> "Sir, I believe in Jesu Christ,
> Which suffered death and harrowed hell,
> As I have heard mine olders tell[1]."

The *Harrowing of Hell* was the most general name of the different Anglo-Saxon and Middle-English verse translations of the apocryphal gospel of Nicodemus.

§ 3. It is noticeable that almost the only translations cited between 1066 and 1400 were those brought forward by Purvey the Lollard, and scholar. The two other Lollard treatises mentioned none, perhaps because their writers were unaware of any: and the friars who wrote the anti-vernacular treatises did not consider the precedents alleged sufficiently important to refute: particularly as the Lollards could not produce any translations except that of the psalter. Purvey, nevertheless, made a gallant effort to produce historical arguments from the

---

[1] *Reliq. Antiq.* I. 43.

period in question. He quoted the words of "the great subtle clerk Lincoln," or Grosseteste, on the duty of preaching[1]:

"If any priest say he cannot preach," he saith, "one remedy is, resign he up his benefice: another remedy is, if he will not thus, record he in the week the naked text of the Sunday's gospel, that he con the gross story, and tell it to his people; that is, if he understand Latin; and do he this every week of the year.... If forsooth he understood no Latin, go he to one of his neighbours that understandeth, which will charitably expound it to him, and thus edify he his flock, that is, his people. Thus saith Lincoln[2]: and on this argueth a clerk and saith: if it is lawful to preach the naked text to the people, it is also lawful to write it to them, and consequently, by process of time, so all the Bible. Also a noble holy man, Richard Hermit, drew on English the psalter, with a gloss of long process, and lessons of *Dirige*, and many other treatises, by which many Englishmen have been greatly edified.... Also sir William Thoresby[3], archbishop of York, did do draw a treatise in English by a worshipful clerk whose name was Gaytrik, in the which was contained the articles of the faith, seven deadly sins, the works of mercy, and the ten commandments, and sent them in small pagines to the common people, to learn this

---

[1] See p. 442.

[2] This sermon of Grosseteste's (referred to elsewhere as beginning: *Scriptum est de Levitis*, see p. 442) has not been printed. There is no reason to doubt its authenticity, however, for his ordination sermons, some of which are printed in the *Fasc. Rer. Exp.*, contain passages very similar in character; cf. *id.* II. 251, for the need of the preaching of the gospel of Christ being the chief cause of the evil condition of the Church; 256, "the work of the salvation of souls...consists of setting forth by word and deed the gospel of Christ, consisting both of the Old and New Testaments"; 260, 265, the first duty of a parish priest is the instruction of his flock; 340, for a letter ordering the archdeacon of Lincoln to assemble the rectors, vicars and parish priests in their deaneries, in order that the bishop, who cannot, as he is bound, preach the gospel of the word of God throughout so large a diocese, may preach to them how they shall teach the people committed to their charge. His visitation articles (see p. 195) enjoined on parish priests to teach the laity the essentials of the faith in English; and when they had said the divine office, to "apply themselves to prayer and the reading of holy scripture, so that by the understanding of scripture they may be ready, as pertains to their office, to give a reason to all who ask them concerning their hope and faith." For Grosseteste's own learning, and familiarity with the scriptures, see p. 182.

[3] Thoresby issued a Latin catechism based on Peckham's canons of 1281 (see p. 196) for his own province in 1357: and with it an expanded English version, made by John Gaytrik, a Benedictine of York, and known as the *Lay Folks Catechism* (EETS, OS, 26, 118). This tract was copied into the bishop's register, and shews that a mediaeval bishop could issue a vernacular tract, when he wished, as an official publication. Forty days' indulgence was granted to those who should learn the tract by heart. The original *Catechism* was expanded later, in one case at least by a Lollard writer, see Wells, 356.

and to know this, of which be yet many a company in England.... Also, Armachan in the book of questions saith that the sacrament may well be made in each common language[1], for so, he saith, did the apostles; but we contend not that, but pray antichrist that we might have our belief in English."

The only other precedent quoted is that of the French Apocalypse, mentioned by the "Lord," in the *Dialogue between a Lord and a Clerk*. "Thou wotest," he says, "where the Apocalypse is written in the walls and roofs of a chapel, both in Latin and French[2]," alluding to the chapel of Berkeley Castle. In the pre-Wycliffite period, such vernacular scriptures as existed were naturally in Anglo-Norman or Anglo-French, the language of the upper classes. A complete Anglo-Norman Bible existed in 1361[3], but must have been rare, for only three manuscripts remain to us. The oldest part of this Bible, apart from the psalter, was the Anglo-Norman Apocalypse, which was also the most popular; there are 84 existent manuscripts[4], including

---

[1] This same passage is alleged in a tract, probably also by Purvey the Lollard, see pp. 270-4. FitzRalph, archbishop of Armagh, was much quoted by Wycliffe and the Lollards, as being a vigorous opponent of the friars. His *De Quaestionibus Armenorum* deals with many matters besides those connected with the Greek schism: the ninth book discusses "that question raised by the Armenians according to holy scripture, whether, namely, any definite form of words is necessary for the consecration of the body and blood of Christ, and what that form is.... No Christian doubts that the sacrament may be made as well in one tongue as in another, since the apostles did this, and since they handed on the tradition of doing this. For Matthew wrote the gospel in Hebrew, John in Greek, Mark in Italian, as did Paul the epistle to the Romans... each without doubt taught that the consecration should be made in those tongues in which they wrote: wherefore it is clear, that consecration can take place in each language,—nay more, for it appears that the gift of all tongues was for this reason conferred on the apostles, in order that they should believe that the form of consecration in this sacrament, as with the other documents of salvation, should be exercised to each nation in its own tongue." Since, FitzRalph continues, the synoptists related different forms of the words of consecration, it is clear that no set form of words is needed, but a certain intention, "thus the sacraments may as well be consecrated in one tongue as in another." (*Summa Domini Armacani in Quaestionibus Armenorum*, Sudoris, J., Paris, 1511, f. 66.)

[2] Pollard, 206.

[3] See p. 221, and Paues, 1902, xix. Jean de Sy's continental version of the Bible, executed in 1355 by order of king John of France, was merely a revision of the old Anglo-Norman Bible, for which see also Berger. For a MS. of Proverbs and Canticles, written by a clerk "in prison" in 1312, see Casley's *Catalogue*, 1734, I. A. xx.

[4] Paues, 1902, xxi; *L'Apocalypse en français*, Delisle, L., and Meyer, P.;

those written both in France and England. Many of them are incorporated with the *Bible Historiale*[1], which largely accounts for the diffusion of the work. This Anglo-Norman Apocalypse was a translation of Gilbert de la Porrée's Latin comment on the Apocalypse, which was arranged in groups of three to five verses, with the gloss following each group; the Anglo-Norman form was itself turned into Middle-English between 1340 and 1370[2]. The "Lord" in the dialogue may have referred to this Anglo-Norman prose Apocalypse, but he is more likely to have been thinking of an Anglo-French metrical version, written in short rhyming verses, which was also popular, and began:

> La vision ke Jhesu Crist
> A son serf monstrer fist, etc.[3]

Mural inscriptions were more frequent in rhyme than in prose, as in the case of the Dance of Death at Bâle, and Holbein's Dance of Death.

It is natural the "Lord" should not have quoted the Anglo-Norman Bible as a precedent, since it was so rare that Trevisa had probably never seen one: but some reference to a French psalter might have been expected, unless he was consciously limiting himself to English, for they were somewhat commoner. Eadwine's *Psalterium triplex*, of about 1120, had an Anglo-Norman, as well as an Anglo-Saxon and Latin version: and the so-called Oxford psalter, of about the same date, became the basis of all subsequent Anglo-French versions[4]. The west midland psalter of about 1350 was translated from a French original, and in the pre-Wycliffite period the Anglo-French psalter was, with the Apocalypse, the best known biblical book in the vernacular.

---

Gilbert de la Porrée died in 1154, and the Anglo-Norman translation of his gloss on the Apoc., of which we have three versions, was made in the thirteenth century.

[1] In 47/70 fourteenth century MSS. (of England and France).

[2] See p. 302.

[3] Ed. by Meyer, P., in *Rom.* xxv. 174 f. C.C.C. Camb. 20 has this Apoc. combined with the Latin text; but some combination of the Latin text with the Anglo-Norman prose version and gloss probably occurs also in some MSS.

[4] Paues, 1902, xx. For possessors of French psalters, see pp. 186, 221. Laud. Misc. 91 is an early fourteenth century commentary on psalms lxviii. to c.; Merton 249 is a thirteenth century comment on certain psalms, the text in Latin, the exposition in French.

The only strict precedent quoted, for English biblical translations, was that of Richard the hermit's psalter, and this is strong evidence that about 1408 it was the only one generally known. It was certainly the earliest biblical book to be translated into English prose after the conquest. The upper classes were mainly French speaking till about 1350, and the south of England, as more in contact with Normandy, more completely so than the north. It was therefore natural that the first local renaissance of Middle-English literature should occur in the north rather than in the south, and this was connected with the lyrical, mystical and didactic works of Richard Rolle[1] of Hampole. Rolle's English psalter is in several ways characteristic of the attitude of mediaeval orthodox translators. The choice of the book was significant, and shews that the aim was increase of devotion in those who said the hours, or the divine office, and not the general instruction of the laity in the New Testament.

Great abundance of ghostly comfort and joy in God comes in the hearts of them that say or sing devoutly the psalms, in loving of Jesu Christ.... Soothly this shining book is a chosen song before God, as a lamp lightening our life, health of a sick heart, honey to a bitter soul.... In this work I seek no strange English, but lightest and commonest, and such that is most like the Latin, so that they that know not Latin, by the English may come to many Latin words. In the translation I follow the letter as mickle as I may; and, there I find no proper English, I follow the wit of the word. In expounding I follow holy doctors, for it may come in some envious man's hand, that knows not what he should say, that will say that I wist not what I said, and so do harm to him[2].

Rolle made the translation for the recluse, dame Margaret Kirkby; and the "holy doctors" which he followed were those of Peter Lombard's catena on the psalter. He did not translate these in their entirety, for the quotation of eight or nine doctors'

---

[1] See *Incendium*, 38, and Miss H. Allen's forthcoming catalogue of Rolle's works. Rolle's life as a wandering hermit approximated much more to that of a Flemish Beghard, than to that of a friar, or enclosed anchorite: and the same charge of vagrancy was objected against him. He was never a priest, though he had spent a year or two at Oxford.

[2] Bramley, *Psalter*, 5. For a later psalter in English verse, based on Rolle, see Carleton Brown, 26. For references to biblical translation occurring in the body of Rolle's gloss, see, for the need of the guidance of the Holy Ghost by translators, Bramley, 61; for a curious interpretation, "Thou shalt raise holy writ, that lay sleeping whilst men understood it nought," *id.* 509.

comments on every verse makes the original Latin very long: instead, he selected a few lines of comment for direct translation in expounding each verse, and gave the substance of the other glosses in his own words, and in much shorter form. The English gloss contains much of Rolle's characteristically exuberant devotion and fervour throughout: and, towards the end, the number of literal translations from Peter Lombard become very few. Rolle's influence was primarily greatest in the north of England, but his translation was copied throughout the fifteenth century by scribes of different dialects, and became the standard English version of the psalms. Trevisa's patron, lord Thomas of Berkley, was one of those to have the psalter copied, in 1415.

It is significant of the attitude of the fourteenth century to biblical translations, that Rolle selected the psalter for translation, that he meant it for use by a religious, and that he did not translate merely the "bare text," but added a long gloss. His choice of Lombard's gloss for translation was merely that of the standard commentary of the age, and as is the case with so much Middle-English literature, had been anticipated by Anglo-French translators. The earliest existent Anglo-French psalter dates from about 1200[1], is accompanied by the gloss of Peter Lombard, and has several variants: but, though Rolle may have seen such a psalter, there is no evidence at present that he made his translation from the French rather than the Latin. He wrote and read Latin very easily, and there are no Anglo-French constructions in his English.

The awkwardness and stiffness both of his translation of the text of the psalter, and of the first Wycliffite version of the Bible, were probably due to the intention of translating a gloss as well as a text. When the Latin gloss so often expounded each word separately, it was most necessary to give a translation as nearly word for word as possible, or confusion would have arisen in translating the gloss. Free translations, "following the wit of the word," were made at the time by preachers in their sermons, and Rolle could have made such a translation had he wished: but the translation of the gloss would have been more difficult,

---

[1] V, *Françaises* [*Versions*]. S. Berger states (p. 42) that the great majority of French biblical MSS. are glossed.

and such a gloss was considered much more advisable in the fourteenth century than the making of a "bare text[1]." It is finally significant that the propriety of Rolle's biblical translations was never questioned, whether in his life-time or later. Translations of the psalter were never considered as quite on a level with those of other parts of the Bible[2]: Rolle's was made with no propagandist aim: it was not meant primarily for lay-people, and it was not a translation of the bare text. The last reason probably explains why it obtained so much more popularity than a contemporary English translation of the psalms, made in the west midlands, of which only three manuscripts have survived to us, and which was never mentioned by contemporaries[3]. This translation was not made directly from the Latin, but from Anglo-French: possibly it was the version bequeathed by a London merchant in 1348, the year before Rolle's death. Another little-copied translation was that of Jerome's *Psalterium Abbreviatum*, which is found in only two manuscripts, and which is, roughly, contemporary with the Wycliffite translations.

It is noticeable that Purvey, in his search for historical precedents for translating the Bible, made no use of those of verse translations: this was no doubt partly because such translations were not widely known, but also probably because the precedent had not the same value. No verse translations, or Bible stories, or "moralisations," or homilies on the gospels, could be appealed to by teachers in support of their doctrine, as in the case of a prose translation: and therefore no verse translation was ever condemned as heretical. Precedents for the translation of the bare text were what Purvey sought, and he

---

[1] For the exemption of this psalter in 1408 see chapter XIII.; and for the Lollards' treatment of it, p. 304.    [2] Though see p. 71 for a prohibition.
[3] Ed. Bülbring, K. D., *Earliest English Prose Psalter*, EETS, OS, 97. The attribution to William of Shoreham has been already discredited, cf. Wells, 403: perhaps the possible early date of Shoreham's ordination strengthens this conclusion. A William de Shoreham was ordained acolyte by archbishop Peckham at Croydon in 1287: CYS, *Reg. Joh. Peckham*, 256. Merton, 249, ff. 117–142, a thirteenth century MS., has a French translation and comment on certain psalms, in which the first verse of the psalm is given in Latin, and an exposition follows in which every three or four Latin words are quoted, then paraphrased in O.F. There is no literal and connected O.F. version in this MS., though the translation could be extracted from the exposition.

included the reference to bishop Thoresby's little books of instruction because they contained translations of certain parts of the bare text of the Bible, namely, the ten commandments and the pater noster. Nevertheless, verse translations and loose renderings of parts of the Bible were made between 1066 and the days of Wycliffe, and had some influence on the laity.

The first verse translation of the psalter was made c. 1300–50 and, like Rolle's psalter, in the north of England. It is the only complete translation which has survived, but there are various contemporary translations, or paraphrases of single psalms[1], and especially the seven penitential psalms. A common version was an east midland paraphrase of the seven penitential psalms, possibly the work of Richard Maidstone, a Carmelite friar, and written about 1370; but, as this poem has an eight line verse to each verse of the psalms, it is a very long and very loose paraphrase of the original. These later verse psalms were not, like the northern verse gospels, close translations written in verse for the instruction of the "lewid," but rather religious *jeux d'esprit*, hardly intended as translations at all. Both during and after the Wycliffite controversy similar verse translations of the psalms were made: the prohibition of 1408 of the translation "alicuius textus Bibliae" seems never to have been interpreted as applying to verse translations of the psalms, and the renderings of Clement Maidstone, Lydgate and Brampton never aroused comment.

Many long poems and compilations included stories from the Bible, and were, in a sense, the successors of Caedmon's paraphrases. The *Cursor Mundi* was a long biblical poem, written about 1300, which included many stories from the Old Testament, though it had a connected plot apart from the biblical narrative. Poems founded on single Old Testament stories were composed between 1350 and 1400, and dealt with such subjects as Adam and Eve, Joseph, etc. The moral poems of *Purity* and *Patience* were mainly composed of Bible stories, and date from about 1370, while that on Susanna was written about 1370–80.

An interesting set of translations is that of the Middle-English verse plenaries, or renderings of the Sunday gospels, with homilies. These usually followed the order of the Church's year,

[1] See Wells, 402–5.

but there was a tendency to combine them so as to form consecutive lives of Christ, or gospel harmonies. The earliest of
these was such a gospel harmony, written about 1200 by the
Augustinian canon Orm, who called his work the *Ormulum*[1] in
reference to his own name. He dedicated it to his brother
Walther,—his brother after the flesh, by baptism, and in holy
religion, and stated in the dedication that he had collected into
his book nearly all the gospels, as they befel in the mass-book
throughout the year. Orm did not, however, translate the gospels in their liturgical order, though his poem was divided up
into portions of about the length of a liturgical gospel[2]. He composed his own gospel harmony, translating first a chapter of one
gospel and then a chapter of another: and to bring his harmony
into relation with the mass-book, he inserted a table of the
opening words of the liturgical gospels before the text. But,
though he wrote the poem to make the gospel known to the
English, there is no evidence that the single manuscript of his
poem was ever copied, or was known to his contemporaries.

The *Ormulum* stands by itself, and had no influence on later
verse renderings of the Sunday and Saint's Day gospels: but the
other verse renderings and homilies were all developments of
the same original cycle,—now generally known as the *Northern
Homily Collection*[3]. It is not impossible that they should have
been actually delivered as sermons in the pulpit on Sundays,
for we have references to the preaching of sermons in verse in
the fourteenth century, especially by the friars[4], and one manu-

---

[1] Ed. Holt, R., Oxford, 1878.

[2] *Id.* LXXXII.–LXXXVII. and table of Latin "texts" at end of dedication.

[3] See Gerould, G. H., *North English Homily Collection*, 1902; and in MLN,
22, 95; *Cat. of Rom.* III 320; Wells, 287–92, 805.

[4] Wycliffe frequently accused the friars of preaching from apocryphal poems
and verse gospels: and sometimes his language implies that they actually
recited them, for the sake of novelty, in the pulpit. The friars "some by
rhyming and others by preaching poems and fables adulterate in manifold
wise the word of God"; they seek new and attractive forms of preaching,
and while the poor priests preach plainly and simply, "the friars preach
feigned words and poems in rhyme" (*Op. Min.* 331). They "dwell upon
apocryphal poems" (*Polem. Works*, I. 41), and in preaching "make use of
rhymes...for they say that unless they add some novelties beyond the
accustomed manner of preaching, there will appear no difference between
subtle theologians...and little lettered country priests" (*Sermones*, I. xvii.;
IV. 266) The abbot of S. Albans in 1426 preached a Latin sermon to the
monastic vicars, the last half being in verse. (*Amundesham*, RS, 229–31.)

script of the gospel homilies, which inserts a Latin passage, has a note that this is to be omitted when the book is read to lay people. It is more likely however that these verse translations and homilies were meant for private study, or to afford material for Sunday sermons by the parish priest.

The earliest form of this set of verse gospels was made somewhere in the neighbourhood of Durham, early in the fourteenth century. It was made with the desire of instructing the "lewid" folk in the meaning of the gospels, just as the *Ormulum* had been. The compiler speaks of his aim in the prologue, without giving his own name; probably he was some Austin canon or parish priest, rather than a monk or friar: the tone of his prologue, with its interest in lay people, is very similar to those of his contemporaries, Maerlant and Jan de Weert in the Netherlands. Just as Robert of Bourne, a Gilbertine canon, translated the *Manuel des Péchiez* for lay people in 1303, so the author of the rhymed gospels took a French book for his model,—the rhymed French gospels of another north-countryman, Robert of Greatham. The latter had made them, between 1250 and 1300, for a certain noble lady, Aline or Eleanor[1], to whom he was chaplain: she was very fond, he said, of listening to *chansons de geste* and history, and as these were mostly untrue or only half true, he made for her a set of gospels, set forth most fairly in Romance, or French, and added a homily or exposition to each gospel. The translations are in jingling verse, easy to learn and remember: and as a *tour de force* for the first Sunday of the year, Robert gave all the lines of this gospel the same ending.

There are some interesting lines in Robert's prologue, which shew that he expected opposition to his work of translation from

[1] This is explained in a prologue, about 300 lines long, most of which is printed by P. Meyer in *Rom.* xv. 298–305. Robert calls his treatise the *Mirror*, says holy scripture is like an apple tree, whose apples only fail to the ground with shaking, and explains its literal and metaphorical senses. From the connexion of the manor of Greatham with the de Montforts till 1264, it is conjecturable that the Eleanor, to whom the gospels were dedicated, belonged to that family, which had more than one member of the name. The prologue, with its side references to frequent opportunities of hearing histories and romances sung by minstrels, suggests that she was a great lady. For a promised discussion of the authorship of the *Mirror*, see H. E. Allen in *Modern Philology*, xiii. April, 1916, 741 n.

certain quarters, just as Maerlant expected and received it for
"unbinding the Bible into Dutch[1]," in the same half-century.

"I will not tell my name as yet," he says, "for the envious to tell
abroad: and so that they may not take from us that good thing, of
which they themselves wish to hear nothing. For it is the custom
of the envious to be grudging, and to cause annoyance. They all
despise the works of others, and seek to prevent holy writings[2]."

"The good thing of which they themselves wish to hear
nothing" is the gospel and its exposition: Robert speaks in the
same prologue of those who hear or recite the gospel, without
understanding the meaning of the Latin[3]: and his words shew
that even in England between 1250 and 1300, while there were
as yet no Bible-reading heretics to cause special alarm, orthodox
feeling, or sections of it, regarded the uncovering of the biblical
text to lay people, even in verse, as probably harmful[4]. At the
end of his book of homilies, however, Robert disclosed his name,
to ask the prayers of his readers:

Here end the Sunday [gospels], shortly related and expounded.
Now let all those who hear and say them pray for Robert of Greatham,
that God may protect his life, and keep him in His watch and ward.

When the unknown north-countryman turned Robert's verse
gospels from French into English,—or composed English verses
largely founded upon them,—he did not translate Robert's prologue, but composed his own. He said nothing in it about
expecting any opposition, or concealing his name, though he
actually made no mention of it, and we are still ignorant of it.
He had in mind readers or hearers of a lower social class than
Robert of Greatham,—the unlettered who came to the parish
church on Sundays to say their prayers, and receive such instruction as they might[5]. For them, he says, he will "undo"
the gospels in English, for they have as great need to know what
the gospel at mass means as learned men, for both were bought
with Christ's blood. When he describes some incident in our
Lord's life, the translation, though in rhymed verse, is fairly

---

[1] See p. 73.
[2] *Rom.* XV. 300, ll. 129 f.; cf. for similar opposition to Aelfric, *supra*, p. 136.
[3] *Rom.* XV. 302, ll. 271–4.
[4] A later prose translator of Robert's prologue into English translated
the lines about the expected opposition, and emphasised them, see chap. XII.
[5] *Metrical Homilies*, Small, 4–5.

close; when the subject was difficult, like the first chapter of
S. John's gospel, the verse was expanded into a loose paraphrase.
The collection was much copied and enlarged during the
fourteenth century, but the tendency of the later manuscripts
was to omit the translations of the gospels themselves, and give
the homilies only, or to add to these lively "exempla" or moral
tales. At the same time when the northern verse gospels were
being composed, an Austin canon, Richard Cricklade, who died
in 1310, was engaged in writing homilies on the gospels in English
to the people[1]; and a fourteenth century manuscript exists
which has the texts of the Sunday gospels in French, and the
homilies upon them in English[2].

The later forms of the *Northern Homily Collection* added a
verse *Legendary*, or lives of the saints. In another verse collection, made in the south of England, the process was exactly
the reverse: the legends of the saints were the earliest material
reduced to rhyme, while homilies on the Sunday gospels were
added later. The earliest form of the collection was made,
probably by the monks of Gloucester, between 1275 and 1300,
though they perhaps used some still earlier English pieces in
making the collection[3]. Their chief Latin sources were the
legends of the saints: but they also used sources which dealt
with the lives of our·Lord and His Mother, and therefore covered
the same ground as many of the gospels for Sunday and the
festivals of Christ. For this reason, and not because the verse
founded on them corresponded to any liturgical Latin source,
they were loosely called a *temporale*[4]. Apocryphal sources as
well as biblical ones were used, particularly the different lives
of Mary, *Gospel of the Infancy* and the *Gospel of Nicodemus*. The
tendency was to form, not a complete set of the gospels for

[1] Stevens' *Monast.* II. 73.

[2] Harl. 6561. For a thirteenth century French verse commentary on the
Sunday gospels, see *Brit. Mus. Cat. Addit. MSS.*, MS. 26,773; for French
verse gospels, Dom. XI. 87.

[3] Though not the *Legenda Aurea*, which was being translated independently into English at this time; Wells, 292.

[4] The northern verse gospels for Sundays and festivals were more correctly
called a *temporale*, for they corresponded to the *proprium de tempore* or
*temporale* of the missal. The contemporary scribe who called this compilation a "temporale" was misleading: he seems to include under it anything
which was not the legend of a saint. For MSS. of the *Northern Hom. Coll.*
and the *Southern Legendary*, see Wells, and Carleton Brown.

Sundays and great festivals, but the complete story of the life
of our Lady and the life of Christ, told consecutively, in verse,
and the tendency of the final and complete form, found only in
a single manuscript, goes farther still. This has a complete Bible
history, in verse, covering the same ground, though more ex-
peditiously, as Peter Comestor had done earlier in Latin, and
the *Cursor Mundi* in much earlier English. It gives a summary
of Old Testament history from the Creation to Daniel: then the
life of our Lady, the life of Jesus, the Passion, the story of
Longinus, the harrowing of hell, and the destruction of Jerusalem. The translation in some places keeps fairly close to the
biblical text, sometimes gives the story in the poet's own words,
without borrowing from any other source, and sometimes inserts
apocryphal matter. The last form of the work was written
shortly before 1400, and illustrates the tendency of orthodox
writers of the period to try to instruct the ignorant in the gist
of the gospel narrative, without translating its letter,—a tendency which was of course strengthened by the edict of 1408.
The number of existent manuscripts shew that all over Europe
some form of gospel harmony, or life of Christ, was considered
the most suitable form for the study of the gospels by devout
lay people: sometimes the life was built up by a rearrangement
of the Sunday gospels, and sometimes the Latin Bible histories
or gospel harmonies were translated into prose or verse[1].

Probably the life of Christ which was most popular for translation throughout Europe was that which was, often, in the
middle ages, attributed to S. Bonaventura[2] (1221-74). It was
more popular, because originally written for the instruction of
a woman, and not, like Peter Comestor's *Historia Scholastica*, or
Clement of Llanthony's *Monotessaron*, for historical study by
clerks.

There is quite as much homily or meditation in this book as
actual narrative. No complete prose translation[3] of it was made

[1] For a verse translation of Comestor, in Anglo-French of c. 1300, see *La
Estorie del Evangelie*, Carleton Brown, 453.

[2] See *Sancti Bonaventurae Opera Omnia*, Quaracchi, 1882, I. xvi. no. 31:
*Meditationes Vitae Christi*, and x. 25, *id.* This spurious work is not printed
by the Quaracchi editors, but is found in the Vatican edition of 1609, Mainz,
VI. 534-401. Bonelli attributed it to the Franciscan, Johannes de Caulibus,
see *Opera*, x. 25, and *Brit. Mus. Cat. Addit. MSS.*, Addit. 36,983.

[3] Bodley, 789, has a prose translation of the Passion.

before the days of Wycliffe: but verse translations of the parts
of it dealing with the Passion were frequent. The commonest
was a very free east midland translation in couplets[1], which
related the story, from the last supper down to the resurrection
and harrowing of hell. This verse translation probably preceded,
and perhaps inspired, a prose translation of approximately the
same section of the *Meditationes*[2], which abridged Bonaventura's
work, and told the story less directly and vividly than the verse
translation. It was used however by Rolle, and quoted in his
*Meditation on the Passion of the Lord*, which is a more fervent
and glowing work, and, of course, much farther from the original.
A later but much closer translation[3] was made about 1400,
apparently in the south of England, beginning, like the early
verse translation, at the account of the last supper. These
partial translations shew the early popularity of this work, which
Nicholas Love translated later, and which was formally approved
by the archbishop for the reading of the devout. Another *Life
of Jesus* has survived in a single manuscript, and was probably
translated from the French about the time of Wycliffe's teaching,
or shortly before 1400[4].

Another life of Christ was occasionally read by the upper
classes in England in the fourteenth century: the original French
form of the beautiful Romantic poem of Guillaume de Deguilleville[5], the *Pèlerinage Jhesucrist*. This Cistercian monk of
Chaaliz[6], who died in 1360, wrote three poems, which in one
sense are the ecclesiastical counterpart of the *Romaunt of the
Rose*, and in another the predecessors of Bunyan's *Pilgrim's
Progress*. The *Pèlerinage de la Vie Humaine*, written in 1330–31,
told how the soul, assisted by the grace of God, is strengthened
by the sacraments, encounters the vices and virtues, and finally

---

[1] Ed. Cowper, J. M., EETS, OS, 60, 1875. The editor attributes it without
sufficient grounds to Robert of Bourne; see Wells, 358. The dialectal and
MS. evidence date it as about 1300–25.

[2] *Privity of the Passion*, Horstmann, I. 198; for Rolle's work, see Wells,
451.

[3] In Laud Misc. 23, ff. 76–102 *b* it is an exact translation of *Bonav.
Meditationes*, Rome, 1588, VI. 399, cap. lxxiv. It is found also in Caius, 669,
ff. 75–.

[4] See Wells, 405.

[5] Cf. Lounsbury, II. 208; *Cat. of Rom.* II. 558–67, for Addit. 22,937.

[6] Chaalis or Chailly in Valois, near Senlis.

the pilgrim passes to a Cistercian monastery. The second pilgrimage was that of the soul after it left the body, the *Pèlerinage de l'Ame*, the third the *Pèlerinage Jhesucrist*[1], written in 1358. These *Pèlerinages* were known to Chaucer, and turned into French prose by a chaplain who dedicated them to the duke of Bedford, regent of France; and the first was also turned into English verse by Lydgate. The English form of the *Pèlerinage de la Vie Humaine*, known as *The Pilgrim*[2], and that of the *Pèlerinage de l'Ame*, known as *Grâce Dieu*[3] were among the books most frequently possessed by the English laity in the fifteenth century. Lydgate did not translate the *Pèlerinage Jhesucrist*, perhaps because of the existent translation of the *Meditationes Jesu Christi*: and so far as is known, no such translation was made of it for English use. Thus this poem was known only to the French speaking upper classes before Wycliffe's day; but the same kind of treatment of the life of our Lord,—its interpretation in the language of fourteenth century chivalry,—prevailed in the miracle plays, which all classes crowded to see. It is therefore not without interest, as shewing a presentation of the gospel narrative widely influential on the fourteenth century laity.

The same instinct for romance made verse translations of the apocryphal gospels and biblical books popular among lay people. The *Gospel of Nicodemus*[4] had been translated into Anglo-Saxon verse by Aelfric, and was again turned into English verse about 1300–25[5]; it was translated into prose seven times,—once by John Trevisa. The *Gospel of the Infancy* gave rise to a poem called

---

[1] The three pilgrimages are edited Stürzinger, J. J., Roxburghe Club, 1897.

[2] *Pilgrimage of the Life of Man, Englished by John Lydgate*, 1426, Furnivall, F. J., Roxburghe Club, 1905. Furnivall states, lxv, that this *Pèlerinage* was independently translated into English prose by William Hendred, friar of Leominster, and thence by an anonymous writer into verse. It is entitled simply *The Pilgrim* in Ff. 5. 30: the title in the fifteenth century MS., Laud Misc. 740, connects it with the *Romaunt of the Rose*.

[3] Translated into English prose in 1413, by R. W., *Cat. of Rom.* II. 580. Verse translation, Caius, 124; part prose, part verse, Kk. I. 7, "liber qui nuncupatur Grace Dieu"; "translated out of French into English with some additions of the translator, 1400," Bernard, *Cat.* no. 2552.

[4] See p. 180 for the Latin form, and contents.

[5] Wells, 326; MLR, x. 222. For the use of apocryphal gospels see *Boekzaal*, 348–53.

the *Gesta Salvatoris*, or *Infantia Salvatoris*, between 1300 and 1350, and the verse life of the Blessed Virgin and our Saviour[1] is of about the same date. English miracle plays drew from these poems, especially the *Gospel of Nicodemus*, to which was due the popularity of "hell-mouth" as a stage accessory and in windows and frescoes.

[1] Ed. Vogtlin, A., Stuttgart, 1888.

# CHAPTER VI

## Pre-Wycliffite biblical study by clerks: (a) the higher clergy, friars, monks

§ 1. Some light is thrown on the origin of the Wycliffite Bible by the evidence of the attitude of earlier and contemporary Englishmen towards biblical study. Two separate questions are involved: whether the teaching of the Church emphasised the duty of priests and lay people to acquaint themselves with the text of the Bible: and whether they were sufficiently educated to do this, either through the Vulgate, vernacular translations, or some other means. How far, in short, were the Lollards justified in claiming that Bible reading was a novelty, both to priests and lay people? The whole point of their championship of English Bibles was to make the "meek and poor and charitable living of Christ" known to the multitude, and thus to provoke a return to the simplicity of life of the apostolic Church: what grounds had they then for asserting that this simplicity of life was generally unknown or unrecognised? The temporary success of their teaching says something for its novelty: the sect of Wycliffites, a contemporary said, "is held in such great honour in these days, and has so multiplied, that you can hardly see two men passing in the road, but one of them shall be a disciple of Wycliffe[1]." If the novelty attracted such attention, it affords some justification for the Lollards' claim that they made the scriptures accessible to those who before were ignorant of them: and raises the question of the place of the Bible in the lives of clerks and lay people before Wycliffe's day.

The Bible had always been the foundation of theological teaching, as much in mediaeval as patristic times. There was no change in the attitude towards it as to a final authority: the question is rather, whether familiarity with it played any necessary part in the lives of the body of the clergy, and of lay people. They were familiar with a theology founded upon it;

[1] Cf. *De Dominio Divino*, Poole, R. L., 1890, XI.

they were familiar with office books which embodied parts of it: but did they make use of the sacred text itself, in their education, or later?

The question of the extent to which biblical study was carried on in England by clerks alone[1] is itself a large one. Three centuries passed between the Norman Conquest and Wycliffe's days, and during them the training and education of the clergy made considerable progress: generalisations true of one century would not be true of another. But till the end of the period bishops had to struggle to get their parish priests well enough educated to be able to read freely the text of the Latin Vulgate: and to refuse ordination to those who could neither read nor write at all. The possibility of Bible reading by clerks was conditioned by education at a grammar or local theology school, and not, in the case of most parish priests, by a theological course at a university. There is much more evidence as to the educational level reached by parish priests in the later centuries than in the earlier: but it should not be assumed that because there are more complaints about the defective education of the clergy in these later centuries, it was therefore worse than in the earlier. The contrary is far more probable. The level of clerical education in Europe steadily improved between the eleventh century and the fourteenth, and it was due to the improved education of some priests that more complaints were made about the ignorance of the rest. It was due to earlier educational efforts that a higher standard was now felt to be possible: and it would be a mistake to suppose, for instance, that because archbishop Peckham complained of the ignorance of priests in his day, fewer priests could read Latin in 1300 than in 1100. On the contrary, fewer complaints were made about priestly illiteracy in 1100, because it was not then recognised as in any way possible that most parish priests should be able to read Latin easily. The efforts of the popes and local bishops to improve the education of ordinands were regular, if not very effective, throughout the two centuries; and the prevalence of complaints in the later ones was not a sign of decadence, but of a higher standard. Until the episcopal registers have

---

[1] It is not proposed to include secular clerks in minor orders in the investigations of these chapters, but only those clerks who were ordained to the priesthood, and monks and friars.

been systematically studied on the subject, no final statements can be made as to the education of English priests during the period, so that attempts at generalisation are difficult and misleading. But, nevertheless, there is already a good deal of evidence available as to the education of priests and their acquaintance with the Bible: evidence of their education at the universities, theological and grammar schools: of the examination of ordinands: the books at their disposal for biblical study: the sermons they gave: the manuals they used: and the books they normally owned. It is convenient to deal first with priests whose education had reached the graduate stage,—those who had sufficient fluency in Latin to use the books contained in the great libraries,—and in the next chapter with those who were not graduates, and were not fluent Latin scholars.

§ 2. The mediaeval parish priest was not normally the graduate of a university. This explains the astonishing difference of intellectual level between the books we know to have been common in libraries for biblical study, and the educational standard required for institution to a living: the gulf between the apparently conflicting statements, that the *Sentences* of Peter Lombard was the normal text-book of theology, and that the minimum knowledge of Latin required for institution to a benefice was: ability to say certain short formulae by heart, and to read the Latin services. The proportion of ordinands who were graduates can be roughly estimated from the bishops' registers already printed, and checked by the record of the number of B.A. degrees conferred by the universities. It is of importance in making even a rough guess at the number of clergy who could have read the Vulgate freely.

Were all the bishops' registers in existence, and were they printed, the total number of graduate ordinands to the priesthood could be told exactly, for the registers stated the candidates' academic standing carefully. But the registers themselves have gaps, are not yet completely printed, and have not as yet been methodically searched[1]: so that final statements as to the numbers of secular priests and their learning, at a given date, are not possible. This is particularly the case, because calcula-

---

[1] The present writer hopes to do this in a future study, for the purpose of giving the history of education in the middle ages a firmer statistical basis.

tion of the number of ordinands from registers already printed
shews that this number fluctuated greatly in different dioceses,
in the same diocese from year to year, and, to some extent, in
all the dioceses for different centuries[1]: so that accurate generalisations cannot be formed from the combination of the records
of a few years in different dioceses and different centuries. There
were twenty-one dioceses in England, and they differed greatly
in size: but, taking Exeter as one of average size, and bishop
Brantingham as ordaining apparently a medium number of
secular priests in a fairly central period of the middle ages,
1370–94, this would give the number of secular priests ordained
each year as 21 × 35, or 735. Again, about 1300, there were
in England 8542 parishes, churches or endowed chapels[2],
served by priests (either the holder of the benefice or his
vicar). If the average post-ordination life of a mediaeval
priest is taken as 25 years, this would give an average of
approximately 302 secular priests ordained per annum. The
number must actually have been larger, for there was in
England a fairly large, though unascertained, number of
priests, other than those who served the parish altars. This is
suggested even by an entry in archbishop Thoresby's register of
1361–2[3], a decade after the Black Death. 302 may thus fairly
be taken as an inferior limit, while the real number of annual
ordinations to the secular priesthood was probably between
that and 735[4]. This contrasts with the small number of B.A.
degrees granted by Oxford and Cambridge together in any year

[1] e.g. Giffard, Worcester (*Reg.* ed. Bund, W.) 1282–90, ordained on average
60 secular priests per annum.
   *Sede Vacante Reg.*, Worcs. (ed. Bund, W.) 1301–1434, averaged 40 s. ps.
in 1301.
   *Sede Vacante Reg.*, Worcs. (ed. Bund, W.) 1301–1434, averaged 20 s. ps.
in 1434.
   Brantingham, Exeter (*Reg.* ed. Hingeston-Randolph) 1370–94, averaged
35 s. ps. p.a.
[2] Cutts, 385.
[3] Cf. A. Hamilton Thompson in *Archaeol. Jour.* 2nd ser. xxi. No. 2, p. 115.
[4] More exact figures could be supplied by calculations from episcopal
registers: but unfortunately at no given date, (e.g. 1250, 1300, 1350 or
1400), is anything like half the area of England accounted for in published
registers. The poll-tax returns of 1377 do not distinguish between clerks
in priests' or minor orders; the returns of 1380–1 underestimated the population, as is shown in E. Powell's *Rising in East Anglia in 1381*, 1896,
pp. 7, 123.

before the Reformation: it is probably safe to say that between 1300–1400 the average did not exceed 100[1], and that it was lower earlier. Hence all the secular priests who were ordained were certainly not graduates of a university: and this is confirmed by the entries in the registers. Of the 812 secular priests ordained by or for the bishop of Exeter between 1370–94, nineteen were M.A.'s; bishop Trillek of Hereford ordained only four M.A.'s among 1741 priests[2]. Hugo de Welles, again, was bishop of Lincoln from 1209 to 1235, and his diocese included the university of Oxford; presentations to livings in the archdeaconry of Oxford might be expected to include a high average of graduates, but of the 156 presentations in sixteen years, only thirteen were made to graduates[3]. The register of Grosseteste[4], his successor, one of the greatest advocates of an educated parish clergy, gives only about the same proportion of graduates, as do other registers.

The normal parish priest was thus clearly not the graduate of a university. Although the large majority of graduates proceeded to the priesthood, only a small proportion of these settled down to pastoral work as their chief occupation. From the stream of graduates were recruited the university professors, the great canonists and civil lawyers, the doctors, and the large number of clerics who became what we should now call civil servants.

[1] The actual numbers of the different degrees granted have only been worked out in the *Fasti Oxonienses* (ed. Bliss, P., 1815), and the Cambridge *Catalogus...et numerus omnium Graduatorum* (1572), after 1500. In 1500, as earlier, the B.A. degree was still the necessary preliminary to all other degrees, except the doctorate of music, which was still in the fifteenth century ranked with the humbler mastership of grammar. Only the regulars received theological or legal degrees without taking the B.A. and M.A. (*Univs.* II. pt ii. 452), and these did not become parish priests: so that the number of B.A.'s granted indicates the largest possible number of graduate secular priests which could have existed. The *Fasti Oxon.* number of B.A. degrees granted gives an average of 43 p.a. between 1503–1526, varying between 20 in 1503 and 70 in 1522. The *Cat. Grad.* has an average of 35 B.A.'s p.a. between 1500 and 1526, varying between 7 in 1500 and 46 in 1524. *The Eve of the Reformation*, Gasquet, F. A., 1905, pp. 38–9, quotes numbers for "the average number of degrees taken by all students" for 1449–59, and 1506–35, which clash with those of the *Fasti Oxon.* and the *Cat. Grad.*; but some, if not all, of this difference would be due to counting the same student three or four times over in successive years, when he took his B.A., M.A., B.D., D.D., or passed from the arts course to civil or canon law, or medicine.     [2] Ed. Parry, J. Y., CYS

[3] *Rot. Hug. de Wellis*, Phillimore, W. P. W., CYS, p. xiii.

[4] Ed. Davis, F. N., CYS.

Some became the domestic chaplains of the greater nobles and bishops, and as members of their households transacted the greater part of the administrative business of the country, while a certain number of them had proceeded to their degrees from the friaries of Oxford and Cambridge, and a few became monks. Many of the graduates who retained fellowships or lectureships at the universities, or who formed part of the royal or some other great household, were assigned livings or cathedral prebends as part of their stipends: but they were not primarily parish priests, never resided continuously in their parishes, and usually put in a vicar to do the parochial work[1]. The resident parish priest had received his education,—if he were not merely an uneducated layman thrust into a living by some lay patron,—in some grammar school, cathedral grammar or theology school, or friary theology school[2]: or possibly he had resided at a university for a year or two without taking his degree[3]. The university graduate could read Latin easily: the examination in Latin at institution to a benefice required something very far short of this, and mediaeval bishops found a difficulty in securing that all parish priests should be able to recite certain Latin formulae by heart, and read and intone the Latin services. Difficulties about illiteracy are constantly found in the registers, and papal indults to ordain illiterate candidates were sometimes granted on a large scale[4]. It seems broadly true to say then, from the evidence of the registers and contemporary writers, that between the Conquest and Wycliffe's day the average parish priest was not a graduate, and probably could not read Latin freely; sometimes, even, he could not translate it at all. The gap between the scholarship of the graduate and non-graduate clergy was great, and it corresponded broadly to that between those who could read Latin freely and those who could not. The two classes in actual life included on the one hand the bishops, university and

---

[1] Episcopal registers give abundant evidence of this, and such a book as the *Testamenta Eboracensia* gives many details of bequests of vestments, altar plate, etc. by some member of the bishop's staff to the church of his prebend, and to the vicar he had appointed to reside there.

[2] See p. 189.

[3] The numbers resident at the universities compared with the degrees granted, shew that many must have stayed a year or two and gone down without taking a degree: the earliest part of the arts course was concerned with Latin, or grammar; see p. 162.　　[4] See CPP, I. 394.

cathedral clergy, friars, and some monks: and, on the other, the parish priests. The education of these two classes, and the extent to which they were familiar with the text of the Vulgate, or would have been benefited by translations of it, differed greatly, and will be considered separately.

§ 3. The education of graduates was not in itself connected with the study of divinity or the Bible; from the very beginning, the training given by Oxford and other universities to the majority of students consisted of the arts course, and had nothing whatever to do with the study of the Bible or theology. Students came up at varying ages, but normally between thirteen and sixteen[1], and the course for the first seven years was the same for all of them if they stayed so long: the lectures and exercises necessary for taking the bachelorship and mastership of arts. All the other courses, theology, medicine, civil and canon law, were post-graduate courses[2], taken by only a small proportion of students. Many left before taking their bachelor's degree, for which four or five years' study was needed, and the majority left on taking their mastership in arts, after another two years[3]. Only religious[4] were exempted from this first seven years' training in arts before other studies, and the course consisted of grammar (i.e. classics), logic, natural philosophy, and nothing else. These "artists," living in halls, colleges or hostels (as the hostels were organised at the end of the middle ages), certainly obtained some partial familiarity with the Bible from the religious exercises prescribed: but nothing from their university course as such. They attended mass each day, and, since they were fairly familiar with Latin, understood and were familiar with the epistles and gospels: there was possibly a certain amount of Bible reading at meals[5], and compulsory attendance at university sermons. But these exercises were on a plane with the hearing of grace before meals, and the singing of the Salve Regina together after the evening potation,—not necessarily performed with much attention. Thus the mediaeval graduate, if he went down after taking his B.A. or M.A., cer-

---

[1] *Univs.* II. 604.  
[2] *Id.* II. 452–8.  
[3] *Id.* II. 455–6.  
[4] *Id.* II. 452; Kellaw's *Reg.*, RS, iv, xc.  
[5] *Id.* II. 620, 625. For a Vulgate bought for reading in hall, see *C.C.C. Descrip. Cat.* XI.

tainly had the ability to read his Vulgate and books of commentaries upon it, but it is quite unlikely that he had ever done so. The wills of such students, and the inventories of their belongings taken by the college or university, afford no instance of a student possessing a Vulgate, or any biblical book[1].

In the early days at Oxford, while the influence of Grosseteste, Adam Marsh and the friars was strong, the friars gave all the lectures upon the Bible at the universities, as well as in their other houses. By Grosseteste's regulation the first morning lecture, or place of honour, was given to the lecturer on the Bible. Roger Bacon complained bitterly that things were worse in his day:

> Even more grievous is it that, in the study of theology itself, holy scripture is too much neglected, and that philosophical wranglings prevail. The expounding of holy scripture consists almost solely in making divisions, solving apparent contradictions, and drawing parallels.... The reading of holy scripture itself is of small account, compared to the study of Peter Lombard's *Sentences*. For he who is lecturing on the *Sentences* has the principal hour for lecturing, according to his will;...but he who is lecturing on the Bible has to beg for an hour for lecturing, according to what shall please the lecturer on the *Sentences*. Also, the lecturer on the *Sentences* can dispute, and is held as a master, but he who is lecturing on the sacred text cannot dispute[2].

Giraldus Cambrensis, Ralph of Beauvais and other scholars[3] also lamented that insufficient knowledge of Latin was often a cause why even the higher clergy were sometimes unable to understand the Bible and service books. Those graduates who had proceeded gradually and in due order through the arts course to other studies, could certainly read the Vulgate and biblical commentaries: but only those who proceeded to the theology degree ever actually studied them in their university course, or owned them as students: and, even in their case, mediaeval scholars complained that more attention was paid to the *Sentences* than to the biblical text itself.

---

[1] Cf. *Mun. Acad.*, Anstey, H., RS, 1868, 543, 557, 592.

[2] *Opus Minor*, Brewer, RS, 328. Cf. Witzel, 18, and the similar complaint of Stephen, bishop of Doornik, †1200: "The study of the sacred books has fallen into neglect among us in the confusion of offices; for scholars applaud only novelties and masters are assiduous for glory rather than doctrine, and they write new fresh little summaries and confirmatory commentaries about theology on all hands, and with them they soothe, retain and deceive their hearers." *Maerlants Werken*, te Winkel, 130.

[3] *Gemma Ecclesiastica*, cap. XXXVII.: "How ignorance of letters is due to the excessive study of secular law and of logic," *Gir. Cambren.* II. 348.

§ 4. The friars did much for the study of the Bible at the universities, and the training of parish priests in their local theology schools[1]: but there is no evidence that in England they made use of biblical translations in either work. From their work for ordinands, and for the laity, it would have been natural to find them the producers, users or supporters of such translations, but the evidence is all against this. They had excellent libraries, and some of the catalogues have survived[2]: but only in one case was an English Bible found among them,—in that of the Cambridge Dominicans at the Dissolution[3]. Each order of friars, moreover, kept records of the literary works of the members of its order, and the lists remain[4]: but there is no mention of any biblical translation among them. In the Wycliffite controversy itself, there is no lack of evidence to shew that they were the chief enemies of vernacular scriptures[5].

The Franciscans' attitude to biblical study was marked by two features, both largely due to the work of Grosseteste and Bacon: the encouragement of the study of the learned languages, as subsidiary to that of the text, and the championship of the literal interpretation, as against the three subsidiary ones. Bacon, who died in 1294, justified the pursuit of all knowledge for the sake of the light thus thrown on the sacred text:

"I wish," he says, "to shew...that there is one perfect wisdom, from whose roots all truth proceeds, and that this is contained in the sacred books; for I say that there is a science which is mistress of all others,...or rather, that there is one only perfect wisdom, which is wholly contained in the holy scripture, which canon law and philosophy ought to interpret[6].... For it must needs be that all knowledge, which is useful and necessary and worthy of the sons of God, should by the will of God be set forth in scripture: and there is gathered together in bud what is unfolded later in leaf, when it is expounded by the canon law and philosophy. Wherefore, all truth is there forced into one spring, which is borne by an abundance of streams into canon law and philo-

---

[1] See p. 192.

[2] *Bibliom.* 79, 80; AM, II. 760; *Henry IV*, III. 445; for the two Franciscan libraries at Oxford, *Bibliom.* 199, at London, 200; Dominicans at London, *id.* 201.

[3] See chapter XIII.

[4] See Dominican, Carmelite, Augustinian, etc. writers, in J. Stevens' two additional vols. to the *Monast.*, London, 1723, II. 197 ff., 165 ff., 218 ff. For friars' translations other than biblical, see W. Herbert's hymns, Carleton Brown, 485; *Rel. Antiq.* I. 86.

[5] See pp. 269, 289.  [6] Witzel, 15.

sophy: and there, in that root, is bound together whatever in canon law and philosophy is elegance of branch, splendour of leaf, beauty of flower, and abundance of fruit." "That alone in philosophy is useful and worthy, which sacred lore deigns to require, as from a handmaiden[1]."

The whole governance of the Church, he says, ought to be founded on the scriptures,—a sentiment in which he antedates the Franciscan, William of Ockham, and the Lollards[2]. The strife and contention in the world and Church nowadays arise because the jurists borrow and derive their decisions from the civil law, instead of from those holy scriptures, which were the true and sole foundation of the canon law.

So fundamental was Bacon's reverence for the Bible as final authority, that he planned the whole of his *Opus Maius* with reference to it. The first two parts dealt with the relation of theology to philosophy; the third, with languages and interpretation; the fourth, with the relation of mathematics, geography and astronomy to the scriptures; the three last with optics and the other experimental sciences. Since in holy scriptures there are things set down from the height of heaven to the very depth, a theologian should know all for the sake of understanding them[3]. He lamented especially the lack of a literal understanding of the text, due to lack of linguistic knowledge[4]:

Above all, the study of languages is neglected, with fatal consequences to theology, which is of necessity founded on writings in foreign languages. For they cannot understand the text, nor know the expositions of the outlines, since all are mingled together in Greek, Hebrew and Arabic.... for they accept an infinite number of errors and superfluities, and what is doubtful as certain, and dark, as self-evident,... and soil theology through faults which proceed from pure ignorance[5].... There are in the world as many correctors, or rather corrupters [of the Vulgate text] as there are readers, for each presumes to know that of which he is ignorant.... For if the letter is in most cases false, and in others doubtful, then it must needs be that the

---

[1] Witzel, 16, 17.
[2] His fellow-Franciscan, William of Ockham, struggled with the same question of authority in the Church, but did not follow Bacon closely enough to be a real link between him and Wycliffe: he was sure rather of the fallibility of the different possible repositories of authority, than convinced that a return to primitive Christianity was possible: see Lane Poole, *Hist. of Med. Thought,* 1884, 277–81.
[3] Witzel, 20.           [4] *Id.* 12, 186, 187.           [5] *Id.* 18, 19.

literal meaning accords with it, and consequently, the spiritual meaning....And one root of this matter is ignorance of the languages from which the text is translated, through which an almost infinite number of words are omitted in the text....For we theologians are ignorant of the alphabets of these tongues, wherefore it follows that we are ignorant of the sacred text[1].

Bacon was the first great mediaeval theologian to emphasise the value of the literal meaning of the sacred text, as against the allegorical, the tropological (historical), and anagogical (mystical). All mediaeval scholars implicitly accepted this fourfold interpretation of the Bible, and it was one of great importance later in the controversy over the lawfulness of translations. But the academic dispute over the relative value of the literal, as opposed to the three other interpretations, began much earlier than the translation controversy in England, was carried on among orthodox scholars concurrently with it, and survived it. The supreme value of the literal meaning, first asserted by Bacon, was again and more clearly asserted by a Norman Minorite, Nicholas de Lyra, who died in 1340. His postill, or commentary, on the Bible became the universal textbook for scholars in the fourteenth and fifteenth centuries, although, even within his own order, theologians hotly opposed his principles. His work is important as the chief link between Bacon's attitude to the Bible, and that of the Lollards,—or, at any rate, that of the first generation of scholarly Lollards. They appealed to Lyra freely to justify their disregard for the secondary interpretations of the text, and Purvey translated and incorporated large portions of Lyra's prologue into his own work.

Lyra explained in the first prologue to his commentary the fourfold interpretation of scripture[2]; and he devoted the second to emphasising the need of understanding the primary or literal one:

Further, it should be noticed that the literal sense, which is the foundation, seems in these modern times to be much obscured; partly through the fault of scribes, who through the similarity of

---

[1] Fr. Witzel considers that Bacon exaggerated the corruption of the text in mediaeval MSS.: but Denifle confirms it: see *Archiv,* IV. 263–311, *Die Handschriften der Bibel-Correctoren des* 13. *Jahrhunderts.* The variations in the text were a great difficulty to mediaeval translators: see an Italian one, p. 46, and Purvey's efforts to get the text of the Latin Bible "somedeal true," p. 258.

[2] Antwerp, 1634; not paginated.

letters have in many places written otherwise than the true text has it; partly through the influence of certain correctors, who have in many places inserted vowel points[1] where they should not be, and begun or ended verses where they ought not to begin or end; and through this the meaning is varied, as we shall make clear, God helping us, when we treat of these places. And partly also it is obscured through our manner of translation, which differs also in many places from the Hebrew books: even as Jerome notices in his treatise on Hebrew problems....Moreover, it should be noticed that the literal sense is much obscured through the manner of exposition traditionally handed down from others: for, though these men said many good things, nevertheless they have touched little on the literal sense, and have multiplied the mystical senses to such a degree, that the literal sense has been entangled among so many expositions, and partly suffocated. Thus they have so much subdivided the text, and read into it so many meanings[1], that they almost bewilder the understanding and memory, and distract the mind from understanding the literal sense. I propose therefore to avoid these and like errors, and with God's help to insist upon the literal meaning, and only occasionally to insert few and short mystical expositions, and that rarely. Also I intend to adduce the declarations as to the literal sense, not only of catholic doctors, but also of Jewish ones, especially of the Rabbi Solomon, who has spoken most reasonably of all the Hebrew doctors.

He then quotes the seven rules for the exposition of holy scripture from Isidore of Seville's *De Summo Bono*. Lyra's postill was almost universally used for the light it threw upon the Hebrew text: but some, even of those who used it, thought it necessary to record their divergence from his views as to the literal interpretation of scripture[2]. The Minorites at Oxford

---

[1] Lyra was predominantly a Hebraist, and was referring to the great changes in meaning made by such a procedure with a Hebrew text. His treatment of Hebrew present and future is interesting: mediaeval scholars apparently understood only imperfectly that Hebrew has only one form for the two tenses. Where the Vulgate, Ex. iii. 14, read *Ego sum qui sum*, Lyra noted that the tense should be future, *Ego ero qui ero*; cf. Lyra, i. 511. See pp. 175–6.

[2] The 1634 edition prints, after the *Postilla*, the *Additions* to it of Paul de Sancta Maria, master in theology. The *Additions*, which were addressed to the chancellor of king John of Castile, were finished by 1429, and stated that "Since the intention of the postillator turned chiefly upon the literal sense: therefore it seemed above all things needful to inquire whether the literal sense is worthier than the other senses of holy scripture: and it appears that it is not worthier." The *Additions* are thus a tract twice as long as Lyra's two prologues, which they traverse, though arguments on both sides are given. To prove that the literal sense is not worthier, Paul claims that: (1) "The letter killeth but the spirit giveth life." (2) The three spiritua

continued to buy many Jewish manuscripts for their libraries and elsewhere[1], owing to the impetus given by Lyra's work to the study of Hebrew, and the wills of mediaeval scholars often record possession of the postill[2].

§ 5. There is no evidence again that monasteries made much use of biblical translations for the training of novices, or the use of the more ignorant among the brethren; and this although there is plenty of evidence that many monks were not well enough educated to read the Vulgate easily. Theoretically, the monks were all a Latin reading class, and had access to libraries of the same type as the colleges and the friaries, or even to more extensive ones. Their primary duty was the recitation of the divine office, and piety required that they should meditate upon the sacred scriptures; moreover, the tradition of learning, and the great libraries, remained to the larger monastic houses after the universities had withdrawn from them the prerogative of scholarship. But monastic records shew that the education of the majority of the monks cannot be measured by that of the few scholars the monasteries continued to produce[3].

The Vulgate was certainly the foundation of every monastic library. The length of the book is much more apparent in manuscript than printed, and it consisted generally of three or four volumes, or sometimes of a set of separate biblical books. It was always placed first in the monastic catalogue, and followed by separate biblical books, the glosses upon them, the longer comments or postills upon them, and then the patristic works more or less closely connected with them. Besides the library

senses are nobler because the other is merely historical. (3) Aristotle says, that if one thing exists for the sake of the other, that other is the greater. (4) Many things in holy scripture are false, if taken literally. (5) Interior things are nobler than exterior: as the interior grace in the sacraments is nobler than the exterior sign. (6) Human and divine knowledge proceed from the less perfect to the more perfect: thus the literal sense, the beginning, is the less perfect. (7) The worthier sense is that which supplies the defects of the other: thus the mystical sense steps in where human understanding fails. These arguments are quoted because they are so similar to those given by opponents of biblical translations. After these *Additions* is printed the reply of an anonymous Minorite, defending Lyra; then Paul de Sancta Maria's reply to him; and then a final defence by Matthew Thoring, minister of the Minorite province of Saxony.

[1] Steven's *Monast.* I. 133.
[2] *Comment. de script. Brit.*, Leland, J., 1709, 322; *Bibliom.* 182.
[3] Cf. PL, 186, c. 1441; 166, cc. 1377–1446.

books, the monastery possessed gospel and epistle books, which were kept separately with the altar furniture, and not always mentioned in the library catalogue[1]. The *textus*, or gospel book for the mass, was usually richly bound, sometimes in gold, like those left to the monks of Bath in 1122, and Peterborough in 1056[2]. Nigel, bishop of Ely, was robbed by the soldiers of Stephen of his precious gospel book[3]; Henry II, when he wished to make a valuable present to the Carthusians of Witham, forced the monks of Winchester to part with a Vulgate which they had just written out with especial care, and which the Carthusians, ignorant of its origin, received with the greatest joy[4]. William Longchamps sold thirteen richly illuminated copies of the gospels for king Richard's ransom in 1199: including one which had belonged to king Edgar. William, the abbot of Malmesbury and historian, stripped twelve gospel books of their rich bindings for the same purpose[5].

The great abbeys all recorded the gifts of their benefactors, and Vulgates and gospel books were given by a succession of such men, ranging from king, abbot, prior or bishop in the early centuries, to the exceptional monk who possessed one or two books before he came, or acquired one after, in the fourteenth and fifteenth centuries. At S. Albans, abbot Paul, who died in 1089, caused to be written for his abbey eight psalters, an epistle book, and three illuminated *textus*[6]; Geoffrey of Gorham, who wrote the earliest miracle play of S. Katherine, copied a psalter for the abbey; abbot Simon gave a Vulgate, c. 1167; abbot John a gospel book and the *Historia Scholastica* of Peter Comestor; abbot Wallingford, two Vulgates[7]. The gifts to the monks of S. Swithun, Winchester, were very similar[8]. In 1283

---

[1] Cf. *Gir. Cambren.* VII. 167; *Rites of Durham*, SS, 8; *Account Rolls of Durham*, SS, II. 426; and cf. the different catalogues of books kept contemporaneously at Durham in CVD.

[2] *Som. Med. Lib.* 39; *Bibliom.* 95; cf. *id.* 61, 62; CVD, 196; *Trans. Bibliog. Soc.* VII. 104.

[3] c. 1133. *Bibliom.* 167.

[4] *Somerset Carthusians*, Thompson, E. M., 59. The Carthusians subsequently returned it, when they learned the heart-burning the incident had caused at Winchester.

[5] *Anglia Sacra*, I. 633; *Bibliom.* 24.

[6] *Lincoln Cath. Stats.* II. 829.

[7] *Bibliom.* 173-82.

[8] *Id.* 156; CVD, 127; *Camb. Univ. Lib. MSS. Cat.* II. 10.

Nicholas Thorn gave to the monks of S. Augustine at Canterbury a "Bible corrected at Paris[1]," and about 1331 G. de Romenal, a monk, gave that house a Vulgate and a *Historia Scholastica*[2]; about the same time John Bocton, a monk of the other Canterbury monastery of Christchurch, gave to his house a Vulgate, a Bible in Latin verse, and a *Historia Scholastica*[3]. The verse Bible may have been the poem *Aurora*, or it may have been that verse history of the Old Testament composed in hexameters by a monk of Canterbury, a manuscript of which we still possess[4]. Abbot Faritius gave Abingdon a textus in 1135[5]; the prior of Rochester gave a psalter written by himself in 1189[6]; Evesham received various Vulgates, textus and psalters in the twelfth century[7]; Bury[8], Durham[9] and Glastonbury[10] all had similar benefactors. The first abbot of Croxton himself copied the greater part of the Bible, and abbot John Howton gave a Bible in nine volumes to its library[11]. The abbey of S. Peter at Gloucester had a benefaction of thirty-five books from Robert Aldsworth of which a list was made between 1263 and 1284; it included five Vulgates, two glossed psalters and one unglossed, a *Historia Scholastica*, and some expositions of the Sunday gospels,—a remarkable list to have belonged at that date even to one of the higher clergy[12]. Rochester was given several Vulgates, from 1108 onwards[13]. Peterborough had a fine library[14]: about 1177 abbot Benedict had a Vulgate in twenty-one volumes, partly glossed, written for the abbey, and in 1272 William Paris the prior had the gospels laid beneath the foundation stone of a new chapel there, as a symbolic act[15]. We possess, besides the catalogue of

---

[1] *Canterbury*, LXXI.
[2] *Id.* 79.
[3] *Id.* 72.
[4] See Bernard, *Cat.* no. 2578.
[5] *Abingdon*, RS, II. 45.
[6] *Bibliom.* 61, 62: and for several other givers of biblical books to the priory.
[7] *Id.* 133–8.  [8] *Bury*, 7, 89.
[9] *Rites of Durham*, SS, 107, p. 8; *Account Rolls*, SS, II. 432; CVD, 117.
[10] Cf. *Joh. Glaston.*, ed. Hearne, II. 443; *Bibliom.* 139, 142· *Som. Med. Lib.* 49.
[11] *Monasticism in Staffordshire*, Hibbert, F. A., 1909, 63.
[12] *C.C.C. Descrip. Cat.* 485.  [13] *Bibliom.* 61.
[14] *Hist. Anglic. Script. Varii*, Sparke, J., 1724, 149. *Trans. Bibliog. Soc.* IX. 23.
[15] *Bibliom.* 96, 98.

Peterborough, lists of the private books of various thirteenth century abbots: Robert of Lindsay, in 1214, had six books, including two psalters, a verse Bible, and Vincent of Beauvais' *Speculum Historiale*, but no Vulgate; abbot Holderness, twelve books, and no Vulgate; abbot Walter, c. 1233, eighteen books including a Vulgate; abbot Robert, eighteen, and no Vulgate; abbot Richard of London, ten, and no Vulgate; abbot Woodford, in 1295, twenty, and no Vulgate. The Templars in London had two Vulgates and an epistle book[1], in 1307. Thus, towards the middle of the fourteenth century, almost all the records of Vulgates which we possess are of those belonging to the monasteries: even abbots of bookish tastes would not necessarily possess one of their own, because the manuscript was too long and too valuable. The monks who did study it must have studied some gloss or commentary on a biblical book much more often than the text of the Vulgate itself, because even the great monastic libraries usually possessed only three or four complete copies each of the Vulgate before the days of Wycliffe. Compared with the total number of monks, this was a very small number, even if the Vulgate were divided into several volumes. It would be quite a mistake to think that each monk had even a copy of the gospels, much less a Vulgate, in constant use for private study[2]. Such familiarity with the gospels as they possessed was almost certainly derived much more from saying and assisting at mass, and hearing the liturgical gospels; while some familiarity with other parts of the Bible would be gained from the lessons at mattins[3].

Thus, though the Latin Bible was certainly studied, to some

---

[1] *Nor. and Norw. Archaeol. Soc.* v. 90.

[2] Cf. *Bibliom.* 26.

[3] The office for mattins consisted of one "nocturn" for a feria, and three for a Sunday or festival, each nocturn including a long passage from the psalms, and three "lessons," from the Bible or the Fathers. The lessons for the ferial office, of a single nocturn, were generally taken from some part of the Bible other than the gospels. When the office had three nocturns, the first three were biblical, but not from the gospels; the second group of three, patristic; and the third group consisted of a verse or two from the gospels, with a patristic homily of three lessons upon those verses. Thus only a verse or two of the gospels was ever read at mattins, though about fifteen or twenty verses of the prophets, epistles, Acts, Apocalypse, etc., were so read, in the biblical nocturn. The "lessons" at the other hours consisted only of a verse or two at each office.

extent, in the monasteries, it was not so studied by all the
monks. It might be said with tolerable certainty that there is
no period in the history of English monasticism, between the
Conquest and the Reformation, when the monks of even the
best managed monastery numbered none but those who could
read Latin freely and easily. The *Usus Ordinis Cisterciensis* made
allowance for illiterates in the twelfth century, and in England
after the Black Death many illiterate persons were received.
The maintenance of houses for monastic students at Oxford and
Cambridge by different orders, or groups of orders, probably did
most for maintaining the scholastic level in the monasteries: but
from the thirteenth century monastic writers sometimes pre-
scribed that disciplinary statutes should be expounded to the
monks *in vulgari*, which shews that they could not all be relied
on to understand even simple Latin[1]. Giraldus Cambrensis relates two stories of unlearned abbots of his own day,—about
1200. Robert of Malmesbury was reported to the pope for
illiteracy by his own monks, and when examined by the pope's
commissioners, and requested to translate a Latin passage into
French, rendered *repente*, "il se repentit." The other abbot was
asked to translate the sentence *Vere dignum et justum est,
aequum et salutare*, and translated *aequum* as "cheval" and
*salutare* as "saillavit"; some considered he ought to be deposed,
but the pope allowed him to remain abbot because he ruled his
house well and maintained good order[2]. The *Speculum Sancti
Edmundi*[3] of archbishop Edmund Rich, a manual of instruction
for "us folk of religion," has a passage where a monk who knows
no letters is told to attain to "contemplation of holy writ" by
listening to sermons: yet the context shews that not the Bible,
but some religious manual would be there expounded to him.

But, although there were always many monks who could not
read Latin freely, biblical translations were very infrequently
found in monasteries before the days of Wycliffe; and this

---

[1] Cf. *Mag. Vit. S. Hugonis*, RS, 37, p. 34.   [2] *Gir. Cambren.* II. 346.
[3] Wells, 346; Horstmann, I. 219, 23, 41. This is the earliest apparent
reference to the reading of vernacular books in refectory, of which I am
aware. But "collation" was primarily a reading, and not a meal. Love's
*Mirrour*, which belonged to the canons of Oseney c. 1450, is divided into
portions, but for meditation, not refectory reading, as is stated in EETS, OS,
133, 1913. pp. 1–4; see *supra*, pp. 152 and 174.

though it was common for a monastery to possess a copy of its rule and constitutions in the vernacular. Besides the evidence afforded by references to gifts of books in the monastic chronicles, where the name of the book and the giver are often carefully stated, there are at least twenty-five existent catalogues and books of monastic libraries for the period[1], which give clear evidence as to what books the monks possessed. Excluding Anglo-Saxon gospel books, a few of which were still preserved in the great abbeys[2], and to which sir Thomas More must have alluded in his words as to the possession of English Bibles, there is not a single reference to the possession of an English Bible, prose psalter[3], gospel book, or any other biblical book. What is true of the monastic libraries, is true also of the five known catalogues of college libraries, and inventories of individuals[4], before Wycliffe's day.

It would perhaps be more reasonable to expect to find French Bibles or psalters in monasteries in this period: but the number of these cases is very small. We know of a French Bible at Peterborough c. 1321, and part of one at Reading[5]; while Christchurch, Canterbury, had four Latin and French psalters, and one of the monks a Latin and French psalter of our Lady. Durham in 1391 had four French psalters, out of a total of twenty-six[6]. Glastonbury had a set of Sunday sermons in French, and the nuns of Barking, c. 1100, a French verse life of S. Catherine[7]. Existent manuscripts of *Bibles Historiales* are commoner than those of French biblical books proper: but the monasteries possessed in nearly every case a *Historia Scholastica* in Latin, and very rarely in French. The small number of these French biblical books would be realised by comparison, not merely with Latin Bibles, but with many of the works of S. Augustine or S. Jerome, which would occur in nearly every monastic catalogue.

---

[1] Dated between 1077 and 1389.
[2] See pp. 137–8.
[3] For a verse psalter at Norwich, see *C.C.C. Camb. Descrip. Cat.* MS. 278; Rolle's own MS. of the psalter was owned by the Hampole nuns.
[4] See p. 20, n. 1.
[5] *Hist. Ang. Script. Varii*, Sparke, J., 170; Royal MS. 1. c. 11.
[6] *Canterbury*, III, 122, 127–9; CVD, 10: for a French *Spec. S. Edmundi* 183; cf. Merton, 249.
[7] *Joh. Glaston.*, Hearne, 443; Ashburnham MS. 112.

Nor is there any evidence that the Bible was used for reading in the refectories of monasteries, or that the refectory reading, at the period, was in any language but Latin. A list of books for refectory reading at Durham about 1100–50 still survives, but the works are all patristic[1]. The *Speculum Sancti Edmundi* implies the reading of a vernacular manual,—or perhaps the exposition of a Latin one,—at collation[2]; the Carthusians of Hinton had in 1343 two books of Latin homilies for refectory reading[3]. The pseudo-Bonaventura's *Meditationes* were divided, not for refectory reading, but meditation, as the author stated[4].

§ 6. The university graduates, with many friars and monks, can thus be roughly classed together as men to whom biblical knowledge was accessible by means of the Vulgate, and Latin commentaries and homilies. In practice the graduates, unless they went on to the study of theology, did not concern themselves with the Bible at all: the biblical literature afforded by the great libraries was used only by those seculars who took a theological degree, by most friars, and by some monks. The biblical literature available for such students included glosses, commentaries, gospel harmonies, Bible histories and compendia of the contents of the Bible, and the apocryphal gospels; besides the large amount of patristic literature which dealt partly with theological problems, and partly with biblical exegesis.

A great step forward in the study of the Vulgate was taken when the Dominicans of Paris, under Hugh of St-Cher, or Hugo of Vienne, with the help of a committee of fifty, compiled the first concordance to it; a work which is the foundation of that in use to-day[5]. The commonest reference books on the Bible were the two glosses, the *Glosa Ordinaria* of Walafrid Strabo, of about 840, and the *Glosa Interlinearis* of Anselm of Laon, of about 1100[6]. The *Glosa Ordinaria* gave brief commentaries drawn from the Fathers upon each verse: it was probably the source of most of the patristic quotations in mediaeval sermons and homilies. A much more elaborate catena of patristic quotations was com-

---

[1] CVD, 9.  [2] See p. 172.  [3] *Som. Med. Lib.*, Hinton.
[4] *Bonav. Opera*, 1609, VI. 401.
[5] See *Concord. Hugonis Cardinalis*, Venice, 1768.
[6] See *Eng. Bible*, Hope Moulton, W., 27.

piled for the psalter by Peter Lombard, and a very much longer one on the four gospels by S. Thomas Aquinas, the so-called *Catena Aurea*[1].

Every library contained also a large number of commentaries on the different biblical books, ranging from those of the Fathers to those of mediaeval theologians themselves. The comments of Origen, S. John Chrysostom, S. Jerome, S. Augustine, the Venerable Bede, S. Anselm, Hugh of St-Cher, S. Bonaventura, and S. Thomas Aquinas were the most frequent, and occur in mediaeval catalogues with almost the regularity of the Vulgate itself: but the works of other mediaeval theologians were also popular. These were sometimes the substance of the lectures delivered at the universities on the biblical text, in the course of graduation in theology, and especially in the case of friars. Typical of such works were the comments of Nicholas Gorham, an Oxford Dominican who wrote postills on every book of the Bible, and Robert Holcote, a Cambridge Dominican who died in the Black Death[2]. But after 1340 the commentary most in demand by what we should now call "scientific scholars" was the above-mentioned work of Nicholas de Lyra, the Franciscan.

Study of the biblical text in the middle ages was based upon these and similar commentaries: but another very popular form of study was the making, reading, expanding, analysing and summarising of biblical harmonies[3]. Harmonies of the gospels were naturally the most widely studied, but compendia of the whole Bible, or harmonies of biblical and secular history, came in for much attention. The few widely known Latin harmonies were generally re-edited by later scholars with the object of

---

[1] See pp. 177, 271. A "libellus de sacris scripturis tractandis" in Bodl. 115 begins: "There are certain rules for the handling of the scriptures," but does not actually treat of mediaeval biblical study: it appears to be a chapter of some patristic work. Digby, 154, ff. 26–, has a Latin tract "On the nature and worthiness and interpretation of the scriptures," but throws no fresh light on methods of study. Nor does Queen's Coll. Oxf. 389, f. 2, which has a fragment "de modo legendi s. scripturas."

[2] See Mandonnet in V, II. 1466.

[3] *Concordancia bibliorum* or *evangelistarum*, generally means a gospel harmony, not a concordance in the modern sense. Cf. *Descrip. Cat. King's Coll.* 77, *Concordancia evangelistarum*, in a 1452 catalogue; and King's MS. 40, *Concordancia Bibliorum*. An *Exempla Bibliorum*, or *Liber de exemplis s. scripturae* means the work of the Dominican Nicholas de Hannapis, patriarch of Jerusalem 1288–91, cf. Addit. MS. 36,984.

making them more and more comprehensive and compendious, while at the same time they were summarised, analysed, and arranged in the form of alphabetical indexes by the diligent scholars of particular libraries[1]. The original forms were widely spread: the later expansions and contractions, though very numerous, nearly always exist as single manuscripts, and must have been the scholastic apparatus of particular students. Of the Latin gospel harmonies[2], the *Diatessaron* of Tatian was the earliest. S. Augustine's tract, *De consensu Evangeliorum*, was not precisely a harmony, but a discussion of the points of similarity and difference in the four gospels; it was very largely used. The first important mediaeval harmony was that of Victor of Capua, which used Tatian's work as a basis: but it was not common in English libraries. The two Latin harmonies most commonly found there were those of Zachary Chrysopolitanus, and Clement of Llanthony. Other gospel harmonies, which confined themselves much less strictly to the Bible narrative, were those attributed to S. Bonaventura, and Ludolphus of Saxony.

The harmony known as that of Zachary Chrysopolitanus was probably written by a "master of the schools" at the cathedral of Besançon in 1134[3]. The manuscripts of this and Clement of Llanthony's harmony generally contain a table for finding the liturgical epistles and gospels in the text, in all probability for private study and not for use at the altar[4]. This shews that the later tables of lessons in manuscripts of Wycliffite New Testaments were much more probably for private study, following this old precedent, than to enable the reader to follow the lessons actually at mass; and much less were they meant to be read aloud at mass after the Latin epistle and gospel.

[1] Cf. for expansion and summary of C. of Llanthony's *Unum ex Quattuor*, p. 177, n. 1; for the Minorite William Norton's alphabetical table of Lyra's glosses, Merton, 12, § 7, written in 1403; for a "compendium" of the *Historia Scholastica* made by the Carmelite Walter Hunt, Stevens' *Monast.* II. 174; for a Bible harmony by an unknown "Malham," also probably a summary of the *Hist. Schol.*, Harl. MS. 3858.

[2] See V, II. 2099. The *Diat.* was used in a Latin translation.

[3] PL, 186, where the harmony is printed; cf. Stowe MS. 8; *C.C.C. MSS.* 475, 27. For a table of lessons, Stowe, 8, f. 190.

[4] Epis. visitations shew that churches had to be provided with gospel and epistle books: gospel harmonies would not have been sufficient.

Clement of Llanthony's harmony was much more popular than any other Latin harmony in England: libraries of any considerable size contained it as a matter of course. The learned Franciscan, William of Nottingham, who died in 1291, prepared a new edition of it, and a certain chaplain of archbishop Arundel was moved to compile a summary and alphabetical table of its contents, which he dedicated to Arundel[1].

The *Meditationes Vitae Christi* of the pseudo-Bonaventura has been mentioned earlier. The *Magna Vita Jesu Christi* of Ludolphus of Saxony was written about 1330, by a friar who became a Carthusian of Strassburg. It had all the doctrinal implications in the life of Christ drawn out to great length: it is more intellectual than the *Meditationes*, and does not merely give patristic glosses verbatim, like the *Catena Aurea*. It was often translated into the vernacular, though not into English,— probably because the English form of the *Meditationes* was then so popular. Besides these well known gospel harmonies, others less well known were probably composed but not copied[2].

Combinations of biblical and sacred history were also popular, especially since universal history was drawn from so few sources besides the Bible. The *Historia Scholastica* of Peter Comestor[3] was so popular, that by 1480 the monks of Christchurch, Canterbury, had accumulated as many as twenty-one copies from different donors. The book had no doctrinal or mystical glosses, but was a summary, in the author's own words, of biblical history and additional information about such person-ages as Herod, Antipater, Archelaus, Augustus, etc. A good many mediaeval scholars occupied their time by making abbreviations of it, especially of the part dealing with the gospels; the tendency was to leave out the secular information, and abridge the events of our Lord's life between the baptism and Passion,—omitting, that is, most of the parables and miracles[4]. It was often translated into the vernacular, the most

---

[1] Laud Misc. 165, ff. 1–588. For Nottingham's harmony and its pro-logue, see Bernard, *Cat.* nos. 1562, 2067; Rawl. C. 572. Thomas Langley gave Nottingham's work to Durham, in 1437, CVD, 119; Christchurch, Canterbury, had two copies of this "gloss on the *Unum ex Quattuor*," *Canterbury*, 95, 105.

[2] Cf. that of brother Jordan, CVD, 182; and *Canterbury*, 159, 165.

[3] PL, 198, c. 1050; Lounsbury, II. 373.

[4] Cf. the summaries in Laud Lat. 109, Univ. 42, Magd. Oxf. 53.

famous case being the French translation by Guyart Desmoulins in 1271. This was later combined with French translations of the biblical books, and was much commoner than these books alone[1].

The *Speculum Historiale* of Vincent of Beauvais carried universal history down to a later date than the *Historia Scholastica*, going down to 1243.

The *Compendium Sensus Litteralis Totius Divinae Scripturae*[2] of Peter Aureoli is a good example of what advanced biblical study meant to theologians of the early fourteenth century. Peter Aureoli was born about 1280, graduated in theology at Paris about 1314, and then became lector in the Minorite convent of Toulouse. Just at the same time, in the Dominican friary, the famous inquisitor of Toulouse was trying to purge France of the Waldensians and the Fraticelli. Aureoli was appointed in 1316 to lecture on the *Sentences* at Paris, perhaps the most honoured theological professorship of the day: and he was made minister of the province of Aquitaine in 1319, and bishop of Aix in 1321, dying however the year after. His treatise divided the Bible into eight parts, and was marked by a strong tendency to rhythmic classification. The seven visions of the Apocalypse are shewn to have been fulfilled by the seven successive periods in the Church's history, from the time of the early persecutions under Julian the Apostate till the day of Judgment. Though the book probably owed its origin to Aureoli's desire that the clergy should be better acquainted with the Bible, that they might cope the better with the Waldensians, it ignored all the questions which the Waldensians raised.

Compendia of Bible history in Latin verse were also often

---

[1] Berger, I–IX.; cf. *supra*, p. 71.

[2] *Compendium...fr. Petro Aureoli Ord. Min.*, ed. fr. Philiberto Seeboeck, Ad Claras Aquas (Quaracchi), 1896, 4s. net. This is an excellent cheap edition of a book most useful to those who wish to reconstruct for themselves university lectures on the Bible at the date. The book was still used in the fifteenth century: cf. Merton MS. 12, which William Romsey, fellow of Merton in 1448, had written "at his own expense," presumably for the use of the college. Richard Barre, bishop of Ely, possessed a *Compendium*, Harl. 3255. The book was very often called a *Breviarium s. scripturae*, cf. Merton 12, f. 21; CVD, XXXIX. 146; Nicholls' *Leicester*, appendix I. 107; *Canterbury*, 168.

found in the libraries, especially a long poem called *Aurora*[1], or from its opening words, the *Quattuor est primus*. This was a paraphrase of the whole Bible in elegiac verse, except Canticles, Lamentations, Job and the Acts, which were in hexameters[2]. Petrus de Riga, its author, was a prior of S. Denis at Rheims, in the late twelfth century, and his poem was praised in fervid language by a canon of Autun, as "filling the heart with light, like the sun shining upon the world[3]." Enthusiasm soon compiled a summary of the poem, also in verse, and "versified Bibles[4]," referring to this summary or the *Aurora*, were frequent in mediaeval libraries. The surprising popularity of the *Aurora* may have been partly due to unfamiliarity with the Vulgate text, or to that craving for theological novelties which so many writers deplored, as tending to oust the study of the Bible itself.

Another less frequent verse harmony was that of the gospels, *Canones Evangelistarum*[5], which had a great effect on the development of miracle plays, and of sacred art in the later middle ages. Another verse harmony which became widely spread in vernacular translations was the thirteenth century *Speculum Humanae Salvationis*[6], which has much comparison of the gospel characters with Old Testament types.

The apocryphal gospels were never, of course, seriously studied for purposes of dogmatic theology: but information from them was incorporated into the *Historia Scholastica*, and especially

---

[1] Extracts are printed in *Polycarpi Leyseri Historia Poetarum et Poematum Medii Aevi*, Halle, 1721, pp. 692–, including principally the *Recapitulation*, sometimes attributed to P. de Riga himself.

[2] *Id.* 696.    [3] *Id.* 748.

[4] Laud Misc. 576; Ll. 5. 15; *C.C.C. Camb.* 107; Bernard, *Cat.* Durham, 541. Quoted as the *Aurora*, Canterbury, 165; five in the 1247 cat. at Glastonbury, *Joh. Glaston.*, Hearne, II. 423–44; *Eng. Mon. Lib.*, Hunter, 6, etc. For *Biblia versifice*, see Canterbury, 104, 109, 114; for *expositiones Bibliae versifice, id.* 129; for two *Biblia versificata, id.* 196–8; for *adaptacio veteris et novi testamenti versifice, id.* Christchurch, no. 246.

[5] Bernard, *Cat.* no. 1853; no. 1953, Canones seu harmonia quattuor Evangelistarum; Rawlinson, A. 384, § 2; cf. Rawl. C. 288, f. 14: Canones Evangeliorum: versus super contenta librorum. The *incipit* is, *Quattuor est primus*.

[6] Printed by Günther Zainer, Augsburg, c. 1470. The author, perhaps Johannes Andreas, in another poem (the *Epithalamium*, Digby, 65, ff. 79–102) refused to give his name. Andreas died in 1348, and was the author of the *Speculum Marie Virginis*, often found in connexion with the *Spec. Hum. Sal.* See Madan, *Sum. Cat.* IV. MSS. 21,778, 22,002. Cf. MSS. C.C.C. Oxford, 161; All Souls, 20; Douce, 204.

into the lives of our Lady which were so popular by themselves, and so frequent a preliminary to lives of Christ. The *Evangelium Nicodemi*, in its Latin form, was perhaps the best known: it is otherwise described as the *Gesta Salvatoris*, or *Acta Pilati de passione et resurrectione Jesu Christi*: sometimes it was described simply as the gospel "found in the praetorium of Pontius Pilate by Theodosius the Emperor[1]." This is a sort of gospel harmony of the Passion and Resurrection, containing little extra-biblical detail in dealing with the Passion, but much in dealing with the Resurrection. In the story of the Passion, the man born blind, Veronica, a woman present at the wedding at Cana, and different spectators of His miracles, plead for Christ at His trial, in a long passage inserted into the narrative at that point. It is from the description of the descent to Hades that the gospel was best known: the saints Carinus and Lenthius, walking in Jerusalem, describe to Nicodemus, Joseph and Gamaliel the descent to Hades, or "harrowing of hell" by Christ, and write it in books of parchment; they then go in procession to Paradise, and are met by Enoch and Elias. Clerks drew from this poem largely in arranging miracle plays, which had a great influence in forming the scriptural conceptions of the less educated classes.

This list of books,—the glosses, commentaries, Bible histories and compendia, practically exhausts the tale of books available for biblical study during the period. The most varied in number and character were the commentaries: the others were stock reference books, found in almost every large library. But though mediaeval scholars had this apparatus available, even the graduate clergy did not always avail themselves of it, or make themselves familiar with the biblical text, as is shewn sometimes by surprising misquotations. The mediaeval habit of quoting from memory may be responsible for some of these, but some are not merely verbal inaccuracies. The knight of La Tour Landry employed two priests and two clerks to help him in editing his collection of edifying tales; but the biblical ones are sometimes surprisingly inaccurate,—the story of Ruth has nothing in common with the biblical narrative except the names. A fourteenth century translator even of the liturgical gospels,

---

[1] *Codex Apoc.* I. 213 ff.

which should have been familiar, could speak of the raising of
Jairus's son, throughout. One chronicler, complaining of the
*Taxatio* of Nicholas IV, stated that " Joseph took all the land
of Egypt, except that of the priests[1]." In some Middle-English
verses for Palm Sunday, "bishop Caiaphas" is mentioned, and a
treatise on dreams refers to David and his "boke of swevenyng,"
or Book of Dreams[2]. Fitzherbert, in his *Book of Husbandry*[3]
quotes S. Paul as recommending economy, " Leste thou spende
in shorte space that thynge, that thou shouldest lyue by long."
The *Speculum Humanae Salvationis*, 1324, mentions Joseph's
sacrifice of his son, instead of Jephthah's sacrifice of his
daughter[4]. Lydgate the monk wrote somewhat later than this
period, and was particularly learned in the scriptures: but he
could represent the Egyptians as suffering from twelve plagues
instead of ten[5].

§ 7. The references of contemporaries to those whom they
considered great biblical students are interesting. S. Hugh of
Lincoln, who died about 1200, had lived with the Carthusians
before his appointment as bishop, and he preserved the same
saintliness of life afterwards. After the recitation of prime, he
had passages from the gospels read aloud in Latin, so that the
four gospels were gone through in the four seasons of the year,
while the other canonical scriptures were read through at night
office and at table[6]. Archbishop Lanfranc was greatly concerned
with the state of the Vulgate text, and ordered it to be carefully
corrected, as did another learned Norman bishop, Gundulph of
Rochester. The great humanist scholar, John of Salisbury, regarded the seven rules of Ticonius, as set forth in the *De Doctrina
Christiana*, as classical for biblical study[7], so did Lyra and
Purvey later. He emphasised the value of the subsidiary meanings of the text[8]; "for although the superficial meaning of the
letter be accommodated to a single sense, a multitude of mys-

---

[1] Capes, 27.

[2] *Rel. Antiq.* 261.

[3] Ed. Skeat, W. W., 1892, p. 99, on which occurs also a wrong attribution
to "Solomon."

[4] *Christian Iconography*, Didron, trans. Millington, 203.

[5] Lounsbury, II. 190.

[6] *Mag. Vita*, RS, 138, 341.

[7] *Policraticus*, ed. Webb, C. C. I., Oxford, 1909, II, 153.

[8] *Id.* 144.

teries lie hid within: and often allegory edifies faith, and history morals, and the mystical meaning leads heavenwards in many manners." Robert Grosseteste, bishop of Lincoln from 1235 to 1253, was a great student of the scriptures himself, as well as their exponent to others.

When king Henry asked him, as if in wonder, where he had learnt the nurture in which he instructed the sons of nobles and peers of the realm, whom he kept about him as pages (since he was not descended from noble lineage, but from humble parents), he is said to have answered fearlessly: "In the house and guest chambers of greater kings than the kings of England": because he had learnt, from understanding the scriptures, the manner of life of David, Solomon, and other kings[1].

Grosseteste's own familiarity with the scriptures is shewn again in his letters, which are full of biblical images, especially from the Old Testament[2]. His constant efforts to improve the learning of his parish priests, and their scriptural knowledge, will be mentioned later[3]: but his care for the instruction of all classes came out in other directions. He wrote to the regent masters of theology at Oxford, warning them to make the books of the Old and New Testaments the fundamentals of their study, "all your reading, especially at such a time, ought to be of the books of the Old and New Testaments[4]," and he spoke elsewhere of the "irrefragable authority of scripture[5]." He wrote to a canon of Lincoln, warning him not to neglect pastoral duties for more advanced theological lecturing:

It is much to be feared that by seeking to teach certain scholars in Paris the subtleties of wisdom, you will thereby refuse to teach Christ crucified to a great multitude of simple souls: for you will not minister to your cathedral scholars solid food [instruction on the *Sentences* and perhaps the text of the gospels and epistles], nor to the simple flock of Christ the milk of simple doctrine [instruction on the commandments, creeds, mortal sins, etc.][6].

Although Grosseteste was probably of all mediaeval bishops the most anxious to extend knowledge of the scriptures, he went no further than his contemporaries in the use of the vernacular for instruction. His circle was French-speaking; he himself

---

[1] EETS, OS, 32, VIII.
[2] *Epistolae*, RS, XLVII.
[3] See p. 195.
[4] *Fasc. Rer. Exp.* II. 393.
[5] *Epist.* 18.
[6] *Fasc. Rer. Exp.* II. 340.

possessed a copy of the *Manuel des Péchiez*[1], and he is said to have translated the pater noster and ave for lay use. He wrote the *Chasteau d'Amour*[2] in French for the instruction of a court lady, and wrote various letters of instruction to the different "Alienores" of the de Montfort family: but his name has never been mentioned in connexion with any French or English biblical translation.

Giraldus Cambrensis was another scholarly ecclesiastic whose views are of interest, because he often insisted on the insufficient knowledge of Latin, which made his contemporary clergy unable to expound the scriptures. His evidence applies to the period of the rise of Waldensianism, for he was born in 1147, and died in 1223. He was certainly vain, but there is no reason to disbelieve the various cases that he cited:

"For you will find," he says, "such defects of learning, not only in the lower priesthood, but even in the higher: in abbots, priors, the deans of great churches, and archbishops.... Also, there is the case of the archbishop who began his sermon thus: *Audite et intelligite, vos omnes qui estis in isto sacro synodo*, and when one of his clerks whispered *a, a*, he was not impatient of correction, but added, *in ista sacra synoda*, and when the clerk still whispered, *o et a*, he repeated for the third time, *in isto sacro synoda*[3]."

The same archbishop, he said, was once presiding over an ecclesiastical court at Oxford, in the presence of many learned scholars, and when the same titter arose over the archbishop's eccentricities in declensions, one of those sitting near rebuked them by saying, "What are you whispering among yourselves? that is the ancient grammatical form," at which they could not suppress the laughter with which they had at first struggled out of reverence to his person. And another time, when S. Thomas of Canterbury was in exile, those English bishops who were considered most eloquent and learned were sent to pope Alexander III, to support the king's case and weaken the archbishop's. And when they were presented, and were relating the arguments which they had planned and thought out, there was not one of them who did not commit a barbarism or solecism in such a

[1] Bernard, *Cat.* no. 2313.                    [2] Wells, 366.
[3] *Gir. Cambren.* II 345, cf. *Visitation of Sarum. S. Francis to Dante*, Coulton, G. G., 298, and Grosseteste's rejection of Passelewe as an unfit and unlearned candidate for the see of Chester, *Epistolae*, RS, lx.

presence: *Oportuit, oportebat, oportebatur, oportuerunt haec fieri,* said one who seemed more eloquent than the rest, but did not actually understand the use of an impersonal verb. *Peace, brother, peace,* said the pope, *for neither should such things have occurred, nor such words have been said.* These and other stories are supported by that decree of the fourth Lateran council, which remarked that ignorance in a bishop was scandalous, and not, for the future, to be tolerated.

Archbishop Peckham, himself a Franciscan and full of the traditions of his order, made great efforts also to improve clerical education, and the sermons of parish priests. In a letter to the bishop of Tusculum, dated 1284, he lamented over the frequent appointments of un-preaching bishops, as elsewhere over the ignorance of the clergy. He described in his letter the seven chief abuses of the Church of his day: the sixth is the "vilipensio Evangelicarum," or small esteem in which the contents of the gospels are held.

For according to the doctrine of saints, a bishop's office consists chiefly in the doctrine of the Word of God, whence the episcopal order is called by the holy Fathers, the "order of preachers": yet in celebrating elections or conferring dignities, no mention is made of the office of preaching; and since in this respect no question is asked as to what the gospels say, but as to what the common gloss clamoureth, the commandments of God are made of none effect for the traditions of men. Hence the study of wisdom is everywhere forsaken, and all men run after those branches of knowledge which bring worldly reward[1].

He himself nevertheless continued the study of the scriptures, and we have in 1283 a correspondence between him and the provincial of the friars preacher, who have, he declares, unjustly detained a Vulgate worth 113 marks (or over £1000 modern money), which he exhorts them to return[2].

Bishop Stapledon of Exeter, in spite of his preoccupation with the royal exchequer, found time to translate the pater noster, ave and creed into French, for lay use[3]; about the same time a "master Adam of Exeter" composed a French exposition

---

[1] *Reg. Johannis Peckham*, RS, 77, Martin, C. T., 1884, II. 696; see also p. 196, for his *Ignorantia Sacerdotum.*

[2] *Id.* II. 542.

[3] *Register*, Hingeston-Randolph, 565.

on the pater noster[1]. Stapledon had a considerable library, for he had two chests made to carry his books, and at his death bequeathed ninety-one volumes, three of which were Vulgates[2].

There is no record of any English ecclesiastic who owned an English or French Bible before the days of Wycliffe, apart from the abbot of Peterborough who gave his monastery a French Bible which had perhaps belonged to him privately. This contrasts with the number of known owners of Vulgates among bishops and the greater ecclesiastics during the same period; for, besides those monks or abbots who caused Vulgates to be written for their houses, there are more than twenty known owners of Vulgates between the Conquest and Wycliffe's day. The wills of lesser personages than great nobles and bishops are infrequent before 1300, so that it is not possible to say whether archdeacons and cathedral dignitaries commonly owned a Vulgate before that date. They would not necessarily own more than the different service books, though they would probably have access to a Vulgate in a library.

Twelve early donors of Vulgates or textus to monasteries were bishops: William de Carilef of Durham, 1095, Gundulph of Rochester, 1108, John of Bath, 1122, Nigel of Ely, about 1133, Hugh Pudsey of Durham, 1194, Longchamps of Ely, 1199, Richard Chandos of Chichester, 1253, archbishop Peckham, 1283, Nicholas of Winchester, 1299, Richard Gravesend of London, 1303, Stapledon of Exeter, 1326, Grandisson of Exeter, 1369[3]. Seven were either cathedral clergy, or connected with the universities. Nicholas, archdeacon of Bedford and canon of Lincoln, gave a large Vulgate to Lincoln minster about 1180; Roger of Ely, dean of York, gave several Vulgates to the university of Oxford in 1225; Thomas de la Wile "master of the schools at Sarum," or chancellor, owned a Vulgate in 1254;

---

[1] Pembroke, 112, f. 71.          [2] Register, 561.

[3] Bibliom. 68 and CVD, 117; Bibliom. 61; Som. Med. Lib. 39; Bibliom. 167 and Anglia Sacra, I. 622; AM, II. 859; Bibliom. 70 and CVD, 118; Anglia Sacra, I. 633; TV, 762; Register Peckham, RS, 77, II. 542; CVD, 127; Hale and Ellacombe in Camden Soc., New Series, x. 1874, 50; Register Stapledon, Hingeston-Randolph, 564; Trans. Bibliog. Soc. VII. 104. For later bishops, see Brantyngham, Register, in 1394; in 1403, Wykeham, TV, 768; 1404, Skyrlaw, CVD, 127; 1416, Mascall, Register, CYS, v.; 1423, Bowet, TE, III. 74, 76; 1435, FitzHugh, North Country Wills, 42; 1437, Langley, CVD, 120.

Henry Melsaneby had a textus about 1260; Michael Northburgh, archdeacon of Suffolk, bequeathed a small Vulgate in 1361; Henry Leicester, fellow of Corpus Christi College, Cambridge, bequeathed one in 1376, and Thomas Farnylawe, chancellor of York, two in 1378[1]. From this time onwards, the wills of canons and other higher ecclesiastics would usually include a Vulgate; and whereas in the earlier cases, all the Vulgates were left to corporations, or were, with one exception, entailed, Vulgates were now sometimes bequeathed to private individuals unconditionally[2].

No recorded will of a secular priest mentions any English or French psalters, or any English or French devotional book, before the days of Wycliffe, though in 1380 John Katerington, canon of S. Mary at Litchwick, gave an English *Legenda* to that church[3], and in 1385 Richard Ravenser, archdeacon of Lincoln, left to lady Isabella Fryskney "the book of Apocalypse which she has of mine[4]," which, from the context, was probably in Anglo-French.

Thus in answer to the question, to what extent the highest and best educated of the secular clergy, the friars and the monks, were familiar with the text of the Bible, it appears that those graduates who proceeded to the degree in theology were usually familiar with it, though an even greater emphasis was laid on their familiarity with the *Sentences*. The training of friars made them, as a class, more familiar with the Bible than any others: the acquaintance of monks with it differed from great knowledge to almost complete ignorance. The Vulgate was so valuable a book that few individuals except bishops possessed it before 1300; but it had become cheap enough for most cathedral clergy to possess one before 1400. There is no evidence in wills for the use of English scriptures before the days of Wycliffe, and there

---

[1] *Linc. Cath. Stats.* II. 787; CVD, XXXI.; *Hist. Antiq. Oxon.* II. 48 and *Bibliom.* 27; Casley's *Cat.* 4; CVD, 196; *London Wills*, II. 61; *C.C.C. Descrip. Cat.* XI.; TE, I. 102–3. For later Vulgate owners, see chapter XIII.

[2] Which shews the greater cheapness of the books in the later periods. Earlier testators sometimes bequeathed the Vulgate to an individual for life, specifying the monastery to which it should pass, or sometimes bequeathed it to an individual and his heirs. The monasteries, or cathedral chapters, were the recipients in most cases.

[3] *Parker Coll.* 34.

[4] *Early Linc. Wills*, 68.

is only a single case of the ownership of a French Bible by a
monastery, and none by a secular priest; the records of the use
even of French psalters are very scanty. There is nothing in the
history of translations in England to shew that they were ever
encouraged by any section of the orthodox: there is no movement, for instance, comparable to that of the Gottesfreunde in
Germany. In that country, a provincial constitution of the
Dominicans had bidden the brothers send their most learned
lecturers to preach in the sisters' chapels: and certain of the
laity were, in consequence, led on to practise lives of meditation
and prayer. In England, the Dominican brothers were not
bound by their constitutions[1] to direct the convents of Dominican nuns, and perhaps in consequence there was no similar
demand for English scriptures among the devout laity. Though
French translations sometimes existed in the libraries of the
greater nobles and ladies, there was no movement to encourage
their use by the priesthood: while, except in the case of the
psalter, no English translation existed.

[1] See *Archiv*, II. 644: Hermann of Minden compiled the Dominican constitutions in question only for his own province.

# CHAPTER VII

## Pre-Wycliffite biblical study by clerks :
## (b) parish priests

§ 1. If the typical parish priest between the eleventh and the fourteenth centuries were not the graduate of a university, where did he get his education, and in what did it consist? If he did not own a Vulgate after he settled down to work in his parish (as in most cases before 1370–80 we have every reason to believe he did *not*), what biblical or theological training did he get before ordination? The questions belong to a post-Tridentine age, which vaguely assumes that theological or biblical knowledge of some sort was always a necessary prelude to ordination, whether acquired in a diocesan seminary, or merely exhibited in an examination before ordination. Actually, the attainments of the mediaeval parish priest should be viewed rather as a link between those of the Anglo-Saxon and the post-Tridentine priest: for, though many mediaeval priests were no doubt better educated than the Anglo-Saxon ones, the minimum educational demands for institution to a benefice seem to have remained the same in both periods: ability to recite a few necessary formulae in Latin by heart, and to read and sing the Latin mass.

It is possible to say with some certainty to what extent a normal parish priest was acquainted with the biblical text before his ordination, because a certain amount of evidence has been already collected as to the educational course in the various schools he might have attended. Since lay patronage was so common, and the minimum standard of education for institution to a benefice so low, the candidate for institution might have attended only an elementary school, or he might have attended any of the various grades intermediate between that and the university. He might have attended the university itself for a year or two, but in that case his studies have been described in the previous chapter.

There is no evidence whatever that biblical translations were

used for instruction in any school of any kind before the days of
Wycliffe (or between his time and the Reformation). Scholars
learned to construe the Latin psalms, ave, or pater noster,
into French or English, but there is no reference to the use of
any biblical translation in school[1]. English ones were non-
existent, but French ones, or *Bibles Historiales*, though expensive
and rare, might conceivably have been used, had it been considered generally desirable that young grammar or theology
scholars should be acquainted with the sacred text: but there
is no evidence at all that French translations were actually
so used. Such acquaintance with the Bible as the mediaeval
parish priest possessed was gained from the Latin Bible, not
from translations.

A mediaeval candidate for ordination might have previously
attended a small parish elementary school, a grammar school, a
cathedral theology school, a friary theology school, or possibly
no school at all. The references in episcopal registers to "enormously illiterate" holders of benefices, or would-be holders,
perhaps refer to some younger sons, educated as lay persons and
not as clerks, and finally provided for by the gift of a living from
some relation or patron: such persons might never have attended
any school. But the majority of resident parish priests were probably the children, not of the nobility, but of small freeholders
or craftsmen, who had availed themselves of the educational
ladder offered by the different schools, and scholarships.

It is now generally recognised that the monasteries rarely had
schools for secular children after the eleventh century, but only
for the "oblates" who were destined to become monks, and who
in most cases never left the convent precincts until they took
the vows[2]. The larger houses had almonry and song-schools
where a small number of boys were maintained, chiefly to sing
treble in the feast-day services: and abbots occasionally received the children of noble parents to be trained in their houses
as pages, as any other great noble might do. But there were no

---

[1] There is no evidence that the north midland glosses were lectures
delivered in school, as Miss Powell suggests, see chapter XII. They were
moreover contemporary with Wycliffe, and probably produced under the
influence of the Wycliffite movement.

[2] Coulton, G. G., *Mediaeval Studies*, x.

schools for secular boys in the modern sense, either for day scholars or boarders.

In the lowest grade of school, the small parish or elementary school, the children indeed learned to read upon the psalter or primer[1], but there was of course no further question of the use of the biblical text. They were "ABC children[2]," as Grosseteste called them, and they were taught largely with a view to their being able to sing in church, like the little clergeon in the *Prioresse's Tale*[3].

At the grammar school again, the next grade, there is no evidence that children learned to translate the Latin Bible before the days of Wycliffe. They learned Latin, which was a step towards it, but the Vulgate was not among the books they used. As late as 1357 the bishop of Exeter reprehended all the archdeacons of his diocese, because clerks, or those who daily repeated mattins and the hours of the blessed Virgin, did not understand what they said. He complained that boys in school, after they had learned to read, or say, even very imperfectly, the pater noster, ave, creed, and the hours of the blessed Virgin, passed on at once to other school books: "And so it happens that when they are grown up they do not understand what they say or read every day." He then ordered, with what effect on the routine of the grammar school is not known, that

boys henceforth should leave other studies, and be made to construe and understand the pater noster, ave, creed, mattins, and the hours of the blessed Virgin, and decline the words there, and parse them, before they go on to other books[4].

Later on, in the middle of the Wycliffite controversy, one writer refers to a practice of translating the epistles and gospels in schools, as well as the psalms[5]: and in this case it is not very

---

[1] *Educ. Char.* 347; bibliog. in A. F. Leach's *Schools of Med. England*, 1915.

[2] And see p. 207. "Pueros abcdarios," *Fasc. Rer. Exp.* II. 402.

[3] ll. 46–9. The frequency, nature, and connexion with the grammar schools of these small schools has not yet been fully worked out. The parish priest, according to his will and ability, sometimes taught small children for nothing, or was sometimes paid to take private pupils.

[4] *Educ. Char.* 317.

[5] In Ii. 6. 26. In the fifteenth century chantry schools also did something for the training of secular ordinands: but though chantries were beginning to be founded before Wycliffe's day, there is no record of the founding of any

clear whether the writer is referring to some grammar, or cathedral theology school.

There were, however, in the thirteenth century, besides the grammar schools, a considerable number of cathedral and friary schools[1], where theology was taught, and it is from such schools that the bulk of the inferior secular clergy must have received their education. Before the rise of the universities, the cathedral schools had been more important than the monastic schools for the training afforded to seculars, but the universities drew from them, as from the monasteries, the best scholars and teachers of the thirteenth century. The papacy, however, saw in the cathedral schools the best means of training the secular clergy, and did what it could to encourage them: the provision of salaries for the grammar master and theology master was always the difficulty[2]. In early days the cathedral school taught both Latin, or grammar, and theology, but by about 1200 the grammar and theology schools had usually become separate. Lectures in the cathedral theology schools were apparently always given in Latin, and the subject, as at the universities, was the *Sentences* of Peter Lombard, and instruction on the elements of the faith. There is no evidence that before the days of Wycliffe the cathedral schools afforded lectures on the biblical text, such as formed a small part of the course for the doctorate of divinity in the universities; or that, as early as this, theology students were taught to translate the Sunday gospels and epistles and make sermons upon them. In Wycliffe's own day, however, such a practice seems to have begun, to judge by the evidence of one of his followers: but how widely it obtained, and whether it were the direct result of the Wycliffite movement, which influenced orthodox teachers as well as avowed heretics, is doubtful.

The Mendicant orders did much, not only for theological study at the universities, but also, apparently, for the training of the secular clergy in their local theology schools. It was the Dominican ideal to have no friary without a lecturer, or qualified

chantry school. Cf. CPP, I. 25, where in 1343 the living of Houghton was appropriated by the bishop of Durham for the maintenance of a parish vicar, resident rector and four chaplains, and four university scholarships.
[1] For the best modern study of these, see *Eng. Franc. Hist.* 158–76.
[2] *Crise Scol.* 42; Coulton, G. G., *Mediaeval Studies*, x, Simpkin, Marshall and Co., 1913.

teacher of theology, and the Franciscans followed in their foot-
steps. Franciscans could not take the degree of B.D. at Paris,
Oxford or Cambridge, unless they had previously lectured at
places reckoned as "studia generalia" in the order; or, in
England, in the friary schools at London, York, Norwich, New-
castle, Stamford, Coventry or Exeter[1]. The records of the
Mendicant orders render it clear that seculars were allowed to
attend these theology lectures[2], intended primarily for the
training of young friars: but Mr Little, in *Studies in English
Franciscan History*, notices the curious lack of evidence that
individual seculars in England had done so[3]. In face of this lack
of evidence, the relative extent to which the secular clergy were
educated in cathedral or friary schools can hardly yet be estimated: but there is no evidence that the training given was
essentially different. The friars too lectured and disputed in
Latin on the *Sentences* of Peter Lombard, with an eye to pastoral
theology: under Grosseteste they "became proficient in doubtful
points of scripture [quaestiones], and subtle moralisations suitable for sermons[4]": but, as at the universities, they taught their
scholars a theology founded on the Bible, and not the biblical
text itself. There is no direct evidence that the friars, for instance, lectured on the Sunday epistles and gospels before the
days of Wycliffe, with a view to their scholars translating and
expounding the text later in sermons. On the contrary, the
manuals of preaching, composed by the friars[5], which were very
popular, commended more novel methods of sermon-making,
likelier to catch the attention of the audience: which renders it
improbable that the friars laid very great stress on the
exposition of Sunday epistles and gospels in their local theology
lectures.

Thus there is on the whole very little indication that any
attention was given to the study of the biblical text by secular
ordinands. Boys learned their letters from the primer, and
possibly, in the days of Wycliffe himself, they construed epistles
and gospels in certain grammar schools: but there is no evidence
that they were otherwise concerned with the text of the Vulgate;
and for its study by means of translations,—such as that re-

---

[1] *Eng. Franc. Hist.* 167.       [2] *Id.* 168–73.
[3] *Id.* 170.       [4] *Id.* 165.       [5] See p. 148 n.

commended for young clerks in the Cologne Bible of 1480,—there is no evidence at all.

§ 2. But, though clerical education was supposed to afford sufficient training in Latin for parish priests to be able to construe the Latin Vulgate and service books for themselves, there are many indications that this standard was never universally reached, and that in many dioceses, at many periods, the gap between theory and practice was very great. There was no effectual examination in letters for the priesthood as such, but the bishop or his official examined candidates for institution o a benefice, and sometimes examined the holders of benefices on visitation. The record of these examinations, in the episcopal registers and elsewhere, shew that the minimum standard was low, and that it was frequently not reached. The examination was *viva voce*, and for a hitherto unbeneficed priest consisted of "reading, construing, singing and speaking Latin," about 1370; while the confirmation of beneficed priests as archdeacons, priors, precentors, etc., at the same date, was generally preceded only by the examination in Latin[1]. The passage selected for examination was generally some portion of the canon of the mass, which shews that the intention was that priests should understand what they read, in this most solemn part of their duties. The council of Oxford in 1222 ordered that priests should be able, at least, to understand the consecration formula in Latin; but at the Salisbury visitation of the same year, the incumbents of five out of the seventeen churches were found unable to do so[2]. Dispensations of non-residence were often given to holders of benefices in order that they might continue their studies, and in such cases the living was really used to provide a university scholarship[3]; but, besides such cases, others are mentioned where the vicar or rector, or candidate for a benefice, was found insufficient in the knowledge of grammar or singing, and was given leave of absence for a stated period in order that he might "learn to chant," "learn music," or "learn

---

[1] Cf. CPL, IV. 175, 194, 6, 9, 222, 363, 401, 2, 413, 4, 421–5, etc.

[2] Coulton, G. G., *Mediaeval Studies*, VII. For references to "enormous illiteracy" on the part of rectors, see *Eng. Franc. Hist.* 161, n. 1, and *Register of S. Osmund*, Jones, W. H. R., in RS, I. 304–6.

[3] Cf. introd. by Tout, T. F., to *Reg. of John de Halton*, CYS, XXXVII.; and CPL, IV. 394, 233, 165, 184, 185, 305, 527, 317, etc.

grammar": that is, pull himself up to examination level. One rector was thus examined three times during his four years' study, and finally rejected for his "ignorance of letters[1]." The "school" the candidate was to attend in such cases was not generally specified, but it was probably not the university; Northampton is mentioned in 1232, and the cathedral school at Lincoln three times[2]. Statistics for the relative frequency of the ability to read Latin on the part of mediaeval parish priests cannot be given here: but the evidence quoted is enough to shew that although the clergy were, in theory, expected to expound the scriptures to their parishioners, they must frequently have been unable to translate the Latin text themselves.

The *Gemma Ecclesiastica* of Giraldus Cambrensis describes in some detail the state of learning and morals among the clergy and laity known to its author: the descriptions would apply mainly to Welshmen, but not solely, since the learned archdeacon was so great a traveller. He represents the parish clergy of about 1180–1200[3] as being frequently illiterate:

We will shew by sundry examples the manner in which parish priests to-day explain to their parishioners the gospels and holy scripture. There is the case of the priest who was preaching to the people a sermon about S. Barnabas, and he said among other things: "He was a good man and a saint, but he used, however, to be a robber." For his authority was that verse of the gospel, namely, "Now Barabbas was a robber," and he did not distinguish properly between Barnabas and Barabbas. Then there is the case of the priest who was preaching about the Canaanite woman, and he said she was partly a woman and partly a dog, because he did not distinguish between *Canaanite* and *canine*. Then, that of the priest who was announcing the feast of SS. Simon and Jude, and said that: "The one was a good man and a saint, and the other the man who betrayed Christ, and we ought not to honour his day for his own sake, but for that of his companion," confusing S. Jude with Judas[4].

He goes on with a string of such stories: those of the priest who could not translate the word *broiled* in *broiled fish and honeycomb*, and rendered it "donkey fish"; and when he was asked

---

[1] *Rot. Hug. de Welles*, CYS, Phillimore, W. P. W., XII., XIII., XIV.; cf. CPL, v. 260.

[2] *Rot. Hug.* XVIII.

[3] He presented the *Gem. Ec.* to Innocent III in 1199.

[4] *Gir. Cambren.* II. 341.

what a donkey fish was, answered that, just as there was a fish
called a dog fish, so also there was a hare fish, and others like
all the other land beasts, and this particular fish was a donkey
fish, but it was not found in those parts. Then, there was the
priest who thought that *altera* was a fish, because they let down
the net on the right side of the ship and took it; and the priest
who gave the same translation for the numerals *five hundred* and
*fifty* in the parable of the two debtors, and on its being remarked
that the lord forgave them both the same amount, added: "but
in one case the coins were Angevin, and in the other, sterling."
There was too the priest who translated *sanctus Johannes ante
portam Latinam* as, *saint John who first brought the Latin language
to England*, and finally, the one who asked master John of Corn-
wall who *Busillis* was? and when master John asked him where,
and in what scripture the name was found, he said, "in the
missal," and ran for his own book, and shewed him *in die*
written at the foot of one column, and *bus illis* at the beginning
of another. Master John took advantage of his question to
bring up the point publicly when he lectured on the morrow in
the schools, and to shew how great a scandal was clerical
ignorance[1].

The anecdotes of Giraldus may have been partly dictated by
vanity, but they are borne out by the evidence of the registers,
and sometimes by the official language of mediaeval bishops.
The most zealous of these for the equipment of the clergy for
their office of explaining the scriptures were probably Grosseteste and Peckham, and their words shew that ability to construe
Latin easily could not be reckoned as general among parish
priests. Grosseteste laid down, as the minimum knowledge
necessary to a priest, only ability to say the ten commandments,
and explain them to his people, with the seven deadly sins: and
to understand "at least simply" the seven sacraments, and the
three creeds[2]. They must be able to teach the children of their
parishioners the our Father, creed, and hail Mary, and, since
"some adults are ignorant of these things, as we hear," to
examine them in them when they come to confession. He also
stated frequently in ordination sermons that the cause of the

[1] *Gir. Cambren.* II. 343.
[2] *Grosseteste*, Pegge, S., London, 1793, 315, in the constitutions.

evil condition of the Church was the failure of the clergy to preach the gospel of Christ[1]: the instruction of his flock was the first duty of a parish priest, and yet:

To-day there are many pastors, bound to feed their hungry flock with the Word of God, who have no food to do it with: for there are many who do not know how to explain to the people a single article of the faith, or commandment of the decalogue[2].

There should be, he concludes, a manual to teach them the most necessary subjects, and in this desire he anticipated Peckham, Quivil and Thoresby, who actually supplied such manuals. Grosseteste's sermon, as quoted by a Lollard, to the effect that priests ought to translate the Sunday gospel for themselves before making their sermon upon it, and that those who could not so translate it should seek help of their neighbours, is not known in its Latin form: but is paralleled in tone by many of his ordination sermons.

Archbishop Peckham, in his constitutions of 1281, dwelt also on the illiteracy of the clergy, and the evils arising from it:

The ignorance of priests precipitates the people into the pit of error; and the folly or boorishness of clerks, who are commanded to instruct the minds of the faithful in the catholic faith, sometimes increases error rather than doctrine....As a remedy for which peril we command and enjoin that each parish priest, four times in the year (that is, once in each quarter of the year), upon one or more holy days shall himself or by his deputy explain to the people in the vulgar tongue...the fourteen articles of the faith, the ten commandments of the decalogue, the two precepts of the gospel, the seven works of mercy, the seven mortal sins, the seven principal virtues, and the seven sacramental graces. And, lest any man should excuse himself from the aforesaid things through ignorance, since all the ministers of the Church are bound to know them, we here give them in a brief summary[3].

The Latin exposition which followed was such as Grosseteste had desired, and very similar to that issued by bishop Quivil of Exeter in 1287[4]. He enjoined that, since ignorance was the

---

[1] *Fasc. Rer. Exp.* II. 251, 256, 260.

[2] *Id.* 265.

[3] Wilkins, II. 54. No translation of the catechism was issued at the time, but archdeacons were ordered to expound it "in the domestic idiom" to the local clergy, who were to teach it to their parishioners in sermons.

[4] *Id.* II. 143, 162.

mother of all errors and ought above all to be shunned by priests, whose office consisted in preaching and teaching, each arch-deacon should inquire which vicars, rectors or priests were "enormously illiterate," and report them. "Enormous illiteracy" was to consist of inability to say by heart the commandments, seven sins, seven sacraments and creed; and, to improve the level of clerical education in his diocese, Quivil not merely issued a tract summarising these matters, as Peckham had done, but ordered each parish priest to possess and use it, under penalty of one mark, payable to the archdeacon. Thoresby's similar tract[1], issued, however, both in Latin and in English, has been mentioned earlier. These tracts, officially issued by archbishops and bishops, throw a twofold light on the question of the biblical knowledge of parish priests. They shew first, that translation or exposition of the Vulgate text was not one of the necessary duties of the parish priest: and secondly, that the minimum knowledge required of them was something very much less than ability to construe the Vulgate text. A tract issued even as late as 1494, written by a theological lecturer at Cambridge full of zeal for clerical education and the study of the scriptures, represents it as not impossible even then that a priest should be unable to understand Latin[2]: and the number of ignorant priests was much greater in 1300 than 1500. So far, the evidence for the education of parish priests, and the duties required of them by the bishops, bears out the Lollards' contention that the text of the Bible, and even of the New Testament, was largely unknown to them and their parishioners at the time. The parishioners knew the great events in our Lord's life, as given in the creeds and expounded thence in the pulpits: but they were not necessarily familiar, through the ministrations of their parish priests, with His teaching, miracles and life, as recorded in the text of the New Testament.

§ 3. When the Waldensian and Lollard heretics complained that the laity were ignorant of the scriptures, since they could not read Latin and were not allowed to read translations, the orthodox answer was always, that it was the duty of the laity to listen to the scriptures, as expounded verbally by the priest,

---

[1] See p. 141.
[2] Melton's *Sermo Exhortatorius*, quoted Gasquet, *Eve of Ref.* 134.

in accordance with holy doctors. By this means unlettered men were to be saved from the dangers of wrongful interpretation, and strengthened in Christian faith and practice. To some extent this answer was justified, for nearly all early mediaeval books of sermons were homilies founded on a text of the Sunday gospel or epistle, and sometimes referring to the contents of the gospel or epistle as a whole: and such books of homilies were written throughout the middle ages. This shews that the tradition of preaching on the Sunday gospel was continuous and widespread: but two circumstances tended to lessen its value as a teaching institution. The first was the infrequency of sermons in the early middle ages, and the second was the tendency to discard the Sunday gospel as a subject in later times. Moreover, it was the one great duty of the priest to teach the faith, and not to expound the Bible, from the earliest middle ages to the Reformation; and it was on this that bishops and synods insisted throughout the period.

The illiteracy of Anglo-Saxon priests rendered impossible the preaching of a compulsory number of sermons in the year. In 1217 bishop Poore, of Salisbury, ordained that each archdeacon was to instruct the "simple priests[1]" within his archdeaconry in simple language on the articles of the faith: they were then to repeat the exposition to their parishioners "frequently, in the domestic idiom." Parish priests, that is, were not yet bound to

---

[1] Mansi, 22, c. 1103, § 3. "Simple priests"=illiterate. All the priests of the archdeaconry were, however, to be present: whether the archdeacon was to make his own exposition in Latin or English is not clear. When sermons were preached at all, there was generally no difficulty in securing that they should be in the vernacular except in the case of Wales or Ireland [or in Slavonic countries]. Giraldus Cambrensis was appointed to preach the crusade in Wales, and spoke so movingly in French that numbers took the cross without understanding his words, De Rebus, 75–6. Grosseteste insisted on the preaching of sermons "in the domestic idiom," and the later popes took some measures to secure vernacular preaching. In 1366, when the English held Gascony, the pope wrote to the archbishop of Bordeaux to ask whether Alexander Dalby, dean of S. John's, Chester, could "so understand the Welsh tongue as to be able to preach in it": since Edward, prince of Aquitaine, wished to have him appointed to the see of Bangor; as the archbishop had "many who spoke Welsh in his diocese," he was to send the pope a private report about it; CPL, IV. 25. An Irish priest was removed from a vicariate in Connor because "he neither understands nor can intelligibly speak the language of the parishioners," id. VI. 425, and complaints were lodged against Robert, bishop of Killaloe, because he was "ignorant of the scriptures and of the Irish tongue," id. VII. 7.

preach every Sunday and holy day, but they were exhorted to preach "frequently." It was probably an advance in practice when archbishop Peckham made it compulsory for priests to preach four times a year at least. Later synods reiterated the injunction for the necessity of sermons, and increased their frequency: but the subjects for sermons remained the same throughout Europe from the twelfth century to the Reformation[1]. They were thus summarised in the prologue to the *Abbey of the Holy Ghost* of c. 1370:

Therefore our father the bishop...has treated and ordained, for the common profit, through the council of his clergy, that each one that under him has cure of souls, openly, in English, upon Sundays, preach and teach them that they have cure of the law and the lore to know God Almighty, that principally may be shewed in these six things:

  (1)  In the fourteen points that fallen to the truth (the creed).
  (2)  In the ten commandments that God has given us.
  (3)  In the seven sacraments that are in holy Church.
  (4)  In the seven works of mercy unto our even-Christians.
  (5)  In the seven virtues that each man shall use.
  (6)  In the seven deadly sins that each man shall refuse.
And he bids and commands in all that he may, that all that have cure or keeping under them, enjoin their parishioners and their subjects, that they hear and learn these ilk six things, and oftsiths rehearse them, till they con them, and sithen teach them their children, if they any have, what time so they are of eld to learn them. And that parsons and vicars and all parish priests inquire diligently of their subjects in the Lenten time, when they come to shrift, whether they know and con these six things: and if it be founden that they con them not, that they enjoin them upon his behalf, and of pain of penance, for to con them[2].

There is no evidence at all among English records that the gospel was ever read in English at the beginning of the sermon till a year or two before the Reformation. The period when the practice began in Germany, between 1500 and 1526, can be quite clearly traced: but there is no evidence for such a practice in England till the year 1538[3]. The absence of reference to such a practice is decisive, because there is so much general evidence

---

[1] See p. 68.         [2] EETS, OS, 26, 2.
[3] The visitation articles of two dioceses then ordered the gospel to be read in the pulpit in English each Sunday, but with accompanying clauses shewing this to be an innovation at the date: see chapter XIV.

about the sermons of the period and their subject-matter, both in the decisions of diocesan synods, the books of sermons prepared for the help of the clergy, and the books to instruct them in the art of preaching. Since none of the three mention any such practice, the weight of evidence against it would seem conclusive.

From about 1300, moreover, when sermons were becoming more frequent, there was a tendency to use other illustrative matter than the gospel in popular preaching, as well as to use the saint's day legends for sermons in place of the saint's day gospels. Both tendencies were part of the growth of popular preaching, as an art in itself, and as a means of moving the congregation to devotion or almsgiving, instead of instructing them in the elements of the faith, or explaining the story of the gospel quite simply in English. The earlier northern rhymed gospels consisted first of the translation of the gospels alone: then of these translations with a moral tale added to each: but in later forms, generally of the moral tales, or *exempla*, alone[1]. The increase of popular preaching was connected with the work of the Franciscans, who were expert, not only in the practice of the art themselves, but in the preparation of books of materials for sermons, and of manuals on the art of preaching[2]. In the thirteenth century Guibert de Nogent wrote a treatise on *How a sermon ought to be made*; Alain de Lisle one on the *Art of preaching*, and between 1210 and 1228 Jacques de Vitry introduced many *exempla* into his popular *Sermons in the Vulgar Tongue*. The *fabliaux* were also used as sources for illustration, both by Odo of Cheriton and Etienne de Besançon in his *Alphabetum Narrationum*, c. 1284[3]. The latter treatise was arranged in dictionary form, so that the would-be preacher could easily find a moral anecdote on Abbess: Confessor: Confusion: and so forth, down to the final one on Zelotipa. These books of ready made sermons, or materials for sermons, were very frequent from the thirteenth century onwards, the most popular of all perhaps being the *Gesta Romanorum*[4]. Several of them have

[1] See p. 149.
[2] *English popular preaching in the fourteenth century*, Toulmin Smith, L., EHR, VII. 25.
[3] EHR, VII. 27, 28; ed. Banks, M. M , EETS, OS, 126, 1905.
[4] EETS, ES, 33.

been printed, and a good description of some of them is given by Mr Little in his *Studies in English Franciscan History*[1]. The stories and sermons deal with the virtues and vices of all classes of society, monks, priests and seculars: but no single story or anecdote can be found to advocate the practice of reading the Bible, either by clerks or lay people, and this is very significant. In the *Alphabetum Narrationum*, for instance, the only tale which mentions scriptural study is that of the abbot Pambo[2], who, while still unlettered, went to another monk to learn to read. He was first taught the verse: *I said, I will take heed to my ways*: and went away to put in practice what he had learnt. This took him the remainder of his life, so that he never returned for a second lesson: the moral of the story being obviously, not the duty of studying the Bible, but of practising virtue. The stories themselves are non-biblical, and the great popularity of these books must have meant a lessening in the biblical character of the sermons delivered[3].

Three features of the preaching of the period are thus clear, and bear upon the question of the biblical knowledge of clergy and laity before the days of Wycliffe. First, that the Sunday sermon was not universal in all parishes before this date, since fourteenth century synods legislated on this point[4], taking measures to provide that the parish clergy should be able to preach them. At the end of the century indulgences began to be granted for attendance at sermons,—though not usually those of the parish priest, but some other ecclesiastic. In 1371 one was granted to all who should hear the sermon in the presence of the duchess of Brittany[5], and in 1372 another to those who heard that of the papal nuncio[6]. Shortly after, the chancellor of Lincoln obtained a holiday from his duties there, on the grounds that he wished to "reside six weeks in his Kentish parish, and recreate his parishioners with sermons[7]." But the Sunday sermon was still not universal. Secondly, for a hundred years before Wycliffe's day there had been a tendency to compose sermons from non-biblical rather than biblical matter, as the

---

[1] 135–157.  [2] EETS, OS, 126, 468.
[3] For Wycliffite statements that the friars preached in rhyme, see p. 148.
[4] For evidence on this point, see G. G. Coulton's *Mediaeval Studies*, 2nd ed. 1915, Appendix, 103.
[5] CPL, IV. 165.  [6] *Id.* 171.  [7] *Id.* VII. 497.

books of sermon materials shew; and thirdly, books on the manner and matter of preaching never suggest that the preacher should make a literal translation of the Sunday gospel in the sermon, or should inculcate the need of Bible reading for the laity at all. This last omission may seem obvious and inevitable when all but the privileged classes were devoid of books, and unable to read: but among the many virtues which different volumes of sermons inculcate on the devout and well-born laity, who could have had plenty of books if they had wanted them, Bible reading is not found.

§ 4. None of the Latin or English manuals composed for the help of the parish priest suggested that it was his duty to study the Vulgate, or to translate its contents to his people in his sermons, or to urge upon them the need of studying it, either by means of translations or otherwise. The Latin manuals were more frequently possessed by the higher clergy than by parish priests: from about 1350 onwards the *Oculus Sacerdotis*[1] of William de Pagula was a book frequently found in libraries, and mentioned in wills. It was divided into four parts; each part was sometimes found separately as the *pars prima, secunda, tertia oculi sacerdotis*, while the fourth was entitled the *Cilium oculi sacerdotis*, or *Priest's Eyelid*; sometimes the different parts were described as the *Pars Dextra*, or *Sinistra Oculi Sacerdotis*[2]. About 1380 John de Burgh, chancellor of the university of Cambridge, wrote another manual modelled upon it, and even longer, called the *Pupilla Oculi*, perhaps the most popular of all fifteenth century manuals[3]. The *Ars praedicandi*[4] of Alain of Lille, and the *Speculum Ecclesiae*[5] of Hugh of St-Cher, were also fairly frequent in English libraries. None of these refers to any duty of the parish priest to instruct his parishioners in the biblical text.

---

[1] Fabricius, III. 181; Syon, 245; *Reg. of Edm. Stafford*, 1395–1419, Hingeston-Randolph, 416, 432; the *Cilium* was bequeathed in 1349, *London Wills*, I. 607 n.     [2] Pembroke MSS. 248, 281; *Bury*, 83.

[3] Fabricius, I. 221; Syon, 191. See *Reg. Stafford*, 394 and 404, where the book is twice bequeathed: once to be used by the ministers of the church of Exeter for their learning. It was bequeathed to the parish church of Swine by Peter the vicar, about 1400, together with the *Speculum Curatorum*, see chapter XIV. Leicester abbey had it in 1492 (Nicholls' *Leicester*, I. app. 106); so *Bury*, 85, and *Parker Coll.* 43.

[4] EHR VII. 27.     [5] Ff. I. 11, § 9.

§ 5. The references to the books owned by particular parish priests, or to their love of biblical study, are very scanty. There is no record of one who owned either an English or French Bible before Wycliffe's day, and the earliest reference to a parish priest who owned a Vulgate is to Hamo, rector of Snaves, who gave one to the abbey of S. Augustine's, Canterbury, about 1300, probably at his death[1]. In 1384 the parson of Snettisham, Stephen Edrich, possessed one[2]; and about 1410 Robert Stoneham, vicar of Oakham, bequeathed one[3]; there are five other cases of rectors or chaplains before 1450, excluding the cathedral and higher clergy[4]. The wills of parish priests before Wycliffe's death are relatively few, because it was not till about 1400 that persons with relatively little to leave made wills at all; nevertheless, it is noticeable that the only books known to have been bequeathed were service books (except the single above-mentioned Vulgate), and also that no English or French psalters or books of devotion are known to have been bequeathed. This emphasises the dependence of the parochial clergy on the gospel for the day, and their own powers of admonition, for the matter of their sermons; and it explains something of the difficulty of synods in enforcing the regular preaching of sermons at all. It agrees with the state of things indicated in Grosseteste's sermon, where he recommended those who said they could not preach, to learn the story of the Sunday gospel the week before, and tell it to the people on Sunday, going if necessary to some neighbour to have the Latin gospel translated for them[5]. In face of this absence of books, it is not surprising that there are no records of parish priests who devoted themselves especially to the study of the scriptures, as there are in the case of monks and of the higher clergy. The parochial clergy were not an order, and no doubt largely for that reason their work was often unrecorded: but the absence of any single mention fits in with the evidence as to their general lack of all except service books. There is no

---

[1] *Canterbury*, LIX.
[2] *Lambeth MSS.*, James, M. R., 20.
[3] *Early Linc. Wills*, 139.
[4] In 1413, rector of S. Andrew Huberd, Eastcheap, *Trans. Bibliog. Soc.* VII. 114; 1423, r. of Rudby, TE, I. 405; 1417, r. of Waldegrave, *Early Linc. Wills*, 125; 1432, a chaplain of York, TE, II. 29; 1446, c. of York, *id.* II. 117.
[5] See p. 141.

evidence that any of the early Anglo-French or Middle-English translators were merely parish priests, although translation from the French was more within their reach than that from the Latin. The *Ayenbite of Inwyt* was translated from the French by a Canterbury monk in 1340[1]; it is unknown what position was held by William of Waddington, who was responsible for the *Manuel des Péchiez* in its French form; but Robert Manning of Bourne, who translated it as the *Handlyng Synne* in 1303, was a Gilbertine canon of the order of Sempringham[2]. William of Nassington, who translated the *Speculum Vitae* into English verse, and perhaps also the *Prick of Conscience*, was advocate of the court of York[3]; Gaytrik was a monk of S. Mary's, York[4], and Walter Hilton was an Austin canon. Richard Rolle was a hermit, as was a certain translator of a sermon of S. Bernard's from French into English[5]; Mirk, an Austin canon of Lilleshall. Only William of Shoreham, the Kentish author of poems on the sacraments, the commandments and the creed, was possibly a parish priest[6]. The evidence as to their education, their books, and their literary work is all against their possessing enough learning before the days of Wycliffe to do much in the way of expounding the Bible to the laity. However hard working and zealous a class they might have been, their proper work was always regarded as the administration of the sacraments, the teaching of the elements of the faith, and the exhortation to lives of virtue; it did not include the personal study of the Bible, or much preaching on the biblical text to their parishioners.

---

[1] Wells, 345.  [2] *Id.* 342.
[3] *Id.* 348, 463.  [4] *Id.* 355-.
[5] Dd. 1. 1.
[6] Wells, 349. The poems are dated by some authorities as between 1375–1400: but may be the work of a William of Shoreham, who was vicar of Chart in Kent c. 1320.

# CHAPTER VIII

## *Pre-Wycliffite Bible reading by lay people*

§ 1. Sir Thomas More would probably have been surprised to learn that, until the days of Wycliffe himself, the language of those lay people who were sufficiently wealthy to own Bibles was French; or that, though they were bi-lingual, English was the language in which they addressed their inferiors, and French the tongue of civil conversation. Edward I swore in English, but he addressed his parliament in French. The upper classes in the time of Grosseteste[1] and the de Montforts were still French speaking, but they were beginning to find English their native tongue, and French an acquired one. A French *trouvère*, writing about 1250, told how a young French squire was received into the earl of Oxford's family to teach his daughter French, which she spoke "not quite so well as if she had been born in Pontoise[2]." French continued to be the language of Parliament and the law courts for a little longer; but in 1362, 1363, and 1364 the lord chancellor first opened parliament by English speeches. In 1362 a statute ordered all pleading at the law courts to be conducted in English instead of French, though the year books continued to be written in French[3]. Wills continued to be written in French or Latin for some time longer: the first English sentence in the collection of *London Wills* occurs in a will dated 1405[4], and directs that a chantry priest should ask for prayers for the founder in English. The grammar schools had already ceased to construe the Latin texts in French, and used English instead; and in 1404 two English ambassadors went so far as to declare to the French ones that they were completely ignorant of that language,—but this may have been due to diplomatic *amour-propre*[5].

---

[1] For his French *Chasteau d'Amour* see EETS, OS, 71, xxxiii.
[2] *Blonde of Oxford*, Camden Soc. 1868, vii.          [3] CHEL, ii. 70.
[4] i. 371. Vows of chastity were taken in French for some time longer: the first English one in the Ely register is in 1407. See EDR, *Arundel*, New Series, 116–39, 153; for 1896, 30; for 1900, 54; for 1901, 58.
[5] De Ryssheton and Swynford, *Royal and Hist. Letters*, ed. Hingeston, F. C., i. lxxvii, lxxxvii, 307; cf. i. lxvii. Knowledge of French had so much died out by 1432, that Oxford regularised the teaching of it; cf. *Univs.* ii. 460.

Thus, till the period of Wycliffe's own influence, and even later, lay people of the upper classes who used translations of the scriptures, or books of devotion, would naturally have had them in French. The last quarter of the fourteenth century saw the beginnings of a revival of vernacular literature all over Europe, and Wycliffe's followers were able to obtain the support they did in favour of biblical translations, because of the coincidence of their championship with this pro-vernacular wave. Had Wycliffe lived a hundred years earlier, his followers would have tried to circulate not English, but French Bibles, among the dukes and knights. No English translation was made before Wycliffe's time, not only because Bible reading was not advocated for lay people, but because the most frequent translators, the chaplains to noble families, would have prepared French translations, had they prepared any.

§ 2. The great majority of lay people were, of course, illiterate, and unable to read or write. This is sometimes obscured by mediaeval writers who deal with social life, and who speak of those of a single class as if that class alone existed. Thus writers like the Knight of the Tower, and those who compiled books of courtesy or manners, speak of the duties of women, or of young boys, when they actually mean only well born women, and the sons of nobles[1]. Thus most of the evidence as to the education of lay people, or their power of reading in after life, applies only to the upper social classes, a very small section of the whole population. There was, in the middle ages, a career open to talent: and those of lowly birth, like Grosseteste, sometimes rose to great positions: but the career lay through the Church, since the student must at least be in minor orders. Those of the lower classes who gained an education did not remain lay people: and those who became really proficient in Latin seldom remained merely tonsured clerks, without proceeding to the priesthood. The majority of lay people were small farmers, farm labourers, personal servants, members of great households, soldiers, and the handicraftsmen of the town: some, but not most of them, might go to a small local *abc* school as children, but they had no further acquaintance with books.

---

[1] Cf. the manuals mentioned, pp. 21–2.

There is almost no evidence that little girls attended the *abc* schools at all, though it is possible that in some cases they did do so[1]. Book-learning was no concern of most English people, before the fifteenth century, at any rate.

There is, however, enough evidence as to how the children of the upper classes were educated, to render it certain that biblical translations played no part in it, either in the case of boys or girls. Noblemen's children were usually sent to some great household to be educated as pages and squires. They were sometimes sent to abbots' or bishops' households, as to those of any other magnate; and the daughters of knights and nobles were sometimes sent to board in a convent, and to be taught letters by one of the nuns. In the fifteenth century treatises were written on the education and training of young pages; and this training, although less elaborate, was probably much the same in earlier centuries. The young page was to learn to take part in the stately routine of the life of a great household, and the knightly exercises of the day: but almost nothing is said about his literary education, certainly nothing of biblical study. Chaucer's young squire, who might have been a contemporary of Wycliffe, was a model of knightly virtues and accomplishments: he could write well, and make songs, and "well portray," or paint on vellum.

The *Book of the Knight of the Tower* dealt expressly with the bringing up of noblemen's daughters, and was accompanied by a companion volume for his sons, which has not survived. The knight of "La Tour-Landry" was a Frenchman of Anjou, who was present at the siege of Calais in 1346, fought against the English in the ensuing wars, and died rather later than Wycliffe: his book was written about 1371[2]. But though it was written by a Frenchman, the life of well born English ladies at the time was much the same as that of his own daughters, and the book was soon translated into English[3]. The knight says in his preface

[1] In England: for the Paris schools for girls, taught by mistresses of grammar, see Jourdain, 127–9. Cf. Hentsch, 62, for the advice given in the *Ancren Riwle*, not to "turn your cloister into a school": the authoress's servant might however teach any little girl in danger of being taught along with boys.

[2] *La Tour-Landry*, VII.

[3] *Id.* I. XIV.

that he means to compile, with the aid of two priests and two clerks, a book of instructions for his daughters, and to collect stories as examples of his admonitions. These stories are drawn from the Bible, the lives of saints, and the fabliaux; the biblical instances, the knight says, have been supplied by the two priests and two clerks. The knight has liberal opinions about the education of his daughters: maidens, he says, should be put to school, to learn virtuous things out of the scriptures[1], like Saint Katharine, who by her wit and clergy, with the grace of the Holy Ghost, surmounted and overcame the greatest philosophers of Greece.

And therefore it is a good example to put young children unto school, and to make them books of wisdom and of science, and books of virtues and profitable examples, whereby they may see the savement of the soul and of the body, by the example of good living of the holy fathers before us: and not for to study in the books that speak of love, fables, and of other worldly vanities.... Howbeit, there be such men, that have opinion that they would not that their wives, nor their daughters, should know no thing of the scripture. As touching unto the holy scripture, it is no force though women meddle not nor know but little thereof: but for to read, every woman it is the better that can read and have knowledge of the law of God, and for to have been learned to have virtue and science, to withstand the perils of the soul[2].

But, though the knight is thus anxious that well born ladies should learn to read, and goes into great detail about the virtues and practices that should find a place in their daily life, it does not occur to him that they should have a Bible or read it. They should, he says, say their mattins immediately on waking[3], and hear as many masses as they may, fasting the while[4]; unmarried maidens should fast three days a week, Fridays if possible on bread and water, and Saturdays and Wednesdays at least eating "no thing that hath received death." They should say their prayers with attention, not twisting their necks round like cranes or tortoises[5], never be late for mass, visit and feed the

---

[1] *La Tour-Landry*, 117: the knight uses "holy scriptures" and "holy writ" in the broader mediaeval sense: e.g. "holy writ saith, 'better were a short orison, said with good devout heart, than great long mattins, said without devotion,'" 7, etc.

[2] *Id.* 118.

[3] *Id.* 7.

[4] *Id.* 8–13, 47.

[5] *Id.* 15.

poor, and practise other pious customs. All these points the knight illustrates at great length with many "examples" or stories: so that it is fair to imagine that, if personal reading of the Bible or gospels had been among the practices of virtuous ladies of the day, he would not have omitted to exhort them to that also. Actually, however, he says nothing of the kind, but insists only on their saying their "mattins" or offices.

Boys who were not sent to some nobleman's house for training, and who nevertheless obtained some sort of education beyond that of the *abc* school, may, after the beginning of the fourteenth century, have attended a grammar school. In the early days of these, probably the great majority of the boys who attended them became clerks or priests in later life: and there is not much evidence to the contrary before the days of Wycliffe. Just about his time, and in the time of William of Wykeham who outlived him by twenty years, some of the grammar schools were beginning to be used for the sons of the landed gentry who were not going to become clerks: that is, they were beginning to assume the likeness of the great public schools, instead of training schools for the clergy. The papal and episcopal registers begin about 1390 to speak of a new class of scholar, "literate laymen": references to them are fairly frequent between 1390 and 1415, which seems to have been the period when the combination of literacy and laity was new. The description is not used earlier, and drops out later, probably because "literate laymen" were more frequent[1]. If a small number of grammar school boys did remain laymen before Wycliffe's day, they were the sons of the landed gentry: and there is no evidence that any grammar school provided biblical teaching.

Well born lay people who could read were thus almost as dependent as the illiterate upon services, plays, and the coloured windows and carvings of churches, for their actual knowledge of the Bible. Sermons dealt mainly with elementary Christian dogma, and with the virtues and vices: but the miracle plays sometimes represented biblical scenes chosen from the whole of the Old and New Testaments. The Chester plays included twenty-four dramas or incidents, each to be acted by a separate

[1] Cf. CPL, IV. 360, 361, 488; V, 247. There are also references to literate laymen in 1414 in DH, *Sodor and Man*, 82, and DH, *Hereford*, 127, 129.

craft-gild: the first was that of the fall of Lucifer; the second the creation and fall; the third, the flood; the fourth, Abraham and Melchisedek; the fifth, Moses, Balak and Balaam; the sixth, the salutation and nativity. The series continued with the events of our Lord's life, and ended with the Ascension, scenes from Ezekiel's prophecy, Antichrist, and Doomsday. It must have been some such series as this that Henry IV watched for four whole days at Clerkenwell, with his wife and son[1]. The plays were not solely biblical; for the Harrowing of Hell, the story of the midwives at the Nativity, etc., were often introduced, with other apocryphal incidents. The verse banns of the Chester plays[2], probably written in the sixteenth century, warned the audience that all the events were not biblical: the monk who composed the plays:

> In pagentes set fourth apparently to all eyne
> the old and newe testament with liuelye comforth,
> Interminglinge therewith onely, to make sporte,
> some thinge, not warranted by any writt,
> which to gladd the hearers, he woulde men to take yt[3].

> .    .    .    .    .    .    .

> the beirthe of Christe shall all see in that stage.
> yf the scriptures a-warrant not of the mydwyfes reporte,
> the Authour telleth his Authour, then take it in sporte[4]!

> .    .    .    .    .    .    .

> As our beleeffe is that Christe after his passion
> descended into hell, but what he did in that place,
> though our Authour sett after his opinion,
> yet creditt you the best learned,—those he doth not disgrace,
> we wishe that of all sortes the beste you ymbrace—
> you Cookes, with your Carriage see that you do well
> in pagente sett out the harrowinge of hell[5].

Besides the apocryphal incidents, the biblical characters tended to be approximated to their representatives of the day: Annas

---

[1] Capes, 373.     [2] See chapter XIII.

[3] *Chester Plays*, pt I. 2. The banns are found in this form only in a MS. dated 1600, but some form may have been written in the fifteenth century: perhaps in 1447, when the plays were solemnly performed in Chester, *id*. I. These verses, if written about 1600, are curious as describing the author as a monk, "moonkelike in Scriptures well seene," or saying of him "For at this daye and ever he deserveth the fame which all monkes deserve, professinge that name."

[4] *Id.* 5.     [5] *Id.* 7.

and Caiaphas appeared as mediaeval bishops, Jezebel persecuted "bishops of holy Church," and Pilate and Herod talked French to indicate their rank. The plays were written in verse, and were merely poems dealing with biblical incidents, not, in any sense, translations: but the origin of the Chester plays seems to shew that they were regarded with some suspicion, as popular English versions of the scriptures. They are described by the manuscript as "The Whitsun playes first made by one Don Randle Heggenet, o Monke of Chester Abbey, who was thrise at Rome, before he could obtaine leave of the Pope to haue them in the English tongue[1]." When the license was obtained, the plays were held in 1327 and 1328[2]; and by about 1350 they must have been regarded by the Church as a useful means of instruction, for another monk of Chester then obtained an indulgence of 1000 days from the pope, and 40 from the bishop, for all who should attend them[3]. The banns shew some reason to think that the plays were intermitted after the prohibition of English translations of the Bible in 1408, but revived again in 1447[4].

§ 3. If the Church had encouraged the laity, or such of them as were wealthy enough to possess books, to read the Bible or the gospels in the period before Wycliffe's death, some traces of this must have survived in the manuals composed for their instruction and the conduct of their life. Those who could have possessed the manuals themselves could have afforded to possess also copies of the gospels, or the Sunday gospels and epistles; so that advice to study such books, in Latin or in translation, could have been given if desirable. The manuals themselves, though addressed to lay people in general, were generally written for the upper classes, and assumed that the reader belonged to them: it would therefore have been natural for the writers to advise study of the Bible, or parts of it, if such had been the practice of the day. The earliest instance of a religious who gave such advice, Otto of Passau, in his *Four and twenty Elders*, might have been paralleled in England.

Actually, however, no exact parallel exists: Otto himself did

---

[1] *Chester Plays*, 1.　　　　　　[2] *Id.* 2 n.
[3] *Id.* 1 n. Dom. Henry Francis obtained the indulgence from Clement VI, between 1342–52.　　　　[4] See chapter XIII.

not write till the year of Wycliffe's death, and his teaching was
the result of a special movement, which had no counterpart in
England. But, though the manuals used in England offer no
instances of the encouragement of Bible reading by the laity in
general, they throw some light on questions connected with it.

The *Lay Folks Mass-Book*, in its earliest form, was about the
earliest of these manuals. It was originally composed by a
Frenchman, Jeremias, archdeacon of Rouen, about 1150[1], for
the benefit of some Norman baron, probably the owner of a
private chapel. The book may have been used in its French
form in England, since French would have been the natural
language for such a book down till about 1350: Jeremias, moreover, passed some time in England[2]. His book, like Robert of
Greatham's gospels, was translated into northern English; in
this case, about 1300: fifty years later, it was recopied by a
south-country scribe[3]. It did not give a translation of the mass
prayers, but instructed the lay person in verse couplets how to
behave, and use his own prayers, throughout, as well as explaining to him the different parts of the service[4]. The pater
noster was not translated:

> It were no need thee this to ken,
> For who con not this are lewid men[5];

but the creed was explained in rhyme. The manual shews clearly
that the gospel was read only in Latin, and that the layman,
though not understanding it, was taught to hear it with the
greatest reverence:

> Both the readers and the hearers
> Have mickle need methinks of lerers,
> How they should read and they should hear
> The words of God so leve and dear:

---

[1] *Lay Folks MB*, XI., XXXII.        [2] *Id.* XL.        [3] Wells, 355.
[4] We possess only the M.E., not the Norman form, of the manual: but
the direction to the reader to answer, *Sed libera nos a malo*, at the end of the
pater noster is a trace of the responses still made by the laity in Jeremias'
day in the use of Rouen: see *Lay Folks MB*, 46, and for other traces of the
Rouen use, XXXII., LXII. The only English used at the mass was that of the
bidding prayers, *id.* 62. For a priest who used a Welsh ejaculation at mass,
see *Gem. Ec.* 33.
[5] *Lay Folks MB*, 46.

> Men ought to have full mickle dread
> When they should hear, or else it read
> .　　.　　.　　.　　.　　.
> But since our matter is of hearing,
> Thereof now shall be our lering[1].

Therefore the gospel should be heard standing, and the sign of the cross should be made at the beginning and end. This book was in use from about 1150 to 1300 in its French form, and down till 1450[2] in English: but none of the manuscripts shew the least trace of any custom of translating the gospel at mass, either after reading it in Latin, or at the beginning of the sermon[3]. Another verse manual for the laity at mass, the *Merita Missae*, makes the point even clearer: the laity are to stand out of reverence, and they will receive grace by simply hearing the gospel, without understanding it; just as an adder is affected by the charm pronounced over her, though she does not understand the words.

> At the gospel were full good
> Steadfastlichë that ye stood,
> 　For no thing that ye stirred it.
> .　　.　　.　　.　　.
> Though ye understand it nought,
> Ye well may wit that God it wrought,
> 　And therefore wisdom were it,
> For worship all God's works,
> To lewid men that been none clerkes:
> 　This lesson, now go lere it.
>
> And why ye should this lesson lere,
> Hearkneth all and ye may hear:
> 　There an adder hauntës,
> Ye well may find, and ye will seek,
> She understands nothing thy speech,
> 　When thou her endauntës:

[1] *Id.* 16, 17. Another MS., written for the use of the Cistercians at Rivaulx, alters this passage to make it useful both to those monks who could read, and those who could not.

> If thou of letter kan,
> To the priest hearken then
> His office, prayer, and pistle:
> And answer thereto with good will,
> Or on a book thyself it read....
> If thou can nought read ne say,
> Thy pater noster rehearse alway.

[2] Wells, 355.

[3] Cf. *Lay Folks MB*, xix. 17, 196, for the old Gallican liturgy, suppressed by Charlemagne, where the responses had been made by the laity in Gallic; and for the reading of the epistle in Old French after the Latin.

> Nevertheless, she wots full well
> What is thy meaning every deal,
>   When that thou her enchauntës.
> So fareth there understanding fails,
> The very virtue you all avails,
>   Through grace that God you grantës[1].

Neither the *Handlyng Synne*[2] nor the *Ayenbite of Inwyt* refer to negligence in reading the Bible as a sin, though each was a collection of warnings against every variety of sin likely to befall a mediaeval layman or clerk. The Anglo-Norman form of the first was in use before 1300[3], and the English after 1303. The *Ayenbite of Inwyt*[4] was in Kentish prose, translated by a Benedictine from a French original. It contained no illustrative stories, but teaching on the subjects which all mediaeval councils, and all mediaeval teachers, considered necessary for the instruction of lay people: the commandments, the creed, the pater noster, and the seven gifts of the Holy Ghost. A midland version of it, the *Book of Vices and Virtues*, appeared about 1400, and is often mentioned in the wills of lay people. This type of book, more than any other, represents the advice of the mediaeval Church to lay people: and the omission of all reference in it to scripture reading is significant. There was no further need to search for further confirmation of the faith in the scriptures, since this type of book had extracted from them the dogma necessary for leading a good life; while the dearness of books and the absence of education made it practically impossible that most lay people should go beyond these manuals.

The *Prick of Conscience* was a very long and very popular poem, perhaps composed from a Latin original of Grosseteste's, but well enough known by 1350 for manuscripts of it to be found in both northern and southern dialects[5]. The author explained in his prologue that he intended his work for those who walked in the darkness of ignorance, but he did not mention the Bible as a guide for them: the motto of the book is the

---

[1] *Lay Folks MB*, 140, 361, 379 n.; Wells, 356. The poem was probably written c. 1400, and used later.
[2] Wells, 342, 345.
[3] The *Manuel des Péchiez*.
[4] *Canterbury*, LXXXIV. 371, no. 1507, LXXVI.–LXXVII.; 371, no. 1536.
[5] Wells, 447.

philosopher's "know thyself," and the book itself was written
in order that men should have guidance, and know:

> And which way they should choose and take,
> And which way they should leave and forsake[1].
>
> . . . . . .
>
> He that right order of living will look,
> Should begin thus, as says the book,
> To know first what himself is.
>
> . . . . . .
>
> There this book is into English drawn,
> Of sundry matter, that are unknown
> To simple men that are unlearned,
> That can no Latin understand.
> To make them themselves first know,
> And from sin and vanities them draw.

The author then states what things he considers it advisable for
the ignorant to know, treating of each in one part of his book:
the wretchedness of man's estate, the unstableness of the world,
death, purgatory, judgment, hell, and heaven. He sometimes
runs through a list of venial sins: but omission to read the
gospels, etc., is not among them[2], any more than it is in the
searching list suggested to lay people by Rolle in his *Form of
Perfect Living*[3]. William Nassington[4], advocate at York, also
concerned himself with the instruction of lay people at the end
of this period, writing about 1375. He translated the Latin
*Speculum Vitae* of John Waldby into short English couplets, and
dealt with the usual points of instruction of the laity: the pater
noster, gifts of the Holy Ghost, seven sins, seven virtues, etc.:
there is nothing about Bible reading. He also turned into verse
the first part of Rolle's beautiful *Form of Perfect Living*: but
neither in paraphrase or original is there any mention of the
subject. It is a sign of the suspicion which all theological books
in the vernacular aroused about the time of Wycliffe's condemnation and after, that a copy of Nassington's *Speculum* was in 1384
formally presented to the chancellor of Cambridge by the
stationers, with whom it had been left by a certain priest to be
bound.

[1] *Pricke of Conscience*, Morris, R., EETS, 1863, 6, 10.
[2] *Id.* 10, 94.          [3] Horstmann, I, 21–5.
[4] Wells, 463.

It was examined for defects and heresies, lest the less literate of the people should by it be negligently deceived and led into error: for four days it was with all zeal and diligence examined and approved in every college around....If it had not been orthodox, it would have been burnt[1].

Nassington explained in the preface that the work was for the benefit of the ignorant:

> Some can French and no Latin,
> That have used courts, and dwelled therein:
> And some can of Latin a party,
> That can French full febelly:
> And some understandeth English
> That neither can Latin nor French:
> But lerid and lewid, old and young
> All understanden English tongue[2].

Another translation from the Latin,—this time into prose, not verse, was made sometime before 1370, and became very popular later: the *Speculum Peccatoris*[3]. The translation is free and shortened; but, as in the other manuals, there is no advice about biblical study, or biblical translations. A less common prose manual, constructed on the usual method of expounding the creed, the seven deadly sins, penance, pater noster, ave, creed, etc., was the *Memoriale Credentium*[4], and it has a similar preface, explaining its composition in English:

Men and women that is in will for to flee sin and lead clean life, take heed to this treatise that is written in English tongue for lewid men that nought can understand Latin ne French, and is drawn out of holy writ, and of holy doctors before this time.

It would have been possible for the writer to recommend the study of English gospels had they existed,—but the tract is silent, like all the others of the date.

Nearly all these manuals of the pre-Wycliffite period, unless they adhered closely to the structure of some tenth or eleventh century Latin tract, were thus constructed on the same plan, and shew quite clearly what was considered the official teaching

---

[1] Wells, I. 36, p. 366.                [2] Ff. 4. 9.
[3] Wells, 458. As with all these translations, the MSS. sometimes have the title in Latin, sometimes translate it. For the original Latin, attributed to various patristic authors by mediaeval scribes, see PL, 40, VI. appendix, coll. 935–91.                [4] See pp. 141, 199.

for the laity. This took the form of a skeleton of theology and the moral virtues and vices, and certainly did not inculcate a personal appeal to the literary sources on which the system of theology and ethics was founded. These manuals all dealt with the same points which Peckham, Quivil and Thoresby had included in their official manuals, and which the laity were supposed to know by heart,—the creed, commandments, Lord's prayer, hail Mary, seven sacraments, etc. So general was the acceptance of this primary scheme of instruction for lay people, that when the Lollards tried to issue their own books of instruction, they made use of exactly the same plan. Thus neither original didactic treatises, nor official summaries, nor unofficial expansions of the summaries,—some of them very detailed,— contain any reference to a possible acquaintance with the text of the Bible or gospels, either in the lists of virtues and vices, or in the summaries of sins of omission and commission grouped under the commandments.

Nearly all these earlier manuals, both official and unofficial, were translations or paraphrases from the Latin, but at the very end of the period, during Wycliffe's own life-time, some original English works appeared. Two of these, both written for lay people, are of interest for the question of Bible reading, the anonymous *Abbey of the Holy Ghost*[1], and Walter Hilton's *Epistle on Mixed Life*[2], both dating from about 1370–80. Both are addressed to those who desire to live a life of special devotion while remaining in the world, and one has and one has not, advice to read the gospels, the difference being due to the spiritual outlook of the writer of the treatises. The *Abbey of the Holy Ghost* breathes the normal spirit of mediaeval piety; it was written for those prevented by some obstacle from entering a religious order, and advises them how they may lead a life of equal piety in the world. Their abbey shall be the abbey of the Holy Ghost, charity shall be its abbess, obedience the walls, and the other monastic virtues the site, pillars and rulers of the abbey. The form of the manual is thus quite original, but the

---

[1] Wells, 368; EETS, OS, 26, 118.
[2] Wells, 461. Perry, G. G., printed the tract from the Thornton MS. in EETS, OS, 20, 1886, as *De Vita Activa et Contemplativa*; Horstmann, I. 264– 92, prints both the Vernon and Thornton texts.

pious practices prescribed are not: there is no mention of Bible reading among them.

The *Epistle on Mixed Life*, on the other hand, was the work of the greatest contemporary English mystic, whose *Scale of Perfection* was the favourite English mystical work among religious of the fifteenth century. The *Epistle* was the first English manual to recommend, almost indirectly, the reading of the gospels to lay people, and it is a curious parallel to the case in Germany, where the same causes produced the same effect. The *Epistle*, though not so common as the *Scale*, is still found in many manuscripts; it was written, according to the earliest, to "a worldly lord, to teach him how he should have him in his state in ordained love to God and to his evenchristians[1]," and it laid great emphasis on the extent to which prayer and contemplation could be practised in a worldly life. The book is the nearest English equivalent to the treatises of the contemporary Gottesfreunde, which were written by mystical teachers for the benefit of disciples still living in the world[1]. Hilton's tract explained first the nature of the active, contemplative, and "medled" or "mingled" Christian lives,—the "medled" being that which sought to cultivate prayer beyond the extent to which it was practised by all good active Christians.

And soothly, as me thinketh, this medled life accordeth most to thee. For sith our Lord hath ordained thee and set thee in the state of sovereignty over other men as much as it is, and lent thee abundance of worldly goods for to rule and sustain specially all those that are under thy governance,...and also therewithal after, thou hast received grace of the mercy of our Lord for to have somewhat knowing of thyself, and ghostly desire and savour of his love: I hope that this life that is medled is best and most according to thee to travail in[2].

Later in the treatise Hilton, like the Gottesfreunde[3], proceeded to recommend the reading of the gospels as a preliminary to

[1] Horstmann, I. 264. The Vernon MS. throughout treats the tract as addressed to a single lord: later MSS. begin: "Brethren and sisters, bodily and ghostly," as in EETS, OS, 20, 19. The whole *Epistle* is often found in the MSS. in connexion with the *Pore Caitiff*, under the name, *Of active and contemplative life*; as in MSS. Ff. 6. 36, Rawlinson C. 69, Ashmole 1286, Douce 288, Bodl. 1843.          [2] Horstmann, I. 271.

[3] Mr G. G. Coulton suggests that English mystics were actually influenced by the German mystics of the Rhine, see *Christ, S. Francis and To-Day*, p. 172; and Mr Summers in *Our Lollard Ancestors*, 71, suggests that

meditation, and to kindle in the soul the fire of love through which it should proceed to higher acts of prayer. He recommended the reading of the Latin gospels, either because no English translations existed, or because his pupil could, as a matter of fact, read Latin. The recommendation is rather vague, but almost certainly refers to the reading of the Gospels.

"A man that is lettered," he writes, "and has understanding in holy writ, if he have this fire of devotion in his heart, it is good to him for to gather him sticks of holy ensamples, and sayings of our Lord, by readings of holy writ, and nourish the fire (of love) with them. Another man unlettered may nought so readily have at his hand holy writ and doctor's saws, and forthi it needeth to him to do many good deeds outward to his evenchristians, and kindle the fire of love with them[1]."

Otto of Passau, the German Gottesfreund, actually advised the reading of the Bible in the mother tongue, and it would be interesting to know exactly why Hilton did not do so, though he was the first English religious to recommend the laity to read the Bible at all. If we knew exactly when the *Epistle on Mixed Life* was written, more light would be thrown on the question. Hilton died in 1395: and the oldest existent manuscript of the *Epistle* seems to date from between 1370 and 1380[2], so that probably the simple reason why translations are not mentioned is because none were in existence, since the Wycliffite were certainly not circulated before 1384. In any case, the lords and ladies who came to Hilton for advice were probably of higher social class than the penitents of the Gottesfreunde, since Hilton speaks of some of them as being "lettered" or "literate," i.e. able to read Latin. This is the only mention of Bible reading

about 1424–30 the Norfolk Lollards had as leaders three travelling foreign priests. I hope to print shortly some notes on the possible connexion of English and continental mysticism: but at present I believe English fourteenth century mysticism to be an independent offshoot of Latin mysticism (like German mysticism itself). Later, there was undoubtedly some interconnexion. Similarly, it would appear that Hilton's advice to study the gospels was an independent result of the same cause as Otto of Passau's advice to read biblical translations: desire to rise to what mystical writers called the "prayer of the affections" through a fresh and vivid realisation of the events of our Lord's life. The point in both cases is, that Bible study was not, at the date, one of the practices normally recommended to the devout, as all the other manuals shew positively: but only in the case of those aspiring to use certain kinds of prayer.

[1] Horstmann, I. 278.                    [2] Wells, 461.

in the *Epistle*: but the passage is of great interest as shewing that the reasons which led the German mystics to recommend biblical translations for the use of the orthodox laity were tending to produce the same result in England. The nearness of the date[1] of the *Epistle* to the circulation of the Wycliffite translations is of interest, as shewing either that Hilton knew of no translations of the gospels, or that he disapproved of translations in general. In any case, he had not behind him, like Otto of Passau, the Gottesfreunde tradition in favour of scriptural translations. Hilton's *Epistle* is finally interesting as the conclusion of the series of pre-Wycliffite manuals for lay people. Whereas none of the earlier manuals suggest Bible or gospel reading for the laity in any shape or form, his does implicitly recommend the reading of the Latin gospels to those who could. But his work was written within a year or two of Wycliffe's death, and was that of a teacher of mystical prayer; not, like all the earlier works, an instruction for good catholic folk in general, who desired to lead lives of merely ordinary activity and devotion.

§ 4.  Judging by wills, and the ownership of surviving manuscripts, very few of the laity possessed books of their own at all, before Wycliffe's day, except a few princes, great nobles, and noble ladies. The number of lay people who bequeathed books was very small compared with that of priests, because the latter possessed breviaries, and sometimes other service books. This is shewn clearly in the two largest printed collections of wills, those of London and York. The London wills are mainly those of lay people, merchants and others, and only roughly one will in a hundred bequeathed a book at all. The York wills are those of northern nobles and squires, with a very large proportion of cathedral dignitaries and canons: here, one will in every three or four bequeaths books, generally service books. Laymen seldom possessed Vulgates: only in five known instances: two givers of Vulgates to colleges or abbeys in the thirteenth century may possibly have been laymen[2]; and two women, Isabella Elmley[3] and Elizabeth de Burgh[4], lady of Clare, possessed

---

[1] One MS. of Hilton's tracts, Ff. 5. 40, f. 126, dissuades from friendship with heretics.

[2] Robert Aldsworth, 1263–84, see *C.C.C. Descrip. Cat.* II. 439, and Nicholas Thorn, c. 1283, *Canterbury*, LXXI.    [3] TE, I. 51.    [4] TV, 58.

Vulgates in 1348 and 1360 respectively, as did John Worstede[1], a London mercer, in 1368. Agnes, sister of Leonfrin, moneyer of Lincoln, left the monks of Bath her psalter, "or the value of the same at the fair of Boston." French Bibles are found in hardly greater numbers; Edward III possessed one, and Richard II[2]. A Yorkshire squire had a French one in 1345[3]; the earl of Warwick left French gospels, psalter and Apocalypse in 1359[4], and a certain John Wells had a French Bible illuminated for himself and his wife in 1361[5]. These numbers are very small compared to the number of existing wills by which books were bequeathed: and it is even more significant that there is no single will which mentions an English Bible before Wycliffe's death at all: nor is there any reference to one in any other historical source.

The references to French psalters and semi-biblical books are also few. A Lincoln lady left a "mattins of our Lady," possibly in French, in 1319[6]; the countess of Salisbury possessed the *Bible Historiale* which was taken from king John at Poitiers[7], and the earl of Devon in 1377[8] left his three daughters one book each, a primer, a psalter, and "a French book," probably also of a devotional character.

The only known owners of English psalters before Wycliffe's death were Robert Felsted[9], a vintner of London, who left a psalter written in Latin and English,—probably Rolle's,—in 1349. English and French devotional books are also very few. The small number of these biblical books explains why no manual which really preceded Wycliffe's day recommended reading of the scriptures at all, and the entire absence of

---

[1] *London Wills*, II. 115; from about 1390 lay lords began to bequeath Vulgates more frequently; cf. also *id.* I. 636.

[2] *Som. Med. Lib.* 48.

[3] Robert Place, TE, I. 10.

[4] *Bibliom.* 193.

[5] *Med. England*, Bateson, M., 321; cf. for French Bibles in the period immediately succeeding Wycliffe, William King, draper of London, 1393, *London Wills*, II. 312; duchess of Gloucester, 1399, *Royal Wills*, 183; Edward Cheyne of Bristol, 1415, *Bedfordshire Hist. Rec. Soc.* II. 33.

[6] *Early Linc. Wills*, 5.

[7] CVD, XXVIII.

[8] *Reg. Brantyngham*, 381; for the succeeding period and French psalters, cf. TV, 148–9, *Royal Wills*, 181–3; TE, I. 179, 271.

[9] *London Wills*, I. 636.

reference to the English translation of any book of the Bible except the psalter is strong evidence of itself that none existed, or rather, that none was ever much copied. Taken in conjunction with the other evidence, it is conclusive against the existence of any such translation.

§ 5. As is natural, there is little mediaeval evidence from contemporary sources other than wills as to the acquaintance of lay people with the Bible. Such as there is, shews that the devout laity who were wealthy enough sometimes possessed a Latin service book, a book of prayers, similar to the priests': they usually, however, said the hours of our Lady rather than those of the breviary. The Knight of the Tower tells a story of a lady of such great holiness, that "her psalter, her mattins or other books of devotion" came to her out of the air[1]; he also often prefaces a gospel story by the words "as ye have heard by the word of God in the Gospel," probably in allusion to sermons. Courtesy books, and books of meals and manners compiled in the second half of the fifteenth century, regard it as certain that every lord who was thus served by pages would have a book of prayers[2]: but this, though possibly true of the period from 1300 till 1400, was not certainly so. It is common for fifteenth century manuscripts to have hail Mary's, our Father's, and the commandments in English or French prose or verse inserted among their contents[3]: and it is likely that, even between 1300 and 1400, the biblical knowledge of many lay nobles was confined to a knowledge of these in French or English, and that, while some possessed them in manuscripts, others did not.

It is almost impossible to quote any instance of lay people who were acquainted with the Bible before Wycliffe's days. The Knight of the Tower's Bible stories are very interesting: but he

---

[1] *La Tour-Landry*, 137. The "books of devotion" would naturally mean primers, or the like: these existed in Latin from the thirteenth century, but were very rare in English till about 1400, *Old Eng. Service Books*, Wordsworth and Littlehales, London, 1904, 251. The editors of this work consider that many more primers remain than any other kind of service book, *id.* 252, apparently because primers were books for the laity, and there were more laity than priests: but evidence from wills shews that, on the contrary, there were many more breviaries, etc. than primers, because so very few lay people possessed the latter, certainly before 1400.

[2] See EETS, OS, 32, 179.          [3] See *Rel. Antiq.*

said expressly that they were found for him and read to him by
his two priests and two clerks:

And I said to them that I would make a book of ensamples, for to
teach my daughters, that they might understand how they should
govern them, and know good from evil. And so I made them extraie
me ensamples of the Bible, and other books that I had, as the gestes
of kings, the chronicles of France, Greece, of England, and many other
strange lands. And I made them read me every book: and there I
found a good ensample, I made extraie it out[1].

Even so, either the priests "extracted" very inexactly, or the
knight edited the extracts very freely: for, though some of the
Bible stories are right as regards their main point, all are very
loosely told, and several differ from the Bible up to the point of
having nothing in common with it except the names. The story
of Ruth, as the knight tells it, is that Ruth so loved and honoured
her husband, that when he died and his sons by another wife
tried to deprive her of her lands, heritage and household furniture, the husband's friends protected her against the sons, because she had so cherished her husband: a story that has nothing
in common with the Bible narrative[2]. Similarly, in the story of
Rahab, the men she saved were not spies, but "certain holy men
come into the town for to teach and preach the people[3]"; and
Samson and Samuel were confused, so that it is said that
Samson's parents were holy and childless people, to whom the
birth of a son was at length promised by an angel: both they
and their child were to practise fasting and penance, "for the
angel said unto them, 'excess and gormandise in eating and
drinking warreth against the body and the soul.'" So "Samson
the fort" grew up and did great battle against the pagans[4].
The knight gives Elizabeth, the mother of S. John Baptist, as
an example of wifely meekness, and tells how if aught happened
amiss in the household, "she would amend it, or keep it secret
unto the time that it were amended, in such wise that her
husband found never occasion of displeasure[5]." He tells also the
story of S. Mary Magdalene from the gospel, adding that she
lived twenty years afterwards in the desert, and was sent
heavenly food by an angel of God[6]; and he goes on to tell the

[1] La Tour-Landry, 3.  [2] Id. 119.  [3] Id. 113.
[4] Id. 115.  [5] Id. 131.  [6] Id. 132.

story of Martha and Mary Magdalene. "Mary had chosen the better service, for she sat at his feet and heard his doctrine and wept, and made sorrow for her sin, and cried him mercy with humble heart. As the good lord said, 'Truth, there is no service that God loveth so much as to cry him mercy, and to be repentant of misliving, and to forsake all sin[1].'"

Langland and Chaucer wrote at the very end of the pre-Wycliffite period, Langland being probably a somewhat younger man than Wycliffe, and Chaucer younger still. Their works throw some light on the education and biblical knowledge of the day. Langland relates how his father and friends had "founden him to school[2]," till he could understand the Latin of the Bible and service books. Like Gower[3], he can scarcely have possessed a Vulgate himself. He quoted freely from the Bible and the Fathers, but like all mediaeval writers, seldom with exactness, since he quoted from memory[4]. In the account of Dowel, Dobet and Dobest, written about 1362, he referred to the translation of biblical passages in sermons: Dobet

> ...is ronne into Religioun . and hath rendred the Bible
> And precheth to the poeple . seynt Poules words,
> *Libenter suffertis insipientes*[5], etc.

Chaucer, again, shews great familiarity with the Old and New Testaments and the Apocrypha, and with persons and passages in them. His interest however is that of the scholar, not the devout monk: and he is familiar with the Bible as he was with the *Storial Mirror* of Vincent of Beauvais, and the other great reference books of the age[6].

---

[1] *La Tour-Landry*, 135.
[2] *Piers Ploughman*, C Text, VI. 36–7; cf. Wells, 252, for his schooling.
[3] See DNB, Gower's will; *P. Plough*. IV. 511–12.
[4] *L'Epopée mystique de William Langland*, Jusserand, Paris, 1893.
[5] B Text, VIII. 90; EETS, OS, 38, p. 129; the editor, IV. 739, explains "rendred" as "construe," "translate." The lines occur also in the A text of 1362, and the editor suggests a reference to metrical translations of the gospels; but these were more common in the north, and A and B texts were southern; cf. *infra*, chapter XII.
[6] Lounsbury, II. 389, 509.

# CHAPTER IX

## Wycliffe as the instigator of a vernacular Bible

§ 1. The value of an English Bible was not the foundation stone in John's Wycliffe's theory for the reform of Church and state, but the practical measure to which his theories led him, at the end of his life. He never included the need of an English Bible among the aims for which he openly and principally contended, but those for which he did contend led him almost inevitably to produce such a Bible. The formal list of propositions for which he was condemned says nothing of the defence of vernacular Bibles, and the list of his works which were burnt at Oxford and Prague has no such item; much less does it specify a translation of the Vulgate itself. Neither have the schedules of heresies and errors, for which his immediate followers were condemned, any mention of the defence of translations of the scriptures: and the fighting treatises of Wycliffe and the early Lollards contend for quite different points. But the heresies for which the Wycliffites were condemned, and the points for which they contended, could only be popularly understood by means of a translation of the Bible: and, actually, the connexion between the Wycliffite theories and the production of an English Bible was closer still.

The old fashioned, popular, idea of Wycliffe as an early John Wesley, primarily concerned to promote the evangelisation of the masses, gives a very false idea of his activities. Wycliffe was primarily a university professor, with far more affinities in character and ability to Peter Abelard, than to John Wesley or Peter Waldo. The predominant powers in his personality were intellectual, not spiritual: and it is curious that one in whom the intellectual side so predominated,—one, for instance, who wrote a treatise on the true nature of prayer and made it consist solely in a completely moral life[1],—should have kindled the genuine religious flame which burnt for a generation[2] in Lollardy. It is

[1] *Sel. Eng. Works*, III. 219.
[2] It was never quite extinguished before the Reformation.

curious both that one who was so much a scholar and so little a saint should have inspired men willing to be burnt for their faith, and that his followers should have lost so soon and so completely his guarded sense of intellectual balance.

Wycliffe took his doctorate of theology in 1372[1]; his brilliancy had before this made him a power in the university of Oxford, and it led him very shortly into politics, and ultimately into the suspicion of heresy. The chief feature of home politics at the time was the struggle of John of Gaunt and the feudal party on the one side, against the clericals, headed by the Black Prince and William of Wykeham. The most disturbing feature of world politics was the captivity of the papacy at Avignon, which lasted from 1308 till 1378, and scandalised Christendom only less than the papal schism which followed. The loss of prestige to the spiritual power led naturally to attempts to increase that of the temporal power, as a means to the reform and leadership of Christendom. Marsiglio of Padua, who died in 1328, had claimed the equality of the temporal and spiritual power in his *Defensor Pacis*: Wycliffe now looked to John of Gaunt and the knights to reform the Church. Whether Wycliffe's theories were influenced by those of Marsiglio is doubtful: but that they were confounded with them by the princes of the Church is assured.

Wycliffe's characteristic theory, his main intellectual lever for the reform of the Church, was that of dominion by grace. Through this he became useful to John of Gaunt, and gained political as well as university eminence. The mediaeval theory of the papacy had assimilated the feudal conception of "dominium" and mediate ownership: just as, in the state, all land belonged to the king, and through him to his tenants-in-chief, mesne tenants, and the peasants who cultivated it, so the papacy had become the final claimant of all spiritual dominion, —the head of the ladder of grace, which descended through archbishops and bishops to the parish priests. The novelty of Wycliffe's theory was that it discarded the idea of mediate dominion or ownership, and not merely with regard to spiritual powers, but temporal possessions. He taught that all dominion, power or ownership, came from God, and that every man was

---

[1] See DNB and Mr H. S. Cronin's *John Wycliffe the Reformer, and Canterbury Hall, Oxford*, RHT, VIII. 55–76.

His tenant-in-chief, owing no vassalage to any mesne tenant. Those who disregarded the laws of God were *ipso facto* dispossessed of dominion,—temporal ownership or spiritual power. Wycliffe's enemies at once exclaimed that such a theory led to social anarchy, if put in practice: but Wycliffe himself propounded it only in his academic Latin writings, and guarded himself from saying that it could at once become the basis for indiscriminate social reform. It was, nevertheless, to be the philosophical justification for some scheme of disendowment, on the ground that the higher clergy were not using the endowments according to the law of God; and it aroused practical hatred on that score.

It also led logically to the demand for a translated Bible. If all men were in immediate relationship to God, and owed Him a righteousness and obedience to His law for which they themselves were responsible, they needed to study His law personally, to satisfy themselves that they were keeping it: and to the Wycliffites, the Bible was preeminently and characteristically "Goddis Lawe[1]." Sooner or later Wycliffe and his followers were bound to see that the doctrine of dominion by grace involved the democratisation, or translation, of "Goddis Lawe." Herein lay one novelty of the Wycliffite translations: their aim at publication. French biblical translations were in use at the time among the highest social classes, in both France and England: the translation of Raoul de Presles was completed for Charles V in 1384, and raised no comment: Wycliffe himself quoted the right of English lords to use French Bibles, as a precedent for his own translations[2]. Had Wycliffe never lived, parts of the Bible would have been translated into English at about this time, and have found a place in the libraries of royal dukes and other noble bibliophiles. The essential novelty of the Wycliffite translations was that they were intended for a wider public, and a lower social class: the knights, in Wycliffe's own

[1] For Wycliffe's conception of the Bible as the supreme law-giver, see R. L. Poole's *Illustrations of the Hist. of Med. Thought*, 1884, 297; for his use of *lex Dei* absolutely as a term for the Bible, F. Wiegand's *De Ecclesiae Notione quid Wiclif docuerit*, Leipzig, 1891, 58; and for his conception of the necessity of a knowledge of the Bible for leading a good life, *id.* 58–91.

[2] EETS, OS, 74, 530.

day, rich merchants a little later, and, finally, agricultural labourers. The latter could not own it for themselves; but, like the early Waldensians, they were taught long passages from it by heart, in Lollard "schools" or conventicles. Thus the need and usefulness of an English Bible was not the foundation stone of Wycliffe's teaching, or of that of his followers: but it was the necessary and inevitable corollary of his doctrine of dominion by grace, and the immediate responsibility of every Christian for following the life of Christ.

§ 2. The weakness in Wycliffe's theory of the immediate relationship of all men to God was soon challenged in its theological as well as its social bearing. He taught, implicitly if not explicitly, that there was no authority for the decision of social and ecclesiastical questions save that of the individual conscience, seeking enlightenment in the Bible, and guided by the early fathers of the Church. Since he disregarded the consensus of findings of individual consciences, as expressed in the visible and historic Church, he left himself open to the objection that the Bible can be very differently interpreted by individuals, and claimed as final authority for widely differing ecclesiastical and social systems. The orthodox recognised perfectly that the Lollards wished to study the Bible mainly to justify their own ideas of reform: Thorpe the Lollard reported archbishop Arundel as saying to him at his trial: "Lo, Sirs, this is the manner and business of this losell and such others, to pick out such sharp sentences of holy scriptures and of doctors to maintain their sect and lore against the ordinance of holy Church! And therefore, losell! is it, that thou covetest to have again the psalter that I made to be taken from thee at Canterbury, to record sharp verses against us[1]!" But the early Wycliffites, who laid stress, not on particular verses of the scriptures, so much as on the whole picture of the simplicity of life of the first Christians, never realised the extent to which the application of different texts could be made to cover widely different conceptions of the Christian life.

The justification for Wycliffe's theories lay in the evident need for reform and reconstruction in Christendom, and the fact that his panacea, of individual appeal to the Bible for guidance in

[1] Pollard, 128.

matters of conduct, had not been tried before, except among the
Waldensian sects, of whom he probably knew little. Ecclesiastical evils of the day were as apparent to devout Churchmen
throughout Europe as to Wycliffe: all deplored the evil of a
captive papacy, and after 1378, of a divided allegiance in the
Church. Churchmen acknowledged and lamented such evils as
the non-residence of parish priests and the worldliness of the
clergy, without perceiving that it was due to absence of training:
ecclesiastics like Courtenay and Arundel lamented and reproved
it equally fiercely. More, probably, than in any other century it
seemed to saint, socialist and sinner that the visible Church had
failed, and that change and reorganisation were needed. The
efforts of oecumenical councils from 1215 onwards—especially
Lyons I and II, and Vienne—shew that it was not merely reformers like Wycliffe who desired radical change, and who even
largely identified the need of reform with the position and policy
of the Curia. So far Wycliffe was justified by his contemporaries
in his estimate of the evil tenor of his days: but he was original
in the insistence of his appeal to gospel and apostolic Christianity
as the standard for succeeding ages. With no perception of the
need for differing organisations for a primitive and developed
Christianity, or for increased complexity of organisation in a
spiritual world power, he contrasted the worldliness, elaborate-
ness, wealth and power of fourteenth century ecclesiastics with
the "meek and poor and charitable living of Christ." He was
novel in insisting that simplicity of life would never be practised
by the masses, till they personally understood the Christianity
of the gospels and the Acts of the Apostles. Devout churchmen
at the time objected to the translation of the scriptures because
it involved their vulgarisation in several senses: a genuine
reverence made them declare that the scriptures should only be
handled by trained men, and not be made freely accessible to the
careless and undevout crowd. With this view Wycliffe was
essentially in opposition: all men needed to know "Goddis
Lawe," all men needed to know the vocation to which they were
called, to follow Christ in His meek and poor and charitable
living, and therefore all men, as far as possible, should have
access to the written story of that life. Probably neither
Wycliffe nor his critics realised that a literal imitation of the

lives of Christ and His apostles would not solve problems of fourteenth century ecclesiastical organisation.

Wycliffe's demand for more Bible study was also justified as to a certain extent novel. The Lollards had some excuse, as has been shewn above, for regarding Bible reading as a new panacea for social and ecclesiastical ignorance: they were novel among Englishmen in asking for a widespread appeal to primitive Christian documents, whether their demand was advisable or inadvisable. The implications of scripture had always been preached by the Church; and, the more devout the ecclesiastic, the more certainly he had always desired their recognition. But it had never been recognised that the mass of men would be better for comparing the teaching of the Church with her primitive documents themselves: the illiteracy of the masses was of course the chief reason why such a course had never been considered. But, even in the case of the clergy, individual Bible study had never been regarded as a necessary duty. A saintly pastoral life was quite possible without it, and depended on the practice of spiritual and moral duties: certainly not on individual attempts to practise new forms of social piety, in supposed imitation of the apostles, regardless of the authority of those who were the apostles' successors and equals. Even to-day the old rule prevails, that no private soldier may read a copy of the king's regulations, if he is on trial for any military offence; an officer may bring the book to his cell and allow him to read, but not to copy, that paragraph of the code under which he is to be tried, and no other paragraph. If such a practice survives to-day, in the interests of discipline, it is not wonderful that a similar one should have appealed to the higher clergy about 1400 as a reasonable measure with regard to "Goddis Lawe": it had not been explicitly necessary before, because "Goddis Lawe" had been practically inaccessible to the Christian "private," and many of the Christian "officers."

Finally, the Wycliffite translations may be justified as a remarkable attempt to produce a scholarly and accurate translation, without any partizan attempt to emphasise particular shades of meaning in certain verses or words by a novel translation: in this it should be distinguished from the versions of the sixteenth century reformers. The translators were among the most learned scholars of the day, and their aim was simply to popularise the connected story of the "meek and poor and charitable living of Christ" and His apostles. They could obtain the picture of this state by a literal and faithful translation, and had no temptation to tamper with the text. The translations were made while Lollardy was still almost solely an Oxford movement, when Lollard literature consisted of little else than the guarded, academic, authority-laden Latin writings of Wycliffe himself; and not under the second generation of Lollards, led by Oldcastle. The accusation that the Lollards falsified the scriptures in their translations was not made by their contemporaries, even by archbishop Arundel when he interdicted their use in 1408; and it is almost entirely due to the addition of their own glosses among the glosses of Rolle's psalter. Even in this case, there were no controversial changes in the translation of the text of the psalter itself: and the very fact that Rolle's psalter was recognised as the only biblical translation which could be used by the orthodox explains the quickness of the Lollards to insert their own teaching among the glosses. The Wycliffite translation was faithful because its authors were scholars, with no special temptation to mistranslate or modify the text.

Thus the weakness of English Bible reading, as the Lollard instrument of Church reform, was that it was not likely to lead to unity among the reformers; while their expedient was justifiable from three points of view; first, the obvious need of some reform at the period; secondly, the novelty of urging a widespread acquaintance with the Bible; and thirdly, the scholarship and accuracy of the translation they produced.

§ 3. The Wycliffite circle at Oxford between 1380 and 1384, the years when the translation of the Bible was conceived and partly or wholly carried out, included some of the most learned scholars of the university, and certainly did not account itself heretical. The chancellor of the university[1] and the other

---

[1] Gairdner, 1. 21, Robert Rigge; also T. Brightwell, J. Aston, and T. Hilman were sufficiently keen Lollards to stand on trial for their opinions, in the year of Wycliffe's condemnation, id. 21–5: many of his admirers no doubt relapsed into passivity without a trial after the chancellor and Brightwell had been condemned by the archbishop for the favour they had shewn to the Wycliffites. Peter Pateshull, the Augustinian, and

authorities were all on the side of Wycliffe: and on the only
occasion when the clerical party had tried to bring him to trial
for his opinions, in 1378, they had not been able to carry it
through. Except for the friars, who had to be reckoned with as
the normal lecturers on theology, the whole university was with
Wycliffe, partly out of admiration for his intellectual powers,
partly out of academic jealousy of episcopal interference.
Wycliffe was openly the protégé of John of Gaunt, who sheltered
from his castle of Leicester the Wycliffite centre in that town.
Leicester is almost due north of Oxford; and fifteen miles south
of it, on the Oxford road, was Wycliffe's rectory of Lutterworth,
given him soon after his first service to John of Gaunt in 1374.
Oxford was the centre of academic Lollardy, where Wycliffe
spent most of his time: Leicester was the centre of popular
Lollardy, and Lutterworth lay on the road between them. The
great abbey of S. Mary of the Meadows at Leicester was infected
by Lollardy; for two of its canons, Nicholas Hereford and Philip
Repingdon, were Wycliffe's most vehement supporters, and
actually spent most of their time at Oxford. The continuator
of Henry Knighton[1] was also a canon of the abbey at the same
time, and therefore likely to be well-informed as to Wycliffe and
his supporters. The hermit, Swinderby, was the leader in the
Lollard "school" or conventicle held at the chapel of S. John
the Baptist at Leicester, and his friends Walter Brute and
Stephen Bell also preached there. Richard Waytestathe,
chaplain of this chapel, was also a member of this Lollard school.
Many Lollard treatises were copied here, by a "parchemyner,"
William Smith, who was later accused of Lollardy for so doing[2].
Thus, while Wycliffe determined in the schools at Oxford on the
sacrament of the altar or the truth of holy scripture, Leicester
was the seat of his patron, John of Gaunt, and the centre of
popular Lollardy.

The two most stalwart followers of Wycliffe at Oxford were
the Leicester canons, Hereford and Repingdon. Hereford was a
regent master in theology and a vehement enthusiast, far less

Peter Clark or Payne, or 'Peter the Clerk' (for whom see pp. 240, 291),
were later prominent Oxford Lollards, as were David Gotray of Pakring,
monk of Byland and master of theology; see Pollard, 119.

[1] See *Knighton*, and DNB, Knighton.
[3] Gairdner, I. 41.

cautious than Wycliffe in his opinions and utterances. Walsingham called him "the most violent of John Wycliffe's followers,
among whom were many notable men[1]," and Hereford went so
far as to maintain in a sermon in 1382 that archbishop Sudbury
had been righteously slain the year before, in the Peasants'
Revolt. He fought very hard for his master's opinions after
Wycliffe's condemnation, and only recanted under the pressure
of imprisonment, and perhaps the threat of worse[2]: but, when
once he had recanted, he left his opinions absolutely and became
firmly orthodox. "Since he forsook and revoked all the learning
and opinions of the Lollards," a clerk heard him say, "he had
had greater favour and more delight to hold against them, than
ever he had to hold with them, while he held with them." He
shewed something of the same capability for enthusiasm when
at the end of his life he entered a Carthusian monastery, after
holding high ecclesiastical office. Philip Repingdon was a
"great clerk" of somewhat similar type: he also made a considerable fight, and was excommunicated before recanting: and
when he became orthodox again, became one of the most
vehement persecutors of the Lollards. A man of a different
type was John Purvey[3], Wycliffe's special disciple and secretary.
He had been ordained priest since 1377, and so was probably
about twenty-eight or thirty in 1382, when Wycliffe was condemned, and he went with him as his secretary to Lutterworth:
as he is spoken of as "doctor" by his contemporaries, he must
just have taken his doctor's degree. All his contemporaries, including the bitterest enemies of the Wycliffites, speak of him as
a great scholar, in terms of special respect. The Carmelite friar
Walden, who was "elected inquisitor general of the faith to

---

[1] See Wykeham's *Register*, II. 338, ed. T. F. Kirby for *Hants. Rec. Soc.* 1896.
[2] Pollard, 165: Thorpe the Lollard was threatened "thou shalt go
thither where Nicholas Hereford and John Purvey were harboured, and
I undertake, ere this day eight days, thou shalt be right glad for to do what
thing that ever I bid thee do." This throws a rather sinister light on
imprisonment in Saltwood Castle.
[3] FZ, 400 n.; Wilkins prints "Purney" throughout. The name is apparently
French (see p. 378 n.). Purvey does not seem to have been Wycliffe's "curate"
at Lutterworth, as is sometimes stated. Leland, *Collectanea*, 1770, III. 409:
"Haec quae sequuntur scripsit Thomas Gascoign, doctor theologiae, Oxon.,
A.D. 1444, edoctus a Johanne Horn octogenario, qui fuit parochialis sacerdos
de Lutterworth quo tempore Wiclivus obiit, A.D. 1384 in die S. Sylvestri."
Apparently John Horn was Wycliffe's curate, Purvey his secretary.

punish the Wycliffites[1]," and wrote the famous "Bundle of
Lollard heresies" and other learned works against them, speaks
repeatedly of Purvey's learning, even expressly calling him
"doctor." "John Purvey," he says, "was called the glossator
and translator of Wycliffe, for he was the continual Achates of
Wycliffe right down till his death, and drank in his most secret
teaching[2]." "Wycliffe's glossator, Purvey[3]," he says in another
place, and in yet another simply, "Wycliffe's glossator[4]," while
the context shews that he means Purvey. He calls him elsewhere
"the Lollards' library[5]" and "the Lollards' librarian[6]," and
"one of Wycliffe's followers, a man of great authority, and a
most notable Doctor, by name, John Purvey[7]." Purvey's whole
career, as well as contemporary references to him, shew that he
was preeminently a scholar, of great breadth of view: while
Hereford and Repingdon saw one side of a question at a time
and saw it intensely, Purvey saw both, to his own undoing.
"John Purvey," said Thorpe the Lollard of Purvey in later life,
"sheweth himself to be neither hot nor cold[8]," and though the
judgment was harsh on a man who recanted his opinions under
threat of burning, and returned to them at great risk, nevertheless Purvey's writings shew a tendency towards moderation and
hair-splitting that partly justified it[9].

Knighton's continuator, the canon of S. Mary's, Leicester,
emphasises the closeness of Purvey's relation to Wycliffe.

The fourth heresiarch was the reverend John Purvey, a simple
chaplain, grave in bearing and countenance, and affecting the appearance of sanctity beyond his fellows. He was dressed and lived
as a common man, and despising rest he gave all his energy to the
work of travelling: and he gave unwearied efforts to lead the hearts
of the people of his sect with deceitful sermons, and in whatever
manner and way he could. And as he strove to be an example of life
and manners to the remnant of his sect, so he imitated and con-
formed himself to the teaching of his master, as an invincible disciple,
and he boldly confirmed the teaching of his master, John Wycliffe, as
a valiant executor in all matters; for he lived with his master while

---

[1] Doct. I. xv.          [2] Id. I. xxviii.          [3] Id. III. 110.
[4] Id. III. 127.
[5] bibliotheca Lollardorum, Hen. IV, I. 179.
[6] librarius Lollardorum, Doct. III. 732.
[7] Doct. I. 619: doctor eximius.          [8] Pollard, 118.
[9] See pp. 284–5.

he was still alive, and was thus watered with his treatises, and drank them the more copiously into his mind, and thus he toiled unweariedly with him [Wycliffe] as his inseparable companion, and was his associate in his doctrines and teaching[1].

When the storm broke on the Wycliffites in 1382, Purvey seems to have acted simply as Wycliffe's secretary, and taken no part in it. The immediate reason of the effort of the clericals to suppress Wycliffe was almost certainly his presentation of seven propositions to parliament early in that year, urging the gradual confiscation of all clerical property by special taxation[2], and not any supposed connexion of Wycliffe with the Peasants' Revolt of the year before: the mob had actually been bitterly hostile to John of Gaunt, Wycliffe's patron, and sacked his palace of the Savoy. Archbishop Courtenay held a council at the Blackfriars' convent at Holborn, condemned twenty-four points of Wycliffe's teaching as heretical, and prohibited Wycliffite preaching. Wycliffe and Purvey retired to Lutterworth: but the archbishop had still to reckon with the authorities of the university of Oxford. Nicholas Hereford preached violent sermons, and the Carmelite friar, Peter Stokes, tried to tie him down to a list of doctrinal errors, without success[3]. Friar Stokes received orders to publish the condemnation of Wycliffe's teaching just before Corpus Christi day, and the chancellor, Robert Rigge, was asked to assist him: but the chancellor refused. Not only that, but the Lollard Repingdon was appointed to preach the sermon before the university on Corpus Christi day: and the chancellor, and the mayor of Oxford, with armed forces, attended in state. Repingdon declared that the duke of Lancaster "had a mind to defend all the Lollards," and justified Wycliffe's teaching: but the archbishop summoned the chancellor and another Lollard to London, condemned him for contempt, and then, at the request of William of Wykeham, pardoned him. The chancellor signed the condemnation of Wycliffe's propositions, and was sent back to publish the condemnation of Wycliffe, Hereford and Repingdon,—a highly unpopular act in the university[4]. Hereford, Aston[5], Alington,

---

[1] *Knighton*, II. 178.      [2] Gairdner, I. 18.      [3] *Id.* 21.      [4] *Id.* 23-5.
[5] Cf. Bernard, *Cat.* 1979, § 14, De Jo. Aston (prob. Ashton) et Nicholas Hereford. There was a John Ashton, fellow of Merton, who wrote a tract

Bedeman and other Lollards had already, on May 21, been prohibited by William of Wykeham from preaching in the parish church of Odiham, and elsewhere in the diocese of Winchester[1], and by July 1 Aston had been imprisoned and had recanted, and Hereford, Repingdon, and Thomas Hilman had been excommunicated by Courtenay. Oxford was still in a ferment, and a disturbance was caused in the church of S. Mary the Virgin when an Irish Cistercian monk preached against the Wycliffites, denouncing them as Lollards. The university authorities suspended him, but the king's council protected him and friar Stokes from more extreme measures.

Nicholas Hereford meanwhile had started for Rome, carrying an appeal which was to prove unsuccessful. When he returned at the end of the year, it was to find that the archbishop had succeeded in crushing Lollardy for the time being. The Leicester Lollards had been cowed by the imprisonment and recantation of Swinderby, the hermit, in July, and the Oxford ones discouraged by the recantation of Repingdon in October and Aston in November. Repingdon threw no backward glances to Lollardy: he became later abbot of S. Mary of the Meadows, chancellor of Oxford in 1397, in 1400 chaplain and confessor to Henry IV, and in 1404 bishop of Lincoln. Hereford was, later, imprisoned in Saltwood castle: and at length, he too was reconciled and taken back to favour. Another Lollard was warned later,

> For the pity of Christ, bethink thee how great clerks Philip Repingdon, Hereford and Purvey were, and yet are, and also B.[edeman], that is a well understanding man: which also have forsaken and revoked all the learning and opinions which thou and such other hold: wherefore, since each of them is mickle wiser than thou art, we counsel thee for the best, that by the example of these four clerks, thou follow them, submitting thee as they did[2].

The archbishop had succeeded in reducing Lollardy to silence in Oxford: the leaders had recanted, and no doubt many who had

on the conjunction of Saturn and Mars, in 1358, Ashmole 393, §§ 36, 37, and a friar John Ashton, who wrote *Quaestiones super sentencias et super canonem missae*, Bernard, *Cat.* Worcs. 877, probably neither of them the Wycliffite. C.C.C. Oxford 240 is late fourteenth century MS. of Bonaventura's *Stimulus Amoris*, written by John Ashton, to whom it belonged.

[1] Wykeham's *Register*, II. 337.
[2] Pollard, 162.

been attracted to their teaching abandoned it without risking a trial for their opinions. Of the Oxford circle, only Purvey remained with Wycliffe at Lutterworth: and various Lollards, like Swinderby, Bell and Brute, continued their preaching at the risk of being burnt as relapsed heretics.

Two causes account for the archbishop's success in this summer of 1382: the real horrors of imprisonment and a shameful death, combined with the archbishop's skill in shewing favour and benignity to those who recanted: and the academic, scholarly characteristics of the first generation of Lollards at Oxford. Though the expedition and regularisation of the punishment of heresy by death by burning was not carried out till 1401, heresy had continuously been punished by burning on the continent, and this was legally possible in England: in fact the first burning of a Lollard was by common law, before the passage of the *De Comburendo* statute. King Richard II threatened sir Richard Stury with a shameful death in 1395, if he did not recant his Lollard opinions. But the conversion of the leading Lollards, the four great clerks, was not solely due to fear or bribery; all early Lollard writings are more guarded, more practical, and less extreme, than those of their followers later. As Purvey himself wrote of the points in dispute between the bishops and the Lollards: "Who that ever granteth all, granteth much falsehood, and who that ever denieth all, denieth many truths[1]." The early Lollards were not men to whom the reasonable or scholarly arguments of their opponents could make no appeal, or who were prepared to hold that their own opinions were right, if Christendom pronounced them wrong. Not only their personal fears or ambitions, but their education and training, was all against their continuing to lead a set of followers who were less learned and more unbalanced than themselves.

Such was the turning point in the last four years in Wycliffe's life: the condemnation of some of his views, and those of his chief followers, in the summer of 1382. Before that time he had lived as the centre of a set of learned clerks at Oxford: afterwards, with his secretary, Purvey, at Lutterworth. It was

[1] See p. 463.

between these years, of 1380 to 1384, that, as passages in his writings shew, he was turning to the idea of producing a vernacular Bible.

§ 4. There is evidence that he did do so, both in the statements of his contemporary and hostile critics, and in his own writings. The man most likely to be well informed on the subject of the biblical translations condemned in 1408 was archbishop Arundel. He was aware of the academic discussion at Oxford over the lawfulness of vernacular Bibles in the years 1400–1407, and he probably chose Oxford for the scene of the prohibition of English Bibles of set purpose. He wrote in 1412 to pope John XXII, relating his efforts to suppress the teaching and followers of "that wretched and pestilent fellow John Wycliffe, of damnable memory, that son of the old serpent, the very herald and child of antichrist," and lamenting that

In these last times, alas,—and we lament it with no small bitterness of heart,—in the most fair garden of the glorious university of Oxford ...there grow together poisoned herbs and infected plants, whose poisoned seeds, too long allowed to ripen in the aforesaid garden, are blown by the wind of pride and scattered abroad into the fair field of the kingdom of England.

After describing Wycliffe's iniquity in seventeen vigorous lines, he specified as the climax of his offences that "to fill up the measure of his malice, he devised the expedient of a new translation of the scriptures into the mother tongue." Arundel was aware that old and unreadable Anglo-Saxon translations existed in abbeys in England, and his words "new translation" indicated the crown of the offence: that the translations were in a tongue comprehensible to all. There is no hint in the letter that the translation was a bad or false one, but the complaint was merely that such a translation had been made at all[1]. Wycliffe, then, "devised the expedient": his secretary, John Purvey, did the bulk of the work.

[1] The words "new translation" cannot be pressed further than I have here indicated. In face of the absolute MS. evidence that no complete Middle-English translation of the Bible, and almost certainly no partial ones, were made before c. 1380 (see chap. XIII. on contemporary partial English versions and their date), it cannot be held that Arundel knew of some other English version, made perhaps between 1300–1380, such as would be comprehensible to men of Wycliffe's generation, and that he was merely rebuking Wycliffe for making one of his own, when this already existed.

The evidence of Arundel is valuable, because it is that of the very man who was chiefly responsible for the "stopping ot scripture" through the prohibitory canons of 1408: but the evidence of Henry Knighton's continuator is of even more value. He was a canon of S. Mary of the Meadows at the same time as Hereford and Repingdon, at the time also when Swinderby the hermit was sometimes the guest of the abbey: and he remained under the new régime, when the converted Repingdon returned as abbot. He might well have had Lollard sympathies before Wycliffe's condemnation: he does shew in his work that he was a partizan of John of Gaunt: but he wrote his account of the doings of the year 1382 later, when Wycliffe had been condemned. His account was not only likely to be well informed, since he was in touch with Hereford and Repingdon, but because it must have been seen later by Repingdon his orthodox abbot.

"In those days[1]," he wrote, of the year 1382, "flourished master John Wycliffe, rector of the church of Lutterworth, in the county of Leicester, the most eminent doctor of theology of those times. In philosophy he was reckoned second to none, and in scholastic learning without rival. This man strove greatly to surpass the skill of other men by subtlety of knowledge and the greatness of his ability, and to traverse their opinions.... This master John Wycliffe translated into English, (not, alas, into the tongue of angels), the gospel which Christ gave to clerks and doctors of the Church, in order that they might sweetly minister it to laymen and weaker men, according to the message of the season and personal need, with the usury of their own minds: whence, through him, it [the gospel] is become more common and open to laymen, and women who are able to read, than it is wont to be even to lettered clerks of good intelligence. Thus the pearl of the gospel is scattered abroad and trodden under foot of swine, and what is wont to be the treasure both of clerks and laymen is now become the jest of both. The jewel of clerks is turned into the sport of the laity, so that that has become the 'commune aeternum[2]' of laymen, which heretofore was the heavenly talent of clerks and doctors of the Church."

The canon is here exactly explaining the orthodox attitude to the Bible at the time. It ought not to be accessible to lay people, but priests should explain passages from the Sunday gospels and epistles in their sermons, not translating them, but telling the

---

[1] *Knighton*, II. 151–2.
[2] A reference to the 'eternal gospel' of abbot Joachim of Flora: which taught that the era of the Father was past, that of the Son passing, that of the Holy Ghost about to be ushered in.

story in their own words, with its moral inferences, "the usury of their own minds." Master John Wycliffe's fault is that he has translated the gospel into English at all, not that he has made an inaccurate or bad translation. Actually, the translations were due rather to Wycliffe's secretary than to Wycliffe, but the canon was justified in speaking of the work "instigated" by Wycliffe as his own.

Finally, the words of John Hus, though not those of a contemporary, have great weight. The intercourse between Oxford and Prague was close; the Wycliffite Peter Payne, who debated with friar Walden at Oxford[1], became the instructor of Jerome of Prague: the latter was at Oxford, transcribed copies of the *Trialogus* and *Dialogus* in 1401–2[2], just when an eminent friar was determining against the lawfulness of vernacular Bibles[3], and took his copies back to Prague. Two other Bohemian Wycliffites, Nicholas Faulfisch and George of Knychnicz were in Oxford in 1407, when the discussion over English Bibles was raging fiercely before its extinction by Arundel[4], and they had copied and personally corrected Wycliffe's *De Veritate Sacrae Scripturae* and two other treatises, and took them back to Prague. Oldcastle corresponded with Hus himself: and the tracts of a Lollard, Clement Folkhirde, were brought to Bohemia in 1410. More Wycliffite treatises exist in manuscript in Prague and Vienna than in England to-day: and all these points justify the acceptance of Hus's evidence as to what was popularly believed by Englishmen of the day. "It is said by the English," says Hus, in a work written in 1411, "that he [Wycliffe] himself translated the whole Bible from Latin into English[5]," and the statement was substantially accurate. Englishmen of the day knew nothing as to whether the work was actually done by Wycliffe or his secretary: they said, naturally enough, that it was "Wycliffe's Bible."

§ 5. Wycliffe's own attitude towards translations of the Bible can be traced from his Latin writings of undoubted authorship, and in one written during the last year of his life there are

---

[1] *Doct.* I. 9.

[2] *Intercourse between English and Bohemian Wycliffites in the Early Fifteenth Century*, Poole, R. L., in EHR, VII. 306.    [3] See p. 289.

[4] See p. 294.    [5] Hus, *Historia et Monumenta*, 1715, I. 136.

distinct references to translations which he or his followers had made, which had roused opposition from ecclesiastical dignitaries[1]: there is nothing, however, in these works to shew that the whole Bible had been published, although the first translation was almost certainly in course of production, and may have been completed. Wycliffe had from the first appealed to the records of primitive Christianity to support his social theories, and passages where he bases his theories on some biblical verse, or claims that the Bible is the final authority for Christian doctrine, would be far too numerous to quote. It is interesting, however, to trace in his works written between 1378 and his death in 1384 his efforts expressly to defend the value of the Bible as the final authority[2]; to shew that the people at large were ignorant of the gospel because of defective preaching; then, that it was necessary for all, even the simplest, to know the gospel, so that they might follow Christ in meekness of living; then, that the gospels ought to be translated into English, for this end; and finally, that it was right that such translations had been made, though prelates raged against them.

Wycliffe wrote his *De Veritate Sacrae Scripturae*[3] within the year 1378[4], primarily to defend the "truth" of holy scripture,

---

[1] See F. D. Matthew's *Authorship of the Wycliffite Bible* in EHR, x. 91–99. This list of quotations dealing with translations, however, cannot be regarded as settling the question, because they are all drawn from English versions of Wycliffe's works, which may have been made by himself or by some disciple, and either within or after his life-time. Wycliffite and Lollard Latin tracts frequently have English counterparts, sufficiently close to shew the source of the English version throughout, but not word for word translations. The English tracts are, naturally, more popular and less measured in language: scholastic references are generally omitted, and the whole tone is generally more violent; additions, interjections, and omissions are frequent. It is often difficult to tell whether the greater violence of general tone, or of interpolated passages, was due (*a*) to the original author's relaxation of caution in addressing an unlettered audience, in translating his own tract, (*b*) to the greater temperamental violence, or less scholarship, of some contemporary who translated the Latin tract, or (*c*) to the fact that the English version was made some years later than the Latin, when the claims of both orthodox and Lollards had increased in bitterness and definiteness. The passages cited by Matthew from some of these English Wycliffite tracts cannot stand *en bloc* as coming from genuine Wycliffe tracts: see pp. 248–9.

[2] For a catena of Latin quotations from Wycliffe's works relative to the need of biblical knowledge for leading a good life, see Wiegand's *De ecc. notione*, 58–91.          [3] *De Verit.* I. xlviii.

[4] As I am informed by Mr Cronin, who will shortly publish a chronological list of his writings. The much shorter M.E. tract, *The holy prophet David*

against those who attacked its apparent errors and inconsis-
tencies, and who pointed out that the literal following of all
biblical precepts was impossible in practical life. In it he insisted again and again that all the faithful were bound to know
the scriptures, to obtain salvation: that their meaning was
apparent, not only to the learned, but to the simple, and that
the first duty of a priest, and in a lesser degree, of all the faithful,
was to preach the gospel. The work was learned and academic;
in it he attacked those "modern doctors" who wished to qualify
the authoritative value of the Bible, characterizing them as
"Lollards[1]" or heretics themselves. Moreover, he defended the
old fourfold interpretation of scripture, with the characteristic
qualification that the three subordinate meanings were also
literal and authoritative if "immediately" drawn from the
Bible: but not if "mediately" or through some later commentator[2]. He called Lyra "a copious and ingenious commentator of
scripture[3]," and like him regarded the literal meaning of scripture as the basis and guarantee of all sound interpretation. He
did not, however, in any way surpass Lyra in his estimate of the
worth of this primary sense, but rather the reverse. "Holy
scripture," he said, "is the preeminent authority for every
Christian, and the rule of faith and of all human perfection";
all priests should have a good knowledge of the Bible, in order
to carry out their pastoral office[4], and all Christians, especially

saith, printed pp. 445–56, takes up exactly the standpoint and arguments
of the De Verit., and I believe it to be Wycliffe's, or at any rate made
between 1378–84. I do not however quote it in this connexion, as Wycliffe's
attitude can be as well illustrated by works indubitably his. For a certain
friar Claxton, doctor of divinity, "who said that holy scripture was
a false heresy," see Rawlinson, C. 411, p. 1.

[1] De Verit. I. xxiii, xxiv: "moderni doctores lolium in universitatibus
seminantes," a very old paraphrase for a heretic, see p. 42. The special argument of Wycliffe's opponents, which he takes most space in refuting, is
that the Bible apparently contradicts itself in places, e.g. as regards the
day of the crucifixion in S. John and the synoptists, etc., and is therefore
untrustworthy; I. xxiv, 275.

[2] Id. I. 119–23. This introduction of the theory of feudal tenure is
similar to that in his theory of "dominium by grace." Cf. Opus Evang.
I. 397, for the "catholic" sense of holy scripture.

[3] De Verit. I. 275, xxxv.

[4] Id. II. 161–4; this might accord with mediaeval theory, but it had
not been reached in mediaeval practice. Cf. II. 147, "for it is further
clear, that this knowledge is above all to be demanded of the faithful, and
especially of priests"; II. 171, 136, 137, "all priests ought, even according to
the canon law, to study the scriptures."

priests and bishops, ought to know in the first place the whole law of scripture[1]. Christ is the power and wisdom of God, Whom no Christian can effectively know except through the scriptures, and therefore every Christian is bound to know them; to be ignorant of the scriptures is to be ignorant of Christ, since Christ is the scripture which we are bound to know, and the faith which we are bound to believe[2].

"For clearly, although they [all Christians] be infants, although they be deaf, although through worldly pride they are ignorant of scripture, yet it behoves them to hear God speaking His law in these scriptures, if they are ever to be saved[3]." "The third fiction is," he continues, "that there is no need to preach, since the Christian faith is widely enough spread, since every old woman knows her creed and pater noster well enough, and this is sufficient for salvation: theologians, they say, are commonly heretics, and so it is prudent to be only 'wise unto sobriety[4].'" "Therefore all Christians, especially secular lords, ought to know and defend the holy scriptures[5]."

Wycliffe returned in his later works to those who, as he said, "attacked holy scripture": "the fathers," he says[6], "studied the scriptures, for they dared not, like foolish modern heretics, call the gospel heretical and damnable," and there are heretics nowadays who try to prove that the faith of the gospel is impracticable from certain sayings of Christ, Who bade a man pluck out his eye and cast it from him, not, however, using the words in the sense they thought[7].

These modern satraps shut up the kingdom of heaven, because they persecute in many ways the true meaning of holy scripture and its professors, so that they say in the schools that holy scripture is utterly false[8].

Besides thus defending the value of holy scripture from its academic assailants, Wycliffe often complained that the increase of popular preaching had tended to thrust the old fashioned sermon on the Sunday gospel into the background. He attacked the friars as being especial offenders in this respect:

---

[1] *De Verit.* II. 137.  [2] *Id.* II. 170.  [3] *Id.* II. 138.
[4] *Id.* II. 179.  [5] *Id.* I. 136.  [6] *Op. Evang.* I. 160.  [7] *Id.* I. 158.
[8] *Id.* III. 38. Many academically subtle and minute arguments about the Bible, or its authority, were answered by Wycliffe,—e.g. he shews that the friars were not justified in saying their order had been founded by Christ because "many things Jesus did which are not written in this gospel," *Sermones*, II., *de sanctis*, 56;—but the real point at issue was that of the interpretation of scripture.

"Do we believe that they who beg immediately after the sermon preach the word of God from a sincere heart, or that they speak, as a rule, from God who lay stress upon apocryphal poems, fables and lies, such as will please their hearers[1]?" "What harm results to the Church, when, as if bending the faith of scripture, they aim at rhymes, flatteries, detractions and lies! For they say that, unless they add some novelties beyond the accustomed manner of preaching, there will appear no difference between theologians subtle in sowing the word of God, and country priests of small learning[2]." "And it is clear how blameworthy they are who hear more eagerly and diligently the deeds of Gentiles and fables of the poets than the gospel of Christ: but more blameworthy are they who preach apocryphal matter to the people[3]."

The friars, he says,

Like the scribes and Pharisees of the old law, tell fabulous stories to the people; and, when accused of silence about the gospel, they say that whatsoever truth is useful to the people is the gospel[4].

They pride themselves on having graduated at the university, and then preach flashy instead of simple discourses:

For some by rhyming, and others by preaching poems and fables, adulterate in many ways the word of God;...the poor priests preach purely and freely the word of God: but the friars preach feigned words and poems in rhyme, and therefore the friars' preaching is acceptable to the people[5].

Wycliffe often dealt with the objection that many of the laity were too simple to have the text of the gospel expounded to them, and asserted that this was necessary for all men, however simple. Sermons ought to be addressed to those "not guided by human praise, but whom experience has shewn to be capable and proficient in the word of God[6]." Every command of the pope should be in harmony with holy writ, "and this is one reason why every catholic ought to know the holy scriptures[7]." True priests ought to reveal holy scripture to their people, and they should not plead the illiteracy of their flock as an excuse for not doing so, since that illiteracy is the result of their own shortcomings: their material cannot be worse than that of the primitive Church, which attained such glorious triumphs: the apostles

---

[1] *Polem. Works*, I. 41.

[2] *Sermones*, I. xvii; IV. 266; this set of sermons was composed between 1380–4: see I. xxvii–xxxiv.    [3] *Id.* III. 120.    [4] *Op. Evang.* III. xi, 7.

[5] *Expositio super Matthaei xxiii*, in *Opera Minora*, Loserth, J., London, 1913, 331.    [6] *Polem. Works*, I. 310–11.    [7] *De Ecclesia*, VI.

themselves were simple and illiterate: the knights of Christ now-adays should preach sharply against such sloth[1]. Wycliffe dealt in another place with the classical argument of those who opposed the opening of the scriptures to the illiterate,—the *Nolite sanctum dare canibus* which had been used by Innocent III in his condemnation of the Waldensian translations at Metz, and was so often quoted by the opponents of the Wycliffite trans-lations[2]. He cited his favourite doctor, S. Augustine, as saying that any man, however conscious of infirmity and sin, may run to hear the words of Christ, Who said, *Ask, and ye shall receive;* gentiles and heathen and even gross sinners should all have the gospel proclaimed to them: the "dogs" of the text are those who tear and disfigure the teaching of Christ, and the "swine" before whom we should not cast the "pearls" are sensualists: but we should not refrain from preaching the gospel because some such men may be among our audience[3]. The "dogs" and "swine" should not be interpreted as meaning the illiterate faithful.

Following on this contention, that the gospels should be ex-plained to the simple, Wycliffe was led to argue that they ought to be translated for this purpose. Probably, at first, he had in mind only that lords and knights should be able to use such translations, and explain them to their households, or that the less lettered priests should use them; it was the followers of Wycliffe, and not Wycliffe himself, who went further, and desired that every man should be acquainted with the gospels, through learning them by heart. Wycliffe was no half-lettered Peter Waldo, to spend his time teaching the gospels by heart in the vernacular, though he did once mention the practice with approval: he wished chiefly to place the English Bible as a weapon in the hands of the "knights." A certain person wrote to Wycliffe, asking him five questions about the love of God, and in particular, what state of life was most fitting for a man who wished to love Him. Wycliffe answered that the man's state might be that of priest or knight or labourer: but all those who were thus in the heavenly way must

carefully study the gospel in that tongue in which the meaning of the gospel was clearest to them: for all the faithful were bound to follow the Lord Jesus Christ, and the more closely they followed

[1] *Sermones*, I. 264–5.    [2] *Op. Evang.* II. 383–8.    [3] See pp. 429, 432.

Him, the more and the better did they love Him; and, since the
deeds and teaching of Christ were more clearly expressed in the
gospel than elsewhere, it was obvious how much the careful study
of this book profited the faithful[1].

Another reference to the need of translations of the Bible occurs
in a tract written especially for knights and secular lords:

Christ and His apostles converted much people by uncovering of
scripture, and this in the tongue which was most known to them:...
why then may not the modern disciples of Christ gather up the frag-
ments of that same bread? The faith of Christ ought therefore to
be recounted to the people in both languages[2].

When Wycliffe again insisted that there was

no man so rude a scholar but that he might learn the words of the
gospel according to his simplicity,...and that these considerations
should move all the faithful to learn the gospel,

he was obviously referring to the learning of some vernacular
translation[3]. In another tract, he shews that his followers had
been called to task by their opponents for translating considerable portions of the gospels in their sermons[4]. Probably even
before the translation of the Bible, or before its publication,
Lollard sermons had tended, like those of the Waldensians[5], to
be preceded by the reading of long passages from the Bible in
English; and from this practice, or alongside with it, arose the
Wycliffite plan to issue an authoritative translation. About
1381[6], in any case, Wycliffe issued a Latin tract, *De nova prae-*

[1] *Op. Minora,* 9. The English translation, which is close, is in *Sel.
Eng. Works,* III. 183–5. The Latin is the original, as can be seen by comparing the concise, scholastic definition of love in ll. 11–13, with the halting
and inexact treatment in English, p. 183: as the translator says, "All these
questions been hard to tell them truly in English." The English may have
been Wycliffe's own work, or translated early, for it adds nothing to the
Latin. "And thus it helpeth here to Christian men, to study the gospel
in that tongue in which they know best Christ's sentence;...he that
sueth Christ most nigh loveth him most, and is most loved of God," p. 184.

[2] *Spec. saec. dom.,* cf. *Op. Minora,* xi, quoted *Johann Wiclif und
seine Zeit,* Buddensieg, R., Gotha, 1885, p. 169, from Vienna MS. 3929,
cf. *Sermones,* I. ix.

[3] *Op. Evang.* I. 92: quin verba evangelica possit addiscere,...istud
moveret quemcumque fidelem ad evangelium addiscendum. The *Op.
Evang.* was written in 1384: cf. I. v.

[4] The translation of single verses would have been no novelty, and
could not have aroused such an opposition.

[5] See p. 27: and for the translation of the whole text of the Sunday
gospels in the course of Wycliffe's English sermons, see p. 317.

[6] See *Polem. Works,* I. 112.

*varicatione Mandatorum*, in which he considered various opinions
and deeds of his enemies as evasions of the ten commandments.
He began by stating that certain men (probably himself and
his followers), "considering that Christ and his apostles wrote
the faith of scripture in different languages," have collected the
teaching of the commandments in Latin and English, dividing
them into sections, for the use of different men[1]. He then explained briefly the contents and divisions of the decalogue, and
in the body of the work shewed how various practices of his
enemies fell under the heading of one or the other sins. The first
practice that he attacked, as an evasion of the first and chief commandment, was the opposition of the friars to the translation of
the gospel: either the translation of long passages in their sermons,
or the proposal to prepare a Wycliffite translation at Oxford.

"Our Pharisees and satraps say," he wrote, "that a man ought
not to preach nor collect together the gospel in the vulgar tongue,
lest perchance suspicion should be aroused from its translation into
English: but [they say that] the seven mortal sins, and the commandments of the decalogue may be explained to the people in
English....And some say that this is the reason why they do not
wish these rudiments of the faith from the gospel to be preached to
the people in English: because, according to the faith, they ought to
live as Christ did, and to follow His manner of life: and when Christ's
manner of life should be disclosed, it would be clearer than daylight
that they are opposed to Him in their lives, and not Christians de-
serving commendation, but rather the chief disciples of antichrist.
And therefore they oppose the turning of the gospels into the vulgar
tongue, so as to hide their baseness[2]."

It is quite possible that some rumour of the Wycliffite translations had aroused this opposition to which Wycliffe referred,
but there can be little doubt that a passage in a tract written in
1383 speaks of the translation of the Wycliffite Bible, or part
of it. Wycliffe argued that those things which are lawful according to God's law, the law of grace, are indeed lawful, though
they may be contrary to the law of man:

---

[1] *Polem. Works.* 116.
[2] *Id.* 1. 126. The "rudiments of the faith from the gospel" cannot
refer to the usual skeleton of theology for lay people,—the commandments, creeds, 7 sins, 7 deeds of mercy, etc., because these always had
been preached in English. The reference is to the disclosing (detegendum),
of His manner of life: practically, the translation of long passages from
the gospels. Buddensieg dates this tract as 1381.

Whence is their folly clearly seen, who wish to condemn those writings as heretical for the reason that they are written in English, and acutely prick sins which disturb this realm[1]. For it is lawful for the noble queen of England, the sister of the emperor, to have the gospel written in three languages, that is, in Czech and in German and in Latin: and it would savour of the pride of Lucifer to call her a heretic for such a reason as this! And since the Germans wish in this matter reasonably to defend their own tongue, so ought the English to defend theirs with reason.

The whole passage shews that Wycliffe was not speaking of controversial tracts written in English, because he distinctly connects the wish of the Germans to defend their own tongue "in this matter," the translation of the Bible, with that of Englishmen. The English translation for which he was responsible was meant mainly for the upper classes, though for those of somewhat lower rank than had possessed French Bibles, or the more frequent French *Historia Scholastica*, before. The Church must be brought back, he argued elsewhere, to the position Christ wished her to occupy: this reformation could not be expected of the secular clergy, and secular lords could do most to secure it:

Temporal lords can study the gospels in the tongue known to them, and bring back the Church to the order which Christ instituted[2].

Wycliffe referred to these translations twice more, in a tract written shortly before his death.

"To-day it is considered very shocking that the gospel is translated into English, and preached to the people, as is manifest in the case of bishops, friars, and their accomplices[3]." "Those who preach the gospel in the form and language in which they are the better understood are brought low: while friars, bishops, and their abettors are shocked that the gospel should become known in English[4]."

While there is no doubt at all that Wycliffe encouraged the writing of scriptural and other works in English, for the instruction of "lewid men," there is some difficulty in deciding whether any of the many popular English versions of his own

[1] *De triplici vinculo amoris*, in *Polem. Works*, I. 168. Wycliffe has declared already, see p. 247, that this was the reason for the opposition to translations. For Anne of Bohemia's different versions of the gospels, see also pp. 278–80.

[2] *Expos. super Matt.*, *Op. Minora*, xliv.

[3] *Op. Evang.* III. 36: hodie multum horretur quod evangelium anglicetur.

[4] *Id.* 115: abhorrent quod evangelium in Anglico cognoscatur.

works were by his own hand. Some of these contain references to the English translations and the opposition they were arousing, but they may have been made in Wycliffe's life-time, or in the years immediately succeeding his death. Before Wycliffe's withdrawal from Oxford in 1382 there was already a nucleus of less educated Lollards at Leicester, and elsewhere. From 1382 Wycliffe and Purvey lived only fifteen miles from Leicester, and it is more likely that the English versions of Wycliffe's works were due to Purvey or the Leicester Lollards, than to Wycliffe himself. Wycliffe's English sermons, for instance, were most probably composed at this time from skeletons or notes; and these twice refer to the progress of the English translations:

> Epistles of apostles been gospels of Christ, for He spake all in them, and Christ may not err....And this moveth some men to tell in English Paul's epistles, for some men may better wit hereby what God meaneth by Paul[1].

Another passage may very probably have been written about 1387, when Purvey was writing his glosses on the English gospels, and was prohibited from preaching in the neighbourhood of Bristol:

> And herefore one great bishop of England, as men say, is evil-apaid that God's law is written in English, to lewid men; and he pursueth a priest, for he writeth to men this English, and summoneth him and travailleth him, that it is hard to him to breathe....But one comfort is of knights, that they savour much the gospel, and have will to read in English the gospel of Christ's life[2].

§ 6.    It will thus be seen that the evidence that the fourteenth century English Bible was really due to Wycliffe is cumulative.

---

[1] *Epistolae dominicales, Sel. Eng. Works,* II. 221; cf. I. 129: "God would that these lords...knew the truth of God's law in their mother tongue"; III. 98: "And sith the truth of God standeth not in one language more than in another...why may we not write in English the gospel?...And so the kindred of Pharisees letteth the Gospel to be learned of the people... writing of the gospel in English, and of good lore according thereto, is a subtlety and mean to the common people, to kunne it the better"; *id.* 100: "it is a rule to Christian men...to kunne...the Gospel and other points of holy writ needful to their souls,...whether it be told to them and written in Latin, or in English, or in French, or in Dutch, either in any other language, after that the people hath understanding." Cf. the *Five Questions on Love,* III. 184, more probably Wycliffe's own work: "it helpeth to Christian men to study the gospel in that tongue in which they know best Christ's sentence."

[2] *Sel. Eng. Works,* I. 209.

There are the references to English translations in his works: there are the words of Arundel, the archbishop who lived through the five-and-twenty years of controversy about the validity of English Bibles, and who finally condemned the Wycliffite translations: there are the words of Knighton's continuator and Walden: there is more contemporary evidence as to authorship than any that could be found, for instance, to prove that Chaucer wrote the *Canterbury Tales*. Finally, there is the argument that none of the contemporaries who mention English biblical translations, or who give a list of them, know of the existence of any translations except Wycliffe's. They do not know of contemporary partial translations, which perhaps existed at the time only in a single manuscript: such ignorance is natural enough. But if, as has been suggested, the so-called Wycliffite Bible were really pre-Wycliffite, it is incredible that those who were seeking for precedents to justify the use of English translations should have been completely ignorant of its existence: for these translations which we now call Wycliffite did not merely exist in scattered manuscripts, but in great numbers.

Trevisa wrote his *Dialogue between a Lord and a Clerk* in 1387, and he clearly knew of no earlier biblical translations save Saxon ones. The absence of reference to the Wycliffite translations may shew merely that by 1387 they were not yet widely enough circulated to have reached Trevisa: but it is much more likely that the raising of the question of biblical translations in the *Dialogue*, was due to the fact that the lawfulness of the Wycliffite translations was already in debate. In any case, Trevisa knew of no recognised Middle-English translations to instance.

Purvey's tract in defence of English Bibles[1] of 1405 could not allege any Middle-English translation of a biblical book as a precedent, though some precedents so wide of the mark as Gaytrik's catechism were made to do service. Two friars wrote against biblical translations between 1401 and 1408[2], and they knew of no earlier precedents than the supposed one of Bede's translation: had the Wycliffite versions been (as has been suggested), really pre-Wycliffite and of recognised origin, they could not have omitted to mention them. Arundel's prohibition

---

[1] Printed pp. 439–45.    [2] Printed pp. 401–37.

of 1408, again, mentioned no translation made in or since the days of John Wycliffe, as a subject of exemption; had any well-known translation existed besides that of Wycliffe, and had its use been regarded as lawful, some reference must have been made to it. Ecclesiastical writers who dealt with the subject of the Lollards, and the ecclesiastical historians of the time, such as Walden and Walsingham, knew nothing of the making of any other translation. The complete absence of contemporary reference to any other version besides the Wycliffite one, when so much was being written at the time on the subject of the lawfulness of biblical translations, renders it most unlikely on that score alone that any other translation ever got into circulation. The definite contemporary ascription of the origin of the translation to Wycliffe and his circle, coupled with the complete absence of evidence that the translations were the work of any one else, is in complete accordance with all the other evidence on the subject. The making of such a work as the Wycliffite translation was a scholastic achievement on quite a different level from the one or two contemporary translations of separate biblical books which were made about 1380–1400, possibly by orthodox people: it is difficult to imagine that no evidence at all on the matter would have survived, if the "Wycliffite" version had been the work of a group of orthodox translators, other than the Wycliffites, at Oxford. In view of the evidence of Lollard authorship of these versions of the Bible, the possibility of authorship by some orthodox but unknown scholar is beside the point: but, even apart from this, there is too much evidence as to the work of secular or religious scholars at the date, for an achievement like the Wycliffite Bible to have passed unnoticed; yet no catalogue or existent manuscript has ever ascribed it to any such orthodox doctor.

# CHAPTER X

*The two versions of the Wycliffite Bible, and the evidence of the* General Prologue *as to the authorship of the second version*

§ 1. The fourteenth century English Bible, as printed by Forshall and Madden in 1850, has two versions, the second closely dependent on the first[1]. The first version is a careful, literal translation of the Vulgate text, in which the order of the English words follows almost exactly the order of the Latin, in the manner of Rolle's psalter, and consequently often gives a poor English translation. For "Dominum formidabunt adversarii eius": "The Lord his adversaries shall dread," is a close literal translation, which almost inverts the meaning. The second version, while clearly dependent on the first, translates more freely, without attempting to preserve the same order of words. The differences of construction follow certain rules, but the most noticeable difference is in the translation of the Latin participles. The first version retains them, while the second turns them into finite verbs; e.g.

(A) And he sente Petre and John, seyinge, Ye goynge make redy pask to us. (B) And he sente Petre and Joon and seide, Go ye, and make ye redi to us the pask[2].

(A) And the breed takun, he dide thankingis. (B) And whanne he hadde take breed, he dide thankyngis[3].

One or other of these translations of the participles is followed constantly throughout each of the versions; and this alone is sufficient to distinguish them, apart from the other variations.

We possess the original manuscript of the first part of the early version, the Old Testament as far as Baruch iii. 20, where it is suddenly broken off and left incomplete[4]. We have also a

[1] Apart from small variants of the versions, of which Professor Craigie kindly informs me that Bodl. 277 and C.C.C. Camb. 147, represent the most important one.

[2] FM, IV. 220.   [3] *Id.* 220.

[4] Bodl. 959.

contemporary copy of it, which also breaks off at Baruch iii. 20, and at the end of which the scribe has written: "Here ends the translation of Nicholas Hereford[1]." The original manuscript is in five different hands[2], so that it was probably made by five different people, unless it was written down at dictation, each scribe using his own dialectal forms. The chief of such differences is the difference in the present participle, where three out of the five used the southern or Kentish "ing," and two the midland "and" or "end"; the first saying, for instance, "loving" and the second "lufand" or "luvend[3]." It seems so unlikely that a scribe writing at dictation should have consistently changed a participle to his own dialectal form, writing "lufand" every time "loving" was dictated to him, that it is on the whole safer to discard the dictation theory, and accept the original manuscript as having been the work of five different people. The last of these five was the same man who finished the second manuscript, the very one which ascribed the translation to Nicholas Hereford: so that his evidence can be trusted. Whether he meant to say that Hereford had been generally responsible for the translation so far, or had been one of the five people who had written it[4], is not clear, but, taking the words at their face meaning, it was the former. From Genesis to Baruch iii. 20 the work was, he considered, the translation of Hereford, the most violent of the early Lollards, and the most prominent in the university after Wycliffe himself. Except for Purvey, Hereford

---

[1] Douce, 369, part i. Explicit translationem [sic] Nicholay de Herford. Most English surnames at the date were place-names, and nearly always used with *de*. At this date the names were actual surnames of families, and do not mean merely that a person of a given Christian name lived in the given town: though the presumption would be that the family came from the town originally. Hereford was of course a canon of Leicester. For a reference to Hereford as a translator in 1393, see pp. 286–8.

[2] See FM, I. xlvii.

[3] The scribes' dialects appear to be: (1) Gen.–Exod., southern, yspoken and *yng*; (2) Levit.–Judges vii. 13 southern or Kentish, heo; (3) Judges vii. 13–II Paral. midland, *ande* and *ende*; (4) Ecclesiasticus i.–xlviii., southern; (5) Ecclesiasticus xlviii.–Baruch iii. 20, midland, *end*. Forshall and Madden unfortunately did not print from this original MS., which is corrected throughout in another hand.

[4] He could not have meant that the last portion alone in Bodl. 959 or Douce, 369, was Hereford's work, for these portions he had himself written; Hereford would scarcely have started copying another MS. if he had been at liberty to complete his own.

persisted in his Lollardy the longest of the academic Lollards, not recanting till some time between 1387 and 1391; the break in the original manuscript must shew where his work was interrupted in the summer of 1382, when he fled to Rome. The second manuscript has a second part, where the Old Testament and most of the New is completed by contemporary hands, in the same method of translation. Thus the first version was the work of the Wycliffite circle at Oxford, Nicholas Hereford played a prominent part in its making, and some members of the Wycliffite circle finished it. It would seem probable, under the circumstances, that Wycliffe's secretary, Purvey, should have been aware of the course of the work from the beginning, should have been one of the five subordinate translators of the early portion, and should have shared in the completion of the later. As a young man of about thirty in 1382, he might well have worked under Hereford, who was of higher standing in the university, and therefore more likely to be entrusted by Wycliffe with the general responsibility of making the translation: but, when Hereford fled the country, it would seem likely that the responsibility of completing the translation would have relapsed to the man who had instigated it, and to the young doctor who lived with him and "drank in his most secret teaching[1]."

As regards the literalness of this early version of the Wycliffite Bible, prefaces to contemporary translations shew that it was not yet decided whether it was permissible to translate from the Latin in any other way, especially when such grave issues hung upon the translation of every word as in the case of holy scripture. Rolle had translated in this way, and his work was the strongest precedent: and a contemporary but uncopied translation of the gospels into north midland adopted the same style of translation. Moreover, there may have been an intention from the first to translate glosses as well as the text; and, since glosses were made on every word, a literal translation would have to be made if such translated glosses were to be of any use. Most elaborate glosses were, as a matter of fact, translated in

---

[1] If the second part of Douce, 369, be found to represent the earliest form of the completion of the early version, there is no dialectal reason against its having been completed by Purvey, since the dialect is southern, and generally similar to that of the *General Prologue* and Purvey's other tracts: see p. 275 n.

connexion with the gospels of this version, and it is likely that
the glossed gospels were at least contemplated when this early
version was made, since this would have been so thoroughly in
accordance with ordinary mediaeval sentiment on the matter.
The fact that Rolle's, the only biblical translation yet made, had
been literal, and the probability that the issue of glosses was
contemplated from the first, explains the literalness of the translation of this version.

§ 2. The second version of the Wycliffite Bible, like the
earlier, has many short English prologues to the translations of
the several books, most of which are merely translations of
prologues in the Vulgate[1], while others are the work of the
English translator[2], and summarise the contents of the true book, or
declare the aim and method of the translator. None of these
short prologues are, however, heretical. It has also a long "prologue for all the books of the Bible of the Old Testament," called
by Forshall and Madden, and frequently by later writers, the
*General Prologue*[3]. This is a long tract in fifteen chapters, which
occupies sixty of the large quarto pages of Forshall and Madden's
edition, and begins "Five and twenty books of the Old Testament been books of faith, and fully books of holy writ." It is
written to incite all men, princes, secular lords, justices and
"men of simple wit" to the reading of "Goddis lawe" and the
Old Testament in particular, and not to spare for any tribulation
or persecution which their enemies may do to them on that
account. The author points out again and again that reading
the Old Testament is useful to all men[4] (a new enough pro-

---

[1] Both S. Jerome's prologues, and the old Latin *argumenta* which are
thought to be earlier than S. Jerome. For an analysis and comparison of
these prologues in the Wycliffite Bible with their Latin originals, see
*Test. Scots*, notes on the prologues of the N. Test.

[2] FM, I. xxix.

[3] Printed FM, I. 1–60: described *id.* I. xxviii, xxxiv. It was printed as a
separate tract in the sixteenth century, but not, like the *Compendious
Old Treatise*, as a part of the propaganda for the spread of Tindale's New
Testament in England (see p. 438). It was printed as the *Door of holy
Scripture*, by J. Gough, in Lombard Street, 1540; and as *The true copy of
a prologue written about CC years ago by John Wycliffe,...the original
whereof is found written in an old English Bible betwixt the old testament
and the new, which Bible remaineth now within the king his majesty's Chamber.*
Robert Crowley, 1550.

[4] "Simple men of wit may be edified much to heavenly living by reading
and knowing of the Old Testament," FM, I. 3; the third book of Kings

position in the fourteenth century); since it encourages them with the examples of those who were persecuted for righteousness' sake[1]. The *General Prologue* is not a translation, but is meant, apart from its propagandist aim, to supply an English equivalent to the famous *Prologus Galeatus* of the Vulgate, and other prologues of S. Jerome. It begins with a statement as to the canonical books of the Old Testament, passes on to a passage reassuring "men of simple wit" that the Bible is not too high and lofty a book for them to read, and gives at some length summaries of the contents of all the books of the Old Testament with the lessons to be drawn from them. It then passes to a long discussion of the old fourfold interpretation of scripture, and ends with a chapter justifying the translation of scripture, describing the method followed in the author's own translation of the Bible, and ending with the familiar note of encouragement against persecution. The *General Prologue* was thus both a scholarly introduction, and a polemical Lollard pamphlet.

The *General Prologue* was written probably somewhat later

should "stir kings and lords to...take council of holy scripture and true prophets, and not to false prophets, be they never so many, and cry fast against one either few true men," 15; I and II Chronicles should "stir Christian kings and lords to...make God's law to be known and kept of their people," 29.

[1] The book of Tobias is singled out for special praise for this significant reason: "Though the book of Tobias is not of belief, it is a full devout story, and profitable to the simple people, to make them keep patience and God's hests,...therefore among all the books of the Old Testament, simple men of wit should read and hear oft this book of Tobias, to be true to God in prosperity and adversity, and...to be patient in tribulation; and go never away from the dread and love of God," *id.* 35. The Song of Songs (of all unlikely lessons), is "to teach men to set all their heart in the love of God and of their neighbours, and to do all their business to bring men to charity and salvation, by good example and true preaching, and wilful suffering of pain and death, if need be," 40. Maccabees "should stir Christian men to hold God's law to life and death: and if knights should use the sword against any cursed men, they should use it against lords and priests principally, that will compel men, for dread of prison and death, to forsake the truth and freedom of Christ's gospel: but God of His great mercy give very repentance to them that thus pursue true men, and grant patience, meekness and charity to them that been thus pursued," 43. "For God's love, ye simple men...answer ye meekly and prudently to enemies of God's law...and hold ye steadfastly to life and death the truth and freedom of the holy gospel of Christ Jesus, and take ye meekly men's sayings and laws, only inasmuch as they accord with holy writ and good conscience, and no further, for life nor for death," 49.

than the second version itself, or at least some years after it had
first been taken in hand; and on the dating of the *General Prologue* hangs the main reason for deciding its authorship, and
that of the second version. It has, among other less definite
allusions to contemporary events[1], a reference to certain evil
conditions resulting from the celibacy of the clergy, as made
known at the "last parliament." The passage is so explicit[2] as
to admit of no doubt that the reference is to the *Twelve Conclusions of the Lollards*[3], which were "presented to the assembled
parliament of the kingdom of England" in the year 1395. This
Lollard petition refers to this evil result of celibacy in its third
"conclusion," and explains in its last one that the matters here
mentioned are set forth at large in another English book; this
"other book," which we also possess, refers to the same specific
evil. The presentation of this Lollard petition was a turning
point in their history[4], and roused the greatest anxiety, not only
on the part of the clergy, but of Richard II himself. The reference in the *General Prologue* is so explicit as to leave no reason
for belief that any earlier or later attack of the Lollards on the
clergy in parliament can be referred to. The *General Prologue*
was therefore written after the parliament of Jan.–Feb. 1395,
and before the next one of Jan.–Feb. 1397. This is in accordance

[1] FM, I. 51: 'But alas, alas, alas, the most abomination that ever was
heard among Christian clerks is now purposed in England,...in the chief
university of our realm, as many true men tell with great wailing;...that
no man shall learn divinity, neither holy writ, no but he that hath done
his fourme in art;...this would be nine year or ten before that he
learn holy writ, after that he can commonly well his grammar." This
reference to some intended effort to enforce an existing statute, as an
anti-Lollard measure, is hardly precise enough to date the tract exactly.
For the difficulties over this same point in 1310, and at other times, when
the friars were anxious for dispensation from it, see p. 162; for an attempt
to revive it in 1387, FM, I. xxiii. There is also a reference to some brawl
at Oxford, "slaying of quick men," which has been interpreted as referring
to a fight between northern and southern scholars in 1389, see *ibid*. But
these references to unimportant events at Oxford,—the first of which was
very probably a "purpose" of the anti-Lollard party there for several
years, and the second of which might refer to any brawl, are not of the
same value as the reference to the important and well known Lollard
petition of 1395.
[2] FM, I. 51: "the second horrible sin is sodomy and strong maintenance
thereof, as it is known to many persons of the realm, and at the last
parliament," with more on the same subject.
[3] See appendix, *Twelve Conclusions*, p. 374.
[4] Trevelyan, 329: "It was the high water mark of Lollardry."

D. W. B.

with the evidence as to the date of the second version of the Bible, with which the *General Prologue* is connected: no manuscript can be dated with certainty as before 1395, but one is dated as written in 1397, and others are of about that date[1]. It is not likely that the second version was the work of a single year, and it may have been the work of many years: but it was probably complete when the *General Prologue* was finished, between Feb. 1395 and Feb. 1397.

The last chapter of the *General Prologue* deals with the need of having the Bible in the vernacular for the use of simple men, and gives an account of the making of the second version, in a passage which throws some light also on the making of the early version, to which it incidentally refers. The writer begins the chapter by giving scriptural reasons for the spreading of the knowledge of holy writ among all people:

> For though covetous clerks be wooed by simony, heresy, and many other sins to dispise and stop holy writ, as much as they may: yet the lewid people crieth after holy writ, to con it and keep it, with great cost and peril of their life.

> For these reasons and other, with common charity to save all men in our realm, which God would have saved, a simple creature[2] hath translated the Bible out of Latin into English. First, this simple creature had much travail, with divers fellows and helpers, to gather many old Bibles, and other doctors, and common glosses, and to make one Latin Bible some deal true; and then to study it of the new, the text with the gloss, and other doctors, as he might get, and specially Lyra on the Old Testament, that helped full much in this work; the third time to counsel with old grammarians and old divines, of hard words, and hard sentences, how they might best be understood, and translated; the fourth time to translate as clearly as he could to the sentence, and to have many good fellows and cunning at the correcting of the translation. First, it is to know, that the best translating is out of Latin into English, to translate after the sentence [meaning], and not only after the words, so that the sentence be as open, or opener, in English as in Latin, and go not far from the letter; and if the letter may not be sued in the translating, let the sentence ever be whole and open, for the words ought to serve to the intent and sentence, and else the words be superfluous or false....At the beginning I purposed, with God's help, to make the sentence as true and open in English as it is in the Latin, or more true and more open than it is in the Latin; and I pray, for charity and for common profit of Christian souls, that if any wise

---

[1] See p. 381.  [2] See p. 276 for this pseudonymic phrase.

man find any default of the truth of translation, let him set in the true sentence and open of holy writ, but look that he examine truly his Latin Bible, for no doubt he shall find full many Bibles in Latin full false, if he look, namely, many new; and the common Latin Bibles have more need to be corrected, as many as I have seen in my life, *than hath the English Bible late translated.*...And whether I have translated as openly or openlier in English as in Latin, let wise men deem, that know well both languages, and know well the sentence of holy scripture. And whether I have done this or nay, no doubt they that con well the scripture of holy writ and English together, and will travail, with God's grace, thereabouts, may make the Bible as true and open, yea and openlier in English than it is in Latin[1].

The writer then goes on to explain at length the manner in which he prefers to translate Latin constructions, and the care necessary for the translation of "equivocal words," or those with double meaning. He goes into these questions in great detail, and emphasises the need of the advice and help of "many fellows" in such a work, explaining that he had had such help at every stage in his translation. He mentions a little later in the chapter that it was common knowledge to his enemies that several others had helped in the translation:

"Let the Church of England now approve," he said, "the translation of simple men, that would for no good on earth, by their witting and power, put away the least truth, yea, the least letter or tittle of holy writ....If they know any default by the translators, or helpers of them, let them blame the default by charity and mercy.... Yet worldly clerks ask greatly, what spirit maketh idiots hardy to translate now the Bible into English, since the four great doctors durst never do this[2]?"

Nevertheless, when he is relating the different processes of making the translation, the writer speaks in the singular throughout: a natural enough record of a piece of work done by a circle of translators, under the leadership of one man. The method was probably the same in the making of "the English Bible late translated," which could have been none other than the one this translator used in making his second version, the work of Nicholas Hereford. That too, to judge from the five hands of the original manuscript, seems to have been the work of "many good fellows and cunning."

[1] FM, I. 57–8.
[2] FM, I. 59: *idiots*, of course, is here used in the common mediaeval sense of *unlearned folk*.

The emphasis the writer of the prologue lays upon the four stages in which he has made his translation, and particularly in the making of his Latin text, suggests whether his account is actually that of the making of both versions, including Nicholas Hereford's and his own: since such elaborate preparations seem uncalled for if the translator were actually going only to "make open" an existing English text. "The English Bible late translated" would be a possible reference to his own work[1], if the *General Prologue* were written some time after the finishing of most of the translation. But the third stage of the translation, as described by the writer, seems to have been only a seeking of advice from old books and doctors about the translation of difficult words, and not a literal translation of the whole Bible. The fourth stage is, of course, the making of a free translation. Moreover, the second version shews that its translator had not merely relied upon the Latin text of his predecessor, but in places used a different one. There are, moreover, no manuscripts of the second version earlier than 1395, the date when the *General Prologue* was written: yet this might have been expected, had the second version been in existence some years earlier ("the English Bible late translated"). It seems then certain that the writer of the *General Prologue* refers only to the making of the second version, and that he made it, using the earlier one, with the express purpose of converting a "construe" of the Vulgate into intelligible English prose.

§ 3.   Two preliminary steps are necessary before determining the authorship of the second version of the Wycliffite Bible. We must shew (1) the connexion of the *General Prologue* with the two versions (that is, that the Bible as printed by Forshall and Madden is the one referred to in the *General Prologue*): and (2) that the *General Prologue* is the work of a single author, and not a glossed or conflate tract.

The reasons for supposing that the *General Prologue* alludes to these particular translations are three. The first is that the *General Prologue* is found in connexion with these translations in the manuscripts, and not in connexion with any other work. The manuscripts of the *General Prologue* are much fewer than

---

[1] In which, in that case, Nicholas Hereford would have been a helper and fellow translator.

those of the translations of the text: partly because the manuscripts of English Bibles seldom contained the whole Bible, and the *General Prologue* was not necessary for completeness' sake[1]: partly because the *General Prologue* was frankly heretical, and would have involved the burning of the Bible if found upon a Lollard: and partly because some of the late fifteenth century manuscripts were no doubt written for orthodox people, probably nuns, in which cases the scribe would not have copied the prologue. Forshall and Madden collated 170 manuscripts of the Wycliffite Bible, and others have been discovered since: but they collated only ten manuscripts of the *General Prologue*. All these ten manuscripts have the *General Prologue* in connexion with the second Wycliffite version, except in one case where the *General Prologue* itself forms the whole manuscript[2]. In three cases it is found with the complete Bible in the second version[3], in another this complete Bible contained it originally[4]; it is found once with the Old Testament only[5], once with the New[6], once with the Old Testament but split up in portions before the books it describes[7], once as a small paragraph only, prefixed to a psalter[8], once as the first chapter only, in the manuscript made for Henry VI[9]. Here the scribe completed the first chapter, which contains heretical matter at the end, but omitted the rest for obvious reasons. Certainly any manuscripts which may have been made originally for orthodox people in the fifteenth century would have omitted it also. Thus, though the manuscripts are few, their rarity is easily understandable, and there is no manuscript evidence at all for supposing that this prologue relates to any other translations than those printed by Forshall and Madden.

[1] MSS. of the whole Bible are comparatively rare, because such books were so large and valuable. MSS. of the New Testament, or part of it, are very much more frequent than the Old Testament, to which the *General Prologue* belongs.

[2] Harl. 1666; in Univ. G. 3, also, it is found as a separate tract, though combined with certain tables, genealogies, and excerpts from the N. Test. in the later Wycliffite version.

[3] C.C.C. Camb. 147, Dublin A. 1. 10, Acland MS.

[4] Claudius E. 11.      [5] Mm. 2. 15.      [6] Kk. 1. 8.

[7] Linc. Coll. Arch. 15: the scribe has arranged it in imitation of Jerome's separate prologues.

[8] Addit. 10,046: copied from Dublin A. 1. 10; other parts are in Worc. cath. F. 172.      [9] Bodl. 277.

The second reason for believing that the author of the *General Prologue* describes the making of the second version, as printed, and refers to the first version as "the English Bible late translated," is that the second of these corresponds exactly to his aim, of a "translation according to the sentence"; and the first to one made "according to the letter." It is easily understandable why a translation made in 1384, more or less according to orthodox precedent in its literal method of translation[1], should have been found inadequate by the Lollard leaders within a few years. In 1382, when the first version was in the making, they had aimed at supplying a book for knights and lords, possibly in most cases with glosses: but, when their aim gradually became democratised, they desired that the most "simple and lewid" should learn their English gospels by heart: and for such a purpose the literal version was thoroughly unsuitable. Lollard preachers in the early days had generally made free translations of biblical verses in their sermons, and it was now seen to be desirable to have such an "open" translation in a written version. The translator says it was his special aim to produce such a version, referring to another existent one which apparently did not meet the case: and the two versions in Forshall and Madden exactly correspond to the situation thus indicated.

The third reason for identifying them, is the close correspondence in the construction of the sentences of the later version with the method of translating described by the author of the *General Prologue*. That this was a matter of debate at Oxford at the time is seen by the treatises of two friars, who argued that the "figures," or grammatical constructions of Latin, could not be adequately rendered into English without violation of the sense, or *vice versa*. First and foremost, the author states that he does not mean to translate the present participle literally, but to turn it into a finite verb. Also, he inverts the order of the Latin words where the English construction demands it; and he has taken especial care with words of double meaning, to give the sense of the original writer. This and some other details he

---

[1] The literal construction is very similar also in the midland gloss on S. Matthew, particularly in the translation of the Latin present participle: Ii. 2. 12, *Haec eo cogitante, ecce angelus domini in somnis apparuit ei dicens, Joseph:* Bot þise þings hym þinkand: lo ane angel of God apperid to him in sleep seyand, Joseph.

explains with examples[1]: and in all cases the second version is translated according to his methods, and his examples appear to be taken from it. These three reasons therefore, the conjunction of this version with the *General Prologue* in the manuscripts, the correspondence of the two versions to the two mentioned in the *General Prologue*, and the close correspondence between the methods of translation of the second and those described in the *General Prologue*, render it certain that the author of that work was the translator of the second version.

It is thus clear that the translations printed by Forshall and Madden are those described by the author of the *General Prologue*: but, since the description occurs in one chapter of the fifteen of the *General Prologue*, it might be questioned whether the prologue was originally written as it stands. The part describing the translation is obviously the work of a careful scholar, with a great zeal for accurate translation: is there any reason to suppose that the distinctively Lollard passages earlier in the prologue are not his, but were inserted later, as for instance the Lollard passages in the version of Rolle's psalter? Internal evidence shews however that the prologue is not a glossed or conflate work[2]. The evidence of the manuscripts is against such a supposition: there is no different version of the *General Prologue*, the final chapter with the description of the translation does not occur separately, and the only part which does ever appear separately is the first chapter, in the manuscript presented by Henry VI to the London Charterhouse[3]. Further, the thought and structure of the *General Prologue* is continuous and orderly, and the only digression is explained by the text itself. The *General Prologue* begins by explaining which biblical books are canonical, and in a single sentence it then passes from ex-

---

[1] FM, I. 57–60.

[2] The prologue to Rolle's psalter has been tacked on to the end of the *Gen. Prol.* in Trin. Dublin 2. 1. 10: but there is no other evidence in the MSS. of any accretion to the original text.

[3] FM, I. xlvii. The chapter ends by exhorting simple men to study the Old Testament, and stating that "pride and covetise of clerks is cause of their blindness and heresy, and depriveth them from very understanding of holy writ,"—a sentiment of sufficiently Lollard flavour to make an orthodox scribe refrain from copying further. Another MS., Harl. 1666, ends imperfectly in the final chapter, but as the end comes in the middle of a sentence, it seems to be merely an unfinished copy.

plaining that all the books of the New Testament are canonical, and therefore to be studied by "Christian men and women, old and young[1]," to explaining that they may study the dark parts of holy writ as well as the open, for the same meaning is in both. "Therefore no simple man of wit be afeared unmeasurably to study in the text of holy writ." There is no gap here between the technical and scholarly definition of the canonical books, and the exhortation for all classes to study all parts of the Bible, which is frankly Lollard: and the same is true throughout the prologue. It continues with a division of Old Testament matter into moral, legal and ceremonial, and continues with a short description of the contents of each book of the Old Testament[2] and Apocrypha, written with the idea of upholding certain Lollard doctrines, and exhorting to steadfastness under persecution. Thus, the book of Chronicles should be specially studied by Christian kings and princes, that they may learn by the example of evil princes and their punishment, and of good princes who "governed well the people in 'Goddis Lawe.'"

But alas, alas, alas, where king Jozophat sent his princes and deacons and priests to each city of his realm with the book of God's law, to teach openly God's law to the people, some Christian lords send general letters to all their ministers and liegemen or tenants, that the pardons of the bishops of Rome, that been open leesings...be preached generally in their realms and lordships, and if any wise man againsayeth the open errors of antichrist,...he be prisoned, as a man out of Christian belief, and traitor of God and of Christian kings and lords.

Hezekiah busied himself in cleansing the house of God: but some Christian lords now defile it, by supporting simonient clerks full of covetousness, heresy and hypocrisy, "to stop God's law, that it be not known and kept and freely preached." Similar morals against idolatry and simony are drawn from the stories of Ahab, Manasseh, etc., so that all this portion[3] serves both as a summary of the contents of the books, and an application of the moral of the stories against the persecutors of the Lollards.

"But it is to wit" (the writer continues without break, after finishing this description), "that holy scripture hath four

[1] FM, I. 2.
[2] Chapters III. to XI., inclusive, out of the fifteen of the whole work.
[3] FM, I. 3-43.

understandings: literal, allegoric, moral and anagogic," and these he explains at length, quoting a sermon of S. Augustine and the seven rules of Ticonius[1] for the understanding of scripture.

"Austin writeth all this in the third book of *Christian Teaching*," he proceeds, "Isidore in the first book of *Sovereign Good* toucheth these rules shortlier, but I have him not now; and Lyra, in the beginning of the Bible, toucheth more openly these rules, but I have him not now; and Armachan in the beginning of his book *de Quaestionibus Armenorum* giveth many good grounds to understand holy scripture to the letter, and ghostly understanding also: but I have him not now."

This lack of books explains the digression which follows, which according to the purpose of the author is little more than padding, but which enables us to fix the date at which the prologue was written.

"Also, no thing may seem to be wiser, no thing of more eloquence, than is holy scripture," he continues; "...but for God's love, ye simple men, beware of pride, and vain jangling and chiding in words against proud clerks of school and vain religious, and answer ye meekly and prudently to enemies of God's law."

Holy living, he says, is needful for the understanding of holy writ: but now no man may learn divinity at the university till he has been regent in arts for two years, or studied nine or ten years at the university beforehand[2]: and horrible practices are to be found among clerks at Oxford, "as is known to many persons of the realm, and at the last parliament[3]." These words refer to the petition the Lollards presented to parliament in 1395[4], which made a great stir. That this whole digression was due to lack of books, and was not a later gloss, is shewn by the sentence with which it was suddenly ended:

Nathless, for Lyra came [of] late to me, see what he saith of the understanding of holy scripture: he writeth thus on the second prologue on the Bible[5],

---

[1] FM, I. 46.  [2] *Id.* I. 51.  [3] *Id.* I. 51; see *infra*, p. 374.
[4] See pp. 375–6.
[5] The writer here translates a passage from Lyra's first prologue on the Bible and the whole of the second, as in the 1634, Antwerp, edition of Lyra's gloss. This long passage, from cap. xiii. p. 52, "John saith in the fifth chapter of the Apoc.," to cap. xiv. p. 55, "Here Lyra rehearseth the sentence of S. Austin and of Isidore in these rules," is merely a translation of Lyra.

and he proceeds to quote the whole of Lyra's long prologue. Having now summarised the contents of the biblical books and devoted much space to the explanation of the four understandings of scripture, he finishes in the last chapter by asserting that it is lawful for the common people to have holy writ, gives the above-mentioned rules for translating different grammatical constructions, and ends on the familiar note of exhortation to patience under persecution. "God grant us all grace to kunne well and keep well holy writ, and suffer joyfully some pain for it at the last."

The *General Prologue* is thus a whole, whose one digression is due to the writer's temporary lack of the books he wished to quote, and which he terminated immediately on receipt of those books; there are no grounds from its internal structure for considering it a glossed or conflate work.

§ 4. It is thus clear that but one person wrote the *General Prologue*, and that he edited also the second version of the Wycliffite Bible. This person was Wycliffe's secretary and literary executor, the leader of the remnant of his sect, the "eximius doctor" John Purvey. For this, the comparison of the *General Prologue* with other documents and data affords sufficient evidence[1]. The *General Prologue* was written by a scholar of undoubted eminence: by a Lollard: and by a persecuted Lollard: and it was finished in 1395. Sufficient is known of all the Lollards to say with certainty that there was no other Lollard doctor or scholar holding out in 1395 except Purvey himself: they had all recanted earlier, and the date of their recantation is known. Moreover, the *General Prologue* is but one of a series of tracts[2] written in the years about 1387 by Purvey, and these tracts or prologues have a forerunner in a chapter dealing with translations, inserted by Purvey when he translated Wycliffe's *De Officio Pastorali*. There is also evidence that the *Thirty Seven Conclusions* is substantially the work of Purvey: and it has so many passages in common with the *General Prologue* that a common authorship is strongly suggested. There are other minor points: and the cumulative evidence leaves no room

[1] See appendix, p. 376, *The identification of the author of the General Prologue with John Purvey.*
[2] See p. 270.

for doubt of Purvey's authorship. Contemporaries who identified his secretary's work with Wycliffe's were justified in believing that "master John Wycliffe" translated the whole Bible, as Hus said they did; and the probability is that Arundel, when he prohibited the use of translations "made in the time of the late master John Wycliffe, or *since*," knew well enough that he was condemning the second version and the glossed gospels made by John Purvey[1].

[1] For Arundel's examination of Purvey's glossed gospels, see p. 279; for his presence at Purvey's trial in 1401, see pp. 284–5; for his unsuccessful attempt to conciliate this eminent scholar by giving him a benefice, p. 289.

# CHAPTER XI

## The controversy about the English Bible 1384–1408, and the constitutions of 1408

§ 1. From 1378 when Wycliffe, writing the *De Veritate*, was declaring that it was the duty of all Christians to be acquainted with the biblical text, till 1408 when Arundel prohibited translations made in his days or later, controversy went on over the lawfulness of translating the text of the Vulgate into the mother tongue. During the whole period the friars were the leaders of the opposition; and, since they were the recognised authorities on biblical study at the universities, and the only lecturers on the biblical text, their opposition carried much weight. The English version of Wycliffe's *De Officio Pastorali*, probably the work of Purvey[1], complained that the friars were the chief enemies of English Bibles: and at the other end of the period we find them bringing their campaign to a successful issue at Oxford. The use of biblical translations was not, like some of the Lollard practices, heretical on the face of it: and it is quite possible that the attitude of the bishops may have been less antagonistic at first than that of the friars[2]. It was an eminent friar who claimed in 1401 that severer measures ought to be taken to enforce the existing custom by which "our enthroned bishops refuse the reading of the Bible to the simple[3]."

We possess an English tract which is the first in this controversy: from its contents, it must have been written about the same time as the *De Veritate*, and probably by Wycliffe himself. It begins *The holy prophet David saith*[4], is written by a Lollard, and is a scholarly and somewhat academic tract, full of citations from the Bible and the fathers: the biblical texts quoted are not taken from either of the Lollard versions, but are apparently translated at sight, as in the English versions of Wycliffe's ser-

---

[1] See p. 378.
[2] Cf. Arundel's attitude in 1394: but Wycliffe stated in the *Op. Evang.* that bishops as well as friars were hostile, see *id.* III. 36.
[3] See p. 408.       [4] Printed, pp. 445–56.

mons[1]. The emphasis in the tract is on the combination of the study of the Bible with a poor and holy life: it repeatedly exhorts the simple to acquaint themselves with God's law, and speaks of the opposition of proud clerks to their doing so. It is almost certainly Wycliffe's own work[2], because of the earliness of its date, and the similarity of its literary style and contents to those of the *De Veritate*; for the simplest person, it says, should be acquainted with the Bible, though it nowhere refers to biblical translations,—a fact which dates it as written c. 1378–80. The Bible, it says, should be studied:

only to edifying of thyself or thy neighbour. Some men will con for that end only that they con, and it is foul curiosity. And some men will con that they be known, and it is a foul vanity; and some men will con, for to sell their cunning for money, or for honours, and it is foul winning....Christian men wonder much on the waywardness of divers clerks, that boasten that they have passingly the cunning of holy writ,...for they feign to study, con and preach holy writ for pride of the word, for covetise of earthly goods, and for womb-joy, to live in delices, bodily ease, and idleness....Such is scripture to a man not willing to live after God: as if any man expounded learning of battle to an earth-tiller, not having will for to fight[3].

The writer then gives a series of numbered steps, which it behoves all men to take: to pray devoutly for a true understanding of the text of holy writ, to do penance that God should grant them this understanding, to believe that His law is true, to enquire meekly of learned and well-living men the true understanding of holy writ, and finally to

read busily the text of the New Testament, and take they ensample of the holy life of Christ, and of His apostles, and trust they fully to the goodness of the Holy Ghost, which is special teacher of well-willèd men....They should see and study the true and open exposition of holy doctors, and other wise men, as they may easily

[1] See pp. 249, 445.
[2] It might be a translation of some Latin work of Wycliffe's, now lost: but it is unlikely to be Purvey's translation, judging by a comparison of its literary style with that of Purvey's other work, and his English gloss of the *De Officio Pastorali*; and from the fact that Purvey did write a series of tracts in defence of translations, in which it is not included.
[3] See p. 448. The passage which is closest to Wycliffe's argument in the *De Verit.* (for which cf. *supra*), is that beginning: "These heretics say cursedly that God is false, and His law is false...the true understanding thereof," p. 450.

see as goodly come thereto. Let Christian men travail faithfully in these six ways, and be not too much afeared of objections of enemies, saying that "the letter slayeth."

The writer then gives a long exposition of what the text, "the letter slayeth," actually means, answers two other objections to the reading of the text of God's law[1], and concludes:

Therefore, notwithstanding these lewid objections, as Christ stretched forth His arms and His hands to be nailed on the cross,.... so all Christian people should stretch forth their arms and hands and all their members to embrace to themselves the law of God.

The points in favour of Wycliffe's authorship, besides the earliness of the date and resemblance in literary style, are the similarity of outlook to that of the *De Veritate*, the fact that the writer deals at length with the argument that "holy scripture is false," which belongs to the quite early stage of the biblical controversy[2] but is not found later, and the improbability that it is a work of Purvey's,—the next most likely conjectural author. The main aim of the *De Veritate* is to disprove the assertion "that holy scripture is false," because it is discordant in parts, and this tract is largely taken up with the same point: but the effect of the *De Veritate* seems to have been so great that the objection was not brought forward later. The tract is found in the manuscript in the closest connexion with three other Lollard treatises, the work of Nicholas Hereford or one of the circle of translators of the first Lollard version[3]

Besides this early tract, and the chapter speaking of the lawfulness of the English translations inserted in the English *De Officio Pastorali*, we have a series of twelve English sermons or tracts[4] by Purvey, defending English Bibles. These must have been written between the years 1382 and 1395: for the first recommends the reading of epistles and gospels, "with exposition,"—an early Lollard demand, probably made before the

---

[1] First, "that lewid men should not intermit of holy writ," because God commanded that only Moses and Aaron should go up into the mount, which signifies holy writ; second, that "since Osa the deacon was slain for putting his hand to the ark, lewid men should not touch holy writ."

[2] See pp. 243-5.    [3] See *infra*, p. 445.

[4] Ii. 6. 26, ff. 1-158, and 2 other MSS. The tracts are written in a coarse upright hand, in a MS. 6″ × 4½″, which contains also the Lollard translation of the *Elucidarium*. Tract II is printed in FM, I. xiv-xv. The whole series, though very interesting, is too long to print in an appendix.

early version was complete;—and it is improbable that the
tracts were written later than the *General Prologue*, which incorporates one of them, and was a long and sufficient apologia
for the time being. The tenth tract is in fact the greater part of
Purvey's epilogue to his gloss on S. Matthew, copied without the
special explanation of Purvey's authorities, and how he had
dealt with Aquinas' gloss, in making his own English one[1].
There is some reason to date this gloss as earlier than 1387[2]:
and if the twelve sermons were written in the order in which
they were copied into this manuscript[3], and the tenth were
written before 1387, this would date the whole series as probably
written between 1382 and 1390. That is, the series would be
roughly contemporary with Trevisa's passage on biblical translations, written in 1387. The preoccupation with the defence of

[1] The original form of the tract is the epilogue on Matthew, printed
p. 457. Ii. 6. 26, p. 98, begins: A dere God, lord of truth...fro þe bigynnynge
of þe world unto þis tyme: printed pp. 460-1, with the variants from this MS.,
which are usually slight verbal expansions, see notes on p. 460. The
scribe of Ii. 6. 26, writing c. 1400-1430, copied a MS. in which the arrangement was the same, with tract x following tract ix without break or
rubrication. This tract (x) is so conspicuously similar in matter and style
to the others of the series, that there are no grounds for supposing it a
solitary work of Purvey's, inserted into an alien collection of sermons.

[2] The epilogue to the gloss on Luke was written in 1387 (see p. 275):
that on Matthew perhaps earlier.

[3] This seems probable, because the references to English translations
as made become successively more definite in the later tracts. An additional
reason for attributing the series to Purvey, is that no one but a Lollard
himself engaged on the work of translation over a number of years would
have written so long a series of tracts on the same subject: the defence
of English scriptures was certainly not one of the usual Lollard theses,
specially before 1408. The biblical quotations are not those of either
Lollard version: but the tracts were issued while Purvey was engaged on
the glossed gospels, and probably before he had turned to the making of the
second version, c. 1390-5. The early version was unsuitable for quotation
in popular sermons: the translations here are often loose, and sometimes
interrupted by the writer's own interpretations. For the mode of translation, cf. p. 43.

Ii. 6. 26, p. 9. Goiþ, seiþ he, al aboute þe world, and preche þe gospel
to euery criature.

EV ȝe goynge in to al the world, preche the gospel to ech creature.

LV Go ȝe in to al the world and preche the gospel to eche creature.

Ii. 6. 26, p. 18. ȝeueþ not þe holy gospel to houndis, ne castiþ not your
margarites a forn þe swyn.

EV Nyl ȝe ȝeue holy thing to houndis, nether sende ȝe your margaritis
before swyne.

LV Nyle ȝe ȝyue hooli thing to houndis, nethir caste ȝe ȝoure margaritis
bifore swyne.

translations is evidence that the writer was himself engaged in making them for several years: and, even without the connexion of one tract with Purvey, it would be difficult to ascribe them to any translator but him. Nicholas Hereford was still a Lollard at the period of their issue: but from 1382–87 he was either on the continent or imprisoned by the archbishop.

The first tract begins:

All Christian people stand in three manner of folk. Some can read and understand, as good clerks and well lettered men: and for them be ordained books of Hebrew, of Greek, and of Latin. Some can neither read ne understand, as lewid people that kunnen no letter,.... Some there be that kunnen read but little, or nought understand, and for them be ordained books of their mother tongue, to French men books of French, to Italians books of Latin corrupt, to Dutch men books Dutch, to Englishmen books of English: in which books they may read to kunne God and His law....And that it is lawful to Christian people to read and kunnen holy scripture,...it is open in many places of God's law, both old and new[1].

The comparative earliness of this tract is shewn by its recommendation only of the reading of the gospels and epistles, and even those with glosses. The author does not contend for the reading of the whole Bible, or the naked text, or the Old Testament, which were later Lollard demands.

But if the ten commandments, the creed, pater noster and ave, that all Christian people ought to kunne, common things of holy writ, gospels and epistles read in church, be well translated and truly, sentence for sentence, with good declaration [i.e. exposition], whoso read it, he shall the better understand it, both in Latin and English[2].

In such a moderate demand as this, Purvey would have found support not only from the jurists of Cologne, who argued in 1398 that the simple and open places in the Bible might be translated for the use of lay people, but also from all others who considered a glossed translation safer than an unglossed. In another tract also Purvey demanded the translation of gospel and epistle at mass itself[3]. Similarly, in Germany, the earliest orthodox

---

[1] Ii. 6. 26, pp. 1, 2.
[2] *Id.* p. 15.
[3] See *infra*; and Ii. 6. 26, p. 87: "those that contrarion the gospel and the epistle and would let it to be preached."

manual to recommend vernacular Bible reading after 1500, re-commended the use of German plenaries or Gospel books[1].

All the tracts in this series deal with this subject of vernacular Bibles: the lawfulness of Bible translations in the abstract, the lawfulness of lords and gentles' possessing them, and the lawful-ness of simple people's possessing and learning them by heart. The second tract begins: "Our Lord Jesu Christ, very God and very man, saith in the gospel[2]"; the third, "Our Lord Jesu Christ made the gospel.... Also Christian men must sue Christ in manner of living as Jesu saith in the gospel...but Christian men know not Christ's life but by gospel: then ought the gospel to be preached that men may know Christ's [life] and follow them thereafter[3]." The fourth begins: "Another sentence commending the gospel in our mother tongue"; the fifth, "An-other sentence shewing that the people may have holy writ in their mother tongue lawfully"; the sixth, "This that sueth sheweth that all those be in great peril that letten the testament of Christ to be known and kept of the people"; the seventh, "This treatise that followeth proveth that each nation may law-fully have holy writ in their mother tongue"; the eighth, "An-other chapter strengthening the sentences that go before"; the ninth, "These be the arms of Antichrist's disciples against true men: *And the letter slayeth.*" The tenth is the above-mentioned epilogue, or lamentation that "Christ's law is laid asleep and little set by of Antichrist and of his false clerks." The eleventh is "A commendation of holy writ in our own language," and the twelfth "A dialogue of a wise man and a fool, denying the truth with fables."

All the tracts seem to be sermons, addressed to such rustic audiences as Purvey might have met with in his pastoral journeys: not to an academic audience. The words "dear friends," "and now, dear friends[4]," occur frequently, and even the last *dialogue* has them occasionally, shewing that an audience was contem-plated. There is an interesting passage shewing that by this writer at least, the foreign word "Lollard" was connected with the English verb "loll."

---

[1] See p. 129.  [2] Ii. 6. 26, p. 43.
[3] *Id.* pp. 49, 52, 56, 80, 82, 91, 93, 98, 102, 116.
[4] *Id.* p. 108.

The most blessed Loller that ever was or ever shall be was our Lord Jesu Christ, for our sins lolling on the rood tree: and of his livery and suit were Peter and Andrew, and other more. These were blessed Lollers, lolling on the right hand of Jesu, with the repentant thief in God's mercy, to whom our Lord behight the bliss of paradise the same day. But good friends, what was the cause that Christ and His suers were lolled thus? Certes for their faithful speaking against the sins of the people, and specially for they spoken against the covetise and sins of untrue bishops, and of false feigned religious.... Now it were to speak of cursed Lollers and untrue, deceiving God....[1]

Elsewhere Purvey complained of the danger of professing Lollardy: a man, he says, may sin grievously, but if he "pay the summoner," he shall be called "a manful man, and profitable to holy Church."

But if a man speak God's word and live thereafter, and faileth not for no persecution ne loss of worldly goods, anon he shall be cursed and put out of the Church, and if he may be caught he shall be burnt as an heretic[2].

The "dialogue between a wise man and a fool" seems to be rather between a faint hearted Lollard, most unwilling to "lose his goods" and adopt the Puritan strictness of the Lollards, and one of sterner metal, who complains of his faintheartedness and finally converts him:

But some say, I pray thee, leave these speeches, and tell me a merry tale of Guy of Warwick, Bevis of Hampton, or of Robin Hood, or of some well faring man, of their conditions and manners.... Let us live as our fathers did, and then good enough; for they were well loved of theaters, wrestlers, buckler-players, of dancers and singers: and they were well willed to have them to the ale: yea, and oft times on Sundays for good fellowship they would dine and drink by night, and go to church after, and so let us do nowadays, and we shall have the blessing of Saint Thomas of Canterbury. Yea, man, and if you have well drunk at home, thy stomach shall wax warm though it be cold weather, and the sweet savour of good ale shall rise into thy brain, and bring thee merry asleep, yea, and though the priest preach then never so false, it shall no more grieve thee than the sound of a mere harp.

Thus the tract, *The Holy Prophet David saith*, and this series of Purvey's, give us the Lollard apologetic for vernacular scriptures down to the writing of the *General Prologue* in 1395. The history of Lollardy between the years 1382, when

---

[1] Ii. 6. 26, p. 116.     [2] *Id.* p. 125.

Wycliffe retired to Lutterworth, and 1408 when his translation was prohibited, was closely bound up with the fortune of Purvey, its leading scholar and probably also its political leader. And throughout that period Purvey gave his labour, to a far greater extent than Wycliffe his master had ever done, to the perfecting and defence of the English Bible.

The first work to be taken in hand was the completion of Hereford's version, broken off at Baruch iii. 20,—that is, with two-thirds of the Bible-and-Apocrypha translated, and Ezekiel, Daniel, the minor prophets, Maccabees and the New Testament as the last third, still left to be done. There is much probability that Wycliffe's secretary was chiefly responsible for the finishing of this first version: and in any case, the Leicester parchemyner was copying the Lollard gospels and epistles by 1384[1]. This points to the completion of the New Testament in that year, or very soon after.

§2. Purvey's next task was one which possibly had been foreseen by the makers of the first translation: the provision of "the doctors'" glosses on part at least of the Bible. Mediaeval opinion demanded it: and when mediaeval opinion was thus satisfied, it might be possible to obtain protection for the book by dedicating it to a royal personage. Purvey took perhaps a year to add a translation of patristic glosses, of portentous length, to each gospel[2]: for he seems to have written the epilogue to the gloss on S. Luke in 1387. If those on Matthew and Mark were written earlier, that on John may have been finished the year after. The epilogue to S. Luke begins:

Therefore a poor caitiff [one of Purvey's usual pseudonyms], letted from preaching for a time for causes known of God, writeth the gospel of Luke in English, with a short exposition of old and holy doctors, to the poor men of his nation, which con little Latin or none, and be poor of wit and of worldly chattels, and nevertheless, rich of good will to please God[3].

---

[1] See p. 232. Till Bodl. 959 is printed, with its dialectal differences, it is not possible to assign any part definitely to Purvey, or even Wycliffe: but the completion of the Bible in that MS., from Baruch iii. 20, has none of those midland or Kentish forms which would be inconsistent with Purvey's authorship.

[2] For the existent MSS. of these glosses, see pp. 256–7.

[3] FM, I. ix. FM believed Wycliffe to have been the author of these glosses on the gospels: but he was never inhibited from preaching, and

This seems to refer to an inhibition from preaching in the diocese of Worcester, which Purvey received in 1387[1]. The bishop's mandate inhibited Nicholas Hereford, John Purvey, John Aston, John Parker and William Swinderby, "who are united in a certain illegal association condemned by the law, by the name or in the rite of the Lollards." Purvey himself was not imprisoned at this time, but he lamented in the epilogue to S. Matthew that other Lollards, continually occupied in studying and teaching of holy writ, were "cursed and forprisoned."

The glosses are founded mainly on the fullest contemporary catena of patristic glosses on the four gospels, the *Catena Aurea* of S. Thomas Aquinas. This is specially the case in the gloss on S. Matthew, where Purvey acknowledged his borrowings from Aquinas in the epilogue. Some of the prologues and epilogues merely discussed authorities, and others lamented the opposition to the spread of holy writ on the part of proud clerks. The glosses are given for almost every word of the text, and are more than ten times as long as the text itself. They are an extraordinary monument of patience and scholarship.

In the epilogues and prologues, which are very similar in matter and style to the *General Prologue*, Purvey described himself by a set of veiled titles, of which the "simple creature of God" of the *General Prologue* is an example. Describing his reasons for entering on the work he says:

"For this cause a sinful caitiff having compassion on lewid men[2]," "this coward sinful caitiff allegeth Jerome on Matthew[3]," "this poor scribbler is not guilty in his conscience that he erred from truth of holy writ and very sentence of these doctors[4]," "this scribbler had travailed with many false books," "this is the desire of this poor scribbler," "therefore a sinful caitiff, letted fro preaching for a time for causes known of God[5]," "this poor caitiff setteth a full sentence of the text together," "therefore a simple creature of God, willing to bear in party the charges of simple poor men, well willing to God's

never made use of the pseudonyms (simple creature, etc., see above), found in the prologues and epilogues to the glosses. That these are genuinely the work of the compiler of the glosses, is shewn by the closeness with which the discussion of authorities and method of translation fits the text of the glosses.

[1] For Lollardy in Bristol, see pp. 357; 379 n. for *Wakefield's Reg.*
[2] Laud Misc. 235, f. 2, col. 1.   [3] *Id.* f. 2, col. 2.
[4] *Id.* f. 264 *b*, col. 1; see p. 457 for next two quotations.
[5] Bodl. 143, f. 3 *b*, col. 2.

cause, setteth a short gloss in English on the gospel of John[1],"
"wherefore a simple creature expoundeth shortly the gloss of Matthew
to lewid men in English tongue[2]."

By the use of these "pseudonyms" Purvey had no serious intention of implying that he was himself unlearned, for he referred continually to the "doctors" he had studied, and in one
case even compared his scholastic equipment not unfavourably
with that of S. Thomas Aquinas:

Whatever doctor or gloss I allege, and tell not specially where, I
take that allegeance[3] of Aquinas on Matthew, for he had many more
originals, both of Greeks and of Latins, than I have now, and I have
many sharp doctors which he had not[4].

In all the prologues and epilogues[5] Purvey set forth his intention, and lamented the opposition to it, in some such words
as those in the epilogue on S. Matthew:

The writer of this gloss purposed to God's honour, and help of
Christian souls, for to tell truly holy writ, and shortly and plainly
the most profitable sentence of these beforesaid doctors: and hitherto,
blessed be God of His great gift and gracious, this poor scribbler is
not guilty in his conscience that he erred from truth of holy writ and
very sentence of these doctors....Alas good spouse of souls, Jesu
Christ: why forsakest thou so much Thy people: that sinful men's
ordinance be openly taught, and maintained by worldly priests and
their fautours: and Thine ordinance, of wilful poverty and great
meekness of clerks, and continual occupation of them in studying
and teaching holy writ, is despised and holden error, and they cursed
and forprisoned that would bring again thy best ordinance[6]!"

Of these prologues and epilogues, one was incorporated by
Purvey or some follower into his set of tracts in defence of
English scriptures, and another by himself into the *General
Prologue*[7].

Meanwhile, under Purvey's leadership, Lollardy continued to
have its representatives at court, among the knights, and among
the poorer classes in the country reached by the travelling
preachers. Personages who were suspected of favouring it, like
Gaunt and to some extent Gloucester, and well-known pro-

---

[1] Bodl. 243, f. 115 *b*, col. 2.
[2] Trin. Camb. 36, f. 7: cf. *Gen. Prol.* cap. xv.
[3] Quotation.         [4] Trin. Camb. 36, f. 7.
[5] See that printed pp. 456–61.     [6] See p. 457.     [7] See pp. 281, 456.

fessors of it, like the earl of Salisbury, and the knights Clifford, Stury, Pecche, Clanvowe, etc., were too powerful to be attacked by the bishops: but in the country districts certain Lollard preachers were tried and forced to recant. At Leicester, William Smith, Wycliffe and Purvey's "parchemyner," did penance in the market place in 1392, and handed over to the archbishop, under compulsion, "the solemn (or well written) books of the gospel and epistles, and other epistles, and doctors in the mother tongue, which he had written, and as he confessed, he had been studiously toiling to write them for eight years[1],"— since 1384, in fact. Such "solemn" books may well have been the fine copies of the Wycliffite scriptures possessed by Gloucester, and probably many of the Lollard knights. The reference to the "doctors" in connexion with the gospels and epistles shews that he had, among other books, copied Purvey's glossed gospels,—the surviving manuscripts of which, especially one which has the text rubricated and written very large, are certainly "solemn" or imposing books.

Through the instrumentality probably of some Lollard at court, these "doctors on the gospels" were presented to the queen. Richard II himself possessed a French Bible[2], according to contemporary custom: but to Anne of Bohemia, who before 1384 read the gospels in Latin, Czech and German[3], French was probably less useful than the language of her adopted country. She was also supposed to be, to some extent, favourable to the Lollards, for her father had founded and encouraged the university of Prague, which gave so favourable a reception to Wycliffe's followers and teaching. Anne died in 1394, and Purvey wrote later[4]:

The bishop of Canterbury, Thomas Arundel, that now is[5], said in a sermon at Westminster, there as were many hundred people, at the burying of queen Anne, of whose soul God have mercy: and in his commending of her, he said it was more joy of her than of any woman that ever he knew, for notwithstanding that she was an alien

[1] FM, I. xxxiii, from Knighton's continuator, the Leicester canon.

[2] Devon, in *Issues of the Exchequer*, 213, calls it a Bible written in the "Gaelic" language, misreading "in idiomate Gallico" (French). Probably it was a *Bible Historiale*.

[3] See p. 248.          [4] See p. 445.

[5] When Purvey wrote, c. 1405: he was archbishop of York in 1394.

born, she had on English all the four gospellers, with the doctors
upon them. And he said she had sent them unto him, and he said
they were good and true, and commended her in that she was so
great a lady, and also an alien, and would so lowlily study in so
virtuous books.

The "four gospellers with the doctors upon them" were certainly Purvey's glosses. There was at the time another set of
English glossed gospels, written in the north midlands[1], but the
description does not fit them with anything of the exactitude it
fits Purvey's. The north midland glosses are throughout a free
comment on the text, in the author's own words: while Purvey's
are exact translations from passages of the "doctors," and as
such he frequently speaks of them in his prologues[2]. Anne sent
them to Arundel for approbation, according to mediaeval
custom: and it is of interest that he thus publicly approved them.
It is most unlikely the copies presented to her contained any
Lollard prologue or epilogue, but it is almost certain that the
gloss on Matthew contained one heretical passage[3]. This however was embedded, without title or marking, in the middle of

---

[1] See p. 310. The translator in the prologue states that he is going to
set forth the "saws of doctors" and not his own opinions, but no references
or doctors' names are given in the text itself, as in the Lollard glosses.

[2] The epilogue to Matthew begins: "Here endeth a short gloss on Matthew
which [is] taken of holy doctors, Jerome, Austin, Ambrose, Gregory,
Bernard, Chrysostom, Grosthead, Rabanus, and other more." The epilogue
to John has: "Some suppose that Parisiensis made this treatise, but I
am not certain thereof; nevertheless, whoever made it, it seemeth that he
allegeth well holy scripture, reason and holy doctors, and this sufficeth
enow to reasonable men"; Lord Dillon's MS. f. 59 b, col. 1. The prologue
to Luke has "he setteth a full sentence of the text together, that it well
may be known from the exposition, afterward he setteth a sentence of
a doctor declaring the text, and in the end of the sentence he setteth the
doctor's name, that men may know how far his sentence goeth. Only the
text of holy writ, and sentence of old doctors and approved, been set in
this exposition." See also p. 458.

[3] The gloss on Luke xvii. 19 has one long heretical digression, which
appears to be original and not an insertion because (a) it arises out of the
subject which is being glossed in the ordinary course, (b) it occurs in all
three of the MSS. in which we possess this gloss (see p. 456). After the
glosses on the healing of the ten lepers, Luke xvii. 19, *thy faith hath made
thee safe*, a long digression on the healing of the leper, and repentance
through faith alone, without confession, is inserted without special marking
or rubric, Kk. 2. 9, ff. 202 b, col. 2—208 b, col. 2. The passage occurs in
Bodl. 143, as can be seen by the beginning, and the marginal references
to authorities: but two folios of the heretical matter, ff. 159 b and 160,
have the text carefully erased with pumice stone. This MS. must have
belonged to an orthodox fifteenth century owner, who wrote on the outside

a very long and cumbrous book, or books, and it is very unlikely that either Anne or Arundel ever discovered it. There is nothing remarkable either in Arundel's praise of a work he probably knew to be Purvey's, for it was episcopal policy to try to win over the scholarly Lollards by argument and benignancy: Hereford had been so won over by 1393. Nor was it contrary to mediaeval consistency to praise a queen for reading the gospels in the vernacular, while two years earlier the scribe who probably wrote her very books was punished as a Lollard. A princess who read the Latin text could certainly, with license, read the English gospels, with the doctors' exposition on them: for a professional scribe, or middle class Lollard, to use the bare text at will was a different matter.

Anne may have had the glossed gospels earlier than 1394, if Purvey finished them by about 1390[1]. Meanwhile, he had already begun another task[2], that described in the *General Prologue* as making the translation of the Bible "as open or openlier in English as it is in Latin." The need of producing a version which could be quoted to the unlearned, and memorised, was now obvious, and Purvey substantially completed it in 1395. Judging by the time needed for such a work, he probably began it when he finished the glosses, 1388–90: but he may, of course, have carried on the two works simultaneously. For the glosses he had used the first or literal translation[1]: and the second version of the Bible which he now made was founded closely upon the first. This he described in the *General Prologue* as "the English Bible late translated," naturally without going

folio, now f. 222 *b*, "Opus fratris Thomae de Aquino a doctoribus diversis extractum et translatum in linguam maternam." Bodl. 243 has the heretical passage on ff. 82–84.

[1] FM, I. viii conjectures that the glossed gospels may have been produced earlier than the EV itself: this cannot be finally decided till the text of the EV is re-edited and compared with that of the glosses: but it is most unlikely, (1) because so large a compilation as the glossed gospels, which is not merely the translation of one Latin gloss, must have taken 4 or 5 years, and this earlier than the making of the EV, which was c. 1380–4! The time-schedule of Wycliffe's Latin works has been so closely worked out by the Rev. H. S. Cronin for a forthcoming book, that it is seen to be practically impossible for Wycliffe or his secretary to have accomplished the glosses before 1380, and the references to Bible reading in Wycliffe's work do not support it. (2) The epilogue to the gloss on Luke strongly points to 1387 as the date of writing.

[2] See p. 258.

more closely into its origin[1]. After he had completed the making of this second version, he wrote a very long prologue to the Old Testament,—the part he was perhaps latest in completing,— the *General Prologue* which has been described elsewhere[2]. Like his prologues and epilogues to the glossed gospels, it contained all the notes on authorities and method which as a scholar he wished to prefix to his work, and it was also the culmination of his series of sermons in defence of English scriptures. While Purvey was writing the tract, and when, after describing the contents of each book of the Old Testament, he was intending to quote from the fathers explanations of the interpretations of scripture, he found himself without the books he needed[3]. He had by him his own prologue to the gloss on S. Matthew, which contained a series of quotations from the *De Doctrina Christiana* of S. Augustine, dealing with the interpretation of scripture. He therefore paraphrased his own translation of the *De Doctrina Christiana*, keeping the order of the passages exactly, but supplying sentences in between, so that nearly the whole of the long prologue[4] was finally embedded.

§ 3. The unexpected death of Anne, for she was only twenty-eight, was a blow to the political hopes of the Lollards: and probably the immunity of the greater Lollards, and the attacks upon the lower, inspired them in an attempt they now made to place their case before parliament. Richard was desolate at the queen's loss, and at her funeral[5] quarrelled with archbishop

---

[1] The writer of the article on *Versions of the Bible, English,* in CE is thus right in dating the glosses as posterior to the EV, but his statement that "the style of the text of the commentary resembles that of the later version rather than the early version," is unjustified. The gospel text does not "resemble" either, but is that of the EV, from a comparison of all the MSS. of the glossed gospels with the EV as printed in FM. If, as the writer implies, certain short biblical verses quoted in the gloss itself "resemble" the LV rather than the EV, that is probably because the editor was here translating at sight, without the need to construe: or quite possibly the making of the LV of the gospels was contemporary with that of the glosses, while the LV of the rest of the Bible was not finished till c. 1395. See appendix, date of LV, pp. 374, 381.

[2] pp. 258–66.    [3] See p. 265.

[4] Laud Misc. 235, f. 1: *Saint Austin saith in the second book of Christian doctrine*...abate soon antichrist's malice, hypocrisy and tyranny; in Harl. 6333, a fifteenth century MS., the scribe has omitted the last, violently Lollard, paragraphs, and then copied the Lollard *Unum ex Quattuor,* etc. See *infra,* p. 303.    [5] 4 Aug. 1394.

Arundel's brother; in December, 1394[1], he sailed for Ireland, and Purvey and the London Lollards thought the time favourable for their attempt. They were sure of some support from the anti-clericals, who desired the confiscation of clerical revenues. Purvey and his friends,—perhaps the Lollard knights who came to London for the parliament,—used a Latin tract of Purvey's, setting forth the opinions of the Lollards under thirty-seven conclusions, and made an expanded and more violent English translation of it, for propaganda purposes[2]. The duke of York presided over parliament, which sat from 27 Jan. till 15 Feb., and in this parliament the Lollard knights, probably with Stury as their spokesman, read a violent document called the *Twelve Conclusions of the Lollards*. This pamphlet recommended those who wished for further information, to seek it in the *Thirty-Seven Conclusions*, which set forth the matter more at large. The Lollards seemed so politically strong that great fear and indignation was aroused among the clerical party, and it was probably now, and in this parliament[3], that a countermeasure was taken: Purvey, whose tale there is no reason to doubt, says that:

It is known to many men, that in the time of king Richard, whose soul may God assoil, into parliament was put a bill,...to annul the Bible that time translated into English, and also other books of the gospel translated into English; which when it was seen of lords and commons, the good duke of Lancaster, John, whose soul God assoil for His mercy, answered thereto sharply, saying this sentence: "We will not be refuse of all men, for sithen other nations have God's law, which is law of our belief, in their own mother language, we will have ours in English, who that ever it begrudgeth." And this he affirmed with a great oath[4].

Probably the violent nature of the Lollard attack had occasioned the change in episcopal, or at least in Arundel's, opinion about the English Bible, and the "other books of the gospel

---

[1] Walsingham, RS, II. 216.    [2] See pp. 375, 379.

[3] The lines following refer to Arundel as chancellor: he resigned the chancery in 1396. It is unlikely that this bill was introduced before Arundel's sermon at Anne's funeral, Aug. 1394: and the only parliament between that and Arundel's resignation of the chancery was this parliament of 1395. The next was Jan.–Feb. 1397; cf. p. 297, n. 4.

[4] See p. 444. For the parliament of 1395, see p. 374; for suppression of scripture-reading London Lollards in 1392, VCH, *London*, I. 218.

translated into English,"—probably the very glosses Arundel
had approved in his sermon six months earlier. Neither the
Lollard *Twelve Conclusions*, nor the bill against translations, received sufficient support from lords or commons to be redrafted
by the royal lawyers, and enrolled on the parliament rolls,
awaiting the royal assent[1]. But the agitation among the clericals
was so great, that archbishop Arundel and the bishop of London
sailed in haste to Ireland, taking with them the *Twelve Conclusions*, and a long Latin answer to each, written by Roger
Dymok, a monk[2]. Richard relinquished his Irish campaign, and
returned and lectured his Lollard courtiers, even taking an oath
of sir Richard Stury the privy councillor to abjure his opinions,
threatening him with a most shameful death if he refused. The
greatest political effort of the Lollards had failed for the time
being: and Purvey returned to the finishing off of the *General
Prologue*, speaking in a digression of this "last parliament," and
transcribing a passage of particular violence[3] from the *Thirty-
Seven Conclusions*. The later version of the Bible had been
practically[4] complete before: and we have a manuscript of
this New Testament dated 1397[5].

§ 4. Between 1395 and 1401 nothing is known of Purvey,
though he probably still made London his headquarters. Gaunt
died in 1399, and the house of Lancaster succeeded Richard II,
but with no favourable results to the Lollards. On May 12,
1400, Henry IV sent a letter to the sheriffs of London, directing
their enforcement of the law that no chaplain, or unbeneficed
priest, should preach without the license of the diocesan: and
certain secular priests of London sent a petition to the king
against the aforesaid letter[6]. This year too saw the burning of
Sawtre, the first Lollard martyr. It was probably on account
of the increased vigilance in London against Lollard preachers,
that Purvey himself was taken and imprisoned, pending trial,
in Saltwood Castle; his trial in London indicates, in lack of

---

[1] See p. 297, n. 4.
[2] Printed EHR, XXII. 292; cf. *id*. XXVI. 738.
[3] See p. 257 n.
[4] But for the translation of certain short prologues from the Vulgate,
see p. 377.
[5] See p. 381.
[6] Digby MS. 98, f. 179 *b*.

other evidence, that he was taken in that diocese[1]. He was cited
for various heresies and errors in the chapter house of S. Paul's
the last day of February, 1401, and he read a recantation of them
at Paul's Cross on March 6th. Lollardy lost its most able
champion. Thorpe the Lollard attributed the recantation to the
horrors Purvey had undergone in Saltwood Castle[2], and the
burning of Sawtre the year before had been enough to make
him shrink. But there was probably another reason which made
constancy like Sawtre's impossible for him: his scholarship and
breadth of view. He belonged properly to the earlier generation
of Lollards under Wycliffe[3], all of whom had submitted to
clerical censure or withdrawn their opinions; and, like Cranmer
later, he was afflicted with a capacity for seeing both sides of
the question. His recantation now, and indecision later, are
illustrated in a tract written later, the *Sixteen Points putten by
bishops ordinarily upon men which they clepen Lollards*[4]. The
Lollards in 1388–9 had described in Latin and English tracts
twenty-five articles falsely attributed to them: Purvey's English
tract is a similar defence against misstatement and misrepre-
sentation. The tract dealt with the Lollard attitude to the
sacrament of the altar, penance, tithes, the pope, images, pardons, etc., and in all of these matters Purvey pursued a *via media*,
noticeable in contrast to the views of the leading Lollards after
1400. After recounting the sixteen disputed points, Purvey says:

> Whoever shall say these sixteen points, be he well ware that in
> every of them is hid truth and falsehood, and who that ever granteth
> all, granteth much falsehood: and who that ever denieth all, denieth
> many truths.... True Christian men should answer advisedly, truly

[1] There is no evidence for any imprisonment of Purvey before this date:
so prominent a Lollard would hardly have been kept in prison indefinitely
without trial, and he was not tried as a lapsed heretic in 1401. The reputed
imprisonment in 1396 (see FM, I. xxiv n. 4, and DNB) rests upon a
mistaken marginal note of bishop Bale in his MS. of the FZ, where he
dated Purvey's confession as 1396 (FZ, 407). Foxe used this MS., and
perpetuated the error, stating that the MS. was itself dated 1396, whereas
it was actually dated 1439 (FZ, ix n. 1, *Hen. IV.* III. 312).

[2] Pollard, 165.

[3] The contrast between the character and views of the first and second
generation of Lollards is well brought out by A. Dakin in *Die Beziehungen
John Wiclifs und der Lollarden zu den Bettelmönchen*, Kingsgate Press,
1911, 68.

[4] Printed pp. 462–5, and see for evidence of authorship p. 461.

and meekly to the points and articles that been put against them[1]....
Christian men should believe that the sacrament on the altar is verily
Christ's body sacramentally and spiritually[2], and more other manners
than any earthly man can tell among us; for Christ, that may not
lie, said, shewing the bread that He held in His hand: This is my
body....Also we grant that shrift of mouth is needful to all such
that been counselled of God for to make it meekly....We suppose
there have been many holy fathers popes sithen saint Peter's time,
(though this name Pope be not said in God's law),...and so we
grant that the pope of Rome should next follow Christ and saint
Peter in manner of living, and if he do so, he is worthily Pope, and
if he contrary him most of all others, he is most antichrist.

Similarly, it is allowed that tithes are sometimes lawful, that
pardons and indulgences grounded in holy writ may be granted,
that laymen of good lives are not priests of office, but only
spiritually, that the pope may make laws, and bishops have
temporal goods in reasonable measure. In the question whether
the chief office of priests is to preach or to minister the sacraments, it is noticeable that Purvey's dictum interjects a demand
for the translation of the gospel and epistle at mass, or at least
their explanation in a sermon.

Also, we grant that priests were ordained of Christ to teach and
preach the people, and not only that, but also to pray, and to minister
the sacraments of God and live well. And of good ordinance of Holy
Church they be ordained by men to say both mattins and masses,
in which be contained both gospel and pistle, and other books of
holy writ, for that end that they should after their reading declare
it to the people *in their mother tongue*.

This tract has been quoted as throwing light upon Purvey's
recantation, orthodoxy, and subsequent relapse. This expression
of his mind, not put forward upon pressure like the articles he
had to retract at Paul's Cross, explains Thorpe's cry: "John
Purvey is neither hot nor cold," and Arundel's anger against
him as a "false harlot:...but come he more for such cause before
me, ere we depart, I shall know with whom he holdeth[3]."

---

[1] Cf. Purvey's adjuration to meekness, p. 265.
[2] Lewis (as he says in Rawl. C. 11, p. 1), copied some of this tract from a
MS. written, he thought, in Henry VI's reign. He did not copy Trin. 333:
and he inverted this clause, putting it "The bread or the host...is not very
God's body."
[3] Pollard, 118.

§ 5. A few other references to the Wycliffite translations, not specially connected with Purvey's career, have come down to us for this period of 1382–1401.

William Swinderby, the hermit of the Lollard school at the chapel of S. John Baptist, Leicester, after a trial for heresy at Leicester, was tried by bishop Trevenant at Hereford in June 1389[1]. The prologue to the account of his trial mentions as the Lollards' greatest offence, their unlicensed preaching, and insistence on the literal interpretation of scripture: "they explain holy scripture to the people literally, in the new-fangled way, otherwise than as the Holy Spirit teaches." There is no reference to translations at his trial, but these words shew the value attached by the Lollards to the text of scripture, as do all other Lollard trials.

That of Walter Brute (or, the Welshman) at Hereford is of great interest for the history of Nicholas Hereford and the early version of the Wycliffite Bible. Trevenant's register describes him as a "litterate layman[2]," and the long written defence he submitted to the bishop shews a good deal of learning[3]. He finally made his submission on Oct. 3, 1393, and the masters of theology before whom he made it included his old leader, Nicholas Hereford[4]. This filled him with such bitterness that he wrote a tract to Hereford, upbraiding him as a traitor and a deserter[5], and making a pointed reference to Hereford's earlier share in the translation of the Bible. The tract begins by arguing that, since no man putting his hand to the plough and looking back is fit for the kingdom of God, and since by the kingdom of God is understood, the knowledge of holy scripture:

[1] *Reg. Johannis Trefnant, ep. Herefordensis* 1389–1404, Capes, W. W., CYS, xx. 231 ff.

[2] *Id.* 278.

[3] Gairdner, I. 38. It is not impossible that he had some share in the translation of the EV: but there is no evidence for his residence at Oxford about 1382.

[4] FM, I. xvii; for Hereford's fierce Lollardy, see Walsingham, II. 159.

[5] See *Reg.* 394–8. The name of the author of the tract is not given in the register, but it is copied in in connexion with the trials of Swinderby and Brute (together with another written in Nicholas Hereford's defence). The author of the tract is alluded to as the "master of the heretic Swinderby, and of other Lollards," p. 398, and it is suggested that it is due to his persuasions that Swinderby has relapsed after his recantation at Lincoln. This points to Brute as the author of the tract upbraiding Hereford.

how can Nicholas Hereford be fit for the kingdom of God, since
he has looked back after putting his hand to the plough, "that
is, to the sowing of the word of God and holy scripture,...as
well by preaching as by affording an example of good works:
nay more, by making clear the knowledge of holy scripture[1]"?
The tract continues with a punning and bitter reference to
Nicholas Hereford and the Nicolaitans, since Nicholas has
"left the infallible knowledge of holy scripture," and no longer
enters into the ground of truth by the exposition of the gospel:
neither does he enter into that knowledge himself, nor suffer
others to enter into it[2].

The tract is followed in the register by a defence of Hereford,
in his name and person, by Thomas Palmer. This friar belonged
to the Dominican house of Holborn, or Blackfriars, the scene of
so many prominent Lollard trials. He wrote many theological[3]
works, and took part in the trial of Oldcastle in 1412[4]. Palmer
began by stating that the Lollard's attack on Hereford has been
sent on to him[5], and that he will answer it in the person of
Hereford, who has been accused of putting his hand to the
plough, and looking back.

The doctrine of S. Gregory shews that a man may lawfully and
unlawfully look back after he has put his hand to the plough:...for
I, after I had put my hand to the plough, looked back lawfully, by
correcting the errors which I had committed by so ploughing.

He then answered the four conclusions put forward by the
Lollard, the first of which is significant in connexion with
Hereford's share in making known the literal text of the Bible
by a translation. The conclusion is that the words of the first
four doctors expounding holy scripture according to the obvious
meaning are without exception true: Palmer answered that the

---

[1] *Reg.* 394. The final sentence cannot refer merely to preaching, for that
is mentioned earlier.

[2] The tract is long and wrangling, and seems to embody arguments delivered verbally between Brute and Hereford, at the trial of the former.

[3] Quoted by Bale, etc. Boston of Bury's list of Westminster MSS. included No 15, a determination of Thomas Palmer, friar preacher, "in
materia scismatis," *Westminster*, 23; cf. p. 293.

[4] AM. III. 334. Foxe wrongly calls him "warden of the Minors," III. 329.
Foxe quotes the letter against Hereford, III. 190, but not Palmer's answer
to it.

[5] *Reg.* 396.

words of holy scripture are to be expounded "sometimes morally, sometimes allegorically, and sometimes anagogically, and not according to the literal meaning of the words,—as in the biblical poems, which in no case are to be interpreted as literally true."

In 1397, again, there is another reference in Trevenant's register to the Lollard translation of the "bare text" of scripture. King Richard, who had busied himself on his return from Ireland with the unorthodoxy of the Lollard knights, wrote to the bishop, enclosing to him a copy of renunciation of heretical opinions by John Croft, a Herefordshire squire, and all his family. Croft swore, apparently at the king's request, that he would never in future read or preach, publicly or secretly, any new doctrine contrary to the catholic faith, nor read or own

English books extracted from holy scripture according to the bare text, with evil intent, by certain persons commonly called Lollards, who oppose the catholic faith and the doctrine of the Roman church. These men try not only to infatuate our simplicity, but make perverse people obstinately to transgress from the wholesome and true understanding of holy scripture and evangelical doctrine and the orthodox faith[1].

This passage shews that Croft and his family had been using the unglossed Lollard Bible, or parts of it, and shews once more the orthodox objection to placing the "bare text" in the hands of laymen. It is noticeable, however, that while Smith at Leicester in 1392, and Croft at Hereford in 1397, were being forbidden the use of English scriptures, Thomas duke of Gloucester died in 1397 possessing a copy of the early version of the Bible[2], and bequeathed it without remark. In 1394 also, John Hopton, a chantry priest of York, bequeathed to the chantry "a book of the gospels in English[3],"—most probably the Lollard gospels. It is just possible that the book was actually the northern *temporale*, or verse gospels and homilies, or the homilies known as the *Mirrur*, or again that it was the north midland glossed gospels described later. According to the custom of wills

---

[1] "Neque libros Anglicos secundum nudum textum de sacra scriptura sinistre extractos per quosdam Lollardos," etc., 148.

[2] *Brit. Mus. Class. Cat. of MSS.*, English Bibles.

[3] TE, i. 196; he was chaplain of the chantry of S. Nicholas in the church of Holy Trinity, Gotheromgate. For partial biblical translations contemporary with the Lollard versions, see pp. 298–318.

of the period, however, the word "gloss" or "rhyme" would usually, in that case, have been inserted. Quite possibly it was a book of liturgical gospels[1], based on the Lollard text. The last case of the bequest of English scriptures before 1408[2] is that of the Wykehamist, John Bount, burgess of Bristol, who in 1404 bequeathed to John Canterbury a "book of the gospels in English, now in the keeping of William Stourton." John Bount seems to have been quite orthodox, judging from his will: yet his possession of English scriptures may not have been unconnected with the preaching of Lollardy in Bristol, which a contemporary ranked with London as a "specially corrupt Lollard centre[3]."

§ 6.  To return to the last phase of Purvey's career, between 1401 and 1408, after which he relapsed into obscurity. He recanted in March 1401, and in August was inducted to the vicarage of West Hythe, "not a mile," as Arundel said, "from Saltwood Castle," where the archbishop could keep a watchful eye upon him. In 1403 he resigned the living, and seems for a time to have led a life which pleased neither the Lollards nor Arundel. Thorpe's interview with Arundel in 1407 shews that Purvey was not then openly professing Lollardy: Arundel shews that his actions or mode of life was in some way highly displeasing to him. He seems to have spent his time between Oxford and London, making fresh efforts in the defence of English Bibles, and stirring up afresh the controversy which had so long raged, in which the friars had taken so large a part.

In 1401 William Butler, a regent (or officially lecturing) master of the Franciscans at Oxford, and later their warden[4], had read a long determination against the lawfulness of any translation of the Bible into the vernacular. The occasion of his action is obscure[5]: but it was in accordance with the consistent

---

[1] See pp. 39, 285.

[2] Till 1408 there was no obstacle to priests or substantial laymen owning English scriptures. Bount left bequests to both Winchester and his Oxford college: see *Great Orphan Book*, ed. Wadley, T. P., 1886, 73.

[3] *Chron. Adae de Usk*, ed. Maunde Thompson, 3; note also Purvey's preaching there, and the Bristol Carmelite Lavenham's familiarity with his errors; for pro-English-Bible agitation in London, 1401, see p. 297.

[4] He was probably elected warden of the Oxford minorites in 1406, though his tenure of that office was reckoned from 1408, cf. *Grey friars in Oxford*, Little, A. G., 254.     [5] See Bale, 1557, *Script. Cat.* p. 536.

attitude of the English friars. His determination was opposed, not to the Wycliffite translations in particular, but to the lawfulness of any translation: its views are utterly opposed to those, for instance, of sir Thomas More later. He took his stand on the broad grounds of the difficulty of translation, and of securing the circulation of correct English texts, and the providential dispensation of the inferiority of the laity: it was no business of the lay folk to read the Bible, and the human intellect, unassisted by the grace of priesthood, was insufficient for it. The earthly hierarchy should be an image of the heavenly, where grace was mediated from the higher to the lower orders. The gospel was not at first given in writing, and the subtlety of the scripture was still too great for it to be read in translations. The determination was based on general principles, not on minor quibbles concerning the interpretation of biblical texts; and it shews great learning in the authorities cited. It is noticeable that friar Butler did not quote Innocent III's letter to Metz, though he quoted from one of Innocent II to S. Bernard on the subject of the heretics Abelard and Arnold of Brescia. Probably he was unaware of the Metz letter; for none of the three English determinations given at Oxford about this time made any use of it. The friars at Oxford had certainly been attacking the Wycliffites on the score of translations before this; but this tract of 1401 is the first which has come down to us[1]. Butler read the determination openly in the schools: but there is no evidence in this case that any other doctor "determined against him."

Before the year 1405 a great debate on the lawfulness of vernacular Bibles was also held at Oxford, between a regent master with strong Lollard sympathies, and the before-mentioned friar Thomas Palmer. There is much reason to believe that the Lollard doctor was Peter Payne, or Peter the Clerk, and that he was stirred up to engage in the debate by Purvey himself, who composed Latin and English records of the debate afterwards, adding arguments of his own. In the Latin version of Purvey's tract *De Versione Bibliorum* he said that the subject debated was:

---

[1] Printed *infra*, pp. 401-18, from Merton 68, "Butler: contra translationem Anglicanam."

Whether, since it was lawful for S. Jerome to translate the sacred canon from Hebrew and Greek into Latin, it is in like manner lawful to translate it into other tongues, less principal and less beautiful? And though in the time of our forefathers this point was never in doubt, now indeed so great a dispute has arisen about it, that two weighty doctors of this university have been spending the whole time of their lectures upon this question. One of them contended by certain arguments for the negative answer to this question, and the other, after him, contended for the affirmative answer, by I know not how many powerful arguments. Neither, however, disclosed to the school what he wished finally to define in the matter. First then I shall recite some arguments from the first doctor, and shall add some more of my own in favour of a negative answer to the article. And thirdly, I shall according to my ability, answer the arguments which are made against the article[1].

The doctor to whom Purvey thus had recourse to defend English Bibles in the schools must almost certainly have been Peter Payne, whom contemporaries mention as the only daring Oxford Lollard at the date[2], though even he could not openly profess his views. He was born about 1380, and introduced at Oxford to the doctrines of Wycliffe, of whom he became a great admirer. He became a regent master of theology shortly before

---

[1] Long quotations from the *De Ver. Bib.* are given in Denis, I. I, col. 842, MS. CCXLIV, f. 195, sufficient to identify the tract with the English version, *Against them that say that holy writ should not or may not be drawn into English*, of Trin. Camb. 333, f. 26, printed *infra*. The reasons for identifying the author of the tract with Purvey are (1) his long anterior connexion with the defence of English Bibles, (2) his secret incitement of the debate would explain Arundel's and Thorpe's attitude to him in 1407, (3) the literary style, fondness of historical precedent, and dialect of the English version is altogether consistent with the same authorship as the *Gen. Prol.* and the epilogues to the Lollard glosses, (4) the English version in the unique MS. immediately precedes the *Sixteen Points*, which there is independent reason for attributing to Purvey, (5) in the Latin version, which has a prologue not found in the English, the author is shewn to be a Lollard scholar (who calls the enemies of English Bibles "antichrist"), and he says he "is fighting alone for the defence of English Bibles." At the date, shewn by references in the Latin version to be between 1399 and 1405, the author could scarcely have been any other doctor than Purvey: his very ignoring of the doctor who actually debated for translations implies both that his own inspiration was behind, and that the debating doctor was not a man of greater status than himself,—though a regent master. Purvey could not have debated himself, as he was not regularly lecturing at Oxford, as both disputants were. (6) The writer of the tract alleges a rarely quoted passage from Fitz Ralph's *De Quaestionibus Armenorum*, in favour of vernacular masses, which Purvey had already dwelt on in his defence of English scriptures. "Also Ardmakan in the *Book of Questions* saith that the sacrament may well be made in each common language: for so, he said, did the apostles," see *supra*, p. 142.　　　　[2] *Doct.* I. 8.

Oct. 5, 1406, and according to Gascoign, it was he who stole the
university seal, and affixed it to the famous spurious letter of
the university in praise of Wycliffe, of that date. He seems to
have defended Wycliffe's teaching as far as he dared, and for a
time avoided punishment, though not suspicion. Thorpe stated
that this "Clerk of Oxford" preached a Lollard sermon at Paul's
Cross in 1407, which a certain "clerk Alkerton" attacked in a
sermon following, at which Thorpe himself was present.

"His sermon was false," said one of Arundel's clerks, "and that
he sheweth openly, since he dared not stand forth and defend his
preaching, that he then preached there." "Sir," answered Thorpe,
"I think that he purposeth to stand steadfastly therein, or else he
slandereth foully himself and many others, that have great trust that
he will stand by the truth of the gospel. For I wot well his sermon
is written both in Latin and in English; and many men have it, and
they set great price thereby. And Sir, if ye were present with the
Archbishop at Lambeth, when this Clerk appeared, and were at his
answer before the Archbishop: ye wot well that this Clerk denied
not there his sermon; but two days he maintained it before the
Archbishop and his Clerks." "That harlot" said Arundel, "shall be
met with, for that sermon. For no man but he, and thou, and such
other false harlots, praiseth any such preaching[1]."

About this time also Peter Payne was incited by "a certain
nobleman to debate at Oxford about pilgrimages, the Eucharist," etc., with the friars, Walden and Befusis, who claimed that
"we came: we were there: but before we had even shaken hands,
Peter the Clerk disappeared, overcome with fear[2],"—probably
of physical, not intellectual danger. This abortive debate was
a parallel with that held with the Dominican Palmer, on what
was, in 1405, a less dangerous subject. Peter Payne became
principal of S. Edmund's Hall in 1410, and retained that office
till 1414, during Oldcastle's rebellion: but in 1415 he was so
vehemently suspected of heretical pravity, that he thought it
advisable to flee to the Wycliffite university of Prague, where he
was made M.A. and had a long and prominent career[3]. The fact
that he was a regent master at the date of the debate, and the
circumstances of his career compared with what is known of
Lollardy at the date, render it practically certain that it was he
who thus championed English Bibles in the schools.

[1] Pollard, 159.          [2] *Doct.* I. 8.
[3] His flight explains the existence of the *De Ver. Bib.* in a unique Vienna MS.

His adversary Palmer had, as has been seen, undertaken earlier the defence of Nicholas Hereford. We have a record of the debate compiled from his side[1], as well as those from the Lollards': it is in Latin, and sets forward first the Lollard arguments, then at much greater length, Palmer's; then the rejoinder, and then Palmer's counter-rejoinder. Palmer set forth as firmly as Butler the unlawfulness of making any translation whatever of the Vulgate; but his arguments, though based chiefly on the inherent inferiority of the laity and their inability to profit by Bible reading, are much less imposing than Butler's. They are longer, more quibbling, subtler, and often based on arbitrary interpretations of biblical texts. His favourites are "Cast not pearls before swine": "And it was said: Write it not," though he uses others much less familiar. The arguments of Palmer's opponent, as stated in his tract, do not coincide exactly with those brought forward by Purvey in the *De Versione Bibliorum*: but, on the other hand, Purvey's tract does not profess to be, like Palmer's, an exact record of the debate: it is the compilation of a scholar who had listened to " I know not how many powerful arguments," and then composed his own treatise. In some cases the arguments in Palmer's and Purvey's tracts are the same. In both, the vernacular defender argued that the law of Moses was recited in the ears of the people (Deut. xxxi.); the apostles were unlettered men, but knew the scriptures; the gift of tongues was given at Pentecost that men of all nations might know the new law; S. Jerome translated the Vulgate; Bede translated the Vulgate into English[2]. Purvey, however, alleged many more English historical precedents than his opponent answered in his treatise. It is so unlikely that two such protracted debates took place, that Palmer was almost certainly Peter Payne's opponent: but each writer on the debate seems to have digested his opponent's arguments somewhat freely.

Purvey's tract gives several points of historical interest. He

[1] See pp. 418–37.
[2] There is, however, no exact correspondence in the arrangement of the points. The chief weight of Purvey's tract lay in the variety of precedent he brought forward: while Palmer's report of the Lollard arguments opposed to him makes it appear that they relied chiefly on a logical proposition: if the faithful are bound to carry out God's law, they must be allowed to familiarise themselves with the book in which it is written.

mentioned that a Fleming, James Merland, "translated the whole
Bible into Flemish," referring of course to the version of Peter
Comestor; that Anglo-Saxon scriptures "be in many abbeys of
England," and that a London man had an English Bible "of
northern speech, and it seemed two hundred years old,"—a
reference, no doubt, to some late Saxon manuscript of the
gospels. He recounted Arundel's sermon at queen Anne's
funeral, and the introduction of the bill against the English
Bible into parliament. He also referred to another Dominican,
who took part in the various heresy trials of the day, and
became superior of Blackfriars in London,—friar John Tille.

"But friar Tille," he says, "that said before the bishop of London,
hearing an hundred men, that Jerome said he erred in translating
of the Bible,—is like to Elymas, the which would have letted a
bishop, or a judge, to hear of the belief, to whom Paul said: O thou
full of all treachery, and of all false teaching, to turn the bishop from
the belief."

Friar John Tille, or Tylle[1], must have preached a sermon against
translations of the Bible at Paul's Cross: and the incident shews
again the hostility of the friars,—in London, as in Zutphen, to
biblical translations.

The result of the wranglings of these two weighty doctors at
Oxford was increased private debating on the subject. "The
very cooks who sod the pottage made good their claim to read
the Bible in Wycliffe's English[2]," and the result was so offensive
to Arundel, that he resolved to put a stop to it.

§ 7.   There was still feeling at Oxford against episcopal inter-
ferences with the rights of the university: Wycliffe's books still
existed in considerable numbers: heretics from Prague came to

[1] Archbishop Chichele wrote to Henry V, 16 Feb. 1418, about the king's
request for a confessor to be sent to him, and about whom he had asked his
messenger to confer with Thomas Fishbourne (see p. 341); Fishbourne had
recommended Thomas Dyss, a friar preacher of Cambridge, "a good man
and sufficient therto,...and a spiritual, and plain to you without fantasy":
and Fishbourne and the archbishop had conferred with "friar John Tylle,"
the provincial of the friars preacher, and obtained his leave to send Thomas
Dyss to the king; *Orig. Letters*, Ellis, H., 1824, Ser. I. i. 4. He had probably
been provincial as early as 1400-1404: see Little, A. G., in EHR, XXXIII.
497. Foxe, AM, III. 583, states that in 1423 John Tylle was one of the four
friars who tried the Lollard, William Taylor; Ussher, XII. 353 calls him
"quidem fraterculus Scillius." See *infra*, p. 443.

[2] *Hen. IV*, III. 433.

Oxford to study them[1], and though a certain testimonial of the university sent to the archbishop on behalf of Wycliffe is now believed to be a forgery, reverence still existed for his intellectual greatness. Walden states that the Lollards still incited the faithful to read Wycliffe's works: "Oh," they say, "but he said many beautiful things,—many useful things. Not all of them were condemned." They asked how particular Lollards could be heretics: "O that man," they say, "how can *he* be a heretic? He preaches holily, he rebukes vices, he busies himself with holy scripture, he proclaims Christ[2]." Above all, Arundel knew that discussion was proceeding at Oxford as to the Lollard tenets, and that laymen and the unlearned were beginning to be familiar with the idea that they could support their private opinions by an appeal to the text of holy scripture; and that it was still contended in the schools that such an appeal was lawful. He therefore went to Oxford, and summoned a synod of clergy in November 1407, to settle particularly the question of English Bibles and English propagandist tracts.

The provincial council of Oxford passed thirteen constitutions dealing with Lollardy[3]. The first reiterated prohibitions against unlicensed preaching, "either in Latin or in the vulgar tongue," and, moreover, limited the subjects of the sermons of parish priests, and other licensed persons, to those enumerated in Peckham's constitution of 1281, the *Ignorancia Sacerdotum*.

By constitution V, no master of arts, or grammar master, was in future to meddle with the sacraments, or any other theological matter when instructing boys or other persons: nor was he to explain holy scripture, except by explaining the text grammatically, according to the good and ancient custom. No one was to read "any tract of John Wycliffe, or any other tract made in his time, or composed more recently, or any that shall be composed," unless it were examined by the university of Oxford or Cambridge.

Constitution VII is headed: That no one shall translate texts of holy scripture into the English tongue. It is the passage which misled sir Thomas More in his theory of the existence of pre-Wycliffite English bibles, and reads:

---

[1] Jerome of Prague, 1401–2; George of Knychnicz and Faulfisch in 1407, see p. 240.　　[2] *Doct.* I. 19, 20.　　[3] Wilkins, III. 314–19.

Also, since it is dangerous, as S. Jerome witnesses, to translate the text of holy scripture from one language into another, because in such translations the same meaning is not easily retained in all particulars: even as S. Jerome, although he was inspired, confessed that he had often erred in this matter: therefore we decree and ordain that no one shall in future translate on his own authority any text of holy scripture into the English tongue or into any other tongue, by way of book, booklet, or treatise. Nor shall any man read this kind of book, booklet or treatise, now recently composed in the time of the said John Wycliffe, or later, or any that shall be composed in future, in whole or part, publicly or secretly, under penalty of the greater excommunication, until that translation shall be recognised and approved by the diocesan of the place, or if the matter demand it, by a provincial council. Whoever disobeys this, let him be punished after the same fashion [as has been indicated above] as an abettor of heresy and error[1].

This clause, from the direct reference to Wycliffe, was probably directed expressly against the two versions of the Lollard Bible: but it rendered illegal also the few partial and contemporary translations, undertaken probably under Wycliffite influence, and described later[2]. The constitutions ended by lamenting that the university of Oxford had brought forth the wild grapes of Lollardy, of which the fathers had eaten, "deeming themselves skilled in God's law," and the children's teeth were set on edge, throughout the whole Church of England. The head of each college was therefore in future to inquire diligently whether any student or inhabitant of the college was infected by the poison of Lollardy.

This measure sufficed both to crush the influence of Lollardy in Oxford, and put an end to Purvey's struggle to uphold the lawfulness of the use of biblical translations. Purvey's own history after the constitutions of Oxford in 1408 is uncertain.

---

[1] Wilkins, III. 317. Lyndwood, *Provinciale*, Appendix, p. 66. The modern contention that *textus* cannot here apply to whole books of the Bible, or to the whole Bible, has already been dealt with on p. 3 above. Cardinal Gasquet's assertion that the mediaeval use of *textus* will not bear this sense is not only untenable on the face of it, but is explicitly contradicted by Lyndwood in his comments on this very constitution of Arundel. Lyndwood's summary, for instance, runs "Holy Scripture must not be transferred into the vulgar tongue, nor may such translations be interpreted until it has been duly examined, under pain of excommunication and stigma of heresy." And in his gloss, s.v. *libri*, he explicitly takes *textus* to refer to the whole Bible, or whole books of the Bible 'ed. 1679, p. 286).

[2] See pp. 302–18.

The Lollard disendowment bill of 1410[1] was partly, at least, his work, for it was quoted by Lavenham when enumerating Purvey's errors. The provision, *inter alia*, for "fifteen universities" to be founded from the funds raised by disendowment, is interesting as coming from him. His fate from now to his death is doubtful: what appear to be his monogram and notes appear in a manuscript belonging to a Lollard priest about 1427[2]. That he suffered imprisonment at some time seems likely, for Walden, who collected the writings of Lavenham and others for the *Fasciculus Zizaniorum*, said of Purvey between 1420 and 1426 "I have in my hands now a book taken from John Purvey in prison[3]." He ended his days in imprisonment or hiding[4].

---

[1] See p. 375.   [2] See p. 378

[3] *Doct.* I. 619. Walden had finished the first two vols. of the *Doct.* in 1426, the third in 1427. This was certainly a different book from the "libellum haereticum" from which Lavenham collected Purvey's errors, FZ, 383, 407.

[4] The DNB states that he was imprisoned by archbishop Chichele in 1421, relying on Foxe's quotation from Walden in AM, III, 285; cf. *Doct.* III. 732. But the reference to Purvey's imprisonment under Chichele does not occur in *Doct.*, or FZ. An entry in Tunstall's *Reg.*, f. 45b, shews that the Lollards, possibly incited by Purvey (*Doct.* I. xxviii), tried in London as well as Oxford to obtain some license for the use of English Bibles. The entry occurs after the mandate, dated 1526, for the handing over of the books of Tindale's New Test., and, according to a marginal note, was "extracted from a book now in the library of the friars preachers [Dominicans], of London." It runs: "There were certain Greeks who came to England with the emperor of Constantinople in the year 1401, which emperor stayed with the lord king Henry, the fourth after the Conquest, in the second year of his reign, and had with him bishops and priests. And when it was asked of them, whether the common people, and the ignorant, in their country, did indeed understand the scriptures, and the divine words [which they] recited together with the learned, they said: 'No: holy scripture is edited in a language totally unknown to the common people, and the common people have a Greek which is totally different from that Greek in which the divine word is retained.' And the king caused this to be preached at Paul's Cross, on the Sunday next before Septuagesima [23 Jan. 1401], by the master of the King's Hall in the university of Cambridge. This was because, a little while before the king returned from Scotland and Wales, many heretics had written various petitions to him, and even in the parliament which followed the feast of S. Hilary [21 Jan. 1401, *Hen. IV*, I. 168], asking that it should be generally permitted to have the Law of God in their mother tongue." For the emperor Manuel II and his visit to Henry IV, Dec. 1400—Feb. 1401, see *Hen. IV*, I. 161-3; for his daily mass according to the Greek rite, *Eulogium*, RS, III. 388; for the wonder aroused because knights as well as clerks took part in the Greek services, "because they were in the vulgar tongue," *Chron. Adae de Usk*, 56; for Richard Dereham, master of the King's Hall, chancellor of Cambridge, 1402, etc., *Hen. IV*, III. 351.

# CHAPTER XII

## *Biblical translations contemporary with the Lollard versions*

§ 1. The last quarter of the fourteenth century would almost certainly have seen the production of some biblical translations in England, even if Wycliffe had not turned the attention of his followers to the popularisation of the biblical text. Continental translations were produced or revised during this period in particular, though they were not scholastic undertakings on the same scale of completeness and thoroughness as the Wycliffite Bible, and though they were not made for popular use. The translations made for Charles V of France and the emperor Wenzel, the revision represented by the Tepl manuscript, the Tuscan gospels, possible translations made by the school of Gerard Groot, all belong to the period of 1375–1400. None of them were quite unglossed "translations according to the naked text," nor was any effort made to popularise them; but their production at this time justifies the surmise that in England too some sort of translations would have appeared, probably glossed, and perhaps at the order of the court.

This probability, together with the certainty that Wycliffite influence pervaded Oxford during the years when the best scholars of the period were being educated, renders it difficult to say whether certain contemporary translations were produced for expressly Wycliffite purposes or not. It was not yet forbidden in England to translate the Bible, though no readable English translations existed, and though the friars were declaiming against such a translation from 1380 onwards. But it is difficult to say whether, in the case of certain partial translations, orthodox zeal alone would have produced the work. In any case, the influence of the partial, contemporary, translations was negligible, compared with that of the Wycliffite versions, judging from the solitary or infrequent manuscripts which have survived to us, compared with the very large numbers of the Wycliffite manuscripts.

Moreover, there is no evidence at all that contemporaries knew of the existence of these partial translations of the New Testament, or could have distinguished between them and the Wycliffite versions. They were not made "before the days of the late master John Wycliffe," and they were therefore on exactly the same footing of legality as the Wycliffite versions, so far as the constitutions of Oxford went; except in so far, as that Arundel deliberately meant to condemn the Wycliffite versions. There is no reason to suppose that any Lollard who obtained a copy of the north midland glossed gospels would have suspected that it was not a Wycliffite copy, or would have objected to it on that score; neither would he have objected to the glosses, as they were little more than alternative renderings of the text. Nor is there any evidence that the orthodox used these glosses in preference to a Lollard text, for apparently they never got into general circulation at all. Their chief interest is linguistic: but the question of the probable authorship of each, by Lollard or orthodox, is of interest in its bearing on the question of the attitude of orthodoxy to vernacular scriptures.

So much translation of classical Latin works was now being accomplished by professional "turners,"—chaplains generally under royal or noble patronage—that the question arises whether any such ever attempted a biblical translation, and, in particular, whether John Trevisa ever did. His *Dialogue between a Lord and a Clerk* is of great interest as shewing the effect of Wycliffite teaching on an Oxford student who did not become a Lollard; and for the theory to which it gave rise, that Trevisa himself produced a translation of the Bible[1].

Lord Thomas of Berkeley is never mentioned by contemporaries as one of the circle of Lollard knights, nor does any suspicion of unorthodoxy attach to Trevisa, his chaplain. The patron's interests seem to have been exclusively literary and scholarly, and although the words of the "lord" in the *Dialogue between a Lord and a Clerk* are actually those of Trevisa, they probably represented Berkeley's sentiments. The *Dialogue* was written in 1387, when the controversy over English Bibles was already

---

[1] Cf. Wells, 206. Trevisa translated a certain Latin sermon of Fitz Ralph, archbishop of Armagh, against the friars, into English, which indicates no love for them.

begun at Oxford, and Trevisa and his patron possibly took the
view of the Wycliffite doctors on the matter, rather than that
of the friars. The question of the lawfulness of translating the
Bible is not raised directly in this dialogue; but the "lord," to
convince the "clerk" that the translation of so learned a book
as the *Polychronicon* was profitable, instanced the making of the
Septuagint and Vulgate translations, and certain Anglo-Saxon
ones. He also mentioned that the gospel and creed[1] at mass
ought to be taught and preached to the people in English: but
he went no further than this. We do not find him saying that
lay people ought to be allowed to use English gospel books;
much less does he demand or refer to a complete English translation of the Bible.

There are no manuscript grounds for attributing any biblical
translation to Trevisa[2]; but a statement, almost certainly mistaken, by Caxton, has been copied successively by many later
authorities. Caxton, in his *Prohemye* to the *Polychronicon*, described the latter as

after the composing and gathering of Dan Ranulph, monk of Chester,
first author of this book, and afterwards Englished by one Trevisa,
vicar of Berkeley, which at the request of one Sir Thomas Berkeley
translated the said book, the Bible, and Bartholemew's *De Pro-
prietatibus Rerum* out of Latin into English[3].

Caxton wrote this in 1482[4], nearly a hundred years after Trevisa
had Englished the *Polychronicon*, in 1387, and there are no

---

[1] "The gospel, prophecy, and right faith of holy church," Pollard, 206,
is probably a loose expression for the liturgical gospels, epistles and Old
Testament lessons, as they occurred at mass, together with the creed; but
the lord was apparently referring only to a loose translation in a sermon, for
he says, "such English preaching is very translation." Cf. the contemporary
homilies described pp. 315–18.

[2] Cf. Mr A. W. Pollard's suggestion in *Records of the English Bible*, 1911, 2,
that Trevisa perhaps finished Hereford's translation after Baruch iii. 20.
But (1) there is no positive evidence of this. (2) It is most unlikely that, if
Trevisa took no part in the translation up to Baruch iii. 20, he would
attach himself to the Lollard scholars in the work *after* the attack on
them in 1382; such a work would have been undertaken only by one
thoroughly in sympathy with them. As to Trevisa's possible participation
in the first part of the translation, under Hereford's general editorship,
there is no evidence: but (*a*) it is doubtful whether he was in Oxford much
after 1376 (see *John de Trevisa*, Wilkins, H. J., Longmans, 1915, 72);
(*b*) there is no evidence that Trevisa was ever sufficiently in sympathy with
the Wycliffites to have undertaken with them a rather risky task.

[3] *Life and Typography of William Caxton*, Blades, W., London, 1861, 1.
194.          [4] *Id.* II. 122.

earlier references to Trevisa's having made a translation of the Bible at all. Moreover, Caxton's assertion is accounted for by his loose reading of the passage in the *Dialogue*, which he was then printing[1], referring to biblical translations: that he was capable of making such mistakes is shewn by his miscopying of the date in Trevisa's note, which described his finishing of his translation[2], thus misdating the work by thirty years. But, much more probably, Caxton was aware of the existence of English biblical manuscripts: like sir Thomas More, thought that since they were good translations they could not be connected in any way with Wycliffe: combined this knowledge with the reference to translations in the *Dialogue*: and offered here his own solution to the problem of the authorship of the Wycliffite Bible. But though the guess was sufficiently clever, it was made a hundred years after the event, and cannot be made to accord with the evidence that the versions which Caxton knew were undoubtedly the work of the Lollards. That he was acquainted with any biblical manuscript which ascribed its authorship to Trevisa is very unlikely, for if so it has disappeared completely, unknown to Trevisa's contemporaries, or to any subsequent librarian or scholar; moreover it would have been as unsafe for Trevisa to sign his name to a biblical translation as for a Lollard. Caxton knew that English Bibles were in existence, but he had no possible means of knowing that the manuscripts went back originally to a version coupled with the heretical *General Prologue*, and beyond that to one for which Nicholas Hereford was largely responsible. His ascription of a biblical translation to Trevisa seems to be merely an unlucky guess at the authorship of the Wycliffite versions, and is unsupported by any earlier evidence.

All the assertions of later writers rest upon this statement of Caxton. Bale and Pits followed him, Bale stating that Trevisa translated the whole Bible, or both Testaments, at the request of lord Berkeley, and even going as far as giving the *incipit* of this translation: but that *incipit* coincides exactly with the dedica-

---

[1] Caxton printed, see *id*. 1. 191, his *Prohemye*, a table of contents, the *Dialogue* (incipit, Sith the time that the great—), the *Epistle of Sir John Trevisa, chaplain, unto Lord Thomas of Berkeley* (an epistle dedicating the *Polychronicon*), and the *Polychronicon*.           [2] *Id*. 195.

tory letter at the beginning of the *Polychronicon*[1]. The translators of James I's Bible followed Caxton, as did later scholars,
the only one who tried to collect evidence on the subject being
Wanley[2]. The latter found a letter from "the prince" (the
future James II?), thanking lord Berkeley for a "very precious
book" of Trevisa's, which had been preserved at Berkeley Castle
for "neare 400 year." Some writers have conjectured that this
"precious book" was an English translation of the Bible, and
have searched for it in the Vatican library, without success[3].

§ 2. Certain other translations, as well as the two versions
and the glossed gospels, were also produced by the Lollards,
notably a new edition of the English translation of the old Anglo-
Norman Apocalypse, a translation of Clement of Llanthony's
*Unum ex Quattuor*, and an edition of Rolle's psalter.

Three Middle-English forms of the Anglo-Norman Apocalypse
are found in fourteenth century manuscripts, the first dating
from about 1340–70[4], and thus preceding the Wycliffite period.
This seems however to have been unknown to the editors of the
second and third versions: the second is founded on a different
French text, and was used by the compilers of the third. This
third version is the so-called Wycliffite Apocalypse, for the

---

[1] Bale, *Script. Cat.* 1557, p. 518. In Anglicum idioma, ad petitionem
praedicti sui domini de Berkeley, transtulit totum Bibliorum opus, sive
*Utrumque Dei testamentum.* Lib. 2. [Incipit] *Ego, Johannis Trevisa, sacerdos.*
The dedicatory epistle begins: *I, John Trevisa, your priest and bedesman,*
cf. Pollard, 209. Ussher, XII. 346, attributes a translation to Trevisa solely
on Bale's authority.

[2] Dibdin's *Topog. Antiq.* 1810, I. 140, 141 n.; and *John de Trevisa,*
Wilkins, 101–109. The CHEL, II. 74, 77 is inclined to attribute an English
Bible to Trevisa, partly on the grounds that when he translated isolated
texts, he did not quote the Wycliffite versions. But almost all mediaeval
writers quoted the Vulgate from memory, in Latin, or when translating
short passages, and this general fact is without significance in Trevisa's
particular case. The "precious book of Trevisa's" is on p. 77 stated to be
"some part of the Bible" apparently through a loose reading of *Notes and
Queries,* V Ser. x. 261–2. Cardinal Gasquet has stated that no English Bible
is now to be found in the Vatican library.

[3] It is possible that Caxton's unconscious change of the dating of the
*Polychronicon,* from 1387 back to 1357, may have made him the readier to
believe that Trevisa had made his Bible earlier than "the days of the late
master John Wycliffe." It is not unreasonable to suppose that Caxton,
following Lyndwood like More, believed that there were mediaeval English
versions anterior to Wycliffe.

[4] Wells, 409; Paues, 1902, xxiv; FM, I. viii. Miss Paues is preparing an
edition of the first version for the EETS.

translation of the text in it follows the later Wycliffite version.
The commentary appears to be merely that of Gilbert de la
Porrée: but some connexion of this version with the Lollards
seems to be shewn by Purvey's insertion of Gilbert de la Porrée's
prologue before his version of the text of the Apocalypse[1].

The circle of early Lollards at Oxford seems also to have been
responsible for the translation of Clement of Llanthony's *Unum
ex Quattuor*, of which some fourteenth and fifteenth century
manuscripts survive[2]. The text of the harmony, which is composed of fairly long passages from the Vulgate arranged chrono-
logically, is said to be that of the early Lollard version: but the
exact relation between them has not been worked out. The
harmony is generally found with two prologues[3], probably
written rather later than the text, both of which are the work
of Purvey. One, beginning *Saint Austin saith in the second book
of Christian doctrine*[4], is part of the prologue to the Lollard gloss
on S. Matthew[5]. The other, *Our Lord Jesu Christ, very God and
very man*[6], is the second of the series of tracts in defence of
English scriptures mentioned earlier. Since the explicitness of
the references to the English scriptures seems to increase pro-
gressively in this series of tracts, it is likely that those which
occur first in the manuscript were actually written first, so that
the second is a fairly early one. This would agree with the

---

[1] *Test. Scots.* This prologue was printed in the Strassburg Bible of 1480,
and some other early printed Bibles.

[2] FM, I. x; Wells, 407; and see p. 273.

[3] Apart from the translation of Clement of Llanthony's own prologue;
e.g., Harl. 6333 has: ff. 18 ff. the two Purvey prologues; then, f. 23 *The
prologue on a book made of four gospels.* Clement, a priest of the church of
Lantonie, etc., which is a translation of Clement's prologue. This MS. was
copied from a Lollard original, since it includes the frankly Lollard second
prologue. It provides an English version of the gospels, epistles, and prophecies, or "lessons" in church, since the places where these occur in the
harmony are marked, and other gospels, etc., not found in the work are
added; f. 298 "Because that certain gospels stand not in order, word by
word, in this story of *One of Four*, that must be sought in divers places,
wherefore hereafter [are] shown some of these gospels as they be read in the
church." 31 gospels follow, taken from the Wycliffite later version. This
arrangement follows the directions in the Latin *Unum ex Quattuor*, which
is also preceded by a table of lessons, and has the beginnings of the liturgical
gospels marked; cf. Dd. I. 17, f. 614, for the Latin table, etc.

[4] FM, I. viii; in *Gen. Prol.* FM, I. 44–49, from Harl. 6333.

[5] In Laud Misc. 235, and Trin. Camb. 36.

[6] Printed FM, I. xiv; see p. 273.

evidence of the text, and date the translation as of approximately the same date as the glosses on the gospels (certainly complete before 1394), and earlier than the completion of the later version.

The Lollards also re-edited Rolle's glossed psalter[1], making no doctrinal change in the text, but introducing their distinctive teaching and attacks on the clergy into the commentary. In one group of manuscripts the bulk and bitterness of the Lollard matter added are much greater than in the other, and this group is probably later in date. It is curious at first sight that the Lollards should have added these polemics to Rolle's work, while nothing of the kind is found in connexion with their own biblical translations: but there were in reality good reasons for their action. The Lollards advocated chiefly and distinctively the use of the unglossed text, and had the greatest reverence for its integrity:

> Let the church of England now approve the true and whole translation of simple men, that would for no good in earth by their witting and power, put away the least truth, yea the least letter either tittle of holy writ, that beareth substance or charge[2].

This seems to have prevented their combining their own translations with any of their polemical writings, except by way of prologue: for the glosses on the Lollard gospels are merely long translations from the fathers. But in the case of Rolle's psalter, the gloss was already there, and was not merely a close translation of the sayings of old doctors[3]: it was therefore more permissible to add to it. Not only this, but after 1408 Rolle's psalter was the one authorised biblical book, and insertions in that book were doubly desirable for purposes of propaganda. Therefore, in contrast to the fresh edition of the Apocalypse, and the translation of the *Unum ex Quattuor*, the Lollard edition of Rolle seems to have been made for the spread of polemic, and not merely for the increased popularisation of the biblical text.

§ 3. The most interesting contemporary translations of the scriptures are those parts of the New Testament published by Miss A. C. Paues. This "biblical version" consisted originally of a "prologue," with the Pauline and catholic epistles, in a southern

---

[1] Wells, 402.    [2] *Gen. Prol.* FM, I. 58.    [3] See p. 145.

or Kentish dialect: but by about 1400 this was combined in two manuscripts with a midland version of S. Matthew and the Acts. Only five manuscripts, containing all or part of this combination, have survived, so that the version was not widely spread; and there is nothing to shew that there was an original connexion between the two parts, the southern and the midland, thus combined in two out of the five manuscripts[1]. Miss Paues also prints a second version of the catholic epistles, in a north midland dialect. The midland Acts-and-Matthew, and the north midland catholic epistles, would seem to be more probably connected with the north midland glossed gospels and epistles, mentioned later[2]. They had no connexion originally with the southern epistles, prefaced by their interesting prologue, as printed by Miss Paues, for had their writer known of the north midland version, he would scarcely have made a fresh translation of the catholic epistles. The two parts are found connected only in two manuscripts, one of which is a copy of the other; while in one out of the five manuscripts the southern epistles are found in connexion with the early Wycliffite version of the gospels. It may be taken as likely that any translator who set to work upon the epistles knew that the gospels were available in English: the Dutch translator of the epistles in 1408 stated in a prologue that there were men who admitted that the study of the simpler part of the New Testament, the gospels, might be useful, but who needed to be convinced in argument that any profit could come of translating the epistles[3]. It may be taken as axiomatic that any teacher anxious to instruct the "lewid" would start by

---

[1] Paues, 1904, xi–xv. Of the five MSS. used by Miss Paues, (1) dated 1400, has the midland Acts-and-Matthew, and the southern prologue-and-epistles, and (2) is a copy of it. (3) is the earliest MS., dating from before 1400, and has the midland Acts, only. (4) has the midland Acts-and-Matthew, and a set of north midland catholic epistles, c. 1400. (5) written soon after 1400, has all the epistles, like (1) and (2), and the four gospels in the early Wycliffite version. It seems to be over-emphasising the connexion between the midland Acts-and-Matthew, and the southern prologue-and-epistles, to term them a "biblical version," since they were merely combined in one manuscript which was then exactly copied. On similar reasoning, if (5) had been once copied, it would be as just to say that yet another biblical version existed, consisting of the early Wycliffite gospels and these southern epistles.

[2] See p. 310.

[3] See p. 99.

translating the gospels, unless they were already available. But there is no evidence that the original translator of these southern epistles intended to combine them with the midland Acts-and-Matthew, any more than with the Wycliffite gospels; if he knew of the existence of any English gospel, as is likely, it was more probably the early Wycliffite gospels that he knew of.

The prologue[1] to these southern epistles is interesting. It begins with a discourse on the Fall, and then proceeds:

(A) Sith every man is holden by Christ's law of charity to love his brother as himself, ye, that have of God's grace more knowing than we have, that be lewid and unkunning, be holden to teach us things that be needful to the health of our souls, that is to say, what thing is pleasing to God, and what displeaseth Him also. And I pray you, pour charité, to teach us lewid men truly the sooth, after our asking.

(B) Brother, I know well, that I am holden by Christ's law to perform thine asking; but natheless, we be now so far fallen away from Christ's law, that if I would answer to thine askings, I must in case underfonge[2] the death. And thou wost well that a man is holden to keep his life as long as he may. And peradventure it is speedful to hold our peace a while forto that God voucheth safe that His will be known: for now the world is full of wickedness, and men have more desire to live in their fleshly lusts in sin than to please God in forsaking sin. And I say thus in certain, that the comonalty of the world hath forsaken God and His hests[3] and herieth false gods....

(A) Lefe brother, I trow full well that the world liveth in much wickedness of sin. But I trow that many men, if they knew how they might please their God, they ne would not spare for dread of no man, ne for love neither, to do thing that were to His pleasing. And I trow that our God be so good and so merciful, that if we acknowledge to Him our sins, and forthink our trespass, and be in full will to offend Him no more, than our hope is that He will forgive us our trespass, if we ask mercy...thou ne shouldest nought spare for dread of thy death to tell us a truth to bring us out of mischief of the death of our soul....Our Lord God also put Himself in peril of death, and underfong the death, to bring us that were His servants out of mischief of sin, and if our Lord put His soul for His servants, it is skilful [reasonable] that one brother put his soul for his

---

[1] The word is retained as it is used in Miss Paues' editions: actually the tract occurs before the epistles in (1) and (2) (though absent in (5), the other MS. of the epistles), and has no reference to the translation of the epistles. The writer only gets as far as discoursing at length about Leviticus: but the tract is unfinished, and some reference to the epistles might originally have been intended. It is therefore only a "prologue" in so far as it occurs before the epistles in two MSS. without referring to the work itself.

[2] Undergo.        [3] Commandments.

brethren;...who that loveth his life in this world, he shall lose his life....And brother, I pray thee for the love that thou shouldst have to God and to thy brethren, that thou answer truly to things that I will ask thee, to health of my soul and other men's souls that be lewider than thou art. And if thou wilt nought, our hope is that God will inform us by some other true servant of His.

(B) Brother, thou hast aghast me somewhat with thine arguments. For though thou ne have not been among clerks at school, thy skills that thou makest be founded in love, that is above reason that clerks use in school: and therefore it is hard for me to againstand thine skills and thine askings[1].

The learned "brother" then describes the giving of the old law on Mount Sinai, and in answer to the question of the inquirer, now and henceforth addressed as "sister," discourses about the old law and the ten "hests" at greater length. He also describes the moral and ceremonial law, and breaks off abruptly in the middle of a sentence, without having mentioned the translations of the epistles, which occur next in the manuscript.

Certain points are clear from this prologue. The "brothers" learned and "lewid," who address each other in it, are literary characters, and do not at all imply that the author of the prologue was himself a monk. The change from "brother" to "sister" shews that the characters are a literary device to give liveliness to the dialogue; like the "John" and "Richard" in a contemporary dialogue concerning the friars[2]. It is much more probable, *a priori*, that if any one asked the translator to undertake this work, it was a "sister" of some sort; but this is no evidence that the writer was himself a monk, for secular priests were sometimes the directors of recluses or the smaller nunneries. The general tone of the tract does not bespeak a monastic origin: there is no apology on the grounds that translations would aid the understanding of the divine office, or the practice of contemplative prayer, much less the specific monastic virtues: while the words of the lewid brother, that if the learned one will not accede to his request, "our hope is that God will inform us by some other true servant of His" are hardly those of one trained in monastic obedience, whose duty would have been to accept unquestioningly the will of his "superior." As a matter of fact,

[1] Paues, 1904, 4–8.
[2] See Trin. 333, § 4.

the word "superior[1]" does not occur in the prologue, and the application of such a term to the learned brother is unjustified. Thus the translations were quite possibly actually written at the request of a "sister," but from the general tone of the tract, more probably by some secular priest or Austin canon than a monk.

The author, from the insistence on the danger of death he incurs by making a biblical translation, must have been writing when English Bibles were considered dangerously heretical,— that is, at a time when the Wycliffite versions were already in circulation, and had aroused fierce opposition from some of the orthodox, especially the friars. For actual heresy the writer might at any date have expected the death penalty, since this was the penalty at common law, and had been exacted even in England[2]. In the Netherlands and the Empire many of the Flemish Lollards, and other heretics, were being sent to the stake just at this time, as they had been throughout the fourteenth century. But it is hardly possible that the writer should have expected the death penalty of heresy for translating the Bible before the Lollards had fought the case for its popularisation, and had been fighting it for some little time. The allusion

---

[1] Paues, 1904, xix, "brother superior" nowhere occurs in the text, and is a misleading term for the "learned brother" in the prologue. A "superior" has definite monastic meaning, but "brother superior" is not found at the date as a monastic term. The lewid brother would have said "father" had he owed the learned brother any sort of monastic obedience, as to a "superior." The term "brother" does probably shew that the writer meant his dialogue to take place between two members of some sort of a community (but just as likely a Lollard "school" as an orthodox order), rather than between learned and lewid secular Christians. But this need not imply that the writer was himself a monk, much less a "superior." Hereford and Repingdon, it is true, were Austin canons, but there is no incongruity in supposing that the early type of scholarly Lollard, of very mild unorthodoxy, should have thrown his dialogue into a form like that of this prologue.

[2] See Henry IV, IV. 314, appendix on the burning of heretics; for heretics in England anterior to Wycliffe, see Inq. I. 113, and for a better and fuller account, Summers, 10–44; and for early cases of heresy in England, see also CPL, III. 1342–62, 138, 227, 231, 253, 432, 565; CPP, I. 115, 216; Kellaw, Reg. in RS, 62, I. 164; Hermits, 89. The editor of Wykeham's Reg. II. 77–9, considers the apostate Benedictine, Margery de Rye, to have been probably an early Lollard: but this is scarcely possible as early as 1369. The Lollard apology, or 25 Articles, in which they offered in 1388–9 to maintain certain theses to kings, lords and commons, refers to a possible death penalty: they will defend them "Yea, by death, if it be justly deemed lawful," Sel. Eng. Works,.III. 457.

to the extreme of persecution in connexion with a biblical translation is exactly similar to the tone of some of Purvey's prefaces
to the glossed gospels, and even to the lament for the persecution
of Bible readers in the *General Prologue*[1]. This would date the
tract as written perhaps between 1388 and 1400, but scarcely
earlier: this date accords also with the linguistic evidence, and
would allow for the union of these southern epistles and the
midland tracts in a manuscript of about 1400. Probably the
period could be still further narrowed to the five years immediately about 1388: for the writer probably knew of the existence
of English gospels, but not of English epistles,—which points
to a date of about 1388, allowing for the writer to have left
Oxford about 1380–5.

The writer was not an extreme Lollard, and yet there are signs
that he was in sympathy with Lollard teaching: perhaps through
a previous education at Oxford. The translation or instruction
in the Bible was to be for the use of the "lewid,"—a very doubtfully orthodox aim; it was a translation of the bare text, without
glosses, which was considered particularly unsafe; the dwelling
on the giving of "Goddis lawe" on Sinai somewhat bespeaks
Lollardy, as does the readiness to expound the details and meaning of the ceremonial law of Leviticus to the lewid; and the
reference to obtaining forgiveness by confession of sins to God
alone sounds suspiciously Lollard. But the writer was certainly
not a convinced Lollard, of the Purvey type: possibly he had
come in contact with Wycliffism at Oxford, for he certainly
sympathised with the Lollard aim of "uncovering" the scriptures to the lewid, but he thinks at first that "peradventure
it is speedful to hold our peace a while, forto that God voucheth
safe that His will be known," though he yields to the lewid
brother's request later. His first thought was, clearly, to wait
and see whether the English Church should settle the matter of
translations by condemning or approving them.

If the writer were southern or Kentish, as the editor of the
edition believes[2], it is much more likely that he should have
been at Oxford, than at any midland or north midland cathedral
theology school, for such schools were mainly attended by local

---

[1] FM, I. 30, 43, 57.　　　　　[2] Paues, 1904, I n. I, xvii.

students. One of the five hands in Nicholas Hereford's original
manuscript appears to be Kentish, and, curiously enough, it is
that of the portion Leviticus to Judges vii. 13[1], which suggests
that the writer may have been the same as that of the prologue.
If such was the case, familiarity with this matter, the Jewish
moral and ceremonial law, may have accounted for the long
dissertation upon them to the lewid brother in the prologue,
written later. This is conjecture: but the probability that the
writer of the prologue was acquainted rather with the early
Wycliffite gospels than with the rare north midland ones, is
serious. As a general result, the examination of the prologue
and the dialect of the epistles would seem to shew that the writer
was a priest of the south country, very doubtfully a monk or
canon regular, who had been influenced by Wycliffite views,
but had remained substantially orthodox, and that he wrote his
prologue about 1388–95.

§ 4. Another group of translations, never widely copied,
seems to have been contemporary with the early Wycliffite
versions, and to have been due to a north midland author, or
group of authors. One of these works has a prologue which
seems to connect the translator with the Wycliffite circle at
Oxford, but the others have no prologues, and therefore no
evidence as to orthodox or heterodox origin, except in so far as
they may be connected in the manuscripts with the one first
mentioned.

The gospels of SS. Matthew, Mark and Luke exist in this
north midland dialect, with a gloss translated mainly from Peter
Lombard[2]. A passage from the Latin text is given, then the
translation, then the gloss, which is quite orthodox and un-
original. The comment on S. Matthew has a prologue:

Here begins the exposition of Saint Matthew.... This work some
time I was stirred to begin of one that I suppose verily was God's
servant, and oft times prayed me this work to begin, saying to me,
that sithen the gospel is rule, by the which each Christian man
ought to live[3], and divers has drawn into Latin, the which tongue

---

[1] Bodl. 959; FM, I xlvii. The prologue as it stands, incomplete, would be
a far more suitable introduction to a translation of Leviticus, which it discusses, than the epistles, which it never mentions.

[2] That on Matthew in two MSS.; those on Mark and Luke together in a
single one. The latter have no prologues. FM, I. x.

[3] This is a typically Lollard phrase: cf. Wycliffe's argument, pp. 242–3.

is not known to each man but only to the learned: and many lewid men are, that gladly would con the gospel, if it were drawn into English tongue, and so it should do great profit to man's soul, about the which profit each man that is in the grace of God, and to whom God has sent cunning, ought heartily to busy him. Wherefore I, that through the grace of God began this work, so stirred as I have said before, by such word, thought in my heart, that I was holden by charity this work to begin: and so this work I began at the suggestion of God's servant, and greatly in this doing I was comforted of other God's servants divers, to such time that through the grace of God I brought this to an end. In the which drawing I suppose there is nothing set against the faith, against health of soul, or else against the worship of God....Wherefore I beseech...them that this work read, that for me they pray the mercy of God,...and that he at whose suggestion I this work began, and they that this work read, and all Christian men with me, through doing of that which is written in this book, may come together to that bliss that never shall end[1].

The reference to "one that I suppose verily was God's servant" points strongly to Wycliffe, and to the translator's having been for a time one of the Wycliffite circle at Oxford, probably at the time when Wycliffe was writing the *De Veritate*, about 1378, or earlier, and before the actual Wycliffite versions had been taken in hand. Arundel says that Wycliffe "filled up the measure of his malice by instigating a new translation of the scriptures," and this sentence in the prologue reads as if he had "instigated" its translator among others. His Latin works for seven or eight years before his death all demanded a popular knowledge of the Bible that led inevitably to the "instigating" of a translation. The phrase "one that I suppose verily was God's servant" suggests that all might not hold him so, and is just one that might have been expected of a scholar who knew that certain teachings of his master had lately been condemned, and who did not therefore wish to prejudice his own work by openly naming the man who had inspired it. It is curious that this man speaks of his inspirer and other helpers as "servants of God," and that the lewid brother in the above mentioned prologue used the same phrase for one who should be willing to translate the scripture for him: "and if thou wilt nought, our hope is that God will inform us by some other true servant of His." The phrase[2]

[1] FM, I. x.         [2] AM, IV. 227.

was thus used by the Lollards, one of whom hoped that a certain bishop would not "trouble the servants of God, but will let them be in quiet." Moreover, the reason put forward by the "servant of God" who urged the making of the translation is exactly Wycliffe's teaching, which he reiterated in all his later works. "The gospel is rule by which each Christian man ought to live" compares exactly with Wycliffe's advice to all Christians

to study carefully the gospel in that tongue in which the meaning of the gospel was clearest to them: for all the faithful are bound to follow the Lord Jesus Christ,...and since the deeds and teaching of Christ are more clearly expressed in the gospel than elsewhere, it is obvious how much the careful study of this book profits the faithful[1].

"The gospel is the rule by which all Christians ought to live" is a typical Lollard proposition, often found in Purvey's writings. Nevertheless, there is no evidence in the prologue that the north midland translator had become a Lollard of an advanced type: he probably took up work at a distance from Oxford, completed his translation there, and lost touch with the Wycliffite circle.

Besides these glossed gospels, a north midland version of the Pauline epistles[2] has survived in a single manuscript. Here the Latin is given in single sentences, followed by a very literal and stiff translation, followed then by occasional short glosses that are not much more than alternative renderings of the word, or explanations of it. There was also the north midland unglossed version of Acts and part of S. Matthew, mentioned earlier, found combined about 1400 with the southern epistles; the editor does not mention that the portion of S. Matthew was connected with, or drawn from, the north midland glossed S. Matthew, and it seems to be a freer rendering than the text of that gloss. There was also a set of north midland catholic epistles, unglossed[3], and found in a single manuscript combined with the portion of Matthew and Acts. It is not at all certain that all these works were connected in origin, though they are in the same dialect, but such may have been the case. In any case, the glossed gospels appear to be the work of one man: the glossed Pauline

---

[1] See p. 245.
[2] *Paul. Ep.* 1–274.
[3] Printed as an appendix, Paues, 1904.

epistles are perhaps connected with him, for they occur only in the manuscript of the glosses on SS. Mark and Luke: and the unglossed Matthew, Acts and catholic epistles appear to have been part of another version, or a revision of the text of the glosses.

The modern editor[1] of the glossed Pauline epistles does not enter into the question as to whether the translator was the same as the compiler of the glossed gospels: she considers it likely that the work was made as an aid to preaching, or for teaching in some divinity school. But we have no reason to assume that between 1380 and 1400 lectures in cathedral divinity schools were given in English: in absence of evidence, it is much more likely that, like those at the university, they were in Latin. Moreover, the lectures at such schools do not seem to have been upon the biblical text. They seem to have formed a course of elementary theology, based on Peter Lombard: though later the council of Constance ordered that the lecturer in theology should expound the Sunday epistles and gospels, for the improvement of the sermons of those, mainly ordinands, to whom he was lecturing[2]. The Lollard Purvey demanded that scholars at grammar schools should learn to construe the biblical text, and if a teacher from Oxford chose himself to introduce such an innovation, in a theology school, such a book as these Pauline epistles would have been exactly what he required: the book is practically a construing of the Latin text into English. There is no need to assume that the hypothetical teacher taught Lollardy in a divinity school, or that he actually used his glosses in delivering his divinity lectures. But he may have had his students in mind in preparing them. The similarity of the north midland dialect in this group of translations rather suggests a common local origin: and the newness of the departure, and scholarship of the glossed gospels, rather suggest an important local divinity school as the place of origin. Putting these inferences together, and till further evidence is collected, the cathedral school of Lincoln might be suggested as the place of origin; the dialect is not northern enough for York. But such preoccupation with the biblical text would have been "advanced"

---

[1] Miss M. J. Powell.    [2] See p. 104.

for the day, and due very probably to the influence of lecturers who had come under the influence of Wycliffite ideals during their studies at Oxford.

The teaching of Wycliffe for the five years or so before his condemnation in 1382, as embodied in the *De Veritate* and some of his other tracts, cannot have been without influence on students who were at Oxford only for a time. Wycliffe's teaching remained strong in his own university for years after his condemnation, but it must have passed out also with students who left Oxford and obtained a prebend in some cathedral, or actually lectured in its school. They would, without becoming active Lollards, remember Wycliffe as "holden of full many men the greatest clerk that they knew then living: and therewith... a passing ruely man, and an innocent in his living," and his followers as "the most godly wise men that I heard of or knew[1]." Of such a type was certainly the author of the north midland glossed gospels: and of such a type was quite probably the author of the southern prologue and epistles, who faced such risk in the making of his translation. In not a single case is there any evidence that any of these translations were made before, or apart from, the influence of Wycliffe: the fact that they contain nothing unorthodox in the text or glosses proves nothing, for the Wycliffite versions themselves contained nothing unorthodox. The north midland glossed gospels are almost certainly the earliest of the group, for the translation was literal and the gloss considerable: but this was made, judging from the prologue, under Wycliffite inspiration. It is not in the least likely that the much freer and unglossed north midland translations of parts of the New Testament preceded the others, in lack of direct evidence to that effect: for this would be an inversion of the usual order in which translations were made at the date. Nor does the earliest manuscript containing part of it appear to date from earlier than 1380–1400[2]. So that the reasons for believing that any biblical version, or part of it[3], substantially preceded the Wycliffite ones, are small: the north

[1] Pollard, 119.
[2] Paues, 1904. xiii.
[3] Apart from the translation of the Anglo-Norman Apocalypse, which dates from 1340–70, see p. 302.

midland glossed gospels are almost certainly the earliest, and
though it is quite possible that they actually antedate the so-
called early Wycliffite one by a year or two, they were written
through Wycliffite inspiration.

But in any case, these contemporary translations are chiefly of
linguistic interest, for they were so rarely copied that they were
unknown to contemporaries. They would come under the ban
of the council of Oxford in 1408 as having been made in the days
of the late master John Wycliffe, or since, without having received any general approbation from a bishop.

§ 5. It will be remembered that Anglo-French and Middle-
English verse paraphrases of the Sunday gospels had been made
in England between 1250 and 1350. These had been originally
accompanied by homilies or expositions, and in the later manuscripts the translation of the text itself was dropped. There are
three interesting sets of prose translations of the Sunday gospels,
with English homilies upon them, all of which belong to the last
quarter of the fourteenth century: that is, were contemporary
with Wycliffe's teaching, or were made shortly after his death.
There is no manuscript or other evidence for dating any of them
earlier than c. 1380, and the set which was probably the earliest
seems to date from about that time. The three sets, all of which
contain translations of the biblical text differing from both the
early and the late Wycliffite versions, are the prose translation of
Robert of Greatham's *Mirror*, the Lollard sermons on the Sunday
gospels connected more or less closely in origin with Wycliffe
himself, and a contemporary set of sermons apparently unconnected with the Lollards. The manuscripts of the Wycliffite
sermons are fairly frequent[1]: but of the other sets only four and
two respectively are known: so that neither set had anything
like the popularity or influence of the Wycliffite versions. The
translation of the text of the gospels was probably made in each
case at sight from the missal or Vulgate, and is an independent
version.

The prose translation and homilies which are modelled upon
Robert of Greatham's *Mirror* contain, apparently, no Lollard
teaching or phraseology, and are found in four manuscripts[2],

---

[1] Wells, 469, mentions 19.
[2] Harl. 5085, Magdalen Coll. Camb. 2498, and C.C.C. Camb. 282, all late

all dating from the end of the fourteenth century, or the beginning of the next. The translator made a fairly close translation
of Robert's prologue[1], and made use of the subject matter of his
homilies, but he apparently made his own translation of the
gospel text, no doubt with Robert's verse translation before
him[2]. The version is not literal, like the early Wycliffite version,
but much freer, and suitable for recitation in the pulpit: the
translation of the whole Sunday gospel precedes the homily. In
translating the prologue the Middle-English editor omitted such
of the French lines as would not apply to his English treatise[3],
so that his version was not a mere English copy of the French
prologue: but he chose to retain the lines (quoted above[4]),
where opposition was anticipated, and to render them somewhat
stronger. This would seem to indicate that he personally expected censure from some quarters, and was writing some time
soon after 1382–4, when the controversy over English scriptures
had begun.

My name ne will I nought name, for the enemies that might hear
it, and might draw your hearts from good, that had will to hear it.
For it is the manner of the enemies for to be grudging and annoyous,
and will blithely coniect[5] the words of holy writ, and will tell it on
their manner, and ne let nought for to blame other; the wicked
ween for to amend it, for to blame the good, and coniect them[6]....
For this werk I do sooth for me and for all men. For all ne have
nought all holy writ. Such hear the gospel and read it, that ne
understandeth nought it, what it saith. And for to do all men for
to understand it, in God I dare take this work in hand, that all men
may understand openly what the gospel teacheth them.

It would appear therefore that this translation and homilies
were made about the time of the beginning of the translation

fourteenth century, and Holkham Hall MS. early fifteenth century. See
H. E. Allen in *Modern Philology*, XIII. April 1916; 741, Paues, 1904, xiv;
and extracts from the prologue, with a specimen of the translation of the
biblical text, in FM, I. xx. The MSS. quoted may go back to an earlier
original, but the language does not suggest it, cf. also *Parker Coll.* 52,
MS. CCLXXXII.

[1] See passages compared in *Mod. Phil.* XIII. 742: in the whole prologue
the resemblance is close.

[2] A comparison of the gospel text as printed in FM, I xx with Greatham's
*Mirror* in Gg. I. I shews no special resemblance in the biblical passages.

[3] *Rom.* xv. 298, ll. 1–6, 68–70, 199–200.          [4] See p. 150.

[5] Cast down, for déprimer. See NED, coniect.

[6] FM, I. xx; the last lines are not a translation of Greatham's lines in
*Rom.* xv. 300, ll. 137 ff.; for the first, see ll. 129 ff., for the last, ll. 275 ff.

controversy, by a scholar who made no departure from orthodoxy in his teaching, but was somewhat apprehensive as to the reception of his work; he does not seem to have been acquainted with the northern English verse homilies, founded on his own model. The Franciscan Butler, and the Dominicans Palmer and Tylle, would doubtless have condemned his work.

The Sunday sermons printed as Wycliffe's[1] are not preceded by translations of the Sunday gospel, but the complete translation of the gospel is given in the course of each homily, which explains a few verses at a time. The text here also is independent, and if the sermons are Wycliffe's own, is his first essay in the translation of the gospel. To have quoted from the early literal Wycliffite version would have been impossible in a passage meant for recitation in the pulpit, and there are no grounds for believing that the second version was begun before his death. But there are serious grounds for doubting whether these English sermons are in Wycliffe's own words, whether they are more than his followers' version of his sermon notes[2], compiled for the benefit of his itinerant preachers. The matter of the sermons, however, follows closely Wycliffe's teaching in his authentic Latin polemical works. Probably the text of the gospels was translated, if not in the original sermon notes by Wycliffe, by Purvey or some Wycliffite before the second Wycliffite version was made. In one case, two sermons are given on the gospel beginning *Egressus Jesus de Templo*[3], and the text of the gospel is twice translated,—each time differently: which confirms the general probability that throughout the translation was made at sight, and not from any earlier translation.

The third set of homilies, apparently orthodox in matter[4], has yet another English text for the gospels themselves. This is

---

[1] *Sel. Eng. Works*, I.

[2] *A priori*, Wycliffe is unlikely to have spent his time writing out vernacular sermons; and the references to persecution in some of the sermons seem to point to their being edited at a time later than Wycliffe's death: cf. the references to the death penalty for heresy, *Sel. Eng. Works*, I. ix; also the reference to a number of translators in *id*. II. 393, "some men would say it [the gospel] in their mother language, as they kunnen."

[3] *Sel. Eng. Works*, I. 235; II. 393.

[4] FM, I. xx; MSS. Kk. 6. 2, Kk. 6. 28. The Camb. Univ. Lib. Cat. states that Kk. 6. 2 is the work of a Wycliffite, but on what grounds is not apparent: a general examination of the MS. does not suggest it. Both MSS. date from about 1400.

given continuously at the beginning of each gospel, but only in one of the two manuscripts. The text is closer to that in the Wycliffite sermons than to either of the Wycliffite biblical versions: but the resemblance is due probably only to the comparative freedom of which the translator felt justified in making use, in a work meant for the pulpit, and not textual study.

Thus of the three late fourteenth century English "plenaries," or gospels and homilies, one is certainly Wycliffite, if not Wycliffe's, and the other two are of apparently independent origin, though the type of sermon approximated to that which the Lollards desired. The Wycliffite work was copied fairly widely: but the other two sets of homilies, judging from the surviving manuscripts, had little influence. The compilation of such a work would have been unlawful in the fifteenth century without episcopal license: and there is no evidence that such was ever given.

# CHAPTER XIII

## Bible reading by the orthodox, 1408–1526

§ 1. The provision of the synod of Oxford in 1408 that no one was to translate, or use the translation of, any text of holy scripture, until the translation should have been approved by the diocesan bishop or the provincial council, seems to imply as possible in future, either the issue of some authorised biblical translation, or the approbation of some private individual's work. If this really floated before the minds of Arundel and his clergy, such a measure was never taken,—to the surprise of sir Thomas More a century later[1]. Friar Butler roundly asserted that the whole hierarchy together had no power to grant a general license for lay people to read a particular translation, and the council of Trent so far endorsed his opinion that lay people were only allowed to use translations by the individual license of their confessors. But it is unlikely that Arundel had any definite intention of taking the lead in such a matter, when no previous English or continental bishop had ever issued an approved translation, and when such an action would have clashed with the conception of the clergy as the teaching branch of the Church. No bishop actually took such a course before the Reformation. The clause may have been intended merely to sanction the old custom of individual license by the confessor: or to placate liberal feeling within the Church: or to shew a scholarly recognition that translations were not, in themselves, wrong. Whichever was intended, no breach in ancient custom ensued: no translation received official sanction[2], but kings and nobles were allowed to possess English Bibles as they had earlier been allowed to possess *Bibles Historiales*. For the first half of the century however there is not only no evidence for lay ownership,

---

[1] See p. 8.

[2] Gairdner's note, I. 109 "Wycliffite Bibles authorised by bishops" is exceedingly misleading, as implying a general license. There is no single known case even of an individual obtaining episcopal license to use one, much less of a general license to use a particular version. See p. 7 n.

but some evidence that English scriptures were too closely connected with heresy for even the greatest to wish to possess them; and it is probable that such manuscripts as were written for use by the orthodox at this time were used by nuns rather than lay people. But when fifty years or so had passed after 1408, and seventy from the death of Wycliffe, confessors and doctors had no means of identifying the actually Lollard versions submitted to them. There was no reason why they should not have approved each manuscript merely on the grounds of its accuracy as a translation: as they probably did, in a few cases. They had not the linguistic skill to know whether the manuscript had been made before the days of Wycliffe or not, even if they knew the exact provisions of the synod of Oxford. Broadly speaking, it is likely that nuns were the most numerous orthodox users of English Bibles between 1408 and 1526, but that between about 1450 and 1526 exalted lay people sometimes possessed them, in complete ignorance that they were Wycliffite. Devotional teaching never laid any stress on their use by lay people in England, and there was certainly no general emphasis on their use even by nuns, though certain nunnery chaplains advised or allowed it. Not only was Bible reading never advised by the hierarchy as a duty, but there is evidence that it was generally regarded as forbidden[1]. The attitude of sir Thomas More's "Messenger" shews that this was so in the sixteenth century, and More would probably have caused quite as much surprise in the fifteenth by stating, on the authority of the synod of 1408, that Bible-reading in general was not forbidden.

English versions of the psalms, however, seem to have been, from the first, an exception to the rule against the unlicensed use of biblical translations. A certain number of people possessed English primers in the fifteenth century, and these books usually included certain psalms[2]. Two partial verse translations of the psalms were being made just at the time of the synod of Oxford: those of Lydgate[3], the Benedictine of Bury, and Brampton[4], a Franciscan recluse in the west of England. Lydgate could

---

[1] See pp. 326–9.
[2] See p. 338 n. Addit. 36683 combines the primer with the Wycliffite psalter.
[3] Psalm 51 and others: see Ashmole, 59, § 39; 48, § 58.
[4] *Trin. Coll. Descrip. Cat.* II. 80; Wells, 404, misdates as 1414.

hardly have been unaware of the prohibition, though Brampton, who wrote in 1413, might well have been: but neither seems to have obtained episcopal license for his poems. Probably the exemption of Rolle's psalter in 1408[1] led to the toleration of all prose texts of the psalter, while for loose verse translations no license was ever regarded as necessary.

§ 2. There is indeed a piece of evidence that Arundel was, in 1408, seriously considering the provision of some English book in which the faithful might study the life of Christ, with due guidance from the doctors. He seems to have decided that an actual translation of the biblical text, however well accompanied by glosses, was impossible, because it afforded the heretics grounds for argument, and for the appeal to isolated texts[2]. He therefore fell back upon a translation of the most popular gospel harmony of the middle ages, the *Meditationes Vitae Christi* then ascribed to S. Bonaventura. The parts dealing with the passion had been used in English verse and prose in the fourteenth century[3], and the whole work was translated into several vernacular tongues at about this date. Arundel in 1410 authorised for general use an English prose translation; and this date, together with a sentence in his authorisation stating that he did it "to the confuting of all false Lollards and heretics," suggests a counter-move to the Lollard efforts to publish the gospels in English. The commonness of fifteenth century manuscripts, and references to this work in catalogues and wills[4], shew that it became the orthodox reading-book of the devout laity, as Arundel probably intended. In any case, his authorisation of the book shews that the licensing, for instance, of a translation of the gospels, would have been a perfectly possible event at the date, and it is significant to note what book he did, in fact, authorise for general use instead.

Nearly all the manuscripts of this book copy a Latin memorandum of Arundel's license, and have notes about the translator and his methods.

---

[1] The author of the Sion *Myroure* thought it superfluous to translate verses of the psalms when the nuns could use Hampole, see p. 339. Ashmole, 61, has another poem, like Brampton's, on the penitential psalms, by a certain Rate, c. 1475–1500.

[2] See his words to Thorpe, p 354.      [3] See pp. 152, 174.

[4] See p. 342.

About 1410 the original copy of this book, the *Mirror of the Life of Christ*, in English, was presented in London by its compiler, to the most reverend father in Christ, and lord, the lord Thomas Arundel, archbishop of Canterbury, for inspection and due examination, before it was made public[1]. And he, when he had inspected it for some days, handed this book back to its aforesaid author, and with his own voice commended and approved it in detail, and by his authority as metropolitan, he decreed and commanded that it should be made public as catholic, to the edification of the faithful, and the confutation of all false heretics or Lollards[2].

The author was the Carthusian Nicholas Love, prior of Mount Grace, at Ingleby, Yorkshire, as is explained by other notes in the manuscript, and one manuscript actually possesses the translator's monogram[3]. The Carthusians of the fifteenth century were active in the spread of religious literature, and regarded this as a duty which they owed to the laity, whom they could not, in their strict seclusion, serve by other active works[4]. Nicholas Love's book was not a close translation of the whole of the *Meditationes Vitae Christi*, but a free translation of such parts as he considered specially suitable for meditation by simple lay people, with additions and explanations of his own. He marked with the initial B those passages which were translated from pseudo-Bonaventura, and with the initial N the passages he had added himself[5], and he followed his original in distinguishing whether the passage narrated was biblical, or founded only on the opinions of the doctors:

S. John said that all the things that Jesu did are not written in the gospel. Wherefore we may, to stirring of devotion, imagine and think divers words of Him, and other that we find not written, so that it be not against the belief: (as S. Gregory and other doctors say that holy writ may be expounded and understanden in divers manners, and to divers purposes, so that it be not against the belief, or good manners). And so what time or in what place in this book is written, that thus did or thus spake our Lord Jesu, or other that are spoken of, and it may not be proved of holy writ, or grounded in express saying of holy doctors, it shall be taken none otherwise than a devout meditation that it might be so spoken or done[6].

[1] Libere communicata: cf. p. 215, *Spec. Vit.*; p. 325, *Fruit of Redemption*.
[2] C.C.C. Camb. 142, f. 2*a*, etc.; Love's *Mirrour*, preface.
[3] Brasenose, e. 9. For an article confusing this work with Deguilleville's pilgrimages, see *Trans. Bibliog. Soc.* VII. 163 ff.
[4] See *Chartreux, travaux de*, V, II. 605.
[5] Love's *Mirrour*, 6; C.C.C. Camb. 142, f. 2*a*.
[6] Love's *Mirrour*, 9; cf. *Bonav. Op.* 1609, 533.

The original *Meditationes* from which Nicholas Love translated contain, on the whole, far more meditation and non-biblical matter than actual gospel narrative,—and a much more detailed account of the nativity, epiphany, fasting and temptations, passion, resurrection and ascension of our Lord than of His teaching or ministry[1]. Nicholas Love followed the same method, though he sometimes omitted long meditations applicable only to a religious, and added others of his own. The general result of his translation was to add meditations of his own on the early and final events of our Lord's life, and still further to abridge the ministry and parables. When he had completed the narrative and meditations down to the temptations, he prefaced his abridgement of his original with the remark:

But for alsomuch as it were a long work, and peradventure tedious both to the readers and the hearers hereof, if all the process here of the blessed life of Jesu should be written in English so fully by meditations as it is yet hitherto, after the process of the book before named of Bonaventura in Latin: therefore hereafter many chapters and long process that seemeth little edification in as to the manner of simple folk, that this book is specially written to, shall be left, until it draw unto the passion, which with the grace of Jesu shall be more plainly contained, as the matter that is most needful and most edifying[2].

Nicholas Love's own passages are generally of much beauty and devotion, and though the work which he produced was far indeed from being a literal harmony of the gospels, its popularity among the orthodox in the fifteenth century can be well understood. In a long prologue he met the Lollards on their own ground by recommending the study of the life of Christ:

[1] The chapters are headed according to the order of events in the narrative, and there is no trace that the order of the Sunday gospels was in any way followed.

[2] Love's *Mirrour*, 100. Many of the chapters omitted from the *Meditationes* form a treatise on the active and contemplative life, following on the discourse on Martha and Mary where it occurs in the narrative. *Medit.* pp. 368–78, or chapters 45–58, are thus omitted by Love: but he actually slips into admonitions of his own to religious, though he states elsewhere that he is writing expressly for lay people; cf. especially, *Mirrour*, 98, his account of Carthusian meals; and 165, *Of silence*, "and other virtuous exercise that longeth to contemplative living and specially to a recluse,...whoso will more plainly be informed and taught in English tongue, let him look the treatise that the worthy clerk and holy liver Walter Hilton, the canon of Thurgarton, wrote in English by grace and high discretion."

For there is no pride but it may be healed through the meekness of God's son: there is no covetise but that it may be healed through His poverty, nor wrath but that it may be healed through His patience: nor malice, but that it may be healed by His charity.... And for this hope and to this intent, with holy writ also are written divers books and treatises of devout men: nor only to clerks in Latin, but also in English to lewid men and women and them that be of simple understanding. Among the which are written devout meditations of Christ's life, more plain in certain parts than is expressed in the gospel of the four evangelists[1]. And as it is said, the devout man and worthy clerk, Bonaventura, wrote them to a religious woman in Latin. The which scripture and writing, for the fructuous matter thereof stirring especially to the love of Jesu, and also to the plain sentence to common understanding, seemeth among other sovereignly edifying to simple creatures: the which, as children, have need to be fed with milk of light doctrine, and not with sad meat of great clergy and of high contemplation. Wherefore, at the instance and the prayer of some devout souls, to edification of such men or women is this drawing out of the foresaid book of Christ's life written in English, with more put to in certain parts, and also with drawing of divers authorities and matters, as it seemeth to the writer hereof most speedful and edifying to them that are of simple understanding.

The *Mirrour* was not only written to supersede the Lollard translations of the gospels, but it also refers in places to the Lollard errors. The loosing of Lazarus from the grave-clothes is compared to that of the sinner, "dead and bounden by the grave-clothes of sin," by confession and absolution: and the scribe emphasised the point by writing in the margin: "Nota de confessione et absolutione, contra Lollardos." Again, in narrating the institution of the Lord's Supper, Love wrote:

These terms I touch here so specially because of the lewid Lollards, that meddlen them against the faith falsely. And moreover the faith of this excellent sacrament...is confirmed by many manner of miracles, as we read in holy books, and hear all day preached and taught. But here laugheth the Lollard, and scorneth holy Church alleging of such miracles[2].

[1] Love's *Mirrour*, 8. Besides the biblical narrative, the pseudo-Bonaventura devotes chapters II. and III. to the strife in heaven between Mercy and Justice, Truth and Peace (much exploited in later miracle-plays and *Piers Plowman*), and the life of our Lady and her seven petitions, "known from her revelations of it to S. Elizabeth." The other non-biblical details at the visitation to S. Elizabeth, the Nativity, etc., are only such as might be supplied by a devout mind picturing the scenes shortly described in the gospels.     [2] Love's *Mirrour*, pp. 180, 208.

Not only did Love deal with the matter in this passage, but he added a separate tract on "the highest and most worthy sacrament of Christ's blessed body" at the end of his *Mirrour*, to the special confutation of the Lollards on this point[1]. On the other hand, the fact that the manuscript purported to be a life of Christ in English seems to have induced some Lollards to possess themselves of it, for in one manuscript the section about the sacrament of the altar is scratched through, and a marginal note says: "Do not beleue thys foleshnes[2]."

Orthodox approval of Bonaventura's *Meditationes* as a reading-book for the devout is confirmed, not only by the Spanish translation made at this time, but by a French one. Jean Gallopes, dean of the collegiate church of Saussaye in Normandy, translated what he called the "golden book of the life of our Lord Jesus Christ according to Bonaventura," and dedicated it to Henry V, and his uncle the duke of Exeter, regent of France at the time, as well as presenting a copy to Henry V[3].

Though Love's *Mirrour of the blessed life of Jesu* was much the commonest in the fifteenth century, two other English lives were composed. Fairly early in the century a Carthusian of Sheen composed an English *Vita Christi*[4], and apologised in the preface for his work as partly unnecessary, since "a man of our order of Charterhouse" had turned Bonaventura's *Vita Christi* into English; he mentioned also the existence of an English "School Story," or *Historia Scholastica*, and said that his two chief authorities were Comestor and Lyra. His narrative keeps closer to the words and order of the gospels than Love's *Mirrour*. The other English life was composed at the end of the century, "for your ghostly comfort that know no Latin[5]" by Simon, the anker of London Wall, who was enclosed in the city church of All Hallows. It was approved as orthodox by FitzJames, bishop

---

[1] Cf. especially *Mirrour*, 321, for his criticism of Wycliffe and his "great clergy" and doctrine of the sacrament.

[2] Camb. Trin. 367, f. 128. There are, apparently, Lollard notes in Univ. 123, since Coxe in *Cat. Cod. Oxon.* attributes the work to "quendam Wiclefistam."

[3] *Parker Coll.* 43, C.C.C. Camb. *Descrip. Cat.* I. 510.

[4] The *Speculum Devotorum*, written for a nun, Gg. I. 6, owned in 1517 by John and Margaret Farmer.

[5] Published by Wynkyn de Worde in 1514 as *The Fruit of Redemption.* *Hermits*, 180.

of London, in 1506, before it was "made public," and was printed four years later by Wynkyn de Worde. Lollard or protestant heresy was just then increasing again in numbers and importance, and this license of a second book dealing with the life of Christ is a curious parallel with that of Love's *Mirrour*.

It is very strong evidence, again, of the attitude of authority in England to vernacular scriptures, in these early days of printing, that several editions both of Love's and Simon the Anker's meditations on the life of Christ should have been printed[1], while no printer ventured to produce any English biblical books, or even a set of glossed Sunday gospels. Manuscripts were there to print from, as easily accessible as Love's *Mirrour*. If the difficulty were the authorisation of the text, for instance, of the Sunday gospels, it would have been possible for FitzJames to read and approve one, as he did Simon the Anker's work; if licenses to read English scriptures had been at all freely obtainable by the devout, such a book would certainly have been printed. The non-printing of such books goes to corroborate More's *Dialogue*, since it shews that the constitutions of Oxford were generally understood to forbid the reading of English scriptures by the laity.

§ 3. The strongest evidence for this is contained in the accounts of various Lollard trials, where the witnesses frequently deposed that they had heard the accused reading in a book of the gospels in English, or some other biblical book, and therefore knew he was a heretic[2]. But there is also other confirmatory evidence, which emphasises the exceptional character of those cases where exalted lay people obtained licenses to have English Bibles.

*Dives and Pauper* is a long tract of moral exhortation in English, written by an author who did not allow his name to appear, though his views were quite orthodox and untainted by Lollardy. He was engaged on the work as early as 1405, though he possibly did not complete it till 1409[3], when Arundel's con-

---

[1] Love's by Caxton c. 1488, Pynson 1495, Wynkyn de Worde 1517 and 1525; Simon's by Wynkyn de Worde in 1514, 1530, 1532; see *Hermits*, 182.
[2] See pp. 353, 366.
[3] *Dialogue of Dives and Pauper*, Pynson, London, 1493; also 1536 ed. For date of the tract, see Richardson, H. G. in *Notes and Queries*, 11th Ser. IV. 321.

stitutions of Oxford had been published. When discoursing on
the ten commandments he remarks—not altogether approvingly
—that "now men say that no lewid folk should meddle with
God's law, or the gospel, or holy writ, and that men are forbidden
to have God's law in their mother tongue[1],"—a sentence shewing
the general impression, and therefore the practical effect, of the
Oxford constitutions. Just as Innocent III did not completely
prohibit vernacular translations in his letter to Metz in 1199[2],
but referred later to this letter as having forbidden them, so the
wording of the Oxford constitutions, however guarded in strict
law, was naturally taken to mean that Bible reading was forbidden to the masses, especially in view of the actual practice
of the hierarchy.

Not merely that, but the mere possession of English books of
piety without a license was sometimes alleged as forbidden by
the 1408 constitutions,—an exact parallel to the suppression of
all German books of devotion by the imperial edict of 1369, for
fear of the connexion of German books with heretical errors. The
abbot of S. Albans governed a great monastic peculiar, and ruled
the vicars of the monastic parishes in place of the bishop. In
1426–7 he held a synod for these vicars, to put forth ordinances
for the prevention of the spread of Lollardy, and in the account
of the synod, the mere possession of English books is mentioned
as a symptom of heresy: the ordinances were expressly passed
"against all false preachers and possessors of books in the vulgar
tongue[3]."

Since the occasion and cause of no small part of this injury is the
possession and reading of books which are written in our vernacular
tongue: we command and enjoin...that all whom ye shall in future
know to frequent the reading of books in the vernacular, as to have
any such books at home, and especially those which might furnish
material or occasion for erroneous and malicious opinions, ye shall
be solicitous to the utmost of your power to take away these books
from such their possessors: and, if your powers seem to you insufficient to procure the final casting out of these books, then ye
shall expressly signify concerning the said books to him who has
fuller or more final authority in the matter[4].

---

[1] See Richardson, *Parish Clergy of the Thirteenth and Fourteenth Centuries,*
in RHT, 3rd Ser. VI. 101, 322.
[2] See. p. 33.          [3] *Amundesham*, RS, 28, I. 223.
[4] *Id.* 225.

The books aimed at were no doubt chiefly Lollard treatises: but the books which above all furnished the Lollards with "material for erroneous and malicious opinions" were English translations of parts of the Bible, and the constitutions were so worded as to include these books. One heretic who recanted confessed to the unlicensed possession of an English theological or devotional book as one of his chief faults:

> I, William Redhead, maltman, of Barnet,...confess that I had in my possession a certain book in the vulgar tongue, in which book are inserted many errors;...I confess that I have gravely offended God and the Church in that I have kept such a book in the vulgar tongue without the previous license and examination of the ordinary[1].

A mandate of bishop Stafford of Wells is more significant still of the usual interpretation of the Oxford constitutions. On August 24, 1431, he issued from Dogmersfield a general mandate to his diocese, which made no mention of Lollard writings, or the spread of any Lollard movement in the diocese, and did not, in fact, expressly deal with Lollardy at all. Yet in one clause he

> forbade that any one should presume in any manner to translate holy scripture, or any part of it, into the English tongue, which is well-known to be our vulgar tongue, nor to [possess] books of scripture translated into the English tongue[2],

without any reference to the possibility of obtaining a special license to do so. Thus in the diocese of Bath and Wells at least, the possession of English translations of the Bible or any part of it, was expressly forbidden by the bishop[3], without his apparently perceiving that he was going beyond the strict letter of the synod of Oxford. This could hardly have been the case if licenses to read English Bibles had been at all frequently granted by other bishops, even to the nobility. Not only this, but

---

[1] *Amundesham*, I. 228. Cf. the charge against certain Colchester possessors of English books in 1414, EHR, XXIX. 102.

[2] The register is unprinted, but the late canon Scott Holmes kindly sent me the following extract, with other information: "Ne quisquam sua temeritate sacram Scripturam seu aliquam eius partem in linguam Anglicanam, quae nostra vulgaris esse dinoscitur, ullo modo transferat, neque libros Scripturae in ydioma Anglicum translatos possideat, per octo dies a tempore monitionis et inhibitionis continue numerandos...."

[3] Capes, 128 "when John Stafford in 1431 threatened with excommunication any who translated the scriptures or copied such, he made no reserve in favour of any accepted version."

Stafford succeeded Chichele as archbishop of Canterbury in 1443, so that his view of the matter became that of the primate of England. His mandate seems in fact to confirm the hypothesis that for forty or fifty years after 1408 the possession of English Bibles by the great was much less frequent than their possession of French *Bibles Historiales* had been in the fourteenth century.

The biblical Chester plays, moreover, lapsed in the first half of the fifteenth century, and were solemnly revived and played again in 1447[1]: it is possible that the omission in the interval was due to the suspicion roused by the Lollards against all biblical narratives in English. The verse "banns" to the play, which were written later but which were possibly founded on some earlier prologue or banns[2], expressed the belief that the "stories of the Testament at this time [were] in a common English tongue never read nor heard," and the author wonders that a monk should have composed them.

Finally, coming nearer to sir Thomas More's own day, an account of the condemnation of a Lollard, written by a cleric, states it as a matter of course that the translation of the Bible is forbidden by the Church. Richard Hun was condemned in 1511, and the scribe who took down the articles of his condemnation wrote under article XIII:

> He defendeth the translation of the Bible in English, and the holy scripture into the English tongue, which is prohibited by the laws of our mother, holy Church[3].

More was actually present at part, at least, of Hun's examination, and the words of the article bear out the contention of the Messenger in the *Dialogue*, that the laity at large regarded the reading of English Bibles as forbidden by the Church.

§ 4. There is no evidence that English Bibles were used, except in very rare cases, by the clergy in the fifteenth and early sixteenth centuries, or that parish priests were now universally competent to study the Vulgate, and instruct their parishioners out of it. Inventories and wills shew that books were relatively

---

[1] *Chester Plays*, 2–9.

[2] The strong approval of the monk, Randall Hignet, and monk-like practices (banns, ll. 20, 21) suggest the fifteenth century rather than 1592, the earliest MS. of the banns: while the dialectal forms of the banns appear sometimes earlier than 1592.

[3] AM, IV. 186.

much commoner and cheaper in 1450 than in 1350: whereas in 1350 a cathedral dignitary might own perhaps a dozen books, all of which he would mention in his will, in 1450 he might not mention his books separately at all, because he had as many as twenty or thirty. The educational system was the same, at the schools and universities. It is true that grammar schools were becoming more frequent, and apparently cathedral schools were now regularly equipped with separate grammar and theology masters; again, a new educational instrument was being constructed in the chantry schools and colleges[1]; but there is still no evidence of the use of biblical translations in any kind of school.

The organisation of *abc* and grammar schools remained roughly the same[2]; the provost and three chaplains of Jesus College, Rotherham, founded in 1480, said daily masses and taught grammar and theology to any scholars who came to them, but no mention is made of any teaching on the biblical text[3]. The universities still laid comparatively little stress on the study of that text, though William of Wykeham laid down in the statutes of New College in 1400 that one of the first aims of the foundation was to be the study of theology[4]. The candidates for admission into monasteries seem not to have received much education before admission, and to have been taught no more afterwards than in the thirteenth century: consequently, when the educational level of seculars slightly rose, monastic ignorance was considered the more reprehensible. The abbot of S. Albans appointed a grammar master from outside c. 1430 to teach the young monks Latin: but S. Albans was a great abbey and still numbered eminent scholars among its monks[5]. But other abbeys were less careful of learning, or less able to pay a

---

[1] *Research Ed.* 17, 42. The earliest cases of chantry priests engaged in teaching printed by Mr Leach are those of two chaplains at Saffron Walden in 1423, and one at Southwell 1475–84: in both these cases the chaplains taught for fees, at their own discretion, and not as one of the duties imposed by the founder of the chantry. For the latter, see Jesus College, Rotherham. For chantry priests who had been doing teaching in 1538 see *Chapels, Chantries and Gilds in Suffolk*, Redstone, V. B., *Suffolk Instit. of Archaeol.* XII. pp. 31, 34, 35, 36: and note the number of chantry priests described as " of small" or "of very small" learning, also VCH, *passim*.

[2] Cf. Ipswich in 1477, *Educ. Char.* 423.

[3] *Id.* 425–9; *Research Ed.* 21. For a biblical student of S. Bartholomew's hospital, Smithfield, see J. Stow's *Survey of London*, 1842, 139.

[4] *Educ. Char.* 351.      [5] *Amundesham*, I. 110, II. 305.

grammar master, and archbishop Warham commented severely in his visitation of 1511 on the ignorance of the Canterbury monks:

Also, a skilled teacher of grammar shall be provided to teach the novices and other youths grammar. For in default of such instruction it happens that most of the monks celebrating mass and performing other divine service are wholly ignorant of what they read, to the great scandal and disgrace both of religion in general and of the monastery in particular[1].

In face of such evidence it will be obvious that English Bibles might have been useful, not only for lay brothers, but many of the monks: but it is curious that, though monastic catalogues compiled between 1408 and 1526 are quite numerous[2], there is not a single case where a catalogue included any English biblical book,—except, of course, Rolle's psalter. We do indeed find that the Charterhouse at Sheen possessed a Wycliffite Bible, presented by Henry VI[3], and that the Dominicans at Cambridge possessed one at the Dissolution[4]: but these are the only known instances. The only English Bibles which monastic libraries possessed, were, according to the catalogues, Anglo-Saxon gospel books or homilies on the gospels: there is not a single instance of an English biblical book, which does not, on investigation, turn out to be a Saxon book, like the gospels at Durham, or the two manuscripts of parts of the Old Testament mentioned in an inventory of S. Paul's cathedral in 1402[5]. This shews that sir Thomas More, when he spoke of "English Bibles fair and old" as possessed by "many old abbeys," was thinking mainly of Anglo-Saxon books, or those of the communities of women[6]. Beyond his apologetic assertion, which does not of course refer exclusively to the libraries of monks, there is a striking lack of

---

[1] *Educ. Char.* 445.    [2] See appendix, *Old Eng. Lib.*, Savage, E. A.
[3] FM, I. xlvii; Bodl. 277, see p. 7 n.
[4] Leland found a "biblia in lingua vernacula" there in 1539; *Collectanea*, III. 16, 51; *Bibliom.* 201.
[5] One Bible, as far as the prophet Zechariah, one ending with the book of Job, described as "veteris Anglicae litterae," *Archaeol.* I. 451; these go back to the 1295 inventory, *id.* 496; and see references, *supra*, pp. 137–8.
[6] Like Sion, Barking, etc. For nunneries possessing English books, see p. 336; among men's houses, Leicester in 1492 had a French Comestor and *Passio Christi*, five secular French books, and no English ones; Canterbury c. 1480 a few French and one English book, Monk Bretton an English *Legenda Aurea* and a *Scale of Perfection*.

evidence that English as distinguished from Anglo-Saxon biblical books were to be found in monks' libraries. Thus neither in the schools or libraries of the monasteries, nor in those for the training of secular priests, is there any evidence for the use of English translations of the Bible.

From the wills of the fifteenth and early sixteenth centuries it may fairly be presumed that all bishops and most cathedral dignitaries now possessed a Vulgate, as the nucleus of a small library; so also did many fellows of Oxford and Cambridge colleges. There are also more recorded cases of the possession of Vulgates by parish priests: but these were rare as compared with those who possessed service books only. It may be worth while here to recapitulate that some 7578 wills dating from before 1526 have been examined[1], and that of these, 338 wills bequeathed service books, and 110 Vulgates. Between 1384, the death of Wycliffe, and 1526, 69 of the testators bequeathed Vulgates: of these, 24 were lay people, generally of noble birth, 23 were bishops or cathedral clergy, 6 were connected with the universities, and 16 only are described as rector, vicar, or chaplain. Neither the higher nor the lower clergy had ever possessed French Bibles, save very rarely, before the Wycliffite period; for such books, never very numerous in England, had been the property of the well born laity. It is not surprising again that there should be no evidence that the clergy possessed such in the fifteenth century, when French had generally ceased to be used, except in nunneries and monasteries.

Clerical or monastic Bible study still frequently took the form of compiling skeletons and lists. Henry Hawkins, of Great Dunmow, compiled a history of the Old Testament from Adam to Ptolemy Philopator, chiefly from Comestor and Josephus, about 1450[2]; and a little later an anonymous scribe, "considering the length and hardness of holy scripture, and namely of the ground of the letter historical, the negligence also of some that might labour and will not," compiled a list of kings, descending from Adam through patriarchs, judges, kings and prophets to Edward IV of England[3]. A good deal of translation from Latin and French works was also accomplished in this century, but

---

[1] See appendix, p. 391; for a French Bible, VCH *London*, I. 225.
[2] Trin. Oxford, 29.     [3] C.C.C. Oxford, 207.

rather of patristic and mystical works than those dealing with
the biblical text. Books called *Examples of holy scripture*, consisting of short paragraphs, generally arranged alphabetically,
of different personages, virtues, etc., mentioned in holy writ, were
relatively common[1]. About eleven cases have been found where
the secular clergy owned or bequeathed English devotional
books,—like those of Rolle, Hilton, or Nicholas Love's *Mirrour*[2]:
one of them was "an English book of the exposition of the gospels."

§ 5. There are five known cases after 1408 when orthodox
priests possessed English translations of the Bible, two of which
are known to be Wycliffite texts. The first is a Dominican friar
and hermit of Newcastle-on-Tyne, John Lacy, who possessed an
early version of the Wycliffite New Testament, written about
1400, without any prologue or heretical matter in it[3]: he may
have obtained it before 1408, or have obtained license to use it.
He bequeathed also in 1420 an English hours of our Lady[4]. The
second is that of Roger Lyne, chantry priest in the church of
S. Swithun, London Stone, who owned a collection of the Sunday
epistles and gospels, unglossed, in the early Wycliffite text,
either before or after 1408[5]. The third is that of William
Revetour, a chaplain of York, and for his day, a great collector
of English books. He bequeathed in 1446 an English book of
miracle plays, and English legendary, the *Prick of Conscience*, a
book on the pater noster, and "a certain book treating of the
Bible, in English[6]." If this is an expression for a complete
English Bible, it would have been an exceptionally valuable
book for a simple chaplain to possess: but the possession of a
book of miracle plays is so unusual as to suggest that William
was personally connected with their production at York, and
needed an English Bible for the instruction of the players. The
fourth case is that of Roger Walton, a priest who owned part

[1] Cf. Bernard, *Cat.* Nos. 2087, 2502.

[2] TE, II. 34, 151, 219; III. 91, 199, 165 n.; IV. 280; *Pembroke Descrip. Cat.*
xxviii; *Trans. Essex Archaeol. Soc.* v. 293; TV, III. 444; Trin. Camb. 352,
f. 134.

[3] Rawl. C. 258, in FM, I. xlix.

[4] S. John's, Oxford, 94.                    [5] Harl. 1710.

[6] TE, II. 117, "quendam librum tractatum [sic: perhaps scribal or
copyist's error for *tractantem*] de Biblia in Anglico." The book was left,
apparently, to a layman: and it appears doubtful whether either Revetour
or the legatee had any other license to use it beyond that of their confessors.

of the later Wycliffite New Testament in Henry VIII's reign[1];
and the fifth, Stephen Tomson, a notary public, who possessed
an Old Testament with the *General Prologue* in 1519[2].

(*a*) There is no doubt that between 1408 and 1526 certain
lay people, of rank eminent enough to be the "friends" of sir
Thomas More, possessed English translations of the Bible. They
were allowed to do so, as earlier nobles had been allowed to
possess French Bibles: though there is no evidence whatever that
the Church "encouraged" them to do so. The practical certainty
that no complete translation existed except the Wycliffite, and
the knowledge that non-Wycliffite partial translations were
very rare, renders it likely that, in the majority of cases, those
who possessed English biblical books possessed them in the
Wycliffite versions, though without the tract known as the
*General Prologue*. The Wycliffite text itself was not heretical,
and not signed by any author's name: any "doctor" who was
willing to license his penitent to use an English Bible at all,
would have licensed a Wycliffite manuscript at almost any time
after 1408, in complete uncertainty that it was Wycliffite. In
four cases we have evidence that the owners of Wycliffite manuscripts had suspicions as to the lawfulness of retaining them, and
deliberately sought to disguise their provenance in order to protect their valuable books: one is a manuscript where the scribe
has dated his work as being finished in 1408, and a contemporary
hand has altered the date to 1308[3]: another, one of the Lollard
glosses on the gospels, to which a contemporary hand has added
as title: "the work of Thomas Aquinas, extracted from divers
doctors, and translated into the mother tongue[4]."

Some of the manuscripts written after 1408, and still preserved
to us, must have been written for Lollard use, as the evidence of
Lollard trials shews. The facts that they have no name, and no
Lollard comments, do not disprove their Lollard ownership, for

---

[1] FM, I. xlix: a MS. written apparently after 1500.

[2] *Id.* I. liv.

[3] FM, I. xlviii, Fairfax, 2. The change of date must have been done
purposely, to safeguard the MS. from the provisions of 1408, "in the days of
the late master John Wycliffe, or since."

[4] Bodl. 143, f. 222 *b*: the MS. which has the Lollard passage, interpolated
among the glosses of the doctors, carefully erased (ff. 159 *b*, 160). See for two
other ante-dated MSS., C.C.C. Oxford 20, and *Rylands Cat.*, Guppy, H.,
1907, 10.

to write such name or marginal comment in the manuscript was dangerous. Many of the epistle and gospel books belonged probably to Lollards, for Purvey argued in one of his tracts that men ought to have the epistles and gospels translated for them: in fact, he took up here exactly the attitude which certain German orthodox teachers took up a century later[1]. The Lollards went to mass, however unorthodox might be their theory of the sacrament: Purvey wrote that "the sacrament on the altar is verily Christ's body sacramentally and spiritually, and more other manners than any earthly man can tell," and he was shocked at the suggestion of Richard of Armagh that the sacrament might lawfully be made in English. The Lollards never devised a new sacrament of their own, like the *consolamentum* of the Waldensians; and the evidence that they ever had celebrations of the Holy Communion, conducted by unconsecrated priests, is scanty. Their midnight gatherings were always, apparently, for Bible reading and exposition, and there is no suggestion in Lollard literature that they repudiated the obligation to hear mass on Sundays and holy days[2]. There is no incongruity, but much probability, in the idea of Lollards possessing gospel and epistle books in English: and among those mentioned by Forshall and Madden which have no distinctive mark of ownership, either by Lollard or orthodox, there is no antecedent probability that they were owned by orthodox lay people. The probability rather is, that they were owned by Lollards, or by nuns.

There is no recorded will of a lay person between 1408 and 1526 which bequeathes an English Bible,—though there were two before,—the Lollard sympathiser, Thomas duke of Gloucester in 1397, and a Bristol merchant in 1404[3]. Two existent manuscripts, however, once belonged to English kings: Henry VI[4], who presented one to the Carthusians of Sheen, and Henry VII[5]. The first was copied from a Lollard manuscript with the heretical *General Prologue*: but the scribe copied only the first chapter; the second was without it. It is significant that in the days of real Lollard danger neither Henry IV, nor that pious king, Henry V, possessed an English Bible: though Henry V

---

[1] Cf. p. 129.     [2] Apart from their general repudiation of canon law.
[3] See pp. 288–9, TE, I. 271, and appendix, p. 398.
[4] FM, I. xlvii.     [5] *Id*. I. xxxix.

used Lydgate's poems on the psalms in his private prayers, and had them sung in Windsor chapel at evensong when he was present[1]. One other manuscript belonged to a lay woman: it is the only known case of non-royal lay ownership after 1408, and it is the only case where some sort of a license appears to have been granted. It is a later version of the New Testament, and on the fly-leaf is a note to the effect that the owner's mother bought it, and that it was "overseen and read"—not by a bishop—but by two doctors, whose names are almost erased[2].

Thus of the known cases of ownership of English Bibles after 1408, five were priests, and three lay people,—two of them kings. This is a very small number compared to the remaining wills, or to the cases of Lollard ownership, which, even in the trials already printed, are mentioned more than eleven times[3].

(b) The evidence that nuns were sometimes licensed to use English Bibles is more explicit. It is still scanty, for it is found only in connexion with two houses, Sion and Barking, at about 1430 and 1400 respectively, and these cannot be taken as altogether typical of the majority of English nunneries at the date. Both were large and important houses, the nuns of Sion especially being drawn from the noblest and best educated classes, while there was at the date of the foundation of Sion some connexion of personnel between the two, for a Barking nun became the first Sion abbess. The majority of English nunneries were smaller, and the nuns less well educated, than at Sion. But though the direct evidence of English Bible reading is small, it is supported by continental analogies. The Bible was preeminently regarded as a book of meditation for the devout, and the Dominican Gottesfreunde had been the first orthodox to advise the use of translations: while two German fifteenth century nunnery catalogues mentioned them[4].

In England Walter Hilton had suggested that lay people aiming at the mixed life, and practising contemplation, should read

---

[1] *Annales of John Stow*, London, 1631, 342; *Trin. Coll. Descrip. Cat.* II 80, MS. 600.

[2] FM, I. lxiii, Ashburnham, 3. The note appears to read: "A lytel boke of...viii. l. vi. s. viii. d. and hit...a holy man...was over seyne, and redd be Doctor Thomas Ebb...al and Doctor Ryve...my modir bought hit."

[3] See pp. 356–70. MSS. mentioned by FM and containing the *Gen. Prol.* were also probably Lollard.     [4] See p. 111.

the sayings and examples of our Lord, presumably from the Latin gospels: so that it is probable that in the fifteenth century English Bibles were used to some extent in the largest and best instructed English nunneries. It was not the case that the best instructed nuns used Latin Bibles, and the most ignorant, English ones: but that the best instructed nuns were allowed to use English translations, perhaps by themselves, perhaps to help in the understanding of the Vulgate, while the smaller nunneries and least instructed nuns almost certainly did not have them at all. Large and flourishing nunneries, where the nuns were drawn from the highest social classes, had the most learned and enlightened directors and confessors, who in some cases obtained licenses for their use of English Bibles; but the directors of small nunneries were often parish priests, or friars who were not eminent scholars in their order, and there is no evidence at all that they encouraged these houses in the use of biblical translations. It is significant, at any rate, that the scanty evidence for the use of biblical translations in nunneries comes to us almost entirely from Sion, the most splendid foundation of the fifteenth century, though possibly also from Barking, another very important house.

One treatise written for nuns comes from the period when the discussion over the lawfulness of biblical translations was in progress, and echoes one of the common arguments about the difficulty of translating without much circumlocution,—afterwards developed at great length by friar Palmer. The author of the *Chastising of God's Children* possibly wrote it for a nun of Barking, since the earliest reference to the book (which dates it as written previously to 1401), is in a *Penitential*[1] of Sibylla Felton, abbess of that house from 1394–1419. The author stated that "some now in these days," as if the custom were modern, "use to say on English their psalter and mattins of our Lady, and the seven psalms, and the litany[2],"—use, that is, an English primer: for the little office of our Lady, the penitential psalms and the litany formed the invariable minimum part of such books,—English manuscripts of which actually begin to be found

[1] Madan, *Sum. Cat.* v. no. 27701; for the reference, f. 145 *b*. The *Chastising* was printed c. 1492, see Ricci, S , *Census of Caxtons*, 110.
[2] Paues, 1904, xxviii.

from this date, and not earlier[1]. He did not state that reading of English gospels was actually practised at the date, but mentioned that it was a disputed subject,—as indeed, in 1401, it was.

Many men reproveth to have the psalter, or mattins, or the gospel in English, or the Bible, because they may not be translated into no vulgar word by the word as it standeth, without great circumlocution, after the feeling of the first writers, which translated that into Latin by the teaching of the Holy Ghost. Nevertheless I will not reprove such translations, ne I reprove not to have them on English, ne to read on them where they may stir you to more devotion, and to the love of God. But utterly to use them in English and leave the Latin, I hold it not commendable, and namely in them that been bounden to say their psalter, or mattins of our Lady.

The rest of the passage shews that the writer was mainly concerned to point out to those bound to the recitation of the little office, that it was not fulfilled by the recitation of the translation from the primer, any more than psalms given in penance could be recited in English; but the passage probably covered an approval of the use of English Bibles for meditation. In connexion with the slight indication that the *Chastising of God's Children* was written for a nun of Barking, it is interesting to find that a Wycliffite manuscript belonged in the fifteenth century to a Barking nun, and probably two Barking nuns in succession. Sister Mary Hastings of Barking possessed a book of English religious treatises, and among them the texts of the apocryphal books of Tobias and Susanna[2]: and its earlier owner wrote her name in it as Matilda Hayle, of Barking. Probably she also was a nun of the same house. The book must have been

---

[1] Some writers (as Mr Manning in the *People's Faith in the Age of Wyclif*, 1916, pp. 10, 46), appear not to realise that the earliest primers, or books of hours, were in Latin. *Prymer*, EETS, p. xxxix, gives the invariable minimum of primers, both Latin and English, as the Hours of the B.V.M., the penitential and gradual psalms, the litany, office for the dead, and the commendations: other prayers and tracts were sometimes added. Emmanuel 246 is a late fourteenth century English primer, as were those described by Carleton Brown, I. 24, 512; and there are no MSS. of English primers earlier than c. 1380. D. II. 82 is a Sarum primer of about 1430: cf. those mentioned in Maskell's *Mon. Rit. Eccles. Ang.; Prymer*, EETS, OS, 105. For owners of primers in Latin, see VCH, *Sussex*, II. 20.

[2] FM, I. xliv, Addit. 10596, which has f. 82, *Sister* Mary Hastings, unnoticed by the editors.

the sister's private property, and not a library book, though it probably became one at sister Mary Hastings's death.

The first evidence for the period after 1408 is that of the *Myroure of our Ladye*, from Sion abbey. This was a community of monks and nuns, founded by Henry V in 1415, but not properly established till the consecration of the second abbess in 1420, at Twickenham[1]. In the meantime, the community consisted of postulants for the Brigittine order, many of whom were already professed monks or nuns from other less strict English orders; the abbess for the first year was a Benedictine nun from Barking, and the mixed community was being trained by Swedish sisters, from the parent house of the Brigittine order. S. Bridget, their foundress, is credited with having made some biblical translation[2] herself, and the order in Sweden encouraged the use of Swedish books of devotion, as it did the study of letters generally: the new community at Sion was therefore likely to be open-minded as regards the use of biblical translations into English. With the neighbouring community of Carthusians of Sheen, it represented the great work of reparation of Henry V for the murder of Richard II: it was very splendidly endowed, and entered by ladies of the highest rank. The brothers at Sion, much fewer in number, included some of the most eminent scholars of the fifteenth century, so that the Sion nuns were looked after by a much abler staff of chaplains than those of any other nunnery in England. The *Myroure* was written between 1421 and 1450: it is a translation of the Brigittine office used by the nuns, together with instructions to aid their understanding and devotion in the recitation of the Latin office. The author referred twice in it to the constitutions of 1408:

And forasmuch as it is forbidden under pain of cursing that no man should have nor draw any text of holy scripture into English without license of the bishop diocesan: and in divers places of your service are such texts of holy scripture: therefore I have asked and have license of our bishop to draw such things into English to your ghostly comfort and profit, so that both our conscience in the drawing, and yours in the having, may be the more sure and clear....Of psalms I have drawn but a few, for ye may have them of Richard Hampole's drawing, and out of English Bibles, if ye have license thereto[3].

---

[1] *Incendium Amoris*, Deanesly, M., pp. 109–29.
[2] V, *Suèdoises* [*Versions*], v. 1876.
[3] *Myroure*, p. 71, p. 3.

The brothers and sisters had separate libraries at Sion, and it would have been of great interest to see whether the sisters' library contained any English biblical translations. Unfortunately, only the brothers' catalogue has survived: and this shews that the brothers possessed no English Bibles when the catalogue was compiled[1]. In 1517, however, an early version of the Wycliffite New Testament was presented to "the master confessor and brethren of Sion" (not to the sisters), by dame Alice Danvers[2], so that henceforward the brothers could have lent the sisters a copy.

The author of the *Myroure* has been conjectured to be doctor Thomas Gascoign[3], chancellor of Oxford, and a great benefactor to Sion: he bequeathed his own library to the brethren. His "if ye have license thereto" is not positive evidence that the sisters did use English Bibles, and it is significant that he says nothing about Bible reading, English or otherwise, in a long section devoted to the "devout reading of holy books[4]." He described the different kinds of books, but even when describing those which "stir up the affections of the soul," he did not, as might have been expected, mention the gospels. The passage is exactly parallel to one of Hilton's, where such a reference is made. He referred to following the lessons, or legend, at mattins, in English, while the Latin was being read: but these lessons were not biblical, and he was obviously referring to the translation and comment on them which he had himself made as part of the *Myroure*[5].

---

[1] See *Syon*, 171, for a partial interlinear gloss; cf. *infra*, p. 418.

[2] FM, I. lxii, no. 156: without the *Gen. Prol.* or any evidence of heresy.

[3] *Myroure*, ix. Gascoign was no doubt much interested in Sion: but it seems a little doubtful whether one of the brothers, perhaps the liturgiologist, Clement Maidstone, is not a more probable compiler of so detailed a commentary on the Brigittine office: especially as he alludes to having obtained a license from "*our* bishop." French was still used in some nunneries in the fifteenth century for directions and rules which the nuns were not expected to be able to read in Latin: but English was used for this purpose at Sion from the first, probably because the Swedish sisters had already one language to learn beside their mother tongue. The *Additions* to the rule of S. Bridget, or local constitutions for the English Brigittines, were drawn up in English, as was the *Martilogium*, or obit book. A Sion *diurnale*, or book of hours, Magd. Camb. 11, has the rubrics in English; and Magd. Camb. 13 is a book of the Latin and English verses and prayers of Jasper Fyloll, apparently a Dominican who in 1518 had passed on to Sion.　　　　　[4] *Myroure*, 65-71.

[5] *Id.* 71: the services for the seven days of the week, including mattins,

A fifteenth century English translation of the penitential psalms is also connected with Sion abbey. The second confessor general, to whom the establishment of the house was really due, who drew up the local rule for the house, and ruled the community till his death in 1428, was Thomas Fishbourn, who had himself in earlier life lived in a hermitage at S. Albans[1]. During this period he had attracted the king's notice through his acquaintance with Eleanor Hull, Elizabeth Beauchamp and other court ladies, who probably resorted to him for spiritual direction. Eleanor Hull, or Hill, did not become a Brigittine nun[2] when Fishbourn was made confessor general at Sion, but one of her pious exercises seems to have been the translation of a long commentary or exposition on the seven penitential psalms, from French into English. The work is very long and laborious[3], and is followed by meditations on the seven days of the week, and certain prayers, all attributed in the manuscript to Eleanor Hull.

Unfortunately we have no English nunnery catalogues to compare with those of Nuremberg and Delft[4]: and their non-existence says little for the size or value of the nuns' libraries at the date. Though it would probably be true to say that nuns used English Bibles more frequently than lay people,—because they needed them for meditation, because of the evidence of the Sion

---

are translated, pp. 72–276. The lessons at mattins were not those of the breviary, but were gone through in the course of one week, and consisted mainly of patristic passages selected in honour of our Lady.

[1] *Amundesham*, RS, I. 27; *Incendium*, 114.

[2] She is not called sister, but Dame Alyanore Hull in Kk. 1. 6, a fifteenth century MS. of this commentary on the psalms, and meditations.

[3] In Kk.1. 6, the commentary occupies ff. 1–148. It begins: f. 2, *"Domine, ne in furore tuo arguas me:* This title is said in the end of the psalms of David. Ye shall understand and know what title meaneth. *Title* is as much as to say as a king, for to open the understanding of the letter of the psalms, and the spiritual significance. For right as we openeth the door of the house wherein we would enter, right so it behoveth by convenable expositions of the title for to enter into the understanding of the psalm of which the title goeth before. And now it is fitting that ye know what psalm is to mean: *psalm*, as the scripture saith, is hymn," etc. Kk. 1. 6 is not the original MS., the note on f. 179 *b, Alyanore Hull drew out of French all this before written in this little book* is copied, since Kk. 1 6 is a large folio; the scribe's name is given on f. 179 *b* as a certain Walter.

[4] See pp. 111, 113. Cf. *King's Descrip. Cat.* MS. 18, for a list of books bequeathed (after c. 1380, since a *Pupilla Oculi* is mentioned) by Peter, the vicar of Swine, to the small Cistercian nunnery of Swine: this has two Latin, but no English biblical books. Cf. *Monast.* III. 424, for Kilburn nunnery, which in 1536 had two English MSS. of the *Legenda Aurea*.

*Myroure*, and because the German and Dutch analogies suggest it,—it is almost certainly an overstatement to say that English biblical versions were at all frequently used in nunneries. There is no single known case where a nunnery library possessed one: John Busch and the Brethren of the Common Life had to fight hard for the right of the sisters' communities to use German or Dutch books, and we hear of no such orthodox champions of vernacular Bibles in England. While the evidence is so slight, it is unsafe to generalise: but it is highly improbable that a majority of the nunneries possessed even an English gospel and epistle book, much less an English Bible.

§ 6. Catalogues of libraries, the wills of private individuals, and owners' names in existent manuscripts, give a fairly safe index to the relative popularity of the English books used by the devout in this period[1]. The mentions of English devotional books in wills are much fewer than those of Latin service-books, but a good many wills between 1408 and 1526 bequeathed either a single English book, or a small collection of them. In lay people's wills, the works of Richard Rolle were perhaps the commonest, and were mentioned at least fourteen times. Nicholas Love's *Mirrour* was bequeathed five times by clergy, and five times by lay people, besides belonging to the canons of Osney and the Sion nuns; probably also this book was sometimes referred to under the vague title of "English meditations on the life of Christ," which occurs fairly frequently. Hilton's works were bequeathed at least nine times, and other English books less frequently mentioned were the *Pore Caitiff*, the second Deguilleville *Pilgrimage*, known in English as *Grace Dieu*, English primers (four times), the *Chastising of God's Children*, an *English book of the Pater Noster*, the *Revelations of S. Bridget*, *Dives and Pauper*, the *Knight of the Tower*, the *Legenda Aurea* in English prose or verse, Suso's *Eternal Wisdom*, and poems like the *Gospel of Nicodemus*, John Awdley's *Concilium Conscientiae*, the *South English Legendary*, and several saints' lives. Books of "vices and virtues" were also fairly common. The wills thus shew the nature of the English devotional books used in the fifteenth and early sixteenth centuries, especially by lay people: and the

---

[1] See appendix, wills, p. 391, and for books bequeathed by clergy, p. 333. It is hoped to print lists of the English books found in wills, shortly.

relative infrequency of English biblical books is striking. Had the use of the latter been generally encouraged by the Church, or had their possession even been regarded as legitimate for the laity in general, some case, or cases, of the bequest of English Bibles by the laity would almost certainly have been found. English Bibles, or English biblical books, were usually far longer and more costly books than tracts of Rolle or Hilton, or Nicholas Love's *Mirrour*, and there would be the more reason to mention them in the testator's will: yet they are not found. There is no reason to suspect that any of these testators who bequeathed English books possessed English Bibles in their little collections, though some, like Cecily, duchess of York, who died in 1495, were of exalted rank and rich enough to do so. The inference is, that the possession of English Bibles was rare, even among the great.

§ 7. Among the frequent manuals for parish priests used during the period, none have been found to recommend the translation of the Sunday gospel as part of the sermon, the use of an English Bible or English gospels in preparing sermons, or the exhortation of parishioners to study the scriptures. No passage has been found which suggests either that priests and chaplains used translations themselves, or advised their use by others.

The Latin manuals mentioned above continued to be the most popular in the fifteenth century, though a few more were written[1]. John Mirk, prior about 1403 of the house of Austin canons in Lilleshall, Shropshire, wrote a *Manuale Sacerdotum*, which he sent with a dedicatory letter to a certain parish priest, saying that he hoped he would soon turn it into English[2].

English manuals now began, however, to be written expressly for parish priests. Mirk translated the greater part of the *Pars Oculi Sacerdotis*[3] into English verse, and into this book of *Instructions for Parish Priests*[4] he put manifold directions for the priest's own life, the direction of his flock, the administration of

---

[1] Cf. the *Speculum Curatorum*, Mm. 1. 20, Balliol, 77; the *Stella Clericorum*, Laud Misc. 206, New Coll. cccIV. f. 94; the *Manipulus Curatorum*, Nor. and *Norwich Archaeol. Soc.* IV. 338, *Linc. Cath. Stats.* ed. 1897, 847; early printed manuals, *Trans. Bibliog. Soc.* VII. 163 ff.
[2] DNB, Mirk.        [3] See p. 202.
[4] Ed. Peacock, EETS, OS, 31, 1868; cf. Wells, 361.

the sacraments, etc., but we find no mention of the study of the Vulgate or its translations. The book is not merely a close translation of the *Pars Oculi*; it may fairly be said to portray the ideal parish priest of about 1400; yet there is no mention of his having any books besides office-books. Mirk, in his zeal for clerical education, wrote also a collection of sermons for the greater festivals, and this *Liber Festivalis*[1] became widely spread in manuscripts and early printed editions. In his prologue, Mirk stated that through his "own simple understanding" he understood well the difficulty in preparing sermons of those who had charge of souls, and "for that many excuse them for default of books and also by simpleness of conning," he had translated this treatise, mainly from the *Legenda Aurea*, for their help. The sermons are sometimes homilies upon texts, sometimes legends of the saints, or sometimes begin with a Bible story: but there is no indication that the gospel was ever to be itself translated at the beginning of the sermon.

An early fifteenth century manuscript[2] has a typical set of sermons for the aid of the parish priest. The text, drawn always from the Sunday gospel, is given in Latin, and the moral implications of the Sunday gospel are then expounded, without any translation of the gospel itself, or even, in this manuscript, of separate verses. Such sermons, or skeletons for sermons, are fairly common: but none of them preface the sermon with a translation of the gospel.

The writers of manuals for the laity generally professed that they aimed at the instruction of the "lewid" or simple: but those who could have owned and read the manuals could have read biblical translations, so that references to these might have been expected, if their use was encouraged. English manuals were not written for the use of agricultural labourers, but for well-born ladies and substantial burgesses; yet even for these, there was no hint of exhortation to study the gospels. There was no reference, as in a few early sixteenth century books in Germany, to their acquainting themselves with the gospels, by means either of attending sermons where the Sunday gospel

---

[1] Wells, 301.
[2] Trin. Camb. 333. This is the MS. which contains the *Against them that say that holy writ*, printed p. 439, but these sermons appear quite orthodox.

was closely translated, or of getting some better educated neighbour to read from some vernacular plenary or gospel book. So far as manuals for the conduct of clergy and laity give evidence, the movement which affected German orthodoxy through the Brethren of the Common Life and their pupils, and which finally recommended the acquaintance of the laity with the vernacular gospels, never touched England at all.

The early fifteenth century manual, *Dives and Pauper*, mentioned earlier[1], remarked almost regretfully that "now men say that no lewid men should meddle with God's law, or the gospel, or holy writ," but in its long discourses on the commandments, creed, etc., said nothing to recommend such meddling. Nor did another manual written about 1400, which discoursed similarly on the commandments, etc., and lamented the general ignorance[2]:

*Here ginnen the ten commandments of God.* Where is any man nowadays that asketh, how I should love God and mine even-Christian? how I shall flee sin and serve God truly as a true Christian man should? What man is that, that will learn the true law of God, which He biddeth every Christian man to keep upon pain of damnation in hell without end? Who knoweth the seven deadly sins and their branches, the seven deeds of mercy bodily and ghostly, and his five wits? as who saith, but few. Unnethe is there any lewid man or lewid woman that can right well say his pater noster, his ave Maria and his creed, and sown the words out readily as they should. But when they play Christmas games about the fire, therein will they not fail.

There were several other fifteenth century manuals for the laity which were simply expositions of the usual skeleton of

[1] See p. 326. The writer translated some verses of the gospels himself.

[2] Laud Misc. 23, § 1, ff. 3–7; 210, ff. 20–93 b; cf. Bernard, *Cat.* no. 2315. The tract is addressed primarily to his mother, and "wit ye well that I desire every man and woman and child to be my mother, for Christ saith: he that doth His Father's will, is His brother, sister, and mother," Laud Misc. 23, f. 20. The author was not a Lollard, but had a grudge against the religious orders, cf. f. 67 b: "Better it were to leave such ordinances of men: therefore His (Christ's) religion is most general, for all men be bound to hold it upon pain of damnation: and most free, for Christ with His convent asketh not twenty marks, as thou wouldest some time have given for me to have been a canon, and they would not receive me for less than twenty pounds. Blessed be Christ with His free convent, that it so ordained, for He loveth no simony, ne asketh of none that will come to His religion pecis (cups), mazers, ne silver spoons, ne whether he be bond nor free, or come of great lords to maintain their possessions." Extracts printed in *Rel. Antiq.* I. 38.

theology and ethics,—creed, commandments, the deadly sins, the works of mercy, etc. Sometimes expositions on the five wits, the four counsels of perfection, the eight beatitudes, the principal joys of Paradise, the principal pains of hell, etc., were added, the whole forming a long list of short homilies[1]. The commonest of these manuals constructed on the official plan, was the *Speculum Christiani*[2] of John Watton, which did for the south of England and the fifteenth century what Gaytrik's treatise had done for the north of England and the fourteenth. Gaytrik's work had been in rhyme, this exposition was in prose, "a treatise in English containing the archbishop's order as to what parsons and vicars ought to teach their parishioners[3]," with the usual syllabus following. Another very common one was the collection of homilies on the creed, commandments, pater noster, etc., known as the *Pore Caitiff*[4], the authorship of which is of special interest, as it has been mistakenly attributed to the Lollards, and even Wycliffe. This was due to the similarity of the way in which the author alludes to himself, to that of Purvey in his prologues to the Lollard comments on the gospel:

"This treatise[5]," he says, "compiled of a poor caitiff and needy of ghostly help of God, shall teach simple men and women of good will the right way to heaven, if they will busy them to have it in mind and work thereafter, without multiplication of many books: and as a child, willing to be a clerk, beginneth at the ground, that is, his A. B. C., so he thus desiring to speed the better, beginneth at the ground of health, that is, Christian man's belief;...but, for the belief's self is not sufficient to man's salvation, withouten good works of charity, as Christ saith by His apostle Saint James, therefore he

---

[1] As in Addit. 10106, ff. 39 *b*–47, where 20 such headings are discussed.

[2] See pp. 196–200.

[3] Sidney Sussex, 55, f. 41; Jesus, 51; Pembroke, 285, f. 51 *b*, which belonged in fourteenth century to Ralph Maynard; Laud Misc. 104; Bernard, *Cat.* no. 1886.

[4] Wells, 482; extracts printed in Vaughan's *Life of Wycliffe* (*British Reformers*), 1852, pp. 382 ff.

[5] Ff. 6. 34, f. 1, early fifteenth century. See Wells, 482. The authorship of this tract has been confused by the supposition that Pecock alluded to its author as "a certain friar," who wrote it "pro suo defensorio" (see FZ, xiii. n. 3), a description which obviously cannot apply to the contents of this treatise. Pecock much more probably alluded to the friar Peckham's *Liber Pauperis contra insipientem novellarum haeresium confectorem*, i.e. William de St-Amour; or possibly to the *Protectorium Pauperis* of the Carmelite, Richard Maidstone, which Walden copied in his MS. of the FZ; cf. FZ, !xxiv.

purposeth with God's help, suyngly to tell the commandments of God, in which the charitable works be contained, that belong to the belief. And, for it is hard to purchase aught of God in prayer till a man verily believe and live after His behests, as He Himself saith in the gospel: Whereto say ye me, Lord, Lord, and do not thilke things that I say? therefore, following after the behests, he thinketh with the help of God to shew shortly the prayer that Jesu Christ taught to His disciples, that is, the pater noster; and after these, some short sentences exciting men to heavenly desire, for thus it behoveth to stigh[1] up as by a ladder of divers rungs, fro the ground of belief unto the keeping of God's hests, and so up fro virtue to virtue till he see God of Sion reigning in everlasting bliss."

After this prologue come homilies on the creed, commandments, pater noster, the counsels of perfection, and a few short tracts, some of which may have been original, while others were certainly extracted or copied from various religious writers, including Rolle and Hilton[2]. There is nothing at all to shew that the author sympathised with Lollardy, and the mystical pieces selected by him as "exciting to heavenly desire" are from the stock authors of mediaeval mysticism. The collection dates from about 1400, or perhaps a few years earlier: but though as far as the date goes the work might be Purvey's, it is unlikely for dialectal and other reasons[3]. In any case, the first tracts on the creed, commandments, etc., follow the normal form, and contain no advice to study the gospels.

---

[1] Climb or rise.

[2] These short tracts, corresponding to the "short sentences exciting men to heavenly desire" of the prologue differ in number and order in different MSS., which have not yet been collated for the establishment of the text. Ft. 6. 34 has, after that on the counsels, *Si quis vult venire post me*, tracts known as *Patience, Temptation, Charter of Pardon, the Soul and the Flesh, De Nomine Jesu* (which incorporates passages from Rolle's *Form of perfect living*, cf. f. 87 *b* and Horstmann, I. 37-8), *Meekness, Active and Contemplative Life* (apparently, Hilton's *Epistle on Mixed Life*), *Chastity*. These tracts are found, with some others, in Rawlinson, C. 69, C. 699, C. 751, C. 882; Ashmole, 1286, Douce, 21587, 288; Bernard, *Cat.* nos. 1843, 2322, 3054; Exeter, 49; Magd. Oxford, 93; Ff. 6. 34; Ff. 6. 55.

[3] (1) The conventionality of the teaching suggests a very early work of Purvey if it were his at all, and the MSS. of the *Pore Caitiff* all appear slightly too late in date for this. (2) Purvey's dialect was of the comparatively uninflected type usual with Oxford scholars at the date, while the original pieces of the *P.C.* are more distinctly southern. (3) Purvey was uninterested in mysticism, and would scarcely have added so many mystical extracts to his collection. Thus the selection of "poor caitiff" as a pseudonym by the author must have been merely a coincidence with Purvey's

§ 8. It will thus be seen that there is no pre-Reformation evidence whatever for the positive encouragement of English Bible reading by the Church, though nuns and lay-women were sometimes given individual licenses to use them. On the other hand, the abundant evidence on fifteenth century Church customs leaves no room for doubt that the gospel was never normally translated at mass. It is interesting, finally, to compare these historical results, and sir Thomas More's scheme in 1528 for the presentation of English Bibles to the orthodox devout of the upper classes[1], with the earliest sets of episcopal injunctions which dealt with the matter in the English Reformation, and which date from the year 1538. Different editions of the English scriptures had been issued between Tindale's New Testament, in 1526, and Coverdale's revised Bible, known as the Great Bible, whose issue was expected in 1538, although it was actually delayed till 1539. The lesser monasteries had fallen, and the English Reformation had begun its course, when in 1538 Cromwell sent to archbishop Cranmer the Royal Injunctions which ordered that a copy of the Great Bible was to be set in a convenient place in every parish church, for parishioners to read. The bishops issued their own injunctions for the carrying out of these Royal Injunctions in their own dioceses, and three of those issued in 1538,—those of archbishop Lee of York, Shaxton of Salisbury, and Voysey of Exeter—are of particular interest with regard to the provisions made for the use of these English Bibles.

They provided for the reading of the gospel and epistle from the English Bible at mass, in the pulpit, with a sermon thereon if possible:

All curates [parish priests]...shall every holy-day read the gospel and epistle of that day out of the English Bible, plainly and distinctly[2].

All...having cures [are commanded to] every Sunday and holy-day continually recite, and sincerely declare in the pulpit, at the

use of similar ones. Cf. Madan, *Sum. Cat.* IV, no. 21947 for John Burton's translation of the *Legenda Aurea*, "drawn out of French into English by a sinful wretch"; E. Underhill's *Mirror of Simple Souls*, 5, "I most unworthy creature and outcast of all other"; index of Holder Egger's *Chron. Salimbene*, for Petrus Peccator, Pietro Peccadore.

[1] See *Workes*, *Dialogue*, 245.　　　[2] Lee, of York: Frere, *Visit.* II. 46..

high mass time, in the English tongue, both the epistle and gospel of the same day (if there be time thereto), or else the one of them at the least[1].

All such of the said clergy, having cure of souls within my diocese, [are commanded to] every Sunday declare sincerely in time and place accustomed, in the English tongue, or in the Cornish tongue where the English tongue is not used, all or part of the epistle or gospel of that day[2].

References to the setting up of the English Bible in the church occur in several of the episcopal injunctions of the date[3]: and also sentences which shew that opposition to the reading of the English Bible by the laity was expected from some at least of the clergy,—a confirmation of the assertion of the Messenger in sir Thomas More's *Dialogue*. Bishop Rowland Lee, of Coventry, had even before the Royal Injunctions of 1538 ordered each parish priest to place a Bible in Latin and English in his church, for any man to read:

And [ye] shall not discourage, but earnestly...admonish every man to read the Bible in Latin or English:...always gently and charitably exhorting them to use a sober and modest behaviour in the reading and inquisition of the true sense[4].

And that ye shall discourage no man privily or apertly from the reading or hearing of the said Bible[5].

That they shall (according to the king's highness' Injunctions) in nowise discourage any man to read in the English Bible,...but shall comfort them therein: nevertheless exhorting them to enter into the reading thereof with a spirit of meekness, etc.[6]

That none of you discourage any lay person from reading of holy scripture, but rather animate and encourage them thereto, so that it be done of them without bragging or arrogancy[7].

That ye, nor none of you, shall discourage any layman from the

[1] Shaxton, of Salisbury, Frere, *Visit.* II. 54.

[2] Voysey, of Exeter, *id.* II. 61. For Edward VI's Injunctions to the same effect in 1547, see *id.* II. 123; for Royal Injunctions to Lincoln minster, 1548, *id.* II. 168; for Cranmer's articles for Canterbury diocese, 1548, *id.* II. 180; and cf. references given under *Gospel*, *id.* I. 274.

[3] See under *Bible*, Frere, *Visit.* I. 224.

[4] In 1537, *id.* II. 20. All these injunctions of 1537–8 enjoining English Bible reading are coupled with clauses for the declaration of the king's Supreme Headship under Christ of the Church of England, the withstanding of the usurpations of the bishop of Rome, etc. This lends no support to any theory that the Bible-reading clauses were merely the recognition of an earlier custom. They were in fact as novel as the other clauses.

[5] *Id.* II. 36, Royal Injunction of 1538.

[6] *Id.* II. 46, York, 1538          [7] Shaxton, 1538, *id.* II. 56.

reading of the Bible in Latin or English, but encourage them that they so read it...and that they be not bold nor presumptuous in judging of matters afore they have perfect knowledge[1].

These episcopal injunctions of 1538 imitated earlier Lollard practice in two other points,—the enjoining of the learning of parts of the Bible by heart, and the use of vernacular prayers. Earlier Waldensians and Lollards had learned the sacred text by heart through the impossibility of providing Bibles for any but the affluent: parish priests were now enjoined to learn long portions of the New Testament by heart for the admonition or comfort of their parishioners.

That every one having cure of souls...do perfectly con without the book the two whole gospels of Matthew and John, and the epistles of Paul to the Romans, Corinthians, Galatians, and other as they stand, with the Acts of the Apostles, and the canonical epistles, after the rate: to con every fortnight one chapter without the book, and the same to keep still in memory[2].

Bonner in 1542 ordered all priests of the diocese of London to learn the whole New Testament by heart[3], and many episcopal injunctions about 1538 made elaborate arrangements for parish priests to read or study one chapter a day, or "confer the English with the Latin[4]." Vernacular prayers had never been explicitly condemned as unorthodox, but the suspicion they aroused in the fifteenth century through their use by the Lollards had been very great[5]: it was now in 1538 ordered in several dioceses that all parish priests were to place in their churches a book comprising the pater noster, ave Maria, creed and commandments in English, for their parishioners to learn[6]; that parish and chantry priests were to teach children to read English, that they might the better learn how to pray[7]; and "from henceforth" not discourage any lay person from the reading of any good books in Latin or English. How real the suspicion of the use of English for books of prayers had become can be seen from the records of some of the Lollard trials[8].

---

[1] Cranmer, 1538, Frere, *Visit.* II. 65. For the royal articles of 1547, inquiring what priests had discouraged the people from hearing and reading of the scriptures in English, see *id.* II. 107, and for later references, *id.* 224.
[2] Shaxton, 1538, *id.* II. 55.   [3] *id.* II. 83.
[4] See under *Bible*, *id.* I. 225.   [5] See pp. 62, 87.
[6] Frere, *Visit.* II. 21, 36, 45, 46, 56, 61, 63, 66.
[7] 1537, *id.* II. 17.   [8] See p. 366.

# CHAPTER XIV

## *The Lollards and English Bible reading*

§ 1. In 1526 Tindale despatched to England the first printed copies of his New Testament, and the old manuscripts of the Wycliffite Bible became no longer text-books for ecclesiastical reformers, but literary curiosities. Lollardy was a continuous, though not an equally powerful movement in the preceding period. It gained in strength till the suppression of Oldcastle's revolt in 1416, when any chance of its political success was crushed. The humbler Lollards were then systematically attacked by the bishops till about 1431, from which time forward there were few Lollard trials till the middle of the century. In 1457 bishop Pecock's orthodox apologetic was itself condemned as Lollardy, after which the embers smouldered for about thirty years. From 1494 onward the movement took a new birth, partly due to a parallel reform movement in Germany, but consciously associated by its professors with the teaching of Wycliffe. Till the beginning of Tindale's activities the Lollards were considered a danger to the Church, and were tried in large numbers. Throughout all the period the records of Lollard trials associate the use of English biblical books with heresy.

It is here proposed to follow the history of the Lollards only in so far as it touches that of the use of English Bibles,—a connexion which has been challenged as non-existent,—and for the sake of comparison between the use of English Bibles by the Lollards and the orthodox, especially in the fifteenth century. Some general considerations must be dealt with as affecting the evidence, which will then be given in its chronological order.

First, since the mere making of an English Bible was not declared unlawful before 1408, no formal mention of their use or possession could be expected in heresy trials earlier.

Secondly, the evidence as to the connexion of Lollardy with the use of English Bibles does not rest solely on those definite instances when Lollards are proved to have owned some biblical book: though, even on this point alone, the evidence is very much more plentiful for them than in the case of the orthodox. Thus, though there were many Lollard trials where the question of English Bibles was not directly raised at all, there was not one in which it was not implied, since the chief question at issue was always the testing of some doctrine by an appeal to the letter of the New Testament. If there were no proven case where a Lollard possessed an English Bible, it would still be impossible to read the records of Lollard trials without recognising that the whole of Lollardy rested upon the popularisation of the New Testament.

Thirdly, there is evidence that, like the early Waldensians, the Lollards practised the teaching and learning by heart of the biblical translations. Manuscripts were relatively commoner in the fifteenth century than in the twelfth and thirteenth, and could be owned by less wealthy people: but there are many cases to shew that Lollard schools were meetings to hear or learn the biblical text. The evidence for the use of English Bibles rests not only on cases of Lollard ownership, but also on the records of these meetings.

Fourthly, there is considerable lack of explicitness in the records, as between ownership of biblical translations, or of books of Lollard doctrine, "Lollard books," "books of their lore," etc. Unlicensed possession of English books dealing with theology had been as definitely prohibited in 1408 as English Bibles, and therefore the mere possession of English books was often cited as suspicious evidence of heresy. In some cases where the possession of "English books" is thus mentioned, they were no doubt Lollard polemical tracts, but in others, from the fundamental nature of Lollardy, they were probably English books of epistles or gospels, or some such biblical translation.

Finally, it is clear that, though the possession of English biblical books was not classed as heresy in itself, it was very often the first sign by which suspicion of heresy was aroused. Witnesses often deposed that they suspected the accused to be a Lollard, because he or she knew certain prayers in English, or the words of the gospels[1], or possessed some English biblical book.

[1] VCH, *Essex*, II. 21.

As one Lollard who destroyed some valuable books out of fear that they would incriminate him remarked, "he had rather burn his books, than that his books should burn him[1]." The willingness to recite verses from the English Bible to a neighbour was often quoted as a sign of heresy. The records of heresy trials justify the assertion in an early fifteenth century Lollard tract: "The third assault of Antichrist is Inquisition, as the prophet saith,...that is to say, Antichrist seeketh and hearkeneth where he may find any man or woman that writeth, readeth, learneth or studieth God's law in their mother tongue[2]."

Thus to some extent it is fair to say that the existence of Lollardy was in itself evidence of the use of English biblical books. Since its existence throughout the fifteenth century is now known to have been continuous in many centres, as the *Victoria County History* shews, some mention will now be made of these centres, apart from explicit proof of Bible reading carried on in them.

§ 2. The Lollard William Thorpe, who was tried by Arundel in 1407, has been mentioned earlier for his account of Purvey: but his history of his own trial brings out also the insistence of all Lollards on the biblical text. Thorpe was a priest[3] who had belonged to the Wycliffite circle at Oxford from 1377 onwards, and travelled about as a Lollard preacher, especially in the north midlands, from 1387. He protested to Arundel:

I believe that all the Old Law and the New Law, given and ordained by the counsel of these three Persons in the Trinity, were given and ordained to the salvation of mankind: and I believe that these Laws are sufficient for man's salvation,

—a typical Lollard assertion as to the sufficiency of the Old and New Testaments. "I submit me," he added, not "to holy Church," but "to be reconciled to be buxom and obedient unto these Laws of God, and to every Article of them[4]." In accordance with this declaration, he alleged against the archbishop the letter of the New Testament on every disputed point; he would not submit and give information as to other Lollards, "for I find in no place in holy scripture this office that ye would now

---

[1] See p. 367.          [2] *Lanterne*, a tract written before 1415, see p. 15.
[3] Pollard, 107: "sir William" is a translation of "dominus," meaning merely our "reverend." Arundel's threat of degradation, *id*. 114, shews that Thorpe was a priest, cf. *id*. 132.          [4] *Id*. 111.

enfeoff me with." He defended his having preached without
episcopal license,

> for by authority of God's Law...I am learned to deem that it is
> every priest's office and duty for to preach busily, freely and truly the
> Word of God: for no doubt every priest should purpose first in his
> soul and covet to take the order of priesthood chiefly for to make
> known to the people the Word of God,

the novelty of which doctrine at the date is explained by the
extent to which lay people were ignorant of the biblical text.
Thorpe then quoted a text from Samuel in support of his argument, and Arundel retorted,

> All these allegings that thou bringest forth are nought else but
> proud presumptuousness,...that thou and such others are so just
> that ye ought not to obey to Prelates,

to which Thorpe answered by more "allegings," and Arundel,
losing patience, cried to the three clerks that stood about him:

> Lo, Sirs, this is the manner and business of this losell and such
> others, to pick out such sharp sentences of Holy Scripture and of
> Doctors, to maintain their sect and lore against the ordinance of
> Holy Church! And therefore, losell, is it, that thou covetest to have
> again the psalter that I made to be taken from thee at Canterbury,
> to record sharp verses against us! But thou shalt never have that
> psalter, nor none other book, till that I know that thy heart and
> thy mouth accord fully to be governed by Holy Church[1].

The lively form of the answer may be due to Thorpe himself,
but all Lollard defences render the truthfulness of the answer
likely: whether Thorpe's psalter were Latin or English, the
Lollards needed biblical texts, and the less lettered ones, translations, for the maintenance of their doctrine, and their attacks
on the lives of prelates. Arundel did not object to the psalter as
a heretical book, but he objected to the Lollard's use of it. His
outburst to Thorpe was justified again and again afterwards
throughout the interview, when on the subjects of transubstantiation, images[2], pilgrimages[3], music in churches, and

---

[1] Pollard, 128.

[2] *Id.* 135, where Arundel recounts the devout practices of those who
make images of the saints, and Thorpe answers: "Sir, I doubt not if these
painters that ye speak of, or any other painters, understood truly the text
of Moses, of David, of the Wise Man, and of other Saints and Doctors, these
painters should be moved to shrive them to God, with full inward sorrow
of heart."

[3] Where, *id.* 139, Thorpe asserts that "examine whoso will, twenty of

tithes[1], Thorpe alleged more scriptural passages, to the prejudice of the existent ecclesiastical organisation.

"Why losell," said the archbishop, "wilt not thou, and others that are confederated with thee, seek out of Holy Scripture and of the sentence of Doctors, all sharp authorities against Lords and Knights and Squires, and against other secular men, as thou dost against priests?"

Thorpe's defence of his Lollardy has been here quoted as typical. He was tried before 1408, so that the question of his possession of English books or Bibles did not expressly arise; but the whole tenor of his defence lay in the citation of biblical passages, and it shews how essential the literal text, in Latin or English, was to Lollardy.

After the failure of Purvey's leadership of Lollardy, as shewn by the constitutions of 1408 and the collapse of the Lollard dis-endowment scheme of 1410, Oldcastle became the avowed leader of the Lollards. His marriage with an heiress had given him large and scattered estates, so that he became of great use locally to the Hereford, Kentish, Norfolk and London Lollards[2], as well as to the party as a whole. An anti-Lollard poem mentions his familiarity with the Bible in the lines:

> It is unkindly for a knight,
> 　That should the kingës castle keep,
> To babble the Bible day and night
> 　In resting time when he should sleep[3].

He was tried in 1414, after a political revolt, at Blackfriars, London, and among his judges was friar Thomas Palmer, the old opponent of English Bibles. Palmer asked him concerning his faith in images, and whether he would worship the cross Christ died upon, to which Oldcastle returned the usual Lollard answer. He was finally executed as a heretic and traitor in 1417.

Meanwhile, Lollards of his political standing were tried in London in considerable numbers, still for "alleging" authorities

these pilgrims, and he shall not find three men or women that know surely a Commandment of God, nor can say their Pater noster and Ave Maria, nor their Credo, readily, in any manner of language."

[1] *Id.* 143, "I know not where this sentence of cursing is authorised now in the Bible."

[2] See W. T. Waugh's *Oldcastle*, EHR, xx. 434, 637.

[3] *Polit. Songs*, RS, ii. 244.

from the Bible in support of new-fangled doctrine. In 1408 John Badby was burned[1]; and in 1415 John Claydon[2], a parchemyner, was apprehended and confessed to the possession of English books, including the *Lanterne of Light*: the canonist, Lyndwood, examined them, and they were declared rankly Lollard. The next year a Lincolnshire heretic was accused of having "a certain book which he, contrary to the former decree of the bishops, did conceal and not exhibit to them[3]." Acts of parliament had already made the possession of Lollard books dangerous, but in 1416 archbishop Chichele, in a letter to the bishop of London, required all bishops and archdeacons to make diligent inquiry, at least twice a year, in every deanery and parish, touching persons suspected of heresy, or "possessing books written in English[4]." The preparation, however, of Lollard books and English gospels still continued, for that same year two priests were accused in London on both counts,—and it is the first case after 1408 when English Bibles are expressly recorded as having figured in a charge of heresy. Ralph Mungin was accused of circulating in the city of London certain books of Wycliffe and Peter the Clerk, especially "the book *Trialogus* and the gospels of John Wycliffe[5]"; he denied the charge of heresy, and was committed to prison. The entry in Chichele's register supports Hus's contention that all Englishmen believed Wycliffe to have translated the Bible: for a copy of the gospels would not have had the heretical *General Prologue*, or any scribal ascription to Wycliffe. The other priest, who had an English New Testament, was also condemned[6]. Lollardy, even at this date, was not dependent on the ministrations of laymen, as the trials of several priests shew[7]. Lollard books seem to have been still mostly copied in London, for in 1424 Richard Baxter

---

[1] Kingsford, 68.

[2] AM, III. 531; Kingsford, 69; *Mem. of London*, Riley, 617. For Richard Baker, burnt about the same time, see Kingsford, 69, 297: and for a Nottinghamshire heretic, 1413, Gairdner, I. 70.

[3] AM, III. 537.         [4] Gairdner, I. 93.

[5] AM, III. 539, from Chichele's register; cf. Ussher, XII. 359, and DNB for Mungin's connexion with Peter the Clerk, or Payne.

[6] AM, III. 538; for William Hervey, accused in 1416 of owning suspected books, see *id.*; for two false accusations of London men, *Mem. of London*, 658, 666.

[7] E.g. William Taylor, Kingsford, 128, Summers, 75; the vicar of Thaxted, Kingsford, 134, 308; Thomas Baggely; and the parish priest of Chedingfold.

was accused of "keeping a school of Lollardy in the English tongue," and of having all the books of that doctrine brought to him from London[1].

In Somersetshire the record of Lollardy was continuous, though not striking, throughout the century, and seems to have originated with Purvey's preaching in the suburbs of Bristol[2], about 1387; a Bristol burgess also was in 1404 one of the few known possessors of an English Bible at the date. No Somerset-shire Lollards were burned, but several abjured. In 1413 John Devenish[3] was accused of Lollardy, and of having placed "a scandalous book of the Lollards" in a vicar's stall. Thomas Smith of Bristol was accused in 1422[4], and in 1429 William Curayn, of Bristol, was cited for heresy for the fifth time, and, imprisoned by the bishop, he confessed that he had held that "every priest was bound to preach the Word of God openly, and that Oldcastle and Wycliffe were holy martyrs." In 1449 John Young, an old and infirm chaplain of S. Cross, abjured similar errors, and agreed to surrender all his heretical books. In 1455 bishop Beckington complained to the duke of Somerset that the duke's tenants at Langport neither "dreaded God nor lived by Holy Church"; they ministered the sacraments and buried the dead themselves, and even alleged the duke's support for so doing, though the bishop refused to believe that this could be true. In 1459 Thomas Cole, a baker, abjured, and in 1475 there were still many heretics in the diocese.

Between 1424 and 1430 more than a hundred persons were arraigned for Lollardy in the diocese of Norwich[5]. In 1429 John Baker was convicted of having a book of the pater noster and other prayers in English[6], which looks as if English primers had fallen under general suspicion, as being English and therefore Lollard. Margery Backster, the wife of a carpenter at Martham in Norfolk, was accused of heresy before the bishop of Norwich

---

[1] AM, III. 585.　　　　[2] See VCH, *Gloucs*. II. 21.

[3] For all these Somerset Lollards, see *id*. 21–4; DH, Bath and Wells, 142, 3, 5, 6; for Bristol Lollards in 1457, Summers, 80–3.

[4] Gairdner, I. 128.

[5] Summers, 71. Lollardy had started early in the eastern counties: Sawtre, the first Lollard to be burned, was a chaplain of S. Osyth's, Walbrook, *id*. 57.

[6] AM, III. 594.

in 1428[1]: another woman deposed against her that Margery had made various attempts to enlighten her as to Lollard doctrines, and said that she "secretly desired her, that she and Joan her maid would come secretly, in the night, to her chamber, and there she should hear her husband read the law of Christ unto them, which law was written in a book that her husband was wont to read to her by night." The "law of Christ," and "Goddis lawe" were still the ordinary Lollard terms for the New Testament and the Bible[2]. In two cases there was even suspicion of Lollardy in connexion with a religious: in 1427 Isabella Hermit, the prioress of Ridingfield, confessed to certain scandalous crimes, but vehemently denied the additional charge of Lollardy; while Bartholomew of Earsham, accused of Lollardy in 1428, seems to have been a monk[3]. In 1429 many more proceedings were taken against Norfolk Lollards: Nicholas Belward, a relation presumably of the Richard who kept a Lollard school, had a "New Testament which he bought at London for four marks and forty pence," out of which he taught others[4]. It was alleged against Richard Fletcher, a member of the same Lollard group, that he had an English book; and against the "daughter of Thomas Moon," "that she was partly of the same sect, and could read English"; William Bate also and his wife "could read English very well, and were of the same sect[5]." John Pert "was of the same sect and could read well"; and Hugh Pie bequeathed to another Lollard "a New Testament which they then called a book of the new law[6]." In the diocese of Canterbury too, two men were detected for Lollards in 1431 through their attendance at a reading of "reprobated books[7]," and in that of Lincoln heresy was to be found. Robert Fleming, bishop of Lincoln, founded Lincoln College in 1427, "with a view to the extermination and destruction of the sects of heretics, who are growing more than is wont[8]."

After these crusades, particularly those of the bishops of Norwich and London between 1429 and 1431, the Lollards were for a time very little heard of. The wars of the Roses in the

---

[1] AM, III. 595. The register from which Foxe transcribed these Norfolk heresy trials is not published. The spelling of surnames from AM is not modernised.   [2] Cf. "book of the new law," AM, III. 538.
[3] DH, Norwich, 147–9.   [4] AM, III. 597.   [5] *Id.* 597.   [6] *Id.* 597.
[7] RS, *Literae Cantuar.* III. 156.   [8] DH, Lincoln, 185.

middle of the century tended to distract attention from them: but although nothing like the same numbers were accused by the bishops between 1430 and 1480 as before and after those dates, nevertheless, records of occasional Lollard trials shew that the movement did not die out. It had travelled to Scotland, and certainly had a continuous existence there through the fifteenth and early sixteenth centuries: John Resly, a Wycliffite from England, was burned in Scotland in 1407[1], and Gerson complained of the influence of Wycliffism there about 1415, in his work on the literal interpretation of holy scripture[2]. "There is opposition to the truth in England, in Scotland, in the university of Prague, and in Germany,...they claim that their sayings are founded on holy scripture, and on its literal sense, and they say that they follow and recognise scripture only,... such heretics are present in England, have destroyed the university of Prague, and have even reached Scotland." A Bohemian Wycliffite, Paul Craw, was burned in Scotland in 1431[3]. Lollardy was again prevalent in 1494, when a raid was made upon the Lollards of Kyle, and in consequence thirty persons were summoned by the archbishop of Glasgow before the king and privy council[4]. A certain Murdoch Nisbet joined this sect about 1500, and when he fled to Germany in 1513 obtained access to Purvey's version of the New Testament. This he carefully copied in his own dialect, between 1513 and 1522, as well as the liturgical lessons from the Old Testament: but his Scots version was made so soon before the appearance of Tindale's New Testament, that it remained in a solitary manuscript. Among other Scottish Lollards, the Gordons of Earlstown had a New Testament in the vulgar tongue[5]. Lollardy persisted, however, elsewhere than in Scotland. John Gardiner was burned in 1438, and Richard Wyche was burned on Tower Hill in 1440. Five Lollards abjured in Surrey in 1441, and there were Lollards at Bristol between 1454 and 1457; two Somersetshire heretics

---

[1] Summers, 57. *Scottish Hist. Rev.* I. 260–73.
[2] *De sensu litterali sacrae scripturae, et de causis errantium*, in *Opera*, Antwerp, 1706, Du Pin, I. 2.
[3] Summers, 72. For intercourse of English and Bohemian Wycliffites at the period, cf. the subsequent career of Peter the Clerk, *supra*, p. 240, who was present at the council of Bâle in 1432.
[4] *Test. Scots.* xii.     [5] *Id.* xxxii.

recanted in 1459[1]. In the diocese of Lichfield, John Woodward of Tamworth abjured Lollard heresies in 1454[2]. The records of the trials of these heretics still remain unpublished in the episcopal registers, so that there is an absence of detail as to their possession of biblical translations or Lollard books: but the record of this in the case of the earlier Lollards is so precise, and the character of Lollardy continued so essentially unchanged, that it is hardly possible to doubt that they too possessed biblical manuscripts. Though a certain proportion of the manuscripts of the Wycliffite versions, written in the fifteenth century and still existent, bear no trace of either Lollard or orthodox ownership, it would not be safe to assume that they were written originally for, or used exclusively by, either party[3]. Some of them have calendars to shew the appointed portions for the Sunday epistles and gospels,—but it was the Lollard Purvey who, unlike any orthodox writer, advocated translations of these portions of the mass, and such manuscripts may well have belonged to Lollards. The evidence for Lollard use of English Bibles is strong where it is almost non-existent for their use by orthodox lay people; and it is very much stronger than for their use in convents.

§ 3. Though Lollardy had been thus dormant for twenty years, the tendency to criticise ecclesiastical institutions and teaching in the light of the letter of the New Testament still pressed heavily upon some minds; for the most conspicuous and original of English fifteenth century theologians was drawn to grapple with it by new methods, which ended finally in his own undoing. Although bishop Pecock wrote his most notable book in defence of orthodoxy against the Lollards, he was in two senses the descendant of Wycliffe and Purvey. He claimed that reason itself must be the guide in the interpretation of the scriptures,—thus facing the crucial problem of interpretation more directly than the Lollards had done—and he did more than any

---

[1] For all this intermediate period, 1430–80, passed over by Foxe, who was presumably without reference to the local episcopal registers, see Summers, 72–87, and VCH.  [2] DH, Lichfield, 169.

[3] The MSS. which contain the *Gen. Prol.* (except the non-heretical first chapter) would presumably have been written for Lollards. Cf. Bodley, 277, written for Henry VI, where the scribe desisted after copying the first chapter.

other man towards making the English tongue a vehicle for theological treatises. The Lollards had written their reasoned theological treatises in Latin, and had been original only in their attempt to issue English paraphrases of them for the instruction of the lewid; Pecock went further, and was the first theologian to write his reasoned treatises in English.

Pecock's career and writings are sufficient in themselves to shew that in the mid-fifteenth century Lollardy was still a force, still claimed the Bible as the sole final authority, and was still a movement in favour of English scriptures. Pecock was ordained in 1422, and in 1431, a period of great activity against the Lollards, was appointed to the mastership of Whittington College[1]. From this time he interested himself chiefly in seeking to convince individual Lollards by argument, and in writing English theological treatises to that end. He sought to prove to them that reason or the "moral law of kind" was the final authority for the interpretation of the Bible, and that reason was on the side of the catholic apologetic,—a theory which commended itself neither to the orthodox nor the Lollards.

"A syllogism well ruled," said Pecock, "is so strong and so mighty in all kinds of matters, that though all the angels of heaven would say that his conclusion were not true, yet we should leave the angels' saying,...and trust more to the proof of thilke syllogism[2]....Certes this inward book...or scripture or law of kind is more necessary to Christian men, and is more worthy, than is the outward Bible and the kunning thereof, as far as they both treat of the more part of God's law to man[3]."

Pecock's personal acquaintance with the Lollards is known from his own words: and his evidence about the prevalence and nature of Lollardy is therefore valuable.

I have spoke oft time, and by long leisure, with the wittiest and kunningest men of thilke said sort, contrary to the Church, and which have been held as dukes among them, and which have loved me for that I would patiently hear their evidences, and their motives, without reprobation. And verily none of them could make any motive for their party as strong as I myself could have made thereto[2]....Two things be the principal causes of heresy in the lay people which be cleped Lollards,...the first is this, overmuch leaning

---

[1] *Repressor of Over Much Blaming of the Clergy*, ed. Babington, C.; RS, 1860, I. xii.    [2] *Book of Faith*, 43.    [3] *Repressor*, 52.

to scripture, and in such manner wise as it long[eth] not to holy scripture to receive[1]....Who that will walk among the people now living in England, far and near, and will attend, hearken, hear and see how diversely divers persons been in their conceits set, he shall, among all the diversities, hear and know that many of the lay people which cleave and attend over unrulily to the Bible...protest and acknowledge that they will not fetch and learn their faith at the clergy of God's whole Church in earth; neither they as for learning and kunning of their faith will obey to the clergy or to the church: but they will fetch and learn their faith at the Bible of holy scripture, in the manner as it shall hap them to understand it[2].

He stated elsewhere also that the Lollards were chiefly in error about holy scripture, believing that no ordinance was to be held a law of God unless it were grounded on the Bible, and that every meek and humble Christian could not fail to understand truly and duly holy scripture[3]. He objected to the Lollards that the Bible gave no information on their cherished tenet of the lawfulness of English translations of the Bible:

Also thou shalt not find expressly in holy scripture, that the New Testament should be written in English tongue to laymen, or in Latin tongue to clerks, neither that the Old Testament should be written in English tongue to laymen or in Latin tongue to clerks: and yet each of these governances thou wilt hold to be lawful[4].

He objected also to the Lollards' emphasis on the practice of Bible reading; they think, he said,

They need nothing unto the school of God's law and service save holy scripture alone, and that thereto holy scripture sufficeth.... They ween themselves for to kun at full and substantially and pithily holy scripture, for that they kunnen by heart the texts of holy scripture, and kunnen lush them out thick at feasts, and at ale-drinking, and upon their high benches sitting[5].

He argued with them that it was reasonable to leave the interpretation of the Bible to the clergy as specialists: just as men who wished to understand charters would appeal, not to laymen, but to "justices or sergeants or famous kunning apprentices of the king's law[6]": and men who had a ship on hand would trust to the wits of carpenters, not to their own: so a "right and

---

[1] *Book of Faith*, 114.      [2] *Id*. 109.      [3] *Id*. 5, 6.
[4] *Id*. 119.      [5] *Repressor*, I. 129.      [6] *Book of Faith*, 228.

due understanding of the high and hard writing of our belief in the Bible" ought to be sought from those trained in divinity.

Pecock had become bishop of S. Asaph in 1444, and of Chichester in 1450: but his Lancastrian sympathies and the dangerous nature of his anti-Lollard apologetic brought him into unpopularity, and finally into suspicion of heresy. He was cited to appear at Lambeth in 1457, and forced to recant his doctrines at Paul's Cross in that year. Finally he resigned his bishopric, and died in captivity in Thorney Abbey.

Although Pecock had no great following among the laity, certain admirers of his books, or possibly Lollards, were proceeded against at about this time. An inquiry was made in 1457 in the diocese of Ely for the possessors of Pecock's writings, and in consequence Robert Sparke of Reach, John Crowd of Cambridge and John Baile of Chesterton were forced to recant their errors as Lollards[1]. In the same year William and Richard Sparke, of Somersham, Huntingdonshire, also recanted[2].

Lollardy in Lincoln[3] at this period was vigorous, but probably unconnected with the teaching or tenets of Pecock. James Wyllys confessed that he had read through the epistles of S. Paul, the Apocalypse, and the gospel of S. Luke in English, and that he had bought the manuscripts from a man of Bristol; and Geoffrey Symeon afterwards acknowledged that he possessed an English book of the holy gospels, which he had of the said James[4]. William Ayleward confessed that he had often "talked of the gospels and holy scriptures, declaring in English the gospel of Nicodemus in judgment, according to the letter[5]." Henry Smith confessed that he had heard Ayleward speak of possessing a copy of the gospel of S. John[6]. John Baron gave a full account of the English books, for the possession of which he was suspected: he had "one of the life of our Lady, of Adam and Eve, and of other sermons, the mirror of sinners, and the mirror of matrimony; the second book of the tales of Canterbury, and the third book of a play of saint Dionise[7]." Geoffrey Simeon,

[1] *Gray's Register*, Ely, f. 130 *b*; cf. EDR, 1907, 42.
[2] *Chedworth's Register*, Lincoln, f. 12 *b*.
[3] *Chedworth's Register*, 1452–71, is not quoted by Foxe, and is unpublished. I am indebted for the following references to Miss C. B. Firth; cf. VCH, *Lincs*, II. 41, 46.  [4] *Chedworth's Reg.* f. 62.  [5] *Id.* f. 61.
[6] *Id.* f. 62.  [7] *Id.* f. 62 *b*.

again, confessed that he had allowed John Goose to read through the English gospel which was in his keeping, and the same John also borrowed a book belonging to a man called Baron. In the latter, Goose acknowledged, was written a confession in English, which had lately been found erroneous by the bishop of Lincoln[1].

§ 4. After the repression of Pecock and his followers, the records of the existence of Lollardy are few for the next twenty years: nevertheless, heresy was to be found in Lincolnshire, Amersham and Henley on Thames in 1462, and a Lollard was burnt in 1466[2]. In Somersetshire Lollardy still persisted, and in 1475 Stillington's register declared that there were still many heretics in the diocese[3]. In London the record of Lollardy is continuous, for in 1489 Stephen Swallow, a layman of the parish of Wylie, abjured his heresies in the presence of the archbishop of Canterbury and four bishops. His heresies were of the ordinary later Lollard type, and he said he had held and taught them for over thirty years[4],—a period extending back to the agitation against Pecock. A Lollard was burnt in 1485, and nine of them abjured their errors at Coventry in 1486[5]. In 1491 John Russell, bishop of Lincoln, "wearied this year 1491 at Oxford with many heretics," copied out with his own hands long extracts from Walden's book on the sacraments, "against the Wycliffites, whose most insane doctrines have infected many of the common people of our English religion." He ordered therefore that these extracts should remain in the registers of his successors, so that they and their assistants might be more prepared for inquisitions into heretical pravity[6]. In 1494 Joan Boughton was burned, openly declaring herself a follower of Wycliffe[7]; she was over eighty, and must have been well to do, for she is described as the "mother of the lady Young," who also held Lollard opinions. In the early months of 1496 five Lollards stood at Paul's Cross for heresy, and in October five stood there

---

[1] Chedworth's Reg. ff. 62, 62 b.          [2] Summers, 86–7.
[3] DH, Bath and Wells, 146.
[4] RS, Literae Cantuar. III. 312–14.          [5] Summers, 87.
[6] Univ. 156. The extracts themselves are in a fifteenth century hand, though the copy of the bishop's note is in one of the seventeenth century. Foxe states that many Lollards abjured, and some were burned, in the diocese of Lincoln under the next bishop, William Smith, 1495–1514, and still more under bishop Longland, 1520–47, AM, IV. 219.
[7] AM, IV. 7.

together, "with the books of their lore hanging about them, which books were at the time of the sermon there burnt, with the faggots that the said Lollards bore[1]." The next year a heretic was burnt at Canterbury[2], and in 1499 fourteen did open penance at Paul's Cross, and an old man was burnt at Smithfield[3], while in 1506 the prior of S. Osyth's and five other heretics did penance at Paul's Cross[4]. In 1506 too William Tylsworth, of the diocese of Lincoln, was burned, and other burnings occurred at Missenden and Amersham[5]. From this time onwards heretics were tried in much greater numbers, and the records of their trials are accessible, so that their use of English Bibles can be studied with some certainty. For these intermediate heretics, however, between about 1430 and 1509, we have only the bare mention of their abjurations or burnings, and no account of their trials. The earlier Lollards, however, before 1431, used English Bibles and learned passages from them by heart, and the later ones, after 1511, used them much more frequently, because books were relatively cheaper. Since there was no change in the character of Lollardy during the intermediate period, it would be rash to infer without evidence that their practice in the intermediate period was not the same. It is thus probable that a certain number of Lollards at any time throughout the century may have been possessors of English Bibles, or single biblical books, for they certainly set store by them. It is unsafe also to argue that there were no Lollards rich enough to own English Bibles; for, apart from the evidence that they gave relatively large sums for them, we possess one or two existent manuscripts of Bibles which almost certainly belonged to Lollards. One of the later versions, for instance, written about 1430, has the whole Bible and the whole *General Prologue*, which would scarcely have been copied by or for any orthodox user; and there is a note in the scribe's hand against a verse in Exodus mentioning the bondage of the children of Israel to Pharaoh, which says: "Thus the peple farith now, for fere of the prelatis more and lesse[6]." Abuse of the tyranny of "prelates" was constant among the Lollards, and

---

[1] Kingsford, 208–11.  
[2] *Id.* 222, 327.  
[3] *Id.* 226, 229, 232.  
[4] *Id.* 261.  
[5] AM, IV. 123. For the Buckinghamshire heretics in 1506 and 1511, see also DH, Oxford, 258.  
[6] FM, I. lvi, C C.C. Camb. 147.

this note and the presence of the *General Prologue* together render the Lollard provenance of the manuscript reasonably certain. Again, the manuscript containing "Pervie's" notes and monogram, written in about 1427, belonged to a Lollard, for besides containing the *General Prologue*, it has a long Latin letter of the parish priest of "Chedingfold," written to cardinal Beaufort in answer to charges of Lollardy[1].

After 1508–9, the references to Lollard ownership of English Bibles are precise and frequent. In 1509 Richard Hillman of Coventry confessed that he had the Lord's prayer and the salutation of the angel, and the creed in English, and "another book he did see and had, which contained the epistles and gospels in English[2]"; and between 1509 and 1519 Christopher the Shoemaker was accused of Lollardy, *inter alia*, because "he read to John Say out of a little book the words which Christ spake to his disciples[3]." Between 1511 and 1521 a long list of abjurations occurred, and it is specially noticeable that the witnesses against the accused always mentioned the possession of English biblical books, or the recitation of English prayers, or even ability to read English, as the principal sign of Lollardy.

James Brewster, who was burned in 1511, confessed to a list of errors which included "having a certain little book of scripture in English, of an old writing almost worn for age," and in the same year William Sweeting was accused of "having much conference with one William Man, of Boxted, in a book which was called Matthew[4]." John Higgs was charged with having in his custody a book of the four evangelists in English, and about 1517 John Southwick was accused of having the book of the four evangelists, a book of the epistles of Paul and Peter, the epistle of S. James, a book of the Apocalypse, and of Antichrist, of the Ten Commandments, Wycliffe's Wicket, etc., in English[5]. Once when "old Durdant," his wife, his son Nicholas Durdant

---

[1] FM, I. lxi, Dubl. A. I. 10.
[2] AM, IV. 135. For his use of English prayers, cf. the accusation against John Smith, 1509, that he held that a man was bound to know the pater noster, etc., in English, *id.* 7; and for the detection of certain Lollards because they had learned the creed, pater and ave, etc., in English, *id.* 225.
[3] *Id.* IV. 217: from Longland's *Reg.*
[4] *Id.* IV. 215, 6. For the Coventry martyrs of 1511, see DH, Lichfield, 177.
[5] AM, IV. 178, 207.

and his son's wife, David Durdant and Robert Carver were at dinner with the witness's children and their wives, he bade a boy there standing to depart out of the house, that he should not hear and tell, and did recite unto them certain places out of the epistles of S. Paul, and of the gospels[1]. It was deposed further that Robert Pope had certain English books, and that John Phips read the gospels in English; moreover, the latter had suddenly burned his books, and when the witness told him "he was foul to blame, for they were worth a hundred marks," John had answered that he "had rather burn his books than that his books should burn him[2]." Nicholas Durdant, it was said, used to read to others parts of the epistles of S. Paul, and the gospels: and he had desired those assembled not to tell that he had any such English books in his house[3], lest he should be burned for the same. John Butler[4] was accused of reading to his brother in a certain book of the scriptures; while Richard Butler[5], presumably the brother, was elsewhere accused of having at divers times "erroneously and damnably read (aloud) in a great book of heresy of Robert Durdant's certain chapters of the Evangelists in English, containing in them divers erroneous and damnable opinions and conclusions of heresy." There can be small doubt that the book from which he read aloud the chapters of the gospels in English was a copy of the later version of the Wycliffite Bible, and that the "damnable opinions and conclusions of heresy" occurred not in the gospels themselves, but in the *General Prologue*.

John and Joan Barret, and John Scrivener, again, were accused of possessing, reciting and lending the gospels of SS. Matthew and Mark, and the epistle of S. James, and others were accused of listening to the reading of a certain epistle of S. Paul. John Newman was present at a reading of the scriptures, and others were accused of learning the pater noster, etc., in English. Alice Brown and John Tracher were accused of teaching and

---

[1] *Id.* 226, 230.        [2] *Id.* 226, 237, from Longland's *Reg.*
[3] He was the son of "old Durdant," the leader of a Lollard school, and owner of Iver Court at Staines. It was deposed against old Durdant, that three Lollards had sat up all night in his house, reading in a book of scripture, and that Joan Cocks had desired Durdant her master "that he, being a 'known man,' would teach her some knowledge of God's law."
[4] AM, IV. 227        [5] *Id.* 178.

learning the beatitudes in English. John Butler and Thomas Geffrey had a scripture book in English, which the bishop took from them: they had also taught and learned from the same. Thomas Man was accused of reading from Genesis, Richard Ashford and others of reading in "a certain little book," whilst Ralph Carpenter had "certain books of the Apocalypse in English, and divers such books." Robert and Jenkin Butler were suspected for "reading two hours together in a certain book of the Acts of the Apostles in English, at Chesham," while the wife of Robert Pope had certain books in English, including an English primer. John Morden and Richard Ashford were accused of having in the house a book of the gospels, and other chapters in English, and Alice Sanders of giving 12d. to buy a certain book in English, and attempting to buy English books at other times. "Geldner the elder" and others had been present at a reading of the epistle of S. James in English, while Thomas Tykill had lent a book of the gospels in English. Joan Gun had instructed another in the epistle of S. James, and Thomas Africh had "held conference in the gospel of S. Matthew[1]." Richard Collins had "a book of Luke and one of Paul," and elsewhere it was stated that he had quite an English library, including several books of the Bible, the hours of our Lady, and the *Prick of Conscience*; his wife Alice Collins was a famous reciter of the scriptures at meetings[2]. Thomas Scrivener had a book of epistles in English, and Bennett Ward and others had the gospels of Matthew and Mark. Edward Pope had the gospel of S. Matthew in English, William Halliday the Acts of the Apostles, Thomas Philip and others had been reading in English biblical books, and John Harris's wife had been "talking of the Apocalypse" and other biblical books. John Edmunds and "many others" had possessed English biblical books, and Robert Collins had been "reading a certain thick book of scripture in English." The wife of Thomas Widemere was accused of reading the Bible in English, and yet another Collins, John, and his wife, "for buying a Bible of Stacey for 20 shillings." John Baker and John Hakker were accused for reading English scriptures, and Thomas Vincent for giving Hakker a book of S. Matthew in English. John Heron

[1] AM, IV. 226–34.    [2] *Id*. 234, 6, 5, 8, 9.

had a "book of the exposition of the gospels fairly writ in English[1]," and Robert Bartlet had read to his brother "a parcel of scripture beginning thus: James, the servant of God, to the twelve kinds." John Jennings was detected because he had carried about certain books in English: and Thomas Chase because he had been heard to recite words from the gospels and epistles. Agnes Ashford also had taught the words of the gospel, the beatitudes, etc., by heart to James Morden.

These cases of Lollardy were nearly all collected from episcopal registers by Foxe, bishop of Hereford, for his *Acts and Monuments*. The later registers have not yet been published: but there is no reason to doubt that when Foxe states that he is quoting an episcopal register, his extracts are accurate copies in the sense that, though he may omit matters inconvenient for his case, he does not insert spurious stuff. This may be verified from the earlier Hereford registers, which have now been published in full[2], and from the Lincoln registers, which have been published in extract[3]. The most interesting case of a Lollard Bible reader related by Foxe from the register of the bishop of London[4] is that of Richard Hun, for sir Thomas More was present at his trial, and inspected his English Bible,—gathering his ideas of the heresy of the Wycliffite versions from the *General Prologue*, which it contained[5]. Hun, a Merchant Taylor of London, was committed to the Lollards' Tower for suspected heresy, and tried on 2 December, 1514. He was accused of various heretical beliefs, and of having in his keeping divers English books prohibited by law, including the Apocalypse in English, the epistles and gospels in English[6], Wycliffe's damnable works, and other erroneous books. After this preliminary examination he was sent back to the Lollards' Tower, where he was found strangled

---

[1] AM, IV. 234–40. The record of Agnes Ashford's trial gives the exact passage from S. Matthew, v., which she taught Morden, and which he went five times to her house to learn; and twice he went to her to learn the beatitudes. Agnes was bidden recite these passages before the bishop, and commanded to teach them no more to any man, and especially not to her children.

[2] CYS, Gilbert, 1375–89; Trevenant, 1389–1404. Cf. VCH, *Bucks.* I. 302.

[3] DH, Lincoln, Venables, E., and Perry, G.; and see *Chedworth's register*, p. 363; VCH, *Bucks.* I. 202–3.

[4] FitzJames, see AM, IV. 173.

[5] See pp. 7, 14.　　　　[6] AM, IV. 184.

next morning: the bishop of London declared he had hanged himself, but the jury, after going into the case with the thoroughness of amateur detectives, gave a verdict of murder. At this inquest, further evidence of Hun's heretical views had been collected by Dr Hed from the prologue of his English Bible, which the bishop kept: and the thirteen articles under which his heresy was tabulated are largely taken from the *General Prologue*[1], which contains plenty of passages which, as sir Thomas More said, "good Christian men did much abhor to hear." The last of these thirteen articles ran:

He defendeth the translation of the Bible and the holy scriptures into the English tongue, which is prohibited by the laws of our mother, holy Church[2].

The bishop of London then had the articles of heresy of which Hun was first accused, and the thirteen articles put forward at the inquest, published at Paul's Cross, and offered to let any man who doubted whether the points were "contained in this book or not" come to him, and examine Hun's English Bible, with its *General Prologue*, for himself,—an offer of which sir Thomas More must have availed himself. Hun was then formally condemned of heresy, and his corpse burned at Smithfield, sixteen days after his death. Foxe expresses his surprise that so early a martyr for the protestant cause should have been in the habit of going to daily mass, and have had his beads in prison with him: but his objection shews lack of historical perspective. Like the early Wycliffites, Hun probably considered himself no heretic, but a devout and enlightened catholic.

Thus the history of English Lollardy between the death of Wycliffe and the introduction of Tindale's New Testament offers ample evidence of its connexion with the use of English Bibles. The historical evidence shews that the Lollards made the English translation of the Bible and consistently practised its use, while no orthodox person or manual ever suggested its use by lay people. Certain noble personages and certain nuns probably had license to read it: but the evidence is much less strong for these than for the Lollards.

§ 5. In the light of the evidence now discussed it is easy to understand sir Thomas More's statement about vernacular

[1] AM, IV. 186.　　　　　[2] *Id*. 186.

Bibles, together with Cranmer's misapprehension, and the reference to English Bibles in the preface to the English Bible of
1609. Caxton, with his special knowledge, had been aware that
manuscripts of English Bibles existed: More, of more exalted
rank, had seen them in the houses of the great, and knew that
they or Saxon manuscripts existed in many old abbeys of
England. Perhaps his generalisation was made from the
Wycliffite Bible at the Carthusian house at Sheen, for More had
friends among the London Carthusians; perhaps he had seen
the copy at Sion. He had to reconcile this fact with the constitutions of Oxford of 1408, and to do so, he had but to accept
Lyndwood's exposition of them. Bibles made before the days of
the late master John Wycliffe were exempted from the prohibition: therefore More jumped to the conclusion that those he
had seen must have been copies of such Bibles. Like Innocent
III in his letter to Metz, like the Cologne jurists of 1398, like
Purvey in his determination, and like master John Wycliffe himself, More would not admit that translations of the Bible could
be heretical *per se*; therefore he fell back on the supposition (to
which much colour was lent by Tindale's work) that Wycliffe's
Bible must have been prohibited because the translation itself
contained heretical matter. He was quite without the oppor-
tunity of knowing that the only Bibles which Arundel actually
excepted in his prohibition in 1408 were unreadable Anglo-Saxon
ones, or that the Wycliffite translation apart from its heretical
prologue was itself an excellent and scholarly version. He did
not even know that, before Wycliffe's day, the only classes in
England who could often have afforded to buy biblical manuscripts were French-speaking. Much less could he have known
that the psalter and Apocalypse were the only books to be turned
into English prose before Wycliffe, and that not fifty years before.

Thus in the history of the Wycliffite Bible two misappre-
hensions have been successively held by certain scholars. These
have assumed first, that there were mediaeval English Bibles
before Wycliffe, and secondly, that the late fifteenth century
manuscripts of the English Bible were copies of these, and not
of the Wycliffite version. The prohibitions of 1408 started the
first theory, by exempting Anglo-Saxon manuscripts and Rolle's
psalter: Lyndwood made the theory more definite: Caxton went

further and attributed the pre-Wycliffite mediaeval Bible to
Trevisa: More followed Lyndwood: Cranmer, anxious to find
precedents for translations, followed him and Lyndwood: and
the preface to the English Bible of 1609 followed them all. Not
one of these writers shews evidence of independent and critical
research. They could not have guessed *a priori*, nor had they
discovered by historical study, that both in Italy and in Germany
orthodox nobles and convents of sisters sometimes possessed
vernacular Bibles derived ultimately from Waldensian translations, without the slightest knowledge of their heretical origin;
or that the use of Wycliffite texts by the orthodox in England
was merely a parallel occurrence.

The attitude of the mediaeval Church to biblical translations
has thus been seen to have been one of toleration in principle,
and distrust in practice. Latin Christianity was founded on S.
Jerome's translation of the Vulgate, and could not well forget it.
The eastern Church preserved the primitive attitude in the
matter, and did not interfere in the making of Russian or Bulgarian translations. The first hostile pronouncement of the
western Church to translations was that of Gregory VII, and
for two important motives. First, he wished to keep Latin as
the speech of all debatable territories between the eastern and
western Churches, and thus to retain those lands for the western
obedience. Secondly, he did more than any other pope to separate the clergy from the laity, and also make them worthy of
forming the teaching branch of the Church. From his time
onwards the orthodox prejudice against lay knowledge of the
biblical text hardened, except in the case of the most exalted
personages, who were always allowed to possess them if they
wished; but popular Bible reading, and the learning of the translations by heart, were found to lead inevitably to their exposition
by lay people, and eventually to heresy. For this reason, the
popularisation of such translations was forbidden in France by
the synod of Toulouse in 1229, and a little later in Spain and the
Empire. Innocent III's letter to Metz, capable of opposite interpretations, was embodied in the *Decretals*. When orthodox, or
semi-orthodox, teachers began to teach lay people the practice
of contemplative prayer, they were the first orthodox religious
leaders to recommend the reading of the scriptures to lay people.

This began in Germany, in 1386: here the teachers recommended translations; in England it began about 1380, by teachers who used the Vulgate. Certain scholars, like the lawyers of Cologne, and the Lollard doctors at Oxford and Prague, contended that biblical translations were lawful: but the far more influential Gerson and the fathers of Constance thought otherwise, and these carried orthodox opinion with them. Only from about 1509, and only in Germany, was there an orthodox movement for the popularisation of the scriptures by means of translating the gospel at mass, and allowing ordinary lay people the use of German gospel and epistle books,—generally glossed, that they might not be exposed to the danger of misinterpreting the bare text. There was no contemporary and similar movement in England: for, while the chief fifteenth century agents of it in Germany,—the Brethren of the Common Life,—were orthodox, the parallel movement of English Lollardy was heretical. Germany was the only country in Europe where orthodoxy allowed the study of biblical translations to lay people before the Reformation, and this only from about 1509 onwards, when the principles of the Renaissance were already bearing fruit, in a soil specially prepared by the earlier efforts of the Waldensians, Beghards, Gottesfreunde, and Brethren of the Common Life. In England, as in the rest of Europe, the great majority of those familiar with the text of the Bible in English were Lollards, and sir Thomas More recognised the general state of affairs when he made his Messenger complain that "the Bible is in so few folks' hands."

# APPENDIX I

1. *The* Twelve Conclusions of the Lollards, 1395, *and the dating of the* General Prologue to the Old Testament.

The passage from the *General Prologue* referring to the "last parliament" (quoted partly *supra*, p. 257), is a close allusion to the third of the *Twelve Conclusions*, and a verbal copy of part of the *Thirty Seven Conclusions*, an expanded treatise to the same effect (see pp. 282–3), issued at the same time. The *Twelve Conclusions* were written in English for presentation to parliament in 1395, and begin: "We poor men, treasurers of Christ and His apostles, denounce to the lords and commons of the parliament certain conclusions and truths for the reformation of Holy Church of England." These twelve conclusions, without the prologue mentioning parliament (Gairdner, I. 43), were also written in Latin and nailed to the door of Westminster abbey and S. Paul's cathedral (a usual mediaeval manner of publishing an academic thesis, cf. the similar action of the Lollard Pateshull in 1387; Trevelyan, 327). The original English form is printed in EHR, XXII. 292, from the MS. of Roger Dymok (see p. 283). The Latin form was copied by Walden; see FZ, 361, and retranslated by Foxe into Elizabethan English, in AM. The third of the conclusions is that referred to in the *Gen. Prol.* (see *supra*, p. 257): "The thirdde conclusiun, sorwful to here, is that the lawe of continence annexyd to presthod, that in preiudys of wimmen was first ordeynid, induceth sodomie in al holy chirche," etc., "quod lex continentiae injuncta sacerdotio, quae in praejudicium mulierum prius fuit ordinata, inducit sodomiam in totam sanctam ecclesiam," FZ, 361.

The question has been raised whether the petition was actually read in parliament, or only circulated among individual lords and commons in London, since the *Conclusions* are not found on the parliament roll. There is however no reason to doubt Walden's statement: "Sequuntur conclusiones Lollardorum... porrectae pleno parliamento regni Angliae, regnante illustrissimo principe Ricardo secundo, anno eius circiter xvii." FZ, 360, Summers, 52, state that sir Thomas Latimer and sir Richard Stury presented the conclusions in parliament, as do Trevelyan, 329, and Gairdner, I. 43. Stubbs, *Constit. Hist.* II. 512 has no doubt that the petition was actually presented in parliament: cf. *Polit. Hist. of England*, IV. 128, and for the parlia-

ment of 1395, *Rot. Parl.* III. 330. At the date, parliamentary
procedure was, of course, much less formal than later: petitions
presented to the king in parliament were redrafted by the royal
lawyers before enrolment on the parliament roll as bills, whether
the petition received the royal assent or not. The *Twelve Conclusions* were no doubt considered too scandalous for redrafting
and enrolment: but this does not disprove the apparent meaning
of the words "porrectae...pleno parliamento," "addressed to
parliament in session," as inferring an actual reading of the text.
Lollard tracts of a nature as offensive to the orthodox had been
circulated vigorously since 1384, and there is no reason to think
the mere circulation of these conclusions as a pamphlet would
have sent an archbishop and a bishop in hot haste to Ireland,
recalled Richard from his campaign, drawn down his wrath on
the Lollard knights, particularly Stury, and occasioned even a
warning letter from the pope to the king. Boniface IX wrote
also to the two English archbishops in Oct. 1395, exhorting them
to greater zeal against the Lollards, and quoting the *Twelve
Conclusions*, not from the Latin form nailed to S. Paul's, but
from the English form addressed to the lords and commons of
parliament: the Lollards, he says, "call themselves poor men of
the treasure of Christ and His disciples" (CPL, IV. 515), thus
quoting the prologue, not found in the Latin form.

The Lollard disendowment bill of 1410 (see Gairdner, I. 64,
Walsingham, II. 282–3, Kingsford, 65, 295, xxxvii) is an exactly
similar case of a bill, stated by contemporaries to have been presented in parliament, and not found enrolled in the parliament
rolls, see *Rot. Parl.* III. 623; here also no doubt because its contents were considered too wild and revolutionary. For petitions
undoubtedly presented and not enrolled, between 1347 and 1401,
see Stubbs, II. 602–10, III. 34; Gairdner, I. 20; *supra*, 297.

The *Thirty Seven Conclusions* is a much longer English tract,
alluded to in the *Twelve Conclusions*: "and though these matters
be here shortly knit, they be in another book longly declared"
(EHR, XXII. 295). They are printed by J. Forshall as the
*Remonstrance against Romish corruptions in the Church*, and
frequently alluded to by modern writers as the *Ecclesiae Regimen*,
from the title given to one MS. by a late scribe. The second
corollary to the third conclusion, or article, sets forth the charge
of sodomy in a paragraph of 32 lines, which agrees almost word
for word with the passage relative to that subject in the *Gen.
Prol.*, FM, I. 51. Comparison leaves no doubt that here the
writer of the *Gen. Prol.* quoted from the *Thirty Seven Conclusions*,
a political pamphlet of 1395; his allusion to the "last parliament" must therefore be to the parliament of 1395.

Bale (*Scriptorum*, 1557, 541), among a list of works he ascribes to Purvey, includes two tracts which may have been different forms of the *Twelve Conclusions*: the *Ad parliamentum Angliae. Prima conclusio est haec, quod* and the *Ad regem et concilium.*

Lewis accepted the reference to the "last parliament" as to the parliament of 1395 (FM, I. xxiii), but FM challenged the dating without due reason. "Imputations of this nature were, no doubt, frequent among those opposed to the celibacy of the clergy, and might very probably have been brought under the notice of parliament previously to 1395," *id.* xxiv. But (1) not merely the sense of the charge, but the wording of the passage in the *Gen. Prol.* is borrowed from the *Thirty Seven Conclusions* of 1395; (2) there was no Lollard agitation in parliament such as can possibly have been referred to for ten years on either side of 1395[1]. The Lollards' agitation in the parliament of 1385 was the nearest anterior one, and had dealt only with the proposal to confiscate certain temporalities of the clergy (*Polit. Hist. of Eng.* IV. 97). The nearest posterior one was the Lollard disendowment bill of 1410. There is thus no record of a Lollard petition or parliamentary agitation between 1385 and 1410, except in 1395: and in neither 1385 or 1410 was the charge of sodomy brought forward, as it was in the unique instance of 1395. For the dates of the parliaments about these years, see Stubbs, *Constit. Hist.* II. 505, 513. FM are here clearly wrong, and Lewis right.

The *Gen. Prol.* was thus certainly written soon after Jan.-Feb. 1395, and before the next parliament of Jan.-Feb. 1397.

2. *The Identity of John Purvey with the author of the* General Prologue to the Old Testament, *and the second Wycliffite version.*

The author of the *General Prologue* was a Lollard, as is shewn in repeated passages against simonient and covetous prelates, references to them as "antichrist," the denunciation of indulgences, needless oaths, image-worship, etc. (FM, I. 2, 3, 29–34, 35, 40, 43, 49, 51, 52, 59, 60). He was also undergoing persecution at the time of writing, and exhorting his followers to undergo it, even to the death. (*Id.* 2, 15, 30, 33, 37, 43, 49, 57, 58, 60.) He was also a scholar of great learning, and quoted freely from learned doctors and particularly Lyra, the best contemporary commentator on the Hebrew text; the description of the four

---

[1] The 25 Arts. of 1388 (see p. 461) do not accuse the clergy of vice, and were not presented to parliament. See also for Pateshull's charges in 1387, *Chron. Ang.* RS, 377; Walsingham, II. 158.

stages of the making of the translation, etc., shews a scholarly care unequalled by any contemporary translator.

The *Gen. Prol.*, as has been established (pp. 374-6), was not finished till 1395: so that this scholarly Lollard was enduring persecution in that year. The only Lollard of sufficient scholarship to have written the *Gen. Prol.* and later Wycliffite version, who had not recanted before 1395, was John Purvey. Hereford, Purvey, Repingdon and Aston were the four most eminent Lollard scholars in 1382: Repingdon and Aston recanted in that year: Hereford was still a Lollard preacher, with Purvey, in the town of Bristol in 1387 (FM, 1. xvii), but he had recanted and received royal letters of protection before 1391. In 1393 he was presiding over the trial of Walter Brute (see p. 286); by 1394 he was chancellor of Hereford cathedral. The other most eminent Lollards, like Swinderby, Bell and Brute, had also all recanted, Brute the latest, in 1393. The only important Lollard scholar, and the only representative of the old circle of Oxford Lollards holding out in 1395, was Purvey, who did not recant till 1401 (*Hen. IV*, 1. 180).

Subsidiary circumstances which are in favour of Purvey's authorship include (1) Walden's and Knighton's references to his scholarship,—the "Lollard's library," etc. (see pp. 233-5). (2) His unique relationship to Wycliffe, as his secretary: if Purvey helped to finish the early version, and was responsible for the later, this explains the belief of the well-informed continuator of Knighton that Wycliffe translated the whole Bible, and Hus's statement that all Englishmen believed Wycliffe to have translated the Bible (see pp. 239-40). (3) The author of the Lollard glosses on the gospels and of the *Gen. Prol.* was the same man, from his use of a set of pseudonyms (see pp. 276-7). There is some reason for attributing these glosses to Purvey (see p. 276), who was "letted fro preaching" in 1387; the glosses were finished before 1394; the time necessary for completing these, and the later Wycliffite version, is allowed for, between 1384 and 1395, and is consistent with what we know of Purvey's career. Neither the Lollard glosses nor the LV could have been the work of a mere Lollard hedge-priest. The writer of the *Gen. Prol.* dealt only with the O.T., and had no occasion to mention his glosses on the gospels (though he incorporated the prologue of one of them, see p. 281): but he says he has made glosses on Job, the major, and part of the minor prophets (FM, 1. 37, 41). This seems to refer to prologues on these books, descriptive of their contents, as the *Gen. Prol.* is for the other books of the O.T., which indicates that the *Gen. Prol.* was regarded as a gloss on the rest of the O.T. The author would thus consider he had glossed all the books of the Bible, but the gospels at far greater length. (4) There are touches in the *Gen. Prol.* consistent with Purvey's breadth of view (see p. 285): e.g. the Oxford scandals are not stated as a certainty, but "deem they that know": the exhortations to accept persecution meekly, and pray for their enemies' conversion, are frequent: the long explanation of the old fourfold interpretation of scripture is quite unrevolutionary. (5) There is evidence that Purvey was interested in the defence of biblical translations. Walden states that Purvey was specially responsible for the translation of Wycliffe's Latin works (see p. 234), and therefore it is probable that the English form of Wycliffe's *De Officio Pastorali* is Purvey's. This is a fairly close translation, the patristic references and quotations being omitted: but chapter 15 in the English form is an interpolation, with no counterpart in the Latin (EETS, OS, 74, 429). It is introduced with some irrelevance to defend the English translation of the Bible,—not one of the normal subjects of Lollard apologetic. The chapter complains that "friars and their fautours say it is heresy to write God's law in English, and make it known to lewid men," and then gives reasons justifying this course. The precedents quoted are mainly the same as those alleged in the fifteenth chapter of the *Gen. Prol.*: the gift of tongues at Pentecost, S. Jerome's translation, the French Bible, and—the only precedent which the translator could then find in English history—the teaching of the pater noster in English, especially in the York play. The following sentence is very similar to that in the *Gen. Prol.* explaining the right method of translation: "Well I wot default may be in untrue translating, as might have been many defaults in turning from Hebrew into Greek, and from Greek into Latin, and from one language into another. But live men good life, *and study many persons God's law*, and when changing of wit is found, amend they it as reason will." The translator of the *De Officio Pastorali* had certainly a special interest in defending biblical translation, and Walden's evidence identifies him with some probability with Purvey. (6) There is also some manuscript evidence pointing to a connexion between Purvey and the Wycliffite versions, if the monogram and notes found in a certain manuscript of Lollard ownership be actually that of Purvey, as Forshall and Madden believed[1]. The name in the monogram, which is small but quite distinct, is spelt J. Pervie[2];

---

[1] Dublin A. 1. 10, see FM, 1. lx.

[2] Professor Craigie calls my attention to the difference in spelling, which seems to him to militate against the identification of this monogram with Purvey's. The mediaeval spelling of proper names often differs considerably,

and the writer has also inserted before marginal notes, corrections and prologues which he added to the original manuscript the common Latin distich:

> Christus homo factus
> J.P. prosperet actus.

The manuscript contains substantially the New Testament in the early version and, following it, the *Gen. Prol.* It has also one or two tables or summaries, and a letter from the curate, or parish priest, of Chedingfold to the bishop of Winchester, answering an accusation of Lollardy which had been brought against him. This was written in or after 1427, and J. Pervie's additions to the manuscript are not earlier. Pervie added various prologues from the later version to the several books of the New Testament, in the spaces left blank for prologues by the original scribe[1], and he also corrected the text in the margin and between the lines. If the monogram is Purvey's, he must have used and corrected the curate of Chedingfold's book: but at the end of his life.

Finally, the evidence on which Forshall and Madden relied to prove Purvey's authorship of the *Gen. Prol.*, though not conclusive, serves as confirmation to the inference from date. The *Thirty Seven Conclusions of the Lollards*, and the passage quoted from it in the *Gen. Prol.*, have been mentioned above[2]. There are also many other long passages so verbally similar as to render it certain that they are quotations from the one book to the other[3]. The *Thir. Sev. Con.* is, on the Carmelite Laven-

even by the writers of their own names: but I have not gone into the records of the Buckinghamshire Purveys to see whether this spelling actually occurs. He is called Pyrvey in 1377 (see FM, I. xxiv): Purueye in Dd. 8. 16, p. 428 (Walden's *Doctrinale*): Peruey in 1387, VCH, *Worcs.* II. 35, from *Wakefield's Reg.* It was at the date usual to initial additions or corrections made to the text: and it is not impossible that Purvey, as a fugitive should have used this book for a time, and made the additions. But the point is immaterial, as the MS. cannot have been that in which Purvey wrote the prologues originally.

[1] The prologue to the gloss on Luke is similarly copied in a blank space, in red ink, in Bodl. 143.

[2] See pp. 257, 374.

[3] They are quoted side by side in FM, I. xxv–xxvii. The *Thir. Sev. Con.* were certainly completed by Feb. 1395, and the *Gen. Prol.* completed shortly after: but probably the first part of the *Gen. Prol.*, the long analysis of biblical books, was begun before the anglicising of the *Thir. Sev. Con.*, in the months preceding Feb. 1395. This appears, because though the passage about clerical vice was quoted (see p. 257) from the *Thir. Sev. Con.* in the *Gen. Prol.*, some of the other parallel passages appear to be quoted from the *Gen. Prol.* in the *Thir. Sev. Con.* (because they occur in the same order, which is that of the biblical books, proper to the *Gen. Prol.*, and not natural, except as a quotation, in the *Thir. Sev. Con.*). That is, the books were prepared together, though the *Gen. Prol.* was finished last.

ham's evidence, a work of Purvey[1], or prepared under his editorship, so that Lavenham felt justified in regarding it as his. The many common passages in the *Thir. Sev. Con.* and the *Gen. Prol.* could thus be explained by common authorship, and the *Gen. Prol.* could be attributed to Purvey on that ground alone, if not with finality, at least with some probability.

Mr Compston in EHR, xxvi. 739, doubts Purvey's editorship of the *Thir. Sev. Con.*[2], on the ground that Lavenham, when reciting Purvey's heresies and errors, cites in three instances errors or authorities not to be found in the *Thir. Sev. Con.*, as printed by Forshall (Purvey on marriage, FZ, 391; the citation of Cestrensis, *id.* 397, § 13; and the Lollard disendowment bill of 1410, in *id.* 393, § 1). It is clear however that Lavenham was quoting, not the *Thir. Sev. Con.* alone, as Mr Compston took him to mean, but Purvey's confession of 1401 (the order of which he follows for the first five sections, cf. FZ, 383–91 with *id.* 400–4), and at least two of Purvey's works, perhaps both written in the book said by Lavenham to have been taken from Purvey in prison (possibly with other minor tracts). The word Lavenham used, "haereticum libellum," implies a political tract, like the *Thir. Sev. Con.*, and Lavenham certainly quoted the latter in some places (cf. FZ, 383, § 1, with *Ec. Reg.* 80; FZ, 384, § 3, with *Ec. Reg.* 79; 389, §§ 2, 3, with 57–8; 379, § 1 with 52). The third instance cited by Mr Compston as not in the *Thir. Sev. Con.* (the Lollard disendowment bill, see Kingsford, 65) is specially mentioned by Lavenham as being quoted from another tract from the one he had been quoting earlier (manifestum est in quodam alio tractatu speciali, FZ, 393). The passage on marriage, not in the *Thir. Sev. Con.*, was probably from the now non-existent tract on marriage, attributed to Purvey by contem-

---

[1] See p. 297.
[2] See Mr H. F. B. Compston's article in EHR, xxvi. 738. He prints a short Latin form of the *Thir. Sev. Con.*, which is more moderate in tone than the longer, English, form. He believes, from this difference in tone, that the expanded English portions are not the work of the original author of the Latin tract. This is less certain than appears at first sight, because the English versions of Latin tracts at the date were always more violent and unmeasured, being intended for a popular instead of an academic audience. Mr Compston's description of the scholarly and moderate author of the Latin conclusions noticeably fits Purvey. The English expansion was intended for use as a political "libellum" in 1395: it would almost certainly have been prepared in collaboration with the London Lollards, of whom Purvey was the "special standard bearer," and perhaps with Stury and Clifford. Whether in Purvey's own words or not, the English form reflects the more popular and violent temper of his followers, rather than his own: but the violence in itself is not enough to disprove Purvey's authorship of the English version. The Latin form may be the form of the work addressed *Ad regem et concilium* (see p. 376).

poraries. Thus Lavenham either quoted an expanded form of the *Thir. Sev. Con.*, to which the Lollard disendowment bill was tacked on, or as is more likely, he quoted a MS. of Purvey's containing the *Thir. Sev. Con.* and other tracts.     These six points, all pointing to Purvey's authorship of the *Gen. Prol.*, taken with the inference from the date of the *Gen. Prol.*, render his authorship of that work historically certain.

### 3. *MS. evidence of the date of the later Wycliffite version.*

The MSS. of the LV which are dated as earliest in the list given by FM are:

6. Royal 1. c. VIII.: Bible: before 1420.
7. Royal 1. c. IX.: Gen.—Job: not later than 1410.
46. Lambeth 25: Pentateuch in EV, remainder of O.T. in LV: c. 1400.
54. Laud 33: Epistles: "perhaps before 1400."
66. Bodl. 554: psalter: c. 1400.
71. Fairfax 2: Bible: dated 1408.
76. Dugdale: Epistles: c. 1400.
83. Gough Eccl. Top. 5: N.T.: c. 1415.
113. Caius 179: Matt. and Mark: "soon after 1400."
114. Caius 343: N.T. and calendar dated 1397. ⎱
119. Emmanuel 1. 2. 13: N.T.; copy of Caius 343' calendar.⎰
122. Jesus Q.B. 13: Matt.—Luke: begins EV, before 1400, continues LV c. 1400.
141. York XVI. N. 7: N.T.: "not much after 1400."
154. Acland: Bible: 1410 "or perhaps earlier."
161. Ashburnham 6: Acts: "not later than 1400."

The earliest dated MS. of the LV is Caius 343, the calendar at least of which has been copied into Emmanuel 1. 2. 13: this appears on careful examination of the two MSS.   Caius 343 (dated by Dr M. R. James as a fourteenth century MS.) has no indication of being an original MS. of the LV: it appears to have been copied by a professional scribe, and there are no corrections or erasures. The same scribe has undoubtedly written the whole MS.; f. 1 has "Here bigynneþ a newe testament...."   The gospels are copied, ff. 1–86, and then a calendar of the saints' day lessons is inserted, before the remainder of the N.T. The calendar is dated by a note of the same scribe as written in 1397. There are no indications that the calendar was not written at the same time as the rest of the MS.: it has incipits from the LV: so that the copying of a N.T. in the LV in 1397 is established.

In Emmanuel 1. 2. 13 the hands of the calendar and N.T. are apparently different, though contemporary. The calendar is here placed at the beginning of the N.T. and has the Sunday as well as the saints' day lessons. The Latin page headings, and certain misreadings, shew that it is copied from Caius 343, and not *vice versa*.

The text of the beginnings and ends of the O.T. lessons quoted in the calendar of Caius 343 are of interest: they are from neither Lollard version, and appear to be a translation made from the *Commune sanctorum* and *Proprium sanctorum* of the missal, not the Vulgate. The months Jan.—April inc. (Caius ff. 86–88) have 13 O.T. lessons, omitting duplicates, and of these eight are certainly from neither version, one resembles the EV, one resembles the LV, and three I cannot identify. The N.T. lessons have been copied by the scribe from the LV, which he had at hand in the MS. It appears likely that he translated the O.T. quotations (which consist only of 3 or 4 words as incipits and explicits), himself. No previous prose translation of the O.T. saints' day lessons, accompanied or unaccompanied by homilies, is known.

FM, 1. xlvii, lv, consider that Bodl. 277 and C.C.C. Camb. 147 (written c. 1440 and c. 1430 respectively) represent a revision of the LV by some scribe. It is possible on the other hand, as Professor Craigie suggested to me, that they go back to a form intermediate between the EV in the glossed gospels, and the LV, as represented by the bulk of the MSS.

4.  *Reformation and post-Reformation writers on the history of vernacular Bibles.*

Cardinal Gasquet brought forward the view that the Wycliffite Bible was the "authorised" version of our catholic forefathers in *The Old English Bible and other Essays*, 1897 and 1908, where he also sought to minimise the hostility of the mediaeval Church to the popularisation of vernacular Bibles. This view hardly does justice to the reasons which made scholars and reformers like, e.g. chancellor Gerson, declare against them. Apart from the historical correctness of cardinal Gasquet's contention (that the Church, speaking generally, encouraged the reading of vernacular Bibles), his theory is one new to orthodox writers on the subject of the attitude of the mediaeval Church. A long string of earlier catholics have sought to shew, not that the Church encouraged biblical translations, but that she did not do so in mediaeval times, and was perfectly wise in not doing so. See p. 385, for the attitude of the Carthusian monk against whom Erasmus wrote; p. 389 for the *Apology* of Frederick Staphylus, translated and published in England in 1565; Jacob van Tombe's *Claer bewys van de warachtige Kerke Christi*, Antwerp, 1567 (quoted *Boekzaal*, 342), where he says that there are many passages hard to be understood in S. Paul's epistles, etc., so that our holy forefathers "wisely decreed that the unlearned laity should not read the Bible," but made for them suitable books of devotion instead. Harney, 216, mentions certain doctors who wrote against biblical translations before the council of Trent: cf. John Driedo, or Nys, †1535, a doctor of Louvain, who wrote a tract denying that S. Paul's epistles could be understood if translated into the vernacular: Matthew Ory, a friar preacher, who wrote a French tract in 1544, denying that holy scripture ought to be communicated freely to all ages, sexes and conditions: and John de Broully, another friar preacher who printed a tract to the same effect. Harney gives, pp. 216–26, details of the works of other writers against translations during the period of the council of Trent: e.g. Perez de Ayala, Van der Bundere, and N. Grenier. James Ledesma and the cardinals Bellarmine and Stanislas Hosius wrote against biblical translations or touched upon them in their works on other subjects; Frederick Staphylus, too, wrote in German against translations, and his work was translated into Latin by the Carthusian, Lawrence Surius; the theologian, Peter Malphus, and others, opposed translations. On pp. 228–41 Harney gives the names of many theologians who opposed them after the council of Trent. In particular, several learned doctors wrote to the same effect when Antoine Arnauld, père Quesnel and the Jansenists desired a more liberal attitude of the Church towards vernacular versions, though without asking for their unlicensed use. Arnauld wrote in 1680 (*Œuvres*, 1783, VIII. no. x), *De la lecture de l'écriture sainte*, against a tract of C. Mallet, *De la lecture de l'écriture sainte en langue vulgaire*, Anvers, 1682. Mallet, doctor of the Sorbonne and archdeacon of Rouen, sought to set forth: *That it is not according to the mind of God or of the canonical scriptures that ignorant people should read holy scripture, but that this is reserved to priests and doctors alone* (Arnauld, *Œuvres*, VIII. 4). Mallet had quoted from a tract published in 1661, *Collectio Auctorum translationes scripturarum in linguas vulgares damnantium* (*Œuvres*, VIII. 3 and 283). Arnauld in several tracts and letters opposed the view that holy scripture ought not to be read by the laity, as did a Belgian writer condemned for Jansenism, John Neercassel, apostolic

vicar-general of the Belgian provinces in 1663, who wrote a
*Tractatus de lectione scripturarum*. The Dominican, Harney, himself then wrote in answer to both Arnauld and Neercassel a learned
history of vernacular versions, treating the biblical, patristic and
mediaeval periods, and claiming that in the latter the Church
had always, with good reason, withheld scriptural translations
from the laity (*De sancta scriptura linguis vulgaribus legenda:
rationabile obsequium Belgii Catholici, per Martinum Harney:
adversus quaedam scripta D. Antonii Arnaldi*, Louvain, 1693).
The Jansenists continued to struggle for biblical translations,
and among the propositions of Quesnel condemned in 1711 were
those advocating the unrestricted right of the laity to use them
(artt. LXXIX. LXXX.: The reading of holy scripture is for all
people; LXXXI., The holy obscurity of the Word of God is not a
reason for dispensing the laity from reading it, and artt. LXXIX.,
LXXXII.–LXXXV. to the same effect; *La lecture de la sainte Bible
en langue vulgaire*, Malon, J. B., 1846, II. 521). In 1793 another
catholic history of biblical translations was written by T. G.
Hegelmaier (*Geschichte des Bibelverbots*, Ulm, 1783), in which,
while the author applauded the more liberal attitude of churchmen of his day towards translations, he emphasised the prohibitory attitude of the mediaeval Church towards them (e.g.
he considers that Innocent III's letter to Metz, 1199, was meant
to discourage lay Bible reading, *Bibelverbot*, 128, and emphasizes
the share of Gregory IX in the prohibitions of the council of
Toulouse, *id.* 135). The encyclical of Leo XII to Spain in 1824
exhorted all pastors to "be instant in season and out of season
...that the faithful entrusted to you...shall be persuaded that
if the sacred scriptures be everywhere indiscriminately public,
more evil than advantage will arise thence" (Putnam, II. 28).
J. B. Malon, canon of Bruges and Librarian of Louvain, wrote
in 1846 the above mentioned history of biblical translations: it
dealt mainly with the post-Reformation period, but did not
question the restrictions laid by the Church upon translations
in the middle ages, or their wisdom: p. v, "La lecture de la sainte
Bible...est utile à tous les fidèles qui la font sous la direction
de l'Eglise, avec un esprit pieux, humble et docile. Elle est
funeste à toutes les personnes qui la font avec orgueil, témérité
et présomption. L'Eglise catholique est dans le vrai, lorsqu'elle
interdit cette lecture aux fidèles qui ne sont pas disposés à s'y
livrer avec fruit." For early Spanish and Italian writers see
p. 50, n. 1.

## 5. *Quotations from Reformation and post-Reformation writers on vernacular Bibles.*

(a)  *Apologia D. Erasmi Rot. adversus Debacchationes Petri Sutoris.* (*Erasmi Opera*, Leyden, 1706, IX. 739.)

Erasmus in this tract defended himself from the attack of a French Carthusian, Petrus Sutor (? Le Couturier), formerly a doctor of the Sorbonne, who had attacked his emendations and paraphrases of the Vulgate text. I am indebted to Mr P. S. Allen for the information that Sutor had published, at Paris in 1524–5, a *De translatione Bibliae et nouarum reprobatione interpretationum*, in chap. 20 of which he attacked Erasmus with great violence. Erasmus answered by publishing this *Apologia* in 1525, in which he recounted many of Sutor's arguments against lay Bible reading, and supplied the answers. Erasmus says that:

When he accuses me for trying afresh to give clearness to the text of the New Testament, he alleges that the old humble and common style was pleasing to the Holy Spirit, and that through it holy scripture can be read and understood alike by the learned and the unlearned [Humanist scholars and their opponents], and therefore he calls it the "common Bible." But if he says this sincerely, why does he in fact blame those who translate the Bible into the vulgar tongue? (ix. 784.)

Sutor has gently derided as incredible Erasmus' assertion that Latin was once the common tongue of Italy, Spain and Gaul, and that the Vulgate was translated for that reason; he has asked "how then the Latin language could have perished there?" and in arguing against popular Bible reading has made use of the popular mediaeval quotation, *Nolite sanctum dare canibus, neque mittatis margaritas ante porcos.* Erasmus answers several of his arguments against vernacular Bibles, *inter alia*:

"The woman," he says, "who is occupied in reading the sacred volumes neglects her domestic duties,"...and perhaps the soldier will be slower to go forth to fight! and a great danger that would be!...And if the sacred volumes ought to be taken from the common people because from this source the Waldensians have fallen into error: so also they ought to be taken from the learned, because Origen and Arius and Wycliffe and Hus have from them also drunk in their heresies.... "It would be a great danger to constitutions of human origin, if the people understood that they were not in the holy books." ..."In many places in the sacred volumes the vices of pastors and princes are reproved, and if the people were to read them, they would murmur against those set over them." (ix. 785–6.)

(b) *An Exhortation to the diligent studye of scripture made by Erasmus Roterodamus. And translated into Inglish.* (1529). Not paginated.

I would desire that all women should read the gospel and Paul's epistles, and I would to God they were translated into the tongues of all men, so that they might not only be known of the Scots and Irishmen, but also of the Turks and Saracens....I would to God that the ploughman would sing a text of the scripture at his plough-beam; and that the weaver at his loom with this would drive away the tediousness of time. I would the wayfaring man with this pastime would expel the weariness of his journey. And, to be short, I would that all the communication of the Christian should be of the scripture; for in a manner, such are we ourselves, as our daily tales are....Neither truly is it meet...sith the reward of immortality pertaineth indifferently unto all men, that only the doctrine should be banished from the secular, and possessed only of a few, whom the commonalty call divines, or religious persons....We cannot call any man a Platonist, unless he have read the works of Plato. Yet call we them Christian, yea and divines, which never have read the scriptures of Christ.... If we covet to withdraw our minds from the tedious cares of this life; why had we liefer learn the wisdom of Christ's doctrine out of men's books, than of Christ Himself, which in this scripture doth chiefly perform that thing which He promised unto us, when He said that He would continue with us unto the end of the world? For in this Testament He speaketh, breatheth and liveth among us in a manner more effectually than when His body was presently conversant in this world. The Jews neither saw nor heard so much, as thou mayest daily both hear and see in the scripture of Christ....What a marvellous world is this: we keep the letters which are written from our friends: we kiss them, and bear them about with us; we read them over twice or thrice. And how many thousands are there among the Christian which are esteemed of great literature, and yet have not once in their lives read over the gospels and epistles of the Apostles....They that profess Saint Benedict's rule... (observe their example), learn it by heart, and drink it into their hearts. Saint Austin's adherents are not ignorant in their rule. Saint Francis' friars do know, observe, and advance their patron's precepts:...Why set they more by their rule which was written of a man, than the whole Christianity by the holy scripture, which Christ did equally preach unto all men?...I would our first and unformed speech should sound of Christ; I would our ignorant childhood should be informed with Christ's evangely....The evangely doth represent and express the quick and living image of His most holy mind, yea, and Christ Himself healing, dying, rising again, and to conclude, all parts of Him, in so much that thou couldst not so plainly and fruitfully see Him, although He were present before thy bodily eyes.

(c) *Censures issued* 17 *Dec.* 1527 *by the Theological Faculty at Paris on certain propositions of Erasmus in defence of biblical translations.*

Mr P. S. Allen kindly informs me that these *Censures* were published as the *Determinatio Facultatis Theologiae in schola Parisiensi super quamplurimis Assertionibus D. Erasmi Roterodami*, by J. Badius Ascensius, July 1531. On f. vii of this book it is stated that the Faculty became disturbed about Erasmus' attitude in July 1526, though Harney's source for supplying the exact date, 17 Dec. 1527, for the pronouncement of the determination, is not clear. The four propositions of Erasmus had (with others) been attacked by N. Beda in 1526, and Erasmus replied in a *Prologus* directed against him in August of that year, and republished in March 1527 (see *Opera*, ix. 442). The quotations given are from Harney, 209–14; cf. Harl. 4381 b. § 9.

Erasmus: *Preface to S. Matthew*: "I would desire that the sacred books should be translated into all languages." *Censure*: "Although the sacred books might be translated into all languages, in that they are in their nature holy and good: yet the great danger of permitting the promiscuous reading of them, when translated without any explanation, is sufficiently shewn by the Waldensians, Albigensians and Turlupins, who have spread abroad many errors through this cause....Wherefore this kind of translation is by law condemned."

Erasmus: *Preface to S. Matthew*: "They cry out, that it would be an outrage if a woman or a tanner should speak of the sacred books." *Censure*: "Rightly is it...esteemed an outrage, that the unlearned and the simple should read the holy books translated into their own tongue...."

Erasmus: *Preface to S. Matthew*: "With my good will, let the husbandman read the holy books: let the smith and the weaver read them." *Censure*: "Holy scripture bears witness that the simple are as children, to be fed, as S. Paul says, with milk....Wherefore it is not a means suitable for these simple people, that they should read the sacred books promiscuously, translated into the vernacular: but the means which befits them is that which the Church has appointed, the hearing of the word of God, and attendance at sermons. Neither is the use of certain of the sacred books prohibited to them, if they are provided with suitable explanations, tending to edification, and if also such books are read by them piously and soberly, without pride and arrogance. Therefore this proposition, set down without any limitation, shews that its assertor is of unsound doctrine."

The fourth proposition was: "Neither shall I forbid to any man the reading of the prophet Ezechiel, or of the Song of Songs, or of any of the books of the Old Testament." *Censure*: "Since, by a *decree* of the apostolic see, the reading of many such books was long since prohibited to the laity: (and to those learned in God's Word among the Jews, the reading of the said books, and of the first chapter of Genesis was prohibited thirty years ago, by the advice of weighty scholars) : the aforesaid proposition is asserted rashly and impudently. For the same cause for prohibiting the reading of such books exists, as there was when the decree of Innocent III was drawn up about these matters, a fragment of which is incorporated in his own words in the *De Haeret.*, as the *Cum ex injuncto.*"

Erasmus answered these censures (Harney, 212–14), in a work printed in 1532 at Antwerp, where he appeared much more ready to accept some restriction of the reading of vernacular Bibles. On the *decree* of Innocent III to Metz, however, he stood firm:

For if the *decree* of that pope, or any other, was at some period brought forward against the rashness of men, I do not consider that it is binding on the whole Church....But if this measure is demanded by the malice of present day men, I will not cavil at the constitutions of popes, or of the Roman see.

### (d) El Nuevo Testamento. Francisco da Enzinas. 1543.

This work was condemned and put upon the index, as the work of a protestant scholar: but Enzinas hoped for recognition at the time of its publication. He dedicated his book to the emperor, Charles V, and pleaded for the recognition of the lawfulness of Spanish translations of the Bible. There are, he says, many opinions that it would be well that holy scripture should be translated into the vulgar tongue, and many to the contrary, with which he does not agree; three reasons have moved him to make the translation.

(1) If the Jews understood the conversion of their forbears, as related in the Acts and the New Testament generally, they would be the more readily converted. For twenty years past, he says (pp. 3 *b*–4), there has been sharp debate in Spain as to the lawfulness of vernacular scriptures, and men of much zeal have striven to prevent the printing of such books.

(2) The second reason is the honour of the Spanish nation. "There is no nation, so far as I know, which is not permitted to read the sacred books in its own tongue, saving only Spain alone" (p. 5). In Italy there are many versions,...in France so many that he cannot count them.... In Flanders and the Rhine towns such new versions are issued almost daily, and that in the most important cities. And so in Germany,...England, Scotland, and Ireland. Spain alone remains lagging behind; wherefore he cannot see why that in Spain is prohibited which is with reason conceded to all the other nations.

(3) If biblical translations were evil (p. 6), or likely to lead to bad results, his majesty Charles V or the pope would have prohibited the possession or printing of such books by law: but though Charles V has made laws with such diligence, he has not made, so far as Enzinas knows, any such law, and therefore this translation is not illegal. He then gives many precedents for the translation of the scriptures: the Jews used Chaldee paraphrases: the early Christians wrote in Greek, then the common tongue of the east: other nations, like the Egyptians, Arabs, Persians, Ethiopians and Latins, all turned the scriptures into their own tongues. Afterwards in the Latin Church:

This custom that the holy scripture should be read in the language which all understood was lost, not because it was not a good custom, but because foreign peoples entered into Europe, and the Latin language became lost in the vernaculars, and they began to use others. But the Church continued to use [Latin] as before. Which custom has remained till recent times: but only in these parts of Europe. In Greece the people retain the ancient custom, and so in Africa, Egypt, Ethiopia, Syria, Palestine, Persia, India, the East and all quarters of the globe. So that it is not a new custom, nor I alone in approving it: nor can it be a bad thing, since it has endured for so long a time in the Church of God, and so many nations approve of it, and the catholic Church holds it for good. (p. 7 b.)

(e) *The Apologie of Fredericus Staphylus, counseller to the late emperor Ferdinandus; Intreating, Of the true and right understanding of holy Scripture, Of the translation of the Bible in to the vulgar tongue. Of disagrement in doctrine amonge the protestants. Translated out of Latin in to English by* THOMAS STAPLETON, *Student in Divinite.* Antwerp. 1565.

*Of the true and right understanding of holy scripture* (p. 32). It is therefore a wonderful slander that these men say of the catholics: "That hitherto the gospel and the word of God hath been banished from the Church, kept in hucker mucker, and at the length under the pope to have been utterly extinguished: but now is revoked into light."

To refute the accusation, Staphylus shews that:

Both now and in all ages, we read the gospel in our churches, we preach the word of God in our pulpits, and interpret it to the people: we express it by outward ceremonies, rites and gestures, such as we have received of our forefathers, even from the primitive Church and the Apostles' time.

*Of translating the Bible into the vulgar tongue* (p. 64). Another thing that the Lutherans object unto me is, that they say, it hath been by my means and counsel procured that the Bible is no more read in the vulgar tongue: especially as Luther translated it. Now although I remember not that I ever said or wrote that the lay men ought not to have the Bible in their vulgar tongue, yet if I had done so, it had been no great trespass. For surely I could never yet find in holy scripture, that the common people ought of necessity to read scripture. But that of the reading thereof much schism and the destruction of many souls hath proceeded, daily experience teacheth us. And holy writ warneth us, where our Saviour thus speaketh: *It is given to you to know the mysteries of the kingdom of God, but to the rest in parables, that seeing yet they see not, and hearing they understand not.* Who are these unto whom our Lord saith: *To you it is given,* etc.? Surely the Apostles and their successors, the rulers of Christ's flock. And who are they that should learn by parables? surely such men, as were better not to know the mysteries, lest misusing them they procure themselves a greater damnation. *For precious stones ought not to be cast before hogs,* and such of all likelihood are the lay ignorant people. ...[The Hebrew text used by the Jews could be read only by the elders, not by the common people], lest peradventure the precious mysteries of the old law should be cast before hogs, the rude and curious people. These threescore and ten elders also very miraculously translated the Hebrew Bible into Greek, before the coming of Christ, they only having the knowledge of the text. So in like wise the threescore and twelve disciples were chosen to read and understand the mysteries of holy writ, unto whom priests have succeeded (as in the principal sees and bishoprics in Christendom we are able to show). Therefore it is evident, that unto priests, pastors and bishops (whom God hath placed to oversee His Church), the grace of the Holy Ghost always assisteth to interpret and expound the mysteries of holy scripture by parables unto the people, as far as for them is requisite. Wherefore the unlearned laymen may well be admonished to refrain from all curious and greedy reading of holy scripture. First, lest rashly and unadvisedly they take upon them the office committed by God to the elders, to priests and bishops;...also, because experience of our time hath taught, how dangerous it is that every lay man, craftsman, labourer or otherwise, all without discretion, should read and examine scripture at their pleasure....[Could ignorant men displace all physicians, and apothecaries, and use their drugs with profit?] Surely so it is of the holy scripture translated into the vulgar tongue and so made common for all men. For the lay man may so read them, and pick out medicines for his appetite: but for lack of skill (as experience hath tried), he will cast himself down....By this similitude the unlearned may gather, how dangerous it is for him to read the scripture in his mother tongue: especially with the intent to interpret it as he shall think best himself....

But here peradventure a man will demand: "Sir, if it be so, that the reading of the Bible in the vulgar tongue be so perilous a matter, how shall the unlearned lay man provide that he be not abused in this case? For many there are among the laity that cannot refrain from reading holy scripture, taking it for a great comfort....What part then of holy scripture might well be permitted them to read?" For the whole corps of the Bible, were it never so well translated, yet I doubt whether it were expedient for the lay [people] to read it. For it might be an occasion of idle and light thoughts, if every girl or young woman should read the stories of Lot and his daughters, of Leah....[Among the Jews it was not thought expedient that every one indifferently should come lightly to high and secret mysteries]: Nor hath it been without the singular disposition and marvellous providence of God that, through all the west Church, the words of His holy sacraments have among so many barbarous nations been kept so long time in the Latin tongue, unknown and strange to the common folk....[Since there are many parts of scripture, not needing to be known, not merely to the laity, but to the inferior sort of clergy, certain bishops of Rome have long ago set certain portions in the breviary, distributed into the seven hours of the passion. This has been translated into German, and the laity may use it, together with homilies from the Fathers, distributed into the Sundays and holy days of the year.]

6. *Analysis of 7578 wills made before* 1526 (*the date of Tindale's printed New Testament*), *to shew the relative frequency of possession of English Bibles, French Bibles, Vulgates, Latin service books, and English and French devotional books; from*

(*a*) Printed collections of wills.
(*b*) Collections of wills printed in archaeological collections, episcopal registers, historical monographs, etc.
(*c*) Single printed wills; single wills in MSS., and references to bequests of books in chroniclers; Lollard trials in *Acts and Monuments*, the *Victoria County History*, episcopal registers, etc.
(*d*) Totals.

## (a) Printed collections of wills made before 1526.

| Name of collection | Dates | No. of wills | No. of book wills | English Bibles | French Bibles | Vulgates | Service books | English devotional books | French devotional books |
|---|---|---|---|---|---|---|---|---|---|
| (1) Testamenta Vetusta | 1189–1526 | 805 | 60 | — | 1: and 1 Spanish | 7 | 48 | 1 glossed psalter<br>1 Life of Jhesu<br>1 legend | 1 legenda aurea<br>2 glossed psalters<br>1 epistles and gospels |
| (2) Bury Wills and Inventories | 1370–1526 | 42 | 8 | | | | | | |
| (3) Testamenta Eboracensia, I.1316–1429 | | 306 | 66 | 1 book of gospels, 1394 | 1 | 8 | 62 | 1 Mirror of S. Edmund<br>1 glossed psalter<br>1 Prick of Conscience<br>1 Grace Dieu | 1 psalter and legend<br>1 glossed psalter<br>1 Barlaam and Josaphat |
| ,, | II.1429–1467 | 232 | 68 | 1 S. Matth. | — | 5 | 70 | 1 "de expositione Evangeliorum"<br>1 Hilton<br>1 "Prick of Conscience"<br>1 "de pater noster"<br>2 Grace Dieu | |
| ,, | III.1395–1491 | 124 | 60 | — | — | 12 | 56 | 1 Hilton<br>2 Life of Christ<br>1 psalter, etc., of Hampole<br>1 Revelations of S. Brigit<br>1 "de pater noster" | |
| ,, | IV.1420–1508 | 167 | 53 | — | — | 4 | 39 | 2 Vita Jhesu<br>1 Speculum Peccatoris | |
| ,, | v. Too late in date | | | | | | | | |
| (4) Lancashire and Cheshire Wills | 1301–1526 | 95 | 3 | — | — | — | 2 | | |

| | Date | | | | | | | Books mentioned | |
|---|---|---|---|---|---|---|---|---|---|
| (5) North Country Wills | Before 1526 | 327 | 25 | — | | 3 | 19 | 1 Prick of Conscience / 1 Chastising of God's Children / 1 Vices and Virtues | 1 Vita Sanctorum |
| (6) London Wills | 1258–1526 | 4002 | 45 | 1 | | 4 | 36 | 1 Latin and English psalter, 1349 / 1 book of Rolle's | |
| (7) Fifty Earliest English Wills | 1387–1439 | 50 | 8 | — | | — | 6 | 1 Pore Caitiff / 1 Story of Joseph | |
| (8) Early Lincoln Wills | 1320–1526 | 522 | 51 | — | | 5 | 41 | 1 book of Richard the Hermit | 2 Apocalypses: probably French |
| (9) Testamenta Karleolensia | 1353–1386 | 157 | 12 | 1 | | — | — | | 1 French book |
| (10) Royal Wills (mainly the same as in *Test. Vet.*). Only those not in *Test. Vet.* mentioned | 1135–1526 | — | — | — | 1 | — | — | | |
| (11) Wills from Doctors' Commons | 1495 | — | — | — | | — | — | 1 Hilton / 1 Life of S. Cath. of Siena | |
| (12) Great Orphan Book, Book of Wills | — | — | — | 1 | 1 | 1 | — | | |
| Totals | | 6829 | 459 | 3 | 4 | 49 | 379 | 32 | 11 |

(b) Collections of wills printed in archaeological journals, episcopal registers, historical monographs, etc.

| Name of collection | Dates | No. of wills | No. of book wills | English Bibles | French Bibles | Vulgates | Service books | English devotional books | French devotional books |
|---|---|---|---|---|---|---|---|---|---|
| (1) Bockett, J. R., Surrey Wills, in Surrey Arch. Coll. I. 180 | 1497–1522 | 7 | | | | | | | |
| (2) Bradford Antiquary, Early Wills, I. 201; II. | 1392–1526 | 39 | 3 | | | | | | |
| (3) Corner, G. R., Southwark Wills, in Surrey Arch. Coll. I. 190 | Before 1526 | 15 | | | | | | | |
| (4) Dashwood, G. H., Stowe-Bardolph Wills, in Norfolk and Suffolk Arch. Soc. II. 97 | 1321–1503 | 11 | | | | | | | |
| (5) Harrod, H., Early Norfolk Wills, in Norfolk and Norwich Arch. Soc. I. 255 | 1478–1522 | 19 | — | — | — | — | — | 1 primer, 1518 | |
| (6) Harrod, H., Extracts from early wills in Norwich Registers, in Norfolk and Norwich Arch. Soc. IV. 317 | 1370–1511 | 24 | 8 | — | — | 1 | 4 | Le doctrine of the herte Book of S. Bridget Hilton Prick of Conscience | |
| (7) King, H. W., Ancient Wills, in Trans. Essex Arch. Soc. IV. 149; v. 286; New Series, I. 148, 165; II. 57; III. 231 | 1414–1526 | 21 | — | — | — | New Test. with Lyra's gloss. | 5 | "my great English book", "Wordys of Goddis Lawe" | 1 Manuel des Pec-chez |

| | Source | Date | | | | | | Notes |
|---|---|---|---|---|---|---|---|---|
| (8) | Malden, H. C., *Ancient Wills*, in *Trans. Essex Arch. Soc.*, New Series, VI. 122 | 1491–1526 | 4 | — | — | 1 | | |
| (9) | Malden, H. C., *Ancient Wills*, and Waller, W. C., *Old Chigwell Wills*, in *Trans. Essex Arch. Soc.*, New Series, x. | Before 1526 | 31 | — | — | | | |
| (10) | Page Turner, F. A., *Bedfordshire Wills*, in *Bedfordshire Hist. Rec. Soc.* II. 3 | 1379–1526 | 9 | — | 1 | 1 | 5 | 1 psalter glossed by Hampole |
| (11) | *Proc. Suffolk Instit. of Archaeol.* I. 248, 267; VII. 196 | 1439–1526 | 32 | | | | | |
| (12) | Sherwood, G. F. T., *Early Berkshire Wills*, in *Berks.Bucks.and Oxon. Arch. Jour.* I. 22, 51, 89; III. 78; IV. 6, 91, 116; v. 49; VI. 23, 92, 119; VII. 28; XI. 47; xx. 82 | 1476–1526 | 55 | | 11 | | | |
| (13) | Tymms, S., *Ixworth Wills*, in *Proc. Suffolk Instit. of Arch.* I. 103 | 1472–1524 | 6 | — | | | | |
| (14) | Plomer, H. R., *Books in wills: extracts from unprinted wills*, in *Trans. Bibliog. Soc.* VII. 99–121 | 1396–1526 | 15 | 15 | — | 6 | | 1 *On contemplation* 1 *Vita Christi*, possibly Eng. 1 *Chastising of God's Children* |

(b) Collections of wills printed in archaeological journals, etc. *contd.*

| Name of collection | Dates | No.of wills | No.of book wills | English Bibles | French Bibles | Vulgates | Service books | English devotional books | French devotional books |
|---|---|---|---|---|---|---|---|---|---|
| (1) Kirby, T. F., *Register of William of Wykeham* | 1366-1404 | 16 | | | | | | | |
| (2) Capes, W. W., *Reg. Johannis Trefnant* | 1389-1404 | 1 | 1 | — | — | 1 | | | |
| (3) *Ely Diocesan Remembrancer*, extracts | 1384-1526 | 13 | — | — | — | 1 | | | |
| (4) Hingeston Randolph, F. C., *Reg. of Edmund Lacy* | 1420 | 1 | | | | | | | |
| (5) Hingeston Randolph, F. C., *Reg. of Walter de Stapeldon* | 1326 | 1 | 1 | — | — | 1 | — | — | Trans. of 10 Commandments, Ave, Creed, etc. |
| (6) Hingeston Randolph, F. C., *Reg. of Edmund Stafford* | 1397-1419 | 59 | | — | — | 1 | | | |
| (7) Parry, J. H., *Reg. Johannis Gilbert* | 1375-1389 | 8 | | | | | | | |
| (8) *Kellawe's Register*, R.S. No. 62 | 1313 | 2 | | | | | | | |
| (9) Hingeston Randolph, F. C., *Reg. of Thomas de Brantyngham* | 1369-1393 | 3 | — | — | — | 1 | — | — | Primer, psalter and devot. book |
| (10) *Peckham's Register*, R.S. No. 77 | | — | — | — | — | 1 | — | | |
| (11) Wigram, S. R., *Cartulary of Monastery of S. Frideswide* | 1265-1400 | 7 | — | — | — | — | 1 | | |

| Reference | Date | | | | | | | Remarks | |
|---|---|---|---|---|---|---|---|---|---|
| (2) Salter, H. E., *Oxford Balliol Deeds* | 1303–1495 | 9 | — | — | — | — | 1 | — | |
| (3) Plomer, H. R., *Abstracts from wills of English printers* | 1492–1526 | 3 | — | — | — | — | — | — | |
| (4) Camb. Univ. MSS. Catalogue | 1501–1526 | 50 | 10 | — | 1 Old Test. | 1 | — | Several | |
| (5) Madan, *Summary Cat. of Western MSS.* | Before 1526 | 4 | 4 | — | — | — | — | 1 English primer, 1446; 1 Clensing of Man's Soul, 1401; 1 Concilium Conscientiae, 1426; 1 Legenda Aurea, 1438 | 1 psalter |
| (6) *Digby MSS. Catalogue* | Before 1526 | 2 | 2 | — | — | — | — | — | |
| (7) James, M. R., *Descrip. Cat. Caius Coll.* | — | — | — | — | — | — | — | 1 Prick of Conscience; 1 Horologium Sapientiae | |
| (8) James, M. R., *Descrip. Cat. C. C. Coll. Camb.* | — | — | — | — | 3 | — | — | 1 Horologium Sapientiae; 1 Vita Jhesu | |
| (9) Bramley, *Rolle's Psalter* | — | — | — | — | — | — | — | 4 Hampole's psalters | |
| (10) *Lincoln Dioc. Docs.* | 1451 | — | — | — | — | — | — | 1 On active life: Life of Christ | |
| (11) Leach, A. F., *Visitations and Memorials of Southwell Minster* | Before 1526 | 23 | 4 | — | 2 | 20 | 16 | — | |
| **Totals** | | 490 | 59 | — | 2 | 20 | 16 | 24 | 6 |

(c) Printed single wills, MS. single wills, and references to bequests in chroniclers.

| Dates | No.of book wills | No.of wills | English Bibles | French Bibles | Vul-gates | Service books | English devotional books | French devotional books |
|---|---|---|---|---|---|---|---|---|
| Before 1526 | 259 | 82 | 3 / 11 Lollard | 3 | 41 | — | 3 | 2 |

(d) Totals

| | No.of book wills | No.of wills | English Bibles | French Bibles | Vul-gates | Service books | English devotional books | French devotional books |
|---|---|---|---|---|---|---|---|---|
| (a) — | 6829 | 459 | 3 | 4 | 49 | 379 | 32 | 11 |
| (b) — | 490 | 59 | — | 2 | 20 | 16 | 24 | 6 |
| (c) — | 259 | 82 | 14 | 3 | 41 | — | 3 | 2 |

Results: in the 7578 wills examined,
6 "orthodox" possessors of English Bibles: 3 of these before 1408,
   in 1394, 1397, and 1404 respectively,
11 (at least) Lollard possessors in *Acts and Monuments*, etc.
9 French Bibles,
110 Vulgates,
395 (more than) bequests of service books,
59 English devotional books, glossed psalters, etc.
19 French ,, ,, ,,

# APPENDIX II. DOCUMENTS

I. *William Butler's Determination against biblical translations*, 1401; *also the burning of English Bibles previous to* 1401.

The friars at Oxford had so long been opposing the lawfulness of English Bibles for popular use, that the delivery of friar Butler's determination in the schools in 1401 needs no special explanation. Bale however makes a curious assertion as to its occasion. In his 1557 ed. of the *Illustrium Maioris Britanniae Scriptorum...Catalogus ...ex J. Lelando...collectus*, p. 536 (Cent. VII. xxxix), he quotes Leland, the *Catalogi Franciscanorum* and some unknown work of Purvey on the subject of William Butler. He quotes Leland as saying: "Legi scripsisse eum a.D. 1401 Determinationis nomine libellum, contra translationem scripturae sacrae in linguam vulgarem: postquam esset in Anglia, (ut testis est Purvaeus) procurantibus fraterculis generale mandatum ut comburerentur....Alexander quintus, Rom. pont., qui et Franciscanus erat, huius factum nefarium confirmavit, damnando scripturas in sermonem vulgarem translatas." Leland (*Scriptorum*, 1709, II. 409) does not give the date 1401, so that probably Bale supplied this from the MS. of Butler's determination, or else the date was in the Franciscan Catalogues. The statement about Bible-burning is attributed to Purvey, which seems almost too curiously appropriate to be a mere guess on Bale's part. He himself attributes to Purvey some tracts which have not survived to us,—but none apparently dealing with this subject: Purvey was not well-known to Bale as a defender of English scriptures, nor hence a likely subject of such a guess. The first part of Butler's determination (see p. 401) is now missing, and may originally have contained some reference to the occasion of the determination: but Bale expressly quotes Purvey, so that it is unlikely that these missing folios were his source.

The tract *Fifty heresies and errors of friars* (*Sel. Eng. Works*, III. 393) is possibly Purvey's, and states that friars pursue poor priests "both to burn them and the gospels of Christ written in English, to most learning of our nation." Cf. *Sel. Eng. Works*, I. 129, an English sermon of [?] Wycliffe's, with its apparent reference to some antivernacular statute: "as the high priests set the stone at the door of Christ's sepulchre, so our high priests dread...that God's law should quicken after this, and therefore they make statutes, stable as a stone, and get grant of knights to confirm them...lest that truth of God's law, hid in the sepulchre, burst out to knowing of the common people. Well I wot that knights took gold in this case."

Hus relates an anecdote with a reference to some edict: but it may just refer to Arundel's constitutions. He says that:

"I heard from a faithful man of honest memory, Nicholas who was called Faulfisch, that when he was travelling in England, he knew a certain cook with whom he used to drink. And when the bishop asked the cook why he read the holy scriptures in the English tongue, contrary to the edict [contra mandatum], he defended himself by an argument drawn from holy scripture. For when the bishop asked him: 'Dost thou know with whom thou speakest?' he answered: 'With a bishop that is but man.' Then the bishop said: 'And dost thou, a wretched little layman dare to argue with me in the matter of holy scripture?' To whom he answered: 'Yea indeed...since the most merciful lord Christ listened calmly to scriptural texts from the devil, why then shouldst not thou, who art less than Christ, hear me, a man?' But the bishop was so angry that he broke off the discussion[1]."

Faulfisch was at Oxford 2 Feb. 1407, when he corrected the MS. of the *De Veritate*, *De Dominio Divino*, and *De Ecclesia*[2], which he took back to Prague, and he returned to Bohemia in 1407, the month not being known. Arundel's synod which dealt with English scriptures did not meet till 7 November, 1407: so that Faulfisch's reference to the "mandatum" would appear to refer to some earlier edict: though it may possibly have been inspired by some conversation between an Oxford cook and Arundel on his short visit, if Faulfisch left at the end of the year.

The evidence is not enough to establish the issue of any edict previous to Arundel's constitutions for the burning of English Bibles: though there is no inherent probability that some were burnt, while Gerson in Paris and the authorities at Oxford were hostile to them; and while the procedure in heresy trials presided over by the English bishops was so similar to that of the continental inquisition. Alexander V had studied earlier as an Oxford Franciscan, and it is not unlikely that the Oxford friars should have sought his help, or that he should have given it. For a late fifteenth century inquisitor's inquiry of the pope, what he was to do with books of the scriptures in German containing no glosses, since it was scarcely fitting to burn them, see *supra* p. 101 n. The episcopal inquisitors in 1400 would possibly have been less scrupulous: and in any case, they might have found plenty of Wycliffite scriptures containing the heretical *General Prologue* to burn. No special edict was needed for the burning of English Bibles before 1401[3].

Bale's statement was followed by Pits, Fabricius, Wadding, and some later writers. Pits, an English Franciscan, writing in 1619, paraphrased Bale from the true mediaeval point of view. In fr. Butler's time, he says, p. 588, "the Holy Bible was translated into the English tongue, and came promiscuously into the hands of workmen and women, and now whosoever could read it reckoned that he

---

[1] *De Ecclesia*, xviii.          [2] EHR, vii. 307.

[3] The episcopal inquisitors certainly took biblical books from the Lollards before 1408: cf. William Smith in 1392 (*supra*, p. 278), and Thorpe's psalter in 1407 (p. 354).

understood it: and hence a great contempt of divine mysteries."
Butler and others sought for a remedy; and hence "a public edict
was made, that all these Bibles translated into English should be
burnt, lest the ignorant multitude should thence by themselves drink
in poison to their souls, whence led by their pastors they might have
drunk things profitable to salvation. When therefore these books
were burned, he put in writing the reason of the deed, and gave to
the light a learned work, entitled, *Contra translationem Anglicanam.*"

This tract is here printed from Merton 68, ff. 202–204 *b*. It begins
imperfectly, and at the bottom of the page a contemporary hand
has written: *Quaere principium huius tractatus fo.* 119 *praecedenti*;
ff. 118, 119, 120 are however cut out, probably because, like the
similar determination of Palmer, they contained first a list of the
Lollard arguments in favour of an English translation, which would
attract notice when Arundel warned the authorities afresh to burn
all Wycliffite books. The handwriting is that of a professional scribe,
who misunderstood and miscopied certain passages.

In this and Palmer's determination, *ae* is printed for the mediaeval
*e*, capitals and a normalised spelling are supplied to proper names,
and *c*'s and *t*'s, *u*'s and *v*'s, *i*'s and *j*'s are normalised. Biblical references are not appended when the scribe gives the chapter reference
correctly.

### Butler, *contra translationem Anglicanam.* (f. 202, col. *1*)

— intellexisse scripturam sacram et eam false composuisse;
et multa secundum illum sensum falsum disputasse in libro *De
moribus ecclesiae catholicae*[1]. Textus vero in quo erravit erat iste:
*Quoniam propter te mortificamur tota die*, ubi translatio Septua-
ginta interpretum sensum habet: *Quoniam propter te morte
afficimur tota die.* Sic constat quod libri si multiplicarentur
essent mendosi, qui cito legentes inducerent ad errorem: ergo,
periculosum esset tales libros scribere. Sed forsan pariformiter
argueret quis: libros in Latina nam[2] esse legendos, cum aequaliter contingeret fore falsos. Huic dico, quod ecclesia ordinavit
universitates in quibus docentur scripturae et scribuntur libri,
qui si falsi sunt, facile possunt corrigi; quae politia non potest
commode[3] servari stante multiplicatione tanta populi; nec
debent praelati hoc admittere, quod singuli ad libitum eorum
legant scripturam in Latinum translatam; quia, sicut experientia
satis docet, hoc fuit multis modis occasio incidendi in haereses
et errores. Non est ergo politicum ut quicunque, ubicunque,
quantumcunque voluerit se det ferventi studio scripturarum.

---

[1] *S. Augustini Opera*, PL, 32, col. 1310. The tract begins in the middle of
the first of the six main arguments of the determination. This was clearly,
that the multiplication of books entailed mistakes in copying, since even
S. Augustine in the work quoted argued concerning a passage where the
principal word had been omitted, as can be verified in the *Patrologia*.

[2] Perhaps for *non*.          [3] MS. *comede*.

Item forsan aliquis diceret, quod scriptura sacra p[er]lecta saltem reficeret gustum affectus pro qualibet eius particula secundum sensum litteralem; sed contra hoc arguit beatus Augustinus, libro *De moribus ecclesiae catholicae*[1], artem tradens in disputando procedendi. Sic dicit: Naturae ordinem habere se, ut, cum aliquid discimus, rationem praecedat auctoritas, ne ratio infirma forsitan iudicetur; ideo hoc efficacius suadeo auctoritate. Nam scribens Augustinus, epistola 39, *Ad Paulinum*[2], de iudicio Dei occulto, quo quosdam approbat ad salutem, quosdam reprobat ad poenam, tandem capit textum *ad Col.*, *Nemo vos seducat*[3], etc., de quo textu Paulinus quaesierat, et notabiliter dicit: Dixisti, inquit Augustinus, ista obscura tibi esse, sed nunc ego, inquit, sine caligine intelligo, atque utinam, inquit Augustinus, praesens de me ista quaesisses, nam in eo sensu quem mihi in his verbis habere videor adhibenda est quaedam pronunciatio in vultu et modo vocis, quae[4] exprimi litteris non potest; ut ex aliqua parte aperiatur quod ideo fuit obscurius quia non recte, ut aestimo, pronunciatur. Cum ergo Paulino instructo in divinis litteris non potuit Augustinus exponere scripturam in his, quomodo a rudibus talibus scriptura sic lecta posset intelligi, sed aliquem sensum ab eis non cognitum [intelligere deberent], et tunc non reficeret gustum, sed potius duceret in errorem.

Item Augustinus Memorio episcopo[5], epistola 55, dicit quod aliquid scripturae difficillime [intelligitur, si] non assit qui disputantium posset separare personas, et pronunciando servare morulas verborum et sillabarum ut omnis exprimatur, sensumque proferant[6] aurium si feriantur genera numerorum. Cum ergo in libro *Ecclesiastes* Salomonis, in quo connectuntur personae sapientes et insipientes et sic personae virtuosae et vitiosae, et sententiae litterarum sunt commixtae, sic quod difficile sit perito theologo illas sententias sic ab invicem distinguere: cum ergo Augustinus consulat Memorio (f. 202, 2) episcopo ut non legat sine doctore libros *Ecclesiastici* [*sic*] ne ipsum legisse paeniteat, si desit qui personas distinguit, qui sonat morulas sillabarum, cum desit talis expressio, qua sensum aurium feriant genera numerorum: conformiter, consulendum est vulgari populo ne scripturam sacram legere cupiant, sed sint secundum Iacobi

---

[1] PL, 32, col. 1311.
[2] PL, 33, col. 639, 640; a letter in which S. Augustine comments on several textual difficulties to Paulinus.
[3] *Col.* ii. 18.     [4] MS. *qui*.
[5] PL, 33, col. 369; whence bracketed words are supplied.
[6] The scribe has *sensus quia*. S. Augustine's words are *sensumque aurium feriant genera numerorum*. Butler himself has taken at least equal liberties with S. Augustine's argument here, which deals directly not with any book of the Bible, but with an abstruse work on music.

consilium[1], *veloces ad audiendum*, et non praesumptuosi aliquatenus ad legendum[2].

Confirmatur, secundo, haec ratio per Aristotelem, secundo *Ethicorum*, sic dicentem: Opus morale, inquit, suscipimus non contemplationis gratia, scilicet, ut sciamus, sed ut boni fiamus. Sed differentia est sacrae scripturae ad alias scripturas, quia ipsa [non] accipit verum et bonum, sed verum ut bonum, et nedum ut bonum morale sed ut bonum gratuitum: ergo talis scriptura est accipienda ut boni fiamus, et sic sciamus ut boni fiamus gratuite. Ergo, cum, teste Ieronymo, aliquid latet in voce quod non latet[3] in cortice litterae, ut patet epistola 33, quae est de omnibus divinae historiae libris[4], in qua exhortatur Paulinum ad addiscendum, et maxime per auditum, et hoc per exempla Pauli, qui didicit ad pedes Gamaliel, qui postea adiit discipulos in Ierusalem ut videret Petrum, ubi misterio hebdomadis et ogdoadis futurus gentium praedicator instruendus erat: quilibet habens zelum fervidum animarum potius deberet consulere ut vulgus addi[s]ceret per auditum, potius quam legendo. Quia ergo, secundum Ieronymum, audire sit modum melius perveniendi ad sacrae scripturae notitiam quam scripturam legere, cum via audiendi sit melior, securior, atque expeditior quam via legendi, et propter paucitatem mediorum tenenda: debet via legendi prohiberi et via audiendi saepissime hortari.

Sed forte obicit quis, quod licet audire sit melius, parum intelligere vulgaribus sit bonum. Hic dico, quod lectio est inductiva in errorem potius quam auditus; quod sic ostendo; nam Augustinus, epistola 58[5], describit errorem, dicens: Non mihi videtur aliquem errare, cum aliquis nescire se scit, sed cum putat se scire quod nescit. Sed sic putare, accidit per legere citius quam per audire; ergo legere periculosum est, saltem vulgari populo. Item Augustinus, *Psalm.* 50[6], ad hoc notans: *Auditui meo*, inquit, *dabis gaudium et laetitiam, et exultabunt ossa*; constat namque ibi, secundum mentem beati Augustini, quod iste textus fuit dictus in persona humilium illuminandorum, et nota quod non dicit *lectioni meae dabis gaudium et laetitiam*, sed *auditui*. Cum ergo gaudium et laetitia non lectioni scripturae sed ipsius scripturae auditui sunt commissa, tenere tantum illam viam est ipsis laicis magis tutum. Nam, dato quod populus legeret ad alium sensum qui non est scripturae, de scriptura non haberet tunc sententiam; secundum Augustinum, epistola 69, *Ad Maximam*[7]; esset de his sicut de illis qui ferramentis medicin-

---

[1] MS. *concilium*.
[2] Cf. *Iac.* I. 19.
[3] *Sic*: but *patet* would seem to make better sense.
[4] PL, 22, col. 541.
[5] PL, 33, col. 924.
[6] PL, 36, col. 593, 594.
[7] PL, 33, col. 1085.

alibus puniuntur, quae utique non ad vulnerandum sed ad sanandum sunt facta. Sic, secundum mentem Augustini, scripturae sunt ordinatae ad sanandum non ad puniendum; ferrum ergo scripturae sacrae non debet dari imperito chirurgico, ne propter artis imperitiam mors sequatur. Cavere ergo summe debent pontifices infulati, qui legere, qui praedicare debent scripturas; ne, unde perveniret utilitas, inde praeveniat mortis calamitas.

Secundo, arguo contra assertionem praefatam ex radice defectus intellectus humanae. (f. 202*b*, *1*) Nam tradit venerabilis doctor Halys, prima parte *Summae*, distinctione secunda, articulo tertio[1], humanae naturae intellectum in duobus deficere propter originalem peccati corruptionem; nam deficit in his quae verissimae sunt et maxime sunt intelligibilia, et in his quae minimae sunt et minime intelligibilia essent; ut patet, inquit, de esse, motus et temporis; et ideo, inquit, sicut sensus deficit in extremis, scilicet in maxime sensibilibus et minime sensibilibus, ita intellectus obtenebratus deficit; et ideo Aristoteles ponit, intellectum nostrum se habere ad perfectissima naturae sicut se habet ad solem oculus vespertilionis[2]. Propter ergo originalem corruptionem pervenientem ex peccato Adae, corruptus est noster modus intelligendi. Et secundum postillatorem Petrum Iohannem[3] super *Gen.* primum, nota naturae fuerunt prius nota Adae in statu innocentiae, ita quod notitia rationis derivatione speciei dimisit discursum rationis. Nam Adam per combinationes qualitatum novit quod combinatio variaret gradum specificum et quod determinaret hoc in tali specie ad diversa individua; sed adveniente corruptione intellectus iam non est nobis cognoscibilis effectus per causam in contingentibus, sed cognoscimus causam per effectum. His praemissis, praemittenda sententia est beati Augustini in sua *Dialectica*[4], quod duo sunt impedimenta veritatis, ne veritas capiatur, scilicet obscuritas et ambiguitas; inter quae hoc interest, quod in ambiguo plurima se ostendunt, quorum quid potius accipiendum sit penitus ignoratur; sed in obscuris parum aut nihil quod attendatur

---

[1] The *Summa Theologica* of Alexander of Hales, ed. Cologne, 1622; tom. 1. p. 10.

[2] *Id.* "intellectus noster se habet ad manifestissima naturae, sicut oculus noctuae ad lumen solis."

[3] Petrus Johannes Olivi, a Spiritual Franciscan, and the author of commentaries on the *Apocalypse* and *Gospel* of S. John, was much influenced by the theories of abbot Joachim. His postills on *Genesis* exist in a Venetian manuscript. He died in 1297, cf. Fabricius, under *Olivus*.

[4] PL, 32, col. 1414, 1415. The work is pseudo-Augustinian, and Butler has taken from it a sentence here and there. Here, as elsewhere, a reference to the *Patrologia* enables us to measure the scribe's too frequent carelessness.

apparet; et amplificat Augustinus dicens quod ubi parum est quod apparet, tunc obscurum est ambiguo simil[e]. Dilucescente caelo quantum oculis satis est, iam omnium viarum deductio clara est; sed qua pergendum sit non obscuritate sed ambiguitate dubitatur. Huius obscuri tria sunt genera: unum quod sensui patet sed animo clausum est; sic patet de vidente malum pictum Punicum[1] et non novit malum Punicum; anima tunc talis, inquit Augustinus, nescit cuius rei pictura sit. Alterum genus obscuri est ubi res animo pateret, nisi[2] sensui clauderetur: sicut est homo pictus[3] in tenebris. Tertium genus obscuri est quando res sensui absconditur, et si sensui nudaretur nihil tamen animo eveniret; quod genus obscuri est obscurissimum; huius exemplum est, secundum Augustinum, quod cum imperitus de malo Punico malum Punicum in tenebris cogeretur cognoscere. Consequenter Augustinus dicit duo fore genera ambiguitatum; primum est in his quae dicuntur, alterum est in his quae scribuntur[4], ut si quis cum audierit *acies*, sive legerit, ignoraret utrum sit militum acies, an ferri, vel oculorum; si quis vero legat scriptum, verbi gracia, *leporem*, dubitabit de penultima an sit media correpta sive sillaba producenda[5]. Cum ergo in scriptura ista concurrunt impedimenta, quantumcunque quis legat in obscuris et ambiguis, prout exemplificat Augustinus, in via non graditur cognitionis. Cum ergo populus sit difficilis intellectus et scriptura sacra sit plena ambiguis seu obscuris, immo, secundum Dionysium, sacris poeticis informationibus; quomodo, quaeso, foret eorum legere medium in via cognitionis sententiae scripturae sacrae? Relinquitur ergo, quod vulgarem populum in scriptura sacra legentem non est medium deducens eos [sic] in notitiam eiusdem scripturae[6], et propter hoc solum consulitur in oppositum opinantibus, scilicet, ut propter maiorem (f. 202b, 2) agendorum cognitionem promoverentur ad practicam spiritualem memoriae actionis.

Confirmatur racio philosophice; nam, secundum Philosophum, pauci sunt vigentes acumine intellectus; et ideo ponit, tertio *Rhethoricae*, quod quanto maior est populus tanto minor vel remotior est intellectus. Ergo, licet politicum fuisset, quod populus vulgaris, quando pauci de lingua fuerunt ad fidem con-

---

[1] Malum Punicum = pomegranate.
[2] MS. *patet, ubi.*    [3] MS. *vinctus.*    [4] MS. *scribimur.*
[5] *Sic*, but Augustine's sense requires *an sit media syllaba corripienda sive producenda*—"whether the middle syllable should be pronounced short or long."
[6] The sentence is ungrammatical, but the sense seems plain: "we are therefore reduced to the conclusion that there is no means of bringing the common people, who read in the holy scriptures, to the knowledge of those same scriptures."

versi, in quacunque natione fuissent, quod tunc sacram scripturam legissent: non tamen sequitur quod modo in eadem
natione foret sic politicum ut omnes modo catechizati fide[1]
possent conformiter scripturam perlegere; et, si inveniatur quod
aliquis doctor[2] approbatorum seu canonizatorum scripturas
sacras alicui populo transtulerit legendas, vel eis legere con-
sul[u]erit, non sequitur modo quod sic staret politicum; quia in
dubio unum est, quod dicit Philosophus, quod quanto maior est
populus tanto remotior est intellectus. Cum ergo optimum
medium ad cognoscendum Deum sit de Deo cogitare et ipsum
Deum suppliciter exorare, et plus proficiunt christiani per haec
duo media quam per lectionem sive per auditum, (ut in epistola
48, *Ad Paulinam*[3], de videndo Deo, docet limpidius Augustinus): mihi videtur quod consulere populum ad haec duo media,
(scilicet, cogitare et orare), foret consilium sanius quam consulere quod scriptura vulgariter translata tradenda sit laicis.

Tertio, principaliter arguo contra praefatam assertionem ex
radice dispositionis hierarchiae angelicae creatae, in qua materia
sic procedam; primo, requiram quomodo acta sit in angelicae
hierarchiae dispositione; quo habito, ex supposito communiter
dato a doctoribus quod perfectio, pro statu viae ecclesiae militantis, sumatur et attendi debeat penes conformitatem ad
ecclesiam triumphantem, concludam oppositum opinantis
praedictam saepius assertionem. Primo, qualiter fiat revelatio,
sive a suprema hierarchia sive a sibi subordinata hierarchia?
Conclusio est Augustini, quod semper fuit actu voluntatis
superioris revelato ad purgationem per actum huiusmodi
collustrandam. Nam disputat et tenet gloriosissimus Augustinus, epistola 48, de videndo Deo, *Ad Paulinam*[4], qualiter Deus
suprema hierarchia sit visibilis, qualiter invisibilis a creatura.
Si quaeris, inquit, si Deus a nobis videri possit, respondebo,
inquit Augustinus, quod ipse potest, quia in verissima scriptura
legitur, *Beati mundo corde, quoniam ipsi Deum videbunt*[5]. Et
si quaeris quomodo videtur a me Deus invisibilis, et inquit
Augustinus Deum esse invisibilem natura, voluntate tamen
visibilem, quia videtur ab altero quando vult et cui vult;
plurimis, inquit Augustinus, non qualis sed quali specie illi
placuit; ex qua sententia liquet Deum esse videndum a creatura
non natura sed sua voluntate. Iam qualiter angeli sint visi-
biles est breviter disserendum, pro qua dicit Augustinus duo-
decimo *Super Genesim ad litteram*[6], declarans quomodo occulte

---

[1] MS. *chatezizati fide*: apparently, "at an early stage of the faith."
[2] A veiled reference to Bede, whose translation of the scriptures was
quoted by the Lollards as a precedent. Cf. the *Compendious Treatise*, p. 441.
[3] PL, 33, col. 596 ff.
[4] PL, 33, col. 612, 613.    [5] *Matt.* v. 8.    [6] PL, 34, col. 473.

miscetur spiritus malus cum spiritu hominis, et exemplificat de uno a[d]reptitio qui, in quadam solemnitate paganorum, fanaticis peractis sacrificiis agitatisque, saltando et ludendo, dixit coram omnibus: In silva, inquit, iuxta nos posita hac nocte quidam a leone perimetur, ad cuius cadaver spectandum tota haec turba est confluxura, et locum huius solemnitatis totaliter desertura. Quod et contigit; et consequenter subiungit Augustinus, quod hoc est differentia inter visionem hominum et visionem spirituum, quod spiritus, etsi nolimus, nos vident, nos autem, inquit Augustinus, imagines existentes (f. 203, *1*) in eis nosse non possumus nisi nobis ostendantur. Nam, ut aestimo, inquit Augustinus, sic habent spiritus in potestate eorum occultare imagines in eis existentes spiritualibus modis, sicut nos interiectis obstaculis quibusdam nostra corpora, ne aliorum oculis videantur, abscondimus; haec Augustinus. Ex qua sententia satis claret quod spiritus solum illuminat ex libera electione propriae voluntatis. Ex istis arguitur, sic noto gratia argumenti, Raphaelum, angelum ordinis inferioris qui debet illuminari de vero sibi obscuro[1] per Gabrielem, archangelum ordinis superioris; et arguitur sic: in ista hierarchia ecclesiae triumphantis illuminatio passiva Raphaelis totaliter dependit a voluntate Gabrielis in ordine causali creato. Sed hierarchia ecclesiae militantis sequi debet hierarchicam dispositionem ecclesiae triumphantis; ergo illuminatio passiva viantium de ordine inferiori dependere debet complete a volitiva viantium in ordine superiori. Sed constat quod legere scripturam vulgariter translatam est actus superioris, et non elicitur neque imperatur a voluntiva personae inferioris ordinis. Ergo talis actus, qui est legere, repertus in inferiori per sacramentum tantummodo purgato hierarchiae celesti [*sic*] penitus est infernus.

Confirmatur quia ratio purgandi per sacramentum a labe peccati originalis vel actualis mortalis contracti est magis necessarium ad salutem quam talem purgatum sacram scripturam cognoscere per lecturam: sed non contingit aliquem purgare se per sacramenta, sed purgatur semper per personam distinctam, baptizantem in sacramento baptismi, et tunc sic, quod personam absolventem, qui actum purgandi reum[2] pure voluntarie exercet, conformiter tamen ad intentionem legislatoris[3],...Ergo conformiter purgatus sed non illuminatus illuminari debet per operationem voluntariam personae illuminantis, qui ut sic est ordinis

---

[1] MS. *obscurum*. The idea of illumination mediated through successive orders of beings is taken from the pseudo-Dionysius' *De Caelesti Hierarchia*: Raphael, says Butler, is lower in rank than the archangel Gabriel. For Raphael, see the book of *Tobit*.     [2] MS. *rerum*.
[3] *Sic*, a line seems to be omitted.

superioris; et ideo christianissimi principes et sanctissimi prae-
sules praedicatoribus quasi suis illuminatoribus, et ut sic eis
superioribus, honorem antiquitus exhibebant.

Confirmatur ratio sic secundo, et noto statum viae angelorum
ante confirmationem in beatudine, et quaero ab opinante
scripturam sacram vulgariter translatam debere tradi laicis ad
legendum: cur debet hoc fieri? Si dicat, prout puto talem dicere
velle, quod tunc inferiores possent quando vellent cognoscere
eis utilia ad salutem et inflammantia affectum ad religiosissi-
mam pietatem: et ego per idem noto unum latentem angelum
ordinis[1] excitatum ad maiorem trinitatis deificae cognitionem et
continentem maiorem obiecti beatifici fruitionem, et quaero si
angeli superioris ordinis permittant angelos inferioris ordinis
speciales habere libros, in quibus per spiritualem lecturam sive
specialem possent cognoscere talia inflammantia affectum, sine
revelatione aliqua ordinis superioris, vel non permittunt? Si
dicitur quod non sunt huiusmodi libri speciales, sed tantummodo
illuminantur per revelationem hierarchiae eis praelatorum: tunc,
cum Deus disposuit ad se parvum principium reducere in infima
per media, et iter ecclesiam militantem per triumphantem, cur
debet aliquis murmurare quod nostri intronizati pontifices non
(f. 203, 2) permittunt suis infimis lecturam sacrae scripturae, per
cognitionem inflammantium ad pietatem, cum hoc in celesti
hierarchia, ubi videtur esse conformis, nullatenus sit repertum?
Et rogo multitudinem celestis patriae ut tales lecturas non permittant in ecclesia militante, quousque doceatur per aliquos
sufficienter, quod sic est in ecclesia triumphante; et ad sic
supplicandum auctoritate beati Ieronymi, qui ponitur in epistola beati Augustini 59, et est *Ad Marcellinum et Anapsycham*[2],
moneo vehementer: Si, inquit Ieronymus, iuxta oratorem, silent
inter arma studia scripturarum, quae studia secundum Ieronymum indigent librorum multitudine, silentio, librariorum seduli-
tate, securitate et otio dictantium. Cum ergo tanta vel maior sit
occupatio populi in agris colendis, in animalibus nutriendis,
servitiis impendendis, quanta sit occupatio militum in armis,
quomodo, quaeso, inter tot varia non nisi[3] silerent studia scripturarum? Videtur ergo bonum Ieronymo vulgari populo laicali
non committere studia scripturarum.

Quarto, arguo contra praefatam assertionem ex radice singu-

[1] *Sic*, perhaps we should supply *inferioris*. Butler is still arguing from
the idea of mediated illumination, based on the *De Caelesti Hierarchia*.

[2] *S. Hieronymi opera*, PL, 22, col. 1086. The scribe has evidently muti-
lated the quotation, which reads, in the PL: Quod si, iuxta inclytum oratorem, (Cicero, *Pro Milone*,) *silent inter arma leges*, quanto magis studia
scripturarum?

[3] *Sic*, something seems to have slipped out between *non* and *nisi*.

laritatis collationis legis evangelii. Docet vero Chrisostomus, *Super Matthaeum, de opere imperfecto*[1], homelia prima, qualiter mundi cordis non indigent auxilio litterarum, sed oportet vitam praebere puram, ut gratia spiritus sancti pro libro fieret nostris animabus; et consequenter deducit quod Noae et Abrahae et filiis suis, et Iobo et Moysi non per litteras loquebatur, sed ipse per seipsum, illorum inveniens mentem puram, et contra dans animum; quare in his Deus Moysi legem dedit, notabiliter scribit: Quoniam, inquit, in malitiae profundum populus in-ciderat Hebraeorum, tunc itaque fieret quod litterae et tabulae fierent; sed hoc, inquit, non factum sanctis veteris testamenti, neque his qui in novo; sed cessante causa, cessat effectus. Cum ergo rationabilitatis malitiarum refrenata [*sic*] fuit causa quare Hebraeis fuit lex data in scripto, ut patet ex Chrisostomo, cum populus christianus iam sit infrenatus laude divina, iuxta idem scripturae: *Infrenabo te laude mea*[2], rationabiliter cessare debet effectus, scilicet, scriptura legis, et ad conformitatem novae legislationis maxime congruum est offerre tabulas cordis; et rationem consequenter addit Chrisostomus: Non, inquit, apos-tolis dedit legem scriptam Deus: sed pro libris promittebat se daturum esse gratiam spiritus sancti: *Is omnium rememorabit vobis*[3]. Et Paulus inquit, hanc excellentiam demonstrans dice-bat, *non nos suscepisse legem in tabulis carnalibus*[4]. Declarat differentiam lationis novi et veteris testamenti, notans quomodo lex vetus scripta fuit in tabulis, et quando et ubi; pro quibus dicit quod vetus dabatur post Egyptiorum destructionem, in eremo in monte Sina, in fumo et igne ascendente a monte, buccina sonante, tonitruis et coruscationibus existentibus; sed in novo, inquit, testamento non sic, neque, inquit, in eremo, neque in monte, neque in fumo, in tenebris nebulae et fulgore, sed incipiente die, in domo omnibus considentibus, cum multa mansuetudine omnia contingebant, quia, inquit, irrationabilibus et effrenatis necesse erat indigentia fantasiae, solitudinis, montis, buccinae, et aliorum, exaltationibus et persuasionibus, neque, inquit, erat necesitas. Nam etsi ibi sonus factus est, hoc non propter apostolos (f. 203*b*, *1*) sed propter praesentes Iudaeos, propter quos et linguae ignis visae sunt; et horum dans rationem subnectit: Sed, inquit, Iudaei post ista visa dixerunt: *Musto pleni sunt isti*[5]; multo magis si nec vidissent haec utique dixissent, et post pauca obiecissent quod apostoli non ascendebant titulos

---

[1] *Pat. Graeco-Lat.* LVII. col. 13, 14. For these homilies, cf. *Fasciculus Joannis Willis Clark dicatus*, James, M. R., p. 85; and *infra* 416, n. 2.
[2] *Isai.* xlviii. 9.  [3] *Ioh.* xiv. 26.  [4] 2 *Cor.* iii. 3.
[5] *Act.* ii. 15.

ferentibus[1] in manibus sicut Moyses; sed ipsum in mente ferentes
textum, ipsi sancti libri [viventes] et leges per gratiam effecti,
tria millia, quinque millia, immo orbis terrarum attraxerunt
populos, Deo loquente omnibus advenientibus per linguas
eorum. Ex quo pro processu satis liquet quod lex gratiae non
conferebatur in Christo legiferis ministris nec ab illis communi-
cabatur nisi advenientibus linguis.

Concordat cum hoc quod Dei sapientia humanata, cum esset
ex tempore duodecim [annorum], reperitur in templo, in medio
doctorum, audiens et interrogans, sed tunc in lege utique legens,
docens per hoc ad Domini legem accedere volentes debere[2] ad
medium doctorum accedere, et non omnium doctorum docen-
tium in templo; sed videte ad quales actus debent procedere,
quia tantummodo ad audiendum et interrogandum, secundum
Christi exemplum, quia hoc a Christo pro cursu aetatis nullatenus est exemplificatum.

Patet ergo singularitas collationis evangelii, quia non dabatur
in scripto: ex quo sic arguo: sapientissimus legislator optime
cuncta secundum tempora disponebat, et notitiam legis[3] gratiae
non nobis nominavit per scripturam sed tantummodo per
gratiam: ergo modus iste communicandi legem per prudentissi-
mum legislatorem est securus, immo securissimus, et tempori
gratiae congruentissimus. Sed modus lectionis est alius modus
a modo praefato: ergo ille modus in laicis non est admittendus,
ratione alicuius perfectionis. Sed ad oppositum opinantibus
ponitur iste modus ratione perfectionis cognitionis; ergo, ex con-
sequenti, ratione alicuius perfectionis; ergo cum iste modus non
sit modus traditus a legislatore perfectissimam legem tradente,
sequitur quod conclusio ad illam perfectionem est inutilis, sic
quod ad eandem perfectionem sine illo modo de communi lege
quis poterit devenire. Confirmatur per argumentum valentium:
Religio communis christiana est perfectissima, quia a perfec-
tissimo legislatore cognoscente quod maxime est commodum
subdito, et maxime diligit subditum; et ideo, inquit, si privata
religio contra communem aliquid perfectionis apponeret, se-
queretur quod iste privatae religionis institutor foret latore legis
communis sapientior, vel in volendo subdito[4] commodum ei
foret magis effectus; quorum nullum est dandum. Per idem
arguo eis, modus quo populus participat fuit perfectissimus:
ergo, per argumentum eorum, quilibet alius modus, qui non est
iste, est superfluus; sed modus iste quem tradit praefata assertio

---

[1] *Sic*, a reference to Chrysostom's text shews that the scribe ought to have
written *non descendebant tabulas ferentes*. From the same source we have
added *viventes* to make the sense clearer.   [2] MS. *debent*.   [3] MS. *regis*.
[4] *Sic* MS.: *subditorum* would seem to make the sense easier.

non est modus legislatoris: ergo quoad omnem rationem perfectionis significabilem superfluus et dimmittendus.

Quinto, arguo contra praefatam assertionem per subtilitatem
ipsius scripturae spiritualis artificii, et contra unum, quod ita
dicunt assertores praefati, qui, ut mihi relatum est, [dicunt] nedum esse utile et conferens[1] scripturam vulgariter translatam
a populo legi, immo quod utile foret et conferens, expositiones
sanctorum doctorum vulgariter transferri et a populo legi.
Potest confirmari haec ratio tamen secundum Gregorium[2], 20
*Moralium*, dicentem quod sancta mater ecclesia sit cum Christo
una persona, et in scriptura sint multa quae intelligenda[3] sunt (secundum doctrinam Ticonii[4] in suis regulis) necessaria, (f. 203*b*, 2)
et maxime ad cognoscendum transitum a capite ad aliquod membrum, et nisi foret transitus contingeret error; cum, per possibile,
sententiam priorem a capite, a quo fit transitus, [attribuat][5] ad
sententiam de membro; et tunc crederetur secundum sententiam
de capite ab aequaliter sicut primam; tunc talis credulitas
tenderet in errorem, quia sic legens illam sententiam crederet
sic dictam esse de capite Christo, quando solum dicitur de
membro.

Item, aliqua sententia dicitur de corpore Christi vero ubi
convertitur sententia de corpore Christi mistico; legens ergo
utramque sententiam, putans verificari de corpore Christi uni-
formiter[6] sumpto, prolabitur in errorem, sed legere expositiones
sanctorum praeservat a casibus huiusmodi sic legentem. Ergo
legere expositiones sanctorum erit omnino inutile[7]. Sed contra
hoc arguitur per sententiam domini Altissiodorensis super
tertium *Sententiarum*, articulo tertio: Quod ingressi in taber-
naculum involverunt vasa tabernaculi, sicut portenda traderent
Coathicis, qui non viderent inquit nec tangerent vasa tabernaculi[8]: in signum quod simplicibus non licet perscrutari
archana Dei, quia talis, inquit, perscrutator *opprimetur a gloria*[9].
Contigit vero videre Deum uno modo per fidem, et sic licet
cuilibet: alio modo per scrutinium, et hoc tantummodo licet
perfectis: sed non est magis[10] scrutinium de Deo quam cognos-

---

[1] Evidently in the sense of *conveniens*, similarly.

[2] PL, 76, col. 251. This is really in Book 23, cap. 1. 2, where Gregory
indulges in a wild flight of allegorical exposition. Butler is quite right in
arguing that an ordinary reader could find no such sense in the Bible.

[3] *Sic*, but the sense seems to require *intelligendo*.

[4] See *supra* pp. 181, 265.     [5] MS. *transitus ad ad sententiam*.

[6] *Veriformiter*?     [7] *Sic*, but we seem to need *utile*.

[8] A comment on *Num.* iv. 15. The *Summa Aurea in quattuor libros
Sententiarum* of William of Auxerre was printed in Paris, 1495; see f. cxcvii
for his argument that the mysteries of the faith should not be explained to
the simple.     [9] *Prov.* xxv. 27.

[10] *Sic*, MS.: *maius* would make better sense.

cendo expositiones doctorum beatorum, in variis sensibus idem veritatis lumen ostendentium. Ergo imperfectis de genere hoc non licet, et ideo, inquit doctor, consequentiam significans, dictum est quod quinque millia plebis percussa sunt, quia plebi, inquit, non licet Deum videre per scrutinium.

Hoc idem ostendit Origenes *Super Leviticum*[1] libro quarto, parte quarta, tractans de veste sacerdotali, ubi notat quod alia veste sacerdos utebatur in exitu ad populum, et alia dum esset in ministerio sacrificiorum. Hoc, inquit, Paulus faciebat, scientissimus pontificum et sacerdotum sapientissimus, qui cum esset in coetu perfectorum, tanquam inter sancta sanctorum positus, et stola perfectionis indutus, dicebat: *Sapientiam loquimur inter perfectos*; sapientiam, inquit, non huius mundi neque [qualem] quisque principum huius mundi cognovit;...sed [tanquam] ad populum exiens mutat stolam et alia induitur longe inferiori quam illa, et dicit: *Nihil aliud iudicavi me scire inter vos nisi Ihesum, et hunc crucifixum.* Vides ergo, inquit Origenes, quomodo mutat stolam, quomodo aliis utpote perfectis praeparat cibos, sed docens alios inferiores lacte potat ut parvulos, alios oleribus nutrit ut infirmos. Et quod idem fecerit Christus ostendit, dicens: Ipse autem pontificum pontifex Ihesus [audi quomodo] primo hoc fecerit, et ista discipulis imitanda reliqu[er]it, nam evangelium refert de eo, *quia in parabolis loquebatur ad turbas, et sine parabola non loquebatur eis*, seorsum autem solvebat ea discipulis. Vides ergo quomodo docuit ea ipse, aliis indumentis uti debere pontificem cum procedit ad turbas, et aliis cum perfectis et eruditis ministrat. Ex quibus patet Origenem velle sentire quod ipsi sacri pontifices et sacerdotes carent communi potestate communicandi scripturas ipsis, et hoc quocunque modo; et cum putam [*sic*] illos in hierarchia ecclesiastica privilegiari, nec ex auctoritate aliquem[2] posse ultra pontificem; videtur tunc quod nulli liceat turbae communicare scripturam sacram ab eis legendam.

Huic sententiae concordat venerabilis doctor de Lyra super 21 capitulo[3] dicens quomodo in populo Iudaeorum [sint] aliqui maiores scripturas legis et prophetarum scientes, et aliqui iuniores, scilicet, laici (f. 204, *1*) vulgares scientes tantum necessaria ad salutem. Nam per omne sabbatum legebatur Moyses, scilicet,

---

[1] *Pat. Graeco-Lat.* XII. 441. The text is here corrected from that source, and omissions are marked.

[2] MS. *aliquis*.

[3] Nicholas de Lyra, a Minorite of the convent of Lire in Normandy, finished his commentary on the Bible in 1330, cf. *Commentaria in universa Biblia*, Antwerp, 1634. The reference is apparently to *Deut.* xxxii. 7, *id.* I. col. 1667.

decalogus datus Moysi, prout dicit Paulus ad Hebraeos; sed
subtilitates scripturarum et dicta prophetarum praefati laici
ignorabant. In cuius, inquit, signum, Herodes sciscitabatur a
scribis de nativitate Christi, et non a populo, quia fuit secretum
prophetale. Haec Lyra. Cum ergo locus nativitatis pertine[a]t
ad articulum fidei de propinquo, et tamen hoc non debuit scire
populus, ex consequente nec alias circumstantias de aliis cre-
dendis sive fiendis. Sed[1] nihil continetur in scriptura sacra nisi
substantia fidei, decem mandata decalogi, vel praedictorum
multiformes circumstantiae, ut patet ex passu superius declar-
ante quare quattuor sunt sensus scripturae: consequens est ut
ipsi laici scripturas cum doctorum expositionibus minime de-
beant legere, cuius tamen oppositum ponet opinio praelibata.

Amplius confirmatur. Nam ipsi Moysi legitur Deus dedisse
tabulas continentes mandata, et non dedit populo tabulas illas
legendas. Et scripturae faciunt mentionem quod sacerdotes
legerunt coram populo in libro legis distincte et aperte ad intelligendum: sed non asserit scriptura quod populus unquam
legerit in libro Moysi. Et tamen, per istos assertores et omnes
rectiloquos, sacra scriptura sufficiens est de utilibus ad salutem.
Tamen modum istum (sup[p]le, quod populus legat in aliquo
ydiomate vel translatione) scriptura non expressit. Miror quomodo predictum modum utilem voluit asserere, ex quo minime
colligitur ex scriptura.

Tertio, confirmatur ratio per Raby Moysen[2], *Directoris*[3]
*Neutrorum*, libro secundo, capitulo XXIX, ponentem quod
sapientes prohibent plana legis[4] populo ne pandarentur, quia
illa plana vel inducunt mali quam pessimam cognitionem, vel
in errorem vel incredulitatem malam in veritatem creatoris, vel
in elationem omnimodam et negationem principatuum legis, et
subvertit. Necessarium est, inquit, cuilibet scienti aliud de his
quod non revelet populo, sicut exposuimus[5]; Sapientes dixerunt

---

[1] *data decalog* expunctuated after *sed*.

[2] Maimonides: the great Jewish commentator who incorporated the
teaching of Aristotle into Hebrew philosophy, as S. Thomas Aquinas did
into Christian (cf. *Maimonides*, Yellin, D. and Abraham, I., London, 1903).
Maimonides' tract on the interpretation of difficult passages in scripture
(the equivalent of the many mediaeval Christian tracts, *de dubiis scripturarum*, etc.) was Latinised as the *Director Neutrorum, Doctor Perplexorum*,
etc.; for an English translation, see *Maimonides' Guide for the Perplexed*,
Friedländer, M., London, 1904, p. xxxi; and for the passage quoted by
Butler, p. 211.     [3] MS. *de duco*.

[4] *Plana legis*: the literal sense of the Scriptures; Maimonides explains
that the Sages used figurative speech in explaining the Creation, and never
discussed it among the common people, lest the literal meaning of the words
should lead them to conceive corrupt ideas of God.

[5] In his commentary on the Mishnah.

a principio libri usque adhuc, quod *gloria Domini est celare
verbum*[1]. Ex quo doctoris passu patet quod eadem est[2] sententia
doctoris, Origenis, et Lyrae: quod non solum populo non est
intimandum de revelationibus originalibus[3], de attributis, vel
de accidentibus eucharistiae, ut exemplificat assertor opinionis
contrariae; immo quod non est licitum intimare populo per
praedicationem multa plana legis; nam si scripturam haberent
quam legere scirent, tunc in disputationem legis de facili possent
prorumpere, quod summe prohibet ius civile.

Nam, ut patet in epistola Innocentis papae ad Senonensem et
Remensem archiepiscopos, et eorum suffraganeos, et ad Ber-
nardum abbatem de Claravalle[4], (et est epistola 33 inter epistolas
beati Bernardi), scripserat quomodo Marcianus, laicus chris-
tianissimus, tamen imperator, tempore praedecessorum eiusdem
Innocentii, prohibuit ne clericus vel militaris cuiuscunque con-
ditionis de fide christiana publice tractare tenetur[5] in posterum.
Haec ille. Nam, secundum ius civile, si talis miles est, militia
privari debet; homo privatus et liber, ex urbe expellatur com-
petenti supplicio subdendus. Haec *de summa trinitate et fide
catholica*, cap. *nemo*[6]. Istis testimoniis non abest[7] ius canonicum
sed constanter ei occurrit, praebens osculum pacificae veritatis,
statuens quod laicus de fide disputans publice vel private ex-
communicandus: *Extra. de haereticis*, cap. *quicunque* [sic] libro
quinto[8]. Ex quibus omnibus testimoniis mihi videtur sequi, quod
propter subtilitatem (f. 204, 2) litteralis artificii ipsius sacrae
scripturae, et haec per doctorum plana testimonia, quod sacra
scriptura nec pro parte eius plana, nec pro parte eius obscura,
nec cum doctorum approbatorum expositionibus quomodolibet
a vulgari populo sit legenda.

Sexto et ultimo, in hac materia arguo contra saepedictam
assertionem ex radice coadunationis corporis Christi mistici.

---

[1] *Prov.* xxv. 2.     [2] MS. *idem ex.*     [3] Or possibly *originibus*.
[4] PL, 179, col. 516. This letter of Innocent II, dated 1140, to the archbishops of Sens and Reims and Bernard of Clairvaux, deals with the condemnation of Abelard and Arnold of Brescia.
[5] *Id.* col. 516, *conetur.*
[6] Butler is apparently citing a passage from the *Corpus Iuris Civilis*
which is quoted in either the *Decret. Greg.* IX., the *Sexti Decret.*, or the
*Clement. Constit.*, the first book of each collection of which is headed *De
summa trinitate et fide catholica*. There is a chapter *nemo* in each of the two
first collections (see Friedberg, II. 753, 954), but neither can be the one
cited; nor could any of the many chapters *nemo* in the *Decretum*. The
scribe's references are often at fault.     [7] *Sic*: abhorret?
[8] This refers to the *de haereticis*, which is lib. v. tit. VII. *Decretalium
Greg. IX*: which does, c. XII., c. XIV., in particular, prohibit lay preaching
(cf. Friedberg, II. col. 784–9). No chapter begins *quicunque*: Butler probably cited the *Cum ex iniuncto.*

Nam apostolus Paulus, *ad Col.* primo, vocat corpus Christi ecclesiam militantem, dicens: *Adimpleo ea quae desunt passionum Christi, pro corpore Christi quod est ecclesia.* Et *ad Ephes.* cap. primo hoc idem dicit de Christo, quod *Deus pater dedit ipsum in caput supra omnem ecclesiam, quae est corpus Christi.* Et ad *Cor.* 12, enumeratis divisionibus gratiarum spiritus sancti, ita dicit: *Sicut unum corpus est et multa habet membra, omnia autem membra, cum sint multa, unum corpus sunt in Christo; etenim,* inquit Paulus, *in uno spiritu omnes baptizati sumus, unum corpus sive Iudei sive Gentiles, sive servi sive liberi*[1]. Et fertur ibidem: *Si totum corpus oculus, ubi auditus? Si totum auditus, ubi odoratus? Nunc autem,* inquit Paulus, *posuit Deus membra sicut voluit; quod si omnia membra essent unum, tunc corpus,* inquit Paulus, *ubi est?* Et idem Paulus *ad Rom.* 12: *Sicut in uno corpore multa membra habemus, omnia autem membra non eundem actum habent: ita multi unum corpus sumus in Christo, singuli autem alter alterius membra*[2]. Ex quibus testimoniis apostolicis irrefragabilibus patet omnes per baptismum Christi in ecclesiam renatos cum distinctis actibus correspondentibus distinctis membris concurrere per unionem spiritus Dei in unionem corporis Christi mistici. Ex qua sententia catholica omnes fideles renati sacramento baptismi sunt membra Christi. Nota tunc membra Christi comparata manibus, dorso, thoraci, ventri et intestinis, cruribus, pedibus, et articulis, et sic de ceteris, per A; et nota omnia membra comparata oculis in eodem corpore per B. Et arguitur sic: ista distincta membra significata per A non possunt in actum convenientem oculis [admitti]; sed litteras legere est actus appropriatus oculis: ergo secundum sententiam apostoli non possunt[3] competere membris significatis per A. Sed totus populus christianus vulgaris est aggregatus ex membris significatis per A: ergo ex radice coadunationis corporis Christi mistici, iuxta mentem apostoli, sequitur populum vulgarem textum sacrae scripturae legere nullatenus sic debere.

Confirmatur quia, dato quod sic facto[4], argumentum apostoli: *Si totum corpus oculus, ubi odoratus, vel ubi pes?*[5] si pedes, quasi populus, scire legem deberent, tunc pedes essent oculi, vel pedes et oculi eundem actum haberent, contra apostolum, ex utraque parte. Ergo et assertio est contra apostolum; et supplico reverentiis vestris, et secundum regulam rationis de ista practica iudicetis: an foret utile [et] conveniens librum ad legendum porrigere pedi vel pedis articulo, vel non? Si decreveritis, quod

---

[1] 1 *Cor.* xii. 12–13.    [2] *Rom.* xii. 4–5.
[3] *Sic*, the grammar would seem to require *potest*.
[4] *Sic*, perhaps the author himself wrote *confirmatur itaque, dato quod sic faciunt, argumentum*, etc.

non, tamen sub zelo animarum hoc agere conentur praefati articuli assertores: quaeso ut omnes articuli a tali incongruo iam declinent[1]! Nam si iam unum pes vel articulus pedis legeret sicut oculus, tunc corpus Christi misticum evacuaretur in sua compositione ab illa caritativa et paternali ac caelica harmonia quae ei (f. 204*b*, *1*) inesse deberet, ut patet ex apostoli sententia superius iam descripta.

Verumtamen qualiter haec membra corporis Christi mistici debent nutriri docet Chrisostomus, Graecorum eximius, [in *Opere*] *imperfecto Super Mattheum*[2], homelia 31, notabiliter, per hunc modum, notans quod presbiter cum venit[3] in templum Dei, sicut, dicit Chrisostomus, medicus ingrediens ad infirmum, statim de stomacho interrogat, et eum componere festinat; quia, si stomachus sanus fuerit, est validum ipsum corpus. Ita, si sacerdotium integrum fuerit, ecclesia florescit; et, si corruptum est, omnium fides marcida est. Et subnectit: Sicut, inquit, stomachus recipiens cibum coquit eum in seipso et per totum corpus dispergit, sic sacerdotes accipiant [*sic*] scientiam per scripturas de Deo, et meditantes apud se toto populo subministrant. Et sicut ministrante stomacho unumquodque membrum suscipit nutrimentum et convertit secundum naturam membri, ut puta quod suscipit iecur totum [*sic*] et sanguinem [*sic*]; sic, quae ascendunt ad pulmonem, flemmata; quod suscipit fel, efficitur bilis; quod in mammillis, efficitur totum lac; sic, inquit, sacerdotes in ecclesia verbum omnes suscipiunt, unusquisque tamen convertit illud secundum proprium cor, ita ut idem verbum in rectis cordibus procedat ad vitam, et in perversis cordibus suscitet ad iracundiam; in aliis operatur dilectionem dulcissimam, scilicet, lac; in aliis flemmata, scilicet, odia nociva totaliter expuenda. Et consequenter exponens hunc textum: *Ex ore infantium perfecisti laudem*[4], distinguitur [*sic*] inter *pastum* per miraculum, et *parata* per scripturam. Ita docet ad propositum pertinenter: lac, inquit, sine labore et opere dentium manducatur, et manducantem sua suavitate delectat. Sic miraculum nec laborem videntibus imponit, sed videntes admiratione delectat et ad fidem nos molliter invitat; panis est perfectionis doctrina et iustitiae, quam accipere non possunt nisi sensus

---

[1] We should venture to translate thus: "If ye decide that this should not be, yet that the champions of the aforesaid article [on scripture-reading] attempt this in their zeal for souls, then I demand that all the toes should now refuse so incongruous an office." It is possible, of course, that the author meant to carry his metaphor all through, and that he intended *articuli assertores* for *champions of the toe*.

[2] *Pat. Graeco-Lat.* LVII. col. 369 ff.; apparently the quotation does not however come from this work.

[3] MS. *plus quam iste*.

[4] *Psal.* viii. 3.

excitati fuerint circa spiritualia; quoniam qui audit necesse habet se tractantibus discutere et meditari, [et] de quibusdam spiritualibus dentibus molere, unde et lex ruminantia animalia munda vult esse. Et sicut, inquit Chrisostomus, si infanti dederis fragmentum panis, quia angustos dentes habet, suffocatur amplius quam nutritur: sic homini [nondum] perfecto in fide et puro sensibus si altiora misteria[1] volueris dicere, eius angusta fides magis scandalizatur quam aedificatur. Sed si viro perfecto dederis lac, quod fauces eius delectat, membra tamen non confortat; sic, si ei miracula ostendis, delectatur quidem aspectu sed nec proficit ad edificationem aut notitiam veritatis; haec Chrisostomus. Ex qua sententia patet quod sacerdotium solum pro toto populo doctrinam hauriet, a quo sicut a stomacho sunt nutrimentum (f. 204b, 2) accepturi.

Quia multi opinantur litteram sacri codicis posse reficere, audiant sententiam Augustini *Super Iohannem*[2], homelia 9, declarantis quomodo hoc fuit initium signorum, quod Christus in nuptiis mutavit aquam in vinum: A prophetiae dispensatione, inquit Augustinus, nulla tempora cessaverunt; vinum, inquit, in aqua quodammodo latet; sic, inquit Augustinus, si in prophetia Christus non intelligitur, ipsa prophetia aqua erit. Lege, inquit Augustinus, omnes libros propheticos non intellecto Christo, quid tam insipidum fatuumque invenies? Sed intellige Christum, et non solum sapit quod legis, sed etiam inebriat, mutans mentem a corpore ut *praeterita obliviscens in ea quae ante sunt extendaris*[3]. Haec Augustinus. Quod autem eunuchus Candacis reginae Ethiopum[4] [in scriptura legebat] quo et eunuchus, ut testatur Ieronimus, non fuit sanctior nec eo studiosior[5], ut patet in epistola 55, cum interrogaret [Philippus] an intelligeret quae legerentur, respondit et *quomodo*, inquit, *possum nisi aliquis me doceret?* et cum sic Augustinus: Prophetia est quid insipidum, immo fatuum[6], tunc pro cognomine habeat nomen pincernae, cuius est bonum vinum diligere. Cernam membra corporis Christi mistici iam inebriata in parte videtur [*sic*] eadem membra aqua insipida, id est, populum christianum pro quadam collatione spirituali reficere. Sed hoc facere nitun-

---

[1] We have ventured to supply *nondum*, and to disregard a contraction mark which the scribe has put over *misteria*, in the interests of what seems the natural sense.

[2] PL, 35, col. 1459.    [3] *Phil*. iii. 13.

[4] Here, again, we have ventured to add three words to complete the sense.

[5] PL., 22, col. 544. Butler or the scribe has misquoted: S. Jerome said, "Ego...nec sanctior sum hoc eunucho, nec studiosior."

[6] So far only Augustine, PL, 35, 1459; the rest of this difficult sentence, and that following, are Butler's.

tur, qui corticem litterae intellectui difficilem ad legendum
populo consulunt. Ego vero pedibus vel manibus ad legendum
libros offerre nolo, nec eis ad manducandum quibus non nutriun-
tur porrigo. Sed purgare stomachum corporis Christi mistici
exhortor in Domino, asserens cum Chrisostomo hoc esse poten-
tissimum medium, ut sub capite Christi eius corpus misticum
nullatenus infirmetur, sed in sanitate Dei perpetuo conservetur.
Ex quibus omnibus plane patet quod ego grosse senserim de
translatione scripturae in quaecunque vulgaria, contra affirma-
tionem eius simplici via occurrens. Quarum prima est ex allec-
tiva conditione sacrae scripturae, secunda est ex defectiva in-
tellectione humanae naturae, tertia est ex hierarchica dispositione angelicae creaturae, quarta ex singularitate collationis
legis evangelii, quinta ex subtilitate scripturae litteralis artificii,
sexta est ex conditione coadunativa concursionis membrorum
corporis Christi mistici. Haec sunt dicta cum omni reverentia
oppositum mihi opinantium vires cognitionis meae nimium exce-
dent[ium], absque inpactivorum verborum misera christianitate
[sic: garrulitate?].

Explicit determinatio fratris et magistri Willelmi Butler
ordinis minorum, regentis Oxoniae. Anno Domini mccccᵒ primo.

2. *Palmer: De translatione sacrae scripturae in linguam
Anglicanam*[1]. (f. 42*b*, col. 2)

1. Utrum[2] sacra scriptura in linguam Anglicanam vel in
aliam barbaricam sit transferenda, et quod sic videtur, nam
licet illam praedicare et docere, igitur et scribere, et haec in
omni lingua eis nota, qui ad servandam illam et observandam
obligantur. Multi Anglici vel barbarici sunt huiusmodi. Igitur,
etc.

2. Sic: omnis lex rite vivendi aliquibus tradita, quae confert
vitam observatoribus et mortem transgressoribus, est in lingua
eis nota habenda. Sacra scriptura est huiusmodi. Igitur etc.
*Scrutamini scripturas in quibus putatis vitam aeternam*[3].

[1] Trin. Camb. 347, f. 42 *b*. The MS. is written in the same hand throughout, and contains several Latin theological treatises, one of which is Woodford's *Contra Trialogum Wiclevi*. On f. 54 *b* occurs a note by the scribe:
Explicit tractatus *de unitate et ordine ecclesiasticae potestatis*, finitus per
manus Cornelii Oesterwic anno domini 1430 in universitate Oxoniae, ad
mandatum Fratris Iohannis Courteys, sacrae theologiae professoris, ordinis
praedicatorum et conventus Exoniensis, tunc regentis universitatis prae-
dictae." A contemporary hand has inserted the title, *Palmer, de translatione*, etc., on f. 42 *b*, and above f. 43, *Palmer, de translatione sacrae
scripturae in linguam barbaricam*. For the delivery of the determination,
see *supra*, p. 293; its probable possession by Sion abbey, cf. *incipit* and
*Syon*, 50.

[2] The points defended by the Lollard doctor, Palmer's opponent, are
given first. [3] *Ioh.* v. 39.

3. Sic: scriptura librorum inventa est in remedium oblivionis, ad iuvandam memoriam, quia labilis est memoria hominis; sed tradere sacram scripturam oblivioni, in qua tota lex rite vivendi continetur veteris et novi testamenti, est maxime periculosum. Igitur illa in vulgari nostro propter labilitatem memoriae est habenda, et sic in illam est transferenda.

4. Sic: nullus rite obligatur ad observandam legem aliquam ignotam; sed utraque lex, nova et antiqua, est vulgo ignota quousque in vulgari habeatur, quia vulgus nullam aliam intelligit nisi propriam et vulgarem. Igitur vulgus non obligatur ad sacram scripturam observandam: ideo licet vulgo habere illam translatam in linguam suam, quam solam intelligit.

5. Sic: iam habetur in Hebraico, Graeco, Latino, Chaldaico et Gallico, et iam necessarium est Anglicam et barbaricam habere illam sicut praedicti. (f. 43, *1*) Igitur aequaliter est habenda a nobis in Anglico sicut et illis in vulgari suo.

6. Sic: dicitur quod Beda venerabilis totam scripturam transtulit in linguam Anglicam, ne lingua sua barbarica videretur, quod non fecisset nisi licuisset. Igitur, etc.

7. Sic: quilibet tenetur vitare peccatum mortale, quod non potest nisi cogitando quale peccatum sit mortale, quod sciri non potest a laicis nisi per doctrinam in lingua propria et vulgari, cum nullam aliam intelligit [*sic*]. Igitur, etc.

8. Sic: non solum tenemur scire quae sunt fugienda sed etiam quae timenda, quae credenda; quae sunt facienda, quae sunt speranda, et alia sacramenta [qualiacunque?], omnia quae necessaria sunt ad salutem. Igitur licet tibi habere in scriptis, et haec in vulgari tuo, quia nullam aliam linguam intelligis; igitur sic curati tenentur praedicare et populum eis subiectum informare de necessariis ad salutem, secundum illud *Marci* ultimo: *Praedicate evangelium omni creaturae*[1]. Sed multi in tanto sunt muti, et aliqui surdi, qui in scientia non possunt uti vocibus secundum scripturas. Igitur licet propter tales habere totam sacram legem in scriptis[2].

9. Sic: quae habentur in vulgari et in lingua eis nota magis movent ad devotionem, ad Deum laudandum et diligendum. Igitur in tali lingua sunt habenda.

10. Sic: omne quod licet modo loqui licet modo scribere; sed utramque legem licet mihi praedicando, disputando, defendendo loqui: igitur licet eam scribere. Nihil valet eam scribere in lingua ignota: igitur scribenda est in lingua eis nota, ut in vulgari nostro.

11. Sic: posset contingere quod nullus Latinus esset inter

[1] *Marc.* xvi. 15.
[2] The scribe now misnumbers by one, omitting nine

barbaros et Anglicos propter guerras vel inimicitias capitales,
et dato quod esset, et nullus eorum sciret linguam nostram, etiam
nec interpretari illam posse [*sic*] nobis, (sicut si unus Hebraeus
vel Graecus esset inter Latinos ignorans Latinam), nulli posset
interpretari in lingua nostra. Igitur nisi haberemus sacram
scripturam in vulgari nostro, non erit nobis via possibilis ad
sciendam illam, et tamen obligamur ad illam faciendam, quia
obligamur ad illam observandam. Igitur irremediabiliter
essemus astricti ad praecavendum [*sic :* praevaricandum?].

12. Sic: *Quaecunque scripta sunt ad nostram doctrinam scripta
sunt*[1]; sed modicum valet scriptura ad nostram doctrinam, nisi
fuerit scriptura in lingua quam intelligimus: sola talis est vulgare
nostrum. Igitur, etc. (f. 43, 2)

13. Sic: scriptura ignota non intellecta modicum valeret ad
nostram correctionem, sed: *Quaecunque scripta sunt ad nostram
correctionem scripta sunt.* Igitur cum tamen scriptura in vulgari nostro tradita est nobis utilis, et ad correctionem nostram
utilis, igitur scriptura sacra, cum sit nobis utilis et tam necessaria
in vulgari nostro, habenda est in scriptis.

14. Sic: *Necesse est impleri omnia quae scripta sunt*[2], *Ioh.* 2,
igitur necesse est impleri omnia quae scripta sunt nobis in vulgari nostro in Anglico, quia haec sunt aliqua scripta, sicut ea
quae scribuntur in Latino, Graeco vel Hebraico; et, si necesse est
omnia scripta in Anglico impleri, necessarium est omnia scripta
in Anglico esse.

15. Sic: *Deut.* 6, sic scribitur de lege[3]: *Audi Israel, Dominus
Deus tuus [unus] est; diliges Dominum Deum tuum ex toto corde
tuo, scribe verba haec quae praecipio tibi hodie in corde tuo, narrabis ea filiis tuis et meditaberis [s]edens in domo tua, ambulans in
itinere; scribes ea in limine et ostiis domus tuae.* Igitur, eadem
ratione, in libris Anglicanis.

16. Sic: *Deut.* 31; Postquam Moyses scripsit verba legis huius
in volumine, decem mandata Dei, praecepit Levitis dicens,
*Tollite librum istum et ponite in latere arcae foederis Domini, ut
sit ibi contra te in testimonium*[4]. Igitur, conformiter, licet nobis
habere legem nostram in vulgari nostro; confirmatur, quia tam
necessarium est nobis Anglicis et aliis barbaris habere legem
nostram in vulgari nostro, sicut Hebraeis, Graecis, aut Latinis
in suo, ut eam sciamus et observemus, cum nullam aliam intelligimus, exceptis paucis litteratis.

17. Sic: secundum regulam rationis omnia intelligimus esse
concessa, quae expresse non sunt prohibita: sed non invenitur in
tota sacra scriptura prohibitum quod ipsa sic transferatur in

---

[1] *Rom.* xv. 14.     [2] Cf. *Luc.* xxi. 22.     [3] Cf. *Deut.* vi. 5–9.
[4] Cf. *Deut.* xxxi. 25–7.

idioma barbaricum. Igitur propositum pro auctoritate notandum est.

1. AD OPPOSITUM, nulla vulgo inutilia sunt in vulgari nostro habenda, quia nocerent plus quam prodessent; sed multa in scriptura sunt huiusmodi. Hugo de Vienna[1], *Ecclesiastici* tertio, Inutilia non sunt investiganda neque habenda neque scribenda, ut quare musca aut pulex tot habet pedes, (f. 43 *b*, *1*) et camelus tantum quattuor et homo tantum duo. Item, *reprobatio quidem fuit praecedentis mandati propter infirmitatem et inutilitatem eius*[2], sed quod est reprobatum non est in vulgari nostro habendum vel scribendum, quia esset causa erroris. Igitur, etc.

2. Non omnis veritas est scribenda in Anglico, quia multae sunt inutiles: sed omnis veritas continetur in sacra scriptura secundum Lollardos, quia continet primam veritatem quae continet omnes alias veritates.

3. Sic multa sunt occultanda et non populo ostendenda, ne nota et usitata vilescerent; unde dicit Carnotensis[3] *Super primum confitenti* [*sic*], quod si in lamina aurea mitrae supremi patris pontificis scribebantur quattuor litterae[4] magni nominis Dei in tetragrammaton[5], *ioth, heo, wach, hoth,* sine[6] apicibus, cum ne notum esset vulgo magnum nomen Dei, quia sic per illud frequenter et horribiliter iurassent, sicut non[7] faciunt christiani,

---

[1] Hugo de Sancto Charo, a Dominican and theologian of Paris, died 1263. He wrote a postill, or short commentary on all the books of the Bible according to the fourfold sense, literal, allegorical, moral and anagogical. The quotation given, and that on p. 9, are printed in the 1502 edition of *Hugonis de Sancto Charo Postilla in totam Bibliam*, pars III., *Ecclesiastici*, iii. 24: *In supervacuis rebus*, scilicet, in eis quorum scientia non est utilis, ut quare musca vel pulex tot pedes habeat et camelus solum quattuor, et homo tantum duos.

[2] *Heb*. vii. 18.

[3] Probably Ivo of Chartres, † 1116, author of the *Panormia* and the *Decretum*, in neither of which, however, can this passage be traced. It might however occur in his (unpublished and inaccessible) comment on the psalms, the word *confitenti* standing for the first word of the psalm. (See *Coll. Canoniques, Ives de Chartres*, Fournier, 1897.) With less likelihood "Carnotensis" might refer to John of Salisbury, author of the *Policraticus*.

[4] MS. esset vulgo magnum nomen Dei, quia sic per illud frequenter, expunctuated.

[5] The sense is clear; many things must be kept secret from the people, and hence the Jews had secret ways of writing the name Jahweh, the four Hebrew letters of which (the tetragrammaton) the scribe attempts to render (yodh, he, waw, he). Lyra's postill on the Bible, with which Butler would have been acquainted (Antwerp, ed. 1634, I. 513, 516), has a note on the tetragrammaton, explaining that the four letters were never vocalised or pronounced. See *Onomastica Sacra*, Lagarde, P., Göttingen, 1883; CE, *Jehovah*.

[6] Nota, crossed out; *apicibus*, vowel points.

[7] MS. *nō*; but the sense seems clearly to require *nunc*.

et multipliciter inhonorassent. Illi enim apices [diversitudine a tergo pro et ex utraque parte per et si debite erat appositione[1]] illis litteris significabunt, *hia, hawe, hia, houe*, quae dictiones in Latino significant, " qui est, qui erat, et qui venturus est." Igitur conformiter, cum multa de scriptura in honore sint habenda, expedit ut a vulgo occultentur ne vilescant.

4. Sic: nulla habenda sunt in vulgari quae simplicibus essent occasio et causa erroris, quia facilius potest vulgus duci in errorem; sed multa de scriptura in vulgari nòstro translata male intellecta ducerent simplices in errorem; nam si Arium, Sabellium, Nestorium et Frontinum et alios haereticos difficultas illius ducat in errorem, et a fortiori simplices in errorem ducet.

5. Sic: nulla sunt revelanda aliquibus qui non sunt talium capaces; sed multarum difficultatum sacrae scripturae non sunt tales laici capaces. Igitur saltem talia in vulgari nostro non sunt scribenda; ideo *Ecclesiastici* tertio: *Plurima sunt supra sensum hominum*, scilicet, transcendunt intellectum et rationem, et *multos supplantavit suspicio*, scilicet, fidei fundamentum (f. 43*b, 2*) subripuit et a veritate deiecit in errorem: *Altiora te ne quaesieris, et qui scrutator est maiestatis opprimetur a gloria*[2].

6. Sic: illa quae diminuunt meritum fidei simplicium non sunt eis in vulgari tradenda; huiusmodi sunt multa in scriptura, unde *Ecclesiastici* 3[3] *Multa abscondita sunt a Domino tibi*; ubi Hugo in glossa reddit causam: Propter, inquit, meritum fidei[4]; quia, secundum Gregorium, fides, inquit, non habet meritum cum humana ratio praebet experimentum[4]. Item, tunc nocerent clericis rudi[bu]s taliter si non aliter trad[er]entur.

7. Sic: stultum est sollicitum esse circa illud quod sine periculo a simplicibus ignoratur; sed multa sacrae scripturae sine periculo a simplicibus ignorantur, quia transcendunt ingenium eorum. Non igitur oportet sollicite illa scribere in vulgari.

8. Sic: multa per praeceptum Dei sunt occulta; non sunt in vulgari scribenda, quia sic possent contra praeceptum christianum omnibus esse nota; sed multa misteria communicata subtilioribus et sapientibus prohibentur scribi, ne nota fiant simplicibus; unde *Apoc.* 10: *Signa*, scilicet, *absconde quae locuta sunt septem tonitrua*, scilicet, misteria Dei, secundum glossam; et, *Noli ea scribere*, scilicet, in publico denuntiare; cuius rationem

---

[1] It is difficult otherwise to extend the scribe's frequent contractions in this passage; yet it is still more difficult to make sense of it. Probably the scribe has written *pro et* by a blunder for *prout*, and *per et si* for *perinde ac si*; possibly also *debite* for *debitum*. However, the general argument seems clear; as the ancient Jews never wrote God's name in full lest it should be desecrated, so we must shew equal economy with God's word.

[2] *Prov.* xxv. 27.                                   [3] Cf. *Ecclesiasticus* xliii. 46.

[4] *In libros Moralium*, see PL, 76, col. 1398, *fides*.

ponit ibi Gorham[1]. Quia infidelibus, foetore malitiae agitatis, blasphemiae plus quam aedificationis materia esset. *Prov.* 23: *In auribus insipientium ne loquaris, quia despicient doctrinam eloquii tui;* et *Daniel* 12: *Tu Daniel, claude sermones et signa librum usque ad tempus.*

9. Sic: aliquae sunt simplicibus nimis ardua et nimis difficilia et alta; non sunt simplicibus communicanda, nam Paulus discipulis scribit[2]: *Tanquam parvulis in Christo vobis lac potum dedi, non escam; nondum enim poteratis, sed nec nunc quidem potestis, adhuc enim carnales estis; Cor. 3: Sed animalis homo non percepit ea quae Dei sunt.*

10. Sic: illa quae simplices nollent observare, sed vellent potius propter duritiam sectam christianam spernere, non sunt admittenda neque scribenda in nostro vulgari; unde Berengarius[3] super illud *Apoc.: Et quae locuta sunt septem tonitrua, noli ea scribere.* In initio fidei, donec praedicatores sancti videntes infirmitatem gentium ad fidem venientium, non sunt ausi [eis] austeriora Christi praecepta committere; ne forte (f. 44, *1*) duritia praeceptorum territi, non auderent ad fidem Christi suscipiendam accedere; et, ut videtur, sic fecerunt Apostoli, *Actis* 15: *Placuit Spiritui sancto et nobis nihil imponere vobis oneris,* scilicet, conversis ad fidem de gentibus, *nisi ut abstineatis vos ab immolatione simulacrorum et sanguine et suffocato et fornicatione.* Igitur duriora legis non sunt infirmis scribenda et revelanda.

11. Sic: secreta non sunt extraneo revelanda, *Prov.* 25: *Secretum extraneo ne reveles;* et *Isaiah*[4], *Secretum meum mihi,* sed tamen amicis meis; *Vos nunc dixi amicos, quia quaecunque audivi a patri meo nota feci vobis*[5]. Igitur talia secreta non sunt extraneis, simplicibus Deum ignorantibus, scribenda, quia ea legere posset aequaliter inimicus sicut amicus.

12. Sic: illa quae scripta non prodessent sed nocerent scribere vulgo non deberent, quia essent contra Christi caritatem; sed talia sunt multa. *Iob* 9: *Verebar omnia opera mea;* antecedens patet, de die mortis, de peccatis, de predestinatione et reprobatione.

---

[1] Nicholas Gorham, or Gorram, a Dominican at Oxford; died 1400; cf. Pits, ed. 1619, p. 571. Gorham's *In Apocalypsim S. Johannis* was printed Antwerp, 1620.

[2] Cf. 1 *Cor.* ii. 14.

[3] Scribe: Bygaius. Berengarius of Tours, the opponent of the doctrine of transubstantiation. His exposition on the *Apocalypse* was a favourite mediaeval commentary, and is printed in the Benedictine edition of the works of S. Ambrose, Paris, 1690, tom. II. appendix. The work is written in seven visions, and the author's name is cryptically indicated in the *Admonitio Auctoris.* The quotation given occurs in col. 542.

[4] *Isaiah* xxiv. 16.       [5] *Ioh.* xv. 15.

13. Sic: caritas est, palam fieri nolle quod noceat agnoscenti; sed multa in scriptura nocerent simplicibus, quia nocerent hereticis valde intelligentibus. Igitur talia non sunt eis scribenda.

14. Sic: omnis transgressio novae legis est peccatum mortale, pro cuius figurae transgressione mors debebatur in lege veteri; sed Aaron et filii videntes quae erant in sanctuario involuta morerentur, unde *Num.* 4: *Cumque involverint involuta, et non tangent vasa sanctuarii ne moriantur: nolite*[1] *perdere populum Caath de medio Levitarum, sed hoc facite eis ut vivant et non moriantur, si tetigerint sancta sanctorum. Aaron et filii eius intrabunt et disponent onera singulorum, et dividunt quid portare quis debeat; alii nulla curiositate videant quae sunt in sanctuario priusquam involvantur, alioquin morientur.* Haec fuit figura quod nulli laici in nova lege deberent videre secreta et sancta involuta in sanctuario sacrae scripturae, de quo sanctuario *Psal.* 72: *Aestimabam ut cognoscerem hoc, labor est ante me, donec intrem in sanctuarium Dei et intelligam in novissimis eorum;* ubi glossa interlinearis[2]: Ordinantur enim qui ineffabilia (f. 44, 2) sacramenta ignorant, et promoti in sacerdotii gradum, ut filii Aaron, scilicet sacerdotes quibus omnia aperta et nuda videre concessum est, unde bonis sanctis Urri percussi sunt, qui viderunt archana Domini, et 50, *de plebe legis,* sexto; et alia figura *Deut.* 22: *Si in terra vel in arbore nidum avis inveneris et matrem pullis desuper incubantem, non tenebis eam cum pullis, sed abire patieris, ut bene sit tibi et longo vivas tempore;* quae figura secundum Gregorium significat, quod sensus litteralis, qui est quasi magister aliorum sensuum, dimitti debet, et pulli eius retineri, allegoriae et anagogiae, quia *littera occidit, spiritus autem vivificat*[3]. Quomodo, igitur, simplices illiterati, vel sola grammatica instructi, illos pullos trium sensuum ignorantes, non errarent habentes magistrum, scilicet litteralem sensum, tamen de pullis non curantes?

15. Sic *Ezech.* 47: *Vir qui habebat funiculum in manu sua mensus est mille cubitos et transduxit me per aquam usque ad genua, et iterum mensus est mille, et transduxit me per aquam usque ad renes, et mensus est mille, et veni ad torrentem quem non potui transire, quoniam intumuerant aquae profundi torrentis, quia non potest transvadari;* quem textum exponit Gregorius de sacra scriptura, et in prologo ponit *Moralium*[4]: Divinus sermo sicut misteriis exercet prudentes, sic [plerumque][5] superficie simplices refovet. Habet in publico unde parvulos nutriat, servat in secreto unde mentes sublimium in admiratione suspendat; quasi quidam [quippe][5] fluvius est planus et altus, in quo agnus am-

---

[1] Scribe, *nolente.*    [2] That of Anselm of Laon, *circa* 1100.
[3] 2 *Cor.* iii. 6.    [4] PL, 75, col. 515.    [5] Supplied from PL.

bulet et elephas natet. Ex istis patet quod scriptura sacra in
aliqua sui parte est ita difficilis quod comprehendi a viatoribus
perfecte non potest, quare non est communicanda simplicibus
in vulgari.

16. Sic: misteria fidei non sunt communicanda simplicibus
nec scribenda; patet *Apoc.*[1]*: Signa,* scilicet, abscondita misteria
fidei, *quae locuta sunt septem tonitrua,* et *noli ea scribere* in pub-
licum[2], deveniant et in malitiam blasphemiae potius quam in
aedificationem convertantur, ut dicit Gorham[3]. Ideo *Matth.* 7,
*Nolite sanctum dare canibus.*

17. Sic: Paulus audivit *archana verba,* (f. 44 *b, 1) quae non licet
homini loqui*[4], quae non erant alia quam divina misteria in sacra
scriptura contenta, quae continet omnia. Igitur non licet omnia
scribere.

18. Sic: causa putata quare Iudaei interfecerint Christum
fuit quia docuit eos intelligere sacram scripturam spiritualiter,
quia *littera occidit, spiritus autem vivificat,* et quando aliqui dis-
cipulorum abierunt retrorsum dixit[5]: *Verba quae ego loquor
spiritus et vita sunt;* spiritualiter intellecta vitam efficiunt
aeternam; unde pro causa mortis eius allegabant: Dixit *quia
possum destruere templum corporis mei, Ioh.* 20 et *Matth.* 26.
Quomodo igitur non errarent simplices, idiotae[6] circa scripturam,
si eam haberent in vulgari idiomate[7] modo, propter malum intellectum Lollardorum et simplicium grammaticam[8] solum intelligentes, [qui] Christi discipulos illam spiritualiter et [*sic*]
exponentes persequuntur? constat quod sic.

[*Additional reasons for and against vernacular scriptures.*]

Pro responsione in hac materia volo ponere alias veritates,
quarum prima est illa: Sacra scriptura in omni idiomate et
lingua quoad aliquam eius partem est habenda; probatur, omne
necessarium omni homini ad salutem est in lingua sibi nota
habendum, ne tradat illud oblivioni quod tenetur scire et observare sub poena damnationis aeternae. Huiusmodi sunt multa in
sacra scriptura contenta; 1 *Cor.* 14: *In ecclesia volo quinque verba
sensu meo loqui, ut alios instruam, quam* [*et*] *decem millia verborum;* ubi Gorham dicit illa quinque verba esse quae sunt

---

[1] *Apoc.* x. 3.
[2] Something seems to have been omitted before *deveniant.*
[3] See p. 423.        [4] 2 *Cor.* xii. 4.        [5] *Ioh.* vi. 64.
[6] The scribe has here expunctuated *scripturam grammaticarum solum
intelligentes.*
[7] MS. *noñe.*
[8] MS. *grammaticarum.*

fugienda, videlicet[1] septem peccata mortalia; quae sunt timenda, videlicet, in[fernales poenae][2]; quae sunt credenda, in simbolo contenta; quae sunt facienda, decem mandata; et quae sunt speranda, praemia aeterna[3]; omnia ista sunt necessaria ad salutem. Igitur haec et consimilia in vulgari sunt habenda et scribenda. Pro illa veritate sunt multa archana, pro parte affirmativa conclusionis adducta.

*Secunda veritas*: non tota sacra scriptura est in omnem linguam et linguagium transferenda; probatur hic per articula ad partem negativam adducta; et iterum, sic. Sacra scriptura in multis locis salvari non potest aliquando incongruitate et falsitate, nisi per figuras et regulas grammaticales, (f. 44 b, 2) sicut ostensum est in quodam tractatu quem vidi, in quo erant omnes figurae grammaticales, et declaratae et quotatae, ubi per eas sacra scriptura in partibus suis sit ab errore servata et defensata. Igitur in nullam linguam quae non regulatur regulis et figuris grammaticalibus est ipsa transferenda. Probatur consequentia quia, si in lingua illis figuris regulata [transferretur][4], esset erronea nisi illis figuris [salvis][4] retineretur; igitur in aliam linguam quae illis non regulatur translata esset erronea, quia non per illas excusaretur. Dicitur forte quia aliae linguae per regulas, proprietates et figuras grammaticales regulantur: Contra, barbarismus est vitium, quod constat in· coniunctione litterarum, et sillabae vel sillabarum [inductione][4] vel eorum accentibus, quo vitio barbari maxime solent uti; sed dicit *Catholicon*[5] de tropis,

[1] MS. *patet*, by an obvious error.
[2] The scribe has written only *in*, leaving a blank for the rest which he apparently could not read.
[3] *Insimul* here expunctuated.        [4] Conjectural emendations.
[5] A general mediaeval term for a Latin dictionary, first used by Jacobus de Voragine, bishop of Genoa (Januensis), for his own work; see *Catholicon Anglicum*, EETS, OS, 75, x. Voragine's work was successively re-edited and enlarged, and printed by Locatellus at Venice in 1495, as the *Catholicon editum a fratre Johanne Januensi*. Under *Tropos* this work gives: "figura moralitatis: modus loquendi: ut cum aliquis loquitur metaphorice vel perifrastice; vel alio tali modo, secundum Hugutionem, et de hoc vide in quarta parte ubi agitur de tropis." "Hugutio" is the title of a book frequently found in mediaeval wills, and refers generally to the gloss on the *Decretals* of Hugutio, bishop of Ferrara, who died in 1212, but also occasionally to a work on grammar, or dictionary, probably by the same Hugutio. (See Fabricius, II. 283.) Hugutio's *Etymologicon* (Ff. 5. 34, fifteenth century) is arranged as a dictionary, and not divided into "parts"; the passage quoted as from the *Catholicon* does not occur as a whole in it, but the explanations given under the different terms appear to be the sources from which the passage was composed: unless Hugutio wrote a separate work on grammar, in four parts, where he collected under *Trope* the information scattered in the *Etymologicon*. The latter under *Tropus* has "tropologia, est enim excusatio vel sensus spiritalis vel moralis, et figurativa intelligentia vel locutio."

quod metaplasmus[1] excusat barbarismum[2], qui est vitium dictionis, scema[3] soloecismum[4], qui est vitium orationis; et tempus[5] improprietatem sillabae excusans [*sic*]. Sed hae figurae non inveniuntur in Anglico, nec in idiomate barbarico; probatur quod alias figuras habent. Similiter circa medias sillabas, ultimarum aliquas addendas, aliquas auferendas litteras vel sillabas, ut patet in *Catholicon*; et pro maiori parte dictiones Angliae sunt monosillabae, sicut *ston, bon, non, don, gon, man, that, math, rat.* Igitur in istis monosillabis non habent locum tales figurae grammaticales, nec possunt orationes et proposi- tiones ab incongruitate et falsitate per eas salvari.

2. Si proprietates unius linguae per regulas grammaticales regulatae non possunt servari in lingua etiam eisdem regulis regulata, a fortiori illae proprietates non possunt servari in lingua barbarica non regulata illis regulis grammaticalibus; sed proprietates linguae Latinae, quae regulatur, ut constat, regulis grammaticalibus, non possunt servari in Graeco linguagio, quod est regulis grammaticalibus regulatum. Unde post prophetiam Sibyllae, quam Isidorus in sermone De Natali subiungit[6], haec de nativitate, passione, resurrectione et secundo adventu eius dicta sunt, ut si quis in Graeco capita eorum versuum dicere voluerit, inveniet *Ihesus Christus Yos theou sother*[7], quod in Latinum trans- latis eisdem versibus apparet [      ]⁸ quod (f. 45, *1*) Graecarum

---

[1] Ff. 5. 34, metaplasmus: formatio vel litterae vel in litteram, vel sillabae vel in sillabam, et ut breviter eius signo aperiatur, metaplasmus dicitur barbarismus, figura in aliquo rationabili de causa in metro vel in prosa facta.

[2] *Id.* Barbarismus est in prosa et in sermone communi vitium; in poemate autem si fiat vel in aliquo metro aliqua rationabili de causa, figura erit et dicetur metaplasmus.

[3] *Id.* Scema, imago vel figura, modus loquendi, scilicet, soloecismus, figura, et fit scema proprie ornatus causa; metaplasmus vero causa necessi- tatis fit vel ornatus in metro, tropus causa utriuscunque tam in metro quam in prosa.

[4] MS. *scolocismum. Id.* Est *soloecismus* quoddam vitium vel quaedam figura; si fit soloecismus in communi sermone, vitium est redarguendum. Si vero fiat in dictamine, vel in poemate, factum in aliqua ratione, figura est et tollerari potest, et vocatur tunc *scema.*

[5] *Id.* Tempus:...dicitur etiam tempus accidens verbi, scilicet, modus signandi.

[6] Not originally: perhaps found in some MS. of the *De Nativitate Domini*, which appears in the early printed editions of Isidore's works, but is rejected by Migne in the PL. The sermon deals with the nativity, passion, resurrection and judgment of Christ; Isidore's other sermon, *De Natali Domini*, does not (cf. *S. Isidori Opera*, Rome, 1797, I. 622: the sermon also appears as cap. 6, lib. I, *De origine officiorum*). The verses of the Sibylline prophecy however do not appear as part of the *De Nativitate Domini* in the printed editions: cf. *S. Isidori Opera*, Cologne, 1617, pp. 367-78.

[7] 'Ιησοῦς Χριστὸς υἱὸς θεοῦ σωτήρ: the capitals (transposed by a blunder here) form ἰχθύς. The scribe has written *sothor.*

[8] The initials of the Latin translation would, naturally, form no such acrostic.

litterarum proprietates potuit non adeo observari. Haec ille. Quomodo igitur proprietates linguae possent in lingua Anglica vel in lingua barbarica, quae regulis grammaticalibus minime regulantur, observari, non video.

3. Sic: orationes, dictiones, propositiones, sillabae multae non possunt plectro linguae formari, nec litteris Latinorum alphabeti sillabicari, sed balbutiendo et de gutture evomendo, quasi grunnitus porcorum vel rugitus leonum exprimendo[1]. Quomodo igitur in lingua tali possent regulae grammaticales fieri et proprietates observari non video. Litterae sufficientes deficiunt ad exprimendum et sonandum Anglicum nostrum; in cuius argumentum aliae litterae minime contentae in alphabeto Latinorum sunt inventae ad exprimendum et servandum Anglicum nostrum: patet[2] h[3] ad ad [sic] exprimendum ha horo et consimilia, et de ȝow ad expressionem talium: ȝe, ȝyth[4], ȝonge, ȝor; et de þorn ad expressionem talium: þero, þat, þorwe, þenne, et huiusmodi.

4. Sic: non solum deficit lingua Anglicana in litteris, sed etiam in dictionibus, nam pro notissimis dictionibus et communissimis in lingua Latina non sunt nomina neque dictiones in Anglico correspondentes; patet de istis transcendentibus, *ens*, *substantia*, *accidens*; et etiam de predicamentis, *quantitas*, *qualitas*, *relatio*, *habitus*; et *positio*, *actio*, *passio*, quando et ubi. Sic de *fallaciis*, sicut de *aequivocatione*, *amphibolia*, quibus non correspondent in Anglico dictiones, non obstante quod illa lingua plus aliis utitur monosillabis, sed vix per circumlocutionem exprimi possunt in eadem.

5. Sic: si tota sacra scriptura sit in Anglicum vel in linguam barbaricam transferenda, aut igitur de verbo ad verbum, aut de sententia ad sententiam. Non primo modo, quia multae dictiones Latinae non habent dictiones in Anglico correspondentes, sed tamen per circumlocutiones exprimi possunt in vulgari nostro; cuius sunt *legio*, 666 [sic][5] et *lustrum*, quod est spatium 5 annorum. Similiter multe partes scripturae salvari non possunt ab incongruitate et falsitate nisi per figuras grammaticales quae non habent locum in lingua Anglicana, et ostensum est igitur, si translatio fieri debet de Latino in (f. 45, 2) Anglicum, non posset in lingua illa ab incongruitate et falsitate salvari. Nec translatio

---

[1] Trevisa's Higden, a work nearly contemporary with this, complains of the "gabbling, chattering, snarling, croaking and hissing" sounds, which characterised some of the English dialects (ed. J. R. Lumby, II. 157).

[2] Apparently for *videlicet*, as later.

[3] The Latin alphabet has *h*: but Palmer possibly here refers to it as being aspirated in English (cf. the exclamations he quotes), and left unpronounced in contemporary Latin, as in Italian. Probably Palmer actually spoke of *w* and the scribe has confused the text: his examples as written might be scribal errors for *wat*, *wors*.

[4] *Sic*: perhaps ȝeȝyth.     [5] From Lyra, Antwerp, 1634, v. 531.

debet fieri de sententia ad sententiam, quia sententia eiusdem litterae Latinae est apud diversos diversa; in quem igitur sensum transferri debet ignoratur. Dicit forte quis, quod habeat sensum litteralem, moralem, allegoricum et anagogicum: transferri tantum debet quoad sensum litteralem. Contra, sensus litterales sunt diversi secundum opinionem diversorum, et stat argumentum sicut prius.

6. Sic 70 interpretes nunquam nisi ieiuniis et orationibus peractis transferrent, et tamen, (dicit Ieronimus,) frequenter erraverunt, sicut Ieronimus hoc idem de seipso confitetur; quomodo igitur generaliter simplices solam grammaticam et vix eam intelligentes in transferendo non errarent?

*Tertia veritas:* sacra scriptura non debet omni publicari quoad omnia, nec ab omnibus occultari quoad aliqua. Probatur, nam Beda dicit misteria fidei christianae non populo pandenda sunt, ne vilescant; nec probis claudenda, ne in totum lateant. Quae item angelus praecepit Iohanni, *Apoc.* 14[1]: *Quod vides in libro scribe, sed quae locuta sunt septem tonitrua, noli ea scribere.* Igitur aliquibus est scribenda, aliquibus non publicanda, secundum diversitatem partium. Similiter Paulus, 2 *Cor.* 12, audivit *archana quae non licet homini loqui.* Igitur nec scribere ea licet.

*Quarta veritas:* sacra scriptura non est malis totaliter communicanda voce vel scriptura; probatur *Matt.* 7, *Nolite sanctum dare canibus,* et Gorham super illud *Apoc.* 10, *Noli scribere quae locuta sunt septem tonitrua:* quia infidelibus, inquit, furore malitiae agitatis blasphemiae potius quam edificationis materia esset; unde *Prov.* 23, *In auribus insipientium ne loquaris, quia despicient doctrinam eloquii.*

*Quinta veritas:* licet ipsa sit revelanda, tamen aliquando ad tempus est occultanda: probatur *Daniel* 12: *Tu Daniel, claude sermones et signa librum usque ad tempus, pertransibunt plurimi et multiplex erit scientia.*

*Sexta veritas:* aperienda est amicis Dei et claudenda inimicis; probatur per glossam *Apoc.* 14: *Noli ea scribere,* inquit, ut amicis pateant et inimicis lateant; et in evangelio[2]: (f. 45b, I) *Vos autem dixi amicos meos, quodcunque audivi a patre meo nota feci vobis.*

*Septima veritas:* secreta Dei celanda sunt a simplicibus et non omnibus manifestanda; probatur *Isaiah* 24, *Secretum meum mihi,* et *secretum meum ne extraneo reveles, Prov.* 25, est gloria Dei celare verbum. [*Id.*]

*Octava veritas:* magis difficillima ad intelligendum et quae excedunt intellectum simplicium non est scripturae demandanda

---

[1] *Apoc.* x. 3.          [2] *Ioh.* xv. 15.

eis[1], ne in errorem inducantur; probatur, quia: *Altiora te ne quaesieris*[2], quae, scilicet, transcendunt intelligentiae tuae rationem; quia *Prov.* 25: *Qui scrutator maiestatis opprimetur a gloria.* Sicut maxima claritas obtendit[3] visum, sic nimia per-scrutatio secretorum Dei obtendit[3] intellectum, et ideo non plus saepe quam oportet, secundum Apostolum: *Quia bestia quae tetigit montem lapidabitur*[4]. Bestia est intellectus humanus simplicium, et mons simplicitas scripturarum, et plura sunt superiora sensus [*sic*] hominum et transcendunt rationem et in-tellectum, et sequitur, multa abscondita tibi sunt a Domino.

*Nona veritas:* multa sunt abscondita a simplicibus et eis non revelanda propter meritum fidei augendum; probatur per Gregorium, quia fides non habet meritum ubi humana ratio praebet experimentum; et Hugo de Vienna super illud *Ecclesi-astici* 3[5], *Multa sunt abscondita tibi a Domino,* in glossa, Propter, inquit, meritum fidei.

*Decima veritas:* nimis ardua ad observanda non erunt simpli-cibus tradenda; probatur, nam Paulus propter eandem causam scribit discipulis: *Tanquam parvulis in Christo lac potum vobis dedi, non escam: nondum enim potestatis sicut nec nunc quidem potestis, adhunc enim carnales estis;* patet 1 *Cor.* 3. Similiter Berengarius super illud *Apoc.* 10: *Quae locuta sunt septem tonitrua, noli ea scribere:* In initio, inquit, fidei, predicatores sancti viden-tes infirmitatem gentium ad fidem venientium non fuerunt ausi exteriora praecepta committere, ne forte duritia praeceptorum territi non auderent ad fidem christianam sustinendam accedere; sic enim fecerunt apostoli, *Actus* 17[6], ubi sic: *Spiritui sancto et* (f. 45 *b, 2*) *nobis nihil imponere vobis oneris, nisi ut abstineatis vos ab immolatis et sanguine suffocato et a fornicatione,* dixerunt apostoli conversis de gentibus ad fidem.

*Undecima veritas:* vana simplicibus et inutilia non sunt eis manifestanda, pro illo *Ecclesiastici* 3: *In vacuis rebus noli scrutari, et in multis operibus eius non eris curiosus*; ubi Hugo de Vienna in postilla[7]: In rebus vacuis, id est, in eis quorum scientia non est utilis, ut quare musca vel pulex tot pedes habent et camelus tantum quattuor et homo solum duo.

*Duodecima veritas:* laicis utilia ad salutem et non alia de sacra scriptura sunt eis tradenda; probatur: *Altiora te ne quae-sieris, et fortiora te ne scrutatus fueris*[8]; sed *quae praecipit tibi*

---

[1] *Sic,* the scribe seems to have transposed *scripturae* from after *difficillima,* and to have changed *sunt* into *est.*

[2] *Ecclesiastici* iii. 22.

[3] *Sic,* by an obvious blunder for *obtundere,* to dull or stupefy.

[4] *Heb.* xii. 20.        [5] *Ecclesiastici* xliii. 36.

[6] *Act.* xv. 28.        [7] See *supra* 421.        [8] *Ecclesiastici* iii. 22.

*Deus, illa cogita semper, et in pluribus operibus eius non sis curiosus....Haec*[1] *sunt praecepta et caerimonia atque iudicia, quae mandavit Dominus Deus vester: Audi Israel, et observa quae praecepit Dominus Deus tuus: diliges Dominum Deum tuum ex toto corde tuo, et ex tota anima tua, eruntque verba haec quae ego praecipio tibi hodie in corde tuo, et narrabis ea filiis tuis, et meditaberis sedens in domo tua et ambulans in itinere, dormiens atque consurgens, et ligabis quasi signum in manu tua; eruntque et movebuntur inter oculos tuos; scribesque ea in limine et ostiis domus tuae.* Ecce quot scribenda erunt praecepta in populo. Vana et inutilia sunt vitanda: *De*[2] *his volo te confirmare, ut curent in bonis operibus qui credunt Deo.* Haec sunt bona et utilia homini: *stultas autem quaestiones et genealogias et contentiones et pugnas legis devita:* talis sunt vobis inutiles et inanes.

*Tertia decima veritas:* Aliqua pars scripturae sacrae in mente non potest extra exprimi, scripta vel voce; probatur quia sicut iubilus mentis potest esse tantus quod propter illius vehementiam extra ostendi non poterit, sic est aliqua pars scripturae in mente tam divina, tam iocunda, quod extra in voce vel scriptura non potest plene et perfecte aperiri: quia *nec oculus vidit nec auris audivit* (f. 46, *1*) *nec in cor hominis ascendit quae praeparavit Deus diligentibus se*[3]*;* et *ad Cor.* 2.

## Pro-vernacular-Bible rejoinder.

Sed illa veritas non est ad propositum, quia hic loquimur de scriptura sacra nobis tradita in canone Bibliae.

1. Contra tamen praedictam veritatem, ut magis appareat articulus, sic: *Qui deliquerit in uno factus est omnium reus,* secundum Iacobum: Sed facilius potest aliquis delinquere contra legem antiquam et etiam novam, nisi habeantur in scriptis, cum labilis sit memoria hominis. Igitur, etc.

2. Sic secretissima Dei et difficillima sunt nobis a Domino tradita, ut articulus Trinitatis, quod una res et una essentia sunt tres personae realiter dictae a qualibet earum, quo articulo nullus est difficilior vel secretior, igitur difficultas vel secretum non impedit.

3. Sic: *Ioh.* 6, *Ego sum panis vivus qui de caelo descendi, si quis manducaverit ex hoc pane vivet in aeternum, et panis quem ego dabo, caro mea est pro mundi vita. Litigabant igitur Iudaei ad invicem dicentes; quomodo potest hic dare carnem suam ad manducandum? durus est hic sermo, quis potest cum audire? Ex hoc multi discipuli abierunt retrorsum, et iam cum illo non ambulabant;* et *Ioh.* 2[4], *Ex nobis prodierunt, sed ex nobis non erant, nam si fuissent ex nobis permansissent.* Difficillima et secretissima eis

---

[1] *Deut.* vi. 5-9.    [2] *Tit.* iii. 8-9; cf. ii. 9.    [3] 1 *Cor.* ii. 9.    [4] 1 *Ioh.* ii. 19.

docuit, non obstante quod capere non voluerunt, sed ex eo recesserunt.

4. Sic: *Matt.* 19: *Dicunt ei discipuli, si ita est, non expedit nubere; qui dixit eis: non omnes capiunt verbum illud, sed quibus datum est; sunt enim eunuchi qui semetipsos castraverunt propter regnum Dei; qui potest, capiat.*

5. Sic: *Ioh.* 6[1]: *Adhuc habeo vobis multa dicere, sed non potestis portare modo; cum autem venerit ille spiritus veritatis, docebit vos omnem veritatem:* igitur docebit omnem veritatem, et secretissimam et difficillimam. Haec contra octavam et nonam veritatem.

Et [item similiter?]: Si fides non habet meritum ubi humana ratio praebet experimentum, tunc [non] expediret doctoribus studere ad fidem defendendam ratione, sicut etiam quod melius docti in fide essent minoris meriti.

Similiter Christus sublimia praedicavit in divinis, *aequalem se faciens Deo, Ioh.* 5, propter quod Iudaei quaerebant eum interficere, sicut ibidem dicitur *Ioh.* 8: *dixit eis, ego principium* (f. 46, 2) *qui loquor vobis, et antequam Abraham fieret* [sic], *ego sum;* propter quod, ut ibi dicitur, *tulerunt lapides ut iacerent in Ihesum.* Igitur sanctum videtur dedisse canibus.

Similiter margaritas videtur posuisse ante porcos conculcandas [quando] Deum se figuratum esse per manna dicebat: *Ego sum panis vivus qui de caelis descendi; non sicut patres vestri manducaverunt manna in deserto et mortui sunt: qui manducat hunc panem vivet in aeternum.* Quam margaritam multi conculcaverunt; dicitur ibi, *durus est hic sermo, quis potest eum audire? et abierunt retrorsum.*

Item, ex hoc quod dedit Iude proditori, qui et canis et porcus fuit, eukaristiam, qua nihil sanctius est in sacramentis. Ex hoc quod ipse alibi videtur[2] contrarium docuisse, ut *Matt.* 14, *Quod dico vobis in tenebris, dicite in* [hoc?] *lumine, et quod in auribus dicite in cubiculis, praedicate in tectis*[3].

Item ex hoc loco: *Nolite sanctum dare canibus, Matt.* 7, videtur [quod] non deberem dare eukaristiam subdito meo quando scio eum esse vel canem per infidelitatem vel porcum per spurcitiam peccatorum; nam si dedero, faciam contra doctrinam Christi; et, si non dedero, faciendo iniuriam. Requiritur in casu isto utrum possim ei dare hostiam non consecratam loco consecratae? quod sic videtur, quia sic incedam in misericordiae via et vitabo ambo praedictas inconvenientias, quia nec dabo sanctum canibus neque perdam peccatorem[4].

---

[1] *Ioh.* xvi. 12.  [2] *dixisse* crossed out.

[3] This is a *cento* of *Matt.* x. 27 and *Luke* xii. 3. Author and scribe between them have produced a result which admirably exemplifies the frequent careless use of the biblical text in the middle ages.

[4] The argument in this paragraph is satirical. Knowing that a refusal of the consecrated host on such grounds is inadmissible, the advocate of ver-

Item, nullo sapiente homine actore fit homo deterior, non enim illa parva culpa vel tanta est ut insipientem hominem cadere nequeant [sic], ut dicitur; sed si dedero ei, fit me actore multo deterior quam fuit ante; patet ex Cor. 11: nullo igitur modo, si sim sapiens, debeo ei dare hostiam sanctam, nec debeo ipsum prodere. Relinquitur illa "via misericordiae," sicut dictum est.

### ANTI-VERNACULAR-BIBLE REJOINDER.

RESPONSIO. Dicendum quod nichil invenitur in factis vel in dictis quod repugnet [     ]: intellectae: Nolite sanctum dare canibus; dicit enim Augustinus, libro secundo De sermoneDomini in monte, nota ibi: unde debet non sanctum dare canibus; neque margaritas posuit ante porcos per se, (f. 46 b, 1) sed propter alios solum, quia non propter eos sed propter alios dixit[1]. Ad aliud quod obicitur de eukaristia data Iudae: adhuc occultum erat discipulis, propter quod et ei dedit etiam eukaristiam, ut dispensaturos futuros huius sacramenti doceret quod propter occultum peccatum non repellerent subditos suos, publice cum aliis hoc sacramentum quaerentes; et hoc propter tres rationes. Prima, ne talis proderetur; secunda, ne scandalum generetur in cordibus aliorum videntium; tertia, ne tales dispensatores haberent libertatem contra bonos malignandi, repellendo eos a communione et infamando eos. Cum igitur dicitur: Nolite sanctum dare canibus, de illis quorum crimina sunt manifesta et notoria intelligendum dico, si ad eukaristiam trahantur; vel, si de aliis, quorum crimina sunt occulta, contendat aliquis hoc debere intelligi, prohibetur non actus dandi, similiter ac[2] in omni causa, sed voluntas; debet enim sacerdos peccatorem occultum primo monere si potest, ut poenitentiam agat, et ad sacramentum accedat; quod si noluerit, debet ei occulte prohibere ne communicantibus publice se immisceat; quod si se immiscuerit, debet dare ei hostiam consecratam voluntate lugubri et nolente, ut dictum est.

Ad aliud, ut dictum est: Praedicate super tecta; respondet Chrisostomus, homelia 23[3], Operis imperfecti: quod non praecepit Christus omnibus omnia dicere, quia sic contrarium huic loco praecepisset, sed praecepit quibus oportuit cum libera propalatione, et in aperto dicere et non in angulo, neque in tenebris, sicut dicunt doctrinae suspectae, quemadmodum Christus observavit Ioh. 18: Ego palam locutus sum mundo.

Ad aliud quod obicitur de eukaristia: patet quod non debet

---

nacular Bibles tries to shew that his opponent's use of the text: Nolite sanctum dare canibus, would as rationally entail it, as it would cover the denial of a translation of the Bible to the ignorant.

[1] PL, 34, col. 1301, "non putandus est [Christus] sanctum dedisse canibus," etc.     [2] MS. &.

[3] Pat. Graeco-Lat. LVII. col. 399.

dari occulto peccatori cum aliis se ingerenti hostia non consecrata propter duas rationes; primo, quia veritati nulla fictio
adiungenda est, quia *nulla conventio lucis ad tenebras*, 2 *Cor*. 6;
et per hoc probat Augustinus [in] *sermone*[1], quod corpus Christi
non fuit factum fantasticum, quia veritas Christus fallere non
potuit. *Ioh*. 13: Nunquam indiget Deus vestro mendacio ut
pro illo loquamini dolos, et ideo in sacramentis ecclesiae quae
sunt sacramenta veritatis, nihil agendum est per fictionem, prae-
cipue in sacramento eukaristiae, in quo Christus (f. 46 *b*, 2), totus
continetur; manifesta enim esset fictio si hostia non consecrata
daretur loco consecratae. Secundo, quia sacerdos hoc faciens,
quantum in se est, fieret populo circumstanti occasio idolatriae,
qui populus licet peccatum idolatriae non incurreret, aestimans
probabiliter hostiam esse consecratam, tamen sacerdos, ex hoc
quod ipse[2] hostiam non consecratam populo exhiberet adoran-
dum, crimen idolatriae incurreret; unde manifestum est quod
in nulla causa faciendum est quod hostia non consecrata ex-
hibeatur alicui tanquam consecrata. Ex istis patet quod illa via
misericordiae non est elicienda[3] sed abicienda, quia in extremo
consistit veritas in proposito.

Ad aliud scilicet, quod nullo sapiente [*sic*] fit homo deterior,
dicitur quod me actore non fit ille deterior, qui me invito accipit
sacramentum, sed seipso per se, et non ego nisi per actus [eius]
et coactus.

Ad aliud scilicet, "fides non habet meritum verum": sed, si
nollent credere nisi haberent rationem pro se; et ad aliud: "qui
deliquerit in uno factus est reus omnium"; quia si[c] omnia
[peccata] remissa per ingratitudinem [irrita] reddunt.

### FURTHER ANSWERS TO THE PRINCIPAL ARGUMENTS OF THOSE WHO DESIRE TRANSLATIONS.

Ad primum principale, cum sic arguitur: Licet totam sacram
scripturam praedicare et docere, igitur et scribere, hic dico:
Primo, negando consequentiam, quia dictum est in Iohannis
*Apoc*. 10: *Quae locuta sunt septem tonitrua, noli ea scribere*; vidit
tamen, audiit et intellexit ea. Secundo nego, asserens quia
*Matt*. 7 dicitur: *Noli sanctum dare canibus, neque margaritas
ponere ante porcos*. Similiter, Paulus audivit *archana verba, quae
non licet homini loqui*, videlicet, praedestinationem beatorum
et reprobationem malorum, nec sibi nec homini licet hoc loqui
propter praesumptionem et desperationem damnatorum. Tertio
dico, quod licet transferri eam liceat, non tamen in omnem lin-

---

[1] The scribe's number is doubtful; the sermon is CCXXXIII in PL, 39, col. 2175.

[2] MS. *ex hoc ipse quidem*.           [3] *Sic*, eligenda?

guam, quia non [in] barbaricam, ut arguendo ad aliam partem ostensum est. Quarto dico, non omnis obligatur ad observantiam omnium in ea contentorum, sed tantum ad praecepta, ut ibi ostensum est.

Ad secundum principale dico, quod lex rite vivendi quoad praecepta, et quoad alia quae conferunt vitam, et quoad illa [quae] necessarie requiruntur[1], est habenda, non tamen quoad alia difficillima et obscura. Secundo dico quod in scripturis aliqua inveniuntur in quibus putamus vitam aeternam habere, et praeter illa sunt multa alia ad quae laici minime obligantur scire vel agere.

Ad tertium (f. 47, 1) dico concedendo quod labilis est memoria hominum, et ideo in omni natione scriptura est habenda in tali lingua in qua potest transferri, ut in lingua Hebraica, Graeca et Latina, et ideo in omni natione requiritur quod sint clerici in aliqua lingua tali periti, qui possunt populo per circumlocutionem scripturas interpretari.

Ad quartum dico, quod licet vulgo per clericos interpretantes habere notitiam scripturae sacrae et habere omnia praecepta eis necessaria, requisita ad salutem; non tamen est eis necessarium ad salutem habere alia difficillima et obscura et ad salutem impertinentia. Secundo dico, si in eis omnia scire esset necessarium ad salutem, esset eis necessarium ad salutem linguam talem addiscere in qua licet eam transferre.

Ad quintum nego consequentiam, quia in linguam Hebraicam, Graecam et Latinam ipsa potest transferri, non tamen sic potest in omnem linguam, quia alphabeto Latinorum non utuntur neque Graecorum neque Hebraicorum, et licet uterentur illo non tamen expediret neque deberet omnia in illa transferri, propter quaedam ante dicta.

Ad sextum, licet Beda transtul[er]it totam sacram scripturam, tamen illius translationem ecclesia non accipit, quia forte erravit, sicut Ieronymus et alii fere omnes qui eam transferre praesumpserunt. Secundo dico, quod Beda non transtulit eam nisi quoad necessaria ad salutem et quoad facilia, quia secundum se totam[2] non potuit transferri in linguam barbaricam, ut in secunda veritate est ostensum.

Ad septimum dico, quod aliquis potest vitare peccatum mortale, licet non cognoscat illud esse peccatum mortale, per inclinationem ad obiectum, unde habitus fidei non solum inclinat ad assensum ad articulum, sed impedit assensum ad haeresim oppositam, licet ignoretur an sit haeresis. Similiter auctor *De fide et legibus:* nota: Sufficit alicui pro sententia ipso ignorante se

---

[1] MS. *quoad illa nc'co requiratur.*
[2] According to its [the Bible's] full contents.

supponat nisi obstaret peccatum aliquod illius, [quo] non cognosceret eam, quia Deus conscientiam illius faceret murmurare vel aliter impediret ne peccaret[1]. Similiter mutus vel surdus posset vitare peccatum, licet nullam linguam intelligeret.

Ad octavam concedo quaestionem adductam, quod licet habere in vulgari omnia nobis necessaria ad salutem.

Ad nonam etiam concedo quaestionem, quia omnia nobis necessaria ad salutem sunt habenda in vulgari, et si aliquis sit surdus et sciat legere, scribatur sibi in nomine Domini quod est (f. 47, 2) necessarium ad salutem.

Ad decimam dico, quod non est generaliter verum, quod magis nota plus movent ad devotionem; quia quandoque vetula est magis devota quam magister in theologia, quia "pluribus minor est ad singula sensus." Similiter, magis nota quandoque vilescunt et facilius veniunt in contemptum: dixit Festus Paulo: *Multae litterae faciunt te insanire*[2].

Ad undecimam, nego assensum, propter illud *Apoc.* 10: *Quae locuta sunt septem tonitrua,* et ratio assignata est superius, in articulo ad partem negativam illius dubii.

Ad duodecimam, dicitur quod[3]: *In omnem terram exivit sonus eorum,* scilicet apostolorum, qui omnem linguam sciverunt et in omni lingua praedicaverunt omnibus quae erant eis necessaria saluti, secundum illud *Marci* ultimo: *Euntes praedicate evangelium omni creaturae,* etc. Alia curiosa scripturae et ardua non oportet quod in scriptis habeantur, nisi a clericis si qui sint, et inter eos, scilicet barbaricos, in lingua Latina Graeca vel Hebraica, vel alia regula et figuris grammaticalibus regulata: sine quibus tamen est salus.

Ad tertiam decimam dico, quod stat quod: *Quaecunque scripta sunt ad nostram doctrinam scripta sunt*[4], licet non intelligamus ea, quia possunt interpretari nobis in lingua nobis nota et probari.

Ad quartam decimam, scripta nobis ignota multa valent ad correctionem nostram, quia possunt nobis interpretari.

Ad quintam decimam: *Necesse est impleri omnia quae scripta sunt de me*[5] dicit Christus; similiter necesse est impleri omnia quaecunque scripta sunt ab hominibus; quae, scilicet, necessaria sunt saluti, et non alia.

Ad sextam decimam, concedo; quae nobis praecepta sunt, habenda sunt in scriptis ne obliviscantur, quia sunt necessaria saluti. Conformiter dico ad septimam decimam: concedo quod

---

[1] The sentence seems corrupt, but the general sense fairly plain; a man is not dependent on the written word to know good from evil in most cases: God guides his conscience, unless he himself obscure the guidance by vice.
[2] Cf. *Act.* xxvi. 24.  [3] *Psal.* xviii. 5.  [4] *Rom.* xv. 4.
[5] Cf. *Luc.* xxii. 22.

tam necessarium est barbaris sicut Graecis, Latinis vel Hebraeis
habere legem christianam in scriptis, quantum ad omnia praecepta in ea et quae sunt necessaria saluti, non quantum ad alia
secreta et difficilia et impertinentia saluti. Etiam, licet illa esset
necessaria saluti, non tamen posset secundum omnem eius partem in linguam barbaricam transferri, quia nulla lingua talis
regulatur regulis et figuris grammaticalibus, ideo aliunde de-
bemus eis providere de notitia scripturae quam per translationem
barbaricam, dando eis donum aliarum linguarum, (f. 47 b, 1)
sicut olim dedit conversis ad fidem.

Ad octavam decimam arguebatur sic: principalis causa quare
non potest transferri in linguam barbaricam videtur esse quod
illa non regulatur regulis grammaticalibus et figuris, cum quibus
non potest sacra scriptura a falsitate et incongruitate salvari;
sed propter ha[n]c causam non deberet ea transferri secundum
aliquam partem eius, nec quoad necessaria saluti nec quoad alia,
quia haec regulae, tropi et figurae sunt [in] omnibus partibus
scripturae sacrae, aequivocationes, cuius oppositum dictum est.
Ad istud dico negando quod omnibus partibus scripturae sunt
illae regulae, tropi et figurae, aequivocationes; quia aliquae
partes quoad sensum litteralem verificantur sine ipsis, et aliquae
non; praecepta autem legis et ea quae necessaria sunt saluti,
aperta sunt et plana: *Iugum*[1] *enim meum suave est et onus meum
leve;* et quae moralia sunt quasi de iure naturali et facilia ad
credendum, unde, *prae*[2] *testimonia tua credibilia facta sunt nimis,*
et ideo non indiget figuris et tropis, vel aliis, [ut] a falsitate ac
incongruitate salventur, ut alia difficilia ibidem contenta. Ad
honorem Dei, qui est benedictus in saecula. Amen. Deo gratias.

3. *Purvey's English version of his treatise, founded on the
debate on biblical translations between the Lollard, Peter
Payne, and the Dominican, Thomas Palmer, at Oxford,
1403–1405.*

Trin. Camb. 333, ff. 26–30 b, from which this tract is printed, is
the only MS. which has the tract complete: a Worc. Cath. MS. has
part, and of this C.C.C. Camb. MSS. 298, § iv; 100, § i; Trin. Camb. 24;
Harl. 325; Vitell. D. 7 are copies[3]. Foxe in his first English edition of
the AM, 1563, p. 452, printed a very mangled version of the tract
(see also 1843, ed. III. 202; IV. 671–6). Foxe's version was not founded
on the complete MS., but on his own transcript of the Worc. MS. (for
which see Harl. 425), and the early printed editions founded on the
Worc. MS., which included those of "Hans Luft," Marlborow in
Hessen, 1530, and Richard Banckes, London [without date; reprinted
in T. F. Dibdin's *Topog. Antiq.*, 1816, III. 257]. Foxe copied the first

---

[1] *Matt.* xi. 30.     [2] *Sic* in MS. *Psal.* xcii. 5.     [3] Cf. *Westminstr*. 34 5.

paragraph from Hans Luft's ed., then inserted two from his own transcript, then followed the printed ed. substantially to the end, but without acquainting the reader that the printed ed. contained about half as much again of new matter as the Worc. MS. (see AM, IV. 671). This new matter, quite out of keeping with the date of the original MS., has hitherto rendered the tract of little evidential value for historical points, drawn, as can now be seen, from Purvey's treatise of c. 1405. The editor of Hans Luft's 1530 ed. was probably Tindale, who published the work as part of his controversy with sir Thomas More. This is inferred because (1) in 1528 More had issued his *Dialogue* (see *supra*, p. 348), with its long discussion of the advisability of vernacular Bibles, directed against Tindale. The latter between 1530–34 was translating the Pentateuch, which was printed for him by Hans Luft, of Marlborow [Marburg], during those years. Tindale did not directly answer More till 1531: but in 1530 Hans Luft printed this *Compendyous Olde treatise shewynge howe that we ought to have the Scripture in Englyshe, with the Auctours*. The preface to the reader renders Tindale's editorship probable: "Consyderyng the maliceousnes of our prelates and theyr adherentes, whiche so furyously barke against the worde of God, and specyally the newe testament translated and set fourthe by mayster William Tyndale, whiche they falsely prechede to be corrupte, That ye may knowe that it is not Tyndale's translation that mouethe them,...I haue here put in prynt a treatyse writen about the yere of our Lorde a thousande fower hundred, By whiche thou shalt playnly perseyue, that they wolde yet neuer from the begyninge admyt any translation to the lay people...." (2) In a similar case, Foxe stated that he printed the MS. of Thorpe's *Defence* against Arundel as edited by Tindale, see AM, III. 249: "the said Master Tindale, (albeit he did somewhat alter and amend the English thereof, and frame it after our manner), yet not fully in all words, but that something doth remain, savouring of the old speech of that time." In the case of the *Compendyous Treatise*, however, Tindale added very long passages. Thorpe's *Defence* was also printed for Tindale by Hans Luft: see 1863 reprint of the *Compendious Olde Treatyse* by Francis Fry, p. 4; *Athenaeum*, Nov. 28, 1919, p. 1260.

Foxe used his transcript of the *Treatyse* for many points in his preface to the *Gospels of the fower Evangelists, translated in the olde Saxons' tyme*, London, 1571. Thus he refers to friar Tille's sermon, in a passage which does not occur in the AM version of the *Treatyse*; he calls him "one friar Scillie," whence Ussher's "fraterculus Scillius" (*Hist. Dogm.* anno 1410).

In this and the following M.E. tracts, þ is printed as *th*, ʒ as *g* or *y* according to the modern spelling of the word, and proper names are given capitals: otherwise the spelling is as in Trin. MS. 333. (Not Purvey's original MS., but written about 1400–30.) Biblical references are not appended when the scribe gives the chapter reference correctly.

*Agens hem that seyn that hooli wrigt schulde not or may not be drawun in to Engliche: we maken thes resouns*[1]. (f. 26)

Ffirst seith Bois[1] in his boke *De disciplina scolarium:* that children schulde be taugt in the bokis [of] Senek; and Bede expowneth this, seying children schulden be taugt in vertues, ffor the bokis of Senek ben morals: and for thei ben not taugt thus in her yougthe thei conseyuen yuel maners and ben vnabel to conseyue the sotil sciense of trewthe, seyinge the wise man: *wisdom schal not entre in to a wicked soule*[2]. And moche ther of the sentence of Bede; and Algasel in his logik seith the soule of a man is as clene myrour newe polichid in wiche is seen sigt liche the ymage of man. But, for the puple hath not konynge in youthe, the[y] han derke soulis and blyndid so that thei profiten not but in falsenes, malice and other vices; and moche ther of this mater. O, sithen hethen philosofris wolden the puple to profeten in natural science, how myche more schulden cristen men willen the puple to profiten in science of vertues; for so wolde God.

Ffor, wane the lawe was gouen[3] to Moises in the mounte of Synay, God gaf it in Ebrew for that al the pupel schuld vnderstonde it, and bad Moises to rede in vnto hem, to the tyme thei vndurstondyn it. And he rede it, as is pleyn in Detronomie 31°. c°. and Esdrias also redde it from morou to mydday, as it is pleyn in his ffirst boke 8°. c°.[4], apertily in the stret; and the eeres of the puple weren entently gouen ther to and thei vnderstoden it. And this thei migt not haue done but if it hadde ben redde in ther modur tonge so that the pupel, hering, felle in to grete wepinge. In Deut.° 32°. c°. it is writen: *Aske thi fadris and thei schullen schewe to thee and thin eldris, and thei schulen sei to thee.* (f. 26b) Also the profete seith *How many things he hath seid unto oure fadris: thei schul make hem knowen vn to her sonnes, and the sones that scholen be borne of hem schulen rise and schullen teche thes things,* to her sonnes. And thus Petre in his first pistile: *Be ye redi to fulfille to eche man that asketh youg in resoun, in feith and hope*[5]. And al so Peter seith: *Euery man, as he hath taken grace, mynyster he forthe to other men*[6]. And in the Apocalips it is writen: *The housebonde, and the wiffe seyn come; and he that hereth seith he cometh*[7]; that Crist (that is heed of holi chirche) is the housbonde, and parfite prechouris and doctouris (that is the wiffe) clepen the puple to the weies of heuene, and iche man that

---

[1] Boethius. For this tract, often attributed to him in the middle ages, see PL, 64, col. 1223 ff. The study of the works of Seneca is there recommended several times, cf. coll. 1225, 1227.

[2] Sap. i. 4.  [3] given.  [4] Esd. lib. II. 8, 3.
[5] 1 Pet. iii. 15.  [6] *Id.* iv. 10.  [7] Apoc. xxii. 17.

herith clepe other. Thus this is confermede in Actus of apostilis, there as the apostilis weren but rude men and fischeris thei [al]legeden the prophecies; as Peter in the first chapiter seid: *The Hooli Goost be the mouthe of Dauid [spake] be[ fore concerning] Judas that was the duke of hem that token Crist*, and more processe there. In the 2º. cº. Peter seith *It is writen be the prophete Joel: It schal be in the last daies seith the Lorde, I schal schede ougt of my spirit vpon iche flesche; youre sones and youre dougtteris schulen prophecie and youre yonge men schullen se viciouns*[1] and more ther in process. Also in the iij. cº. James seith, allegginge the profecie: *Aftur thes things I schal turne agene [and] I schal make vp the tabernacle*[2]. And thus the apostilis, that ben clepid ydiotes be scripture, allegeden here and in many other placis the profecies. And of this it is notabile that the lewde puple in the olde lawe knewe of the lawe notwithstandig that God for synne hadde departed the tunges of hem, as it is opon in the ij. chapitur of Genesis. If god wole, he loueth not less vs cristen men in thes daies than he dide (f. 27) the pupel in the olde testament, but better, as he hath scheued be the mene of Cristis passioun and be the newe parfite lawe gouen to vs; and herfore on the witsondaie he gaf to many diuerse nac[i]ouns knowing of his lawe be [their] one tunge, in tokene that he wolde alle men knewe his lawe, to his worschipe and her profite. Ffor, as it is writen in the boke of Numbers, the 11. cº., wane Moises had choson seuenty elder men and the spirite of God rested on hem and thei profecieden, twey men, as Eldad and Medad, profeciden in castelis[3], and on seid to Moises: *Sir forbede hem* and he seide *Wat, enviest thu for me? w[h]o schal lette that alle the puple profecie, if god gif hem his spirite?* and in actus of apostilis, the 11º. cº., seith Peter, wane he had cristened Cornelie, and his felowes repreued hym therof, for he was an hethen man, he seid to hem, *If God hath gouen to hem the same grace that he hath geuen to vs, wiche beleuen in our Lorde Ihesu Crist, w[h]o am I that may forbede God.* And sent Poule seith in Iº Cor. 14º. cº. *I wole euery man to speike with tunges more forsothe to profecie.* Also he seith: *I schal preye with spirit and I schal preie with mynde*, that is with affeccoun and with vndurstandinge; and this is myche better than al onli to haue deuocioun in wordes and not in vndurstanding. And this preueth the texte aftur, that seith: *how schal he sei amen vpon this blessing that wot not wat thu seiste?* and on this seith the doctor Lire[4]. If the puple vnderstood the preyour of the prest, it schal the better be lade in to God and the more deuoutelie

---

[1] Act. ii. 17.        [2] *Id.* xv. 16.
[3] Num. xi. 26, "in the camp."
[4] Nicholas de Lyra; see *supra*, p. 166.

answere *amen*. Also in the same chapeter he seith: *I wole rather fyue wordes be spoken to the vndurstanding of men, than ten thousand that the[y] vnderstonden not.*

Also seuenti doctouris, with outen mo, by fore (f. 27*b*) the incarnacioun translatiden the Bibile into Greek ougt of Ebrew; and aftur the ascencoun many translatiden al the Byble, summe into Greek and summe into Latyne. But seint Ierom translatide it out of Ebrew in to Latyne: w[h]os translacioun we vsen most. And so it was translated in to Spaynesche tunge, Frensche tunge and Alemayne; and other londes also han the Bibel in ther modur tunge, as Italie hath it in Latyn; for that is ther modur tonge, and be many yeeris han had. Worschipful Bede in his first boke *De Gestis Angulorum* 2°. c°.[1] tellith that seint Oswold kyng of Northeumberlond axide of the Scottys an holi pischop Aydan to preche his puple, and the kynge of hym self interpreted it on Englische to the puple. If this blessid dede be aloued[2] to the kynge of al hooli chirche, how not now as wel augte it to be alowed a man to rede the gospel on Englische and do ther aftur? It was herde of a worthi man of Almaine, that summe tyme a Flemynge (his name was James Merland)[3] translatid al the Bibel into Flemyche, for wiche dede he was somoned before the pope of grete enmyte, and the boke was taken to examynacoun and trwly apreued[4]; it was deliuered to hym agene in conficioun[5] to his enmyes. Also venerabile Bede, lede by the spirit of God, translatid the Bibel or a grete parte of the Bibile, w[h]os originals ben in many abbeis in Englond. And Sistrence in his fifte booke[6] the 24. c°. seith the euangelie of Jon was drawen into Englice be the for seide Bede; wiche euangelie of Ion and other gospellis ben y[e]t in many placis, of so oolde Englische that vnnethe can any man rede hem; ffor this Bede regnede an hooly doctor aftur the incarnacoun seuene hundered (f. 28) yeer and xxxij. Also a man of Loundon, his name was Wyring, hadde a Bible in Englische of northen speche, wiche was seen of many men, and it semed too honndred yeer olde. Also seint Poule seith: *If our gospel is hid it is hid to hem that schal be dampned*[7]*;* and eft he seith *he that knoweth not schal not be knowen of God.* Also Cistrence in his sext bok the i. c°. seith that Al[f]rede the kynge ordined opone[8] scolis of diuerse artes in Oxenforde; and he turnede the best lawes in to his modir tunge, and the sawter also[9]; and he regned aftur the incarnacioun eigt

---

[1] PL, 95, col. 119.

[2] Allowed.

[3] See *supra*, p. 71.

[4] Approved.

[5] Confusion.

[6] Higden's *Polychronicon*, RS, VI. 224.

[7] 2 Cor. iv. 3.

[8] Open, public. See *Polychronicon*, VI. 354.

[9] See *supra*, p. 135.

hundered yeer and seuenti and thre. Also seint Thomas [Aquinas] seith that barbarus is he that vnderstandith not that he redeth in his modor tunge and therfore, seith the apostile[1], *If I knewe not the vertu of the voice to wome I speike, I schal be to hym barbarus and he that speiketh to me barbarus,* that is to sey, he vnderstandith not that I sey, ne I vnderstande not wat he seith. Sum men thenkyne hem to be barbaros wiche han not propur vnderstan[din]ge of that thei reden, to answere therto in her modor tunge. Also he seith that Bede drew in to Englische the liberal artis, leste Engliche men schuldon be holden barbarus. This seint Thomas, *super primum posecicorum*[2], exponens hoc vocabulum Barbarus. Also the grett sutil clerk Lyncolne[3] seith in a sermon that bigynneth *Scriptum est de leuitis*; If (he seith) any prest seie he can not preche, oo remedie is, resyne he vp his benefice; another remedie is, if he wol not thus, record[4] he in the woke[5] the nakid tixt of the sonndaie gospel, that he kunne the groos story and telle it to his puple; that is, if he vndurstonde Latyne; and so [do] he this euery woke of the yeer, and for sothe he (f. 28 *b*) schal profite wel. For thus preched the lord seyng, Joh. 6⁰, *The wordes that I speike to youg ben spirit and lyf.* If for sothe he vnderstode no Latyn, go he to oon of his neigtboris that vnderstandith, wiche wole charitabily expone it to hym; and thus edifie he his flock, that is his puple. Thus seith Lyncolne, and on this argueth a clerk and seith: If it is leueful to preche the naked text to the pupel, it is also lefful to write it to hem; and consequentliche, be proces of tyme, so al the Bibil. Also a nobil hooly man, Richerde E[r]myte[6], drewe oon Englice the sauter, with a glose of longe proces and lessouns of *dirige* and many other tretis, by wiche many Engliche men hau ben gretli edified. And if he were cursed of God that wolde the puple schulde be[7] lewder either wors than thei ben. Also sire Wiliam Thorisby[8], erchebischop of York, did do to drawe a tretys in Englisce be a worschipful clerk w[h]os name was Gaytrik; in the wiche weren conteyned the articulis of the feith, seuene dedli synnes, the werkes of mercy and the comandements; and sente hem in smale pagynes to the comyn puple to lerne this and to know this, of wiche ben yit manye a componye in Englond.

---

[1] 1 Cor. xiv. 11; quoted in the work attributed to S. Thomas in the Parma, 1867 ed., *In octo libros Politicorum expositio*: tom. XXI. 369. This work the 1882 editors reject as spurious (tom. I. col. cclxiii).

[2] For *Politicorum*.       [3] Grosseteste. For this sermon, see *supra*, p. 141.

[4] Let him think over (recordor).                      [5] Week.

[6] Richard Rolle of Hampole. See *supra*, p. 144. "Dirige," Rolle's Latin *Novem lectiones mortuorum.*

[7] *lerned* expunctuated. Apparently some words missing.

[8] See *supra*, p. 196.

But ther ben summe that seien: If the gospel were on Engliche, men mygten ligtly erre therinne.    But wel touchith this holi man Richad Hampol suche men expownyng this tixte: *Ne auferas de ore meo verbum veritatis vsquequaque*[1], ther he seith thus: Ther ben not fewe but many wolen sustene a worde of falsenes for God, not willing to beleue to konynge and better than thei ben.    Thei ben like to the frendes of Job: that, wiles thei enforsiden hem to defende God, they offendeden greuosly in hym; and, thoug suche ben slayne and don myracles, (f. 29) thei neuertheles ben stynkyng martirs.    And to hem that seien that the gospel on Enliche wolde make men to erre, wyte wele that we fynden in Latyne mo heretikes than of ale other langagis; ffor the *Decres*[2] rehersith sixti Latyn eretikes.    Also the hooli euangelistis writen the gospell in diuerse langages, as Matheu in Indee, Marke in Ytalie, Luck in the partyes of Achaie, and John in Asie aftur he hadde writun the Apocalips in the yle of Pathomos; and al thes writun in the langage of the same cuntre, as seith Ardmakan[3].    Also Ardmakan in the *Book of questiouns* seith that the sacrament mai wel be made in iche comoun langage; for so (as he seith) diden the apostilis.    But we coueteyten not that, but prey Anticrist that we moten haue oure bileue in Englische.    Also we that han moche comyned with the Jewis knowen wel that al mygty men of hem, in wat londe they ben born, yit they han in Ebrew the Bible, and thei ben more actif of the olde lawe thane any Latyn man comonli; yhe, as wel the lewde men of the Jewes: as prestis.    But it is red in comyne of the prestes, to fulfille ther prestes office and to edificacoun of porayle[4] that for slouthe stoudieth nogt.    And the Grekis, wiche ben nobel men, han al this in ther owne langage.    But yit aduersaries of trewith seien, wane men rehersen that Grekis and Latyns han al in ther owne langage, the clerkis of hem speiken grammaticalliche and the puple vnderstondith it not.    Witte thei that, thoug a clerke or another man thus lerned can sette his wordis on Engliche better than a rewde man, it foloweth not her of that oure langage schuld be destried[5].    It were al on[e] to sei this, and to kitte[6] oute the tunges of hem that can not speke (f. 29b) thus curiosly.    But thei schulde vnderstonde that "grammaticaliche" is not ellis but abite[7] of rigt spekyng and rigt pronounsyng and rigt wrytinge.

But Frere Tille[8], that seide before thi buschop of Londoun,

---

[1] Psal. cxviii. 43.  The quotation from Rolle is loose, cf. Bramley, *Psalter*, 416.

[2] Gratian, *Decretum*, cf. Æ. Friedberg's ed. 1878, Leipzig.
[3] See *supra*, p. 142.          [4] poor people.
[5] destroyed.                    [6] cut.                    [7] the habit.
[8] See *supra*, p. 294.

heerynge[1] an hundrid men, that Jerom seide he errid in trans-
latyng of the Bibel, is lyk to Elymas, the wiche wolde haue lettid
a bischope or a Juge to heere the byleue; to w[h]om Poule seid:
*O thou ful of al trecherie, and of al false teching* to turne the buschop from the beleue, *thou schalt be blynde to a tyme*[2]. This [is]
writun in the Dedus of the apostilis 13°. c°. Ffor Jerom seith
in the prolog of Kynges: I am not knowyng to my self in any
maner me to haue [erred, in] changyng any thinge from the
Ebrew trewith. Wel I wot, he seide sum tyme that holy writ
was false aftur the letter. But aftur, wane Austyn hadde writen
to him, and he to him agen, he grauntid wele that it was trewe,
as he rehersith in a pistile, and in the Prolog of the Bible; and
was glad and ioyeful of his translacoun; and therfor, wane he
hath rehersithd al the bookis of the Bibel, thane he seith in the
Prolog of Penteteuke[3]: I praie the, dere brother, lyue amonge
these, haue thi meditacoun in these, knowe noon other thing
but these. But Jerom hadde many enemyes for translating of
the Bibel, as he rehersith in the ffirst Prolog, to his enemyes
thus: Whi art thou turmented be [*sic*] enmeye? what stirist
thou the willes of vnkunnynge men agens me? if it semeth to the
that I haue erred in myn translacion: aske the Ebrew councel, with
the maisteris of diuerse citees[4]. In the secunde Prolog he seith
this: We seeyn (rehersing the sentence bifore), leest we ben seen
to holde oure pes agens the ba[ckbi]tourus[5]. And in the same he
seith: We, hasting to oure contre, schullen passe with (f. 30) a
deffe eere to the dedely soungyis of the mermaidens. And thus in
many prologis he scorneth his enemyes and lettith not his hooly
werk. But [he] seith: *I seide I schal kepe my weies that I trespas
not in my tounge: I haue put keping to my mouthe wane the
synfulman hath stande agens me*[6]. These ben the wordis of Ierom
rehersing the profigte.

Also it is knowen to many men that in the tyme of Kyng
Richerd, whose soule God a soile, in to a parliment was put a
bille[7] be assent of two erchebischopis and of the clergie to anulle
the Bibel that tyme translatid in to Engliche, and also other
bokis of the gospel translatid in to Engliche; wiche, wanne it
was seyn of lordis and comouns, the good duke of Lancastre Ion
(w[h]os soule God asoile, for his mercy) answered ther to sharpely,

---

[1] in the hearing of.
[2] Act. xiii. 10, freely applied to fourteenth century events.
[3] Actually, in the *Prologus Galeatus*.
[4] Actually, in the prologue to the Pentateuch, *Ad Desiderium*.
[5] calumniantibus tacere. *In Iosue Praefatio*.
[6] Vulg. Psal. xxxviii. 2.
[7] AM, IV. 674, reads "Bible," from a mistake in the 1530 ed. of the *Compendyous Treatise*. See *supra*, p. 437.

seying this sentence: we wel not be the refuse of alle men; for, sithen other naciouns han Goddis lawe, wiche is lawe of oure byleue, in ther owne modur langage, we wolone haue oure in Engliche, w[h]o that euere it bigrucche; and this he affermede with a grete othe.

Also the bischope of Caunturbiri, Thomas Arrundel, that nowe is, seide a sermon in Westimister[1] there as weren many hundred puple, at the biriyng of quene Anne, (of w[h]os soule God haue mercy); and, in his comendynges of hir, he seide it was more Joie of hir than of any whoman that euere he knewe; ffor, not withstanding that sche was an alien borne, sche hadde on Engliche al the foure gospeleris with the docturis vpon hem[2], and he seide sche hadde sent hem vnto him, and he seide thei weren goode and trewe, and comended hir in that sche was so grete a lady and also an alien, and wolde so lowliche studiee in so vertuous bokis. And he blamed in that sermoun scharpeli the necligence of prelatis (f. 30b) and of other men, in so miche that summe seiden he wolde on the morowe leue vp his office of chaunceler and forsake the worlde; and than it hadde be the last sermoun that euere thei herde.

## 4. *Wycliffe's* [?] *tract: The holi prophete Dauid seith....* (f. 1)

This tract, printed from Ff. 6. 31, § 3, is followed in the MS. by four other Lollard tracts, which follow each other without *incipit*, *explicit* or title, and give the appearance at first of forming a single treatise (ff. 1–16 b, *The holy prophet David saith*; ff. 16 b–27, *Meekness*; ff. 27 b–35 b, *Here sueth the sayings of divers doctors upon the xxvi chapter of Matthew*; ff. 36–42, *Chrisostom and some other doctors here*). The MS. contains also another Lollard tract on the *Four errors which letten the very knowing of holy writ*, and the hand of these tracts is c. 1380–1400. The literary style, as well as the manner of quoting the Bible, differentiates *The holy Prophet David saith* from the four which follow it (see p. 268), which use the EV. [Cf. f. 27 b: "Forsooth them supping, Jesu took bread and blessed and brake" = EV (the LV has: "and while they supped"); cf. also f. 28 b, "And he, taking the cup, did thankings"; f. 29 b, "the disciples supping Jesu took bread,"..."the disciples eating Jesu took bread, and he blessing brake and gave it to them"..."and the bread taking, he did thankings and brake"; f. 30, "and he doing thankings...," all EV.] It is so rare to find quotations from a particular biblical version in mediaeval tracts, that these quotations would seem to imply a very close acquaintance of the author with the EV, such as would have been possessed by Nicholas Hereford or one of the original circle of translators, e.g. John Aston, who "taught and writ accordingly and full busily, where, when, and to whom he might" (Pollard, 119). *The*

---

[1] See p. 278.          [2] Purvey's English patristic glosses, see *id.*

*holy prophet David saith* was written, however, probably before the making of the first Lollard version, and by Wycliffe (see *supra*, p. 270).

The holi prophete Dauid seith in the persone of a iust man: *Lord, how swete ben thi spechis to my chekis*[1]*;* that is, to myn vndirstondyng and loue; and the prophete answerith and seith: *Tho ben swettere than hony to my mowth.* Eft[2] the same prophet seith in the persone of a iust man: *Lord I was glad of thine spechis as he that fyndith many spoilis eithir praies*[3]. Eft the same prophete seith: *The domes of the Lord ben trewe and iustified in hem silf; tho ben more desireable than gold and precious stones, and swettere than hony and hony comb; ffor whi? thi servant kepith tho, and moche rewarde is to kepe hem*[4]. Therefor he seith: *Moche pees is to hem that louen thi lawe: and to hem is no sclander*[5]. For thei gyuen no sclandre to othere men: bi euel dede ne bi yuel word; and thei ben not sclandrid for tribulacion and persecucion; but thei suffre gladli and ioiefulli (f. 1b) tribulacion and persecucion for the laue of God. Eft the same prophete seith: *Blessid is the man that gede not in the counceil of vnfeithful men, and stood not in the wei of synners, and sat not in the chaier of pestelence* (that ys, pride eithir wordli glorie), *but his wille is in the lawe of the Lord, and he schal hawe mynde bi nygt and bi day in the lawe of the Lord*[6]. Ffor, as the same prophete seith: *Lord, thi word is a lanterne to my fet* (that ys, to rule myne affeccions and myne werkis), *and thi word is ligt to my pathis*[7] (that is, myne thowttis and myne counceilis). And eft he seith: *The comaundement of the Lord is ligtful, and ligtneth iyes of the sowle*[8]; that is, resoun and wille; and eft he seith: *The declaryng of thyne wordis gyueth goostli ligt, and gyueth vndirstondyng to meke men*[9].

Ffor thise auctorites and siche othere (f. 2) sum men of good wille redin besili the text of holi writ, for to kunne it and kepe it in here lyuynge and teche it to othere men bi hooli ensample. And for the staat that thei stondyn ynne, and for this werk, thei han the blissyng of God, as he seith in the gospel, Luc. xi°: *Blessid ben thei that heryn the word of God and kepin it;* and in the first c.[hapter] of Apocalips seynt Joon seith: *He is blessid that heerith and redith the wordis of this prophecie, and kepith tho thyngis that ben writen ther ynne.* But othere veyn men besie hem faste to studie to kunne the lettre of Goddis lawe and thei bisi hem nat treuli to kepe the sentence ther of. And therfore thei disceyuen hem self and in maner sclaundren the lawe of God. Ffirst thei schulde studie to kunne wel the trewe sentence of Goddis lawe,

---

[1] Psal. cxviii. 103.    [2] again.    [3] Psal. cxviii. 162.
[4] Psal. xviii. 11.    [5] Psal. cxviii. 165.    [6] Psal. i. 1.
[7] Psal. cxviii. 105.    [8] Psal. xviii. 9.    [9] Psal. cxviii. 130.

aftirward to kepe it in werk and thanne to speke therof (f. 2*b*)
mekeli and charitabli to the edificacion of othere men; for if thei
iangelyn oonli of this blessid lawe to schewe here cunnynge
abowe othere men and kepe not it opynli in here wirkis but doon
opynli the contrarie, thei ben contrarie to hem silf and this
cunniynge turnyth hem to more dampnacion. Ffor Crist seith
in the gospel, Luc. xij°: *A seruaunt that knowith the wille of his
lord and dooth it not schal be betyn with many betyngis.* James
seith in the iiij. c.: *It is synne to hym that can good and dooth it
not.* And Poul seith, *Kunnynge makith a man proud*[1], that is
nakid kunnynge withoute goode werkis, whanne it is medlid
with pride veyn glorie and boost. Sich men semen to do goos[t]li
auoutrie with the word of God, for there thei schulde take of the
Hooli Goost trewe vndirstandyng of hooli writ bi gret meknesse
and hooli praier, to brynge forth very charite and goode werkis.
Thei takyn the nakid[2] (f. 3) vndirstondynge bi presumcion of
mannes witt, and bryngen forgt pride veynglorie and boost, to
coloure here synnes and disceiue sutilli here negebours. Siche
maner of peple schulden takyn hede what Poul comaundyth, to
*kunne no more than nedith to kunne, but to kunne to sobirnesse*[3];
that is as moche as perteyneth to saluacion of thin owene sowle,
eithir to edificacion to othere mennes.

And Bernard expounneth this auctorite, *On Cantica,* xxxvj.
sermon, and writith thus: "To vndirstonde to soberness, is to
kepe most wakyngli what it bihoueth to kunne more and
sunnere[4]. The tyme is schort: ech trewe science is good in it
silf, but thou that hastist for the schortness of tyme to worche
thyn owne helthe, with drede and tremblyng, do thi besynesse
to kunne sunnere and more tho thyngis that ben ner to helthe.
Alle metis (f. 3*b*) ben goode wiche God hath fourmed, natheles
yif in takynge hem thou kepist not maner and ordre thou makist
hem not goode. Ffele ye also this thing of sciences wiche I seie of
metis. Poul seith: *He that gessith hym silf to kunne ony thyng,
woot not yit, hou it bihoueth hym to kunne*[5]. Poul appreueth not
a man that can manie thyngis if he cunne not the maner of
kunnynge. Poul hath set the fruit and profit of science in the
maner of kunnynge; the maner of kunnynge is that thou wete
by what ordre, by what studie, and for what entent it behoueth
to kunne alle thyngis. Bi what ordre that thou kunne: first
that thyng that ledith riphere[6] to helthe. Bi what studie, that

---

[1] I Cor. viii. I.          [2] *word* expunctuated.          [3] Rom. xii. 3.
[4] sooner.          [5] I Cor. viii. 2.

[6] *Sic,* apparently, the comp. of "ripely"; cf. EV, 2 Macc. vii. 37: "more
rijply for to be maad helpful," and NED, *Ripely.*

thou lerne more brennyngli that thyng that ledith greetliere to the loue of God and negebour. Ffor what ende, that thou lerne not to veynglorie, (f. 4) eithir to coriouste[1], eithir to ony sich thyng, but oneli to edifiyng of thi silf or of thi negebour. Sum men wollen kunne for that ende oneli that thei cunne, and it is foul coriouste. And sum men wolen cunne that thei be knowen, and it is a foul vanyte. And sum men wolen cunne for to sille here kunnyng for mony eithir for honowris, and it is foul wynnynge. Sum men wolen kunne for to edifie here negebours and that is charite. Sum men wole kunne that thei hem silf be edified, and that is prudence: thise tweyne laste ben preciable. Of alle the othere heere thei James seiynge: *Synne is to hym that can good and dooth it nat*[2]*:* as mete undefied[3] gendrith yuele humours and corrumppith the bodi and not nourischith, so moche kunnyng had in mynde, if it is not defied bi charite, whanne the soule is not maid good bi (f. 4b) witnessynge of the lyf of vertues, thilke kunnynge schal be arettid[4] into synne, as mete that is turnyd into schrewid and noiful humors. Wher a man that can good and not dooynge good, schal he not haue bolnyngis[5] and turmentis in his conscience, as who seiyhis, wher he schal not hawe in hym sylf answere of deeth, and of dampnacion. How ofte the word of God that is seid schal come into his mende: as who seighis: *Ffor a seruaunt that knowith the wil of his lord and dooth it not schal be betyn wit many woundis.* Al this is the sentence of Bernard[6].

Therfore alle men that wolen stodie hooli writ scholden studie to this entent, to know here owene freelte and defautis and eschewe deedli synnes and to kepe wilfulli the comaundements of God, and to do the werkis of merci and gewe hooli ensample (f. 5) to here negebours; wherfore the wise man seith: *Sone thou that desirest wisdam, kepe rigtwisnesse and God schal gyue it to the*[7]. And eft: *Sone, thou that neigist to the seruice of God, stonde in drede and rigtwisnes, and make thi soul redi to temptacion*[8], bi Godis grace and thyn owene besynesse. Ffor the *drede of the lord is bigynnyng of wisdom*[9]. And seynt Gregor seith: Hooli writ is to us to se therynne our defautis and amende hem, and to se goode ensamplis of hooli fadris, and to kepe tho in oure lyuynge.

Cristene men wondren moche on the weiwarnesse of diuers clerkis that bosten that thei han passynly the cunnynge of hooli writ, sithyn thei makyn hem self moost vnable therto: for thei

---

[1] Curiosity.  [2] Iac. iv. 17.  [3] Undigested.
[4] Accounted.  [5] Swellings.  [6] PL, 183, coll. 967–9.
[7] Ecclesiastici i. 33.  [8] *Id.* ii. 1.  [9] Prov. i. 7.

feynen to studie kunne and preche hooli writ for pride of the
word, for couetise of ertheli goodis, (f. 5 b) and for wombe ioie, to
leve in delices, bodeli ese and ydilnesse. Agenes hem seith God,
Prou. xijᵒ. c. *He that suyth ydilness is most fool,* and the lord
Ihesu seith Mt. xjᵒ. c. *Ffadir, lord of heuene and of herthe and
knoweleche to the,* that is I herie the, *for thou hast hid thise thyngis,*
that is preuites of hooli writ, *fro wise men and prudent of the
world, and thou hast schewid tho to meke men.* And Crisostom
seith that good leuynge is a lanterne to brynge men to veri vndirstondyng of holi writ, and with oute good lyuyng and the drede
of God no man is wise. And the wise man seith, Sapienc. ijᵒ.
*Wisdom schal not entre into an yuel willid soule nether schal duelle
in a bodi suget to synnes*[1]; sithen these grete synnes bifore seid
makyn the dewel to dwell and to regne in the sowle of siche
veyn clerkis; no wondir, (f. 6) though he brynge hem to gostli blind-
nesse and fals vndirstondyng of hooli writ. These men semen
grete foolis, that poisone hem self bi the mystakynge and vndirstondynge of the hoolsum mete of hooli writ, and thei bind hem
silf bi ropis of deedli sinnes, and betake hem prisoneris to the
deuyl, and bryngen the chayn of deedli synne aboute here nekk:
wherbi thei schollen ben hangid in helle; and therfore hooli writ
seith, Prou. v. c. *The wikkidnesses of an yuel man takyn him, and
ech is streigtli bounden with the ropis of hise sinnes.* Thise men ben
grete foolis in alle maner, for if thei han verili the vndirstondyng
of holi writ, and doon wetyngli and custumabli ther-agenes,
their goon lyuynge doun to helle as seynt Austin seith on this
word on the salm: *Descendant in infernum viuentes*[2], and if thei han
not the trew vndirstonding (f. 6 b) of hooli writ and bosten that
thei han it passande alle othere men, thanne be thei open foolis,
fouli disseyued of the deuel the world and of there fleisch.
Pryncipali thise clerkis ben grete folis that with sich lyuynge
prechyn opynli the lawe of God, ffor as Crisostom seith on
Mᵗ v. c. on that word *Vos estis sal terre, vos estis lux mundi:* he
that lyueth yuele opynli in knowyng of the peple, and prechith
the laue of God, dampnyth hymself, sclandrith othere men and
blasfemeth God.

Siche proude clerkis and blyndid in peyne of here synnes
schulden taken hede what Crist seith in Mᵗ xxiijᵒ. c. to the blynde
Saduceis, where Mᵗ writith thus: *Ye erren, ye kunne not the
[s]cripturis neither the vertu of God*[3], wheron Crisostom writith
thus in the xxxviij omelie, Wisli[4] Crist repreueth first the
necligence of hem, for thei redden not. (f. 7.) The secunde tyme

---

[1] Sap. i. 4.
[2] Psal. liv. 16.
[3] Matt. xxii. 29.
[4] Wisely.

he repreueth here ignorance, for thei knewyn not God; ffor the science of God cometh of diligence of redynge: truli ignorance of God is dougter of necligence. Treuli if not alle men redynge knowyn God, how schal he know that redith not? thanne men redynge knowe no treuthe, whanne thei redyn not wyllynge to fynde treuthe. He that redith scriptures of God and wole fynde God, and his good lyuynge is maad as the legt of lampe bifore hise iyen of his herte, and openeth the wai of treuthe. Treuli he that hastith not to leue worthili to God and redith of God, sekith not God to his helthe, but onli the kunnynge of God to ven glorie. Therfore thoug he rede euere he schal neuere fynde; as neithir philosophiris founden, wiche sougten for the same (f. 7 b) cause. Gessist thou that prestis of Saduceis redden not scripturis? but thei mygte not fynde God in hem, for thei wolde not lyue worthili to God; ffor goode wordis mygte not teche hem, the which here yuele werkis taugten, that is blyndid in errour. Ffor whi; sich is scripture to a man not willynge to lyue aftir God, as if ony man expounne lernynge of bataile to an erthe teliere[1] not hauynge will for to figte. And so agenward[2] of a knygt, thoug he here aldai wordis of his declaryng he mai no thing vndirstonde or take, for he hath no desire to his lore: ffor where is mannes desire, there his witt is dressid: this is the sentense of Crisostom[3].

But of all foolis blyndid of the deuel thise ben most folis, that seyn and mayntenen opynli that holi writ is fals. Ffor Dauid seith: *Alle the* (f. 8) *comoundementis of the lord ben feithful: tho ben maid in treuthe and equite*[3]. And eft, Dauid seith to God: *The begynnynge of thynne wordis is treuthe;* and eft he seith to God: *Thi laue is treuthe,* and eft, *Alle thyne comaundementis ben treuthe.* Item God seith, the viij. c. of Prouerbis, *Alle myne wordis ben rigtful, and no schrewid thyng and no weiward thyngis is in hem, tho ben rigtful to hem that vndirstonden, and thei ben euene to hem that fyndyn kunnynge.* Also in the xxxc. of Prou. holi writ seith: *Euery word of god is a scheld of feir*[4] that is purid in treuthe and charite, *to hem that hopyn in hym,* and Jon seith in the ende of Apocalips: *Thise wordis of the lord ben most feithful*[5], and oure lord Ihesu seith, *The lord is feithful in alle hise wordis and he is hooli in alle hese werkis*[6]. But thise heretikes seyn cursidli (f. 8b) that God is fals and his lawe ys fals, for if the lawe of God is fals, as thei seyn opynly, thanne God is fals sithen he is auctour of this lawe; and yit these folis seyn agens hem self, whanne thei seyn

---

[1] earth-tiller.    [2] on the other hand.
[3] Psal. cx. 8: cf. cxviii 160; *id.* cxli.; *id.* lxxxvi.
[4] Shield of fire; *purid,* purified.
[5] Apoc. xix. 9.    [6] Psal. cxliv. 13.

that hooli writ is fals: ffor yf it is holy, it is nat fals in ony maner, and agenward if it is fals, it is not hooli. Thise heretikis mys vndirstonden hooli writ and they clepin her owuene errour hooli writ, and thus the deuyl blyndith hem an disseywyth hem and be-iapith hem: as a drunke man demeth of a candele to be tweyne or thre, so these foolis demen that hooly writ hath many false vndirstondyngis where it hath oonli trewe vndirstondyng aftir the entent of the Hooli Gost. Therfore seynt Jerome and Ysedere seyn[1]: 24° q. 3°. c°. *heresis* et c°. *quidam*: Who euere vndirstondeth hooli writ othirwise than the Hooli Goost askith, of whom is wreten, he may be clepid an heretik; and seynt Austyn seith in his (f. 9) epistil to Jerom: If ony part of holy writ were fals al were suspect. Thise heretikis wolden menyn thus, that the text of hooli writ is fals, but here fleischli vndirstondyng is trewe and of auctorite, and thus thei magnefien hem self and her errour more than God and hooly writ. And thus thei ben opyn anticristis and moost perilous heretikis that euere risen vp agens hooli chirche, but as blasfemers of God were stoned of al the peple bi Goddis doom in Moises lawe, Leuetici xxiiij, so alle cristene men schulde stone thise heretikis and blasfemers bi stonis of the Gospel, that is scharp and opyn repreuynge, and castynge out of cristene lond.

But leue we alle thise cursidenessis biforeseid, and comforte we cristine peple to take trustili and deyutously[2] the text of hooly writ and the trewe vndirstondyng therof. Cristene men schulden preye deuoutli to God, auctor of al wisdom and kunnynge, that he giue to (f. 9b) hem trewe vndirstondyng of hooli writ. Thus seith the wyse man: *Lord, giwe thou to me wysdoom that stondith about the setis*[3], that I wete what failith to me and what is plesant befor thee in al tyme. The secund tyme, thei schulde meke hem silf to God in doynge penaunce that God opene to hem the trewe vndirstondyng of his lawe, as he openede witt to hise apostolis to vndirstonde hooli scripture. The thridde thei schulden sugette hem self to the wille of God, and bileue stidfastly that his laue is trewe, and trust feithfuli in Goddis help, and for this thei schullen haue the blissyng of God and the blesse of hewene, and schullen graciousli be herd in here preier; for God dispicith not the praier of meke men and he herith the desire of pore men that knowen verili that thei haue no good but of God. The fourthe tyme thei schulden meke hem self to here bretheren, and enquere mekeli of euery lerned man and speciali (f. 10) of wel-wellid[4] men and weel lyuynge the trewe vndirstondyng of hooli writ, and be thei not obstinat in ther owne wit but gyue

---

[1] In Gratian's *Decretum*.     [2] duteously.
[3] Sap. ix. 4.     [4] willed.

stede and credence to wiser men that han the sperit of wisdom
and of grace. The fifthe tyme, rede thei besili the text of the
newe testament and take thei ensample of the hooly liyf of Crist
and of hise apostilis, and truste thei fuili to the goodnesse of the
Hooli Goost, whic is spesial techere of wel willid men. Ffor
Crist seith in the gospel to hise disciplis: *The Hooli Goost schal
teche you al treuthe that is necessarie to helthe of soulis*[1]; and Joon
seith in his epistil: *That anoyntyng*, that is grace of the Hooli
Goost, *techith yow of all thingis that perteyneth to helthe of sowle*[2].
The sixte tyme, thei schulden see and studie the trewe and opyn
exposicion (f. 10 b) of hooli doctours and othere wise men as thei
may eseli and goodli come therto.

Lat cristene men trauaile feithfulli in thise vj weies, and be
not to moche aferid of obiectiouns of enemyes seyynge that *the
lettere sleeth*. Thise enemyes menyn thus: that the lettere of
hooli writ is harmful to men, and fals and repreuable[3], sithen
that it sleeth men by deeth of synne; but sekirli thei mystaken
the wordis of hooly writ, and here mystakyng and weiward
menynge and here wickide lyuynge bryngen in deeth of soule
that is synne. But agens here fals menynge Crist seith in the
gospel of Joon vi. cap. *The wordis wiche I haue spoken to you ben
sperit and liyf*, and in the same chapetre seynt Peter seith to
Crist, *Lord, thou hast wordis of euerlastyng liyf*. Poul seith
ij° T[h]ess. ij. that *the lord Ihesu bi the spirit of his mouth*, that
is his hooli and trewe wordis, *schal sle anticrist*, and the prophete
Isaie seith xj. c. that *God by the spirit of his lippis schal* (f. 11)
*sle the wickid man*, that is anticrist. Thanne sithen the wordis of
Crist ben wordis of euerlastyng liyf, that is, brynge trewe men to
euerlastyng blisse, and sithen thise wordis schulyn sle anticrist,
the wordis of Crist been ful hooly and ful migty and ful profitable
to trewe men. But Poul menyth thus by auctorite of the Hooly
Goost, whanne he seyth, *the lettere sleeth*, that cerymonyes eithir
sacrifices of the elde law withoutyn goostli vndirstondyng of the
newe lawe sleeth men bi errour of mysbileue; ffor if men holden
that bodeli circumcisioun is nedful now as it was in the elde
testament, it is errour and mysbileue agens the treuthe of the
gospel. Also if men holden that the sacrifice of bestes is nedful
now as it was bifore Cristis passioun, it is errour and mysbeleue
agens Crist and his gospel. Therfore this lettere vndirstonden thus
fleischli sleeth (f. 11 b) the mysvndirstonders; therfore Poul seith,
*the sperit quickeneth:* that is goostli vnderstondyng of ceremonyes
and sacrifices of Moises lawe quekeneth men of rigt bileue, that
now in stede of bodeli circumsisioun takyn baptym taugt and
comaundid of Crist, and in stede of sacrifices of bestis in the elde

---

[1] Ioh. xvi. 13.     [2] I Ioh. ii. 27.     [3] reprovable.

lawe takyn now Crist and his passioun and hopyn to be sawid
therbi with his mercy and here owene good lyuynge. Also the
lettere of the newe testament sleeth rebel men that lyuen ther
agens custumabli with-outtyn amendyng in this lif; ffor Crist in
the gospel seith to sich a rebel man, *The word wich I haue spoke
schal deme hym*, that is dampne hym, *in the laste day*[1]. Also God
seith: *I schal sle false men and rebel agens my lawe and I schal
make to lywe feithful men that kepyn my lawe*. Thanne thoug the
letere sleeth in maner beforseid, it sueth not therfore that the
lettere is fals and harmful to men, as it suith not that God (f. 12)
is fals and harmful in his kynde, thoug he sleeth iustli bi deeth of
bodi and of soule hem that rebellen fynaly agens his lawe. Also
this sentence, *the lettere sleeth*, schulde more make aferid proude
clerkis, that vndirstonden the trewthe of Goddis lawe and lyuen
custummabli ther agens, than symple men of witt that litil
vndirstonden the lawe of Crist and bisie hem to lywe weel in
charite to God and man; ffor thise proud clerkis the more thei
cunne Cristis lawe the more they make hem self dampnable for
here hig[h] cunnyng and here wickid lyuynge, and the symple
men for here lytyl cunnyng groundyn hem silf the more in
meknesse, and bisie hem to lerne the wei of saluacioun. Thus
thoug thei haue not tyme and leiser to turne and turne agen the
bokis of Goddis lawe to cunne the lettere therof, thei han and
kepyn the fruit and the veri sentence of al the lawe of God,
thourg kepyng of duble charite, as seynt Austyn seith (f. 12*b*) in
a sermoun of the preisyng of charite; and of ech symple man the
hooli prophete Dauid seith thus: *Blessid is the man whom, lord,
thow hast taugt, and hast enformyd hym of thi law*[2], that is charite;
and Deuteronomye it is seid, that *a lawe of fier*, that is charite,
*is in the rigt ho[n]d of God*[3].

The secunde obiectioun is this: proude clerkis seyn that lewid
men schulden not entirmete of[4] hooli writ, for in the xix. c. of
Exodi God (f. 13) comaundith vndir peyne of deth that neithir
beeste neither man, (out-takyn[5] Moyses and Aaron), stie[6] into the
hille where God apperid, and be this hille thei vndirstonden hooli
writ, which no man schulde touche but onli clerkis that ben
vndirstonden by Moises and Aaron. But this lewid obieccion
lettith as wel prestis as lewid men to entirmete of hooli writ,
which they vndirstonden to entre in to the hille, ffor in the same
chapetre aftirward God comondith that prestis schulde not stie
in to the same hille; therfore thei take fleischli and weiwardli
this hille to vndirstonde therbi hooli writ. Ffor God comandith

---

[1] Ioh. xii. 48.        [2] Psal. xciii. 12.        [3] Deut. xxxiii. 2.
[4] meddle with.        [5] except.        [6] ascend into

[by] Josue c. i., that was duk[1] of the peple and of the lenage of
Effraem [that the people] schulde studie both nygt and dai the
lawe of God, and the same charge God gyueth to the kyng in
the xvij. c. of Deuteronomye. Also God seith generali to the
peple of Israel, Exodi xij. that *the laue of God be euere in here
mouth*, and the wiseman seith, Eccl. vj. to ech man, *Al thi
tellyng be in the comaundementis of God*, and oure lord Ihesu seith
to hise apostlis, Marc. vltimo. *Preche ye the gospel to eueri
creature*, that is to euery staat of men, and God comaundith in
Moises lawe that tho bestis that chewe not code be demed
vnclene; that is that alle thei that tretyn not and thinke not and
speke not of the lawe of God, after that thei han herd it, ben
vnclene bi Goddis doom and vnable to[2] blisse. Therfore Dauid
(f. 13 b) seith: *I schal blesse the lord in al time: his heriynge*[3] *schal be
euere in my mouth*. It is of fendes weiwardnesse to forbede cristene
men to fede here soulis on Goddis word, ffor God seith Deut.º
viij. *A man liwith not in bred alone, but in ech word that cometh
forth of Goddis mouth*, and the same sentense is confermid bi
Crist Ihesu in the gospel, M[t] iiijº. Thanne sithen Ihesu Crist
ordayneth his word to be sustynaunce of mennys sowlis, it is a
fendis condicion to refreine cristene men fro this goostli mete,
sithen with-outyn it thei mowe not liuen in grace neither comen
to bliss. Also God seith, Amos viij. *I shall send hungyr on the
herthe: not hungir of breed neithir thourst of watir, but to heer the
word of God:* as it were a gret cruelte to with-holde bodeli mete
and drynk fro hungri men and thoursti, and tho withholderis
schulde ben gelti of bodeli (f. 14) deeth of the same men, so it is a
moche grettere cruelte to with holde goostli mete, that is Goddis
word, fro cristene men that hungryn and thoursten therafter, that
is, desiren it gretli to kunne and to kepe it to teche it othere men
for the staat that thei stonde inne; and thise witholders ben
cursid of God and been sleeris of mennys soulis. Ffor God seith,
Prou. xjº. *He that hideth whete shall be cursid among the peple*.
But skilefulli[4] cristene men reden and stodien hooli writ to
cunne it and kepe it, for Crist seith in the gospel, M[t] xxijº *I have
maad redi my mete, my bolis*[5] *and my volatilis ben slayn and alle
thyngis ben redi: come ye to the weddyngis;* wher on Crisostom
writeth thus: what euere thyng is sougt for helthe of soul, now
al is [ful]fillid in [s]cripturis; he that is vnkunnynge schal fynde
there that he owith to lerne; he that is rebellour and synnere
schal fynde there the scourgis of doom to comynge, which he

---

[1] leader.        [2] unfit for.        [3] praise. Psal. xxxiii. 2.
[4] reasonably.
[5] bulls, Matt. xxii. 4. Both Wycliffite versions have *volatilis*, fowls,
through confusion with the correct *altilia*, fatlings.

owith to drede; he that trawailith schal fynde there (f. 14 b) the glorie of biheste of euerlastynge liyf, and while he etith this scripture, that is bileueth kepith and holdeth in mynde, he schal be more sterid to good werk; he that is of litil corage and sike in his soule schal fynde there mene metis of rigtwisnesse, and thoug thise mene metis makyn not the soule fat, that is parfit in goostli lyuynge, natheles tho suffre not the soule to die; he that is of grett corage and feithful schal fynde there goostli metis of more continent liyf, that is mor parfit liyf, and thise metis bryngyn him nig[h] to the kynde of angels; he that [is] smetyn of the deuil and woundid with synnes schal fynde there medicinable metis that schullen reparaile him to goostli helthe bi penaunce. Nothyng faylith in this feste that is nedful to helthe of mankynde: that is hooli [s]cripture.

The thridde lewde obieccion is this: Goddis lawe tellith, ij⁰ Reg. vj⁰. that Oza the dekene[1] was sodeynli slayn by Goddis veniaunce, for he heeld forth his hond and touchide (f. 15) the arke of God whanne it was in perel to falle, and by this arke wordli clerkis vndirstonden hooli writ; thanne sithen this dekene Oza was slayn of God for he touchide the arke whanne he hadde leyn with his howne wif in the nygt before, as diuerse doctoris seyn, moche more lewid men schulden han more weniaunce[2] of God if thei touchyn the arke, that is hooli writ, whanne thei ben in grettere synnes thanne this dekene was inne. This obieccion of wordli clerkis is so lewid and so opynli groundid on falshede that it nedeth noon answere, no but for men of litil vndirstandyng. It is knowe bi the text of Moises lawe that the dekenes schulde bere the arke of God on here schulders, as it is writen, Num. vij⁰., this dekne hadde this veniaunce for he putte the arke on vnresonable bestis to bere it, whanne he (f. 15 b) schulde haue bore it on his owene schuldres, and not for he lai bi his owene wif in the nigt bifore. Ffor no text of Goddis lawe nethir ony doctur of auctorite tellith this cause of liynge bi his wif, as seynt Jerom and Lire seyn on the same lettere; but this storie that the arke was put on vnresonable bestis and that the veniaunce of God cam sodeynli on him that putte it on the bestis figurith this treuthe: that the hige veniaunce of God schal com on hem that putten the cure of mennys soulis on flescli foolis and vnkunnynge of Goddis lawe, and not wilful to trauaile aboute helthe of mennys sowlis; wich cure schulde be put oneli on hooli men and kunnynge of Goddis lawe, and wilful to performe the goostli cure and ensample of Crist and hise apostilis. Ffor as Gregor and Grosted seyn, to make vnable curatis is the higeste wikkidnesse and tresun agens (f. 16) God, and is like synne as to crucifie Crist.

[1] deacon.          [2] vengeance.

Therfore not withstondynge thise lewide obieccions, as Crist strecchid forth hise armes and hise hondes to be nailid on the cros, and hise leggis and hise feet also, and bowide doun the heed to schewe what lowe he hadde to mankynde, so alle cristene peple schulde strechyn forth here armes and hondis and alle here menbris to enbrace to hem silf the lawe of God thourg veri bileue and trewe obedience therto, and trewe mayntenaunce therof to here lyues ende. Ffor Crist seith in the gospel: *If a man knowlechith me be for men, thanne I schal knowleche him bifor my fader and his angelis. And eft if a man schame me and myne wordis, I schal schame him bifore the aungelis of God*[1].

## 5. *Purvey's Epilogue to his Comment on S. Matthew's Gospel.*

For the date and authorship of this comment or gloss, see *supra*, pp. 275–8. The text of the gloss is found in Laud Misc. 235, ff. 263 col. 1–264 *b* col. 1; Trin. Camb. 36, ff. 7–104, and in Lord Dillon's MS. ff. 1–264. It has two prologues and this epilogue: one prologue Purvey embedded in the *Gen. Prol.* (see *supra*, p. 281), and the epilogue largely coincides with one of his set of tracts in defence of biblical translations (see *supra*, p. 273).

The prologue *Saint Austin saith in the second book of Christian doctrine* (cf. FM, I. viii) occurs in Laud Misc. 235, ff. 1 col. 1–2 *b* col. 1, and as a "prologue to the gospel of Matthew" in a collection of prologues to the gospels in Harl. 6333 (printed from this MS. in FM, I. 44–49). The original form of the prologue is probably that of Laud Misc. 235 (*Saint Austin saith...abate soon Antechrist's malice, hypocrisy and tyrantry*), where Purvey gave a free translation of Ticonius' seven rules for the understanding of scripture, as quoted by S. Augustine in his *De Doctrina Christiana*, and continued "For this cause a sinful caitiff, having compassion on lewid men, declareth the gospel of Matthew to lewid men in English," with complaints against those who persecuted the Lollards. The first part of the prologue he paraphrased, and in many sentences copied, when in writing the *Gen. Prol.* he had completed his analysis of the biblical books of the O.T., and explained the traditional four interpretations of scripture. He was without the books he needed (see *Gen. Prol.* FM, I. 48), and therefore recopied his own quotations from the *De Doct. Chris.*, pp. 44–49, stopping short when the references to S. Matthew's gospel began. [This prologue and its counterpart in the *Gen. Prol.* cannot be independent translations of the *De Doct. Chris.*, because the translation is not continuous, and the same lines are selected for translation in the same order. The prologue could scarcely have been copied, reversing the order, from the *Gen. Prol.*, because its verbal quotations from the *De Doct. Christ.* are more direct: pro-

[1] Luc. xii. 8.

logue, "Austin saith thus, 'Be thou ware that thou take not figurative speech to the letter, for hereto pertaineth the apostle's word, saying, the letter slayeth, truly the Spirit,' that is, ghostly understanding, 'maketh it to live'"; *Gen. Prol.* "It is to beware in the beginning that we take not to the letter a figurative speech, for then, as Paul saith, the letter slayeth, but the spirit, that is, ghostly understanding, quickeneth," etc. (see FM, I. 44).]

The second prologue (*The Holy Ghost saith by the prophet Zachary...
and come by God's mercy to the endless bliss of heaven. Jesu king of
mercy, of peace and charity, that sheddest thy precious blood for the love
of men's souls, grant this end. Amen*) precedes the text in Trin. Camb.
36, f. 7, and Lord Dillon's MS., f. 1 b. In the part describing the
writer's method of quotation from holy doctors (Lord Dillon's MS.
f. 7), it is almost a paraphrase of Purvey's prologue to the gloss on
Luke.

The epilogue, which is here printed from Laud Misc. 235, ff. 263
col. 1–264 b col. 1, in this MS. follows the text of the gloss. The
first part describes the use of authorities in the gloss on Matthew;
the last part (not divided by any break) is a lament for the opposition
of antechrist to the preaching of the gospel, and is found among
Purvey's tracts in defence of English scriptures in Ii. 6. 26, p. 98
(cf. FM, I. xiv).

The MSS. of Purvey's glosses on the other gospels are: S. Mark,
Lord Dillon's MS.; S. Luke, Kh. 2. 9, Bodl. 143, Bodl. 243; S. John,
Bodl. 243, Trin. Camb. 36. For Purvey's pseudonyms in all of them,
see *supra*, p. 276.

## Epilogue. (f. 263, col. 1)

Blessyd be almygti God in trynyte: here endith a schort glose
on Matheu, whyche [is] takun of holy docturis, Jerome, Austyn,
Ambrose, Gregori, Crisostom, Bernard, Grosthed, Rabanes, and
othere mo, as is teld in the first prologe[1]. The writer of this glos
purposide to Goddis onour and helpe of cristen soulis, for to telle
treuly holy writ, and schortly and pleynly the moste profitable
sentence of these byforeseid doctours; and hidurto, blessid be
God of his grete gyfte and graciouse, this pore scribeler is not
gilti in his concience, that he erride fro treuthe of holy writ and
very sentence of these doctouris. If ony lerned man in holy writ
se this glos: dispise he not it without good examinacoun of olde
origynalis of doctouris; for this scribeler hadde trauelid with[2]
fals bookis, to see many and chese the beste and clereste sentence
acordynge with holy writ and resoun. If ony lerned man in holy
writ fynde ony defaute in this glos: sette he in the trewe and
cler sentence of holy doctouris; for this is the grete desire of this
pore scribeler.

[1] The writer was thus aware that there were two prologues: see *supra*.
[2] *many* expunctuated.

Wondre not, lernide men, though Rabanes be myche alleggid in this glos, for he was an old doctur almest of sixe hundrid yeeris agon, (f. 263, 2) and hadde plente of olde docturrs whiche he rehersith in his book thoroughout, and in it seith of himself; and yit he touchith no but pleyn mater, whiche may lightly be prouyd by holy writ and resoun. Therfore men holden the sentence profitable and trewe, though he hadde spokun no word therof; but we knowen it the betere for his writynge and declarynge.

We geuen greet credence to these olde holy doctouris, namely Austyn, Crisostom, Ierom, Gregorie, Ambrose and suche olde seyntis, namely marterid for holy writ, and that for thre causes. Oo cause, for her oldenesse and holynesse. The secunde cause is, for her grete kunynge and trauel in holy writ, and so long approuynge, holy chirche approuynge of her bookis for goode and trewe. The thridde cause and moste of all is this: for thei acordiden so myche with holy writ and resoun in spekynge and lyuynge, and weren euere meke and redy to be amendid, if ony man coude fynde defaute by holy writ or resoun in her writynge; and thei chargiden neuere neither constreynede ony man to take her bookis, but comaundiden men to byleue not to her bokis, no but in as myche as thei weren groundid in holy writ expresly, or in pleyn and sufficient resoun. Wherfore seynt Austyn, souereyneste of oure Latyn docturis, seith on the lxvi salm, the firste vers: If Y seye, no man byleue it; if Crist seith, wo to him that byleueth not. Eft[1] Austyn on the firste pistil of Ioon, in the ende, seith thus to his aduersarie: If Y seie, dispise it; if gospel spekith, be thou war. Eft Austyn in the firste book of the trynyte seyth thus: Who euer redith (f. 263 b, 1) these writyngis, where he is certeyn with me, go he with me, seke he with me; where he knowith his errour, come he agen to me; where he knowith myn errour, he agenclepe[2] me: so entre we togidere in to the weye of charite, goynge to him of whom it is seid: seke ye euer the face of hym. Y haue made this couenaunt pitouse and sikere byfore youre lord God, with alte hem that reden tho thingis that y write, and in alle my writyngis, and moste in these in whiche the unyte of trynete is sought. Also if he that redith my writyngis undirstondith othere men in that word, in whiche [he] undirstondith not me: leye he my book asidis, or cast awey, if it semeth good to him; and geue he trauel and tyme to hem that he undirstondith. Also he that redith my writyngis, and seith: Y undirstonde what is seid, but it is not seid treuly: afferme he or proue his sentence as it plesith, and reproue he my sentence, if he may; if he schal do this with charite and treuthe,

---

[1] again.          [2] contradict.

and schal make this knowen to me, if Y dwel in lyif, Y schal take the most pituouse [sic] fruyt of this my trauel. Also in the viii booke of the trynyte Austyn seith: Alle the bildyngis or makyngis of Goddis bookis [a]risen for [that] feith, hoope and charite to be bildid in mannes soule. Eft Austyn seith in the first bok agenes Faustus in xi. cº.: The excellence of autorite of the olde testament and newe, is departid from bokis of latter men, whiche confermed in tyme of the postlis, by successiouns or aftercomyngis of bischopis, and bryngynge forth of cristen chirches, is set hig[h]ely as in sete to whiche alle feithful and pitouse [sic] undirstondyng (f. 263 b, 2) serueth; there if ony thing myssownynge styre[1]: it is not leuful to seie. The autour of this book helde not treuthe, but if he may seie; The bok is fals, or interpretour or translatour erride. Or thou undirstondist not for-sothe in litle werkis [2] of lattere men that ben conteyned in bokis without noumbre, but in no maner euened[3] to the alle holyeste excellence of canoun scripturis, or reulis of holy writ, yhe in whiche euer of hem the same treuthe is foundun: netheles the autorite is fer uneuene treuly in these lattere mennes bokis; if ony thingis in hap ben gessid to discorde fro treuthe, for thei ben undirstondun as ben seid: netheles the reder or herer hath there fre demynge[4] bi whiche ether he approue that that plesith, or reproue that that offendeth, and therfore alle siche thingis, no but[5] they be defendid or mayntened by serteyn resoun, or by the ilke autorite of holy writ, that it be schewid either on alle maner to be so, or that it mygte be don so: that thing that is disputid or told there, if it displesith to ony man, or he wole not bileue: he is not reproued. But in the ilke hignesse of holy scripturis, yhe of a profete or postle or gospeler is declarid by the ilke confirmacoun of reule to have set ony thing in his letteris: it is not leueful to doute that it is soth; elles no book schal be by whiche the sekeness of mannes ignoraunce schal be gouerned, if the moste leueful autorite of these bookis either dispisid be al don aweye, either forbodun[6] be confoundid.

A litil byfore (f. 264, 1) in the same chapitre Austyn seith: We ben amonge hem of whiche the postle seith: and if ye undirstonden in other maner ony thing, also God schal schewe it to you, whiche kynde of lettris, that is of latere seyntis is to be red, not with nede of byleuynge, but with fredom of deniynge; and in the secunde book, xii. c., many men han writun manye thingis of the lettris of holy chirche that is not writ not by autorite of reule, but by sum studie of helpyng or lernynge.

---

[1] arise.  
[2] in detail the works.  
[3] comparable to.  
[4] freedom of judgment.  
[5] unless.  
[6] forbidden.

Also Austyn seith thus, and the comyn lawe rehersith him in
thre maner. Y geue this onour to holy writ, that I dar not seie
that ony of tho autours erride in writynge; if Y fynde in tho
bokis ony thing contrary to treuthe: Y dar seie noon other
thinge, than that the bok is fals, either the translatour erride,
or Y undirstonde not it. Y rede so other writeris or expositouris,
that hou greet euer holynesse or doctryn they hau, not therfore
Y gesse it to be sothe, for thei feeliden or undirstonden so, but
for thei mygten proue to me by other autours, that is, of holy
writ, either by resoun of reule ether probable that it is soth, that
thei seyen. Al this seith Austyn.

Also seynt Ierome on the secunde c. of Ionas the profete seith
thus: Y undirstonde this, that Crist schal be thre dayes and thre
nygtis in the herte of erthe, that a part of the firste day be takun
for al the day, and the Saterday hole and the first part of the
Sunday for al the Sunday. If ony man betere interprete the mys-
tries of this letter, sue thou his sentence. Eft Ierome on xxiii. c.
of Mattheu: For [that] this seiynge hath not autorite (f. 264, 2)
of holy scripture, it is dispisid.

A[h]¹ dere God, lord of treuthe, my litle wit suffisith not for
to wondre on the blyndenesse and pride of sum prestis, whiche
constreynen² cristen men for to byleue to her lawes, statutis and
customes by peynes of dampnacioun, as they feynen, and by
bodily peynes, thorou blyndenesse of cristen kyngis and lordis,
whanne cristen men knowen not the ground of these lawis,
nether in holy writ, nether in resoun; but thei semen agenes
Cristis techyng and lyuyng³ and his postlis, and brougt yn for
pride and coueitise of worldly⁴ prestis, for to charge more the
puple⁵ in cost than Crist and his apostlis ordeyneden.

Alas! gode Ihesu, louer and sauyour of⁶ mennes soules: whi
ben⁷ newe statutis of worldly⁴ prestis magnefied aboue thyn holy
gospel, confermed with⁸ preschous blood and treuthe of thi
godhed?

Alas! gode spouse of cristen soulis, Ihesu Crist⁹: whi forsakest
thou so myche thi puple, that sinful mennes ordenaunce ben
openly taugt and maytened by worldly⁴ prestis and her fau-
tours¹⁰: and thyn ordenaunce, of wilful pouerte and greet¹¹

---

¹ The principal variants henceforth given from this tract as in Ii. 6. 28,
pp. 98 ff.          ² contrarion.
³ P. 105. And thei that wolden brynge yn agen this lord thi best ordinaunce: been slaundred pursued cursed and prisond. And peyned to the
deeth of bodi.
    ⁴ prelates and.          ⁵ pepel, throughout.          ⁶ of feithful.
    ⁷ ben these.          ⁸ with thin.
    ⁹ A few lines extra: sin hath great maistry, etc.          ¹⁰ mainteneris.
    ¹¹ grettistn.

mekenesse of clerkis, and continuel[1] ocupacioun of hem in
studiynge and techyng holy writ, is dispisid and holdun errour,
and they holdun cursid and foreprisoned that wolden brynge
agen thi beeste ordenaunce?

Alas, alas, alas! ye cristen puple, whi suffre ye worldly[2]
prestis to robbe[3] you of Goddis word, sustenaunce for youre
soules, and of your worldly goodis[4] by vertu of deed leed or rotun
wex, getun[5] thorou symonye[6]? be ye war, for Crist seith, *if the
blynde ledith the blynde: they bothe fallen in to lake*[7]: and certis, ye
schulen not be excusid by ignoraunce[8] of Goddis (f. 264 *b, 1*) lawe,
for ye mygten kunne[9] it if ye wolden seke it of godly disyre, and
good lyuynge after kyndely[10] resoun writun of God in youre
soulis; and as bisily seke it of trewe prestis, as ye seken worldly
goodis of worldly men. Therfore eche cristen man and woman
bisie hym in all his mygtis to lerne and kepe Goddis heestis[11],
to ocupye his wittis in spekynge[12] of Cristis gospel, for therynne
is all comfort and sikirnesse of cristen soulis, for to come to the
blisse of heuen. Crist Ihesu, kyng of mercy, wysdom and charite:
make thi puple to knowe verily and kepe feithfuly thyn holy
gospel: and to caste awey antecristis errours, and veyn bondis
that tarieth many men fro feith and charite, and cumbren
many men in endeles dispeyr[13].

## 6. *Purvey's Sixteen Points.*

Purvey's authorship of this tract may be assumed from (*a*) its
following immediately Purvey's *Agens hem that seyn that hooli writ
schulde not or may not be drawun in to Engliche*, in the unique MS.
Trin. 333, ff. 30 *b*–34. The tracts are by the same scribe, and would
appear to have been copied by him from the same MS. (*b*) The
noticeably moderate and scholarly character of the articles, combined
with the late date of post 1400, strongly suggest it. The moderation
is seen by comparison with an earlier Lollard tract of the same sort,
in which *Twenty-five points* are discussed, *These bene tho poyntus that
worldely prelates at tho suggestione of freres putten on (impute to) pore
Cristen men, and what thai graunten ande what thai denyen*, printed
*Sel. Eng. Works*, III. 454–96. These were circulated in 1388–89 (see
*id.* 454), and while explaining the Lollard position, did not attempt

---

[1] fruytful.
[2] prelates and.
[3] bereve.
[4] and oure this thei spoilen you of.
[5] dead lead or rotten wax, gotten.
[6] extra words.
[7] ditch.
[8] unkunning.
[9] knowe.
[10] natural.
[11] commandments.
[12] longer spekynge.
[13] Ii. 6. 26, p. 102, after *endless despair*, has Jhesu mercy! Jhesu helpe!
for now is tyme of nede: as gret as euer was fro the bigynnynge of the world
unto this tyme. Amen.

to minimise or split hairs, as the *Sixteen Points* do. The traces of
north-midland dialect in the *Twenty-five points* (gafe; dos, sais) would
not support Purvey's authorship of that tract: but the southern
dialect of the *Sixteen Points* is consistent with it. (*c*) The attitude of
compromise adopted throughout the tract, and the greater moderation than that of the *General Prologue*, would well suit a Lollard
leader who had persuaded his conscience to a recantation, like Purvey:
and exactly fits Thorpe's description of Purvey in 1407 as "neither
hot nor cold" (see *supra*, p. 285).

*Thes ben the poyntis wiche ben putte be bishcoppis ordinares
vpon men, which thei clepen Lollardis.* (f. 30*b*)

The ffirst, the brede or the oost[1] in the auter sacrid of the
prest it is very Goddis body: but it is the same bred in kynde
that it was before. The secunde that schrift of mouthe is not
nedeful to helthe of soule, but only sorowe of hert doth awey
euery synne. The thred that no man is holdoun to tithe in
manere nowe vsed of the chirche but such tithis and ofiringes
be[2] the lawe of God schuld be deled to the pore nedi men. The
fourte that ther is no pope, nether was any sith the tyme of seint
Peter the pope. The ffifte that neither bischoppis neither popis
curs byndith any man not but him that is ffirst cursed of God.
The sexte that neither pope nether bischoppe may graunt any
pardoun, but the lest prest hath as myche power to graunte
suche pardoune as the pope. The seuent that ther schulde be
bot oo[3] degre aloone of prestehod in the chirche of God, and
euery good man is a prest and hath power to preche the worde
of God. The eigte that neither the pope may make lawes, neither
bischopis constitucouns, and that no man is holden to kepe suche
lawes and constituciouns made be bischopis or popis. The
nynthe is that it is agens the lawe of God that bischopis and
other prelatis of the chirche schulden haue temporal possessions,
for by Goddis lawe thei schulden go oon fote preching the worde
of God. The tente that is that prestis weren not ordeyned to
sey massis or mateynes, but onli to teche and preche the worde
of God. The eleventhe that it is not leful (f. 31) to preye to seint
Marie neither seientis seying the latanye[4] or other orisouns, but
onli to God men owen[5] to preie. The tuelfthe that neither crosse
ne ymages peynted or grauen in the worschip of God or any other
seyntes in the chirche schuld be worschipid, and thoug a man
sauye[6] before him the same crosse were on Crist sufferred deth
he schulde not worschipe it, ffor as it is seid al that worschipen
the crosse or ymages ben cursed and done mawmentri[7]. The

---

[1] host.                [2] by.                 [3] one.
[4] litany.              [5] ought.              [6] saw.
[7] idolatry.

thrittenete it [is] not medeful neither leueful to go on pilgrimage. The ffourtenete that it is not leueful to sustene ligttis in the chirche before the crucifix, neither before any other ymages. The ffiftenete that it is not leueful to sle any man neither in dome[1] neither ougt of dome, neither Sarsines[2] neither paynemes be batel as knyttes done, wane thei asailen the hooli londe, for it is seide in the Gospel that thou schalt not sle. The sixtenete that exorsismes don in the chirche as halowing of the watur, brede, and salt and askis[3] and such other ben pure craft of nigromancie wiche is the worschiping of the fende.

Who euer schal see thes sixtene poyntes be he wele ware that in eueriche of hem is hidde trewthe and falsehed, and who that euer grantith al, grauntith myche falsehede, and who that euer denyeth al, denyeth many trewthes. Therfore witte wel this, that wane a coupulatif[4] is madde, thoug ther be many trewthes, if it afferme a falshed it schal be denyed altogidur: falsenes is so venemus. Trewe cristen men schulden answere here aviseliche, trewliche, and mekeliche to the poyntis and articulis that ben put agens hem. Aviseliche that thei speike not vnkonnyngliche, trwliche that thei speike not falseliche, and mekeliche that thei speike not prowdeliche in her answere, and than schalt be grace in ther speiking or answering be the helpe of Crist. (f. 31 b)

Ffor cristen men schulden beleue that sacrament on the auter is verrely Cristis body sacramentli and spirituali and mo other maners than any erthely man can telle amonge vs, ffor Crist that mai not lye seid schewyng the bred that he helde in his hande: *This is my bodi;* and therfore seith Jerom in his epistile to Elbedie: Here we: the brede that Crist brack and gaf to his discipulis to ete was his owne bodi, for he seide, *This is my body:* and so be oure beleue it is both Cristis bodi and bred of lyfe, and so God forbede that we schulde seie that this blessid sacrament were but breed, for that were an heresye, as to sey that Crist is man and not god. But we seyn that it is bothe brede and Cristis body, rigt as Crist is both God and man, as seint Austin seith; and seint Hillari seith, the bodi of Crist that is taken of the auter is figure, sith bred and wyne ben seen withougt-forthe[5], and it is verri trewthe, sith Cristis body and his blood is beleued withinne forthe: *hec ibi*[6].

Also we graunteyn that schrifte of mouthe is nedeful to al suche that ben counselid of God for to make it mekeliche. But yut very contricoun is more nedeful, ffor whi? withougten schirft of mouthe may a syneful man be saued in many a caas. But

---

[1] judgment.          [2] Saracens.
[3] ashes.          [4] copulative.
[5] outwardly.          [6] I.e. "here ends my quotation."

withougten veri contricioun of herte, mai no syneful man of discrecioun be saued. Therfore seith the comyn lawe, as autorite witnesses, the wylle of a man is rewarded, not the werke. Will is in contricoun of hert and werke is in scrifte of mouthe, therfore it is certeyn clerer thane ligt, that synnes ben forgeuen be contricioun of hert: *hec ibi.* Therfore very contricioun is the essencial parte of penance and confecioun of mouthe is the accidental parte, but natheles confessioun of hert (f. 32) done to the hige prest Crist is as nedeful as contricoun.

Also we graunten that men ben holden and boundoun be the boonde of manis lawe and counsel, not contrarie to goddis lawe, to paie tithus and offrynges to curatis in al trewe manere nowe vsed, for that ende that curatis do ther office as God hath comanded hem; and if thei lyuen as curatis schulden, and spenden the goodis of the chirche to Goddis worschippe in hem self and other pore puple, thane ben the tithus paied to the pore men and nedi, for thei hem self ben pore.

Also we beleuen that our lord Ihesu Crist was and is cheffe bischoppe of his chirche, as seint Peter seith, and schal be vnto the dai of dome; and we supposen that ther han ben many hooli faderris popis sithen seint Petrus tyme, thoug this name pope be not seid in Goddis lawe: as seint Clement, seint Clete[1], and other many moo. And so we graunten that the pope of Rome schulde next folowe Crist and seint Peter in maner of lyuynge, and if he do so he is worthily pope, and if he contrarie hem moost of al other, he is most anticrist.

Also we graunten that neither bischoppis curse ne popis bynden any man anemptis[2] God, but if that bonde acorde with the bonde of God: and if a man is vnrigtfuly cursed of the pope or of the bischope, for Goddis cause, if he suffer it pacientli, he schal fare myche the better for the curse: and thei that cursen schullen fare myche the wers. Ffor as seint Austin seith, I seie not this foole hardili: that if any man is cursed wrongfulliche it schal harme hym rather that curseth thane him that sufferith this curse, ffor the Hooly Goost puttith no such peyne of curse to any man vnderserued.

Also we graunten that bothe the pope (f. 32 b) and bischoppis moun[3] lefully and medefully[4] graunte such pardouns and indulgence as ben grunded in hooli write and that in thre maners. Oon is that thei moun bi ther office denounce or schewe the wille of God houg he forgeueth synne, and that trewe denounsi[n]g is forgiuyng be ther office of presthode. In the secunde maner thei

---

[1] Clement and Cletus, both early popes whose names occur in the canon of the mass.          [2] with regard to.
[3] may.          [4] lawfully and profitably.

moun forgeue and relese penance folily[1] enioyned to men, and
foly avowes[2] and boondis that men haue bounden hem self with,
and that is clepid indulgence or dispensacioun.  And in the
thridde maner thei moun [forgeue] trespas that men han doun
agens hem in as myche as lith in hem, and so it is vndurstanden
that Crist seith in the gospel: *Forgeueth, and it schal be forgiuen
to yow*, and thus what euer synnes they schullen forgiue, thei
ben forgeuen, and what euer thei lo[o]sen vpon the erthe it
schal be losed in heuene.  Netherles [the] sale [of] pardouns that
smacchen[3] symonye maketh bothe the graunter and hym that
bieth it acursed of God.

Also we graunten that the state of prestis schulden be oon in
very vnite, and the order is al oon as anempte the substance,
both in the pope and bischopis and symple prestes.  But the
degrees in hem ben diuerse, both heier and lower.  And as God
hath graunted hem the keies of power and knouyng of his lawe,
so al prestes of office[4] han euene[5] power of ordere of presthode.
But summe passen other in power of iurisdiccioun and in excellence of the keies, kunnynge, and thoug lewde men ben good
lyueris and wise men, yit ben thei not prestes of office, ne thei
be not bounden to preche of office: al be yit that thei be prestes
spirituali, as seith Crisostom and Lyncolne, and so thei may teche
ther wyfes, ther children and ther seruantis to be of good maners.

Also we graunten that popis mown medefully make lawes and
(f. 33) decres, and bischoppis constituciouns, and kings statutis,
so that thilke lawes and ordinaunce further men to kepe the lawe
of God: and than men ben holden to kepe hem, and if thei make
any lawes contrarie to Cristis lawe, men ben as grettly bounden
to agenstande thoo wicked lawes as thei ben bounden to keep
ther good lawes; and therfore seith God be Ezechiel the prophete:
*Nil ye go[6] in the comaundements of your faders, neither kepe ye ther
doomys, neither be ye defouled in her mawmentis.  But kepith my
mandementis and my lawes and my domes.*

Also we granten that bischoppis acordyngly with Goddis lawe
mown haue temporal goodis and possessiouns in resunable
mesure, so that thei spenden hem as goddis awmyners[7], and not
holding hem as wordely[8] lordes: ffor Crist seith in the gospel: Ye
schullen not haue lordschipis as lordes and kynges of the puple[9],
and seint Peter seith: *Be ye not hauynge lordschipe in the clergye[10]*;
and so thoug boschoppis ride or go, so thei do wel ther office thei
ben excused.

---

[1] foolishly.                     [2] vows.                         [3] smack of.
[4] ex officio.                     [5] equal.
[6] Walk ye not. Ezek. xx. 18.                                     [7] almoners.
[8] worldly.                       [9] Cf. Marc. x. 42.             [10] 1 Pet. v. 3.

Also we graunten that prestes weren ordeyned of Crist to teche
and preche the puple, and not onli that but also to preie and to
mynyster the sacramentis of God and lyue wille; and of goode
ordinaunce of hooli chirche thei ben ordeyned be men to seie
bothe matynes and messis, in wiche ben conteyned gospellis and
pistillis and other bokis of hooly wrigte, for that ende that thei
schulden aftur ther redinge declare it to the puple in ther modur
tounge. Ffor seint Poule seith: *I wole that alle prestes speike with
langages*, as ben orisouns and lessouns in Latyn, *But more I wole
that thei preche*[1].

Also we graunten that it is both leueful and medeful to preie
to oure lady and to alle halownus[2], so that the entent of oure
preiour be do principally to Goddis worschipe. And in oure
preiour we schulden not thenke that our lady or other seyntis
mown graunte any (f. 33b) thing of hem self. But thei knowen
Goddis wille and preien that it be fully don and so ther preier is
herde. And so the letanye is rigt good and it be wel vsed. But
wane prestis or religious singen the latanye for pride, for ipocrisie,
or for couaitise, than thei plesen not God but the fende and the
worlde, wiche ben the maistris that thei serueu.

Also we beleuen that neither the crosse that Crist was don
vpon, neither any other Roode or ymage maad of mannys hand,
schulde be worschipid as God ne as resonabel creaturis. ffor wo
so euer worschipith hem so doth mawmentrie and is cursed.
But natheles the making of ymages trewly peyntid is leueful,
and men mowen leuefuliche worschippe hem in sum manere as
signes or tokones; and that worschipe men done to hem, if thei
louen hem and vsen hem to that ende that thei ben ordeyned
fore, (as clerkis don her bokis), dispising the avowes, preiers and
sacrifice and misbeleues vnlawfully don to hem.

Also we graunten that it is leueful and medeful to go on
pilgrimage to heuen warde doing werkes of penance, werkis of
rigtfulnes, and werkis of mercy, and to suche pilgrimage allen
men ben boundun after ther power wile thei lyuen here, ffor the
prophete seith in the sawter booke: *Lorde, be thow not stille, for
I am a straunger and a pilgrime as alle my fadris weren*[3]. Suche
pilgrimage may we wel do without scheching[4] of dede ymages
and of schrynes.

Also we graunten that it is leueful in mesure [to have] ligttis
before ymages and holde torchis before the auter so that it be
doune principally for the worschip of God and not to the ymages,
and other werkis of rigtwissenes and of mercy to be not left
therfore; ffor Crisostom seith thei that honouren chirchis don a

---

[1] 1 Cor. xiv. 5.　　　　　[2] saints.
[3] Psal. xxxviii. 13.　　　[4] seeking.

goode werke if thei kepine other werkis of rigtfulnes. But men schulden as wel (f. 34) sette suche ligte in the chirche thoug the ymages weren aweye, as thoug thei weren there, or ellis the loue that thei gyuen ymages smacchen mawmentrie.

Also we graunten that it is leueful to sle men in dome and in batellis, if tho that doun it han autorite and leue of God, and if thei sleen any man Cristen or hethen agens the autorite of God thei ben acursed and breken the comaundement of Good, and so it is like that fewe or none ben nowe slayne be the autorite of God.

Also we graunten that halowing of holy watur, of brede, salt, and asken ben leueful, for thei ben deuougte preiers and blessings and ther is noon exorsisioun don on holibred but a preier as good as our gracis; and not alle exorsisiouns ben craft of nigramancye and worchinge of the fende, ffor Crist and his apostilis vseden the office of an exorciste in casting ougt of fendes to mannys saluacoun. Natheles tho that setten her bileue that euery drope of hooli watur doth awey a synne, and taketh none heede how hali watur is a token that we haue euer more nede of repentance in hooly chirche alle the wile we lyuen, ben foule bigilid.

# INDEX

Titles of treatises, etc., are given under the author's surname, where known; religious houses under the order to which they belonged.